▲ Piskarov Cemetery (5km)

Ploshchad
Lenina Ⓜ Finland
Station

V Y B O R G S I D E

Museum of Russian
Political History

Cruiser
Aurora

Lenin ⊙

Kresty
Prison

Peter's
Cabin

ULITSA KUBYSHEVA

PIROGOVSKAYA NABEREZHNAYA

PETROVSKAYA NABEREZHNAYA

ARSENALNAYA NABEREZHNAYA

River Neva

LITEYNIY MOST

NABEREZHNAYA KUTUZOVA

NABEREZHNAYA ROBESPERA

Smolniy Complex

SHPALERNAYA ULITSA

Bolshoy dom

ZAKHAREVSKAYA
ULITSA

Marble
Palace

Summer
Palace

Museum of
the Defence
of Leningrad

ULITSA CHAYKOVSKOVO

POTEMKINSKAYA ULITSA

PR. CHERNYSHEVSKOVO

Tauride
Gardens

Marsovo
Pole

Summer
Garden

Museum of
Decorative &
Applied Arts

FURSHTADTSKAYA

ULITSA

SADOVAYA ULITSA

MIKHOVANA

Ⓜ Chernyshevskaya

KIROCHNAYA ULITSA

ULITSA PESTELYA

MANEZHNIY PER.

Church
of the Saviour
on the Blood

Engineers'
Castle

Preobrazhenskiy
Church

ULITSA RYLEEVA

Suvorov
Museum

ULITSA RADISHEVA

SAPERNIY PEREULOK

Russian Museum
& Ethnographic
Museum

Circus

BASKOV
PEREULOK

ULITSA MAYAKOVSKOVO

ULITSA VOSSTANIYA

NABEREZHNAYA KANALA GRIBOEDOVA

NABEREZHNAYA REKI FONTANKI

UL. BELINSKOVO

Nekrasov
Museum

ULITSA NEKRASOVA

PL.
ISKUSSTV

Nevskiy
Prospekt

ITALYANSKAYA ULITSA

KARAVANNAYA ULITSA

ULITSA ZHUKOVSKOVO

Sheremetov Palace

LIGOVSKIY PROSPEKT

3-YA SOVETSKAYA

GRECHESKIY PROSPEKT

Nevskiy
Prospekt Ⓜ

Kazan
Cathedral

Gostiniy
dvor Ⓜ

Gostiniy
Dvor

N E V S K I Y   P R O S P E K T

2-YA SOVETSKAYA

SUVOROVSKIY PROSPEKT

ULITSA

Aleksandriinskiy
Drama Theatre

SADOVAYA ULITSA

ULITSA LOMONOSOVA

Beloselskiy-
Belozerskiy
Palace

Mayakovskaya
Ⓜ

Ploshchad
Vosstaniya

Apraksin
dvor

River Fontanka

VLADIMIRSKIY PROSPEKT

ULITSA RUBINSHTEYNA

Dostoevskaya
Ⓜ

Ploshchad
Vosstaniya Ⓜ

Moscow
Station

NABEREZHNAYA REKI FONTANKI

Vladimirskaya
Ⓜ

Arctic &
Antarctic
Museum

PUSHKINSKAYA

LIGOVSKIY PROSPEKT

Militia
Museum

Alexander Nevskiy Monastery

ZAGORODNIY PROSPEKT

SVECHNOY PEREULOK

DOSTOEVSKOVO

Dostoevsky
Museum

KUZNECHNIY
PER.

MARATA

Bread
Museum

Rimsky-Korsakov
Museum

RAZYEZHAYA ULITSA

ULITSA

Gumilev
Flat
Museum

N

Vitebsk
Station Ⓜ Pushkinskaya

Theatre of
Young Spectators

ULITSA MARATA

TROITSKA UL.

Ligovskiy
Prospekt

0   500 m

...ion

D0009313

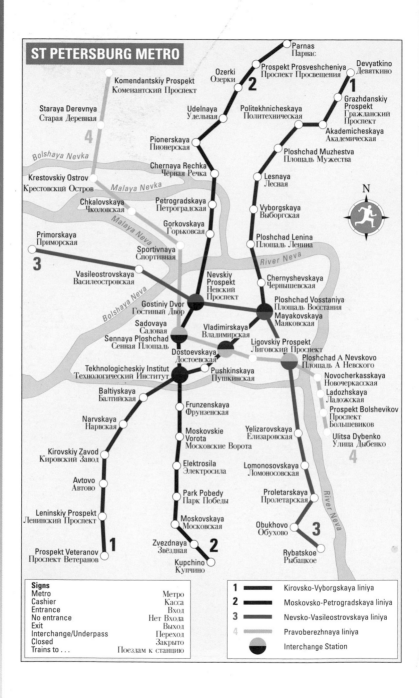

ST PETERSBURG METRO

Parnas
Парнас

Prospekt Prosveshcheniya
Проспект Просвещения

Devyatkino
Девяткино

Ozerki
Озерки

Komendantskiy Prospekt
Комендантский Проспект

Grazhdanskiy Prospekt
Гражданский Проспект

Staraya Derevnya
Старая Деревня

Udelnaya
Удельная

Politekhnicheskaya
Политехническая

Akademicheskaya
Академическая

Ploshchad Muzhestva
Площадь Мужества

Pionerskaya
Пионерская

Bolshaya Nevka

Chernaya Rechka
Чёрная Речка

Lesnaya
Лесная

Krestovskiy Ostrov
Крестовский Остров

Malaya Nevka

Petrogradskaya
Петроградская

Vyborgskaya
Выборгская

Chkalovskaya
Чколовская

Gorkovskaya
Горьковская

N

Primorskaya
Приморская

Malaya Neva

Sportivnaya
Спортивная

Ploshchad Lenina
Площадь Ленина

River Neva

Vasileostrovskaya
Василеостровская

Bolshaya Neva

Nevskiy Prospekt
Невский Проспект

Chernyshevskaya
Чернышевская

Gostiniy Dvor
Гостиный Двор

Ploshchad Vosstaniya
Площадь Восстания

Sadovaya
Садовая

Vladimirskaya
Владимирская

Mayakovskaya
Маяковская

Sennaya Ploshchad
Сенная Площадь

Dostoevskaya
Достоевская

Ligovskiy Prospekt
Лиговский Проспект

Tekhnologicheskiy Institut
Технологический Институт

Pushkinskaya
Пушкинская

Ploshchad A Nevskovo
Площадь А Невского

Baltiyskaya
Балтийская

Novocherkasskaya
Новочеркасская

Frunzenskaya
Фрунзенская

Ladozhskaya
Ладожская

Narvskaya
Нарвская

Prospekt Bolshevikov
Проспект Большевиков

Moskovskie Vorota
Московские Ворота

Yelizarovskaya
Елизаровская

Ulitsa Dybenko
Улица Дыбенко

Kirovskiy Zavod
Кировский Завод

Elektrosila
Электросила

Lomonosovskaya
Ломоносовская

Avtovo
Автово

Park Pobedy
Парк Победы

Proletarskaya
Пролетарская

Leninskiy Prospekt
Ленинский Проспект

Moskovskaya
Московская

River Neva

Obukhovo
Обухово

Prospekt Veteranov
Проспект Ветеранов

Zvezdnaya
Звёздная

Rybatskoe
Рыбацкое

Kupchino
Купчино

Signs

Metro	Метро
Cashier	Касса
Entrance	Вход
No entrance	Нет Входа
Exit	Выход
Interchange/Underpass	Переход
Closed	Закрыто
Trains to . . .	Поездам к станцию

1 — Kirovsko-Vyborgskaya liniya
2 — Moskovsko-Petrogradskaya liniya
3 — Nevsko-Vasileostrovskaya liniya
4 — Pravoberezhnaya liniya
● Interchange Station

Contents

An Imperial city colour section following p.144

The Soviet heritage colour section following p.272

Peter & Paul Fortress

Hermitage

Colour maps section following p.464

◄◄ The Griboedov Canal ◄ The Winter Palace

Introduction to

St Petersburg

Where were you born?
St Petersburg.
Where did you go to school?
Petrograd.
Where do you live now?
Leningrad.
And where would you like to live?
St Petersburg.

S t Petersburg, Petrograd, Leningrad and now, again, St Petersburg (in Russian, Sankt Peterburg) – as this tongue-in-cheek catechism suggests, the city's succession of names mirrors Russia's history. Founded in 1703 as a "window on the West" by Peter the Great, St Petersburg was for two centuries the capital of the Tsarist Empire, synonymous with hubris, excess and magnificence.

During World War I the city renounced its Germanic-sounding name and became Petrograd, and as such was the cradle of the revolutions that overthrew Tsarism and brought the Bolsheviks to power in 1917. Later, as Leningrad, it epitomized the Soviet Union's heroic sacrifices in the war against Fascism, withstanding almost nine hundred days of Nazi siege. Finally, in 1991 – the year that the USSR collapsed – the change of name, back to St Petersburg, was deeply symbolic, infuriating the wartime generation but delighting those who pined for a pre-revolutionary golden age; a dream kept alive throughout the years of Stalinist terror, when the poet Osip Mandelstam (who died in a labour camp) wrote: "We shall meet again in Petersburg . . ."

St Petersburg's sense of its own identity owes much to its origins and the interweaving of myth and reality throughout its history. Created by the will of an autocrat, on a barren river delta on the same latitude as the southern tip of Greenland, the Imperial capital embodied Peter the Great's rejection of Old Russia – represented by the former capital, "Asiatic" Moscow – and his embrace of Europe. The city's architecture, administration and social life were all copied or imported, the splendid buildings appearing alien to the indigenous forms and out of place in the surrounding countryside. Artificiality and self-consciousness were present from the beginning and this showpiece city of palaces and canals soon decreed itself the arbiter of Russia's sensibility and imagination. Petersburgers still tend to look down on the earthier Muscovites, who regard them in turn as snobbish. As the last tsar, Nicholas II, once remarked, "Remember, St Petersburg is Russian – but it is not Russia."

For all that, the city is associated with a host of renowned figures from Russian culture and history. It was here that Tchaikovsky, Stravinsky and Shostakovich composed; Pushkin, Dostoyevsky and Gogol wrote their masterpieces; Mendeleyev and Pavlov made their contributions to science;

As the last tsar once remarked, "St Petersburg is Russian – but it is not Russia."

▼ A "Red Granny"

5

"Walruses" and ice-fishing

Russians are proud of their **"walruses"** (*morzhi*) – intrepid bathers who break holes in the ice to swim in rivers throughout the winter. You can see them on the Neva bank of the Peter and Paul Fortress any day, joined by less hardy swimmers once the water warms up. This rugged tradition has spawned some great Olympic champions. Another quintessentially Russian sport is **ice-fishing** on frozen rivers, lakes or seas. Every year, hundreds of fishermen have to be rescued from ice floes on the Gulf of Finland or the Sea of Okhotsk. Many are equipped only with an ice-drill and rod, a stool and plastic tent – and, of course, vodka.

and Rasputin, Lenin and Trotsky made history. So, too, are various buildings and sites inseparable from their former occupants or visitors: the amazing Imperial palaces outside St Petersburg, where Peter and Catherine the Great led the field in exuberant living; the Yusupov Palace, where Rasputin was murdered; Finland Station, where Lenin returned from exile; and the Winter Palace, the storming of which was heralded by the guns of the cruiser *Aurora*, now moored along the embankment from the Peter and Paul Fortress – itself a Tsarist prison to generations of revolutionaries.

Today, "Piter" (as it's affectionately known) casts itself as Russia's cultural capital. For its three hundredth anniversary in 2003, much of the centre underwent a facelift when President Putin (a Leningrader by birth) hosted a G8 summit. While the city has never looked finer or been so tourist-friendly as now, homelessness, alcoholism and poverty are still visible reminders of the human cost of Russia's embrace of capitalism. Yet the city has endured far worse in its history, and there are plenty who are doing well or anticipate a brighter future.

What to see

St Petersburg is Russia's second largest city, with a population of five million and an urban sprawl of over 1400 square kilometres, across islands and peninsulas delineated by the **River Neva** and its tributaries. The metro covers most parts of the city of interest to visitors, but the historic centre is best explored on foot – easily done with a decent map, given the abundance of landmarks.

St Petersburg's major islands and "mainland" districts are juxtaposed in the magnificent panorama of the Neva Basin. On the south bank of the Neva, the golden dome of St Isaac's Cathedral and the needle-spire of the Admiralty loom above the area **within the Fontanka** (Chapter 1), whose vibrant main axis, **Nevskiy prospekt**, runs past a slew of sights culminating in the Winter Palace. The seductive vistas along the Moyka and Griboedov waterways entice you to wander off in search of the Mariinskiy ballet, the spot where Rasputin was murdered, or the setting for *Crime and Punishment*.

Two museums here rate a chapter each. The **Hermitage** (Chapter 2) boasts superlative collections of Rembrandt, Spanish masters, French Impressionists and Post-Impressionists; treasures from Siberia, Central Asia, India, Persia and China – plus the sumptuous state rooms of the Winter Palace, which forms part of the complex. If homegrown art is lacking there, that's because it's in the **Russian Museum** (Chapter 3), which runs the gamut from folk art and icons to Futurism and Socialist Realism.

▼ Queuing for food is a thing of the past – but prices are a worry for many

Opposite the Admiralty, on the spit or Strelka of **Vasilevskiy Island** (Chapter 4), the Rostral Columns and Naval Museum proclaim a maritime heritage bequeathed by Peter the Great. Nearby is the **Kunstkammer** of anatomical curios founded by Peter as Russia's first museum and still the city's most ghoulish tourist attraction. Farther along the embankment stand the Academy of Arts and the palace of Prince Menshikov.

Completing the panorama is the **Peter and Paul Fortress** (Chapter 4), its bastions surrounding a soaring cathedral where the Romanov monarchs are buried, and a Prison Museum attesting to the dark side of its history. Beyond its moat, the city's zoo and mosque mark the onset of the residential **Petrograd Side**, with its Art Nouveau buildings and flat-museums commemorating the opera singer Chaliapin and the Bolshevik "martyr" Kirov, whose name was given to the archipelago that forms its hinterland. The **Kirov Islands** are the city's summer playground, with boating lakes, the Zenit Stadium and Yelagin Palace to explore.

Back on the "mainland", the area beyond the Fontanka is designated **Liteyniy, Smolniy and Vladimirskaya** (Chapter 6), after the three localities that define its character. Its finest sights are the Smolniy Cathedral, near the Institute from where the Bolsheviks orchestrated the October Revolution, and the Alexander Nevsky Monastery, in whose cemeteries many of the city's most famous personages are buried. However, don't neglect the atmospheric Vladimirskaya district, where Dostoyevsky's apartment and the Pushkinskaya 10 artists' colony are located, along with an assortment of odd museums.

St Petersburg's beauty is tinged with melancholy.

Further out, the industrial **Southern Suburbs** (Chapter 7) are dignified by grandiose Soviet architecture such as the House of Soviets and the Victory Monument, and Tsarist triumphal arches that were re-erected in the euphoria of the Soviet Union's victory over Nazi Germany. Aside from these, there's the lovely Art Nouveau Vitebsk Station, an Outdoor Railway Museum and an atmospheric cemetery, the Literatorskie mostki.

The **Vyborg Side** (Chapter 8) of the Neva is similarly industrial but noteworthy in other ways. Anyone interested in the city's revolutionary past should visit Finland Station, where the first ever Lenin statue still stands, and the cruiser *Aurora*, preserved as a relic of 1917, is moored. Kresty Prison and the Piskarov Cemetery are sombre reminders of the victims of Stalin's purges and the hundreds of thousands who died during the Blockade. Only the Buddhist temple strikes a lighter note.

Just outside the city, the **Imperial palaces** (Chapter 9) are among Russia's premier attractions, particularly Peterhof with its magnificent fountains, and the Catherine Palace at Tsarskoe Selo with its fabled Amber Room. Though both deserve a full day each, it's possible to combine Tsarskoe Selo with another palace, Pavlovsk, if you're willing to dash around.

The island naval base of **Kronstadt** (Chapter 10) is best known today for an annual rave staged in an offshore sea fort. While the **Gulf coast** has several beach resorts that come alive in summer, the real draw for city dwellers are the forests, lakes and weekend *dachas* (cottages) of the Karelian Isthmus. This region once belonged to Finland and was previously contested by Russia and Sweden, as is evident at **Vyborg**, near the Finnish border.

On Lake Ladoga, the prison-fortress of **Shlisselburg** (Chapter 11) is a poignant reminder of those who suffered there in Tsarist times and its resistance to the Nazi Blockade, while the **Valaam** archipelago attests to the centuries-old monastic tradition in Russia's northern lakes, whose isolation gave rise to the amazing wooden churches of **Kizhi** Island in Lake Onega.

▼ Zakuski

Ladoga is linked to the great inland waterways of Russia, which once enriched **Novgorod** (Chapter 12). Its medieval Kremlin, parish churches and outlying monasteries merit a full day's exploration, while local hotels are cheap enough to make an overnight excursion from St Petersburg quite feasible.

When to go

St Petersburg lies on the same latitude as the Shetland Islands and Anchorage, Alaska, but its **climate** is less harsh than you'd imagine. Summers are hot and while winters may be cold by Western European standards, they rarely compare with the cold of winter in Moscow, let alone Siberia.

New Year and January is the best time to come. The city looks magical covered in snow and days can be gloriously sunny. Arts and music lovers will find plenty to enjoy; party animals can revel in the nightlife; and visitors needn't queue to get into the Hermitage or the Imperial palaces (though they'll have to forgo seeing the fountains at Peterhof). New Year occasions shopping and merrymaking, much as Christmas does in the West, and it's worth sticking around to catch the traditional Russian Orthodox Church celebrations of both holidays, in early January.

Spring is chiefly rewarding for the rituals and candle-lit processions marking Orthodox **Easter**, when cathedrals are so packed that people wait for hours to get in. (Christmas services are as splendid yet not nearly so crowded.) Whereas Easter is a moveable feast whose date can be foretold, the amazing sight of **ice floes** grinding their way down the Neva may not occur until April or even early May, depending on the spring thaw.

The most popular time is **summer**, especially during the intoxicating **"White Nights"** (mid-June to mid-July). While it's hard to resist nights turned to days and weeks of festivities, there's a downside to visiting then. Accommodation is costlier; there are queues for the Hermitage and Imperial palaces; and the ballet dancers at festivals are rarely top class. Days are baking hot and nights sultry with the occasional downpour providing relief from the humidity. In August, everyone who can afford to leaves the city, if only to stay in a *dacha* (cottage) in the surrounding countryside.

By mid-September **autumn** is under way, with cloudy skies and falling temperatures. In October theatres reopen and the Mariinskiy starts its new season, making this one of the best times for ballet and opera lovers prepared to risk the first frosts (and sometimes snowfalls), though there can also be warm and sunny days, when the city looks especially beautiful in the soft northern light. It's best to **avoid** coming in November, December or February, when the weather is uncertain and cultural offerings are patchy.

Finally, make sure you **bring** the right gear. Lots of layers, a hat and waterproof footwear with non-slip soles are essential for winter. A compact rainproof jacket will protect you from showers in spring or autumn. Shorts and T-shirts are fine for summer, but pack long trousers or a skirt for visiting churches, the ballet, or dining out – and a mosquito net to drape over your bed if you're unsure that your lodgings have screens on the windows.

Monthly temperatures and average monthly rainfall in St Petersburg

	Jan	Feb	Mar	Apr	May	June	July	Aug	Sept	Oct	Nov	Dec
Max. temp. (°C)	-7	-5	0	8	15	20	21	20	15	9	2	-3
Min. temp. (°C)	-13	-12	-8	0	6	11	13	13	9	4	-2	-8
Rainfall (mm)	35	30	31	36	45	50	72	78	64	76	46	40

things not to miss

It's not possible to see everything that St Petersburg has to offer on a short trip – and we don't suggest you try. What follows is a subjective selection of the city's highlights, shown in no particular order, ranging from the peerless art collection of the Hermitage to the sumptuous palaces on the outskirts, all arranged in colour-coded categories to help you find the very best things to see, do and experience. All entries have a page reference to take you straight into the guide, where you can find out more.

01 The Hermitage Page **175** • This stupendous museum boasts masterpieces by artists from Rembrandt to Matisse, prehistoric Siberian mummies and curios such as the Kolyvan Vase, displayed in a complex incorporating the Winter Palace, with its fabulously ornate decor.

02 Dvortsovaya ploshchad (Palace Square)

Page **74** • The boldest of St Petersburg's public spaces juxtaposes the rampant triumphalism of the General Staff building and the Alexander Column with the Baroque effusions of the Winter Palace.

03 Mariinskiy Theatre

Page **366** • Watch world-class ballet and opera performed in a magnificent auditorium under the baton of maestro Gergiev, by the company better known abroad as the Kirov.

04 Yusupov Palace

Page **108** • A waxworks tableau of Rasputin's murder in the cellar where it happened, a glamorous theatre, as well as sumptuous apartments mirroring generations of aristocratic taste, make the Yusupov Palace irresistible.

05 Kunstkammer

Page **156** • Peter the Great's collection of grotesqueries was Russia's first museum and remains one of the city's most popular tourist attractions.

06 Cruiser Aurora

Page **178** • The warship whose guns heralded the October Revolution has been preserved as a museum – though some say that a sister ship was substituted for the original. Decide for yourself.

07 White Nights Page **45** •
Several weeks in midsummer when twilight is as dark as it gets, and half the city stays up partying, toasting the Neva bridges as they rise to let ships sail upriver in the small hours.

08 Georgian cuisine Page **339** •
The healthiest and tastiest of Russia's diverse culinary traditions, owing to its emphasis on fresh herbs, vegetables, pulses, nuts and garnishes such as pomegranate seeds – but Georgian food has plenty to offer carnivores, too.

10 Pavlovsk Page **265** • Created for Tsar Paul, Pavlovsk Palace is surrounded by a vast Romantic park, full of Antique follies and especially lovely in autumn.

09 Novgorod Page **307** • This medieval city celebrates its pagan roots with bonfires and revelry on the Night of Ivan Kupala (July 6).

11 **FortDance** Page **369** •
A midsummer rave party in an abandoned plague laboratory and naval fort, way out in the Gulf of Finland. How cool can you get?

12 **St Isaac's Cathedral** Page **97** •
Decorated inside with 14 kinds of marble, jasper, malachite, gilded stucco and mosaics, the cathedral's golden dome offers a stunning view of the inner city.

| ACTIVITIES | CONSUME | EVENTS | NATURE | SIGHTS |

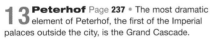

13 **Peterhof** Page **237** • The most dramatic element of Peterhof, the first of the Imperial palaces outside the city, is the Grand Cascade.

14 **Tsarskoe Selo** Page **254** • The Catherine Palace at this Imperial suburban estate contains the mirrored Great Hall and the fabled Amber Room.

15 **Kizhi** Page **304** •
Built entirely of wood, the amazing Church of the Transfiguration is twice the height of St Basil's in Moscow, and situated on a remote island in Lake Onega.

15

16 Orthodox choral music
Page **364** • Inseparable from the Byzantine rituals of the Orthodox faith, this is best heard at the Preobrazhenskiy Church, whose choir includes many singers from the State Kapella.

17 Church of the Saviour on the Blood Page **83** •
A standing rebuke to foreign architecture and revolutionary ideas, built on the spot where Alexander II was fatally injured by a nihilist's bomb; its onion domes evoke St Basil's Cathedral in Moscow, and its interior is entirely covered in gilded mosaics.

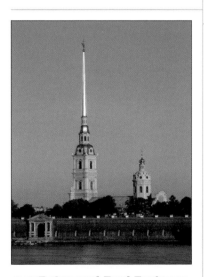

18 Peter and Paul Fortress
Page **167** • The kernel from which the city developed, the fortress contains a cathedral where the Romanovs are buried and a prison museum denouncing their tyranny.

19 Russian Museum Page **137**
• The world's largest collection of Russian art runs the gamut from medieval icons to Futurist art, by way of nineteenth-century works such as Vasnetsov's *A Russian Knight at the Crossway* (pictured).

Basics

Basics

Getting there

St Petersburg's peripheral location in northeastern Europe means that the quickest and easiest way to get there is by flying. There are direct flights from almost every European capital; the flight time from London is three hours. If you have more time, then travelling overland from Finland, the Baltic States, Germany or Poland (accessible by low-cost airlines) becomes an attractive option, with approaches by train, bus or car and ferry. While St Petersburg still lies beyond the scope of low-price airlines or rail passes, and the need to obtain a visa makes it hard to take advantage of last-minute offers, you should be able to save money on both tickets and Russian visas by booking months ahead of time. For short visits to St Petersburg, a package tour may well be cheaper than doing things independently, once you've taken the cost of accommodation and visas into account.

Booking flights online

Many airlines and discount travel websites offer you the opportunity to book your tickets online, cutting out the cost of middlemen and often giving you a discount at the same time. Good deals can often be found through discount or auction sites, as well as through the airlines' own websites – though some can't distinguish between St Petersburg in Russia and its Florida namesake, even if you input the right airport code, LED. Another thing to bear in mind is that many online deals permit little or no flexibility, so your flight dates need to mesh with the dates of your Russian visa, which may take several weeks to obtain (see p.29).

Online booking agents and general travel sites

ⓦ www.ebookers.com (in UK)
ⓦ www.expedia.com
ⓦ www.joewalshtours.ie (in Ireland)
ⓦ www.lastminute.com (in UK)
ⓦ www.northsouthtravel.co.uk (in UK)
ⓦ www.opodo.co.uk (in UK)
ⓦ www.orbitz.com (in US)
ⓦ www.statravel.com
ⓦ www.trailfinders.com (in UK)
ⓦ www.travelcuts.com (in Canada & US)
ⓦ www.travelocity.com ⓦ www.zuji.com.au (in Australia) ⓦ www.zuji.co.nz (in New Zealand)

Flights from Britain and Ireland

Between them, British Airways (BA) and the Russian airlines Aeroflot and Rossiya operate 5–10 **direct flights** a week from London to St Petersburg. Rossiya's fares are lowest (from £183 including taxes), with Aeroflot's starting at £210 during low season, £260 in high season (June, July, New Year and Easter), and BA's from £280 (low season) and £310 (high season). If you're planning to visit **Moscow** as well, all these airlines fly there daily, as do bmi and the Russian carrier Transaero. Fares can be as low as £190 throughout the year – for Moscow, there isn't a high season as such.

You might get a better deal on an **indirect flight** to St Petersburg via another European city, eg Air Baltic via Rīga, Lufthansa via Frankfurt, KLM via Amsterdam, Air France via Paris, Austrian Airlines or Lauda Air via Vienna, CSA via Prague, SAS via Stockholm, Alitalia via Milan, or Finnair via Helsinki. Some offer connections from Birmingham, Manchester, Glasgow or Edinburgh.

Also investigate **low-cost airlines** such as bmi, easyJet and Ryanair for **cheap fares to Finland, Estonia or Latvia**. A return flight to Helsinki, Tallinn or Rīga can cost as little as £50, with departures from a range of UK airports. From any of these capitals it's easy – and inexpensive – to travel overland to St Petersburg (as detailed on p.26). As you'll end up spending time (and money) in whichever city you arrive at you probably won't economize in the end – but you'll be able to see a lot more on a limited budget.

There are **no direct flights to St Petersburg from Ireland**, so the best you can hope for is an indirect flight via another hub city. Dublin offers more choice of routings and lower prices than Belfast, so travellers from the North may do better by flying to London or Manchester for an onward connection. For departures from Dublin, the cheapest routing is usually KLM via Amsterdam (from €260), which tends to be well below fares on Aeroflot, Air France or BA.

Flights from the USA and Canada

There are **no direct flights** to St Petersburg **from the US or Canada**. In the US, Aeroflot flies from New York, Washington DC and Los Angeles to Moscow and has several same-day onward flights to St Petersburg (about thirteen hours journey), but you may well do better with other **one- or two-stop flights** offered by the major European carriers, that allow you to depart from any number of US gateways. Excluding taxes, **fares** from Eastern gateways range from $620 in low season to $1160 during summer; from the West Coast, upwards of $1255/$1490 during low/high season. In Canada, fares from Toronto or Montreal start at C$1050/C$1710 in high/low season (excluding taxes).

Alternatively, you may wish to travel to a European city and make your way **overland** from there. Helsinki is the closest foreign capital to St Petersburg, just six hours away by train; Berlin is a more distant (36 hours by train or coach) gateway. If St Petersburg is part of a longer European trip, you'll also want to check out details of the Eurail pass (see p.24). US and Canadian citizens should obtain a Russian **visa** before leaving home, as they may not be able to in Europe (see p.29).

Flights from Australia and New Zealand

Flight time **from Australia and New Zealand** to St Petersburg is over twenty hours, and can be longer depending on routes. Some entail touching down in Asia, and all involve changing planes at a European gate-

way for the last leg to St Petersburg. Given the length of the journey, you'd be better off including a night's stopover in your itinerary – some airlines include one in the price of the flight. There's a plethora of airline combinations online, so shop around and be flexible.

Return **fares** to St Petersburg from eastern gateways range from around A$1650 in low season (mid-Jan, Feb, Oct & Nov) to A$1720 in high season (June–Sept, Christmas & New Year). Fares from Perth or Darwin cost A$200–400 more. From Auckland you can fly to Seoul with Korean Airlines and then on to Moscow and St Petersburg. Alternatively, you could fly into Moscow instead – it costs A$300–600 less than to St Petersburg and is feasible with two flights rather than three. For the best results online, input the code for Moscow's Domodedovo airport (DME). Be sure to get a Russian **visa** before you leave home (see p.29).

Airlines

Aeroflot UK ☏020/7355 2233, US ☏1-888/340-6400, Canada ☏1-416/642-1653, Australia ☏02/9262 2233, ⓦ www.aeroflot.co.uk, ⓦ www.aeroflot.com.

Air Baltic UK ☏01293/555 700, ⓦ www.airbaltic.com.

Air Canada US and Canada ☏1-888/247-2262, ⓦ www.aircanada.com.

Air China Australia ☏02/9232 7277, ⓦ www.air-china.co.uk, ⓦ www.airchina.com.cn.

Air France UK ☏0870/142 4343, US ☏1-800/237-2747, Canada ☏1-800/667-2747, Australia ☏1300/390 190, ⓦ www.airfrance.com.

Alitalia UK ☏0870/544 8259, Ireland ☏01/677 5171, US ☏1-800-223-5730, Canada ☏1-800/361-8336, New Zealand ☏09/308 3357, ⓦ www.alitalia.com.

American Airlines US ☏1-800/433-7300, ⓦ www.aa.com.

Austrian Airlines UK ☏0870/124 2625, Ireland ☏1800/509 142, US☏1-800/843-0002, Australia ☏1800/642 438 or 02/9251 6155, ⓦ www.aua.com.

British Airways UK ☏0870/850 9850, Ireland ☏1890/626 747, US and Canada ☏1-800/AIRWAYS, Australia ☏1300/767 177, New Zealand ☏09/966 9777, ⓦ www.ba.com.

bmi UK ☏0870/607 0555 or 0870/607 0222, Ireland ☏01/407 3036, US ☏1-800/788-0555, ⓦ www.flybmi.com.

CSA (Czech Airlines) UK ☎0870/444 3747,
Ireland ☎0818/200 014, US ☎1-800/223-2365,
Canada ☎416-363/3174, ⓦwww.czechairlines.
co.uk.
Delta US and Canada ☎1-800/221-1212, ⓦwww.
delta.com.
easyJet UK ☎0905/821 0905, ⓦwww.easyjet.com.
Emirates Australia ☎02/9290 9700, New Zealand
☎09/968 2200, ⓦwww.emirates.com.
Estonian Air UK ☎020/7333 0196, Ireland
☎01/8444 300, US ☎1-800/397-1354, Canada
☎1-416/221-3508, ⓦwww.estonian-air.ee.
Finnair UK ☎0870/241 4411, Ireland ☎01/844
6565, US ☎1-800/950-5000, Australia ☎02/9244
2299, ⓦwww.finnair.com.
Garuda Indonesia Australia ☎1300/365 330
or 02/9334 9944, New Zealand ☎09/366 1862;
ⓦwww.garuda-indonesia.com.
JAL (Japan Air Lines) Australia ☎02/9272 1111,
New Zealand ☎09/379 9906, ⓦwww.jal.com or
ⓦwww.japanair.com.
KLM/Northwest Airlines UK ☎0870/507 4074,
Ireland ☎1850/747 400 US ☎1-800-225-2525,
Australia ☎1300/303 747, New Zealand ☎09/921
6040, SA ☎11/961 6767, ⓦwww.klm.com.
Korean Air Australia ☎02/9262 6000, New
Zealand ☎09/914 2000, ⓦwww.koreanair.com.
LOT (Polish Airlines) UK ☎0845/601 0949, Ireland
☎1890/359 568, US ☎1-800-223-0593, Canada
☎1-800-668-5928, Australia ☎02/9244 2466,
New Zealand ☎09/308 3369, ⓦwww.lot.com.
Lufthansa UK ☎0870/837 7747, Ireland
☎01/844 5544, US ☎1-800-645-3880, Canada
☎1-800-563-5954, Australia ☎1300/655 727, SA
☎0861/842 538, ⓦwww.lufthansa.com.
Qantas Airways Australia ☎13 13 13, New
Zealand ☎0800/808 767 or 09/357 8900, ⓦwww.
qantas.com.
Rossiya Airlines UK ☎020/7493 4612, ⓦwww.
pulkovo.ru.
Ryanair UK ☎0871/246 0000, Ireland ☎0818/303
030, ⓦwww.ryanair.com.
SAS (Scandinavian Airlines) UK ☎0870/6072
7727, Ireland ☎01/844 5440, US and Canada ☎1-
800-221-2350, Australia ☎1300/727 707, ⓦwww.
scandinavian.net.
SN Brussels Airlines UK ☎0870/735 2345, Ireland
☎01/844 6006, US ☎1-516-740-5200, Canada
☎1-866-308-2230, Australia ☎02/9767 4305,
ⓦwww.flysn.com.
Swiss UK ☎0845/601 0956, Ireland ☎1890/200
515, US ☎1-877-FLY-SWIS, Australia ☎1300/724
666, New Zealand ☎09/977 2238, ⓦwww.swiss.
com.
Transaero UK ☎0207/727 4100 or 0870/770
2852, ⓦwww.transaero.ru.

Virgin Atlantic US ☎1-800-821-5438, Australia
☎1300/727 340, ⓦwww.virgin-atlantic.com.

Tours

Given the price of flights to and hotels in
St Petersburg, there's a strong incentive to
look for a **package tour** – an easy way of
cutting the cost and trouble of organizing
a trip. Tours sold in Britain usually include
flights, but many US, Canadian, Australian
and New Zealand operators quote land-only
prices – assuming that travellers will make
their own way to Russia via Europe or Asia
– though they're happy to sell you a return
flight if you wish. Anyone planning to join a
tour later should be sure to obtain a Russian **visa** before leaving home unless *certain*
of getting one in another country (see "Red
tape and visas", p.29).

Many UK operators sell three- or four-day
city breaks in St Petersburg (or Moscow);
prices are competitive and there's a range
of accommodation, so you can pay as little
as £400 if you're flexible about when you fly
or where you stay. Most US and Canadian
operators only offer St Petersburg with Moscow on an eight-day **twin-centre** tour, featuring an overnight train journey between the
two; for this sort of trip expect to pay around
£900 in the UK (including flights), $2660
($1980 land-only) in the US, or C$2950
(C$1700 land-only) in Canada.

To see more of Russia's heartland, you
can visit the **Golden Ring** of towns and
monasteries beyond Moscow: Sergiev-
Posad, Vladimir, Suzdal, Kostroma, Uglich,
Preslav-Veliky and Yaroslavl. For an eight- or
nine-day tour, expect to pay from $3880
($3180 land-only) in the US, C$2825 (including flights) in Canada, A$3120 (land-only) in
Australia. Some also feature Novgorod (see
p.307) as part of a circuit between Moscow
and St Petersburg.

A more leisurely approach is a Volga
cruise between Moscow and St Petersburg.
A typical tour involves three days in each
city, three or four days visiting Yaroslavl,
Kostroma and Uglich, and a brief look at the
wooden churches of Kizhi (see p.304) or the
holy isle of Valaam (see p.297). Expect to
pay from £1060 in Britain (including flights),
$4700 in the US, C$4100 in Canada, or
A$2230 in Australia (land-only). Other cruises

include St Petersburg among several Baltic capitals, sailing down the Volga as far as Rostov Na Don, or from Kiev to Odessa.

Trans-Siberian Railway operators offer a bewildering variety of tours, starting or finishing in Moscow, Beijing, or the Mongolian capital, Ulan Bator. Check what's on offer in the way of side trips: some include forays into Buryatia or around Lake Baikal, or staying in a yurt on the Mongolian Steppes. For a basic twelve- or thirteen-day tour, land-only prices start at £800 in the UK, $5700 in the US, C$2675 in Canada and A$2540 in Australia. Some of the same companies also do **Silk Road** tours visiting the ancient cities of Kashgar, Bukhara and Sammarkand, en route to Moscow, Beijing or Ulan Bator. Land-only prices start at £1000 in Britain, $6100 in the US, A$2540 in Australia – you can pay a lot more for tours along the same routes **by deluxe private train**, arranged by firms like GW Travel.

Adventure tours of the Russian Far East, Lake Baikal and the Altay Mountains of Siberia or northern Karelia are increasingly popular. These are usually sold from Britain or the US with flights included. You can go bear- and **volcano-watching** in Kamchatka (from £1825 in the UK, $7800 in the US), **dog-sledding** in the Urals (from £1320 in the UK) white-water **rafting** and horse-riding in the Altay (from £1310 in the UK), or on a **snowmobile** safari to Kizhi (from £870 in the UK).

A scarier thrill is **flying a MiG** fighter at Nizhniy Novgorod. Jets have dual controls so passengers can try their hand at manoeuvres under the control of an expert pilot. In the US, Incredible Adventures charges $21,000 to ride a state-of-the-art MiG 31 to the edge of "near space" at over twice the speed of sound, while in Britain, Go Russia offers hi-jinks in an older MiG 21 from £2870. Clients must pass a physical examination before booking.

Other **specialized tours** are aimed at **ballet** or **music** fans (with backstage visits at the Mariinskiy and/or Bolshoy theatres), **art** lovers (behind the scenes at Tsarskoe Selo and other Imperial palaces) or those into **World War II** battlefields or relics of the **Gulag**. See the listings below for an idea of what's on offer.

Specialist tour operators

Abercrombie and Kent UK ☎0845/618 2200, ⓦwww.abercrombiekent.co.uk; US ☎1-800/554-7016, ⓦwww.abercrombieandkent.com; Australia ☎03/9536 1800; New Zealand ☎0800/441 638; ⓦwww.abercrombiekent.com.au. Upmarket cruises from Moscow to St Petersburg and around the Baltic capitals (tours start in the US), twin-centre (Australia/NZ) and city breaks (UK); all include flights.

Adventure Center US ☎1-800/228-8747, ⓦwww.adventure-center.com. Agent for adventure specialists Dragoman, offering the Trans-Siberian Railway, the Silk Road and Moscow–St Petersburg, plus an 11-week road tour of Russia and Mongolia.

Australians Studying Abroad Australia ☎1-800/645 755, ⓦwww.asatravinfo.com.au. A 24-day arts tour featuring Moscow, Yaroslavl, Suzdal, Abramtsevo, Pskov, Novgorod and St Petersburg; flights included or land-only.

Beetroot Backpackers UK ☎020/8566 8846, ⓦwww.beetroot.org. Budget tours of St Petersburg, Moscow and Novgorod; Christmas and New Year's parties in Russia; affiliated to Trans-Siberian Experience (see below).

Bentours Australia ☎02/9247 3381, ⓦwww.bentours.com.au. Baltic and Moscow/St Petersburg cruises, tours of Karelia and the Golden Ring, as well as Trans-Siberian trips (some escorted, others not).

Cosmos Tourama UK ☎0871/622 4344, ⓦwww.cosmostourama.co.uk. Mainstream tour operator with twin-centre cruises (including Kizhi), city breaks, and a cruise from Kiev to Odessa.

Dragoman UK ☎01728/861 133, ⓦwww.dragoman.com. Two- to six-week overland tours of the Caucuses, Central Asia and China, in a customized truck.

Eastern Europe Travel Centre Australia ☎02/9262 1144 ⓦwww.eetbtravel.com. Moscow, St Petersburg, the Golden Ring, Kiev, and a river cruise are among the options.

Exeter International US ☎1-800/633-1008 or 813/251-5355, ⓦwww.exeterinternational.com. St Petersburg–Kizhi–Moscow cruises, backstage at the Mariinskiy Theatre or the amber workshop at Tsarskoe Selo, and other deluxe tours.

Gateway Travel Australia ☎1800/700 333, ⓦwww.russian-gateway.com.au. Russia/CIS specialists offering Trans-Siberian trips, cruises from St Petersburg to Valaam and Kizhi, and an eclipse-watching tour in 2008.

General Tours US ☎1-800/221-2216, ⓦwww.generaltours.com. Twin-centre tours, cruises via Kizhi, and the Trans-Siberian to Beijing, priced land-only.

Geographic Expeditions US ☎ 1-800/777-8183 or 415/922-0448, ⊛ www.geoex.com. Adventure tours of Kamchatka and Siberia; Moscow–Golden Ring–St Petersburg packages; flights from the US included.

Go Russia UK ☎ 020/8434 34961, ⊛ www. justgorussia.co.uk. City breaks and adventure tours (snowmobiling, dog-sledding, volcano-watching), flying MiGs and World War II battlefield trips.

GW Travel UK ☎ 0161/298 9410, ⊛ www.gwtravel .co.uk. Tours in vintage private trains from Moscow to St Petersburg and Vladivostok; to Mongolia for the Naadam festival; and from Moscow to Beijing via the Silk Road.

Innovative Travel New Zealand ☎ 03/3653 910, ⊛ www.eetbtravel.com.au. Agents for the Eastern Europe Travel Centre (see above).

Interchange UK ☎ 020/8681 3612, ⊛ www. Interchange.uk.com. Tailor-made individual tours from Britain to anywhere in Russia.

Incredible Adventures US ☎ 1-800/644 7382 or 800-FLY-MIGS, ⊛ www.incredible-adventures.com. MiG flights, freefall, HALO parachuting, Cosmonaut or Special Forces training at Russian military bases.

Intourist UK ☎ 0870/112 1232, ⊛ www.intourist. co.uk. Does a vast range of tours and tailor-made holidays throughout Russia and the CIS.

Intours Corporation Canada ☎ 1-800/268-1785, ⊛ www.tourussia.com. St Petersburg, Moscow, the Golden Ring, Siberia and the Russian Far East, plus cruises to Rostov Na Don, Kiev and Odessa.

Mir Corporation US ☎ 1-800/424-7289, ⊛ www. mircorp.com. The Silk Road, the Trans-Siberian and the Golden Ring by private train, and tours focusing on Siberian shamanism or the Gulag Archipelago, all priced land-only.

On the Go Tours UK ☎ 020/7371 1113, ⊛ www. onthegotours.com. Group and tailor-made tours to Russia and China.

Passport Travel Australia ☎ 03/9500 0444, ⊛ www.travelcentre.com.au. Trans-Siberian and Silk Road travel; MiG flying; a Murmansk and Lapland tour and a river cruise are among their packages.

Pioneer Tours and Travel US ☎ 1-800/369-1322, ⊛ www.pioneerrussia.com. Customized individual tours, special-interest and educational tours to Russia and the CIS.

Russian Gateway UK Ltd UK ☎ 0874/461 812, ⊛ www.russiangateway.co.uk. Tours to St Petersburg, Moscow, Novgorod and Yekaterinburg; cruises and school tours.

Russia House UK ☎ 020/7403 9922, ⊛ www. therussiahouse.co.uk; US ☎ 202/364-0200, ⊛ www.russiahouse.org. Arranges visas, tickets and accommodation in Russia, mainly for business travellers.

Russian National Group US ☎ 877/221-7120, ⊛ www.russia-travel.com. Affiliated to the Russian National Tourist Office in New York. All kinds of tours, including Moscow–St Petersburg cruises. Visa support, hotel and flight bookings in Russia.

Scantours Inc US & Canada ☎ 1-800/223-7226, ⊛ www.scantours.com. Scandinavian ferry agent selling Baltic and Russian river cruises featuring St Petersburg.

Scott's Tours UK ☎ 020/7383 5353, ⊛ www. scottstours.co.uk. Discount flights to Russia and the CIS, city breaks, visa support and other services.

Trans-Siberian Experience UK ☎ 020/8566 8846, ⊛ www.trans-siberian.co.uk, Australia ☎ 1300/654 861, ⊛ www.trans-siberian.com.au. Trans-Siberian specialists in individual, small group and adventure travel in Russia, Mongolia, China and Tibet.

Travel for the Arts UK ☎ 020/8799 8350, ⊛ www.travelforthearts.co.uk. Deluxe tours for music lovers, scheduled for the Russian Orthodox Easter and the Stars of the White Nights festival.

Visit Russia UK ☎ 020/7495 7570, ⊛ www. visitrussia.org; US ☎ 1-800/755-3080, ⊛ www. visitrussia.com. Offshoot of the Russian National Tourist Office, offering visa support, flights, hotel bookings and a wide range of tours throughout the CIS.

Voyages Jules Verne UK ☎ 0845/166 7003, ⊛ www.vjv.co.uk. City breaks, twin-centre tours and a Baltic cruise visiting St Petersburg.

By train and ferry

Travelling **by train** from London to St Petersburg takes three days and three nights, and for those not entitled to student or youth discounts, costs more than flying. There isn't a direct train, and going by rail only really makes sense if you're planning to visit St Petersburg as part of an extensive European odyssey, which could involve travelling by ferry some of the way. Trains to St Petersburg from Helsinki, Tallinn and Rīga are covered on p.26.

The route

To reach St Petersburg **from Britain**, you must catch a night train to Berlin that connects with an onward service to Russia. The 6.35pm Eurostar from London St Pancras to Brussels Midi arrives two hours before the departure of the comfortable *nachtzug* to Berlin at 11.41pm, arriving at the Hauptbahnhof at 8.10am next day. This allows you a few hours sightseeing in Berlin before boarding a direct sleeping car to St Petersburg attached to the *Moskva Express*, which runs daily except Saturday from late May to early October, and on Wednesday, Thursday, Friday and Sunday the rest of the year. It leaves Berlin at 3.22pm and arrives at St Petersburg's Vitebsk Station at 6.20am two days later. You can check the departure times on the Hauptbahnhof's website, ⓦhttp://bahn.hafas.de).

The **route** goes **through Germany, Poland and Belarus**. Be sure to have transit **visas** for Poland (if required) and Belarus (see box on p.27) before leaving. None is issued at border crossings, and visa-less passengers may be forced off at Brest on the Polish–Belarus border, where trains are jacked up in order to change to the wide-gauge Russian tracks (meant to make it difficult for invaders to use the network). Bring food and drink for the whole journey, since there's nothing available in Russian wagons except hot water from the samovar, and the odd can of beer.

Longer routes **via Denmark, Sweden and Finland** are also feasible if you fancy seeing something of Scandinavia and travelling some of the way **by ferry**. From Britain, you can take a DFDS Seaways ferry from Harwich to Esbjerg in Denmark, then a fast train to Copenhagen and another on to Stockholm, where you board a luxurious Silja Line ship leaving at 5pm, arriving in Helsinki next morning (four days after leaving London). For details of this and other routes, see the Finland and Russia sections on ⓦwww.seat61.com. Ferry operators are listed opposite.

journey with a return ticket on Eurostar and the Brussels–Berlin train, and buy a ticket from St Petersburg back to Germany using a local agent agent, such as Svezhy Veter (see listings below).

Eurostar and Brussels–Berlin are covered by an inclusive return **fare** of £160, while the journey from Berlin to St Petersburg costs about £80 one-way, £160 return. On top of this there's a sleeper supplement of £20 each way (which gets you a berth in a three-bed compartment), and the cost of a Belarus transit visa (see p.27).

There are various European rail passes, but none covers Russia, Belarus or the Baltic States. With **InterRail**, for example, their Global Pass can take you as far as Warsaw or Helsinki; the onward fare to St Petersburg is about the same from either city (about £60/£40 in first/second class), but the journey from Helsinki is much faster and doesn't require a Belarus transit visa. A ten-day pass costs £352/£259/£172 travelling first/second class/student rate; for a one-month pass, the rates are £583/£431 and £288. InterRail isn't valid in the UK, though you're entitled to discounts in Britain and on Eurostar and cross-Channel ferries. To qualify for the pass you must have been resident in Europe for six months.

North Americans, Australians and **New Zealanders** who don't qualify for InterRail can obtain a **Eurail pass**, which comes in various forms, and must be bought before leaving home. For more information, and to reserve tickets, contact Rail Europe or STA Travel in North America, Trailfinders in Australia or Walshes World in New Zealand (see below).

Tickets and passes

You cannot buy **tickets** to Russia online, only by phone from certain UK rail agents, up to sixty days ahead. The best ones to call are Deutsche Bahn's UK office, or Real Russia, which don't charge for quotes (unlike European Rail). It is possible to book the entire outward journey to Russia by using the computer reservation system for trains starting in Germany, but booking a return journey may be impossible in Britain. In that case, ask them to book you the outward

Rail contacts

European Rail UK ☎020/7619 1083 (bookings) or 0901/235 0105 (enquiries; premium line), ⓦwww. europeanrail.com. Charges £5 for each quote (refunded against your ticket purchase) and £20 booking fee.
Europrail International Canada ☎1-888/667-9734, ⓦwww.europrail.net. Agent for Eurail passes.
Eurostar UK ☎0870/518 6186, ⓦwww.eurostar. com. Latest fares and discounts (plus online booking) on the London–Paris and London–Brussels Eurostar service, and add-on fares from the rest of the UK.
Finnish Railways Finland ☎358 + 9/2319 2902,

@ internationaltickets@vr.fi, 🅦 www.vr.fi. Bookings for the Sibelius and Repin trains from Helsinki to St Petersburg.

German Railways (Deutsche Bahn) UK ☎ 0870/243 5363, 🅦 www.bahn.de. Competitive fares for any journey from London across Europe; their website can't give prices for tickets to St Petersburg, but does allow journey-planning.

International Rail UK ☎ 08700/847 410, 🅦 www. international-rail.com. Agent for all European railways and rail passes, and many others worldwide.

Rail Europe UK ☎ 0870/584 8848, 🅦 www. raileurope.co.uk, US ☎ 1-877/257-2887, Canada ☎ 1-800/361-RAIL, 🅦 www.raileurope.scom/us. Ticket agent for European passes and journeys as far as Warsaw, owned by SNCF (French Railways).

Real Russia UK ☎ 020/7100 7370, 🅦 www. realrussia.co.uk. Rail bookings to/from/ within Russia, visa support and other tourist services.

STA Travel UK ☎ 0870/1630 026, US ☎ 1-800/781-4040, Canada ☎ 1-888/427-5639, 🅦 www.statravel.co.uk, 🅦 www.statravel.com. Student and youth fares, InterRail and Eurail passes.

Svezhy Veter Russia ☎ 3412/450 037, 🅦 www. sv-agency.udm.ru. Russian travel agency with a user-friendly website in English, for international and domestic rail bookings.

The Man in Seat 61 🅦 www.seat61.com/Russia. htm. This wonderful site features virtually all the information you might need to plan a journey from London to Russia or other European countries, by train or ferry.

Trailfinders UK ☎ 0845/058 5858, Ireland ☎ 01/677 7888, Australia ☎ 1300/780 212, 🅦 www.trailfinders.com. Student discounts and advice on rail travel; agents for Eurail.

Walshes World New Zealand ☎ 09/379 3708. Agent for European railway passes and tickets.

Your Train (aka Poezda.net) 🅦 www.poezdanet/ en/. Russian rail bookings website, with timetables and other useful information, in English.

Ferry contacts

DFDS Seaways UK ☎ 0871/522 9955, 🅦 www. dfds.co.uk. Operates the *Dana Sirena* from Harwich to Esbjerg, and acts as the UK agent for Tallink-Silja Line.

Emagine Ltd UK ☎ 01942/262662, 🅦 www. emagine-travel.co.uk. Agents for Viking ferries from Stockholm to Helsinki and Helsinki to Tallinn.

Ferry Centre St Petersburg ul. Vosstaniya 19 ☎ 327 33 77, 🅦 www.paromy.ru. Russian agents for Tallink-Silja, Viking, DFDS and other Scandinavian lines.

Tallink-Silja Line 🅦 www.tallinksilja.com/en. Deluxe ferries from Stockholm to Helsinki, catamarans

from Helsinki to Tallinn, and occasional cruises to St Petersburg.

Viking Line 🅦 www.vikingline.fi. Luxury ferries between Stockholm and Helsinki and Helsinki and Tallinn.

By coach

There are no direct services from Britain to St Petersburg, nor can Eurolines in Britain book **coaches** from Berlin or Frankfurt (readily accessible from the UK by low-cost airlines). The journey will probably cost as much as flying once hidden costs are taken into account – so this approach is better suited if you're travelling around (or based on) the continent and you'd like to visit Russia and the Baltic States, but don't fancy using (or qualify for) an InterRail or Eurail pass.

Services **from Germany** to St Petersburg are operated by Eurolines Russia, an affiliate of the European-wide bus consortium Eurolines. You can book seats through their German agent, Deutsche Touring (🅦 www. touring.de), but not through their own website (🅦 www.eurolines.ru, in Russian only). Coaches leave from Berlin's central bus station (Tues & Sat at 11.55pm; 14hr; €95 one-way) and the main train stations in Frankfurt (Tues; 48hr; €120) and Stuttgart (Sat; 45hr; €130), arriving outside St Petersburg's Baltic Station.

Another, more roundabout, route is to go from Germany **via Estonia**. Eurolines Estonia (🅦 www.eurolines.ee) runs coaches to Tallinn from Berlin (daily; 26hr; €90 one-way), Munich (Sun; 35hr; €104), Frankfurt (Mon–Fri; 34hr; €104), Cologne (Thurs, Wed & Sat; 35hr; €107) and Stuttgart (Mon–Fri; 38hr; €107). From Tallinn, you can continue on to St Petersburg by coach or by train (see "Travelling from Finland, Estonia or Latvia", p.26).

A still longer route is from Germany **via Latvia**, using the Eurolines Estonia service to Rīga from Berlin (Wed & Fri; 22hr; €78 one-way), Frankfurt (Wed & Fri; 32hr; €93), Munich (Wed; 32hr; €93), Cologne (Thurs; 33hr; €93) or Stuttgart (Wed & Fri; 34hr; €96). From Rīga there's a Eurolines Russia coach to St Petersburg (see "Travelling from Finland, Estonia or Latvia", p.26).

Although coach fares are extremely cheap, you have to consider the cost of transit visas for Belarus (see box opposite), and will also need to obtain a Russian visa in advance (see p.29).

Coach contacts

See also under "Baltic travel contacts" below.

Deutsche Touring Germany ☎ 30/306 7210 or 69/4609 2780, ⊕ www.touring.de. Agents for Eurolines Russia in Germany; their multi-lingual website allows online booking.

Gosia Travel UK ☎ 020/7828 555. London agent for Ecolines services on the continent.

Travelling from Finland, Estonia or Latvia

Travelling **from Helsinki** to St Petersburg offers the widest choice of transport, and was for many years the most popular approach with those travelling around Europe **by train**. Although none of the European rail passes is valid for services to St Petersburg, the fare is reasonable: €81/ €51 one way in first/second class, with discounts for under-16s and over-60s (50/30 percent). There are two **trains** daily: the Finnish **Sibelius** (departing at 7.27am) and the Russian **Repin** (at 3.27pm) – both are comfortable and do the 350-kilometre journey in six hours, stopping at Vyborg (see p.221) en route to St Petersburg's Finland Station. Details can be found on Finnish Railways' website ⊕ www.vr.fi.

Alternatively, there are three daily **coaches** from Helsinki, operated by Finnord, Ardis and Sovavto. The three companies are represented in the main bus station by MH-Booking (☎+ 358 0 607 718) and have identical routes, stopovers and vehicles – the only difference is their livery. They leave at 9am, noon and 11pm and arrive in St Petersburg 8–9 hours later, where they stop at Finnord's office and/or the *Grand Hotel Europe* before terminating at the *Park Inn Pulkovskaya Hotel* in the southern suburbs. One-way fares range from €38–45.

Travelling **from Tallinn**, the Estonian capital, is increasingly popular with backpackers. An overnight **train** run by GoRail is the best option, departing daily at 10.25pm and arriving in St Petersburg's Vitebsk Station at 7.25am next day. Depending on the time of year the one-way fare is €33–42 in a four-bed cabin (*a coupe*), €16–22 for a seat. Bookings can be made at GoRail's office in Tallinn Station. This is a lot comfier than the 8–9hr journey on a Eurolines Russia (3 daily; €21 one-way) or Eurolines Estonia (Mon, Tues, Wed, Thurs & Fri; €25) **coach** terminating at St Petersburg's Baltic Station. Tickets for both services are sold by MootoReisi AS (☎372/680 0909) in Tallinn's bus station.

Travelling **from Rīga**, the Latvian capital, is the longest of the three journeys to St Petersburg. It takes at least fourteen hours on a Eurolines Russia (☎371/721 4080) or Ecolines (☎371/721 4512) **coach** (2–3 daily) from the bus station (where both firms have offices); the one-way fare is €23. The overnight **train** (12hr 30min), departing at 7.30pm, is a lot comfier but the one-way fare for a berth in a four-bed compartment is €78. Details can be found on the Latvian Railways website (⊕ www.ldz.lv).

Anyone approaching St Petersburg via Finland, Estonia or Latvia should be sure to obtain a **Russian visa** beforehand, as they are not issued at border crossings, and are not easily available to non-EU citizens at the Russian consulates in Helsinki, Tallinn or Rīga.

Baltic travel contacts

Ecolines St Petersburg, Podnezdnoy per. 3 ☎325 21 52, ⊕ www.ecolines.net. Operates a daily bus to/from Rīga; their office is behind Vitebsk Station, near the Ecolines bus stop on Zagorodniy prospekt (see map on p.192). Their international website allows online bookings.

Eurolines Russia St Petersburg, Admiral Business Centre, beside the Baltic Station ☎441 37 57, ⊕ www.eurolines.ru. Buses to the Baltic States and Germany, leaving from the square outside the station (see map on p.214). Website in Russian only; no online booking.

Finnord/Ardis St Petersburg, Italyanskaya ul. 37 ☎314 89 51. Ticket agents for both coach lines to Helsinki.

GoRail Tallinn, Toompuiestee 37 ☎+358 631 0043, ⊕ www.gorail.ee. Their Estonian/Russian website doesn't allow bookings, but you may be able to buy a train ticket from outside Estonia through ⊕ www.reisieksperert.ee.

Sovavto St Petersburg, Park Inn Pulkovskaya Hotel,

Belarus transit visas

All foreigners crossing Belarus by road or rail require a **transit visa**, which must be obtained in advance from a Belarus consulate abroad; ask for a double-entry visa if you're returning by the same route. You have to submit your passport with a Russian visa already in place to apply for a Belarus transit visa.

Belarus consulates

UK 6 Kensington Court, London W8 5DL ☏020/7938 3677, ⓦhttp://belembassy. org/uk. Single-/double-entry transit visa £44/£79 in 5 working days, £79/£149 in 48 hours.
US 1619 New Hampshire Ave NW, Washington, DC 20009 ☏202/986-1604; 708 Third Avenue, 21st Floor, NY 10017 ☏212/682-5392; ⓦwww.belarusembassy.org. Single/double-entry transit visa $50/$100 in 5 working days, $90/$190 in 48 hours.
Canada 130 Albert St, Suite 600, Ottawa, ON K1P 5G4 ☏613/233-9994, Ⓔbelamb@igs.net.
Australia/New Zealand No consulates; apply in Europe.

---

pl. Pobedy 1, ☏740 39 85, ⓦwww.sovavto.ru. The hotel is the terminus for all three coaches to/from Helsinki.

Coming from Moscow

Visitors taking the Trans-Siberian Railway or InterRailing around Europe will almost inevitably reach St Petersburg **from Moscow**. Of the fifteen-odd **trains** from Moscow's Okyabryskaya (formerly Leningrad) Station, the fastest are the evening *Aurora* (Wed & Sat) and trains #164 (Mon, Tues, Thurs, Fri) and #166 (Wed & Sat), which take about five hours, arriving shortly after 11pm. However, most people prefer an **overnight train** (8–9hr) arriving between six and nine o'clock next morning, namely the *Smena*, *Nikolaevskiy Express*, *Krasnaya Strela*, *Express* or *Afanasiy Nikitin*, which depart around midnight with the city hymn playing on the platform and smartly uniformed guards waving batons. Their unisex sleeping cars are overheated but otherwise comfortable, with mineral water, sweets and paper towels provided gratis. Fares on the "named" (*firmeny*) trains are around R1350 for a bed in a four-berth cabin, R2600 in a two-bed *spalniy vagon*. On "numbered" night trains you can get a bed in a four-berth cabin for as little as R750. The least crowded, most helpful booking office is at Leningradskiy prospekt 1, by the Belarus Station, which has some English-speaking staff. Bring your passport, since **tickets** are sold to named individuals only, and conductors make identity checks before allowing passengers on board. Alternatively, tickets may be ordered through any of Moscow's hostels, travel agents or hotels, for a surcharge.

Red tape and visas

Bureaucracy has always been the bane of Russia, and visas are the greatest deterrent to would-be visitors; the system seems designed to make you spend money to get round the obstacles it creates. Visas must be obtained in advance from a Russian consulate in the country where you hold citizenship or have right of residence. If you're not travelling on a package tour, this requires some kind of visa support, which is available from B&B agencies, hostels and hotels in St Petersburg for their guests, or from specialist travel agents or visa brokers abroad. Then there's the fee for the visa itself – which varies from country to country according to type of visa and the speed at which it's issued – plus an extra sum if you pay an agency to deliver and collect your documents at the consulate rather than applying by post and allowing more time for the process, or wasting time queuing in person. At the minimum, you're looking at £45/€70/$100/C$75/A$85 for a visa, and could spend a lot more if you're in a hurry. Note that children travelling on their own passports will also require a separate visa.

Visas

There are various kinds of **visa** (all in the form of a one-page sticker in your passport), and it's important to know which will suit you best. It's perfectly acceptable to use a tourist visa for a business trip, or a business visa for a vacation, if it's more convenient or works out cheaper that way. Russian officials don't care which kind you travel under providing the stated purpose of the trip matches the type of visa, all the paperwork is in order, and you don't overstay. Broadly speaking, a tourist visa is the cheapest, simplest option for a single visit of up to one month, while business visas are for those wishing to stay longer or travel back and forth without getting a new visa each time. However, regulations can (and do) change, upsetting the calculus; check consulate websites and the visa forum on Way to Russia (🌐 www.wayto-russia.net) for the latest facts.

Tourist, business, student or private visas each require some kind of supporting documentation from Russia, generically known as **visa support** – the exact form varies according to the type of visa. Most consulates accept faxed or emailed visa support for tourist and single- or double-entry business visas. Visitors on package holidays get this from their tour operator; many hotels in Russia can provide it if you make a booking with them for the duration of your stay; or local agencies can supply it for €20-30, without obliging you to stay at (or pay for) a hotel. If you're planning to stay in a flat or with friends, make sure that the **agency** providing your visa support has an office in the city where you're arriving in Russia, to register you (see "Migration cards and registration").

A single-entry **tourist visa** is valid for an exact number of days up to a maximum of thirty, covered by a tourist voucher and confirmation of pre-booked accommodation in Russia for the entire period. If you're going on a package tour, the formalities can be sorted out for you by the tour operator, though they may charge extra for this. If you're travelling independently, visa support can be provided by specialist travel agents in your own country (see "Getting there", p.22), or by some agencies, hostels and hotels in St Petersburg (fees vary; see Chapter 13, "Accommodation"). You have to email or fax them the following information: nationality, date of birth, passport number and date of expiry, length of stay at the hotel or hostel, date of arrival and departure from Russia, and credit card details. The support documentation should be faxed or emailed to you the following day (or the originals sent by post, if your consulate demands it). The procedure is essentially the same if you buy your visa support from a travel agency in Russia or online.

A single- or double-entry **business visa** (specify which you want at the outset) is valid for up to 90 days. There is no obligation to pre-book accommodation, so you can rent a flat or stay with friends if you wish. You don't have to be doing business in order to get one; you simply need to provide the consulate with a stamped letter of invitation (or fax or email in some cases) from an organization in Russia that's accredited to the MID (Ministry of Foreign Affairs) and MVD (Ministry of the Interior). There are lots of foreign and Russian travel agencies and visa brokers that can provide this for a fee. **Multi-entry** business visas valid for a year are now only issued to people who have travelled to Russia before on a single- or double-entry business visa (enclose a copy of this with your application), and only allow you to stay up to 90 days within a 180-day period.

Foreigners wishing **to live in Russia** without spending an equivalent time abroad must now leave every 90 days to obtain a new business visa in another country. Otherwise, the only solution is to obtain a Russian residence permit, or a work permit from a local employer – which isn't an option for most people – or to come here on a student or private visa. A **student visa** is issued to people who come to study at a Russian school or institution, whose "foreign department" will post or fax an invitation directly to the consulate. A **private visa** is the hardest kind to obtain, requiring a personal invitation (*izveschenie*) from your Russian host – authorized by the PVU (see p.31) – guaranteeing to look after you for the duration of your stay. A faxed copy is not acceptable, so the original has to be posted to your home country, and the whole process can take three or four months to complete. By law, foreigners wishing to stay in Russia for longer than three months must obtain a **doctor's letter** certifying that they are not HIV-positive, and submit the original with their application – make a copy to take to Russia, as the letter will not be returned by the consulate.

If you are planning only to pass through Russia en route to another country, you can apply for a **transit visa**, valid for a 72-hour stopover in one city. You'll need to show a ticket for your onward journey from Russia, and a visa for the destination country (if required).

Russian consulates abroad

Australia 78 Canberra Ave, Griffith, Canberra, ACT 2603 ☎ 02/6295 9474, ⊛ www.australia.mid.ru; 7–9 Fullerton St, Woollahra, Sydney, NSW 2025 ☎ 02/9326 1866, ⊛ www.sydneyrussianconsulate. com.

Canada 52 Range Rd, Ottawa, Ontario K1N 8J5 ☎ 613/236-7220, ⓔ ruscons@rogers.com, ⓕ 613/238-6158; 175 Bloor St East, South Tower Suite 801, Toronto, Ontario M4W 3R8 ☎ 416/962-9911, ⊛ www.toronto.mid.ru; 3655 Avenue du Musee, Montréal, Quebec H3G 2EL ☎ 514/843-5901, ⊛ www.montreal.mid.ru.

Ireland 186 Orwell Rd, Rathgar, Dublin 14 ☎ 01/492 3525, ⓔ russian@indigo.ie.

New Zealand 57 Messines Rd, Karori, Wellington ☎ 04/476 6113, ⓔ eor@netlink.co.nz.

South Africa Butano Bldg, 316 Brooks St, Menlo Park 0081, PO Box 6743, Pretoria 0001 ☎ 12/432 731.

UK 5 Kensington Palace Gdns, London W8 4QS ☎ 020/7229 8027, ⊛ www.rusemblon.org; 58 Melville St, Edinburgh EH3 7HF ☎ 0131/225 7098, ⓕ 0131/225 9587.

US 2641 Tunlaw Rd, NW, Washington, DC 20007 ☎ 202/939-8907, ⊛ www.russianembassy.org; 9 East 91st St, New York, NY 10128 ☎ 212/348-0926, ⊛ www.ruscon.com; Green St, San Francisco, CA 94123 ☎ 415/928-6878, ⊛ www.consulrussia. org; 2323 Westin Bldg, 2001 6th Ave, Seattle, WA 98121 ☎ 206/728-1910, ⓕ 206/728-187.

Applying for a visa

The current situation is that you can only apply for a visa **in the country where you hold citizenship** or a country where you can prove **right of residence** for 90 days. EU citizens can thus apply for a visa in any EU state, but will need to prove right of residence to apply in the US or Australia, as will North Americans, Australians or New Zealanders anywhere abroad. This ruling is a huge blow to Trans-Siberian tourism, and Russia chat forums are buzzing as operators try to figure out a response – see ⊛ www. waytorussia.net for advice if you are facing this difficulty.

Aside from that, your **passport** must be valid for at least six months after your intended date of departure from Russia, and contain at least one blank page for the visa to be stuck into place. Some consulates have a website with a downloadable **application form** and detailed instructions on what documents to send. Others steer you towards visa brokers, with the consulate taking a cut of the profits. Apply as far ahead as possible, because the cost of processing your application rises the faster it's done.

With all applications, you need to submit a photo (signed on the back) and your passport. Applying to the consulate rather than through a travel agent or visa broker, you'll also need to include the fee (money order only by post, or cash in person, no cheques), plus a prepaid SAE envelope (preferably registered) for postal applications. Postal applications are preferable to delivering or collecting in person, when you may have to queue for ages outside the consulate, but will add three or more days to the **visa-processing times** given below. These refer to working days (excluding weekends and Russian holidays) *after* the day on which your application is received – though at some consulates you can get a visa in 48 hours or even on the same day if you're willing to pay enough. Just be sure to submit the right documents to support your application, which can differ in small but crucial details from country to country.

In **Britain**, applications from England, Wales and Northern Ireland are handled by the London consulate; one in Edinburgh deals with Scotland. Forms can be downloaded from ⓦ www.rusemblon.org. Applications for a tourist visa require the original tourist voucher, and a fax or copy of the confirmation from an accredited Russian or foreign travel agency. Applying for a business visa, a fax or photocopy of your invitation is required, plus a letter of introduction from your employer (or yourself, if self-employed, in which case you must also submit copies of bank statements for the last three months). For a transit visa, you need to include both the original and a copy of your ticket for onward travel from Russia. The fee for a single-entry (tourist or business), double-entry or multi-entry visa is directly related to the speed of processing: £45/£55/£110 for seven working days; £95/£105/£160 for same-day processing.

With the exception of Britain, Ireland and Denmark, **other EU countries** have signed an agreement with Russia on a unified tariff, with all types of visa costing €35 for seven days processing, €70 for three days. Though some consulates nudge applicants towards a visa broker by refusing to accept postal applications, in theory these tariffs apply to EU citizens in any country, even outside the EU. Citizens of the **Schengen states** (Austria, Belgium, France, Germany, Holland, Italy, Portugal and Spain) must also fill in and submit an **insurance card** (downloadable from ⓦ www.russianvisas.org) with their application.

In the US, you must apply to the Russian consulate that has "jurisdiction" over your home state. Separate application forms for US citizens and other nationals are downloadable from ⓦ www.ruscon.com. If not delivered in person, all documents must be posted (and returned) using a certified courier. It's left to the consulate's discretion whether applicants can send a fax or photocopy of their invitation, or must submit the original – it's wiser to follow the latter course if the consulate hasn't specified. There's a flat fee of $100 for any kind of visa in six working days. Otherwise, the cost of a single-/double-/multi-entry tourist or business visa is $150/200/300 in three working days; $200/250/350 next day; and $300/350/450 for same-day issue.

In Canada, three consulates hold jurisdiction over different states, two with websites from which you can download the application form. Canadians must have three blank pages in their passport and include a photocopy of the page with their personal details. The original voucher and confirmation is required for a tourist visa, and the original invitation for a double- or multi-entry business visa. Applying by post or in person, the fee must be paid with a money order (no cash or cheques). A single-entry tourist or business visa costs C$75 in fourteen working days, C$150 in seven days, C$180 in three days, C$210 next day, and C$300 the same day. For a double-entry visa the rates are: C$100, C$175, C$205, C$235 and C$325; for a multi-entry, C$205, C$290, C$305 C$335 and C$425.

In **Australia,** copies of the tourist voucher or business invitation are okay for a single-

or double-entry visa, but multi-entry visas require the original document. A single-/double-/multi-entry visa costs A$85/A$140/A$350 in fifteen working days; A$110/A$170/A$370 in ten days; A$140/A$200/A$400 in five days; A$170/A$255/A$430 in two days; A$200/A$285/A$460 in one day; and A$400/A$485/A$600 for same-day issue.

Migration cards and registration

On arrival in Russia, foreigners must fill out a **Migration card** (*Migratsionnaya karta*) similar to the "landing card" given to non-EU citizens arriving in Europe, which will be stamped by an immigration official. Your stated reason for travel should correspond with the type of visa you are travelling under (tourism, business, etc); you also need to specify the organization that issued your invitation and your address in Russia (if you don't know, put the name of any hotel in St Petersburg). Guard the card as carefully as your passport, as you'll need to produce it when leaving Russia; make a photocopy to show if you're stopped by the police (see p.49), or lose the original.

By law, all foreigners are supposed to **register** their visa within 72 hours of arrival (excluding weekends and public holidays, but including the day when you arrive, even if this is after office hours). It used to be a stamp on your visa or Migration card, but is now a slip of paper (which should be photocopied as a precaution). Hotels are legally obliged to register guests (and may charge a small fee) however they obtained their visa support, but for those visitors who opt for homestay or flat rental only the company that issued their invitation can legally register them (and has a responsibility to do so), so it's vital that it has an office (or accredited partner) in St Petersburg. Similarly, hostels may register only guests who got their visa support from the hostel (or its partner). If renting from a private landlord, they must provide you with a letter to submit to the Passport and Visa Service or **PVU** (*Passport i Viza Upravlenie* – still universally known by its old acronym, **OVIR**), at Nevskiy prospekt 78 (☎327 30 23; Mon–Fri 9.30am–6pm), which charges R1000/R1500 to register a tourist/business visa. For more on this, see ⓦwww.waytorussia.net.

While not registering within the 72-hour limit is an infringement for which the police can detain you up to three hours and/or fine you R1000 (under Federal Law #195-FZ, Article 18.3), officers have been known to try to extort more during ID checks (see p.48). The easiest way to get belatedly registered is to check into a hotel for one night. This might not cover your whole time in Russia, but at least you'll have some evidence of registration. Some tourist agencies may be willing to register you for up to 30 days at a fictitious address for around R600. When it comes to leaving Russia, immigration officials may not even bother asking for your registration slip – but there are enough tales of people being stopped, fined or missing their plane to make it wise to get properly registered.

Currency declaration and customs

Another form available at the airport and border crossings is the **currency declaration**, for listing valuables brought into and out of Russia. You don't need one and can simply walk through the Green customs channel unless you're carrying over $3000 in cash, in which case you must declare it on a form and get it stamped going through the Red channel. This also goes if you're travelling with hypodermic needles, bring a prescription for them and declare them under "Narcotics and appliances for use thereof". GPS devices may not be brought into Russia.

Export controls change so frequently that even customs officials aren't sure how things stand. The main restriction is on exporting antiques and contemporary art, though it's unclear where they draw the line between artwork and souvenirs (which aren't liable to controls). However, you can be fairly sure of encountering problems if you try to take out antique icons, samovars, porcelain or jewellery. Permission to export contemporary art and antiques (anything pre-1960, in effect) must be applied for to the Ministry of Culture at Malaya Morskaya ul.17 (Mon–Fri 11am–2pm; ☎ & ⑨571 03 02), but you would be advised to ask the seller to do the paperwork for you, if possible. If the export is approved, you can be liable for tax of up to one hundred percent of the object's value. Pre-1960 books must be approved by the Russian National Library, using the entrance on Sadovaya ulitsa by the cross-roads with Nevskiy prospekt (Tues 3–6pm, Thurs 4–6pm & Fri 10am–noon).

Health

Visitors to St Petersburg are advised to get booster-shots for diphtheria, polio and tetanus, but there's no need to be inoculated against typhoid and hepatitis A unless you're planning to visit remote rural areas. Though there's no danger of malaria, mosquitoes can be fierce during the summer months, so a mosquito net or a locally available repellent is advisable. The most likely hazard for a visitor, however, is an upset stomach or the disruption of their biorhythms during the midsummer White Nights.

Giardia and heavy metals

St Petersburg's water supply is extracted from the polluted River Neva, and its anti-quated filtration plants are unable to deliver tap water free of the parasitic bacteria **Giardia lamblia** (to which the locals are largely immune). To avoid giardia, use only bottled water for drinking and cleaning your teeth, or use tap water that has been boiled for fifteen minutes. If ingested, giardia may cause acute diarrhoea, which should be treated with 200mg of Metronidazole (Flagyl) three times daily for fourteen days. In Russia this drug is called Trikapol and comes in 250mg tablets; it's used by Russians for treating body lice, so you may get a funny look when you ask for it in a pharmacy.

Also present in the water supply are **heavy metals** such as lead, cadmium and mercury. Brief exposure to these substances shouldn't do you any harm, but long-term residents may suffer from skin complaints and apathy as a result. Simply boiling the water is not enough: you need to leave it to stand for a day and avoid drinking the dregs. If you're staying for a long period of time, a proper water filter makes life easier; imported models are sold all over town. Alternatively, you can buy spring water in five-litre bottles from most food stores, and bottled mineral water is available everywhere.

Mosquitoes and ticks

St Petersburg's waterlogged basements are an ideal reservoir for **mosquitoes** (*komari*), present throughout the year in most buildings and particularly noxious in summer. The best solution for a good night's sleep is to bring a mosquito net, but, failing that, you should invest in an anti-mosquito device that plugs into an electric plug socket (known by the generic name of Raptor), which is sold at local pharmacies, supermarkets and household goods shops.

More seriously, forested areas such as the Karelian Isthmus beyond St Petersburg are potentially infested with encephalitis-bearing **ticks** (*kleshy*) during May and June. Russians take care to cover their heads, shoulders and arms at this time of year when walking in forests, so you should do the same or, failing that, check all over your body (particularly your neck and shoulders) for signs of burrowing ticks. If you find them, press around the tick's head with tweezers, grab it and gently pull outwards; avoid pulling the rear of the body or smearing chemicals on the tick, which increases the risk of infection and disease.

White Nights, bootleg liquor and sexually transmitted diseases

Anyone coming in June or July is liable to be affected by the famous **White Nights**. The sun barely dips below the horizon for a few hours, so the sunlight is still strong at ten in the evening and a pearly twilight lasts through the small hours of the night, playing havoc with your body clock. Locals are used to it and revel in the annual shift to a 24-hour consciousness, but newly arrived foreigners often find it hard to pace themselves when the general attitude is "Let's party!" If you're here for only a few days it's OK to burn the candle at both ends, but anyone staying for a week or longer will inevitably make deep inroads into their sleep-account. This particularly applies to young children, who may find it impossible to sleep when they should, with sunlight streaming in through the thin curtains of hotels or flats.

If you drink alcohol, it's hard to avoid the national drink, vodka – and frankly, you can't hope to relate to Russia without at least one vodka-fuelled evening with Russians. Getting drunk and speaking *dushe po-dushe* (soul-to-soul) goes with the territory. Unfortunately, so does **bootleg liquor** – a hazard that can be avoided by following the advice on p.341.

Torrid White Nights, vodka and a rampant sex industry make St Petersburg one of the most hedonistic cities on earth. Just keep in mind that the large number of intravenous drug users and prostitutes has made it Russia's worst nexus of **AIDS/HIV**, so you would be rash to have any sexual encounter without using a condom. In the event of being found to be HIV-positive or carrying an infectious disease such as syphilis or hepatitis, you risk being incarcerated in a locked isolation ward and treated like a subhuman. If you suspect you're infected, seek treatment outside Russia.

Pharmacies, doctors and hospitals

For minor complaints, it's easiest to go to a high-street **pharmacy** (*apteka*), which stocks a wide range of Western and Russian products; most are open daily from 8am to 9pm and identifiable by the green cross sign. It goes without saying, however, that if you are on any prescribed medication, you should bring enough supplies for your stay. This is particularly true for diabetics, who should ensure that they have enough needles.

The standard of **doctors** varies enormously, so seek recommendations from friends or acquaintances before consulting one. Some Russian specialists are highly skilled diagnosticians who charge far less for a private consultation than you'd pay in the West, while private dentistry is so much cheaper that savvy foreigners often get their teeth fixed while they're here.

If your condition is serious, public **hospitals** will provide free emergency treatment to foreigners on production of a passport (but may charge for medication). However, standards of hygiene and care are low compared with those in the West and horror stories abound. Aside from routine shortages of anaesthetics and drugs, nurses are usually indifferent to their patients unless bribed to care for them properly. Long-term expats advise, "Get an interpreter first, then a doctor." On the whole, however, foreigners rely on private **clinics** (see below) with imported drugs and equipment, and American-standard charges – a powerful reason to take out insurance. As a last resort, Helsinki is only an hour's flight or six hours' drive from St Petersburg. Many foreign clinics have their own ambulances, and can arrange medical evacuations. For a public **ambulance phone** ☏03 and demand "*Skoraya pomosh*" – the more urgent you sound, the better the chance of a speedy response.

Healthcare in St Petersburg

American Medical Clinic nab. reki Moyki 78 ☏740 20 90, ⓦwww.amclin.ru; Sadovaya metro. All medical and dental services; family practice; medical evacuation. Daily 24hr.

Euromed Suvorovskiy pr. 60 ☏327 03 01, ⓦwww.euromed.ru; Ploshchad Vosstaniya metro. Family practice, dental and emergency. Direct billing to major European insurance companies. Daily 24hr.

Medem International Clinic & Hospital ul. Marata 6 ☏336 33 33, ⓦwww.medem.ru; Mayakovskaya metro. Full service medical and dental clinic with family practice and direct billing to insurance companies. Daily 24hr.

Medi Clinic Nevskiy pr. 82 ☏777 00 00, ⓦwww. emedi.ru; Mayakovskaya metro. Dentistry, cosmetic and corrective eye surgery. Daily 8am–10pm.

Petropharm Nevskiy pr. 22 ☏314 54 01, Nevskiy Prospket/Gostiniy Dvor metro. Downtown branch of a city-wide chain of pharmacies, open 24hr.

Information

Russian tourist offices abroad are few in number and poorly stocked with maps and brochures, and St Petersburg's local tourist office is not much better. If you want to do some research or whet your appetite for the city before you go, it's worth checking out the various websites below.

St Petersburg's **City Tourist Information Centre** (Mon–Sat 10am–7pm; ☎310 288 22) has a walk-in pavilion near the Hermitage (see map on. p.80), where you can pick up a free copy of *The Official City Guide* and/or *St Petersburg In Your Pocket* and a map of the city. Staff might be willing to delve into their ledgers to supply information that's not in these publications, or may simply refer you to their head office at Sadovaya ulitsa 14/52 (same hours), which is even less used to bestirring itself. For all their bragging about strategic plans for tourist development, the city's bureaucrats seem incapable of setting up a user-friendly tourist office.

Alternatively, there's the old standby of using the service desks at such downtown hotels as the *Astoria, Radisson SAS Royal* and the *Grand Hotel Europe* – or their counterparts at St Petersburg's hostels (for addresses, see Chapter 13) – which are usually willing to help out even if you're not staying there.

The best source of information about what's on are local **publications** such as *St Petersburg in Your Pocket* (updated monthly), *The Official City Guide* (bimonthly), the twice-weekly *St Petersburg Times* and the monthly magazines *Where St Petersburg* and *Pulse*, available for free at hotels, clubs and restaurants frequented by foreigners. If you can read Russian, it's worth checking out the monthly listings magazines *Afisha*, *Vash Dosug* and *Time Out Peterburg*, which are sold at newspaper kiosks.

Websites

There are myriad **websites** about Russia; the trick is finding ones that are up to date, relevant and accurate. Official **tourist sites** are often hijacked, left untouched for years, or change address without leaving a link to the new site. This leaves the field clear for sites belonging to tourist agencies and hotels, which have more of an interest in providing up-to-date info – though this can't be taken for granted. Commercial tourist sites such as ⓦhttp://petersburgcity.com, ⓦwww.inyourpocket.com, ⓦwww.spbtourguide.com and ⓦwww.waytorussia.net may not be perfect, but by visiting them all you can get an idea of the city, panoramic views, practical info, hotel discount rates, special offers, weather reports, and diverse links. Details of **what's on** in the city can be obtained from the *St Petersburg Times* website (ⓦwww.sptimes.ru), but aside from a few flagship institutions, such as the Mariinskiy Theatre (ⓦwww.mariinsky.ru), the Hermitage (ⓦwww.hermitagemuseum.org) and Russian Museum (ⓦwww.rusmuseum.ru), it is rare for the English-language version of any museum or concert hall website to be up to date – whereas the Russian version is likely to be. For some **historical perspective**, check out ⓦwww.alexanderpalace.org, a lavishly illustrated historical site devoted to the Imperial palaces and the Romanov dynasty.

Arrival

Most visitors arrive by air and enter the city via a grand Stalinist thoroughfare that whets your appetite for the historic centre. If you're not being met at the airport, the taxi ride will be your first introduction to Russian-style haggling and driving. Arriving by coach from Helsinki, you'll cross Petrograd Side and the River Neva – another scenic curtain-raiser. The sea approach holds some appeal, with vistas of shipyards as you steam towards the Sea Terminal on Vasilevskiy Island, or the Neva basin in the heart of the city. Arriving by train, you'll be pitched straight into things.

Airports

Pulkovo-2, St Petersburg's **international airport** (☎704 34 44), is 17km south of the city centre. Exchange some cash or make an ATM withdrawal before leaving the terminal so you have enough rubles to get into town. The cheapest method (R15–20) is a **bus** (#113, #213) or **minibus** (#3, #13, #113), running every 15 minutes until midnight to Moskovskaya metro, from where you can continue your journey. Alternatively, there's the 24-hour **Pulkovo Express** bus (R70), terminating at Pushkinskaya metro (Vitebsk Station), nearer the centre.

If you have a lot of luggage or don't feel up to dealing with public transport immediately, most hotels or hostels will meet guests at the airport by prior arrangement; some do so for free if you book three nights' stay. Otherwise you're at the mercy of licensed or unofficial **taxis** (see p.38), whose drivers ask anything from R1500/€45/$50; R750/€35/$45 is fair for a ride into the centre, but be sure to agree the price beforehand. A cheaper option is to take a bus or minibus to Moskovskaya metro and then a taxi from there into the centre (about R200).

Should you fly in from Moscow, you'll arrive at **Pulkovo-1**, the **domestic airport** (☎704 38 22), 15km south of the city, served by the Pulkovo Express (see above) and minibus #39, which stops at Moskovskaya metro, Moscow Station and the *Moskva Hotel* (see p.332) before terminating at Ladoga Station. Taxi fares are much the same as from Pulkovo-2.

In the future, passengers may find themselves using **Pulkovo-3** airport (cur- rently under construction) and may be able to travel into the city **by metro** (if the new over-ground line gets the go ahead).

Leaving St Petersburg

When leaving St Petersburg, allow plenty of time to get to the international airport in order to arrive at least an hour and a half before your flight is scheduled to depart. Give yourself at least an hour from the centre, using the Pulkovo Express or any of the buses or minibuses from Moskovskaya metro (see above).

Check-in opens ninety minutes before take-off for Western airlines and two hours before for Aeroflot flights; desks close forty minutes before departure. Luggage and passengers are scanned *before* entering the check-in hall, and may have to queue for thirty minutes in order to get through. Beyond lies passport control and a final cus- toms check; if you filled in a customs decla- ration and went through the Red channel on arrival (see p.31) you'll have to do the same on departure. Pulkovo-2 is non-smoking throughout – once you enter the terminal, there won't be a chance to light-up until you arrive at your destination.

Train stations

St Petersburg's train stations are linked to the city centre by a fast, efficient metro system, and named after the direction from which trains arrive. Trains from Moscow pull into **Moscow Station** (Moskovskiy vokzal), halfway down Nevskiy prospekt, one stop from the downtown area by way of the metro interchange Ploshchad Vosstaniya/ Mayakovskaya. Coming from Tallinn or Rīga you'll arrive at the **Baltic Station** (Baltiyskiy vokzal) beside the Obvodniy Canal and Baltiyskaya metro, while trains from Berlin or Warsaw end up at **Vitebsk Station** (Vitebskiy vokzal), near Pushkinskaya metro. Trains from Helsinki now once again terminate at the historic **Finland Station** (Finlyandskiy vokzal), served by Ploshchad Lenina metro, having for some years used the **Ladoga Station** (Ladozhskiy vokzal) east of the Neva – linked to the centre by Ladozhskaya metro – which handles trains from Northern Russia. All these mainline stations have exchange offices and/or ATMs.

Bus terminals

Eurolines Russia and Eurolines Estonia coaches from Germany, Estonia and Latvia terminate on the square outside the **Baltic Station** (Baltiyskaya metro), near the Eurolines office (see map on p.214); Ecolines services from Riga and points west outside the **Vitebsk Station** (Pushkinskaya metro); and Finnord, Ardis and Sovavto coaches from Finland drop passengers at the Finnord/Ardis office at Italyanskaya ulitsa 37 and the *Grand Hotel Europe* or *Astoria Hotel* in the centre, before terminating at the **Park Inn** *Pulkovskaya Hotel* in the Southern Suburbs (see map, p.214). Buses from other Russian cities such as Novgorod arrive at the **Bus Station** (Avtovokzal) near the Obvodniy Canal (see map, p.214). To reach the centre from there, walk a few blocks west (left) along the canal to catch a taxi (R150) or any minibus up Ligovskiy prospekt, alighting either at the metro station of the same name, or further north at Ploshchad Vosstaniya metro, beside Moscow Station.

Cruise boat moorings

Some Baltic cruise boats dock at the **Sea Terminal** (Morskoy vokzal) on the Gulf coast of Vasilevskiy Island, 4km west of the centre (R200–300 by taxi, or minibus #151 to Vasileostrovskaya metro and continue from there). Other, upmarket cruise ships moor in the **Neva basin** instead – usually within fifteen minutes' walk of the Winter Palace, off the Angliyskaya naberezhnaya to the west of the Admiralty, or near the Mining Institute on the other side of the Neva. Just make sure your boat isn't docking in the **shipyards** of the Narva district; taxis aren't allowed inside the gates and there's no public transport into the centre. If you come on a river cruise from Moscow, you'll disembark at the **River Terminal** (Rechnoy vokzal) on prospekt Obukhovskoy oborony, five minutes' walk from Proletarskaya metro, which can take you into the city centre.

City transport and tours

St Petersburg is a big city, which means that sooner or later you're going to want to make use of its cheap, efficient public transport system. As well as the fast metro network, there are minibuses, buses, trolleybuses and trams (in that order of usefulness). Taxis are likely to prove expensive if you don't negotiate a price at the outset. In the city centre during rush hour, you may well make faster progress on foot.

Tickets

On buses, trams and trolleybuses, **tickets** (*talony*) are sold by the conductor (or the driver on commercial vehicles); with a **flat** fare on all routes, there's no need to state your destination. Retain your ticket in case of plainclothes inspectors, who can fine you R150 for travelling without a ticket. On minibuses you simply pay the driver; no ticket is issued.

The system on the **metro** is different, insofar as you can either buy metro **tokens** (*zhetony*) from the cashier (each token is valid for one journey, with as many changes of line as you wish), or various kinds of magnetic **cards**. A *proezdnoy bilet* valid for ten, twenty or sixty journeys within a thirty-day period is a worthwhile investment for short-term visitors, to avoid queuing for tokens all the time. A monthly *yediniy bilet* (valid for the metro, buses, trams and trolleybuses) is only worth it if used extensively, and doesn't cover minibuses. Passengers touch them to the scan-disc aboard vehicles, or on the turnstiles in metro stations.

Although **fares** are liable to increase in line with inflation, public transport is still affordable for the locals and great value for tourists. A metro *zheton* costs R14, a thirty-ride *proezdnoy bilet* R480, a minibus ride in town R14–20 and a trip to Peterhof or other suburban destinations R40–70.

The metro

St Petersburg's metro is the deepest in the world, due to the city's many rivers and swampy subsoil. Its former name, "The Leningrad Metro in the name of Lenin with the Order of Lenin", gives you an idea of the pride that accompanied its construction, which began in the 1930s. There are four **lines** (see the colour map at the back of this book) covering over 100km, with some sixty stations. Outlying stations are still being constructed, and there are plans to build an entirely new over-ground line linking Obukhovo and Prospekt Veteranov metro stations with Pulkovo airport, Petrodvorets (Peterhof) and Pushkin (Tsarskoe Selo).

Stations are marked with a large "M" and have separate doors for incoming and outgoing passengers. Most carriages and stations now feature bilingual route maps, but all other signs are in the Cyrillic alphabet; the metro map in this book gives the Cyrillic characters for each station and common signs you'll encounter on the metro.

The network covers most parts of the city you're likely to visit, except for the Smolniy district and the western end of the downtown area within the Fontanka. Depending on the line, trains run daily from 6am till midnight or slightly later, with **services** every one to two minutes during peak periods (8–10am and 5–7.30pm), and every three to five minutes at night. Note, however, that certain underground walkways linking crucial **interchange stations** may close earlier – in particular, between Mayakovskaya and Ploshchad Vosstaniya, or Gostiniy Dvor and Nevskiy prospekt. Where two lines intersect, the station may have two **separate names**, one for each line, or, alternatively, be numbered (as at Tekhnologicheskiy Institut or Ploshchad Aleksandra Nevskovo stations). To change lines you must follow the переход signs up or down an escalator or along a passageway, except at Tekhnologicheskiy Institut, where the two southbound lines are on parallel platforms (as are the northbound ones), so you simply cross the central concourse.

Owing to the depth of most stations, almost nobody walks up the vertiginous **escalators,** although the left-hand side is designated for that purpose. The older lines boast a system of "horizontal lifts", whereby the **platforms** are separated from the tracks by automatic doors that open in alignment with those of the incoming trains – a bit of Stalinist wizardry that's been abandoned on the newer lines. Many of the station vestibules and platforms are notable for their **decor**, especially those on the downtown section of the Kirovsko–Vyborgskaya line, adorned with marble, granite, bas-reliefs and mosaics. It's worth travelling almost to the end of the line to see the glass columns at Avtovo station.

Since the platforms carry few signs indicating which station you are in, it's advisable to pay attention to the Tannoy **announcements** (in Russian only) in the carriages. As the train pulls into each station, you'll hear its name, followed by the words *Sleduyush-chaya stantsiya* – and then the name of the *next* station. Most importantly, be sure to heed the words *Ostorózhno, dvery zakry-vayutsya* – "Caution, doors closing" – since they slam shut with great force. Should anyone ask if you are getting off at the next stop – *Vy vykhodite?* – it means that they are, and need to squeeze past.

Minibuses

Minibuses (*marshrutnoe taxi* or *marshrutki*) are the most useful form of surface transport. Faster than buses, trolleybuses or trams, they carry only as many passengers as there are seats; can be flagged down at designated bus stops, or drop you off at any point along their route (tell the driver *ostanavites, pazhalsta*). Handiest for tourists are the **#187** – running the length of Nevskiy prospekt, past Gostiniy dvor and the Hermitage and on to the university on Vasilevskiy Island – and services to the outlying Imperial palaces from metro stations in the southern suburbs.

Minibuses carry a Cyrillic **signboard** listing their termini and the main points (and metro stations) along the route, and are usually numbered. The **prefix K-** indicates that the minibus is operated by a private company, whose fares are slightly higher than on municipal services. While some minibuses follow the same route as buses with an identical number, don't assume this to be the case. The most useful *marshrutka* routes are listed where appropriate in the text.

Buses, trams and trolleybuses

Visitors have less reason to use the city's overcrowded buses, trolleybuses and trams – the last being the slowest of the lot – with the exception of a few **scenic routes** for sightseeing (if not during rush hour). **Bus #22** crosses the city from the Smolniy Institute via St Isaac's Cathedral to the Marriinsky Theatre, while the **#46** from Marsovo pole runs up Kamennoostrovskiy prospekt to Kammeniy Island, on the Petrograd Side. Trolleybuses still run along Nevskiy prospekt – unlike trams – and offer some convenient routes across the Neva; for example, **trolleybus #10** runs from ploshchad Vosstaniya through the city centre and across Vasilevskiy Island to Primorskaya metro. **Trams** are being phased out in the centre, but the **#3** still offers an interesting ride along Sadovaya ulitsa, from the Summer Garden to the Haymarket district, and on April 15 a special memorial tram **#0** runs from Finland Station, along Liteyniy prospekt and through the centre, to commemorate the resumption of services after the first winter of the Siege of Leningrad.

Stops are relatively few and far between, so getting off at the wrong one can mean a lengthy walk. Bus stops are marked with an "A" (for *avtobus*); trolleybus stops with what resembles a squared-off "m", but is in fact a handwritten Cyrillic "t" (for *trolleybus*). Both are usually attached to walls, and therefore somewhat inconspicuous, whereas the signs for tram stops (bearing a "T", for *tramvay*), are suspended from the overhead cables above the road.

Taxis

St Petersburg's traditional **official taxis** – yellow Volgas – are being edged out by private firms with newer foreign cars in diverse liveries – but two rules still apply. Never get into a cab without agreeing the fare (nobody uses meters), and don't take a taxi parked in front of a hotel, restaurant or tourist attraction (walk down the road to find a cab). To avoid the "taxi mafia" at the airport, arrange a car before you arrive.

Many locals don't bother with official taxis at all – a habit dating back to Soviet times – instead **hitching rides in private vehicles**, whose drivers earn money as *chastniki* (moonlighters). You simply stand on the kerb and flag down any likely looking vehicle heading in the right direction. When one stops, state your destination and what you're willing to pay ("*Mozhno* [say the destination] *za* [say the sum in rubles] *rubley?*"); the driver may haggle a bit, but R200–300 should get you to most places in the centre. Don't get into a vehicle which has more than one person in it, and never accept lifts from anyone who approaches you. Women travelling alone would be best advised to give the whole business a miss.

Taxi companies

Svetlana ☎702 14 14, ⊛www.taxi-svetlana.spb.ru.
Taxi Blues ☎271 88 88, ⊛www.taxiblues.ru.

Driving

You don't really need a **car** in St Petersburg, since public transport is cheap and efficient. Traffic is heavy and many Russian motorists act like rally drivers, swerving at high speed to avoid potholes and tramlines. Bear in mind also that some drivers are likely to have purchased their licence, rather than passed a test. Driving yourself therefore requires a fair degree of skill and nerve.

To drive a car in St Petersburg you are required to carry with you all of the following **documents**: your home driving licence and an international driving permit with a Russian-language insert (available from motoring organizations); an insurance certificate from your home insurer, or from your travel company; your passport and visa; the vehicle registration certificate; and a customs document asserting that you'll take the car back home when you leave (unless, of course, you rented it in St Petersburg).

Petrol (*benzin*) is cheaper than in Western Europe. Foreign cars require 95 octane (4-star) or 98 octane (premium), but most Russian models use 92 octane (3-star) fuel. Lead-free petrol and high-octane fuel suitable for cars fitted with catalytic converters are sold at Neste-Petro and BP service stations, which take major credit cards as well as rubles. At all gas stations, you pay before filling up. If you **break down**, 24-hour emergency repairs or tow-away is provided by A24 (☎320 90 00), Avtoliga (☎326 00 00, ⓦwww.avtoliga.info) and LAT (☎001).

Rules of the road – and the GIBDD

Rules and regulations are often ignored unless there are traffic cops around. Traffic coming from the right, or onto roundabouts, has **right of way**, while **left turns** are only allowed in areas indicated by a broken centre line in the road, and an overhead sign. If you are turning into a side street, pedestrians crossing the road have right of way. **Trams** have right of way at all times, and you are not allowed to overtake them when passengers are getting on and off, unless there is a safety island.

Unless otherwise specified, **speed limits** are 60km (37 miles) per hour in the city and 80km (50 miles) per hour on highways. It is illegal to drive after having consumed *any* **alcohol** – the rule is stringently enforced, with heavy fines for offenders. **Safety-belt** use is mandatory (though many Russians only drape the belt across their lap, and drivers may be insulted if you belt up), and **crash helmets** are obligatory for motorcyclists. Take extra care when driving in **winter**

(between Oct and March), when snow and ice make for hazardous road conditions.

Rules are enforced by the **GIBDD**, a branch of the Militia (see p.49) recognizable by their white plastic wands tipped with a light, which they flourish to signal drivers to pull over. Empowered to levy on-the-spot fines, they're notorious for regarding drivers as a source of income. If you're unlucky enough to get fined, it's easier to pay there and then: if not, you'll have to surrender your licence and reclaim it when you pay at the local police station. Unless your Russian is fluent it's better not to argue, but concentrate on negotiating a lower fine.

Vehicle crime is on the increase and Western cars are a favourite target – never leave anything visible or valuable in your car. Guarded parking (*avtostoyanka*) is available at all top hotels (free for guests) and in many locations around the city centre.

Car rental

If you have Russian friends or acquaintants, asking around may well get you a car with a driver for less than you'd pay for self-drive hire at a car rental agency. A foreign car is preferable to a Russian one if you're driving yourself. Many rental agencies insist on payment by credit card and require the full range of documentation (see above) for self-drive rental. The only international agencies represented in St Petersburg are Hertz and Avis, which have desks at the *Grand Hotel Europe* and the *Moskva Hotel*.

Local rental agencies

Avis pl. Aleksandra Nevskovo, Moskva Hotel, ☎600 12 13. Mercedes, Opals and Skodas for rent, with or without driver; also hires sat-nav devices and child seats.

Avto-Izyumoff ul. Lizy Chaykinoy 10, Petrograd Side ☎716 76 75, ⓦwww.easymove.ru. Cars, limos and minibuses, with or without drivers.

Hertz Malaya Morskaya ul. 23 ☎326 45 05; Pulkovo-1 and -2 airports. Cars with or without driver. CCs only (Amex, Visa, MC, DC, JCB).

Rex Konyushennaya pl. 2, office 206 ☎320 66 62, ⓦwww.relux.spb.ru. Mercedes cars and minibuses with drivers.

Beware of the bridges

Whether travelling by car or on foot, you should always bear in mind that, between early April and mid-November, the **Neva bridges** are raised late at night to allow ships to pass through, severing the islands from the mainland. It's a spectacular sight as they swing open, and one that draws many spectators to the embankments during the White Nights. Always allow an extra five minutes if aiming to get across a bridge, as they can open or close early and there is invariably a crush of cars waiting to race across during the brief interval that some of them come down again. Conversely, they may stay open all night if there's a naval holiday or too many ships. For up-to-date **information** on bridge opening hours (in Russian), phone ☎063 (8am–10pm).

Birzhevoy most 2–4.55am.
Blagoveshenskiy most 1.25–2.45am & 3.10–5am.
Dvortsoviy most 1.25–4.35am.
Grenaderskiy most 2.45–3.45am & 4.20–4.50am.
Liteyniy most 1.40–4.45am.
Most Aleksandra Nevskovo 2.20–5.10am.
Most Petra Velikovo 2–5am.
Sampsonievskiy most 2.10–2.45am & 3.20–4.25am.
Troitskiy most 1.40–4.50am.
Tuchkov most 2–2.55am & 3.35–4.55am.
Volodarskiy most 2–3.45am & 4.15–5.45am.

Cycling

Cycling is seen in Russia as more of a leisure activity than a means of transport, and St Petersburg's potholed roads, tramlines, manic motorists and air pollution are enough to put most people off, but the picture isn't all bleak. The Kirov Islands (see Chapter 5) are relatively car-free and a pleasure to cycle around; every Friday night there's a **mass bike ride** across the city, starting from Dvortsovaya ploshchad at 11pm; and there are **bike tours** from late May until mid-autumn. BikeTour's Sunday morning guided tour in English takes in Smolniy, Kresty Prison, the Cruiser Aurora and St Isaac's Cathedral (R800 including bike), or you can **rent** a bike with an mp3 player (R400) from Velocity for a self-guided tour. Riders with more stamina might cycle to Tsarskoe Selo (25km), which is agreeably rural once you get beyond Pulkovo airport. You can carry your bike aboard the train for the journey back to St Petersburg. If you're leaving your bike somewhere, be sure to secure it with a Kryptonite or other U-shaped lock, rather than just a chain and padlock.

Bike tours and rental

BikeTour Goncharnaya ul. 7 ☎717 68 38, ⓦwww. biketour.spb.ru. A joint venture by Skat Prokat (see below) and Peter's Walking Tours (see p.42), their tour starts at the above address, just off pl. Vosstaniya, at 10.30am on Sun.

Skat Prokat Goncharnaya ul. 7 ☎717 68 38, ⓦwww.skatprokat.ru. This shop rents mountain bikes (R400 plus R3000/R6000 deposit with/without documents), does repairs, sells second-hand bikes, and takes online bookings.

Velocity Nevskiy pr.3 (in the yard) ☎922 63 83, ⓦwww.velocity-spb.ru. Rents bikes, maps and mp3 players for self-guided tours (R4500 deposit); close to Dvortsovaya ploshchad for the mass bike ride and open all night Fri & Sat.

Tours

Cycling aside, there are heaps of other **tours** available, covering all the main attractions inside and outside the city, plus more esoteric themed tours. Price-wise, there's generally a big difference between the regular scheduled tours aimed at Russian tourists – which are OK for sightseeing the city or reaching one of the Imperial palaces provided you've got your own guidebook – and the excursions arranged for foreigners, which are usually a lot dearer, and booked for groups or individuals on an ad hoc basis.

Coach tours

Local tourist agencies offer **coach tours** of the city and its environs, with commentary in Russian. The most accessible have kiosks outside Gostiniy dvor on Nevskiy prospekt (see p.70), where you can compare schedules and prices and buy tickets (the addresses given below are for the firms' offices). All tours depart from Dumskaya ulitsa, beside Gostiniy dvor (see map on p.65). City sightseeing tours (*obzornaya ekskursiya*) run more or less hourly, day and night, for around R300. Aside from days when the site is closed there are 6–8 tours daily to Peterhof (R1200–1400), Oranienbaum (R650–850), Gatchina (R750–850), Tsarskoe Selo (R1200–1660), Pavlovsk (R800–1000), and the last two combined (R1600–1850); plus once or twice a week to Schlisselburg (R600–750), Kronstadt (R400–600), Vyborg (R700–900) and Novgorod (R750–1000). Two firms also run tours **in English**: Eclectica-Guide's 90-minute **city tour** costs R550, and its excursions to Peterhof and Tsarskoe Selo R1880 each, while Davranov Travel does a two-hour city tour for R500 plus R300 an hour for an interpreter. Except for city tours the price should include some if not all **admission tickets**, for which foreigners pay more than Russians do (see "Museums", p.55).

Tour operators

Baltia Tour Kuznechniy per. 3, office 3 ☏ 575 80 00, ⓦ www.baltia-tour.spb.ru. Some of the cheapest coach tours to the Imperial palaces, Kronstadt, Vyborg and Novgorod.
Davranov Travel Italyanskaya ul. 17 ☏ 571 86 94, ⓦ www.davranovtravel.ru. A wide range of tours at slightly higher than average prices, including a city tour in English.
Eclectica-Guide Nevskiy pr. 44, office 3 ☏ 710 55 29, ⓦ www.eclectica-guide.ru. A city tour, Tsarskoe Selo and Peterhof in English, plus many other excursions in Russian.
Paritet Plus Nevskiy pr. 44, office 11 ☏ 710 59 43, ⓦ www.paritetplus.com. Cheap tours, in Russian only.

Boat tours

One of the pleasures of St Petersburg is cruising its waterways, navigable from mid-May till late September. **Cruises** vary in length from 45–90 minutes and may travel the River Moyka, the Griboedov Canal or the River Fontanka as far west as New Holland,

or the grand Neva basin from Vasilevskiy Island to the cruiser *Aurora*. With the large **enclosed boats** that Russians call *kater* (cutters), the view is better if you sit outdoors on the stern deck. For a 90-minute **tour in English** (R400), track down Anglo Tourismo on the Fontanka (see map, p.62), whose boats sail at noon and 8.30pm, with a **night cruise** (R450) at 12.30am to see the Neva bridges being raised. If you don't mind commentary in Russian, other firms run trips (R300–400) departing at 30-minute intervals from 11.30am to 8pm (till the small hours during the White Nights). You'll find them north of Kazanskiy most and south of Politeyskiy most just off Nevskiy prospekt (see map, p.62); at the Lion Quay near the Admiralty (see map, p.94); the Commandant's Pier of the Peter and Paul Fortress (see map, p.170); and the Strelka embankment near the Kunstkammer (see map, p.155).

Alternatively, you can rent a small motorboat, advertised as **water-taxis**, from the moorings alongside Politseyskiy most or Kazanskiy most. You hire the entire boat (plus driver) for a negotiable sum: R1000–1500 an hour according to the size of the boat (4–10 passengers). The route can be flexible, there's no commentary and you can bring along booze and caviar to complete the experience. Boats can be booked in advance by paying a small deposit, but are easily engaged at a whim. If you go boating at night, stick to the canals rather than cruising the Neva basin, where collisions with larger ships are possible, especially in the not completely unlikely event that your motorboat captain happens to be drunk.

Other operators run **hydrofoils** (known as *Raket* or *Meteor*) from the Hermitage pier near the Winter Palace (see map, p.63) across the Gulf of Finland to Peterhof (see p.240) and Strelna (see p.235). Day **excursions** by hydrofoil from the Finland Station pier to Schlisselburg (p.297) and from the Angliyskaya naberezhnaya pier to Valaam (p.302) are also feasible.

Tour operators

Alien Shipping Angliyskaya nab. 4 ☏ 327 54 54, ⓦ www.alienshipping.ru (in Russian only). Day-excursions by hydrofoil to Valaam.
Anglo Tourismo nab. reki Fontanki 64, 400m

south of Anichkov most ☏ mobile 7921/989 4722, ✉ anglotourismo@yahoo.com. Twice-daily canal tours in English and a night cruise on the Neva, with reductions for students.

AstraMarine Admiralteyskaya nab. 2 (Lion Quay) ☏ 320 08 77, ✆ www.boattrip.ru. Canal tours, boats to Peterhof and cruises in the Gulf of Finland, slightly dearer at weekends, with reductions for children and students.

Driver Admiralteyskaya nab. 2 (Lion Quay); Commandant's Pier (Peter and Paul Fortress); Universitetskaya nab. 3 (Kunstkammer) ☏ 716 58 86. You can catch four different river and canal cruises from any of their three piers.

Russian Cruises Nevskiy pr. 51, 2nd floor ☏ 325 61 20, ✆ www.russian-cruises.ru. Hydrofoils to Peterhof and Shlisselburg; cruises to Valaam and Kizhi.

Walking tours

St Petersburg's hidden curiosities are revealed by **walking tours**. Peter's Walking Tours has a team of enthusiastic guides who set the standard for others to match. They do a daily 4–5 hour ramble (R430 per person) through the centre, starting at 10.30am from the *St Petersburg International Hostel* (see p.335); a Friday-night pub crawl twice a month from May to September (R430 excluding drinks), also starting from the hostel; and a 5–6 hour Siege of Leningrad tour every Saturday from May to September, leaving from the *Quo Vadis* Internet café on Nevskiy prospekt (see p.53) at 11am (R500). There's no need to book – just turn up. A Rasputin Walk, Dostoyevsky's St Petersburg, a Communist heritage tour and other themed walks can be arranged for a minimum group booking of R3200 (up to eight people; R400 for each extra person).

Another firm, VB Excursions, also does a *Crime and Punishment* walk (R750), a revolutionary St Petersburg tour (R560), a vodka pub crawl (R700 excluding drinks) and a visit to the notorious Kresty Prison (see p.223) by prior arrangement.

While walking is by far the best way to enjoy the historic city centre, there are few pedestrian zones and you should always be aware of traffic. Cars may cut across the pavement en route to (or emerging from) the courtyards of buildings, and motorists pay no attention to pedestrian crossings without a traffic light. Even when the green man is showing, cars can turn in from side streets.

Tour operators

Peter's Walking Tours ✆ www.peterswalk.com. Does scheduled tours, and many others by prior arrangement.

VB Excursions Avtogennaya ul. 6, office 415 ☏ 928 07 39, ✆ www.vb-excursions.com. Prearranged tours, including one of Kresty Prison.

Helicopter tours

St Petersburg's layout is best appreciated from the air, though helicopters can't fly directly over the centre, but range over the river from the Peter and Paul Fortress to the Smolniy. Flights leave from behind the Golovkin Bastion of the fortress at weekends (April–Oct) and last about fifteen minutes. Seats can be booked on the spot or through Baltic Airlines (Nevskiy pr. 7/9, office 12 ☏ 104 16 76, ✆ www.balticairlines.ru), which also offers a sightseeing flight over Peterhof at weekends and on public holidays. Each trip costs R1000 per person.

The media

The city's major hotels sell a limited range of foreign newspapers, generally a day or more old. Local English-language papers are useful for finding out what's on and the St Petersburg Times features some national and international news, but to keep up with world events it's better to go online, or tune into foreign radio or satellite TV.

The press

If you can understand the language, the **Russian press** holds some surprises for those who remember it from olden days. *Pravda*, the Communist Party daily, fell into the hands of "Greek swindlers who claimed to be Communists" in the mid-1990s, and now only a rebel version exists in cyberspace. *Izvestiya*, once the organ of the Soviet government, is now a popular daily owned by the energy giant Gazprom, and the erstwhile Young Communists' daily, *Komsomolskaya Pravda*, has become a tabloid rag owned by the oligarch Potanin. The elite peruse *Kommersant*, owned by the steel tycoon Alisher Usmanov, or *Nezavisimaya Gazeta*, independent by name and allegiance. Liberal-minded Russians also read *Novaya Gazeta*, whose investigative journalism has become more cautious since the murder of its reporter, Anna Politkovskaya. Russia's angry dispossessed buy *Sovetskaya Rossiya* or *Zavtra*, both unashamedly far-right, xenophobic hate-sheets. A more amusing read, *Limonka*, published by the National Bolshevik Party, is a vehicle for the ego of its leader, Limonov.

The best-selling **local papers** in St Petersburg are *Smena*, *Sankt-Peterburgskie Vedomosti* and *Chas Pik*, the last having the fullest listings of **what's on** (augmented on Fridays by a separate supplement, *Pyatnitsa*). *Afisha* and *Pulse* are cooler, lifestyle-listings magazines, which, like the more family-oriented, pocket-sized *Vash Dosug*, are published every month, staggered to overlap each other.

Foreign newspapers aren't widely available, but you're sure to find a selection in major hotels and newsagents on Nevskiy prospekt. Many foreigners prefer the **local English-language press**, which is better distributed, free and will tell you what's going on locally. The doyen of the pack is the *St Petersburg Times* (published Tues & Fri), which is good for local news and features, and has a useful **listings** and reviews section in the Friday edition. The style magazine *Pulse* carries excellent club and exhibition reviews, and the glossy magazine *Where St Petersburg* contains tourist-related features, news and listings. All are free and available from hotels, shops and restaurants frequented by foreigners. The *St Petersburg Times* was one of the first papers in the world to go online, later followed by *Neva News* and *Pulse* (see below).

Russian media online

Afisha ⓦ www.afisha.ru/spb/. Monthly style and listings magazine, in Russian only.

Kommersant ⓦ www.kommersant.com. English edition of the business-oriented Russian daily.

Moscow Times ⓦ www.themoscowtimes.com. The paper isn't distributed in St Petersburg, but is worth reading if you're going to Moscow, or for its national news.

Neva News ⓦ www.nevanews.com. Since going out of print, this lightweight rival to the *St Petersburg Times* has survived online.

Novaya Gazeta ⓦ http://novayagazeta.ru. Online English version of the liberal Russian daily paper.

NTV ⓦ www.ntv.ru. News, features and schedules for the NTV channel, in Russian only.

Pravda.ru ⓦ http://english.pravda.ru. English-language edition of the erstwhile Communist Party paper, in cyberspace.

Pulse ⓦ www.pulse.ru. Monthly St Petersburg style and listings magazine, produced in English and Russian.

RIA Novosti ⓦ www.rian.ru. Multilingual, state-owned Russian International News Agency.

Russia Today ⓦ www.russiatoday.ru. State-funded satellite TV station, broadcasting in English.
St Petersburg Times ⓦ www.sptimes.ru. The city's oldest English-language newspaper; its archives accessible by subscription.

TV and radio

Television in the Yeltsin era was outrageously biased, yet rivalry between media moguls made for some plurality and criticism. Putin ended that by using Gazprom and LUKoil to prise the networks from their owners and assert direct or indirect control. **Channel 1** (formerly ORT) is the nation's favourite for its soaps, game shows and classic Soviet films; **NTV** for its slick thrillers, drama and documentaries; the Moscow-based private **TV3** and **Ren-TV** and the state-owned **Rossiya** channels lag behind in popularity. St Petersburgers also watch the local **Kultura** channel

and cable stations delivering **OTV** (European news and documentaries), **MTV-Russia**, and **Sky**. Abroad, you may be able to watch the English-language satellite channel **Russia Today**, launched by the Kremlin in 2005.

As far as **radio** goes, cafés and drivers tune into one of the many FM music stations. The most popular are Europa Plus (100.5 FM), Eldoradio (101.4), Radio Maximum (102.8) and Rocks FM (102.0). Russkoe Radio (107.8) and Retro FM (88) are devoted to Russian music of the 1960s, 1970s and 1980s, and Radio Chanson (104.4) offers a mixture of easy listening from France and Russia. For classical music, tune in to Radio Kultura (89.3). Should you have a short-wave radio, it's possible to pick up the BBC World Service (see ⓦ www.bbc.co.uk/worldservice for frequencies).

Holidays and festivals

On national holidays, banks and most state institutions are closed (including Russian consulates abroad), but restaurants, museums and public transport functions as normal. Festivals of one kind or another occur throughout the year but you can seldom obtain details far in advance. Some holidays and festivals are celebrated by fireworks, or by the lighting of the flames on the Rostral Columns on the Strelka.

National holidays

National holidays (*prazdnik*) have been a contentious issue since the end of Communism. Most of the major Soviet ones are still observed, but **May Day**, once a nationwide compulsory march, now sees only die-hard Communists and anarchists take to the streets, while National Unity Day (**November 4**), instituted by Putin to replace the November 7 anniversary of the Bolshevik Revolution, has been hijacked by the far right. A bigger change in 2006 was the declaration of an extended **New Year** holiday (**January 1–5**) almost right up to the Russian Orthodox Christmas (**January 7**), in recognition of the fact that most Russians skipped work anyway, being hung over: in practice,

of course, many people take January 6 off too. Two holidays hardly changed since Soviet times are International Women's Day on **March 8**, when Russian men give flowers to their spouses and female acquaintances and make a big fuss of doing the housework for one day of the year; and Victory Day on **May 9**, marked by military parades. Defenders of the Motherland Day on **February 23** is more low-key, while Russian Independence Day on **June 12** – the anniversary of Russia's secession from the Soviet Union – has become a feel-good event that tries to please everyone, called Russian Flag Day. While the Russian Orthodox Christmas is once again a national holiday, Good Friday is still a working day, much to the Church's annoyance. As Easter is a moveable feast according to the Orthodox calendar, it may coincide with public holidays in May, giving rise to an extended holiday period of three to four days. If public holidays fall at the weekend, a weekday will often be given off in lieu.

Festivals

No publication or website gives the full run-down of the city's festivals throughout the year. Some events are sure to occur at a certain time, but others drift across the calendar, or vanish in some years. The best you can usually hope for is a month's notice in *The Official City Guide*, *Where St Petersburg*, *Pulse* or the *St Petersburg Times*. Nearer the time, events are advertised by posters and banners on the streets.

There are numerous **music festivals**, from jazz (March, April & Nov) to indie or avant-garde (April) – but classical music, ballet and opera claim centre stage during the ten-day **St Petersburg Spring** (May), the **Stars of the White Nights** and the **Palaces of St Petersburg** festivals. These last two run from early June to the end of July or August, through the famous **White Nights** (*Belye nochy*) when the city parties into the small hours, with revellers thronging Nevskiy prospekt and the Neva embankment, where the raising of the bridges from 1.55am onwards occasions much popping of champagne corks. You can rely on nights being short and celebratory for at least two weeks on either side of the "official" White Nights between June 11 and July 2, with a one-day carnival sometime during that period. Other events around the same time include the **Festival of Festivals** international **film** bash, a two-day **beer festival** on Dvortsovaya ploshchad (first weekend in June), the ceremonial opening of the **Fountain Season** at Peterhof (first Sat or Sun), and the **Tsarskoe Selo Carnival** at Pushkin (last Sat in June).

St Petersburg celebrates its own foundation on **City Day** (May 27) with brass bands and jolly games at various locales, especially the Peter and Paul Fortress, from which the traditional fireworks display is launched. **May Day** parades went out of fashion during the 1990s but are coming back, while **Victory Day** (May 9), commemorating the surrender of the Nazis in 1945, is still fervently marked by the older generation, with a parade of war veterans down Nevskiy prospekt and wreath-laying ceremonies at the Piskarov Cemetery. The **Siege of Leningrad Day** (Sept 8) and the **anniversary of the breaking of the Blockade** (Jan 27) are also big days for World War II veterans, but not public holidays, while the approach of **Navy Day** (last Sun in July) is heralded by the appearance of warships and subs in the Neva basin. On the day itself, motorboats ferry families out to open days on the warships, while their crews drink and brawl ashore (not a time to wander the streets), and the Rostral Columns are lit at night, augmented by a fireworks display. **Airborne Forces Day** (Aug 2) sees parachute displays, benefit concerts and drunken veterans roaring around town in armoured cars. Thankfully, **Defenders of the Motherland Day** (Feb 23) is limited to wreath-laying ceremonies at selected sites, while **Russian Independence Day** (June 12) is enlivened by a pop concert on St Isaac's Square, followed by fireworks.

Indie bands, DJs and performance artists converge on St Petersburg for the **SKIF** festival in April, while ravers flock to the **Fort-Dance** party at Fort Alexander off Kronstadt (see p.285) and **Castle Dance** at Vyborg (p.290) in late July or early August. Come mid-October, celebs and fashionistas from Russia and abroad attend the St Petersburg **Fashion Week**.

Despite all the Christmas trees and bunting, Russians ignore the Western Christmas in the rush to prepare for **New Year** (*Noviy God*). This remains a family occasion until midnight, when a frenzied round of house-calling commences, getting steadily more drunken and continuing until dawn. As you cross the Neva, watch out for the blazing torches atop the Rostral Columns. In residential areas, you may see people dressed as *Dyed Moroz* (Grandfather Frost, the Russian equivalent of Father Christmas) and his female sidekick, *Snegurochka* (Snow Maiden), who do the rounds wishing neighbours a Happy New Year (*s Novim Godom!*).

The **Russian Orthodox Christmas** (*Rozhdestvo*) starts at midnight on January 6 and goes on until dawn the following day. The choir, the liturgy, the candles and the incense combine to produce a hypnotic sense of togetherness, or *sobornost*. Despite their

Calendar of holidays, festivals and events

Note: National holidays are marked with an asterisk.

January
New Year's Day (January 1)*.
Orthodox Christmas (night of January 6/7)*.
Old New Year (night of January 13/14) according to the Julian calendar, celebrated by traditionalists.
CIS Cup indoor finals or semi-finals, if any St Petersburg team is in the running (sometime in January).

February and March
Defenders of the Motherland Day (February 23)*.
Maslenitsa Traditional feast of pancakes, celebrated at Novgorod (one week before the beginning of Lent, usually in late Feb).
Buddhist New Year (late February/early March).
International Women's Day (March 8)*.
International Festival of Jazz Dance and Music (early March).
Prokofiev Young Violinists contest at the Kapella (second half of March).
Russian Championship qualifying matches (late March onwards).

April and May
Russian Cup qualifying matches (early April onwards).
Festival of Russian Theatres from all over the CIS (mid-April).
SKIF festival of indie and avant-garde music, DJs and performance artists from Russia and abroad (April).
Orthodox Easter – not a public holiday, but a major celebration (date varies).
International Labour Day/Spring Festival (May 1 and 2)*.
Climbing for Everybody festival on the Karelian Isthmus (first half of May).
Victory Day (May 9)*.
Sonorous Nightingale children's festival at Vyborg (early or mid-May).
St Petersburg Spring international festival of classical music (mid-May).
Religious procession by water to the St Nicholas Skit on Valaam (May 19).
Day of Slav culture at Novgorod (May 24).
City Day festival in St Petersburg (May 27).

June–August
Stars of the White Nights international festival of ballet, opera and classical music (early June till early Aug).
Fountain season at Peterhof ceremonially opens (first Sat or Sun in June).
Sadko Folklore Festival at Novgorod's Museum of Wooden Architecture (first weekend in June).
Beer festival on Dvortsovaya ploshchad (first weekend in June).
International Arts Festival of music, graphics and poetry at Peterhof and Oranienbaum (early June).
Festival of Festivals international film festival (throughout June).
Russian Independence Day or Russian Flag Day (June 12)*.
Tsarskoe Selo Carnival at Tsarskoe Selo/Pushkin (see p.255), outside the city (last Sat in June).

emotional charge and Byzantine splendour, Orthodox services are come-and-go-as-you please, allowing non-believers to attend without embarrassment, but women should cover their heads and wear a skirt. The high point of the Orthodox calendar, though, is **Easter** (*Paskha*), when worshippers exchange triple kisses and the salutation "Christ is risen!" – "Verily He is risen!" For both Easter and Christmas celebrations, the principal churches and the Alexander Nevsky Monastery are packed to the gills.

White Nights Marathon starting from the Hermitage (end of June).
Sand Sculptures festival on the beach beside the Peter and Paul Fortress (end of June/early July).
Sound of the Bells bell-ringing festival at the Peter and Paul Cathedral (late June/early July).
Palaces of St Petersburg chamber music and fireworks at Peterhof, Tsarskoe Selo and Pavlovsk (June and July).
LUKoil Cup Formula 1600 racing (first Sun in July).
Night of Ivana Kupala revels at Lake Ilmen near Novgorod (June 6/7).
White Nights Swing international jazz festival (early July).
Open Look (or Open View) festival of modern dance (early July).
Baltic Cup windsurfing championships at Zelenogorsk on the Gulf of Finland (second half of July).
Musical Olympics for visiting soloists (second half of July).
Baltic Regatta international sailing week, at the Central/River Yacht Club on Petrovskiy Island (second half of July).
Knights' Tournament at Vyborg Castle (last weekend in July).
Navy Day (last Sun in July).
FortDance at Fort Alexander off Kronstadt, and **Castle Dance** at Vyborg (late July/early Aug).
Russian Cup matches between current contenders for the cup at the Petrovskiy Stadium (June/Aug).
Airborne Forces Day (Aug 2).
Golf National Cup at Solechnoe (first week in Aug).
Sailing Week (Aug).
Consecration of the water at Valaam (Aug 14).
Festival of the Kizhi Volost on Kizhi (Aug 23).
Window on Europe film festival at Vyborg (throughout Aug).

September
Siege of Leningrad Day (Sept 8).
Ice hockey season begins.
Sacred Music Festival in Novgorod (late Sept).
Early Music Festival at the Kapella and the Menshikov and Sheremetiev palaces (late Sept till mid-Oct).

October and November
Baltic House Festival of drama (Oct).
St Petersburg Open international tennis tournament, at the SKK (Oct).
Fountain season at Peterhof closes (first or second week in Oct).
Festival of Spanish Music at the Hermitage Theatre (first half of Oct).
St Petersburg Fashion Week (mid-Oct)
National Unity Day (Nov 4)*.
Autumn Rhythms international jazz festival (mid-Nov).

December
Winter folklore festivities at Novgorod (Dec 7–9 and Dec 20 until mid-Feb).

Less obviously, the **festivals of other faiths** are celebrated in their places of worship. The synagogue on Lermontovskiy prospekt comes alive at Rosh Hashana, Yom Kippur, Hanukkah and other Jewish festivals; the mosque on the Petrograd Side is the focus for Ramadan celebrations (dates vary); and the Buddhist temple across the river from Yelagin Island is at the heart of events during the sixteen-day Tibetan New Year festival, *Tsagaalgan* (late Feb/early March).

Trouble and the police

St Petersburg's lurid reputation for mafia killings and police corruption is based on fact, but exaggerates its effect on everyday life. Personal security is generally in inverse proportion to personal wealth; those with most to fear are local politicians or rich businessmen. The average citizen – or visitor – is no more likely to be a victim of crime than in any other large European city. Pickpockets are the main hazard, on Nevskiy prospekt and on the metro.

Avoiding trouble is mostly common sense. Keep your money in a money-belt under your clothing, don't carry cameras or other valuables in a bag on your back, and keep a low profile. Don't travel with luggage on the metro or talk loudly in your own language, as this will identify you as a foreigner to gangs of **pickpockets** active in the centre, whose tactic is to surround their victim(s) just before the carriage door closes. Sensible precautions include making photocopies of your passport and visa, and noting down travellers' cheque and credit card numbers. If you have a car, don't leave anything in view when you park it, and take the cassette/radio with you. Luggage and valuables left in cars make a tempting target and foreign or rental cars are easy to spot. Vehicles get stolen, too; use guarded car parks, or park in the inner courtyards of buildings.

Changing money with street hustlers is a sure way to get ripped off, and the regular police (Militia) couldn't care less about these instances. Getting blind drunk or going back to strange flats with prostitutes is asking for trouble, and neither the Militia nor foreign consulates have much sympathy in such cases. If you're unlucky enough to be robbed you'll need to **go to the police**, if only because your insurance company will require a police report. There are Militia posts in every metro station, which should be able to help, or try the local precinct office. Few Militia speak any language but Russian; try the phrase *Menya obokrali* – "I've been robbed".

Generally, the law in Russia is Janusfaced. Bribery is widespread, and few Russians expect cops or judges to be honest. Many regard the police as a predatory force

with links to organized crime – a suspicion confirmed in St Petersburg in 2003 with the arrest of two dozen senior detectives, dubbed "Werewolves" by the local press for having "gone over to the dark side". Police corruption at a lower level is manifest in petty **shakedowns**. They can demand ID and, if not satisfied, take you to a Militia station and hold you for up to three hours. Some use this as a licence to hassle people, especially those with darker skins (on grounds of "security") or tourists who might pay a "fine" when something is found to be "wrong" with their documents. It's best to carry a photocopy of your passport, visa, Immigrant Card and registration at all times, and be ready to point out that your visa and registration are in order. If you have a mobile (cell) phone, pull it out and tell the officer you'd like to call your consulate (see p.51) to have somebody meet you at the police station. Do not surrender your passport. In a funnier case of cops on the take, police are known to wait in the Mikhailovskiy Gardens for nocturnal revellers to relieve themselves; they then pounce, threatening arrest unless a "fine" is paid (100 rubles suffices).

Racism

While not all Russians are racist, **racism** is a casual and common phenomenon, mostly directed against Roma, Chechens, Azerbaijanis and Central Asians, but also Africans and Arabs. Anyone dark-skinned can expect to be stopped by the Militia in metro stations, and some clubs have been known to refuse entry to black people. Worse is the risk of **assault** by neo-fascist skinheads; St Petersburg has been dubbed "Russia's racist murder capital". Some embassies advise

Emergencies

☏ **02** Militia
☏ **578 30 14** Militia hotline for foreigners

their nationals to stay indoors on April 20 (Hitler's birthday) and November 4 (National Unity Day), when neo-fascist gangs are out in force. In any case, it's safer to avoid neighbourhoods outside the city centre after dark – an out-of-the-way hotel is inadvisable.

The police

The Ministry of the Interior (MVD) maintains several law-and-order forces, all of them armed and with a high profile on the streets. Foremost are the regular police, or **Militia** (*Militsiya*), in blue-grey uniforms with red bands on their caps, or jumpsuits and parkas in shades of grey. Militiamen are much in evidence around metro stations, where they often conduct spot ID checks.

The other main branch of the Militia is the **GIBDD**, or traffic police – still universally known by its former title, the GAI – who you're likely to run into only if you're driving or happen to be involved in an accident (see p.39). They wear Militia uniforms emblazoned with a badge, armband or large white letters reading ДПС (standing for *Dorozhno Patrulnaya Sluzhba*, or Highway Patrol Service).

Some checkpoints are also manned by the **OMON**, a paramilitary force charged with the responsibility of everything from riot control to counter-insurgency. In St Petersburg, they guard important state buildings, patrol crowds and lend muscle to Militia crack-

downs on Mafia gangs. Dressed in green or grey camouflage, with a patch on the back reading ОМОН, and toting Kalashnikovs or pump-action shotguns, they look fearsome but are unlikely to bother tourists unless they get caught up in a raid of some kind. Should you be so unlucky, don't resist in any way – even verbally. The same goes for operations involving **RUOP**, the smaller Regional Force Against Organized Crime, whose teams wear civilian clothes or paramilitary uniforms like the OMON's, only the patch on the back reads РУОП.

Aside from maybe having your passport scrutinized by a plainclothes agent at Pulkovo airport, you shouldn't have any contact with the once-feared KGB in its post-Soviet incarnation as the **Federal Security Service** (FSB) unless you get involved in any kind of activism or high-tech acquisitions. The FSB has now regained the powers of the KGB in the 1970s, thanks to its former boss, President Putin, but it no longer intervenes in the lives of ordinary Russians, who are happy to ignore it. Visitors are free to do likewise, or saunter past the Bolshoy dom (see p.196) out of curiosity (taking photos is not advised).

You're far more likely to encounter **private security guards** in banks, stores, clubs or restaurants. They are allowed to carry guns, but have no powers of arrest and you're not legally obliged to show them ID. However, since many wear paramilitary garb, you may find it hard to distinguish them from the OMON (who have full police powers); private guards usually wear an ОХРАНА badge.

Travel essentials

Addresses

In Russian **addresses**, the street name is written before the number. When addressing letters, Russians start with the country, followed by a six-digit postal code, then the street, house and apartment number, and finally the addressee's name; the sender's details are usually written on the bottom of the envelope. The number of the house, building or complex may be preceded by *dom*, abbreviated to *d*. Two numbers separated by an oblique dash (for example, 16/21) usually indicate that the building is on a corner; the second figure is the street number on the smaller side street. However, if a building occupies more than one number (for example, 4/6), it is also written like this; you can usually tell when this is the case as the numbers will be close to each other and will both be even or odd. *Korpus* or *k.* indicates a building within a complex, *podezd* (abbreviated to *pod.*), an entrance number, *etazh* (*et.*) the floor and *kvartira* (*kv.*) the apartment. **Floors** are numbered in American or Continental fashion, starting with the ground floor, which Russians would call *etazh 1*. To avoid confusion we have followed the Russian usage throughout this book.

Cyrillic addresses

alleya	аллея
bulvar	бульвар
dom	дом
dvor	двор
etazh	этаж
kvartira	квартира
korpus	корпус
most	мост
naberezhnaya	набережная
pereulok	переулок
ploshchad	площадь
podezd	подъезд
prospekt	проспект
sad	сад
shosse	шоссе
ulitsa	улица

The main **abbreviations** used in St Petersburg (and in this book) are: ul. (for *ulitsa*, street); nab. (for *naberezhnaya*, embankment); pr. (for *prospekt*, avenue); per. (for *pereulok*, lane) and pl. (for *ploshchad*, square). Other common terms include *most* (bridge), *bulvar* (boulevard), *shosse* (highway), *alleya* (alley) and *sad* (garden). In the city centre most of the streets now have **bilingual signs** (Cyrillic and Latin script), which make it easier to find your way around.

Visitors should be aware of the quintessentially St Petersburg distinction between the **main entrance stairway** (*paradnaya lesnitsa*) of an apartment building, and the subsidiary entrances off the **inner courtyard** or *dvor*. Traditionally the former was for show, with handsome mirrors and carpets, while the real life of the apartments revolved around the *dvor*. In Soviet times the grand stairways were gradually reduced to the darkened, shabby stairwells of today, but the *dvor* never lost its role as the spiritual hearth of St Petersburg life.

Airlines

All the airline offices listed below (except Korean Air and Rossiya) are centrally located, within walking distance of Gostiniy Dvor/ Nevskiy Prospekt or Ploshchad Vosstaniya/ Mayakovskaya metros.

Aeroflot ul. Rubinsteyna 1/43 5 ☎ 438 55 83.

Air France Malaya Morskaya ul. 23 ☎ 336 29 00.

Alitalia Nevskiy pr. 30, office 4 ☎ 334 44 51.

American Airlines Konyushennaya pl. 2, office 412 ☎ 740 30 75.

Austrian Airways Nesvkiy pr. 32, ☎ 331 20 25.

British Airways Malaya Konyushennaya ul. 1/3a, office 23-b ☎ 380 05 26.

Delta Bolshaya Morskaya ul. 36 ☎ 571 58 20.

Finnair Malaya Konyushennaya ul. 1/3a ☎ 303 98 98.

KLM Malaya Morskaya ul. 23 ☎ 346 68 68.

Korean Air Pulkovo-2 airport ☎ 336 56 46.

LOT Karavannaya ul. 1 ☎ 273 57 21.

Lufthansa Nevskiy pr. 32 ☎ 320 10 00.

Rossiya ul. Pilotov 18, korpus 4 ☎ 704 37 38;
Moskovskaya metro.
SAS Nevskiy pr. 25 ☎ 326 26 00.
SN Brussels Stremyannaya ul. 10 ☎ 748 30 20.
South African Airways Stremyannaya ul. 10
☎ 740 38 20.
Transaero Liteyniy pr. 48 ☎ 579 64 63.

Cigarettes

Nearly all Western brands of cigarettes are
available, though many of the packets sold
at kiosks are made under licence (or coun-
terfeited) in Russia or Turkey. It is normal to
be approached by strangers asking for a
light (*Mozhno pokurit?*) or a cigarette. While
museums, most theatres and public transport are no-smoking (*ne kurit*) zones, Russians puff away everywhere else, and see
nothing wrong with it. However, many fast-
food chains have a no-smoking policy.

Consulates

Australia (Honorary) Italyanskaya ul. 1 ☎ 325 73
33; Nevskiy Prospekt metro. Mon–Fri 9am–5pm.
Britain pl. Proletarskoy diktatury 5 ☎ 320 32 00,
ⓦ www.britain.spb.ru; minibus #147 from Nevskiy
pr. Mon–Fri 9am–5pm.
China nab. kanala Griboedova 134 ☎ 114 76
70; Sadovaya metro. Visa section Mon, Wed & Fri
9.30–11.30am.
Estonia Bolshaya Monetnaya ul. 14 ☎ 702 09 20;
Gorkovskaya metro. Mon–Fri 10am–noon.
Finland Preobrazhenskaya pl. 4 ☎ 331 76 00,
ⓦ www.pietari.com; Chernyshevskaya metro.
Mon–Fri 9am–3.30pm.
Latvia 10-ya liniya 11 ☎ 336 34 54;
Vasileostrovskaya metro. Mon–Fri 9.30am–noon.
Lithuania ul. Ryleeva 37 4 ☎ 327 30 97;
Chernyshevskaya metro. Mon–Fri 9am–noon.
Netherlands nab. reki Moyki 11 ☎ 334 02 00;
Nevskiy Prospekt metro. Mon–Fri 10am–12.30pm.
USA Furshtatskaya ul. 15 ☎ 331 26 00, ⓦ www.
stpetersburg-usconsulate.ru; Chernyshevskaya
metro. Mon–Fri 9am–5.30pm.

Costs

For visitors, **costs** in general terms compare
well with major cities in Western Europe; you
can eat, drink, travel and go to concerts or
clubs for less than in Paris or London. The
chief exception is accommodation, with
relatively few decent hotels for under €60
a night. If you're staying longer than a few
weeks, renting a flat works out much cheaper.

Another factor is discriminatory ticket pricing at
museums, palaces, the Mariinskiy Theatre and
other major attractions, whereby foreigners pay
up to four times what Russians do. While the
Hermitage or Russian Museum charges seem
fair enough, others are unjustifiably high; to see
everything at Peterhof costs about €85, unless
you have a **student card**.

ISIC cardholders get a 30–50 percent
reduction on museum and palace admission
charges and free entry to the Hermitage. Student
cards issued in Russia entitle you
to Russian student rates, which are even
lower. With proof of student status, you can
buy an ISIC card at most of St Petersburg's
hostels (see p.334) or language schools (see
"Study", p.57).

For package tourists with prepaid accommodation including full- or half-board, €40
a day should suffice for tickets to museums and palaces, buying gifts and the odd
snack or drink. Independent travellers will, of
course, have to add accommodation costs
and food on top of this figure. Staying in a
modest hotel and sticking to inexpensive
bars and restaurants, you could get away
with a total daily budget of €140, but
patronizing fancier establishments will easily
triple or quadruple this figure. Alternatively, if
you rent a flat and live as Russians do, you
could spend €55 a day or less on the whole
works, including lodging, food and drink.

Cultural Institutes

American Corner Mayakovsky Public Library,
nab. reki Fontanki 46 ☎ 571 15 89; Dostoevskaya/
Vladimirskaya metro. Aside from US newspapers
there isn't much to attract tourists. Mon–Fri
9am–7.30pm.
Goethe Institut nab. reki Moyki 58 ☎ 314 40 15,
ⓦ www.goethe.de; Sadovaya/Sennaya Ploshchad
metro. Organizes film showings and lectures, and
diverse extramural events. Mon–Thurs 3–6pm.
Institut Français nab. reki Moyki 20 ☎ 571 09
95, ⓦ www.ifspb.com; Nevskiy Prospekt metro.
Has a lending library (free membership) and organizes
all kinds of cultural events, from French films and
concerts to Bastille Day celebrations. Mon & Wed
2–6.30pm, Tues & Thurs 2–8pm, Fri noon–5pm.
Prince Galitzine Memorial Library nab. reki
Fontanki 46 ☎ 571 13 33, ⓦ www.galitzinelibrary.
ru; Dostoevskaya metro. This charitable foundation
has an extensive collection of books about Russia
in English. Tourists are welcome to use the reading

room. Mon–Fri noon–7pm, Sat 1–5pm. Closed the last Thurs of each month and during Aug.

Disabled travellers

The needs of disabled citizens in Russia were largely ignored in the past, and the chronic shortage of funds has hindered progress even now in places where attitudes have changed. There is **wheelchair access** to the *Novotel*, *Radisson SAS Royal*, *Park Inn Pribaltiyskaya* and *Park Inn Pulkovskaya* hotels; the *Grand Hotel Europe* and *Nevsky Palace* are accessible throughout, and the *Ambassador* has excellent disabled facilities. Of the city's museums, only the Hermitage and the Russian Museum have ramps or lifts for wheelchairs. **Transport** is a major problem, since buses, trams, trolleybuses and the metro are virtually impossible to get onto with a wheelchair, and the suburban train systems only slightly better. Of the theatres and museums, only the Teatr na Liteynom is wheelchair-accessible.

Drugs

Grass (*travka*) and cannabis resin (*plastylin*) from the Altay Mountains are commonplace on the club scene, as are acid, ecstasy and heroin. At some clubs, the merest whiff will draw the bouncers; at others, dope-smokers are stolidly ignored. However, the legal penalties are draconian, so it's best to avoid all drugs entirely.

Electricity

Electricity in St Petersburg conforms to the standard Continental 220 volts AC; most European appliances should work as long as you have an adaptor for Continental-style, two-pin round plugs. North Americans will need this plus a transformer.

Etiquette

Despite the creeping Westernization of manners, Russians observe the distinction between the formal (*vy*) and informal (*ty*) "you", and expect to be called by their patronymic (see "Language", p.430) if they are older than you, or you are meeting in a formal situation. Visiting a Russian household, you should remove your shoes and put on slippers (*tapochki*) offered by your host. On

public transport, young men are expected to offer their seats to children or the elderly. For other cultural hints, see "Superstitions" (p.57).

Gay and lesbian travellers

While sexual relations between men over 16 were decriminalized in the early 1990s, Russian society remains extremely **homophobic**. In recent years, the Liberal Democratic Party has tried to criminalize both gay men and lesbians (ignored under Soviet law); a Deputy from another party tried to ban the distribution of the film *Brokeback Mountain*; and Moscow's Mayor Luzhkov vowed never to permit a Pride march. Most Russian gays and lesbians adopt a low profile and seldom come out to family and friends. That said, attitudes in St Petersburg are more liberal than elsewhere in Russia, and the city has a flourishing **gay scene**. Two good websites to check out are ⓦwww.english. gay.ru (the Moscow-based gay, lesbian and transgender group Gay.Ru) and ⓦwww. krilija.sp.ru (the St Petersburg Human Rights Centre for Gays and Lesbians, PO Box 108, St Petersburg 191186; ☏312 31 80). Besides articles about gay life and history in Russia, links and listings, the former can put you in touch with gay or lesbian guides and the latter with a gay/lesbian travel agency. See p.360 for clubs in St Petersburg.

Insurance

Medical insurance is obligatory for citizens of Australia and the Schengen states (Austria, Belgium, France, Germany, Netherlands, Portugal and Spain), and is strongly advisable for other nationalities.

Travel insurance is also worth having in the event of unforeseen curtailment or cancellation of your trip. Cover for lost or stolen baggage or valuables is often fairly minimal but some "all risks" home insurance policies provide more generous backup. Rough Guides has teamed up with Columbus Direct to offer you travel insurance that can be tailored to suit your needs. Products include a low-cost **backpacker** option for long stays; a **short-break** option for city getaways; a typical **holiday-package** option; and others. There are also annual **multi-trip** policies for those who travel regularly. Different sports

Internet Cafés

Café Max Nevskiy pr. 90/92, 2nd floor ☎273 66 55, ⓦwww.cafemax.ru; Mayakovskaya metro. Two hundred terminals, gaming zone, Wi-Fi, IP telephony, print centre and café-bar; student discounts. There's also a branch in the Hermitage Museum (p.117). Open 24hr.

Consay Ligovskiy pr. 63 ☎764 57 452, ⓦwww.consay.sp.ru; Ligovskiy Prospekt metro. Open 24hr.

Free Time ul. Lomonosova 2 ☎448 52 78; Gostiniy Dvor/Nevskiy Prospekt metro. Popular with students and clubbers. Open 24hr.

Indigo Internet Nevskiy pr. 32 (in the yard); Nevskiy Prospekt/Gostinniy Dvor metro. Basement den to the left, behind St Catherine's Church. Daily 11am–11pm

Quo Vadis Nevskiy pr. 76 (entrance on Liteyniy pr.) ☎333 07 08, ⓦwww.quovadis. ru; Mayakovskaya metro. Café, chill-out zone and Wi-Fi; the starting point for Peter's Walking Tours (see p.42). Daily 9am–11pm.

Virus Kronverksiy pr. 46 ⓦwww.virus.spb.ru; Gorkovskaya metro. A Petrograd Side Internet club that's popular with gamers. Open 24hr.

can usually be covered if required. See ⓦwww.roughguidesinsurance.com for eligibility and purchasing options. Alternatively, UK residents should call ☎0870/033 9988; US citizens should call ☎1-800/749-4922; Australians should call ☎1-300/669 999. All other nationalities should call ☎+44 870/890 2843.

If you need to make a claim, you should **keep receipts** for medicines and medical treatment, and in the event you have anything stolen, you must obtain an official **theft report** (*spravka*) from the police (see p.48).

Internet

You can go online at numerous **cafés** in St Petersburg, many of which are open 24 hours (see box above). Hourly rates vary, but are rarely more than R70 at peak times and as little as R30 after midnight, with premium rates for higher-speed and broadband links. At most places the staff speak some English and can reset the onscreen language format so that you don't have to grapple with instructions in Cyrillic. The Russian word for @ is *sobachka* (literally "dog"). To use a laptop in Russia, you'll require an (American) Bell lead for your modem that can connect directly to a five-pin Russian telephone plug, or a UK/Russian adaptor. Users can either open an account and pre-pay, or use pay-as-you-go scratch **cards** sold at CD shops and phone kiosks. These can be time-limited, with credit for anything from

1–100 hours, or charge by the megabyte. On the back there will be a dial-up number (*nomer telefona*), log-in (*imya polzovetelya*) and password (*parol*). Some brands such as Zebra (see "Phones") require you to register on their website before you get your password. If you don't have a digital line, make sure your dial-up setting is on pulse, not tone. With Windows XP, you can get pulse-dialling by preceding the Internet access number with a capital "P". **Wi-Fi** "hot-spots" exist at Pulkovo airport, train stations and the sea terminal, hotels, clubs and cafés. Two local Wi-Fi providers are Comset (ⓦwww. set3.ru) and Quantum (ⓦwww.wifizone.ru). There are computer dealers all over town – though warranty agreements on hardware or software bought abroad don't apply within Russia. Pirated software is widely available in shops and markets.

Laundry

Stirka (Kazanskaya ul. 6 ☎314 53 71; daily 10am–11pm) is a launderette-café with a snack bar, sound system and sofas, where you can drink a beer or smoke a *shisha* while waiting for your wash (five kilos costs R150). Clothes can be washed, ironed and delivered in three days by Garant, with branches (daily 9am–8pm) at Manezniy per. 3 (☎579 52 50), Sadovaya ul. 29 (☎310 60 28), and Suvorovskiy pr. 24 (☎271 57 69). Dry cleaners include Super-Dry (Kuznechniy per. 10 ☎710 80 67; daily 11am–7pm) and Russkiy

Ostrov (nab. kanala Griboedova 55 ☎571 78 77; Mon–Fri 10am–8pm, Sat 10am–7pm).

Lost property

Anything you might lose is unlikely to end up at the lost property depot (*stol nakhodok*) for Moscow Station (Nevskiy pr. 85 ☎768 40 43; daily 24hr), but there's slightly more chance of it being recovered at the city-wide Centre for Lost Documents (Bolshaya Monetnaya ul. 16 ☎336 51 09; Mon–Fri 10am–6pm), or the 24-hour offices at Pulkovo-1 (☎723 83 61) and Pulkovo-2 (☎324 37 87) airports.

Mail

The state postal service is unreliable, so visitors wishing to send (or receive) important post should use an express mail or courier firm. Post International, Westpost, the *Nevsky Palace Hotel* and the *Grand Hotel Europe* offer an **express delivery** service via Finland or Sweden, which can take anything from three to five days and costs about R100 per letter, or there are **international courier** services, whose rates are higher. With all of these services it pays to shop around for the best deal (see listings below).

St Petersburg's **main post office** (*glavniy pochtamt*) is at Pochtamtskaya ul.9 (Mon–Sat 9am–7.30pm, Sun 10am–5.30pm ☎312 83 02), a few blocks from St Isaac's Cathedral (see map, p.94). Branch offices (*pochta*) are generally open from 9am to 2pm and 3 to 7pm and can be identified by the blue and white sign depicting a postman's horn. If you want only **stamps**, it's easier to go to the postal counters in a big hotel rather than queue in a post office, although there's a heavy mark-up on the price.

American Express cardholders can use their client mail service, which is more reli-able than the **poste restante** in public post offices.

Maps

The **maps** in this guide should be sufficient for most purposes, but if you need more detail, or are staying outside the centre, it's worth investing in a detailed street plan. If you can read the Cyrillic alphabet, it's best to buy a locally produced map once you arrive. The fold-out *Polyplan Map of St Petersburg* features all major sights and covers the whole city, while the pocket-sized *Atlas S-Peterburg S kazhdym domom* identifies the street number of every building (making it invaluable for locating clubs, restaurants and residential blocks). Both can be found at local bookshops (see p.372 for addresses) for about R150, along with a little booklet mapping transport routes, *Sankt-Peterburg Ves Transport* (R50).

Foreign maps in English sold abroad include a detailed, laminated *Lonely Planet* map; an *Insight Map* which confusingly gives the names of sites in Russian, in the Latin alphabet; and outdated, unwieldy *Falk plan* or *Freytag & Berndt* maps – only the last two are commonly found in St Petersburg. At a pinch, visitors can also use the colour maps in the free *Official City Guide* or *Where St Petersburg* magazine (see p.43).

Marriage agencies

The Internet and foreign-language press are full of advertisements by agencies offering to supply **Russian brides** for foreign men. A lot of them are purely aimed at extracting money from hapless foreigners, and even where "genuine", many of the women are simply planning to divorce their spouses as soon as they gain a foreign residency per-

---

Express mail and courier services

DHL Nevskiy pr. 10 ☎325 61 00, ⊛www.dhl.ru.
Federal Express Nevskiy pr. 30 ☎449 18 78; per. Grivtsova 6 ☎325 88 25.
Garantpost Moskovskiy pr. 109, ☎325 75 25, ⊛www.garantpost.ru.
Pony Express Parkovaya ul. 4, office 326; ul. Marata 47–49, office 201 ☎499 72 52, ⊛www.ponyexpress.ru.
Post International Nevskiy pr. 34, 2nd floor ☎570 44 72, ⊛www.postoperator.ru.
TNT Sofiyskaya ul.14 ☎718 33 30, ⊛www.tnt.ru.
Westpost Nevskiy pr. 86 ☎336 63 52 or 275 07 84, ⊛www.wespost.ru.

mit or passport. For a real relationship, find someone yourself.

Money

Russia's **currency**, the **ruble**, has been enviably stable since its revaluation after the crash of 1998, buoyed by rising energy prices. The **denominations** in circulation are coins of 5, 10 and 50 kopeks (100 kopeks = 1 ruble) and 1, 2 and 5 rubles; and notes of 5, 10, 50, 100, 500, 1000 and 5000 rubles. The designs are the same as pre-1997 banknotes, which are no longer legal tender and are occasionally palmed off on tourists. Though rubles are the only legal currency, some hotels, tourist agencies and a few restaurants still quote prices in euros, dollars or **"standard units"** (*uslovnye yedenitsy*, abbreviated to УЕ, which can mean either currency paid in rubles at the going **rate of exchange**. At the time of writing this was approximately: £1 = R50, €1 = R35, $1 = R25. With a few exceptions, all the local prices in this book are in rubles. To find out the Central Bank rate, check the financial section of the *St Petersburg Times*, or the currency converter website ⓦwww.xe.com. The designation code for Russian rubles is "RUR". Inside Russia, ruble prices are written with a Cyrillic р or руъ followed by a decimal point and a к for kopeks – so that 80р.50к means eighty rubles and fifty kopeks.

Rubles can't be obtained abroad; you must change money or draw on your plastic in Russia. Changing money with street hustlers is a sure way to be cheated, and there's no reason to change money anywhere other than in a **bank** or a **currency exchange** (*obmen valuty*). **Banking hours** are usually Monday to Friday 9am to 6pm; Sberbank and Citi Bank also open at weekends. Exchange bureaux work long hours, often around the clock. Rates vary a bit, but commission should be negligible. Banks and exchanges may refuse banknotes with any tears, scribbles or stains, and US dollars issued before 1999. Euros and dollars can be changed anywhere; other currencies depending on how much they're in demand. You may need to show your passport when exchanging money.

Many banks and exchanges give **cash advances** on **credit cards** or debit cards.

bank	Банк
currency exchange	обмен валюты
convertible currency	СКВ
standard units	УЕ
ruble	рубль
buying rate	покупка
selling rate	продажа
exchange rate	курс

Visa, Eurocard, MasterCard, Maestro and Cirrus are widely accepted; Diners Club, JCB, Union and American Express, less so. Money can be paid out in dollars or rubles. Cash advances are treated as loans, with interest accruing daily, plus a 2–5 percent local commission charge. It is more economical to use a **debit card** for withdrawals from **ATMs** (*bankomat*), as there are no interest payments and the transaction fee is modest. You can **pay** by card in most hotels and restaurants, but in shops it may depend on whether the single member of staff who knows how to swipe cards is working that day. Always keep the **receipts** from ATM withdrawals or card transactions, and be sure to know the overseas hotline number for reporting **lost** or stolen cards.

Travellers' cheques aren't worth the trouble; only large banks such as Sberbank and Alfabank will cash them, and charge 3–6 percent commission. **American Express** cheques are the only brand that can be replaced in Russia if lost or stolen, and only 2 percent commission is charged if they are cashed at their **office** in St Petersburg (Malaya Morskaya ul. 23 ☎326 45 00; Mon–Fri 9am–5pm). All transactions require your passport. **Wiring money** to Russia is expensive but easily done via Western Union, available at American Express, most banks and some exchange bureaux (see ⓦwww.westernunion.ru for a full list).

Museums

Opening hours for museums tend to be from 10 or 11am to 5 or 6pm. They are closed at least one day a week on a regular basis, plus one day in the month set aside as a *sanitarniy den* or "cleaning day", but generally open on public holidays except for New Year's day. Full opening hours are detailed in the text.

Direct dialling codes

To St Petersburg
From Britain ⓣ00 7 812
From Ireland ⓣ00 7 812
From the US and Canada ⓣ011 7 812
From Australia and New Zealand ⓣ0011 7 812
From Moscow ⓣ8 (pause) 812

From St Petersburg
Australia ⓣ8 (pause) 10 61
Ireland ⓣ8 (pause) 10 353
New Zealand ⓣ8 (pause) 10 64
UK ⓣ8 (pause) 10 44
US and Canada ⓣ8 (pause) 10 1
Moscow ⓣ8 (pause) 495

Admission charges are higher for foreigners than for Russians, ranging from R70 for minor museums, to R300 for major attractions such as the Hermitage and the Russian Museum, or as much as R500 for some of the Imperial palaces. A **student card** entitles you to a thirty- to fifty-percent discount at most museums, and free admission to the Hermitage. Many places require you to buy a permit for **photography** (cameras R50–100; video R100–150; no discounts) or leave your camera in the cloakroom (*garderob*), and some make visitors put on felt or plastic **overshoes** (*tapochki*) to protect their parquet floors.

At some museums you can rent an **audio-guide** (*player*) at the ticket desk (*kassa*), or arrange a **guided tour** (*beseda*) through the excursions bureau in English or other foreign languages. There are no hard and fast rules about how far in advance you should book a tour, and a lot may depend on the museum's staffing rosters. Some museums have set rates for tours; others prefer to negotiate on an ad hoc basis.

Phones

Public phones are now mostly found at metro and mainline stations, and rarely on the streets in the centre. Green-and-white **SPT phones** may be used for local, intercity and international calls; SPT **phonecards** (*telefonaya karta*) are sold at kiosks, post offices and branches of Sberbank. Pre-paid **Zebra cards** (also sold at kiosks and Sberbank) are the cheapest way of making international calls, and also serve as pay-as-you-go Internet cards.

Europeans using the GSM system can use their own **mobile phones**, but Americans must rent a special phone from their cellular dealer before leaving; in either case "roaming" in Russia is expensive. Anyone intending to use a *mobilnik* extensively will save money by getting a Russian SIM card from a local dealer (you'll need to show your passport, visa and registration). Providers include MegaFon (ⓦwww.nwgsm.com), MTS (ⓦwww.spb.mts.ru), and Tele2 (ⓦwww.spb.tele2.ru) – the last two websites are in Russian only. Most offer subscribers a choice between seven-digit direct-dial numbers and ten-digit federal numbers; calling the latter, you need to dial 8 first.

To **make an international call** dial 8, wait for the tone to change and then dial 10, followed by the country code, city code (omitting the initial zero) and subscriber number. To call anywhere in Russia, or most of the former Soviet republics (except the Baltic States), dial 8, pause, and then the city code (including any zeros). Calls placed through the international operator (ⓣ079/073 for outside/inside the CIS) cost more and may take time to come through.

Visitors staying a while may prefer web-based, or **IP, telephony**, provided by Peterstar (ⓦwww.comset.net/en/), Skylink (ⓦwww.skylink.ru) or WestCall (ⓦwww.westcall.spb.ru); the last two sites are in Russian only.

Always bear in mind the **time difference** when calling Russia from abroad. Lines are at their busiest during UK or US office hours, but you'll have fewer problems getting through at, say, 7am in the UK – which is 10am in St Petersburg. Conversely, should you phone St Petersburg after 3pm UK time, everyone will have already left the office (it's acceptable to call people at home up until 10pm, local time).

Photography

Most museums require visitors to buy a **permit** (camera R50–100; video R100–150) at the ticket desk if they wish to photograph indoors. Using flashes or tripods is prohibited. Elsewhere in the city, **avoid** taking photos of army barracks (indicated by pictorial signs), foreign consulates, the headquarters of the secret police (see p.196) or anywhere on the metro – or your camera could be confiscated. Most Internet cafés (see p.53) can burn images onto CDs for a modest sum, while Agfa, Fuji and Kodak Express outlets for **film** and one-hour processing services can be found all over the centre. When leaving the country put films in your pocket, as Russian filmsafe X-rays do not always live up to the name.

Prostitution

Prostitution is not illegal in Russia, and most large hotels, expensive clubs and restaurants have their quota of prostitutes. Foreign males on their own or in a group are likely to be approached; invitations to dance are the usual pretext, which can cause confusion over women's motives if they flirt with you at a disco.

Religious buildings

Churches and other places of worship are open for services, if not all day. It often depends on how valuable their icons are and whether there are enough parishioners, since few churches can afford to hire guards. **Orthodox churches** celebrate the Divine Liturgy (*Bozhestvennaya Liturgia*) at 8am, 9am or 10am Monday to Saturday, and at 7am or 10am on Sunday and saints' days; most also hold services at 5 or 6pm daily, some with an *akafist* or series of chants to the Virgin or saints. Both services last about two hours. Additional services are held on saints' days (*Prestolniy prazdnik*). Orthodox believers cross themselves with three fingers (first the head, then the stomach, followed by the

right shoulder and then the left). Tourists are required to **dress** appropriately in church (no shorts, short skirts or bare shoulders); some monasteries require women to wear a long wraparound skirt and a headscarf. St Petersburg's synagogue, mosque and Buddhist temple have their own dress codes. Details of services in Christian, Muslim, Jewish and Buddhist places of worship appear in the Friday edition of the *St Petersburg Times*.

Study

Several local language schools offer **Russian lessons**, with one-to-one or group tuition. Comparing what's on offer, note the size of the group and if teaching materials are included in the weekly rate (which some schools quote in euros). For example, EducaCentre charges €195/€255 per person for twenty/thirty lessons in groups of six; CREF R18,000/R15,000 for forty hours' tuition in groups of two/five people, or R30,000 one-to-one; and the Swiss-managed Liden & Denz €215–260 for twenty lessons, with a weekly supplement of €60 from June to September. All schools below can provide visa support and some may also arrange accommodation.

Superstitions

Russians consider it **bad luck** to kiss or shake hands across a threshold, or return home to pick up something that's been forgotten. Before departing on a long journey, they gather their luggage by the door and sit on it for a minute or two, to bring themselves luck for the journey. When buying flowers for your hostess, make certain that there's an odd number of blooms; even-numbered bouquets are for funerals. It's considered

---

Language schools

CREF Malodetskoselskiy pr. 24 ☏712 63 27, ⓦwww.cref.ru. Teaches French and English to locals, as well as Russian to foreigners.
EducaCentre Maliy pr. 87, Petrograd Side ☏974 03 73, ⓦwww.educacente.net. Offers specialist tuition in business or literary Russian, as well as standard language courses.
Herzen State Pedagogical University nab. reki Moyki 48 ☏314 78 59, ⓦwww. herzen.spb.ru. Students can stay in the University hotel behind the Kazan Cathedral (R275–750 per day according to the type of room) or a hostel on Ligovskiy prospekt (R3750 per month).
Liden & Denz Transportniy per. 11, ☏325 22 41, ⓦwww.lidenz.ru. Under Swiss management with lots of corporate clients.

unlucky to whistle indoors, or to put a handbag on the floor.

Time

St Petersburg uses Moscow Time, which is generally **three hours ahead of Britain** and **eight hours ahead of US Eastern Standard Time**, with the clocks going forward one hour on the last Saturday of March and back again on the last Saturday of October.

Tipping

In **taxis**, the fare will usually be agreed in advance so there's no need to tip; in **restaurants**, no one will object if you leave an extra ten percent or so, but in most places it's not compulsory. Check, too, that it hasn't already been included. In those places where a service charge is compulsory, it ranges from **ten to fifteen percent**; the exact figure will be stated on the menu.

Toilets

It's generally okay for non-customers to use the toilets in restaurants and hotels, since public toilets (*tualet* or WC) are few and far between – despite efforts to boost numbers by locating Portaloo-type cabins in parks and squares. There is a small charge, which

includes a wad of toilet paper given out by the attendant. Otherwise, make for the nearest *McDonald's*. Men's facilities are marked M; ladies, Ж. You can buy toilet paper (*tualetnaya bumaga*) in any supermarket or pharmacy.

Women travellers

Sexual harassment is no worse than in Western Europe, but the tendency of Russian men to veer between extreme gallantry and crude chauvinism – and of Russian women to exploit their femininity – makes for misunderstandings when foreigners are involved. Russian men often make a big deal of kissing hands on being introduced, opening doors and pulling out chairs for them. Foreign women may feel under-dressed wearing combats, fleeces or trainers, as Russians favour figure-hugging clothes, high heels and full make-up; nose-studs, lip rings and other such jewellery may draw comments. Political correctness has barely a toehold in Russian society, and Russians of both sexes regard striptease acts as normal entertainment in clubs and restaurants. Russian women feel secure enough to flag down cars as taxis (see p.38), but foreign women shouldn't risk it.

The City

The City

Within the Fontanka

T he heart of St Petersburg is circumscribed by the seven-kilometre-long River Fontanka and the broader River Neva, which separates it from Vasilevskiy Island and the Petrograd Side. Concentrated on this oval of land **within the Fontanka** are some of the city's greatest monuments – the Winter Palace, the Admiralty and the Bronze Horseman, the Engineers' Castle, the Summer Palace and Garden, and the cathedrals of St Isaac and Our Lady of Kazan – as well as the art collections of the Hermitage and the Russian Museum; the Mariinskiy Theatre (better known as the Kirov); the Gostiniy and Apraksin bazaars; and a whole host of former palaces associated with the good, the bad and the downright weird.

The area is defined by a fan of avenues, chief among them Nevskiy prospekt, which radiate from the Admiralty, interwoven with canals spanned by elegant bridges. The area's historical associations practically peel off the walls: here, unbridled rulers and profligate aristocrats once held sway, poets were driven to suicide, murderers wept in remorse and revolutionaries plotted assassinations.

There are enough sights within the Fontanka to keep you busy for days – as well as most of the city's theatres, concert halls, banks, airline offices and swankiest hotels. All in all, you're likely to spend much of your time in this area, and largely judge St Petersburg on the strength of it. Finding your way around is relatively easy, with bilingual street-signs and street plans posted around the major tourist sites. With regard to **addresses**, remember that even numbers are always on the south side of the canal or river, odd numbers on the opposite (north) embankment. On Nevskiy prospekt, however, even numbers are on the north side of the avenue, and buildings are numbered starting from the Admiralty.

Nevskiy prospekt

Nevskiy prospekt is St Petersburg's equivalent of the Champs Élysées or Unter den Linden – an imperial thoroughfare whose name is virtually synonymous with that of the city. Like St Petersburg, the avenue is on an epic scale, running all the way from the Admiralty on the banks of the Neva to the Alexander Nevsky Monastery beyond the Fontanka – a distance of 4.5km – and measuring up to 60m wide in places. Yet, at the same time, it is intensely human in its foibles and failings, juxtaposing palaces and potholes, ballerinas and beggars – as Gogol wrote in *Tales of Good and Evil*, "What a rapid phantasmagoria passes over it in a single day!"

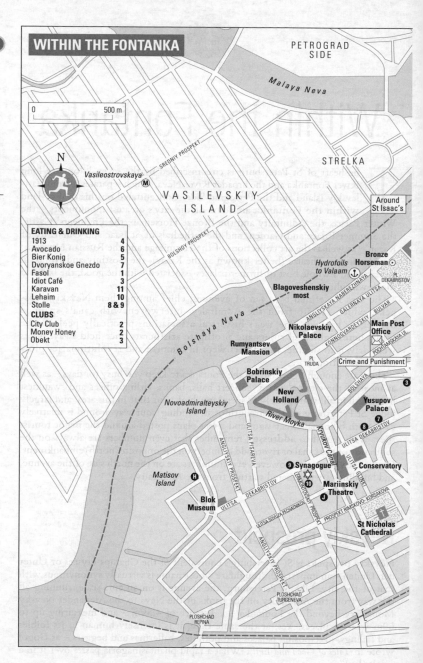

WITHIN THE FONTANKA

PETROGRAD SIDE

Malaya Neva

STRELKA

VASILEVSKIY ISLAND

0 — 500 m

N

Vasileostrovskaya Ⓜ

SREDNIY PROSPEKT

BOLSHOY PROSPEKT

Around St Isaac's

EATING & DRINKING

1913	4
Avocado	6
Bier Konig	5
Dvoryanskoe Gnezdo	7
Fasol	1
Idiot Café	3
Karavan	11
Lehaim	10
Stolle	8 & 9

CLUBS

City Club	2
Money Honey	2
Obekt	3

Bolshaya Neva

Hydrofoils to Valaam ⚓

Bronze Horseman ⊙

PL. DEKABRISTOV

ANGLIYSKAYA NABEREZHNAYA

Blagoveshenskiy most

GALERNAYA ULITSA

KONNOGVARDEYSKIY BULVAR

Main Post Office

POCHTAMSKAYA UL.

Nikolaevskiy Palace

PL. TRUDA

Crime and Punishment

BOLSHAYA

Rumyantsev Mansion

❸

Bobrinskiy Palace

Novoadmiralteyskiy Island

New Holland

River Moyka

Yusupov Palace

❼

ULITSA DEKABRISTOV

❽

KRYUKOV CANAL

ULITSA GLINKI

ULITSA PISAREVA

ANGLIYSKIY PROSPEKT

Matisov Island Ⓗ

DEKABRISTOV

❾ **Synagogue** ✡

LERMONTOVSKIY PROSPEKT

Conservatory

❿ ✡

Mariinskiy Theatre Ⓙ

Blok Museum

ULITSA

ULITSA SOYUZA PECHATNIKOV

ANGLIYSKIY PROSPEKT

PROSPEKT RIMSKOVO-KORSAKOVA

St Nicholas Cathedral ✝

PLOSHCHAD TURGENEVA

PLOSHCHAD REPINA

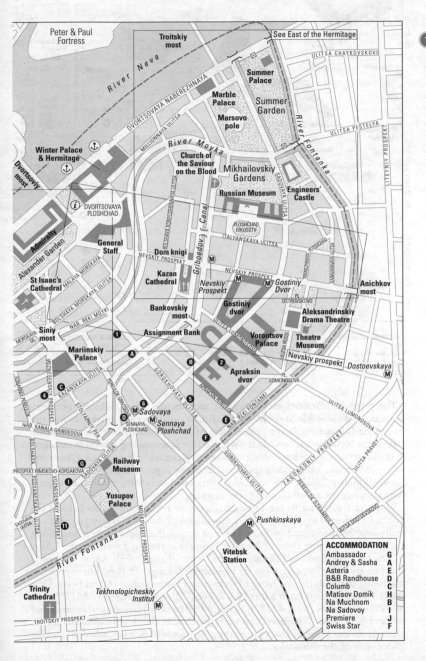

Peter & Paul Fortress

Troitskiy most

See East of the Hermitage

ULITSA CHAYKOVSKOVO

River Neva

Summer Palace

Marble Palace

Summer Garden

Marsovo pole

DVORTSOVAYA NABEREZHNAYA

River Fontanka

ULITSA PESTELYA

LITEYNIY PROSPEKT

MILLIONNAYA ULITSA

River Moyka

Winter Palace & Hermitage

Church of the Saviour on the Blood

Mikhailovskiy Gardens

Engineers' Castle

Dvortsoviy most

Russian Museum

BOLSHAYA KONYUSHENNAYA ULITSA

SADOVAYA ULITSA

DVORTSOVAYA PLOSHCHAD

PLOSHCHAD ISKUSSTV

Admiralty

General Staff

Dom knigi

ITALYANSKAYA ULITSA

MANEZHNAYA

KARAVANNAYA ULITSA

Alexander Garden

NEVSKIY PROSPEKT

Kazan Cathedral

Nevskiy Prospekt

Nevskiy Prospekt

Gostiniy Dvor

Anichkov most

St Isaac's Cathedral

MALAYA MORSKAYA

BOLSHAYA MORSKAYA ULITSA

Bankovskiy most

Gostiniy dvor

OSTROVSKOVO

PL

MORSKAYA UL

NAB. REKI MOYKI

Assignment Bank

Aleksandrinskiy Drama Theatre

Siniy most

PEREULOK GRIVTSOVA

Vorontsov Palace

Theatre Museum

Mariinskiy Palace

GOROKHOVAYA ULITSA

ULITSA LOMONOSOVA

ULITSA ROSSI

Nevskiy prospekt

Dostoevskaya

VOZNESENSKIY PROSPEKT

KAZANSKAYA ULITSA

Apraksin dvor

PL. LOMONOSOVA

ADMIRALTEYSKIY

ULITSA LUMONOSOVA

NAB. KANALA GRIBOEDOVA

STOLYARNIY PER

Sadovaya

Sennaya Ploshchad

NAB. REKI FONTANKI

PROSPEKT RIMSKOVO-KORSAKOVA

SENNAYA PLOSHCHAD

GOROKHOVAYA ULITSA

ZAGORODNIY PROSPEKT

ULITSA PRAVDY

Railway Museum

SADOVAYA ULITSA

PEREULOK DZHAMBULA

BOLSHAYA PODYACHESKAYA

VOZNESENSKIY PROSPEKT

Yusupov Palace

MOSKOVSKIY PROSPEKT

ULITSA DOSTOEVSKOVO

SADOVAYA ULITSA

Pushkinskaya

River Fontanka

Vitebsk Station

Trinity Cathedral

Tekhnologicheskiy Institut

TROITSKIY PROSPEKT

ACCOMMODATION	
Ambassador	G
Andrey & Sasha	A
Asteria	E
B&B Randhouse	D
Columb	C
Matisov Domik	H
Na Muchnom	B
Na Sadovoy	I
Premiere	J
Swiss Star	F

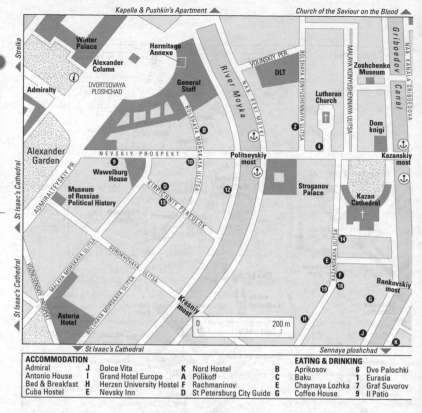

Map labels:
Kapella & Pushkin's Apartment ▲ | Church of the Saviour on the Blood ▲

Strelka ◀
Winter Palace
Hermitage Annexe
Alexander Column
VOLINSKIY PER.
Griboedov Canal
NAB. KANALA GRIBOEDOVA
DLT
Zoshchenko Museum
Admiralty
DVORTSOVAYA PLOSHCHAD
General Staff
River Moyka
NAB. REKI MOYKI
BOLSHAYA KONYUSHENNAYA ULITSA
MALAYA KONYUSHENNAYA ULITSA
Lutheran Church
Dom knigi
Alexander Garden
NEVSKIY PROSPEKT
Politseyskiy most
Kazanskiy most
St Isaac's Cathedral
ADMIRALTEYSKIY PR.
Wawelburg House
Museum of Russian Political History
KIRPICHNIY PEREULOK
Stroganov Palace
Kazan Cathedral
St Isaac's Cathedral
VOZNESENSKIY PROSPEKT
MALAYA MORSKAYA ULITSA
GOROKHOVAYA ULITSA
BOLSHAYA MORSKAYA ULITSA
KAZANSKAYA ULITSA
Bankovskiy most
Krasniy most
Astoria Hotel
0   200 m
St Isaac's Cathedral ▼ | Sennaya ploshchad ▼

ACCOMMODATION				EATING & DRINKING	
Admiral	J	Dolce Vita	K	Nord Hostel	B	Aprikosov	6	Dve Palochki
Antonio House	I	Grand Hotel Europe	A	Polikoff	C	Baku	1	Eurasia
Bed & Breakfast	H	Herzen University Hostel	F	Rachmaninov	E	Chaynaya Lozhka	7	Graf Suvorov
Cuba Hostel	E	Nevsky Inn	D	St Petersburg City Guide	G	Coffee House	9	Il Patio

The prospekt manifests every style of **architecture** from eighteenth-century Baroque to *fin-de-siècle* Style Moderne (Russia's own version of Art Nouveau), its skyline culminating in the golden spire of the Admiralty. Nevskiy's **streetlife** reflects the New Russia: bemedalled war veterans promenading alongside teenagers in the latest fashions; cadets linking arms in beery camaraderie; barefoot gypsies and wild-eyed drunks like *muzhiks* (peasants) from the pages of Dostoyevsky. During the midsummer "White Nights", when darkness barely falls, the avenue is busy with people, even at two o'clock in the morning.

While you're bound to use public transport to reach some sights beyond the Fontanka (covered in Chapter 6), the downtown stretch of Nevskiy prospekt can really only be appreciated on foot. The least demanding approach involves taking the **metro** to Gostiniy Dvor or Nevskiy Prospekt station, and **walking** the 1.5km to Dvortsovaya ploshchad (Palace Square) – an itinerary with Kazan Cathedral and two stunning canal vistas as its highlights. A longer (2.4km) but even more rewarding option is to start from Mayakovskaya metro station, 600m beyond the River Fontanka, then catch a **bus** (#3, #7 or #22), **trolleybus** (#1, #5, #7, #10 or #22) or **minibus** (#47, #128, #147 or #187) or walk up to Anichkov most and proceed from there. Whichever approach you choose, the chief **landmarks** are the glass cupola and globe of Dom knigi; the green dome of Kazan Cathedral; and the gilded spire of the Admiralty.

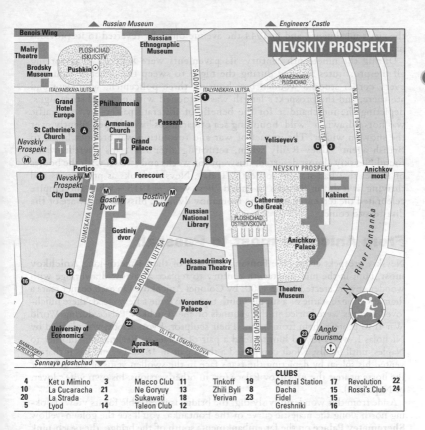

								CLUBS			
4	Ket u Mimino	3	Macco Club	11	Tinkoff	19	Zhili Byli	Central Station	17	Revolution	22
10	La Cucaracha	21	Ne Goryuy	13	Zhili Byli	8	Yerivan	Dacha	15	Rossi's Club	24
20	La Strada	2	Sukawati	18	Yerivan	23		Fidel	15		
5	Lyod	14	Taleon Club	12				Greshniki	16		

This account progresses from Anichkov most on the Fontanka towards the Winter Palace and the Admiralty. To describe Nevskiy prospekt's sights roughly in the order in which they appear, it switches from one side of the road to the other more often than you're likely to do in practice, and merely alludes to various **turn-offs** that receive fuller coverage later in the text.

Some history

Like so much in the city, the prospekt was built during the reign of Peter the Great under the direction of a foreigner, in this case the Frenchman Jean-Baptiste Le Blond, who ploughed through 4km of forests and meadows to connect the newly built Admiralty with the Novgorod road (now Ligovskiy prospekt). It was constructed by Swedish prisoners of war, starting from opposite ends in 1712; when they met in the middle it was discovered that they intersected the Novgorod road at different points, hence the kink in the road near what is now ploshchad Vosstaniya. Despite this imperfection, the grand view suggested its original title, the "Great Perspective Road", changed in 1738 to Nevskaya perspektivnaya ulitsa, after the River Neva to which it leads, and shortened to its present name twenty years later. The Bolsheviks renamed it "25 October Avenue" (after the date of the Revolution), but this was effectively ignored by the city's inhabitants, and in 1944 the avenue officially reverted to its previous name.

During the nineteenth century, its pavements were kept clean by forcing all the prostitutes arrested during the night to sweep the street at 4am. On every corner stood a wooden box housing three policemen, who slept and ate there, and the prospekt's length was festooned with pictorial store signs, depicting the merchandise for the benefit of illiterate passers-by. All traffic was horse-drawn, a "wild, bounding sea of carriages" which sped silently over the snow in winter. The impact of war and revolution was brought home to British agent Sidney Reilly when, returning after the tsar's overthrow, he found Nevskiy almost deserted, unswept for weeks and strewn with the bodies of horses that had starved to death. Today, Nevskiy looks as prosperous and thriving as it did in Russia's so-called "best year" – 1913 – when the Empire celebrated the tercentenary of the Romanov dynasty, blissfully unaware of the disasters to come.

From Anichkov most to Passazh

Nevskiy prospekt crosses the Fontanka by way of the 54-metre-long **Anichkov most**, built in the mid-nineteenth century to replace a narrow drawbridge with wooden towers erected in the 1700s by Colonel Anichkov. On each corner rears a dramatic bronze statue of a supple youth trying to tame a fiery steed: these much-loved **statues** were buried in the grounds of the Anichkov Palace during World War II to protect them from harm. Their sculptor, Pyotr Klodt, was plagued by Nicholas I, who ordered him to send a pair of horses to Berlin, then another to Naples, until finally, Klodt completed a third pair in 1850. Legend has it that he vented his spleen by depicting the tsar's face in the swollen veins of the groin of the horse nearest the Anichkov Palace (or, in other versions, his own wife's lover, or Napoleon).

Aside from this wonderfully sly dig, the bridge is irresistible for its **view**. Looking north along the majestic curve of the Fontanka, you'll see the golden-yellow **Sheremetev Palace** on the far embankment: south of the bridge, the peach-pink **Beloselskiy-Belozerskiy Palace** faces the cream Anichkov Palace across the river. Such **colours** are typical of St Petersburg architecture; brick and stucco were the main building materials (marble, granite and other stone had to be shipped in), and bright or pastel colours provided relief from the city's bleak climate and winter snows.

While the two palaces beyond the Fontanka house museums (described in Chapter 6), the **Anichkov Palace** – officially the Palace of Youth Creativity – is home to over 100 after-school clubs, as in Soviet times, when it was called the Palace of Pioneers and Youth. The site was once an encampment commanded by Colonel Anichkov; in 1741, Empress Elizabeth built a palace here for her lover, Alexei Razumovsky (a Ukrainian chorister nicknamed "the night-time Emperor"), which Catherine the Great presented to her own favourite, Potemkin. Her successor, Alexander I, built the **Kabinet** annexe to house his Chancellery, but after 1817, the palace was exclusively a winter residence for heirs to the throne, second only to the Winter Palace. Two Classical **pavilions** festooned with gilded statuary – now containing a Versace shop – are a relic of the gardens that once ran beside Nevskiy.

▲ Statue on Anichkov most

Ploshchad Ostrovskovo

Following Russia's victory over Napoleon, Alexander I chose the Russian-Italian architect Carlo Rossi to create a unified scheme for the city centre, incorporating the Admiralty, Winter Palace, state ministries and splendid public buildings. Rossi created a series of ensembles that became the focal points of the city: the General Staff building; the Mikhailovskiy Palace and Philharmonia; and St Petersburg's first public library and theatre. The latter stand on a square laid out in 1828–34, which some still call Aleksandrinskaya ploshchad (after Nicholas I's wife Alexandra), rather than **ploshchad Ostrovskovo** (as the Soviets renamed it in honour of the dramatist Nikolai Ostrovsky), or fondly refer to as "Katkin sad" ("Katya's Garden"), after the **statue of Catherine the Great** that was erected here in 1873. Matvey Chizhov and Alexander Opekushin sculpted the ermine-robed empress almost twice as large as the figures of her favourites and advisers clustered around the pedestal, including Prince Potemkin – who grinds a Turkish turban underfoot as he chats to Marshal Suvorov – and Princess Dashkova, the first president of the Russian Academy of Sciences. Somewhat surprisingly, this is the only statue of Catherine in St Petersburg.

Along the right-hand side of the square is the dove-grey Ionic facade of the **Russian National Library** (Mon–Fri 9am–9pm, Sat & Sun 11am–7pm), crowned with a figure of Minerva, goddess of wisdom, and garnished with statues of philosophers. This Rossi-built extension of St Petersburg's first public library, opened in 1814, holds such treasures as Voltaire's library (purchased by Catherine the Great) and a postage-stamp-sized edition of *Krylov's Fables*, so clearly printed that it can be read with the naked eye.

Catherine the Great

Catherine the Great of Russia (1729–96) always disclaimed that sobriquet, insisting that she was merely Catherine II, but posterity has insisted upon it. She was born Princess Sophie of Anhalt-Zerbst, in northern Germany, on May 2, 1729, and married at the age of 15 to the 16-year-old Russian heir apparent, Peter. The marriage was a dismal failure, and the belated birth of a son and heir, Paul, probably owed more to the first of Catherine's lovers than to her husband, the future Tsar **Peter III**. Notwithstanding this, Catherine strove to make herself acceptable to the Russian court and people, unlike her husband, who made his contempt for both – and her – obvious, until their worsening relations made conflict inevitable. On July 28, 1762, with the assistance of the Orlov brothers and the support of the Guards, Catherine staged a coup, forced Peter to abdicate, and proclaimed herself ruler; Peter was murdered by the Orlovs a few days later.

Her reign was initially characterized by enlightened absolutism: works of philosophy, literature and science were translated into Russian; hospitals, orphanages, journals and academies founded; roads, canals and palaces built. The Crimea was annexed to Russia, in which quest she was greatly assisted by Prince Potemkin, who planted the Tsarist flag on the shores of the Black Sea, having beaten back the forces of the Ottoman Empire.

Later, however, the French Revolution turned her against any hint of egalitarianism and towards the Orthodox Church. Meanwhile, she lost her taste for older, masterful lovers such as Orlov and Potemkin, opting for ever younger, more pliable "favourites". Estimates of their number range from 12 to 54, and although Catherine was no more promiscuous than the average male European sovereign, she was judged by the standards set by the Habsburg Empress Maria Theresa, the so-called "Virgin of Europe". For more about Catherine's life, see the accounts of the Winter Palace (p.78), Peterhof (p246), Tsarskoe Selo (p.255) and Oranienbaum (p.250).

Behind the statue of Catherine stands Rossi's *tour de force*, the **Aleksandri-inskiy Drama Theatre**, its straw-coloured facade decorated with a columned loggia topped by a statue of Apollo in his chariot, and flanked by niche-bound statues of the muses Terpsichore and Melpomene. The theatre company here can trace its history back to 1756, making it the oldest in Russia. While Gogol's *The Government Inspector* caused a sensation at its first staging in 1836, Chekhov's *The Seagull* was so badly received at its premiere in 1896 that he fled the theatre to wander anonymously among the crowds on Nevskiy.

The Theatre Museum and ulitsa Zodchevo Rossi

Behind the theatre, at no. 6, the **Theatre Museum** (Mon & Thurs–Sun 11am– 6pm, Wed 1–7pm; closed Tues & the last Fri of each month; R100) exhibits items belonging to the opera singer Chaliapin, the choreographer Pepita and other stars of the Russian stage; Rimsky-Korsakov's annotated scores and Tchaikovsky's letters; costume sketches by Bakst and a half-life-sized replica of a Constructivist stage from the 1920s. Models of the Mariinskiy stage and antique devices used to create sound effects are displayed in the children's section. Ask an attendant to open the **ballet room**, holding costumes from the first production of *The Sleeping Beauty*. From September to May, **concerts** are held here, employing the piano on which Tchaikovsky once played; for details, phone ☎571 21 95 or see the Russian-language version of the website Ⓦwww .theatremuseum.ru.

Next door stands the **Vaganova School of Choreography**, whose alumni include such ballet stars as Anna Pavlova, Tamara Karsavina, Vaslav Nijinsky, Galina Ulanova, Rudolf Nureyev and Mikhail Baryshnikov. Its origins go back to 1738, when J.B. Landé began to train the children of palace servants to take part in court entertainments, though it wasn't until 1934 that a modern curriculum was implemented by Agrippina Vaganova (1879–1951), the "Empress of Variations". Over two thousand young hopefuls apply to the school every year, of which only ninety are chosen to undergo its gruelling regime.

The school is on **ulitsa Zodchevo Rossi** (Master-builder Rossi Street), the most perfectly proportioned of his creations: exactly as wide as the height of its buildings (22m) and ten times as long, with every facade, paving stone and lamppost perfectly mirroring those on the opposite side of the street. At the far end is the crescent-shaped **ploshchad Lomonosova**, another of Rossi's designs, whose severe buildings used to house the Tsarist ministries of the Interior and Public Instruction. The area is busier at night than it is by day, thanks to *Rossi's Club* at the end of the street and other **clubs** on nearby ulitsa Lomonosova and Dumskaya ulitsa.

Malaya Sadovaya, Yeliseyev's and Passazh

Returning to Nevskiy, you can cross the avenue by an **underpass** at the junction with Sadovaya ulitsa, and turn right up the ramp on the far side to emerge near **Malaya Sadovaya ulitsa**. This short pedestrianized street is home to some cute **statues:** cast your eyes to the second-floor ledges of the houses 20m off Nevskiy, to espy a male **black cat**, destined never to meet the female **white cat** across the way. At street level there's a bronze figure of the great St Petersburg photographer **Karl Bulla**, with his tripod camera and bulldog, and a marble **sphere** spun by a fountain. The latest addition is a model of a **loudspeaker** on the corner of Nevs-kiy, recalling the public-address system that broadcast news and air-raid warnings during the Siege of Leningrad.

On the opposite corner of Malaya Sadovaya stands the famous pre-revolution-ary food store **Yeliseyev's**, baldly designated "Gastronom No. 1" during Soviet times. Designed by Yuri Baranovsky in 1902–3, it's one of the most stunning Style Moderne buildings in the city; the interior of the delicatessen has a lofty ceiling with gold filigree work, festooned with crystal fairy lights, while from the walls wrought-iron flowers burst forth, culminating in a gracefully drooping chandelier. Alas the store is now closed and in legal limbo, since its buyers' plans to gut the interior under the guise of "refurbishment" were blocked.

Returning to the underpass and crossing Sadovaya ulitsa, you'll find the northern side of Nevskiy rife with hoardings advertising two emporiums on the same block. At no. 48, **Passazh** (Mon–Sat 10am–9pm, Sun 11am–9pm) is a 180-metre-long, galleried shopping arcade built in 1846 for St Petersburg's upper classes, selling porcelain, antiques, shoes and cosmetics. Its canary-yellow walls are offset by maroon marble surrounds, topped by a glass canopy like that of GUM in Moscow. More opulent but less elegant is the Yeltsin-era **Grand Palace** (daily 11am–9pm) at no. 44, a quadruple-level marbled mall of French and Italian designer stores. Both malls run through to Italyanskaya ulitsa, off ploshchad Iskusstv (p.91).

Gostiniy dvor to the Griboedov Canal

Directly across Nevskiy stands the grand-daddy of St Petersburg's malls, the eighteenth-century **Gostiniy dvor** (daily 10am–10pm, Wed & Thurs till 10.30pm), whose columned arcades extend for 230m along the prospekt. Having taken over sixty years to build, it took its name and inspiration from the *gostiniy dvory* or merchants' hostels of Old Russia, which offered lodgings and storage space as well as a bazaar where each product was allocated a specific area – there was even one for the sale of stolen goods, which buyers entered at their peril. The **interior** is nearly a kilometre in circumference with hundreds of shops on two floors – now mostly boutiques selling furs, designer clothes or jewellery – while the external gallery offers fine views of the surrounding area. During maintenance work on the gallery in 1965, over 300 pounds of gold hidden by merchants was discovered.

Outside the dvor on Nevskiy, you'll see **"Red Grannies"** selling far-left and far-right newspapers, and people touting **coach excursions** around St Petersburg and to the Imperial palaces, run by tourist companies with **kiosks** on the forecourt (see p.40 for details).

Dumskaya ulitsa

Dumskaya ulitsa, on the dvor's western side, is one of the few downtown locations that rates a **warning**, as short-change artists lurk outside Luigi Rossa's elegant Neoclassical **Portico**. The street is named after the former seat of the **City Duma**, or pre-revolutionary municipal government, one of the few elected institutions in Petrograd until it was suppressed by the Bolsheviks in October 1918. The Duma's triple-tiered red-and-white **tower** was erected in 1804 to give warning of fires, and later adapted for semaphore and heliograph signalling between St Petersburg and the Imperial palaces outside the city; ironically, it caught fire in 2000 and has yet to be repaired – billboards mask the damage. At night, the far end of the street resounds with the cries of revellers outside *Dacha*, *Revolution* and other **clubs** in the vicinity (see Chapter 15).

From the Armenian Church to St Catherine's

In Tsarist times Nevskiy prospekt was dubbed the "Street of Tolerance", owing to the variety of non-Orthodox denominations that were allowed to build their churches here. Across the road from Gostiniy dvor stands the **Armenian Church** (Armyanskaya tserkov), an azure Neoclassical edifice, built in the 1770s by the German-born architect Felten, and set back from the street in its own courtyard. Converted into a workshop during Soviet times, it has now been restored as a place of worship, with a simple yet elegant decor of pastel colours and fake marble. Notice the fountain in the yard, resembling a silvered bouquet of pomegranates and grapes.

Near the church, the broad, tree-lined **Mikhailovskaya ulitsa** forms a grand approach to ploshchad Iskusstv and the Mikhailovskiy Palace (which contains the Russian Museum; see p.137) beyond. The whole of the western side of the street is occupied by the deluxe **Grand Hotel Europe** (Yevropeyskaya), built in 1873–75 but greatly altered by the Art Nouveau architect Fyodor Lidval. Turned into an orphanage after the Civil War, it was totally refurbished in the 1980s by a Swedish–Russian joint venture.

Further up the prospekt, amid the next block and set back slightly from the street, **St Catherine's Church** (Kostyol Svyatoy Yekateriny) was St Petersburg's main Roman Catholic church. Its steps have now been taken over by street artists, and inside it harbours the tombs of **General Moreau**, a Frenchman who fought on the Russian side against Napoleon, and **Stanislaw Poniatowski**, the last king of Poland. Enthroned by his erstwhile lover, Catherine the Great, Poniatowski subsequently died fighting the Russians near Leipzig, but was buried in St Petersburg. In 1938, his remains were repatriated and secretly interred in eastern Poland, before being dug up yet again and transferred to Warsaw's Royal Castle, where they remain to this day, stashed away in a coffin out of sight, since many Poles regard him as a traitor.

At the end of the block, on the corner of the Griboedov embankment, **Nevskiy Prospekt metro station** is a focal point for teenagers, old women selling cigarettes, and boozers, who dub it "the climate" (*klimat*), because of the warm air blowing from its vestibule – a blessing during the Russian winter.

Crossing the Griboedov Canal: Dom knigi

The broad **Kazanskiy most** (Kazan Bridge) carries Nevskiy prospekt across the **Griboedov Canal** (kanal Griboedova). Originally called the "Krivushchy" ("twisting river"), it was canalized and embanked under Catherine the Great and henceforth nicknamed the "Katinka Kanavka", or "Catherine's Gutter", flowing as it did through the heart of the notorious Haymarket district, until the Soviets renamed it after the writer Alexander Griboedov (see p.210). It's worth lingering to admire the superb **views** along the canal. To the left, beyond the colonnades of Kazan Cathedral, you might be able to glimpse **Bankovskiy most** (Bank Bridge), with its gilded griffons (see p.101), while to the right are the multicoloured onion domes of the **Church of the Saviour on the Blood** (p.83). If the view tempts you onto the water, **waterbuses** depart from a jetty near Kazanskiy most.

Looming above the bridge's northwestern corner is the former emporium of the American sewing-machine company, Singer, now St Petersburg's most famous bookstore, **Dom knigi** (daily 9am–10pm). Designed by Pavel Syusor and completed in 1904, its Style Moderne exterior is distinguished by a conical tower topped by the Singer trademark: a giant glass globe, which used to light up at night. Before the Revolution, women worked at sewing machines in the windows to pull in the crowds. Today, the bookshop has been reduced to two floors and the upper storeys are offices; a much larger Dom knigi at Nevskiy prospekt 62 is now the flagship emporium.

Kazan Cathedral

Kazan Cathedral (Kazanskiy sobor) is one of the grandest buildings in the city, its curvaceous colonnades embracing Nevskiy prospekt like the outstretched wings of a gigantic eagle. The cathedral was built between 1801 and 1811 to house a venerated **icon**, Our Lady of Kazan, reputed to have appeared miraculously overnight in Kazan in 1579, and brought by Peter the Great to St Petersburg, where it resided until its miraculous disappearance in 1904. Although the cathedral was erected during the reign of Alexander I, its inspiration came from his father Paul, who decreed that it should be designed and executed by Russian artists, despite being modelled on St Peter's in Rome.

During Soviet times, it housed the infamous **Museum of Atheism**, whose foundation in 1932 coincided with a period of anti-religious repression in Leningrad. Containing over 150,000 exhibits, from Egyptian mummies to pictures of monks and nuns copulating, it was used to prove Marx's dictum that "religion is the opium of the people". Renamed the Museum of Religion during perestroika, it was moved out in 1999 and is now located near St Isaac's Cathedral (see p.97). There are daily **services** in the cathedral (Mon–Sat 10am & 6pm, Sun & holidays 7am, 10am & 6pm), which at **Easter** overflows with believers greeting each other with the salutation *Kristos voskres!* (Christ is risen!) and replying with the traditional answer *Voistine voskres!* (Verily, He is risen!)

The exterior

The semicircular **colonnade** is made up of 96 Corinthian columns hewn from Karelian granite, and largely unadorned with sculptural decoration: it's easy to miss the **bas-reliefs** at either end of the colonnade – depicting *Moses Striking the Rock* and *The Adoration of the Brazen Serpent* – and the bronze **statues** hidden in the porticoes of (from left to right) St Vladimir, John the Baptist, Alexander Nevsky and St Andrew. The bronze **doors** facing the prospekt are worth inspecting at close quarters: an exact copy of Ghiberti's doors for the Florentine Baptistery, which Michelangelo allegedly described as "splendid enough to serve as the gates of paradise".

In 1837, two **statues** by Boris Orlovsky were erected at either end of the colonnade: to the west, **Michael Barclay de Tolly**; to the east, **Mikhail Kutuzov**, the hero of Tolstoy's *War and Peace*. The Scottish-born General de Tolly's contentious policy of strategic retreat before Napoleon's armies prompted his replacement by the one-eyed Field Marshal Kutuzov, who used to close his good eye and pretend to sleep so that his aides could express their opinions freely. Public opinion forced Kutuzov to engage the vastly superior French troops at the Battle of Borodino (1812), which produced no clear winner despite horrendous casualties on both sides - but his "scorched earth" strategy was vindicated by Napoleon's retreat after the burning of Moscow.

The interior

The cathedral is **open** to sightseers (11am–5pm, Sun & holidays noon–5pm, closed Wed; free) outside prayer times, but visitors should behave with decorum. Depending on which part of the interior is being refurbished, the entrance may be on the left or the right of the colonnades facing Nevskiy, and the first sight you might see is the **tomb of Marshal Kutuzov**, overhung with captured Napoleonic banners. He was buried here with full honours, on the spot where he had prayed before setting off to war. The object of his prayers was the icon **Our Lady of Kazan**, or *Derzhavnaya* (Sovereign), which reputedly disappeared in 1904, to reappear miraculously in Moscow on the day of Nicholas II's abdication, where the woman who found it dreamt of being told that the divine power vested in the tsars had now returned to the Mother of God. In the latest chapter of this long-running mystery, Our Lady of Kazan is now thought to be one and the same as an icon now in the possession of the Prince Vladimir Cathedral on the Petrograd Side (see p.185).

On towards the Moyka

Other, lesser sights are distributed on either side of the prospekt as it approaches the River Moyka. Diagonally opposite the cathedral, set back behind a beer garden, the mid-nineteenth-century **Lutheran Church** (Lyuteranskaya tserkov) was built in a vaguely neo-Romanesque style unusual for St Petersburg. After being converted into a swimming pool (complete with diving boards and spectators' stands) in the late 1950s, it has now been returned to the Lutherans, who are slowly restoring it, as related by an exhibition in the lobby (Mon–Fri 10am–2pm & 3–6pm). During the late 1840s, Mussorgsky was a pupil at the eighteenth-century **Peterschule** (officially School No. 222) next door.

The Stroganov Palace

Across the prospekt, the pink-and-white facade of the **Stroganov Palace** (Stroganovskiy dvorets) overlooks the intersection of Nevskiy and the River Moyka. Built by Rastrelli in 1753, it's a fine example of Russian Baroque, paying homage to the carved window-frames of peasant cottages, whilst flaunting its owner's status with Doric columns and pediments emblazoned with the Stroganov coat of arms. Though hard to see from street level, this features a bear's head flanked by sables – the Stroganovs owned vast tracts of Siberia, and earned a fortune from salt trading (their chef also invented the dish beef stroganoff). The palace now belongs to the Russian Museum and its restored state rooms exhibit **Tsarist porcelain** from the Gardner and Lomonosov factories (10am–6pm, Mon till 5pm; closed Tues; R300). Downstairs is a separate **waxworks exhibition** (daily 11am–8pm; R150) of figures from Russian history, entered from the courtyard, which also has a restaurant and a shop masquerading as a Chocolate Museum.

The adjacent **Politseyskiy most** (Police Bridge), spanning the Moyka, was the city's first iron bridge, constructed in 1806–8 to the design of Scotsman William Hastie. Originally called the "Green Bridge" after the colour of its outer walls, it was subsequently renamed the "Police Bridge" and then, after the Revolution, the "People's Bridge", before reverting to its second name in 1992. Moored to the north and south of the bridge are motorboats and larger vessels for **private or scheduled canal trips** (see p.41).

Beyond the Moyka

Beyond the Moyka, billboards obscure the edifice known as the "House with Columns", where the Italian architect **Giacomo Quarenghi** lived after arriving in Russia, before designing the Hermitage Theatre for Catherine the Great. Previously this was the site of a wooden palace built for Empress Elizabeth as a temporary home while Rastrelli constructed the Winter Palace; dismantled in 1765, its site was purchased by the merchant Yeliseyev brothers, whose mansion subsequently housed the Institute of Marxism-Leninism and is now an exclusive restaurant (see p.351).

On the other side of Nevskiy stands a yellow-and-white building with colonnaded arcades at either corner which formerly housed the fashionable *Café Wulf et Béranger*, frequented by the poet Pushkin, who met his second here en route to his fatal duel with D'Anthès in 1837. It later became the *Restaurant Leiner*, where Tchaikovsky is supposed to have caught cholera, and today contains the shamelessly touristic **Literaturnoe Café**.

At this point, you'll probably be lured off Nevskiy towards the Winter Palace by the great arch of the General Staff building (see p.76), leaving behind the **Wawelburg House** which dominates the corner of Nevskiy and Malaya Morskaya ulitsa. A monument to 1900s capitalism, this granite pile was designed to resemble both the Doge's Palace in Venice and the Palazzo Medici-Riccardi in Florence. The stone was imported from Sweden by the banker Wawelburg, whose initials appear on the shield crowning the pediment and above the service entrance on Malaya Morskaya, once St Petersburg's equivalent of Wall Street (see p.100).

If you stick with the prospekt all the way to the needle-spired Admiralty (see p.93), watch out for a couple of buildings on the right-hand side as you go. Outside the 1930s secondary school at no. 14 is a stencilled **warning sign**, in blue and white, which reads: "Citizens! In the event of artillery fire, this side of the street is the most dangerous!" During the Siege of Leningrad, such signs were posted on the northeastern sides of main thoroughfares after ballistic analysis determined that they were most at risk from Nazi shellfire. A little further on, at nos. 8 and 10, stand the **oldest houses** on the prospekt, dating from the early 1760s and decorated with griffons and medallions.

To the Winter Palace

The best way of **approaching the Winter Palace** (which houses the Hermitage – see Chapter 2) is to turn right off Nevskiy prospekt at **Bolshaya Morskaya ulitsa**, whose northern end was designed by Rossi to lie along the Pulkovo meridian (the Tsarist equivalent of the Greenwich meridian), so that at midday, the houses cast no shadow. The beauty of this approach becomes obvious as the street curves beneath the triple arch of the General Staff building – also designed by Rossi – and you first glimpse Dvortsovaya ploshchad, its towering Alexander Column set against the facade of the Winter Palace – it's been called "the greatest compliment ever paid by one architect to another", so eloquently does Rossi's design introduce and frame the open space and buildings of Dvortsovaya ploshchad.

Dvortsovaya ploshchad (Palace Square)

The theatrical expanse of **Dvortsovaya ploshchad** (Palace Square) is inseparable from the city's turbulent past. Here, the Guards hailed Catherine as empress on the day of her coup against her husband Peter III, while later rulers revelled in showy parades. It was also the epicentre of the mass demonstration on what became known as "**Bloody Sunday**", which marked the beginning of the 1905 Revolution. On January 9, Father Gapon, head of a workers' society sponsored by the secret police, led thousands of strikers and their families to the square, bearing religious banners and portraits of the tsar and the tsaritsa, seeking to present a petition to Nicholas II (who was actually at Tsarskoe Selo). The Preobrazhenskiy Guards opened fire without warning, killing hundreds (the police figure was "more than thirty"). At the outbreak of World War I, however, much of the hostility felt towards "Bloody Nicholas" was submerged in a wave of patriotism, and hundreds of thousands of people sank to their knees and bellowed "God save the tsar" as he emerged from the Winter Palace.

Despite this, within three years Tsarism had been swept away in the **February Revolution** of 1917. The determination of Kerensky's Provisional Government to continue the war enabled the Bolsheviks to mobilize support by promising "Peace, Bread, Land" and launch a second revolution. On October 25, 1917, the square witnessed the famous **storming of the Winter Palace**, immortalized (and largely invented) in Eisenstein's film *October* – more people were injured during the making of the film than in the event itself. Having taken over all the key installations, Lenin announced the resignation of the Provisional Government at 10am. In fact, the first real exchange of fire didn't take place until 9.40pm, followed by blank shots from the cruiser *Aurora*, anchored downriver. Sporadic gunfire continued until around 10pm, when the Cossacks defending the palace deserted en masse, leaving only a few-score officer cadets and members of the Women's Battalion to continue resistance. They were persuaded to lay down their arms and, in the early hours of the morning, a large group of Bolsheviks entered by a side entrance and made their way through the palace's interminable rooms to arrest the Provisional Government.

Eisenstein's version of events was filmed in 1928, but by then the myth of the mass charge across the square was already part of Soviet folklore, thanks to the spectacles staged in honour of the **first anniversary of the October Revolution**, when artists including Nathan Altman and Marc Chagall transformed the square by covering the Alexander Column, the facades of the Winter Palace, and the General Staff with sculptures and canvas plastered with avant-garde art. For the **third anniversary** (1920), under the glare of giant arc lights, a battalion of Red Army troops and thousands of citizens pretended to storm the palace, while fifty actors dressed as Kerensky (who was, in fact, absent at the time of the assault) made identical speeches and gestures, on a stage backed by Futurist designs.

In 1991, the square was at the centre of events during the referendum on the city's name, when groups of people congregated to argue the merits of Leningrad or Petersburg. During the attempted **putsch** in August that year, Mayor Sobchak addressed some 150,000 citizens who assembled here to protest against the coup. Though political rallies still occur here, the square is more used to tourists, skateboarders and people offering horse-and-carriage rides or coach excursions to the Imperial palaces outside the city – plus the occasional beer or music festival.

The Alexander Column

Napoleon had hardly begun his 1812 retreat from Moscow when it was decided that a triumphal column should be erected in the middle of the square. However, work on the **Alexander Column** (Aleksandrovskaya kolonna) didn't begin until 1830, when Auguste de Montferrand, the inexperienced architect in charge of building St Isaac's Cathedral, landed the job. Crowned by an angel, whose face is supposedly modelled on Alexander I's, the monument is 47.5m high, one of the tallest of its kind in the world. The **bas-relief** facing the Winter Palace depicts two figures representing the Niemen and Vistula, the two great rivers that Napoleon crossed on his march to Moscow, together with the simple inscription, "To Alexander I from a grateful Russia".

Its construction entailed Herculean efforts, rewarded by a faultless climax. After two years spent hewing the 600-tonne granite monolith from a Karelian rock face, and a year transporting it to St Petersburg, the column was erected in just forty minutes using a system of ramps, pulleys and ropes, pulled by two thousand war veterans (as shown in an animated film in the Peter and Paul Fortress, see p.172). More than a thousand wooden piles had to be driven into the swampy ground to strengthen the foundations and, so the story goes, Montferrand insisted the mortar be mixed with vodka to prevent it from freezing. Amazingly, the column isn't attached to the pedestal at all, but stays there simply by virtue of its weight.

The General Staff building

To complete the architectural ensemble around the square, Alexander I purchased (and demolished) all the private houses that faced the Winter Palace, and in 1819 commissioned Rossi to design a new headquarters for the Russian Army **General Staff** (Generalniy shtab) building. The edifice frames one side of the square in a gigantic yellow arc, its sweeping facade interrupted by a colossal **arch** commemorating the Patriotic War against Napoleon. The underside is covered in armorial bas-reliefs; above the arch, Victory rides her six-horsed chariot, while two Roman soldiers restrain the horses from leaping over the edge. The whole structure was so large, rumours spread that it would collapse, prompting Rossi to declare, "If it falls, I fall with it" – he proved his point by standing on top of the arch as the scaffolding was removed. At one time the General Staff building also served as a prison: Griboedov spent four months here in 1826 as a suspected Decembrist, and Lermentov was held for five days before being exiled to the Caucasus for having written his *On the Death of a Poet* about Pushkin.

As the diplomat Samuel Hoare observed, "true to Russian type, the facade was the best part of the building", concealing "a network of smelly yards and muddy passages that made entrance difficult and health precarious". At the outbreak of World War I, work often came to a standstill "owing to a perfect covey of saint's days and national anniversaries". Confusion also prevailed at the Foreign Ministry, housed in the eastern wing of the building, where, following the Bolshevik seizure of power, the head of the Petrograd Cheka (forerunners of the KGB), Moses Uritskiy, was assassinated in August 1918.

Since being given to the **Hermitage** to house its Impressionist and Post-Impressionist collections and contemporary art, the second floor of the Foreign Ministry has been used for temporary exhibitions, with the third floor divided between the Post-Impressionists **Pierre Bonnard** and **Maurice Denis** and **Empire Style decorative art**. However, both floors are due to close in 2008 when the rest of the building is converted into exhibition space (including a **Saatchi Room** of contemporary art) – possibly to reopen in 2011. When it

The Winter Palace and the Hermitage

Although begun as separate buildings, the **Winter Palace** and the **Hermitage** are now effectively one and the same thing. Catherine the Great created the first Hermitage and its embryonic art collection, and though "respectable" citizens were admitted after 1852, it became fully accessible only following the October Revolution – its collection swollen with Old Masters, precious objects and dozens of Impressionist masterpieces confiscated from private owners. Originally occupying only the eastern annexe, today the Hermitage's paintings take up most of the rooms in the Winter Palace. For a full account of the Hermitage collection and state rooms, see Chapter 2.

does, opening hours and admission charges are likely to be the same as for the Hermitage (see Chapter 2).

The Winter Palace

The **Winter Palace** (Zimniy dvorets) is the finest example of Russian Baroque in St Petersburg, and at the time of its completion was the largest and most opulent palace in the city. Its 200-metre-long facade features a riot of ornamentation in the fifty bays facing the square, including two tiers of pilasters, a balustrade peppered with urns and statuary, and the prominent vertical drains so characteristic of the city. From this ultimate symbol of power, the autocrat could survey the expanse of Dvortsovaya ploshchad or gaze across the Neva to the Peter and Paul Fortress. As the journalist Alexander Herzen wrote of the palace, "Like a ship floating on the surface of the ocean, it had no real connection with the inhabitants of the deep, beyond that of eating them."

The existing Winter Palace is the **fourth structure** of that name, all of them built within half a century of each other. The first two, created for Peter the Great on the site of the present Hermitage Theatre, reflected his penchant for Dutch architecture; their remains were discovered during restoration work and are now open to the public. In 1730, Empress Anna commissioned a third version (on the site of today's west wing) by Bartolomeo Rastrelli, but her successor Elizabeth was dissatisfied with the result and ordered him to start work on a replacement. This was intended to take two years to build and cost 859,555 rubles, though in the event it took eight years and cost 2.5 million, obliging Elizabeth to open a network of beer halls to finance the excess. What you see now is not entirely what Rastrelli had in mind. Originally the **facade** was painted an icy turquoise blue with white trimmings; this was given a uniform coat of Venetian red in the nineteenth century, but is now sage-green and white. A fire in 1837 caused enormous damage but, in typically Russian fashion, "neither money, life nor health was spared" to restore it completely – the court was re-established there within fifteen months.

The Small and Large Hermitages and the Hermitage Theatre

Once Rastrelli had completed the Winter Palace, new buildings were gradually added to the east wing, becoming ever more austerely Neoclassical in style. The first addition was the long, thin annexe known as the **Small Hermitage** (Maliy Ermitazh). Directly inspired by Peter the Great's Hermitage at Peterhof, it was given the same, somewhat ironic, name – anything less "hermitic" would be difficult to imagine. It was built as a private retreat for Catherine the Great and it was here that she began the Imperial art collection that would eventually become the world's largest art gallery.

The **Large Hermitage** (Bolshoy Ermitazh), to the east, is made up of two separate buildings: the "Old Hermitage", facing the River Neva, was built to house the rapidly expanding Imperial art collection, and in the mid-nineteenth century this was augmented by the "New Hermitage", designed as Petersburg's first purpose-built public art gallery. Its best exterior features are the ten giant granite **atlantes** which hold up the porch on the south facade, their rippling, polished muscles glistening in the sunlight.

Beyond stands the **Hermitage Theatre** (Ermitazhniy teatr), built in 1775–84 by Quarenghi as a private theatre for Catherine the Great. Once a fortnight she would fill it with the capital's diplomats; otherwise, the average audience of private guests rarely reached double figures. The theatre was built directly over the **remains of Peter the Great's Winter Palace** (see p.79), and joined to the rest of the complex

The palace in history

The Winter Palace is as loaded with history as it is with gilt and stucco, having been a winter residence for every tsar and tsaritsa since **Peter the Great** (not to mention the court and 1500 servants). Though Peter always preferred to live at Monplaisir, he died in the second Winter Palace – the first of several Imperial demises of note associated with the building.

The first tsar to inhabit the present structure was **Peter III**, who lived with his mistress, Elizabeth Vorontsova, in the southeastern corner of the second floor, while his wife, the future **Catherine the Great**, resided on the other side of the courtyard. On assuming the throne, Catherine redecorated and took over Peter's quarters, giving her lover, Grigory Orlov, the rooms directly beneath her own. Decades later, following a visit by the last of her paramours, Platon Zubov, she was found unconscious on the floor in her bedroom and later died. Given that she was then 67, it's difficult to believe the scurrilous legend (probably a Prussian invention) that she died whilst attempting to copulate with a stallion (which supposedly crushed her when the harness suspending it from the ceiling broke).

Despite the choice of luxurious apartments available, **Nicholas I** picked himself one "no larger than a Bloomsbury dining room", furnished with barrack-like simplicity, where he worked, ate, slept and entertained his mistresses – and eventually died of influenza in the middle of the Crimean War. In contrast, his wife Alexandra spared no expense in the adornment of her state room – the emerald green and gold Malachite Drawing Room.

Alexander II also chose to reside in a remote corner of the palace, furnished not with the Rembrandts or Rubens at his disposal, but in the simple, tasteless, bourgeois fashion of the day. In 1880 a bomb was planted below the Imperial Dining Hall by a member of the revolutionary Narodnaya Volya; eleven soldiers died, but the tsar – who had taken a break between courses – survived. A year later, however, another attempt on his life succeeded, and he died of his wounds in his apartment in the southwestern corner of the palace.

Nicholas II lived in the apartments above the Malachite Room until 1904, when increasing unrest forced the Imperial family to retreat to Tsarskoe Selo, only returning to the capital for state functions. At the outbreak of World War I, he pledged before five thousand people in the palace's St George's Hall that he would "never make peace so long as the enemy is on the soil of the fatherland", just as Alexander I had when Napoleon invaded the country in 1812. For much of the war, the great state rooms on the second floor were occupied by a hospital for invalids established by the tsaritsa, and during the February Revolution, loyalist troops made a brief last-ditch stand there.

In July 1917, the **Provisional Government** made its fateful move from the Mariinskiy Palace (see p.99) to the Winter Palace. Kerensky took over the tsaritsa's old rooms, and even slept in her four-poster bed. His ministers conferred in the Malachite Drawing Room and were arrested by the Bolsheviks in an adjacent dining room in the early hours of October 26. Party activists quickly put a stop to looting, except in the Imperial wine cellars, where every unit on guard soon got roaring drunk – and twelve people drowned. By 1922, most of the palace had been given over to the Hermitage art collection, while another part housed the Museum of the Great October Socialist Revolution between the wars.

by a covered passageway which passes over the **Winter Moat** (Zimnaya kanavka), originally dug to surround Peter's palace. The views, as you look beneath the overhead passageway to the Neva beyond, and inland across the canal, are some of the loveliest in the city.

The Winter Palace of Peter the Great and Preobrazhenskiy Barracks

In 1976, workmen uncovered a sizeable remnant of the original **Winter Palace of Peter the Great** (10.30am—6pm, Sun till 5pm; closed Mon; R200), sometimes known as "Peter's Hermitage". To visit it, you must buy a ticket in the lobby of the Hermitage before heading for the entrance at Dvortsovaya naberezhnaya 32 (just beyond the Winter Moat) – an audio-guide is included in the price. The remains consist of part of a courtyard flanked on two sides by arcaded galleries and private apartments used by Peter and Catherine I, including a reconstruction of Peter's turnery and a life-size wax figure of the tsar by Carlo Rastrelli.

Beyond the Winter Moat, to the south of the Hermitage Theatre, are the former **Preobrazhenskiy Barracks**. As the first regiment of the Imperial Guard, whose colonel was always the tsar himself, the Preobrazhenskiy was the most powerful of the "toy" regiments established by Peter at Preobrazhenskoe, the summer estate outside Moscow where he spent his youth. During the uncertain decades following his death, the Guards became de facto kingmakers, whose allegiance was essential for any ruler. This could be alienated by seemingly trivial matters – such as a change of uniform – as Peter III discovered when the Preobrazhenskiy cast off the Prussian-style garb introduced by him, and donned its old uniform of bottle-green and scarlet to salute Catherine's coup.

The view from the embankment

There are more magnificent views from **Dvortsovaya naberezhnaya** (Palace Embankment) across the widest part of the River Neva. To the north, the gilded spire of the Peter and Paul Cathedral soars above its island fortress; to the west, the rust-red Rostral Columns stand proudly on the Strelka; while to the east, the river curves around past the Summer Garden and runs beneath bridges to the Petrograd and Vyborg sides. In summer, this is also the place from which to catch **hydrofoils to Peterhof**, the great Imperial palace beside the Gulf of Finland (see p.240 for details).

In Tsarist times this spot was the scene of the **Blessing of the Waters** or "Jordan Feast" on January 6. The ceremony took place in a chapel erected for the occasion on the frozen Neva, and tradition required the court to appear in silk stockings and shoes, without winter coats: Alexander I contracted frostbite in three of his fingers at one such event. As for ordinary folk, the most devout had their newborn babies baptized through holes in the ice. Sometimes the priest lost his grip, or the infant caught pneumonia, but the parents were generally ecstatic, believing that the child had gone straight to heaven. More bizarrely, in 1739, Empress Anna Ioannovna ordered a palace built of ice upon the frozen Neva, where Prince Golitsyn was obliged to consummate a forced marriage on an icy bed, while Anna watched from the warmth of the Winter Palace. A replica of the **Ice Palace** was built on Dvortsovaya ploshchad in 2006, and might be recreated again in the future.

East to the Summer Garden and Palace

There are several possible routes from the Hermitage to Peter the Great's Summer Garden, the most direct being along either Millionnaya or the Neva embankment. Alternatively, you could follow the curve of the Moyka, taking in **Pushkin's Apartment** and the nearby church where he lay in state. Either way, you can't avoid **Marsovo pole**, where the Imperial troops used to parade. On the far side of

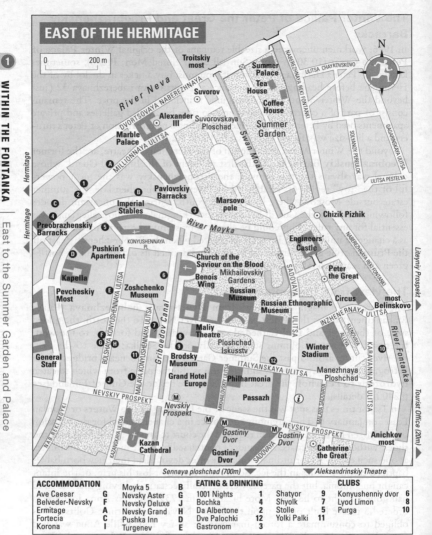

EAST OF THE HERMITAGE

0   200 m

ACCOMMODATION				EATING & DRINKING				CLUBS	
Ave Caesar	**G**	Moyka 5	**B**	1001 Nights	**1**	Shatyor	**9**	Konyushenniy dvor	**6**
Belveder-Nevsky	**F**	Nevsky Aster		Bochka	**4**	Shyolk	**7**	Lyod Limon	**8**
Ermitage	**A**	Nevsky Deluxe	**J**	Da Albertone	**2**	Stolle	**5**	Purga	**10**
Fortecia	**C**	Nevsky Grand	**H**	Dve Palochki	**12**	Yolki Palki	**11**		
Korona	**I**	Pushka Inn	**D**	Gastronom	**3**				
		Turgenev	**E**						

this, surrounded by water, is the **Summer Garden**, the most romantic of the city's parks and home to Peter's **Summer Palace**.

Millionnaya ulitsa

The first private houses in St Petersburg were built across the Neva on Petrograd Side in 1704, followed shortly afterwards by an elegant street of houses on this side of the river, dubbed **Millionnaya ulitsa** (Millionaires' Street) after the members of the royal family and the wealthy aristocracy who made it their home during the nineteenth century. Today, a new generation of Russian millionaires are buying up the old palaces and knocking through the walls to create huge luxury apartments, though they're outwardly indistinguishable from the shabby communal flats that occupy the rest of the buildings.

Of the various **palaces** on Millionnaya, few are architecturally outstanding, but many were at the centre of the cultural and social life of the Russian aristocracy before the Revolution. The grandest buildings, predominantly on the left-hand side, have their main facades on the Neva, so to appreciate them fully (and to follow the account given below) you will need to walk along the embankment for part of the way.

The Italianate building at no. 26 on the embankment is **Grand Duke Vladimir's Palace**, easily identified by its griffon-infested portal. A notorious hedonist, Vladimir was one of the most powerful public figures during the reign of his nephew, Nicholas II, but it was Vladimir's wife, Maria Pavlovna, who really set Petersburg talking. One of the tsar's most outspoken aristocratic critics, she hosted a popular salon, but left the city in the winter of 1916–17 vowing, "I'll not return until all is finished here" – and never did. It's worth trying to get inside the palace – now owned by the Academy of Sciences – to see its sumptuously gilded stairway, flanked by huge Chinese vases.

Further along is **Grand Duke Michael's Palace** (no. 18), an over-wrought neo-Baroque building that is so big that one of his sons used a bicycle to visit his sister-in-law in another part of the palace. At **Putyatin's House** (no. 12), on March 3, 1917, another Grand Duke Michael – Nicholas II's brother and named successor following his abdication the previous day – renounced his right to the throne, formally ending the Romanov dynasty.

Next door at no. 10, the architect Stakenschneider built himself a suitably majestic home. Here, in 1843, the French writer **Balzac** met a Polish countess, Éveline Hanska, whom, a decade earlier, he had promised to marry once her husband died – but though the count had already passed away by this time, Balzac managed to delay the marriage until 1850, just five months before he himself expired.

Along the Moyka

An alternative route east from the Winter Palace is to follow the **River Moyka**, which describes a graceful arc before joining the River Fontanka. Both rivers resemble canals, being embanked and adorned with handsome railings and flights of steps. The first bridge is **Pevcheskiy most**, or "Singer's Bridge", named for the nearby **Kapella** building, home of the Imperial Court Choir (now the Glinka Choir) established by Peter the Great. Various famous Russian musicians, including Rimsky-Korsakov and, of course, Glinka, worked here, and the Kapella concert hall boasts some of the best acoustics in the city (see p.365). On the other side of the river, a sculpted plaque on the facade of no. 31 commemorates the city's first democratically elected mayor, **Anatoly Sobchak**, who lived there from 1960 until his death in 2000.

Pushkin's apartment

Just up from the Kapella, a wooden doorway at no. 12 leads to the garden-courtyard of **Pushkin's apartment** (Muzey-kvartira A.S. Pushkina; 10.30am–5pm; closed Tues & the last Fri of each month; R200). The admission price includes an audio-guide to the second-floor apartment that he leased for his wife, their four children and her two sisters in the last unhappy year of his life (1836–37). The most evocative of its eleven rooms is the poet's **study**, containing a replica of his library of over 4500 books in fourteen languages, and a portrait of his teacher and fellow poet, Vasily Zhukovsky, given to Pushkin on the publication of *Ruslan*

Alexander Pushkin

Among Russians, **Alexander Pushkin** (1799–1837) is the most universally esteemed of all the great writers: "In him, as if in a lexicon, have been included all of the wealth, strength, and flexibility of our language", wrote Gogol. While the difficulty of translating his subtle "poetry of grammar" means that Pushkin is rarely lauded with such passion outside Russia, in his homeland he is not only seen as the father of Russian literature but as a national martyr.

Born in Moscow, Pushkin was educated at the Imperial Lycée in Tsarskoe Selo (see p.264), where he excelled in fencing, French and dancing. His first major poem, *Ruslan and Lyudmila*, caused an enormous stir in 1820, as did his subsequent political poems, for which he was exiled to the provinces. Drinking, gambling and sex characterized this period, during which Pushkin wrote his "southern cycle" of poems which, he admitted, "smack of Byron", to whom he is often compared. In 1826, the new tsar, Nicholas I, allowed Pushkin to return to St Petersburg and met him personally, appointing himself as the poet's censor. In 1831, Pushkin married the St Petersburg beauty **Natalya Goncharova**, the tsar making him an officer cadet so he could attend court functions, which Pushkin disliked (unlike Natalya).

His untimely death at the age of 38 was due to a French officer, **D'Anthès**, the adopted son of the Dutch ambassador, Heeckeren. D'Anthès set tongues wagging with his advances towards Natalya; some believe he acted at the tsar's bidding, as an *agent provocateur* or a panderer. Pushkin received anonymous letters mocking him for being a cuckold, which he concluded had been sent by Heeckeren. He challenged D'Anthès to a duel (January 27, 1837) at Chernaya Rechka (see p.227), where the Frenchman was shot in the hand, and Pushkin was fatally wounded. The doctor posted notices outside the door of his apartment to keep his admirers informed about their hero's condition, until he died after several days in extreme agony.

Pushkin's second in the duel was an equerry, so his **funeral** took place around the corner in the Equerries' Church on February 1, 1837 (though it was misleadingly announced that it would be held at St Isaac's Cathedral). Since Pushkin was officially persona non grata at the time, a decree was issued forbidding university professors and students from attending. Nevertheless, the city's intelligentsia turned out in force, as did the diplomatic corps. Three days after the funeral, Pushkin's body was removed in secret and laid to rest at his country estate.

and Lyudmila, with the dedication "To the victorious pupil from the vanquished master". Pushkin kept a "blackamoor" figure on his desk to remind him of his African great-grandfather, Abram Gannibal, whom he immortalized in his last, unfinished novel, *The Negro of Peter the Great*. In the Russian fashion, the clock in the study was stopped at the moment of Pushkin's death (2.45am), while in the nursery you can see the waistcoat that he wore at the duel (complete with bullet hole) and a candle from his funeral service (see below). In another part of the building is a separate exhibition entitled **Pushkin's life and Creative Work** (same hours; R100).

Konyushennaya ploshchad and the Church of the Saviour on the Blood

Pushkin's funeral service in the Equerries' Church at the Imperial Stables on **Konyushennaya ploshchad** drew such crowds that cab drivers needed no other directions than "To Pushkin!" Inside the church, souvenir hunters tore his frock coat to shreds and snipped curls from his hair and sidewhiskers. Under Communism, the stables were taken over by the state removals company and the square became little more than a turnaround for trams; now the church has been restored and the trams banished, while a stream of coaches brings tourists to admire the memorial to another untimely death.

The **Church of the Saviour on the Blood** (Khram "Spas na krovi"; 10am–8pm; closed Wed; R300) was begun in 1882 on the orders of Alexander III to commemorate his father, Alexander II, who had been slain on the site the year before. It was decreed that the tabernacle should be on the spot where his blood had stained the cobblestones – hence the church's unusual name and the fact that it juts out into the Griboedov Canal. Architecturally, it was a slap in the face for Classicism, built in the neo-Russian style to resemble St Basil's in Moscow, with gilded, faceted onion domes like psychedelic pineapples, and a facade aglow with mosaic scenes from the New Testament, and 144 coats of arms representing the provinces, cities and towns of the Russian Empire, united in grief at the murder of the tsar (the achievements of whose reign are described on plaques) – giving it the most flamboyant **exterior** of any building in St Petersburg.

Like so many churches, it was closed in the 1930s and turned into a storeroom, gravely damaging the interior; in 1970 it became a museum of mosaics, before being closed once again for over two decades. Since it reopened in 1997, the church has become one of the city's foremost tourist attractions, owing to its amazing **interior**, entirely covered in **mosaics** based on paintings by Nesterov, Vasnetsov, and other religious artists of the era. From Christ and the Apostles in the cupola to the images of saints and biblical scenes on the walls and pillars, framed by wide decorative borders, the total area covered amounts to over seven thousand square metres.

The site's visual drama is enhanced by the florid **Style Moderne railings** of the nearby Mikhailovskiy Gardens, cast from aluminium, which at that time was worth more than gold. You can have yourself photographed with people in eighteenth-century costumes or enjoy a five-minute ride around ploshchad Iskusstv in a horse-drawn carriage. Among the **buskers** in the vicinity, look out for the guy who plays a carpenter's saw with a violin bow.

The assassination of Alexander II

The **assassination of Alexander II** (March 1, 1881) followed numerous previous attempts on the tsar's life by the revolutionary Nihilist organization, Narodnaya Volya (People's Will). Their original plan involved digging a tunnel from below what is now Yeliseyev's food store and packing explosives beneath Malaya Sadovaya ulitsa, along which the tsar was expected to drive to a review at the Imperial Riding School. Although he unintentionally avoided this attempt by taking a different route, the revolutionaries had learned from previous failures, and had posted a backup team of bombers. As the Imperial party returned along the Griboedov embankment, **Nikolai Rysakov** hurled his bomb, killing a Cossack and mortally wounding himself and a child, but only denting the axle of the tsar's carriage. Ignoring the coachman's urgings to drive on, Alexander began berating his would-be assassin, who – in response to the tsar's assurance that "I am safe, thank God" – groaned, "Do not thank God yet!" As Alexander turned back towards his carriage, another terrorist, **Ignaty Grinevitsky**, threw a second bomb, which found its target. The tsar was carried off bleeding to the Winter Palace, where he expired shortly afterwards; Grinevitsky himself died of his wounds a few hours later. Legend has it that Alexander had a plan for constitutional reforms in his pocket at the time of his murder; if it's true, the Nihilists scored a spectacular own goal, since his successors were utterly opposed to any change whatsoever.

Malaya Konyushennaya and the Zoshchenko Museum

Though something of a detour, it's worth sidetracking to **Malaya Konyushennaya ulitsa**, an attractive street between Konyushennaya ploshchad and Nevskiy prospekt which has been pedestrianized and adorned with a cast-iron **Metrological Pavilion**, built in 1997 according to the nineteenth-century designs of Nikolai Pansere. If nothing else, it provides an excuse to cross the Griboedov Canal by a footbridge from where there's an excellent – and photogenic – view of the Church of the Saviour on the Blood.

Also on Malaya Konyushennaya ulitsa is the **Zoshchenko Museum** (10.30am–6.30pm; closed Mon & the last Wed of each month; R100), reached by entering the courtyard of no. 4/2, passing through a door on the left and up a stairway to the third floor, to find flat #119. This tiny two-room apartment was the last residence of the satirist Mikhail Zoshchenko (1894–1958), whose life mirrored the fortunes of many writers of that era. Born into an academic Petersburg family, he volunteered for the army in 1914 and was gassed at the front. Returning home after the February Revolution he tried many professions before starting to write in 1921, and won a wide following with his short stories, whose style was copied by generations of Soviet comedians and movie actors. His novel *Before the Sunrise* was an attempt to exorcize his depression through psychoanalysis. Although unscathed by the purges of the 1930s, Zoshchenko fell victim to the postwar *Zhdanovshchina* (see p.92); expelled from the Writers' Union for "hooligan representations", he was reduced to dire poverty. The museum contains a collage of humble personal effects and period artefacts, and preserves his bedroom, where his widow lived until 1981.

Around Marsovo pole

Back on the River Moyka, beyond Konyushennaya ploshchad, the **Marsovo pole** (Field of Mars) was a parade ground for the Imperial Guards from the earliest days but didn't acquire its name until the great military reviews of the nineteenth century. Its western side is flanked by an incredibly long yellow facade with three Doric porticoes, that was formerly the **Pavlovskiy Barracks**. Founded by Tsar Paul in 1796, the first recruits of the Pavlovskiy Guards regiment were allegedly chosen for their snub noses – Paul being so ashamed of his own pug nose that his face never appeared on coins ("My ministers hope to lead me by the nose, but I haven't got one", he once remarked). Nor was the selection of guards on the basis of physical appearance so unusual – all the Preobrazhenskiy and Semyonovskiy Guards were respectively blond and brunette.

Following the overthrow of Tsarism, Marsovo pole changed character completely. On March 23, the 180 people who had died in the February Revolution were buried in a common grave in the centre of the field, dignified two years later by the erection of a granite **Monument to Revolutionary Fighters**, one of the first such works of the Soviet era. Lofty epitaphs by Commissar Lunacharsky adorn the gravestones, and an **Eternal Flame**, lit on the fortieth anniversary of the Revolution, flickers at the centre – it's now a popular place for newlyweds to have their photo taken. Heroes of the October Revolution and the Civil War were buried here too, including the head of the Petrograd Cheka and the editor of *Krasnaya Gazeta*, both assassinated in 1918 by Socialist Revolutionaries. In 1920, sixteen thousand workers took part in a *subbotnik* (day of voluntary labour), transforming the dusty parade ground – dubbed the "Petersburg Sahara" – into the manicured park that exists today, where sunbathers gather on sunny days.

The Marble Palace

As a retirement present for her former lover Count Grigori Orlov, who orchestrated her seizure of power, Catherine the Great built him the costliest palace in the city. Designed by Antonio Rinaldi, and faced with green and grey marble, which had recently been discovered in enormous quantities in the Urals, it quickly became known as the **Marble Palace** (Mramorniy dvorets; 10am–5pm, Mon till 4pm; closed Tues; R300). However, Orlov died before it was finished (he never lived there) and Catherine repossessed it for the crown, whereupon it gradually fell into ruin till it was refurbished in the late nineteenth century by Grand Duke Konstantin, its last resident. After the Revolution it was turned into the city's main Lenin Museum, with the famous armoured car from which Lenin spoke outside the Finland Station standing proudly in its courtyard, until the museum was closed after the 1991 coup.

Now, the courtyard contains a **statue of Alexander III** that once stood near the Moscow Station. The clodhopping horse and hulking rider were widely ridiculed in Tsarist times; even their sculptor, Pavel Trubetskoy, reputedly said, "I don't care about politics. I simply depicted one animal on another." At first the Bolsheviks let the statue remain with a sarcastic inscription by poet Damian Bedniy – but in 1937 it was taken away and spent the next six decades in storage or buried underground, till it was exhumed and erected here in 1994. In 2007 it was joined by the **First Rider**, a statue of a giant kid astride a Tyrannosaurus-Rex, by Finnish artists.

Architecturally, the palace is a link between Catherine's Baroque city and Alexander I's Neoclassicism, with elements of both on the exterior. All that remains of Rinaldi's original interior are the main staircase of grey and blue marble with allegorical statues in niches, and the fabulous **Marble Hall**, featuring a dozen hues of stone, offset by gilded chandeliers and a parquet floor. Today, the palace is a branch of the Russian Museum, used to display a rotating selection of works from the **Ludwig Collection** of modern art, donated by the German chocolate king, Peter Ludwig. Picasso, Beuys, Rauschenberg, Warhol and Basquiat are among the foreign artists featured alongside the St Petersburg neo-Academist Olga Tobreluts and the Muscovites Ilya Kabakov and Erik Bulatov. On the floor above you'll find temporary exhibitions by contemporary artists, or antiques from the Russian Museum's storerooms.

Suvorovskaya ploshchad

At the northern end of the park, abutting Troitskiy most (Trinity Bridge), **Suvorovskaya ploshchad** is named for the Russian general **Alexander Suvorov** (1730–1800), whose bronze **statue** stands on a granite plinth at the centre of the square. Suvorov, a veteran of the Italian campaigns against Napoleon, was a portly man, though he is portrayed here as a slim youth in Roman garb, representing Mars, the god of war. Don't believe the urban myth that the statue is made from recycled rods from Sosnovy Bor nuclear reactor – for this to be true, the reactor would had have to have been running in 1801, when the statue was cast.

On the east side, by the embankment, the late eighteenth-century building where the satirical writer Ivan Krylov once lived stands beside a green mansion which housed first the Austrian and later the **British Embassy**. In March 1918 the diplomatic corps followed the Soviet government to Moscow, leaving a contingent in Petrograd. After an attempt on Lenin's life, the Cheka raided the building in search of counter-revolutionaries, whereupon the British naval attaché, Captain Cromie, killed a commissar and was shot dead himself. The remaining British officials were arrested, but the ambassador was already in Vologda, courting White generals. Such intrigues were nothing new; two hundred years earlier, an English ambassador fostered the conspiracy to murder Tsar Paul at the Engineers' Castle (see p.89).

The Summer Garden

The **Summer Garden** (Letniy sad; daily: May–Sept 10am–10pm; Oct–March 10am–8pm; closed during April; free) is the city's most treasured public garden. Less than a year after founding the city in 1704, Peter the Great employed a Frenchman, Le Blond, to design a formal garden in the style of Versailles, with intricate parterres, a glass conservatory, and orange and lemon trees. Sixty marble statues of scenes from Aesop's *Fables* adorned numerous fountains, their water drawn from the Fontanka. After a flood in 1777 wrecked the garden, it was reconstructed under Catherine the Great, who preferred the less formal, English-style garden that survives today.

Notwithstanding the dress restrictions introduced during the reign of Nicholas I, which remained in force until the Revolution, the Summer Garden has always been popular with Petersburgers. Among those drawn here were Pushkin, Gogol and Tchaikovsky, while the novelist Goncharov used the garden as a setting for a meeting between the ill-starred couple, Oblomov and Olga, in his book *Oblomov*. The garden's popularity with lovers dates back to the early nineteenth century, when **marriage fairs** took place here on Whit Monday. The participants were mostly from the lower classes, "dressed in a great deal of finery badly put on, and a great many colours ill-assorted", as one English traveller sniffily observed.

Surrounded on all sides by water, the garden is best approached from the Neva embankment, through the tall, slender wrought-iron grille, designed by Yuri Felten, whose father had come to St Petersburg from Danzig as a cook for Peter the Great. The northern half of the garden features over eighty **Baroque statues**

▲ Fishing in the Neva

(mostly replicas of the originals, due to vandalism), which are encased in insulated boxes over winter, to prevent them cracking from the cold. One of the finest is **Cupid and Psyche**, on a platform that juts out into the Swan Moat, depicting the moment when Psyche falls in love with Cupid, as she leans over his sleeping figure, holding a lamp to his face. Of historical interest is a bust of **Queen Christina of Sweden** (the fifth statue on the right as you walk straight ahead from the main gates): Christina ruled Sweden for just ten years (1632–42) before her secret conversion to Catholicism (which was proscribed in her homeland) was discovered, forcing her to abdicate. In the centre of the park is a large memorial to the satirical writer **Ivan Krylov** (1769–1844). Like Aesop, Krylov used animals in his fables to illustrate human foibles, and many of his characters decorate the statue's pedestal, some of them playing musical instruments.

The Summer Palace

In the northeastern corner of the garden stands the **Summer Palace** (Letniy dvorets; May–Oct 11am–6pm; closed Tues & the last Mon of each month; R300) that Domenico Trezzini began in 1710 for Peter the Great. A modest two-storey building of bricks and stucco – one of the first such structures in the city – the new palace was really only a small step up from the wooden cottage in which Peter had previously lived on the other side of the river. Its position, at the point where the Fontanka joins the Neva, suited Peter's maritime bent; the seating area with benches, now laid out to the south side of the palace, was originally a small harbour.

The palace was equally divided between husband and wife: Peter occupied the first floor, while Catherine took over the top floor. Information on each room is posted in English and Russian and the decor, though not original, has been faithfully reproduced. The tsar's **bedroom** is typically modest; his four-poster bed is significantly shorter than he was, since in those days the aristocracy slept propped half-upright on pillows. Next door is Peter's **turnery**, where he would don a leather apron and spend hours bent over his mechanical lathes, presses and instruments; notice the huge meteorological device, connected to a weather vane, which measures the strength and direction of the wind.

In Petrine times, major banquets were held at the Menshikov Palace on Vasilevskiy Island (see p.158); the **dining room** here was used for less formal gatherings. Having taken his seat, Peter would blithely tell his guests, "Those of you who can find places may sit where you want. The rest of you can go home and dine with your wives" –

Court life in Petrine times

Along with Monplaisir at Peterhof, the Summer Palace is still faintly redolent of court life in Petrine times. Peter lived here with little pomp, preferring to lounge around in old clothes, attended only by a couple of servants and two valets (whose stomachs he used as pillows on long journeys). This informality nearly cost him dearly, as an attempt was made on his life by an Old Believer (religious dissident) during a meeting in the palace reception room. Peter's hospitality was legendary – and feared. The most important summer celebration was the anniversary of the Battle of Poltava (June 28), when Peter himself served wine and beer to his veterans. Sentries were posted at the gates to prevent guests from fleeing when the huge buckets of corn brandy were brought on for compulsory toasting, which wouldn't stop until all the guests were blind drunk – something the foreign ambassadors were particularly wary of. Dancing and drinking would continue until dawn, though "many simply sank down where they were in the garden and drifted into sleep".

prompting much "cuffing and boxing" which he enjoyed immensely. He also loved practical jokes, such as concealing dead mice in the soup, or having dwarves burst forth from mounds of pâté. The **kitchen** was unusually modern for its day, plumbed with running water from the nearby fountains, and – most importantly – opening directly onto the dining room: Peter liked his food hot, and in large palaces dishes would usually be lukewarm by the time they reached the table.

The **top floor** was the domain of Peter's wife, who became Empress **Catherine I** upon his death. She was one of the most unlikely people to end up ruling Russia, having started life as a Lithuanian peasant girl, but had a good influence on Peter – insisting that women be present (and remain sober) during his drinking parties, and that the men could get drunk only after nine o'clock. She was also one of the few people unmoved by his violent temper. On one occasion, Peter smashed a Venetian mirror, shouting, "See, I can break the most beautiful object in my house," to which she replied, "And by doing so, have you made your palace more beautiful?"

The Tea House, Coffee House and Swan Lake

South of the Summer Palace stands the **Tea House** (Chayniy domik), a simple Neoclassical pavilion built in 1827. Damaged by fire in 1981, it has since been restored and is now an exhibition hall. Carlo Rossi's nearby **Coffee House** (Kofeyniy domik), on the site of an old grotto from Petrine times, is now a souvenir shop and café. At the southern end of the garden is the **Swan Lake**, enlivened by said birds, and on its far side, by the entrance/exit to the gardens, stands a giant red porphyry **vase**, a gift from the Swedish king Karl Johan to Nicholas I.

South of the Moyka

Across the Moyka from the Summer Garden looms the **Engineers' Castle** – a building forever associated with the murder of Tsar Paul, and now a branch of the Russian Museum. Its dramatic facade and spire lure sightseers onwards in the direction of the main **Russian Museum** on ploshchad Iskusstv, while the shady **Mikhailovskiy Gardens** behind the museum offer a respite from the traffic along Sadovaya ulitsa.

Crossing the road from the garden to the castle, you'll notice people peering over the embankment where the Moyka joins the Fontanka. They're paying homage to **Chizik Pyzhik**, a tiny statue of the Siskin bird whose green and yellow plumage was likened to the uniforms of law students in Tsarist times, giving rise to the ditty: "*Chizhik Pyzhik, gde ty bil? Na Fontanke vodku pil*" ("Chizhik Pyzhik, where have you been? On the Fontanka drinking vodka"). The first monument to be erected in the glasnost era by an individual rather than an organization, it has since become a kind of good-luck talisman, at which Russians throw coins – even when the statue has been stolen, as it is from time to time.

The Engineers' Castle

The pensive poet casts a glance

At the palace buried in oblivion,

A tyrant's menacing memorial

Deserted in the mists of sleep.

Alexander Pushkin, *Freedom*

Few buildings in St Petersburg are so imbued with myths and the character of their original owner as the Mikhailovskiy or **Engineers' Castle** (Inzhenerniy zamok; for opening times see p.90). Tsar Paul commissioned this fortified residence shortly after he assumed the throne in 1796; to clear the site, he had the wooden palace that Rastrelli had built for Empress Elizabeth – in which he himself had been born and raised – burnt to the ground: an act pregnant with significance for a man plagued by rumours of illegitimacy, who wanted nothing more than to erase the memory of his hated mother, Catherine the Great.

Paul employed Vincenzo Brenna to construct the building (named the Mikhailovskiy Castle after the Archangel Michael appeared in a vision to one of Paul's guards) and, in a deliberate snub to Catherine's taste for a unified aesthetic, specified a different style for each facade. He happily plundered much of the building material (and most of the furniture) from the palaces his mother had built, and insisted that his monogram appear throughout the palace – over eight thousand times, according to one account.

Paul moved into the castle in February 1801, even before the paint was dry. To allay his fear of being murdered – as his father had been – it was surrounded by a moat with drawbridges protected by cannons, and had a secret escape passage reached by a trapdoor near his bedroom. In the event, he spent only forty days here before his worst fears were realized and he was strangled in his bedroom (see box below).

The assassination of Tsar Paul

The origins of the **conspiracy** against Paul are murky. Count Pahlen, head of foreign affairs and the police, was ideally placed to prepare a coup and had good reasons for doing so, but the English ambassador, Lord Whitford, secretly gave money to buy support and may even have proposed the plot to Count Zubov – another key conspirator – under the cover of an affair with Zubov's sister, Olga. However, animosity towards Paul ran so deep that almost everyone who was anyone ended up playing some kind of role in the conspiracy.

Paul had already alienated the nobility and the Guards by curtailing their privileges. His own diplomats were aghast at him sending a force of Cossacks to expel the British from India without consulting anyone, and inviting the sovereigns of Europe to settle their differences by hand-to-hand combat. His impulsiveness and erratic behaviour were the talk of St Petersburg; "the Emperor is literally not in his senses", Whitford reported to London. With the prospect of a European conflict looming, it was in both the Russians' interests and England's to have Paul replaced by a less bellicose monarch. Pahlen even obtained the consent of Paul's heir apparent, the future Alexander I, whose only proviso was that his father's life be spared.

At midnight, March 11–12, 1801, some sixty conspirators set off in the rain for the castle. En route they quenched their thirst with champagne, but were almost scared off by a flock of crows while creeping through the Summer Garden. Paul's false sense of security in the castle had led him to replace the guard of thirty well-armed men with just two unarmed hussars, a valet and a sentry. One of the hussars resisted but was quickly dealt with; the tsar, having vainly tried to hide, was arrested in his nightshirt and cap. Then several soldiers who had got lost burst into the room and lunged at him, upsetting the night-light and plunging the room into darkness. In the confusion, Paul was knocked unconscious and strangled with his own sash.

When Paul's death was officially ascribed to apoplexy – as his father's had been – Tallyrand quipped, "Really, the Russian government will have to invent another disease." Meanwhile, Alexander promised the Guards: "During my reign, everything will be done according to the principles of my beloved grandmother, Catherine the Great." All Paul's reforms and innovations were revoked – his mother had triumphed yet again, from beyond the grave. (See the box on p.271 for more about Paul's life.)

As the scene of a regicide the castle was subsequently shunned by the Imperial family and later given to a military engineering academy, where Dostoyevsky was enrolled at the age of sixteen. After the Revolution, it was used to house libraries, institutes and record offices. Restoration began in the 1980s, and the palace subsequently became a branch of the Russian Museum. *Objets d'art* from its vast collection are displayed in the restored state rooms which you can wander during **visiting** hours (10am–6pm, Mon till 5pm; closed Tues; R300). To see other parts of the palace such as the site of Paul's murder, you'll need to book a **guided tour** in Russian five days ahead (☏ 313 41 73; R2400 group rate).

The castle's **exterior** was inspired by the chateau of the Prince de Condé at Chantilly, which Paul had seen on his European tour, and painted an apricot colour that matched his mistress's gloves. A holy woman is said to have foretold that Paul would live as many years as there were letters in the inscription above the portico on the south face – a prophecy fulfilled when he died at the age of 47. The octagonal inner courtyard contains a recently installed **statue of Paul** enthroned, wearing thigh-boots and holding the Imperial orb and sceptre – a pose that delighted him, but which cruelly underlines the futility of his ambitions.

Inside the museum you can see a model of the moats and drawbridges that originally defended the castle. A grand fake marble staircase graced with a copy of the *Dying Cleopatra* (the original is in the Hermitage) ascends to the **state rooms**. Gilding and caryatids abound in the burgundy throne room of his wife, Maria Fyodorovna, and in the state dining hall, where Paul ate supper two hours before his murder. In his day, the barrel-vaulted Antique Gallery boasted statues, now in the Hermitage, solid bronze doors and four tapestries based on Raphael's work that were a gift from Louis XVI and hung in the Raphael Gallery. Now, eighteenth- and nineteenth-century portraits, landscapes and allegorical paintings from the Russian Museum's collection are hung in these galleries and a suite of rooms that once belonged to Paul's son Konstantin.

Paul's own suite was long ago carved up into a warren of passages comprising the "backstage" of the museum, which can only be seen on a tour. Although his bedroom was converted into a chapel to efface the scene of the crime, you can still see the backstairs used by his assassins. One reason they got this far was that they included an officer charged with reporting urgent news to the tsar at any time of the day or night. Paul's fate was sealed by his final error – he ran to hide in his mistress's bedroom rather than making for the secret passage, and found his line of retreat blocked. The tour ends downstairs in a charming **church** with artificial marble columns, where the composer Glinka got married.

Beyond the Engineers' Castle

South of the castle, Rossi laid out the triumphal **Klenovaya alleya** (Maple Alley) on the site of Paul's former parade grounds. At the top end is an equestrian **statue of Peter the Great**, erected by Paul and sporting the pithy inscription *Pradyedu pravnuk* ("To great grandfather from great grandson"), intended to quell persistent rumours of his illegitimacy. To the south stand two **pavilions** designed by Rossi to house sentries guarding the approach to the castle.

To the east, on Belinskovo ploshchad, St Petersburg's **State Circus** (Tsirk) occupies the late nineteenth-century premises of the Cinizelli Circus, whose traditions it maintains. In the opposite direction, across Inzhenernaya ulitsa, the **Winter Stadium** (Zimniy stadion) was originally the Mikhailovskiy Manège – an Imperial riding school built by Rossi in the 1820s. During the Revolution, the Manège served as the headquarters of the Armoured Car Detachment, a pro-Bolshevik unit that sped around in Austin armoured cars, clad in black leather. From the triangular **Manezhnaya ploshchad**, outside the stadium, where teenagers hang out drinking until the small hours, **Italyanskaya ulitsa** (Italian Street) leads west to ploshchad Iskusstv and the Russian Museum.

Ploshchad Iskusstv and the Mikhailovskiy Gardens

Early in the nineteenth century, Carlo Rossi designed a palatial square and thoroughfare off Nevskiy prospekt, every facade conforming to an overall Neoclassical plan. Both were originally named after the Mikhailovskiy Palace that dominates the square, but in Soviet times the latter was renamed **ploshchad Iskusstv** (Square of Arts) owing to the many artistic institutions located here, and is still known as such today. A **statue of Pushkin** reciting his poetry, by the city's leading postwar sculptor, Mikhail Anikushin, was erected in its centre in 1957.

Besides the Mikhailovskiy Palace you might consider visiting the **Brodsky Museum** (11am–5pm; closed Mon & Tues; R300) at pl. Iskusstv 3, in the palatial former home of Isaak Brodsky, a leading Socialist Realist painter responsible for such gems as *Lenin in the Smolniy*. It displays his collection of 600 minor works by Repin, Levitan, Kramskoy and other "Wanderers" plus over 200 of his own pictures. Next door on the corner of Italyanskaya ulitsa stands a recreation of the **Stray Dog cabaret**, where Mayakovsky, Akhmatova and other Futurists and Acmeists hung out before the Revolution – nowadays just a tourist trap for coach parties.

The Mikhailovskiy Palace: the Russian Museum and Russian Ethnographic Museum

Amazingly, while Rossi was overseeing the General Staff building, he was also working on the **Mikhailovskiy Palace** (Mikhailovskiy dvorets). The two epitomize the Russian Empire style of Alexander I's reign, one rampantly martial and the other coolly Neoclassical, with a relentless parade of Corinthian columns across a pale yellow facade. Sadly, little remains of Rossi's interior, save the main staircase and the austere "White Room" inside what is now the **Russian Museum**, occupying the central and western wings of the palace. This vast repository of Russian art is a must-see for any visitor, and rates a chapter of its own (see pp.137–150).

In the early 1900s, the palace's east wing and stables were replaced by an annexe to house the museum's ethnographic collections, which eventually became the **Russian Ethnographic Museum** (10am–6pm; closed Mon & the last Fri of each month; R300; Ⓦ www.ethnomuseum.ru). The museum is deeply Soviet (or Tsarist) in its inclusion of myriad peoples that once comprised the Soviet Union (or Tsarist Empire), their unity symbolized by a giant **frieze** of peasants and workers from every nation of the former USSR, in the main hall.

The museum is divided into four sections. **European Russia** focuses on Russian peasant life and wedding rituals, rooted in paganism; their fellow Slavs, the Ukrainians and Belarussians; the Finno-Ugric Mordvinians, Udmurty, Mari and Komi whose language is related to Estonian, Hungarian and Finnish; and the horse-breeding Kalmyks, related to the Mongols, whence comes a felt *yurt*.

In the **Caucasus and Crimea** section, much is made of the traditions of hospitality and feasting among the Christian Ossetians and Georgians (Stalin's folks); the Muslim Crimean Tartars (whom he deported en masse to Kazakhstan); and the jewellery and embroidery of the Armenians and Azerbaijanis – pointedly omitting the Chechens from the peoples of the North Caucasus. In contrast to these sedentary, mostly highland peoples, the semi-arid steppes of **Central Asia** sustained nomadic pastoralist cultures such as the Turkomens and Kazakhs, while the Uzbeks also had a sophisticated urban civilization in the oases on the Silk Road from China.

Perhaps the most interesting section, however, is **Siberia and the Far East**, covering subjects ranging from shamanism among the Buryats (who remained semi-nomadic until after the Revolution but have since settled around Lake Baikal and are now Buddhists) to the reindeer herders, hunters and fishers of the taiga and the Far North – the Evenki, the Nanaytsy and the Chukchi (the butt of racist jokes in Soviet times).

Though captioning in English is minimal, most exhibits speak for themselves; a **guided tour** in English (☎570 54 21; R1070 group rate) can be arranged. There's also a **Children's Centre** (Sun 11am–5pm; ☎570 53 20), where instructors teach **handicrafts** such as weaving, printmaking and pottery.

Behind the palace are the **Mikhailovskiy Gardens**, where St Petersburgers used to picnic and play badminton at three o'clock in the morning during the White Nights. Alas, since the gardens were transferred to the ownership of the Russian Museum a few years ago, its lawns have been declared out of bounds (obliging sunbathers to hang out on Marsovo pole instead), and outdoor **concerts** are no longer held here, rendering the place somewhat lifeless.

The Maliy and the Philharmonia

On the western side of ploshchad Iskusstv stands the **Maliy Opera and Ballet Theatre** (Maliy operniy teatr) – previously known as the Mikhailovskiy – the city's main opera house after the Mariinskiy. While the building appears to be part of Rossi's masterplan, it was actually designed by the architect Bryullov – although Rossi was responsible for the square's other great musical institution, the **St Petersburg Philharmonia**, on the corner of Mikhailovskaya ulitsa, which was originally the concert hall of the Salle des Nobles.

Of all the figures associated with these institutions, the one closest to the hearts of the city's intelligentsia is **Dmitri Shostakovich** (1906–75), whose opera, *Lady Macbeth of Mtsensk*, was premiered at the Maliy in 1934 to great critical acclaim, only to be denounced by *Pravda* as "Chaos instead of Music" less than two years later. After years during which his music swung in and out of official favour, Shostakovich scored his greatest public success with his Seventh Symphony – the "Leningrad Symphony" – during the Blockade of the city in World War II. He wrote the first three movements whilst serving as an air warden (breaking off composing whenever the sirens sounded), before being evacuated to Kuybyshev, where he completed the work, which was broadcast nationwide from here on August 9, 1942. Yet despite his commitment to the war effort, he was one of the first victims of the postwar cultural purge known as the *Zhdanovshchina*, being accused of "formalist perversions and anti-democratic tendencies" in his art, and his relations with the Soviet authorities remained uneasy until his death in 1975.

Other notable events at the Philharmonia have included the premieres of Beethoven's *Missa solemnis* (1824) and Tchaikovsky's Sixth Symphony – the latter conducted by the composer just a few days before his death in 1893. It was here, too, that the American dancer Isadora Duncan made her Russian debut a few days after "Bloody Sunday" in 1905.

The Admiralty and the Bronze Horseman

The whimsical medusas cling angrily,

anchors rust like discarded ploughs –

and, lo, the bonds of three dimensions are all sundered

and opened are the seas of all the world.

Osip Mandelstam, *The Admiralty*

Standing at the apex of Nevskiy prospekt, the **Admiralty** building (Admiralteyst-vo) is one of the world's greatest expressions of naval triumphalism, extending 407m along the waterfront from Dvortsovaya ploshchad to ploshchad Dekabris-tov. Marking the convergence of three great avenues that radiate across the city centre – Nevskiy prospekt, Gorokhovaya ulitsa and Voznesenskiy prospekt – its golden spire draws you naturally towards it on any walk along Nevskiy. Once there, you'll want to take the time to stroll in the **Alexander Garden** and explore the neighbouring ploshchad Dekabristov, which is dominated by the **Bronze Horseman**, the city's renowned statue of Peter the Great. This part of town is shown on the map on p.94.

The Admiralty

The **Admiralty** was originally founded by Peter the Great in 1704 as a fortified shipyard, with a primitive wooden tower and spire. A ban was placed on building in the vicinity to maintain a firebreak – hence the open spaces that still surround the edifice. As the shipyards moved elsewhere, and the Admiralty became purely administrative in function, Andreyan Zakharov was commissioned to design a suitable replacement.

Built in the early 1820s, the key feature of the existing building is a central **tower** rising through tiers and columns and culminating in a slender **spire** sheathed in gold. Like the spire of the Peter and Paul Cathedral, it asserted the city's European identity – differentiating its skyline from the traditional Russian medley of onion domes. It also enabled the tsar to scan the streets for miles around, using a tele-scope, to check whether they were being laid out according to plan. Topping the spire is a gilded **weather vane** shaped like a frigate, which has become the emblem of St Petersburg, appearing on everything from medals to shopping bags. Another piece of symbolism is encoded in the building itself, whose plan corresponds to the Greek and Cyrillic initial letter of Peter's name – Π – as does the form of the arched tower facing the Admiralty Garden.

The Admiralty's **facade** swarms with Neoclassical sculptures and reliefs, glorify-ing Russia's maritime potency. The archway of the main entrance is flanked by trios of nymphs bearing globes, representing the triple aspects of the goddess Hec-ate. A frieze below the entablature shows Neptune bequeathing his trident to Tsar Peter, while statues of Achilles and other heroes embellish the ledge below the col-onnade. This in turn is topped by statues of the four seasons, winds and elements, and the mythological patrons of shipbuilding and astronomy, Isis and Urania.

The **porticoes** of the 163-metre-long side wings are similarly adorned, with reliefs of deities rewarding Russian bravery or artistry with laurel wreaths. Two lesser archways on the **embankment** side feature the Genii of Glory, a pair of angelic figures blowing trumpets (a symbol of St Petersburg); sadly, the river-front facade is marred by a row of late nineteenth-century apartment buildings. North along the embankment towards Dvortsoviy most (Palace Bridge) you'll notice a statue of **Peter the Shipbuilder**, a gift from the city of Amsterdam, where Peter

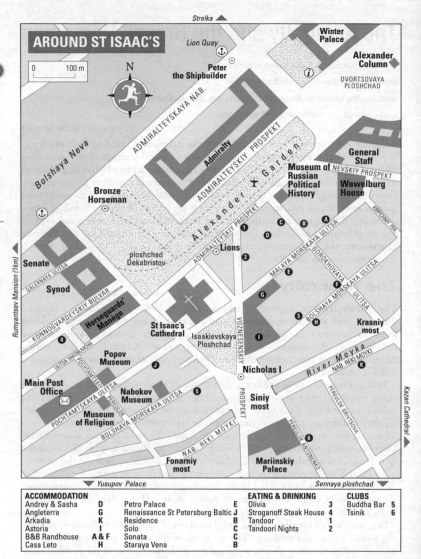

AROUND ST ISAAC'S

0 — 100 m

N

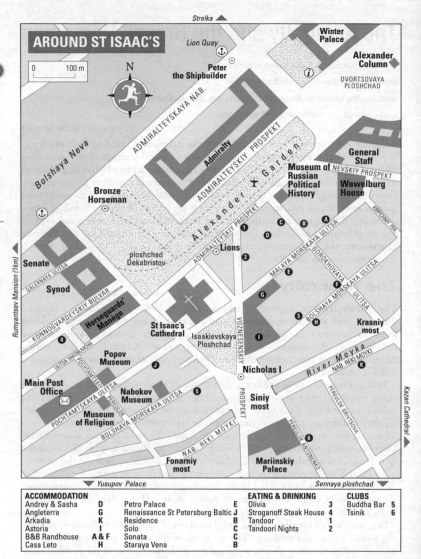

ACCOMMODATION, EATING & DRINKING and CLUBS map of Around St Isaac's showing: Strelka, Lion Quay, Peter the Shipbuilder, Winter Palace, Alexander Column, DVORTSOVAYA PLOSHCHAD, Admiralty, Admiralteyskaya nab., Bolshaya Neva, Bronze Horseman, Alexander Garden, Admiralteyskiy Prospekt, General Staff, Nevskiy Prospekt, Museum of Russian Political History, Wawelburg House, Kirpichny Per., Lions, Malaya Morskaya Ulitsa, Gorokhovaya Ulitsa, Bolshaya Morskaya Ulitsa, Senate, Galernaya Ulitsa, Synod, Konnogvardeyskiy Bulvar, Horseguards' Manège, ploshchad Dekabristov, St Isaac's Cathedral, Isaakievskaya Ploshchad, Krasniy most, Popov Museum, Ulitsa Yakubovicha, Pochtamtskiy Pereulok, Nicholas I, River Moyka, Nab. Reki Moyki, Main Post Office, Nabokov Museum, Pochtamtskaya Ulitsa, Bolshaya Morskaya Ulitsa, Museum of Religion, Siniy most, Voznesenskiy Prospekt, Pereulok Grivtsova, Pereulok Antonenko, Kazan Cathedral, Nab. Reki Moyki, Fonarniy most, Mariinskiy Palace, Yusupov Palace, Sennaya ploshchad, Rumyantsev Mansion (1km)

ACCOMMODATION					EATING & DRINKING		CLUBS	
Andrey & Sasha	D	Petro Palace	E		Olivia	3	Buddha Bar	5
Angleterre	G	Renaissance St Petersburg Baltic	J		Stroganoff Steak House	4	Tsinik	6
Arkadia	K	Residence	B		Tandoor	1		
Astoria	I	Solo	C		Tandoori Nights	2		
B&B Randhouse	A & F	Sonata	C					
Casa Leto	H	Staraya Vena	B					

worked as a common shipwright to learn the skills needed to build a Russian navy.

The Alexander Garden and prospekt

Largely obscuring the Admiralty, the wooded **Alexander Garden** (Aleksandrovskiy sad) leads towards ploshchad Dekabristov, toddlers and lovers mingling with officers from the naval college. On Sunday afternoons in summer, a navy **brass band** plays near the Zhukovsky statue. Other Russians honoured with monuments here include Glinka, Lermontov and Gogol (near the fountain), but the most engaging of the statues commemorates General Nikolai Przhevalsky (1839–

88), whose intrepid journeys in Central Asia are symbolized by a saddled camel. There's a bizarre legend that Przhevalsky was the real father of Iosif Dzhugashvili – better known to history as Stalin.

Admiralteyskiy prospekt, beside the park, rates a mention for two buildings. The grey-and-white Neoclassical pile at no. 6 was the headquarters of the Imperial secret police for over fifty years before the Revolution and, from December 1917 until March 1918, the headquarters of the Bolshevik Cheka, led by "Iron" Felix Dzerzhinsky. Since 1995 it has housed a small branch of the **Museum of Russian Political History** (Mon–Fri 10am–5.30pm; R100) covering the history of the secret police in three rooms on the second floor. One room re-creates the interior as it was during the reign of Alexander III, with a curtained-off door through which agents could enter in secret to report to their chief. The others contain photographs of leading *Chekisti* and famous foreign spies like Reilly, plus memorabilia such as bulletproof vests and KGB medals – but unless you understand Russian, it will interest only hardcore espionage buffs.

Two blocks further along Admiralteyskiy prospekt is the **Lobanov-Rostovskiy House**, a massive wedge-shaped mansion built in 1817–20. The columned portico facing the prospekt is guarded by two stone **lions** immortalized in Pushkin's poem *The Bronze Horseman* (see below).

Ploshchad Dekabristov

Ploshchad Dekabristov – an expanse of fir trees and rose beds merging into the Alexander Garden – is largely defined by the monuments that surround it, and known for the event recalled by its name, "Decembrists' Square". The **Decembrists' revolt** began on the morning of December 14, 1825, when a group of reformist officers marched three thousand soldiers into the square in an attempt to force the Senate to veto the accession of Nicholas I and proclaim a constitutional monarchy. Alas, the senators had already sworn allegiance to Nicholas and gone home, while the officers' leader, Prince Trubetskoy, never showed up. The revolt turned from farce to tragedy as the tsar surrounded the square with loyalist troops. When labourers on St Isaac's Cathedral started pelting them with bricks, Nicholas feared that the revolt could spread and ordered his troops to attack. By nightfall the rebellion had been crushed and interrogations were under way; Nicholas attended the trials and dictated the sentences. Five ringleaders were hanged and 130 officers stripped of their rank and exiled in fetters to Siberia. Although the soldiers had only been obeying orders, with little or no idea of the revolt's aims, dozens were forced to "run the gauntlet" of a thousand men twelve times – that is, to be clubbed twelve thousand times.

The Bronze Horseman

Once on the square, your eyes are inevitably drawn to the famous equestrian statue of Peter the Great, known as the **Bronze Horseman** (Medny vsadnik), which rears up towards the waterfront. Of all the city's monuments, none has been invested with such poetic significance: a symbol of indomitable will and ruthless vision. The statue made its literary debut in Pushkin's epic *The Bronze Horseman* (1833), an evocation of the Great Flood of 1824. In the poem, the only survivors are a poor clerk, Yevgeny, who climbs on top of one of the lions outside the Lobanov-Rostovskiy House to escape the floodwaters, and the statue of the Horseman itself, which comes to life and pursues him through the city. The radical journalist Herzen regarded the statue as a symbol of tyranny, whereas Andrei Bely likened it to Russia on the verge of the apocalypse: "Your two front hooves have leaped far off into the darkness, into the void, while your two rear hooves are firmly implanted in the granite soil."

Peter the Great

Peter the Great (1672–1725) was responsible for irrevocably changing Russia's character, turning it from an ultra-parochial, backward country to an imperial power to be reckoned with. In childhood, he had experienced at first hand the savagery of Old Muscovy, when several of his family were butchered by the Kremlin Guards during a power struggle between the Naryshkin and Miloslavskiy clans. Secluded in Preobrazhenskoe, outside Moscow, he began to form his own "toy" regiments and mingle with the isolated foreign community: unlike most Russians, he was anything but xenophobic (styling himself "Peter" rather than "Pyotr"). He also taught himself to sail, and his enthusiasm for maritime affairs and Western ways was given full rein after the death of his elder brother and co-tsar, the feeble-minded Ivan V.

In 1697–98, Peter embarked on a **Grand Tour** of Europe, travelling incognito to be free of the burdens of protocol, so that he might concentrate on studying shipbuilding in Holland and England, where he worked on the docks as an apprentice. His aim was to create a Russian navy in order to drive back Charles XII of Sweden and secure a Baltic "Window on the West" – the genesis of **St Petersburg** itself. When he wasn't poring over plans, inspecting the navy, founding institutions or leading his armies into battle, Peter enjoyed a riotous lifestyle with cronies such as Menshikov (p.159) and Lefort. Together they formed the "Drunken Synod", whose parties parodied the rituals of the Orthodox Church, reflecting his crude sense of humour and his dislike of Old Russia – though the former was somewhat mitigated by his astute second wife, **Catherine I** (p.88).

Amongst Peter's innovations were the Kunstkammer, or "chamber of curiosities", Russia's first public museum (p.156), and the imposition of a tax on those who wore beards and caftans, after Peter proclaimed them backward and impractical. His Westernizing reforms and lukewarm devotion to Orthodoxy alienated nobles and commoners alike – but the beheading of the Kremlin Guard (1698) and the execution of his own son, **Tsarevich Alexei** (p.171), dissuaded further rebellions. Opinion remains divided over Peter's achievements. Whereas most Russians see him as a great ruler who advanced the nation, others blame him for perverting its true, Slavic destiny, or setting an autocratic precedent for Lenin and Stalin. Unlike them, however, Peter's sheer *joie de vivre* makes him hard to dislike, for all his brutality.

The statue was commissioned by Catherine the Great to glorify "enlightened absolutism" – an ideal that she shared with Peter the Great (see box above). This served to emphasize her place as his true political heir (she had, after all, no legitimate claim to the throne) – hence the canny inscription "To Peter I from Catherine II", which appears on the sides in Latin and Russian. The French sculptor, Étienne Falconet, was allocated the finest horses and riders in the Imperial stables, so that he could study their movements. Later, he sketched them held motionless on a special platform, while a cavalry general of similar build to Peter sat in the saddle. The statue wasn't completed until 1782 (Falconet complaining of arrears in his salary), with disaster narrowly averted during the casting stage, when a foundry man tore off his clothes to block a crack in the mould, preventing the molten metal from escaping. Its huge **pedestal** rock was brought from the village of Lakhta, 10km outside Petersburg; Peter had supposedly surveyed the city's environs from this 1600-tonne "Thunder Rock", sculpted by the waves over millennia. A trampled serpent (symbolizing evil) wriggles limply down the back of the pedestal.

As a visit on any sunny day will confirm, the statue is a customary spot for newlyweds to be photographed, before drinking a toast on the Strelka (see p.154) to celebrate their nuptials, often hiring stretch limos or Hummers for the occasion.

The Senate and Horseguards' Manège

The colossal ochre-and-white **Senate and Synod** building on the far side of ploshchad Dekabristov was constructed in the mid-nineteenth century to replace an old mansion that had formerly housed both institutions. Peter established the Senate (1711) to run Russia in his absence, and the Holy Synod (1721) to control the Orthodox Church, and both had assumed a more permanent role by the time that Rossi designed these new premises. Echoing the General Staff, a resplendent arch unites the twin buildings, which now contains offices of the Presidential administration.

Further south stands the former **Horseguards' Manège** (Konnogvardeyskiy manezh), built as an indoor riding school at the beginning of the nineteenth century. The architect Quarenghi felt that its prime location called for a temple-like portico fronted by the Sons of Zeus reining in wild horses, which was copied from a similar arrangement outside the Quirinale Palace in Rome. In 1840 the naked youths were removed after the Holy Synod objected to their presence within sight of St Isaac's Cathedral, and they were reinstated only in 1954. The Manège was used for concerts in Tsarist times (Johann Strauss conducted here), but is now the **Central Exhibition Hall**, used for both modern art and trade exhibitions.

St Isaac's Cathedral and around

Looming majestically above the rooftops, **St Isaac's Cathedral** (Isaakievsky sobor) – one of the city's premier tourist attractions – is visible from way out in the Gulf of Finland, but is too massive to grasp at close quarters. It stands on its own square, **Isaakievskaya ploshchad** (St Isaac's Square), and it's from the centre of this that you'll get the best view of the cathedral. By day, its gilded dome is one of the glories of St Petersburg's skyline; at night, its gigantic porticoes and statues seem almost menacing, like something dredged up from the seabed. Its opulent interior is equally impressive, as is the wonderful view from its colonnade. During World War II, the cathedral appeared on Luftwaffe bombing maps as "reference point no. 1", and the park to the south was dug up and planted with cabbages to help feed the famished city.

The Cathedral

The **Cathedral** (10am–8pm; closed Wed; R300) is the fourth church in St Petersburg to have been dedicated to St Isaac of Dalmatia, a Byzantine monk whose feast day fell on Peter the Great's birthday (May 30). The previous one on this site was judged too small even before its completion, so a competition to design a replacement was announced after Russia's victory over Napoleon in 1812. By submitting no fewer than 24 designs in various styles, a young, unknown architect, Auguste de Montferrand, impressed Alexander I into giving him the commission, though he soon required help from more experienced architects. The tsar insisted that the walls of the previous church be preserved, causing huge problems until he relented three years later, at which point everything was demolished and work began again from scratch. Many reckoned that construction (1818–42) and decoration (1842–58) were deliberately prolonged, owing to the popular superstition that the Romanov dynasty would end with the cathedral's completion – more likely, the delays were caused by Montferrand's incompetence.

During Soviet times the cathedral was a Museum of Atheism, where visitors could see an enormous Foucault's pendulum that supposedly proved the falsity of religion by demonstrating the earth's rotation; and although it has been reconsecrated as a place of worship it is still classified as a **museum**. The ticket kiosks to the east of the cathedral also sell separate **tickets** for the colonnade (R150), and **photo** permits for each (R50/R25; video R25/R50). Due to its popularity with sightseers, the colonnade is also open **at night** (daily 7pm–4.30am; R300), when tickets are sold by the entrance to the cathedral, beneath its south portico.

The interior

The cathedral's vast **interior** is decorated with fourteen kinds of marble, as well as jasper, malachite, gilded stucco, frescoes and mosaics. An 800-square-metre painting by Karl Bryullov of the Virgin surrounded by saints and angels covers the inside of the cupola, while biblical scenes by Ivan Vitali appear in bas-relief on the huge bronze **doors** and as murals and mosaics elsewhere (all labelled in English). Malachite and lazurite columns frame a white marble **iconostasis**, decorated by Neff, Bryullov and Zhivago, its wings flanking the gilded bronze doors into the **sanctuary**. Only the monarch and the patriarch were admitted to the sanctuary, whose stained-glass window is contrary to Orthodox tradition (though perfectly acceptable elsewhere in an Orthodox church). At the back of the nave are vintage scale-models of the cathedral, its dome and the scaffolding used to erect the portico. Montferrand is remembered by an outsized cast-iron relief, copied from a figure on the extreme left of the western portico – which was all the honour that he received for dying on the job after forty years. His widow begged that he be interred in St Isaac's crypt, but the tsar refused to sully it with the tomb of a non-Orthodox believer and sent his coffin home to France.

The dome and colonnade

The cathedral's height (101.5m) and rooftop statues are best appreciated by climbing the 262 steps up to its **dome** – the third largest cathedral dome in Europe. This consists of three hemispherical shells mounted one inside the other, with 100,000 clay pots fixed between the outer and middle layers to form a lightweight vault and enhance the acoustics. Nearly 100kg of gold leaf was used to cover the exterior of the dome, helping push the total cost of the cathedral to 23,256,000 rubles (six times that of the Winter Palace). The sixty men who died from inhaling mercury fumes during the gilding process were not the only fatalities amongst the serf-labourers, who worked fifteen hours a day without any holidays, since Nicholas believed that "idleness can only do them harm". Dwarfed by a great **colonnade** topped with 24 statues, the dome's wind-swept iron gallery offers a stunning panoramic view of central St Petersburg. The *kolonada* has its own entrance beneath the south portico, so visitors must exit the cathedral on the Neva side and go back round again.

Around Isaakievskaya ploshchad

On the eastern side of Isaakievskaya ploshchad, the pinkish-grey **Astoria Hotel** is famous for those who have – and haven't – stayed there. Built in the early 1900s, its former guests include the American Communists John Reed and Louise Bryant, and the Russian-born Anarchists Emma Goldman and Alexander Berkman. It's said that Hitler planned to hold a victory banquet here once Leningrad had fallen, and sent out invitations specifying the month and hour, but leaving out the exact date.

Adjacent to the *Astoria* is a smaller, butterscotch annexe named the *Angleterre*, where the poet **Sergei Yesenin** apparently slashed his wrists and hanged himself in December 1925, leaving a verse written in his own blood. In 1998, however, evidence emerged suggesting that Yesenin was killed by the secret police. The theory is that Trotsky ordered him to be beaten up, to dissuade Yesenin from planning to emigrate, but the *Chekisti* entrusted with the job killed him by accident, and faked a suicide to cover it up – the poem being written by the *Chekist* commander Yakov Blumkin.

At the centre of the square prances a haughty, bronze equestrian **statue of Nicholas I**, known to his subjects as "the Stick" (*Palkin*) and abroad as the "Gendarme of Europe". Sculpted by Klodt, its granite, porphyry and marble pedestal is adorned with figures representing Faith, Wisdom, Justice and Might (reputedly modelled on Nicholas's daughters); bas-reliefs depict the achievements of his reign, and four lamp-stands flaunt screaming eagles. His daughter Maria objected to the horse's backside facing her Mariinskiy Palace, as did the clergy to it facing St Isaac's Cathedral – the latter won in the end.

Further west stand a trio of buildings with diverse antecedents. The **Myatlev House** (no. 9) is the oldest on the square, dating from the 1760s, its medallioned facade bearing a plaque attesting to the fact that the French encyclopedist Denis Diderot stayed here from 1773 to 1774 at the invitation of Catherine the Great. When he fell on hard times, she bought his library but allowed him to keep the books and be paid for "curatorship" until his death. The house is named after a later owner, the poet Ivan Myatlev. Alongside stands a brown granite building that served as the German Embassy until the outbreak of World War I, when a mob tore down its statues, flung them in the Moyka and looted the building in an orgy of hysterical patriotism.

Next door at no. 7, the **Vavilov Institute of Plant Breeding** is proud of preserving its collection of 56,000 edible specimens throughout the Blockade – when 29 of its staff died of malnutrition – and of its founder, Nikolai Vavilov (1887–1943), Russia's greatest geneticist. The memorial plaque fails to mention that he was arrested, tortured, accused of heading a nonexistent opposition party, and died in prison during Stalin's time. Around the side of the building, on the Moyka embankment, a tetrahedral granite **obelisk** marks the level of the worst floods in the city's history – the five-metre watermark is at chest height, and a mark well above head level can also be seen.

Siniy most and the Mariinskiy Palace

Isaakievskaya ploshchad's southern end continues across **Siniy most**, the Blue Bridge, which is so wide that you hardly realize the Moyka is flowing beneath it. Like the Red and Green bridges further along the Moyka, the Siniy gets its name from the colour of its river-facing sides. Until Alexander II abolished serfdom in 1861, serfs were bought and sold here in what amounted to a slave market. On the far side of the bridge, the building (no. 66) on the corner of the Moyka embankment was once the residence of John Quincey Adams, the United States' first Ambassador to Russia, and later its sixth President.

Further south, the **Mariinskiy Palace** (Mariinskiy dvorets) flaunts the tricolour and crest of the Russian Federation, and the five awards bestowed on Leningrad during the Soviet era – a schizoid heraldry reflecting the palace's history. Built for Maria, the favourite daughter of Nicholas I, it later became the seat of the State Council; the Council of Ministers met here while Tsarism was falling, as did the Provisional Government before it moved into the Winter Palace. Since 1948 it has been the equivalent of City Hall, a largely rubber-stamp institution. The area beyond here is covered under "West of St Isaac's" (p.105) and "Between the Yusupov Palace and the Blok Museum" (p.108).

Between Nevskiy and Voznesenskiy prospekts

If you don't reach St Isaac's Cathedral by way of the Admiralty and ploshchad Dekabristov, you'll probably approach it along one of the streets or canals between Nevskiy and Voznesenskiy prospekts. These two avenues delineate a central wedge full of contrasts and vitality, encompassing the old financial district along Bolshaya and Malaya Morskaya, the faded beauty of the Moyka and Griboedov embankments, and bustling Sadovaya ulitsa and Sennaya ploshchad.

Malaya and Bolshaya Morskaya

Before the Revolution, financiers and aristocrats congregated in the banks and clubs of **Bolshaya Morskaya** and **Malaya Morskaya**, a pair of streets dubbed "**the City**". In 1918, these were nationalized or shut down, leaving only imposing facades as a reminder of their heyday. Post-Soviet hopes of reviving this as the financial district foundered on the fact that most buildings contained communal flats and were terribly decrepit inside, so while airlines and fast-food joints have taken over the street-facing floors, the upper and rear sections are still virtual slums. That said, as these streets are the nexus of downtown St Petersburg, you're bound to pass this way often, and there are several buildings with picturesque features or historic associations.

On **Malaya Morskaya ulitsa**, no. 10 is known as the "**Queen of Spades' House**", having once been the residence of Princess N.P. Golitsyna, who is thought to have been the model for the countess in Pushkin's short story *The Queen of Spades*. A former society beauty, she was an old woman in Pushkin's day, when she was nicknamed "Princess Moustache". *The Queen of Spades* was later turned into an opera by **Tchaikovsky**, who occupied the Empire-style block diagonally across the street at no. 13, on the corner of Gorokhovaya ulitsa. It was here that he died on October 25, 1893, most likely from cholera contracted from a glass of unboiled water that he consumed in the *Restaurant Leiner* on Nevskiy prospect. (The theory that he committed suicide to avoid a scandal over his love affair with his nephew is now largely discredited, following research showing that homosexuality was generally tolerated in Russian high society at that time.)

A block further on, a plaque at no. 17 remembers **Gogol**, who lived there from 1833 to 1836, during which time he wrote such short stories as *The Nose*, *Nevskiy Prospekt* and *Diary of a Madman* – set in a St Petersburg where "everything breathes falsehood" – and his satirical drama *The Government Inspector*. Despite the play's success, Gogol felt misunderstood and victimized, and left the city two months after its premiere. His last years were marked by religious mania and despair: lapsing into melancholia, he ate only pickled cabbage and, suffering from cataleptic fits, died after being mistakenly buried alive in a Moscow cemetery – as was discovered years later when his body was exhumed, and claw marks were found inside the coffin.

Running parallel to Malaya Morskaya a block to the northwest, **Bolshaya Morskaya ulitsa** is more notable for its architectural extravagances. At no. 24, voluptuous brown granite pillars and an inscription identify the pre-revolutionary emporium of the jewellers **Fabergé**. It was Carl Fabergé (1846–1920) who turned a small family firm into a world-famous company with branches in Moscow, Kiev, Odessa and London. In 1884 Alexander III commissioned him to design a jewelled Easter egg for the empress – the first of 56 Imperial Eggs exchanged by the tsar and tsaritsa every year until the fall of the Romanovs. Still more intricate was the Grand Siberian Railway Egg, produced to mark the completion of the line to Vladivostok, which contained a tiny clockwork replica of the Trans-Siberian Express. Many such creations were smuggled abroad after the Revolution; in 2004, a Russian oligarch paid $90 million for nine eggs and 180 other pieces, which he donated to the Kremlin Armoury Museum in Moscow.

Also notice the **Bank for Foreign Economic Affairs** (no. 29), resembling a scaled-down Winter Palace, and a statue of Mother Russia succouring a widow, child and pensioner, crowning the former **Rossiya Insurance Company**, past Gorokhovaya ulitsa. The continuation of Bolshaya and Malaya Morskaya beyond St Isaac's Cathedral is described on p.105.

Along the Moyka embankment

Walking along the **River Moyka embankment** (naberezhnaya reki Moyki) from Nevskiy prospekt to Isaakievskaya ploshchad takes longer, but its melancholy charm is hard to resist – the sooty tan, beige and grey facades like a Canaletto canal vista painted by L.S. Lowry.

Turning off Nevskiy prospekt by the Stroganov Palace (see p.73) brings you to the eighteenth-century **Razumovskiy Palace**, while further along is the old **Foundling House** (Vospitatelniy dom) for abandoned babies, which by 1837 was taking in 25,000 children a year, before farming them out to peasant familes for "nursing". Today, both buildings belong to the Herzen Pedagogical Institute.

Immediately beyond, the Moyka is spanned by **Krasniy most**, or Red Bridge, carrying Gorokhovaya ulitsa across the river. Of the four similar wrought-iron bridges built across the Moyka in the early nineteenth century, it alone retains its original form, featuring four granite obelisks topped with gilded spheres. From Krasniy most, it's 400m along the embankment to Siniy most at the bottom of Isaakievskaya ploshchad (see p.99).

Along the Griboedov Canal

The winding **Griboedov Canal** (kanal Griboedova) makes a fairly indirect approach to St Isaac's, but the views are so lovely you hardly notice the distance. At the very least, you should walk as far as Bankovskiy most, the first footbridge off Nevskiy prospekt. Here, the south bank of the canal is thronged with students from the **University of Economics**, which is easily identified by the wrought-iron railings and curved wings of what was previously the Assignment Bank. The bank lent its name to the picturesque **Bankovskiy most**, or Bank Bridge, whose suspension cables issue from the mouths of four griffons with gilded wings – in ancient Greece, these mythical creatures were thought to be the guardians of gold. Its designer, Walter Traitteur, also built Lviniy most (Lion Bridge), further along the canal (see p.108 for a description of this and other sights beyond Voznesenskiy prospekt).

Beyond this point the canal runs beneath **Muchnoy most** – a wrought-iron footbridge – and the humped **Kamenniy most** (Stone Bridge), which carries Gorokhovaya ulitsa across the canal. Looking north up the avenue from the bridge you can see the Admiralty spire; in the other direction, the Theatre of Young Spectators. In 1880, the People's Will planted dynamite beneath the bridge in an attempt to kill Alexander II as he rode across, but the plan failed.

Soon after Kamenniy most the canal becomes tree-lined and veers left, passing beneath the arched, wrought-iron **Demidov most**. South of here the embankment opens on to **Sennaya ploshchad**, which was the setting for *Crime and*

Punishment (see below). Thereafter, the canal switchbacks through a residential area, spanned by a pair of bridges with gilt finials, and under **Voznesenskiy most**, decorated with bundles of spears and gilded rosettes, which carries Voznesenskiy prospekt across the Griboedov Canal.

Sadovaya ulitsa

The longest of the routes between Nevskiy and Voznesenskiy prospekts is quite unlike the others. Thronged with people and traffic, the two-kilometre length of **Sadovaya ulitsa** is notable for its once palatial edifices standing cheek by jowl with seedy communal apartments. You can ride all the way along Sadovaya from Gostiniy dvor to Sennaya ploshchad and on to the St Nicholas Cathedral by tram #3 or #14.

Originally bordered by country estates (hence its name, "Garden Street"), Sadovaya became a centre for trade and vice in the nineteenth century, when its markets and slums rubbed shoulders with prestigious institutions – much as they do today. The initial stretch is flanked by the Gostiniy dvor (p.70) and, further on, by the old **Vorontsov Palace**, set back from the south side of the street behind ornate railings. Built between 1749 and 1757 by Rastrelli, this later housed the elite *corps des pages*, an academy for boys from the highest ranks of the nobility, whose students included Rasputin's assassin Yusupov, the anarchist Prince Kropotkin, and several of the Decembrists. Today it serves as the Suvorov Military Academy, whose cadets cut a dash in their black-and-red uniforms.

On the next block stands the **Apraksin dvor**, a labyrinthine complex of cheap shops and *ateliers*. Built by Corsini in the 1860s, it took its name from an earlier warren dedicated to Peter the Great's admiral, Fyodor Apraksin, which *Murray's Handbook* described in the 1870s as crowded with "a motley populace", all "bearded and furred and thoroughly un-European". At night, the yard rocks to the sound of bands playing at *Money Honey* (see p.357).

Sennaya ploshchad – and Dostoyevsky's "Crime and Punishment"

As Sadovaya ulitsa nears the Griboedov Canal it opens onto **Sennaya ploshchad** (Hay Square). Flanked by apartment blocks from the 1930s, when the square was remodelled and its eighteenth-century Church of the Assumption demolished to build a metro station – both optimistically called ploshchad Mira (Peace Square) – this St Petersburg equivalent of Skid Row was facelifted for the city's tercentenary and now has shopping arcades instead of shabby kiosks, but retains a whiff of its disreputable past. In Dostoyevsky's time it was known, and functioned, as the **Haymarket**, embodying squalor, vice and degradation. Here, infants were sold to be mutilated by professional beggars, and ten-year-old prostitutes rented out for fifty kopeks a night. Thousands of people slept outdoors, huddled around fires, trading their shirt for a bite to eat or a gulp of vodka. Local tenement blocks provided lodgings for tradespeople, clerks, prostitutes and students, who thronged the pubs on every corner.

The Haymarket was the setting for *Crime and Punishment*, whose feverish protagonist, Raskolnikov, finally knelt in the square in atonement for his murder of the moneylender Alyona Ivanova. **Dostoyevsky** knew the area well, for he lived in several **flats** on nearby Malaya Meshchanskaya ulitsa (Petit-Bourgeois Street) – now Kaznacheyskaya ulitsa: at no. 1 from 1861 to 1863, before he took a spa-cure at Wiesbaden; at no. 9 in April 1864; and finally at no. 7 on the corner of Stolyarniy pereulok, from August 1864 till January 1867 (as attested by a plaque).

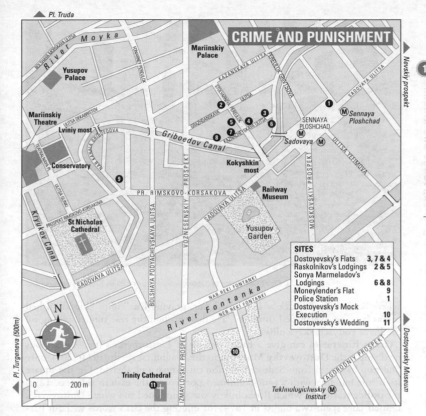

CRIME AND PUNISHMENT

SITES

Dostoyevsky's Flats   **3, 7 & 4**
Raskolnikov's Lodgings   **2 & 5**
Sonya Marmeladov's
   Lodgings   **6 & 8**
Moneylender's Flat   **9**
Police Station   **1**
Dostoyevsky's Mock
   Execution   **10**
Dostoyevsky's Wedding   **11**

It was at this flat that he met Anna Snitkina, a stenographer to whom he dictated the final instalment of *Crime and Punishment* (parts had already been serialized) and the whole of *The Gambler*. Four months later they were married. His brother, too, lived on the street; together they published *The Times* and *Epoch* reviews, neither of which prospered.

Although Dostoevsky referred to streets by their initials, his descriptions are precise enough to locate the fictional abodes of his characters, though most of the courtyards have now been gated, to prevent sightseers leaving graffiti. **Raskolnikov's lodgings** were on Stolyarniy pereulok ("S—Lane"): either at no. 5 on the corner of Grazhdanskaya ulitsa – whose stairwell has the requisite thirteen steps that he descended "like a cat" from his attic – or no. 9, with its yardkeeper's lodge, where he espied the axe that he stole for a murder weapon. Similarly, there are two possibilities for the saintly streetwalker **Sonya Marmeladov's lodgings**, namely no. 63 or no. 73 on the Griboedov embankment, which she patrolled for clients in the novel (there's a café named after her at no. 79).

You can trace the circuitous **murder route**, from Stolyarniy pereulok across Kokushinskiy most ("K—Bridge"), down Sadovaya ("S—Street") and along what is now prospekt Rimskovo-Korsakova, to the **moneylender's flat** on the Griboedov Canal. House no. 104 fits the bill perfectly, but its inner yard is no longer accessible, to stop sightseers climbing the stairs to flat #74, fingered as the place

▲ Courtyard at one of Dostoyevsky's former flats on Kaznacheyskaya ulitsa

where Raskolnikov struck at her "thin, fair, graying hair" until "blood gushed out as from an overturned tumbler". He fled through the rear tunnel exiting on Srednaya Podyacheskaya ulitsa.

Other itineraries can give a fuller picture of Dostoyevsky's life. An obvious next stop is the **Dostoyevsky Museum** in the Vladimirskaya district (p.207), only one stop by metro from Sadovaya station on Sennaya ploshchad. On the square itself, the building with a four-columned portico on the eastern side (no. 12) is the **police station** to which Raskolnikov was summoned and where Dostoyevsky himself later spent two nights in 1874, for quoting the tsar's words without permission in his journal *The Citizen*. He enjoyed the seclusion of his cell, rereading Hugo's *Les Misérables* and reflecting on the turns his life had taken within a mile or so of the Haymarket. At 28, he belonged to the **Petrashevsky Circle** of utopian socialists who met in the house of Mikhail Butashevich-Petrashevsky, on **ploshchad Turgeneva**, until their arrest in 1849. Though Dostoyevsky hid his role in setting up an illegal printing press, he and twenty others were sentenced to death for treason. Their mock execution on **Semyonovskiy plats**, across the river, presaged years of hard labour in Siberia, where his beliefs changed utterly. And his marriage to Anna – which set him on the path to fatherhood and financial security – was consecrated at the **Trinity Cathedral**, not far from the execution ground. The last two are shown on the accompanying map but described in Chapter 6.

The Railway Museum and Yusupov Garden

Besides the Dostoyevsky trail there are a couple of minor sights 100m or so beyond Sennaya ploshchad. At Sadovaya ulitsa 50, the **Railway Museum** (Muzey Zheleznodorozhnovo Transporta; 11am–5pm; closed Fri & Sat & the last Thurs of each month; R70; ⑩www.railroad.ru/cmrt in Russian) retains a statue of Lenin hailing the railway workers and a model of an armoured train used in the Civil War. The rooms also contain intricate scale-models of bridges and locomotives (including some futuristic bullet trains that were never built), and a walk-through section of an old "soft class" sleeping carriage, with velvet upholstery and Art Nouveau fixtures, including a bathtub. You can see the model railways in action during free guided tours (posted in the lobby), but for real-life trains you can't beat the Outdoor Railway Museum near the Obvodniy Canal (see p.217).

In summer, the adjacent **Yusupov Garden** (daily 6am–11pm) is perfumed with the smell of lilac trees and thronged with sunbathers. It was originally the grounds of a **Yusupov Palace** on the Fontanka that later became an engineering institute; the Yusupovs bought another palace beside the Moyka, where the last of the dynasty murdered Rasputin (see p.108). He might be pleased that the Tea Pavilion of their old pile on the Fontanka now houses one of St Petersburg's top restaurants, *Dvoryanskoe Gnezdo* (see p.351). See pp.111–114 for details of the St Nicholas Cathedral and other sights beyond the Griboedov Canal.

West of St Isaac's

The area **west of St Isaac's** has fewer obvious sights than the quarter between the Moyka and the Fontanka, so it pays to be selective. Apart from the Nabokov Museum on Bolshaya Morskaya ulitsa, and the Popov Museum and Museum of Religion on Pochtamtskaya ulitsa, there's not much to see until you hit ploshchad Truda and New Holland, roughly 800m beyond Isaakievskaya ploshchad. However, there is a nice feel to the locality, whose leafy embankments and residential character give it a genteel atmosphere and make for pleasant evening walks during the summer. The area is shown in detail on the map on p.94.

Along Bolshaya Morskaya ulitsa

Such attractions as there are in the immediate vicinity present a discreet face to the world, particularly along **Bolshaya Morskaya ulitsa**. Several big names in pre-revolutionary Petersburg lived on the northern side of the road, where Montferrand built mansions for the industrialist Pyotr Demidov (no. 43) and the socialite Princess Gagarina (no. 45). The latter is now the **House of Composers** (Dom kompozitorov), whose picturesque coffered hall can be admired under the pretext of visiting the restaurant in the building.

Next door, the **Nabokov Museum** (11am–6pm, Sat & Sun noon–5pm; closed Mon; R100; Ⓦwww.nabokovmuseum.org) occupies the birthplace and childhood home of the great Russian writer, unfairly best known abroad for his novel *Lolita*. Opened in 1997, it is the foremost centre for Nabokov studies in Russia, hosting events ranging from jazz concerts and exhibitions of contemporary art to an annual Bloomsday (June 16) honouring Joyce's *Ulysses* (the two writers admired each other's work). Besides some of Nabokov's personal effects and first editions, visitors can see the oak-panelled library and walnut-ceilinged dining room that he lovingly described in *Speak, Memory*. The Nabokov family was immensely wealthy and epitomized the cosmopolitan St Petersburg intelligentsia: the children all spoke three languages and their father helped draft the constitution of the Provisional Government, only to be killed in Berlin in 1922 in the act of shielding the Kadet leader, Milyukov, from an assassin. Guided tours in English can be booked on ☎315 47 13.

On the anniversary of Nabokov's birth (April 22 by the New Calendar), the museum organizes an **excursion** (€30 per person for a minimum of five people) to the family's country estate, 70km from St Petersburg, whose mansion is being reconstructed following a fire in 1995. Nabokov knew it as Vyra, but it is nowadays called **Rozhdestveno**.

Along Pochtamtskaya ulitsa

Pochtamtskaya ulitsa, running parallel to Bolshaya Morskaya, takes its name from the **Main Post Office** (Glavniy pochtamt; Mon–Sat 9am–7.45pm, Sun 10am–5.45pm), with its distinctive overhead gallery spanning the street. Designed by Nikolai Lvov in the 1780s, the post office originally centred on a stable yard whence coaches departed to towns across Russia, measuring their distance from the capital from this spot; the Style Moderne hall, with its ornate ironwork and glass ceiling, was created by the conversion of the courtyard early last century. The gallery displays a **Clock of the World**, whose outer face shows Moscow time (in relation to which, all Russian time-zones are defined), while the inner face gives the hour in other major cities around the world. A replica got trashed during the high-speed tank and car chase in the Bond film *Goldeneye*.

On the northeast corner of the crossroad, the **Popov Museum of Communications** (10.30am–6pm, closed Sun & Mon; R50) was founded in 1876 as the Telegraph Museum to enlighten Russians about this foreign technology – twenty years before Russia could boast of its own revolutionary invention. Russians regard **Alexander Popov** (1859–1906) rather than Marconi as the inventor of the radio, since Popov transmitted a signal in the laboratories of St Petersburg University on March 24, 1896, almost a year before Marconi – but news of his achievement was slow to leave Russia. The museum has a vast collection of Tsarist and Soviet stamps, switchboards, radios and satellites, some only viewable on guided tours (R600 for up to five people; ☎571 00 60). The admission charge includes use of their Internet centre.

The **Museum of Religion** (11am–6pm; closed Wed & the last Fri of each month; R120; Ⓦwww.relig-museum.ru, in Russian) on the opposite corner of Pochtamtskiy pereulok features artefacts representing the religions of ancient Egypt, Greece and Rome, Judaism, Buddhism, Islam and Russian Orthodox Christianity – most of them from the old Museum of Atheism (see p.72). Ironically, many of its curators were devoutly religious and used the museum to safeguard holy relics until atheism ceased to be state policy.

From Konnogvardeyskiy bulvar to the Nikolaevskiy Palace

Just around the corner from the Popov Museum, the broad, tree-lined **Konnogvardeyskiy bulvar** runs from the Triumphal Columns near the Horseguards' Manège to ploshchad Truda, 650m southwest. Laid out in 1842 along the course of an old canal, Konnogvardeyskiy bulvar (Horseguards' Boulevard) got its name from the Lifeguards' barracks off what is now called **ploshchad Truda** (Labour Square). Here stands the huge Italianate **Nikolaevskiy Palace**, built by Stakenschneider for Grand Duke Nicholas, but used as a boarding school for young noblewomen until after the Revolution, when it was allocated to the city's Trade Union Council as a Palace of Labour. Nowadays, its grand **ballroom** is used for nightly "folklore" concerts (p.364), and you should at least nip inside the lobby to see the vast double staircase, while a visit to room 44 on the first floor will reward you with the sight of the ornately panelled **Moorish Smoking Room**.

From ploshchad Truda you can head towards New Holland or the Neva embankment, via an underpass and dismal subterranean shopping mall. En route to New Holland, you'll pass the crumbling red-brick **Kryukov Barracks**, earmarked as the future site of the Naval Museum (see p.154).

From New Holland to the Neva

Early in the eighteenth century, a canal was dug between the Moyka and the Neva, creating a triangular islet later known as **New Holland** (Novaya Gollandiya). Surrounded by water, it was an ideal storage place for flammable materials such as timber, which could be transported by barge to the shipyards. In 1763, the wooden sheds were replaced by red-brick structures of different heights, for storing timber vertically, with a great **arch** spanning a canal leading to a basin in the centre, later used for the first trials of Krylov's design for a non-capsizeable boat. Owned by the Navy until 2004, this long-neglected backwater is now the site of a $300 million **redevelopment** project headed by the British architect Norman Foster. His design envisages a star-shaped, roofed amphitheatre and an opera house, flanked by galleries, hotels, offices and luxury apartments, incorporating the brick facades of the timber yards and naval prison: the plans include eight bridges linking the development to the Hermitage and the Mariinskiy Theatre. The project is scheduled to be completed by 2010, resurrecting what was once a fashionable quarter of the city.

On the Moyka embankment to the south, Nicholas I's sister, Grand Duchess Kseniya, lived at no. 108, while Grand Duke Alexei occupied a palace (no. 122) near the naval shipyard on Novoadmiralteyskiy Island. To the north, the golden-yellow **Bobrinskiy Palace**, on Galernaya ulitsa, was built for the illegitimate son of Catherine the Great and Grigori Orlov, who was smuggled out of the Winter Palace at birth, wrapped in the fur of a beaver (*bobyor* in Russian) – hence the surname under which he was raised by foster-parents until Catherine brought him to court as Count Bobrinskiy.

Along the Neva embankment

Further north, the Neva embankment is lined with mansions from the eighteenth century, when it was first called the **Angliyskaya naberezhnaya** (English Quay), as it is again now. This fashionable promenade was the centre of St Petersburg's British community in the nineteenth century. Its Soviet-era name – Red Fleet Embankment – alluded to the bombardment of the Winter Palace by the cruiser *Aurora* at the outset of the Bolshevik Revolution. On the night of October 25, 1917, the *Aurora* steamed into the Neva and dropped anchor near the middle span of Blagoveshenskiy most (better known as the Lieutenant Schmidt Bridge), trained its guns over the roof of the Winter Palace and at 9.40pm fired the (blank) shots that "reverberated around the world". The event is commemorated by a granite **stela** carved with a picture of the *Aurora*. In summer, giant cruise liners moor just beyond the bridge.

The main point of interest is **Rumyantsev Mansion** (Osobnyak Rumyantseva; 11am–6pm, Tues till 5pm; closed Wed & the last Thurs of each month; R100) at Angliyskaya naberezhnaya 44. Barring a single room on the mansion's history, the second floor is devoted to **the Siege of Leningrad** (ask for an English-language handout). A model anti-aircraft position and a life-sized bomb shelter represent the defence of the city; dioramas portray the effort to survive during winter, when water had to be drawn through holes in the ice and firewood scavenged from snowdrifts to feed the tiny makeshift stoves known as *burzhuiki*. Supplies arrived by the "Road of Life" across Lake Ladoga, enabling Leningrad to carry on until the Blockade was broken in January 1944. You can also see a copy of the diary of 11-year-old Tanya Savicheva, recording the deaths of members of her family. A magnificent oak staircase leads upstairs to an exhibition on the **New Economic Policy** (NEP) of the early 1920s, when capitalism was briefly restored to revive the devastated economy – represented by colourful posters, cartoons, advertising and fashions from that time.

Between the Yusupov Palace and the Blok Museum

The area between the Yusupov Palace and the Blok Museum knits together several strands in the city's cultural history, being the site of the **Conservatory** and the **Mariinskiy Theatre** (home of the Kirov Ballet); the **synagogue** and the much-loved **St Nicholas Cathedral**; the fabulous **Yusupov Palace**, where Rasputin was murdered; and the former **residence of the poet Blok**. It's a ten- to fifteen-minute walk from St Isaac's to the Yusupov Palace, and not much further to the Mariinskiy, from where it's just a few blocks to the cathedral or the synagogue. From here, a further fifteen-minute walk or a short tram ride takes you to the Blok Museum, set somewhat apart on the western edge of the Kolomna district. The Mariinskiy and St Nicholas Cathedral can also be reached by following the Griboedov Canal as it bends around beyond Voznesenskiy prospekt. This route takes you past the beautiful **Lviniy most**, or Lion Bridge, whose suspension cables emerge from the jaws of four stone lions with wavy manes.

The Yusupov Palace on the Moyka

The **Yusupov Palace** (Yusupovskiy dvorets; daily 10.45am–5pm; April–Oct closed the first Wed of each month; ⓦwww.yusupov-palace.ru) on the Moyka embankment (not to be confused with the palace of the same name on the Fontanka – see p.105) is famed as the scene of Rasputin's murder by Prince Yusupov, but deserves a visit in its own right as the finest palace in St Petersburg, embodying the tastes of four generations of nobles and rivalling the residences of the tsars, but on a more intimate scale. Situated at naberezhnaya reki Moyki 94, between the Pochtamtskiy and Potseluev bridges, the building still belongs to the Union of Educational Workers, which used it as a headquarters and clubhouse during Soviet times, but now functions as a museum and may even be rented for parties – Mick Jagger celebrated his sixtieth birthday here.

The museum offers two kinds of **guided tours** every day. If you're not able to do both, opt for the general tour (R400) of the ceremonial rooms and theatre that runs every hour on the hour; it's in Russian but the price includes an audio-guide in other languages. The cellar where Rasputin was murdered is covered by a separate tour at 1.45pm (R200), also in Russian. You can also book a tour of the private apartments of Princess Zinaida and Irina, and a bus excursion covering Rasputin's haunts in St Petersburg (☎314 88 93; cost varies with the size of the group).

The ceremonial rooms

The magnificent **ceremonial rooms** were created or reworked by each successive Yusupov as they came into their inheritance, so the diversity of styles is matched by the personalities behind them, from Boris – who started the ball rolling in the 1830s – down to his great-grandson Felix in the 1900s. Tours begin with a suite of rooms designed in the 1860s by the Italian Ippolito Monighetti for Boris's son Nikolai, featuring a *faux marbre* billiard hall, an embossed **Turkish study** and an extravagant **Moorish dining hall** with gold filigree arabesques and "blackamoor" figures holding incense vases. After his wife died, Nikolai slept in a small study-bedroom linked by a private staircase to the apartments of his daughter, Zinaida, whose portrait by Serov hangs downstairs. There is also a **buffet room** with embossed leather walls and ceramics standing in for the pilfered family silver; notice the crane-headed walking sticks in the corner.

Ascending the voluptuous marble **State Staircase**, flanked by allegorical statues of Asia, Africa, Europe and the Americas symbolizing hospitality beneath a chandelier holding 130 candles, you reach the classical rooms designed by Andrei Mikhailov for Prince Boris in the 1830s, with green, blue and red **drawing rooms** preceding a **large rotunda**, a white colonnaded **concert hall** and a **ballroom** with a barrel-vaulted ceiling that's really a *trompe l'oeil* canvas hung from chains. After these were completed, Boris had an entire wing built to house the **art collection** amassed by his own father, Nikolai, at Arkhangelskoe outside Moscow, including the **Canova Rotunda** – which contains the celebrated *Cupid and Psyche* and *Cupid with a Bow and Quiver* by the sculptor after whom it is named – and a lovely private **theatre** where Glinka's opera *Ivan Susanin* was premiered in 1836 by the Yusupov troupe of freed-serf actors, who also served as oarsmen on the Moyka and the Neva. The Renaissance-style **Tapestry Hall** that Boris added in the 1840s and the coffered **Oak Dining Room**, commissioned by Zinaida in the 1890s, fit harmoniously into the ensemble.

The cellar

Although small and plain compared to the rest of the palace, few visitors can resist visiting the site of **Rasputin's murder**, where a waxworks tableau portrays the events of December 16, 1916. The deed was planned by Prince Felix Yusupov, the ultra-monarchist Vladimir Purishkevich, the tsar's cousin, Grand Duke Dmitri, Dr Lazovert (who obtained the cyanide) and Guards' Captain Sukhotin. The last four waited in Yusupov's study while the Prince led Rasputin – who had been lured to the palace on the pretext of an assignation with Yusupov's wife Irina – to the cel-

Rasputin

Born in the Siberian village of Pokrovskoe in 1869, **Grigori Rasputin** later added ten years to his age to enhance his image as an elder and the prefix Noviy ("New") to his surname (derived from the word for "dissolute"), but never lost the reputation of being a libertine: his wife said of his philandering, "it makes no difference, he has enough for all". Wanted for horse-rustling, Rasputin sought refuge in a monastery, emerging as a wandering holy man, who claimed to have made a pilgrimage to Mount Athos in Greece but was really involved with a heretical sect called the *Khlysty*. His preaching attracted influential patrons, from provincial Kazan to the salons of St Petersburg, where he was introduced to the tsar and tsaritsa in 1905. He impressed the royal family by alleviating the internal bleeding of their haemophiliac son, Alexei, whom conventional physicians had been unable to help. In 1907, Alexei had a severe attack while Rasputin was in Siberia. Alerted by telegram, he replied, "the illness is not as serious as it seems. Don't let the doctors worry him" – and from that moment on Alexei began to recover.

As Rasputin's influence at court increased, his enemies multiplied. Although he opposed Russia entering World War I, he was blamed for the mistakes of the corrupt ministers appointed on his recommendation. His orgies in Moscow and Petersburg were a public scandal; it was whispered that he kept the tsar doped and slept with the empress (or her daughters). Aristocratic and bourgeois society rejoiced at his murder, but the peasants were bitter, believing that Rasputin was killed because he let the tsar hear the voice of the people. Rasputin himself prophesised that should he be killed by the nobility, the monarchy would not survive – true to his words, the February Revolution occurred less than three months after his death. Although Rasputin's corpse was subsequently dug up and burnt by soldiers, the Museum of Erotica (p.197) exhibits what it claims are his genitals, supposedly removed at the autopsy.

lar, where two rooms had been furnished and a table laid with cakes and bottles of sweet wine, laced with cyanide. The poison, however, failed to have any effect, and so Yusupov hurried upstairs, fetched his revolver and shot Rasputin from behind. Yusupov relates how he left Rasputin for dead, but when he returned later, Rasputin leapt up and tried to strangle him, before escaping into the courtyard, where Purishkevich finished him off with four shots. When the coast was clear, the body was driven across the city and dumped, bound but unweighted, into the Malaya Nevka – but instead of being carried out to sea, the corpse was washed ashore downstream and found on January 1, 1917.

The results of the autopsy remained unknown until the publication of Edvard Radzinsky's *The Rasputin File,* which used hitherto secret documents to argue that Yusupov invented the tale of Rasputin's supernatural vitality to make his own role seem more heroic, and that no trace of cyanide was found (perhaps because Dr Lazovert substituted a harmless chemical, as he swore on his deathbed). In 2004, historian Andrew Cook advanced yet another theory – that Rasputin was shot by a British intelligence officer, Oswald Rayner, to stop him persuading the tsar to seek peace with Germany. Whatever the truth, the putative conspirators escaped remarkably lightly, the Grand Duke being exiled to Persia and Yusupov to his estates in the Crimea, while the others weren't punished at all.

The private apartments

By prior arrangement (see p.108) you can also tour the **private apartments**, which are as grand as the ceremonial rooms, but smaller. **Princess Zinaida's suite** was designed by Monighetti and redone by Alexander Stepanov after she inherited the palace in 1890. Her Rococo **Porcelain Boudoir** and **White Drawing Room** are perhaps the finest rooms in the palace, with an intimacy also characteristic of the **Henri II Drawing Room** – none of which bears any trace of her estranged husband, but bespeak an enjoyable widowhood. She eventually moved out after her son, Felix, married the tsar's niece, Princess Irina, and the couple commissioned their own apartments, designed in the Neoclassical style by Andrei Vaitens and Andrei Beloborodov, and finished only a year before the Revolution. **Irina's suite** is notable for its **Silver Bathroom**, while **Felix's suite** contains an exhibition on the history of the Yusupov family, which was of Tatar origin. Before fleeing Russia they hid much of their jewellery in the palace cellars, to be discovered by the Communists: to sustain Felix's spendthrift habits in exile, Irina opened a fashion house catering to Russian émigrés, and later won the vast sum of £25,000 in damages from MGM, for defaming her character in the film *Rasputin the Mad Monk.* (Meanwhile, the Grand Duke took up with Coco Chanel, helping her to launch Chanel No. 5.) A **ballroom** and a delightful **winter garden** complete the tour.

The Mariinskiy Theatre and Conservatory

Teatralnaya ploshchad (Theatre Square), southwest of the Yusupov Palace, is home to two of St Petersburg's most revered cultural institutions: the Mariinskiy Theatre and the Conservatory. The **Mariinskiy Theatre**'s exterior is as graceless as its interior is lovely, a pea-green chest enclosing an auditorium upholstered in blue velvet and silver brocade, ablaze with lamps and chandeliers. Yet backstage is so cramped that staff have only forty percent of the space required by law, and in 2003 the outmoded technical systems were cruelly exposed by a fire that destroyed its entire collection of historic stage sets. Since then, the set workshop has been rebuilt as a 1100-seat **concert hall** for symphonic performances, and a new 2000-seat **second stage** (*vtoraya stena*) is to be constructed across the Kryukov Canal from the old theatre. However, clearance work is already behind schedule and the controversial, multi-canopied design by Dominique Perrault (designer of the National Library in Paris) has been endlessly revised at the insistence of St Petersburg's governor, chief architect and the Kremlin, making it impossible to complete by 2008, as was envisaged.

The Mariinskiy was established in 1860 (though ballet performances didn't start until twenty years later); its **golden era** was at the turn of the last century, when audiences watched Anna Pavlova, Mathilde Kshesinskaya and Vaclav Nijinsky dance, and heard Fyodor Chaliapin sing. Most of the company's stars left shortly before or after the Revolution, but following a lean period, it gained new popularity in the Soviet era thanks to composers Prokofiev and Khachaturian, and dancers such as Galina Ulanova. Having suffered in the 1980s, today it flourishes under the direction of Valery Gergiev, far eclipsing its old rival the Bolshoy Theatre in Moscow. The company remains best known abroad as the **Kirov**, a title bestowed on it in 1935, when numerous institutions were renamed in honour of this Bolshevik "martyr"; but natives of the city have always called it by its affectionate diminutive, "Mariinka". For information on dancers, performances and tickets, see p.366.

Opposite the Mariinsky stands the **Conservatory**, the premier institution of higher musical education in Russia, founded in 1862 by the pianist and composer Anton Rubinstein – though the building wasn't completed until the 1880s. Rubinstein hated Russian music and ran the institution on conservative, European lines, though his regime relaxed sufficiently to allow the premieres here of Mussorgsky's *Boris Godunov* (1874), Borodin's *Prince Igor* (1890) and Tchaikovsky's *The Sleeping Beauty* (1890). Tchaikovsky was one of the Conservatory's first graduates, while another, Shostakovich, taught here in the 1930s. Since 1944 it has been named after the composer Rimsky-Korsakov, whose **statue** stands near the building (as does one of Glinka, after whom the street crossing the square is named).

Leading figures in the world of music and drama once lived close to the Conservatory: the choreographer **Michel Fokine** at no. 109 on the Griboedov Canal; ballerina **Tamara Karsavina** at no. 8 on the Kryukov Canal; while ulitsa Glinki 3–5 was the family home of **Igor Stravinsky**, until he married his first cousin – contrary to Orthodox custom – and had to leave home to spare his family the shame.

The St Nicholas Cathedral

Looking down ulitsa Glinki you'll see one of the loveliest **views** in the city: the golden onion domes of the St Nicholas Cathedral, superimposed against the blue cupolas of the Trinity Cathedral beyond the Fontanka (see p.212). Traditionally known as the "Sailors' Church" after the naval officers who prayed here, the **St Nicholas Cathedral** (Nikolskiy sobor) is a superb example of eighteenth-century Russian Baroque, by Savva Chevakinsky. The exterior is painted ice-blue, with white Corinthian pilasters and window surrounds, crowned by five gilded cupolas and onion domes. Its low, vaulted interior is festooned with icons and – as at other working cathedrals – you might find a funeral in one part of the nave and a baptism in another going on simultaneously. In Tsarist times, the lofty free-standing **bell tower** used to harbour a flock of pigeons, fed "with the rice which the pious place there for the dead". Legend has it that the bells of St Petersburg ring whenever someone makes an offering pleasing to God. A fairy tale relates how two waifs intended to donate a crust of bread and a one-kopek coin, but the boy gave the bread to a sick beggar and stayed to nurse him, telling his sister to go on alone. When she arrived at St Nicholas just before closing time, the offering tables were laden with gold coins and gifts, but – as she put her kopek down – the bells tolled across the city.

It's worth carrying on to the junction of the River Moyka and the Kryukov Canal, behind the cathedral, where you can see at least **seven bridges** at once, more than from any other spot in St Petersburg. They frequently appear in *White Nights*, Dostoyevsky's most romantic novel.

West to the Synagogue and Blok Museum

The **Kolomna district** beyond the Kryukov Canal was once full of wooden houses, inhabited by tradespeople, clerks and workers at the iron foundry on Matisov Island – the setting for Pushkin's *Little House in Kolomna* and Gogol's *Portrait*. This humble social profile might explain why St Petersburg's synagogue was sited here, though by that time the district was becoming gentrified thanks to its proximity to the Mariinskiy and the Conservatory – until the Revolution threw the process into reverse. Today, grim 1930s blocks line the way to the docks along **ulitsa Dekabristov**, so there isn't any point in **walking** beyond the synagogue, just past the Mariinskiy's concert hall. To reach the Blok Museum, ride **bus** #6 or #22 from Teatralnaya ploshchad down ulitsa Dekabristov, alighting when it turns off at Angliyskiy prospekt.

The Synagogue

St Petersburg's synagogue stands discreetly off ulitsa Dekabristov, its corkscrew-ribbed cupola poking above the rooftops on the corner of Lermontovskiy prospekt. Jews were the most oppressed minority within the Tsarist Empire, where they

Within the Fontanka

Streets and squares

Admiralteyskaya naberezhnaya	Адмиралтейская набережная
Angliyskaya naberezhnaya	Английская набережная
Angliyskiy prospekt	Английский проспект
ploshchad Belinskovo	площадь Белинского
Bolshaya Konyushennaya ulitsa	Большая Конюшенная улица
Bolshaya Morskaya ulitsa	Большая Морская улица
ploshchad Dekabristov	площадь Декабристов
Dvortsovaya naberezhnaya	Дворцовая набережная
Dvortsovaya ploshchad	Дворцовая площадь
Gorokhovaya ulitsa	Гороховая улица
kanal Griboedova	канал Грибоедова
Isaakievskaya ploshchad	Исаакиевская площадь
Italyanskaya ulitsa	Итальянская улица
ploshchad Iskusstv	площадь Искусств
Kaznacheyskaya ulitsa	Казначейская улица
Konnogvardeyskiy bulvar	Конногвардейский бульвар
Konyushennaya ploshchad	Конюшенная площадь
Lermontovskiy prospekt	Лермонтовский проспект
Malaya Konyushennaya ulitsa	Малая Конюшенная улица
Malaya Morskaya ulitsa	Малая Морская улица
Marsovo pole	Марсово поле
Mikhailovskaya ulitsa	Михайловская улица
Millionnaya ulitsa	Миллионная улица
naberezhnaya reki Fontanki	набережная реки Фонтанки
naberezhnaya reki Moyki	набережная реки Мойки
Nevskiy prospekt	Невский проспект

were largely confined to the Pale of Settlement and barely tolerated in the capital prior to the reforms of Alexander II. Not until 1893 was the community secure enough to build a synagogue and cultural centre, in the Moorish style of synagogues in Eastern Europe. Unlike there, the city's Jewish community escaped the Nazi genocide, but its religious and cultural life was severely restricted for most of the Soviet era. Perestroika both strengthened and diminished it, inaugurating freedoms and opening the floodgates of emigration to Israel. Although far-right parties still foment anti-Semitism, the pogroms that were feared in the early 1990s never materialized and Israel no longer seems a desirable alternative to life in St Petersburg, where Jewish organizations are flourishing as never before. There's an informative exhibition on Jewish history in the foyer of the **Great Synagogue** (Bolshaya sinagoga), whose magnificent prayer hall, with its stucco squinches and stalactite mouldings, has been restored with donations from the Saffra family and others from the diaspora. Besides the celebration of Jewish holy days, it hosts a **Klezmer music festival** in June, and has an excellent restaurant in the basement (see p.350). The enclave also includes a **Small Synagogue** used for everyday worship and a *Yeshiva* that dispenses cheap meals to Jewish pensioners. To enter either synagogue men must wear a skullcap.

The Blok Museum

The Symbolist poet **Alexander Blok** (1880–1921) belonged to the so-called "Silver Age" of Russian poetry, which lasted from the beginning of the last century to the mid-1920s, by which time many of its greatest talents had died,

ploshchad Ostrovskovo	площадь Островского
Sadovaya ulitsa	Садовая улица
Sennaya ploshchad	Сенная площадь
Stolyarniy pereulok	Столярний переулок
Suvorovskaya ploshchad	Суворовская площадь
Teatralnaya ploshchad	Театральная площадь
ploshchad Truda	площадь Труда
Voznesenskiy prospekt	Вознесенский проспект
Metro stations	
Gostiniy Dvor	Гостиный двор
Nevskiy Prospekt	Невский проспект
Sadovaya	Садовая
Sennaya Ploshchad	Сенная площадь
Museums	
Blok Museum	музей-квартира А.А. Блока
Russian Ethnographic Museum	Русский тнографический музей
Hermitage	рмитаж
Museum of Religion	музей Религии
Museum of Russian Political History	музей политической истории России
Nabokov Museum	музей Набокова
Popov Museum of Communications	музей Связи им. А.С. Попова
Pushkin Museum	музей-квартира А.С. Пушкина
Railway Museum	музей Железнодорожного транспорта
Rumyantsev Mansion	особняк Румянцева
Russian Museum	Русский музей
Theatre Museum	Театральный музей
Zoshchenko Museum	музей М.М. Зощенко

killed themselves, or been forced into internal exile by official hostility. Blok's first poems expressed his passion for Lyubov Mendeleyeva, the actress daughter of the scientist Mendeleyev, whom he married in 1903. Later, Blok told Stanislavsky, "Russia is the theme of my life", a theme that reached its apotheosis in the winter of 1918 with *The Twelve* (*Dvenadtsat*), a fusion of religious imagery, slang, revolutionary slogans and songs. Watched over by Jesus Christ, a dozen Red Guards march through a blizzard and the maelstrom of the Revolution, whose imperative Blok voiced as:

Comrades, take aim and don't be scared,

Let's blast away at Holy Russia.

The Twelve caused a sensation amongst his fellow poets, yet the Bolsheviks barely acknowledged it, perhaps because, as Kamenev admitted, "it celebrates what we, old Socialists, fear most of all". For the last two years of his life, Blok suffered from scurvy, asthma, delirium and depression. Sensing his end, he wrote bitterly, "Dirty rotten Mother Russia has devoured me as a sow gobbles up her sucking pig." Gorky tried to get him into a Finnish sanatorium, but he died on August 20, 1921.

In 1980, his former apartment at ulitsa Dekabristov 57, overlooking the Pryazhka Canal, was turned into the **Blok Museum** (11am–6pm; closed Wed & the last Tues of each month; R70). Having collected a pair of slippers from the downstairs lobby, you can visit an exhibition of Blok's childhood drawings, photos of the poet and first editions of his work on the floor above. Two floors up, Blok and Lyubov's **apartment** is preserved much as it was when they lived there, with their brass nameplate on the door, and an antique telephone and hat stand in the hall. Finally, after going back down to the first floor, you'll be admitted to a room containing Blok's stubbled **death mask** and a sketch of Blok on his deathbed, drawn on the last page of his writing pad. The apartment hosts **concerts** of chamber music (☎713 86 31 for details) and commands a lovely **view** over the Pryazhka.

Across the road, the ballerina **Anna Pavlova** (1881–1931) lived in the apartment building on the southwestern corner of ulitsa Dekabristov and **Angliyskiy prospekt** (formerly named prospekt Maklina after John Maclean, one of the leaders of Scotland's "Red Clydeside", as a mark of international solidarity in 1918). The restoration of its traditional name pays tribute to the Britons who contributed to the city's development in olden days.

The Hermitage

Many tourists come to St Petersburg simply to visit the **Hermitage** (Ermi-tazh; рмита), one of the world's great museums. To visit all 350 exhibition rooms would entail walking a distance of about 10km and, at the last count, the collection contained over three million items – it was calculated that merely to glance at each one would take nine years. The museum owns more than 12,500 sculptures, 16,700 paintings, 624,000 drawings and prints, and 298,000 works of applied art, plus 784,000 archeological exhibits and a mil-lion coins and medals, and although only a small percentage of these is on show, it's still more than enough to keep you captivated.

The Hermitage has excellent examples of Italian High Renaissance art, as well as unparalleled groups of paintings by Rembrandt, the French Impres-sionists, Picasso and Matisse – not to mention fabulous treasures from Siberia and Central Asia, Egyptian and Classical antiquities, and Persian and Chinese artworks, among others. Last but certainly not least, there is the interior of the **Winter Palace** itself, with its magnificent **state rooms**, where the tsars once held court and the Provisional Government was arrested by the Bolshe-viks (the history of the Winter Palace is related on p.78).

The history of the Hermitage

Although Peter the Great purchased maritime scenes during his visit to Holland, and his immediate successors commissioned portraits by foreign and Russian artists, the Hermitage collection really began with **Catherine the Great**, who saw how other monarchs set store by their art collections and began accumulat-ing one to enhance her own prestige. A shrewd and lucky buyer, she bought 225 Old Masters in 1794 from the Prussian merchant Gotzkowski, after her rival Frederick the Great had turned them down for lack of cash; 600 paintings from Count Brühl of Saxony (1769); 400 first-rate pictures from the Crozat collec-tion (1772); 198 Flemish and Italian masterpieces formerly owned by the British Prime Minister Walpole (1779); 119 canvases (including nine Rembrandts and six Van Dycks) from the collection of Count Baudouin (1781); 250 Roman busts and bas-reliefs from a director of the Bank of England; and 1200 architectural drawings coveted by Emperor Joseph. She also commissioned Wedgwood and Sèvres dinner services, furniture, portraits and some 32,000 copies of antique cut gems – making her one of the greatest art collectors of all time.

Catherine invited select guests to **parties** in the Small Hermitage that she built to display her art collection, and composed "Ten Commandments" for their behaviour, ranging from "All ranks shall be left outside the doors, simi-larly hats, and particularly swords", to "Eat well of all things, but drink with moderation so that each should be able always to find his legs on leaving the doors". Anyone who violated the rules had to drink a glass of water and read aloud from the poem *Telemachiad* – a far cry from draining a chalice of port, as Peter the Great had punished breaches of etiquette. Though restricted to a small circle, these parties set a precedent for her successors to display the Imperial art collection – on which they, too, spent lavishly.

Catherine's grandson, Alexander I, cannily acquired 98 pictures from Napoleon's wife Josephine – many stolen from other collections – right under the noses of fellow sovereigns attending the Congress of Versailles in 1815. With Nicholas I's purchase of the collection of Napoleon's stepdaughter, the Russian monarchy could at last boast of owning the finest art collection in Europe. Moreover, in 1852, Nicholas decided to open the Hermitage to "decent citizens" on certain days, and appoint professional curators, making it more like an institution than a private hobby.

After the October Revolution, the Winter Palace and Hermitage became a state **museum**, which both benefited and suffered from Bolshevik policies. Its collection grew threefold as a result of artworks **expropriated** from the Yusupov, Shuvalov, Stroganov, Rumyantsev and Steiglitz collections, plus Impressionist paintings and works by Picasso and Matisse, owned by the Moscow millionaires Shchukin and Morozov. Yet the Hermitage had to surrender many outstanding pictures to Moscow's Pushkin Museum of Fine Arts, and allow the foreign **sale** of major works by Rembrandt, Rubens and Van Eycks in the 1920s and 1930s, when the regime needed hard currency to buy imported machinery – though staff did manage to prevent the sarcophagus of St Alexander Nevsky from being melted down for its silver.

In 1941, staff evacuated 45 carriage-loads of items to Sverdlovsk before the **Blockade** of Leningrad began. As the able-bodied were drafted to fight or dig trenches, invalid or aged curators and attendants strove to protect the thousands of remaining treasures and the building itself from incendiary bombs, shells, ice and damp, during months without electricity or heating. Some two thousand people lived in the palace's cellars, which served as a bomb shelter. While scholars continued their research and gave lectures by candlelight, guides described the works that normally hung in the rooms for the benefit of troops on leave from the front, affirming the values of scholarship and civilization in the face of hardship and Nazi aggression.

Although the Hermitage was patched up and secretly acquired priceless "**trophy art**" seized by the Red Army in Europe (see p.127), Party ideology and xenophobia cramped its style and limited contacts with foreign museums and scholars for much of the postwar era. In Brezhnev's time, pictures from its collection were often presented to "friends" of the Soviet Union – leading to the widely believed (but false) rumour that the local Party boss, Grigori Romanov, borrowed an Imperial dinner service for his daughter's wedding party, and that several pieces were broken.

More **recently**, the Hermitage's director, **Mikhail Piotrovsky**, has signed **agreements** with museums abroad to exhibit treasures from the Hermitage in return for income and art loans; new humidity-control and fire-detection systems, and UV-filtering on the windows, have been installed in most of the rooms; and a full, digitalized inventory of its vast collection is under way. In 2005, one of the curators was found to have been stealing silver artefacts and selling them in antique shops. Plans to move the Impressionist and Post-Impressionist collections into the General Staff building have been put on hold till 2009.

Visiting the Hermitage

Although the Hermitage's **opening hours** (10.30am–6pm, Sun till 5pm; closed Mon) are similar to other museums in St Petersburg, the **queues** during the summer months are in a league of their own, stretching as far as the Alexander Column. If you're around then, it's well worth **booking online** through the Hermitage's website, to receive an email voucher that lets you jump the queue and go straight to collect your ticket, using the main entrance in the courtyard of the Winter Palace, accessible from Dvortsovaya ploshchad. Tour groups may face a short wait at the group entrances on Dvortsovaya ploshchad and the Neva embankment. **Disabled access** is via the ramped group entrance on the square, with a lift just inside; wheelchairs are available and museum porters will carry people up stairs where no lifts or ramps exist. Phone (℡710 90 79) the day before to explain which areas of the museum you wish to visit.

The Hermitage's own **excursions bureau** (℡571 84 46; 10.30am–4pm; closed Mon), up the stairs to the right as you pass through the gates on the square, offers a variety of **guided tours** in different languages, which should be booked a day or two ahead – but the cost (R1500 for up to ten people) is likely to be prohibitive for one or two people and doesn't include the price of admission. Failing that, you should turn up on Dvortsovaya ploshchad an hour before the museum opens and be prepared to stand in line. Generally speaking, the Hermitage is far less crowded after 3pm, when many groups have come and gone.

Tickets sold **online** come in two forms: a regular one covering the Winter Palace and Hermitage ($17.95), and a combined ticket ($29.95) valid for two days, that includes the nearby General Staff annexe and Peter's Winter Palace (see p.79), plus the Menshikov Palace on Vasilevskiy Island (p.158) and the Porcelain Museum on prospekt Obukovskoy Oborony (p.220). Both types also include a permit for photography. Otherwise, you can buy a ticket **in the lobby**, valid for the Hermitage only (R350). There is **free entry** for under-17s and students, which applies to everyone on the first Thursday of each month. A permit for **photography** costs R100 (R350 for video cameras).

You can get a free **floor plan** from the **information desk** in the centre of the lobby, or print one from the touch-screen displays located around the museum (which, in theory, can show you the quickest route to any section). English-language plans adhere to the British convention for numbering floors (ie ground floor, then first floor) rather than the usual Russian and US system, whereby the ground floor is called the first floor; they also display the buildings the other way up from the plans in this book. In the first-floor Rastrelli Gallery are **shops** selling souvenirs, art reproductions and **books** related to the Hermitage, plus an **Internet café** that allows free access to the Hermitage **website** (Ⓦwww.hermitagemuseum.org). This features highlights of the collection and information on which sections are closed at present, temporary exhibitions, lectures and other events.

In the gallery leading to the Jordan Staircase you can hire a three-and-a-half-hour-long **audio-guide** for R300 plus ID as security; the paperback guides (R350) sold in the shops are less useful in practice. Some shops take **credit cards** (Visa, MasterCard or Maestro); or you can get rubles from the **ATM** and the **exchange** office in the lobby. **Toilets** (only on the first floor, near the café, a cloakroom and the Jordan and Council staircases) are quite grungy and often lack toilet paper. Beware of ending up far away from the **cloakroom** where your coat or bag is stashed near closing time, as they start barring access to some wings half an hour beforehand.

Touring the collections

It's impossible to see all the finest works in the Hermitage during a single visit, so concentrate on what interests you most rather than wandering aimlessly from room to room. To help you plan your visit and for ease of reference, the main **collections** are listed in the box below and the rest of this chapter is arranged along similar lines.

The State Rooms are a must and few would miss the Impressionists, Post-Impressionists, Rembrandt or Leonardo – but beyond that everyone has their own preferences, so it's tricky to suggest an **itinerary**. If you're planning a **whole day** at the Hermitage, it makes sense to visit far-flung "specialist" sections like the Siberian artefacts first (they're likelier to close early), and devote the afternoon to the State Rooms and artworks that tour groups focus on (which are most crowded in the morning). If you have only a **few hours**, a minimalist itinerary might go as follows. Visit the State Rooms on the second floor of the Winter Palace first; pass through the Pavilion Hall of the Small Hermitage and whizz around the Italian, Flemish, Dutch and Spanish art on the second floor of the Large Hermitage, before nipping upstairs to the Impressionists. Finally, head downstairs to the first floor to see the Hall of Twenty Columns, the Kolyvan Vase and the Classical antiquities on your way out.

Bear in mind that some rooms may be closed for restoration, or open erratically owing to lack of staff, so if you want to see a particular section it's worth checking in advance. Once you're inside the Winter Palace, it's hard to know where one building ends and another begins, and direction signs can be misleading. However, almost all rooms are numbered, usually on a plaque

Where to find what in the Hermitage

This checklist gives the floor and room numbers of the **main permanent exhibitions**. Those marked by asterisks may be open at irregular times as staff numbers allow; the ones in bold type are especially recommended.

Archeology and Siberian artefacts	Winter Palace first floor 11–27
Central Asian artefacts	Winter Palace first floor 55–66*
Classical antiquities	Small & Large Hermitages first floor 101–131
Dutch, Flemish and Netherlandish art: 15th–18th century	Large Hermitage second floor 245–254, 258, 261 & 262
Egyptian antiquities	Winter Palace first floor 100
English art: 17th–19th century	Winter Palace second floor 298–300
French art: 15th–18th century	Winter Palace second floor 272–289
French art 19th & 20th century (trophy art)	Winter Palace second floor 143 –146
German art: 15th–18th century	Winter Palace second floor 263–268*
Italian art: 13th–16th century	Large Hermitage second floor 207–230
Italian art: 16th–18th century	Large Hermitage second floor 231–238
Modern European art	Large Hermitage third floor 314 350
Numismatic collection	Large Hermitage third floor 398–400*
Oriental art and culture	Large Hermitage third floor 351–397*
Russian art and culture	Winter Palace second floor 151–173
Russian palace interiors	Winter Palace second floor 175–187
Spanish art: 16th–18th century	Large Hermitage second floor 239 & 240
State Rooms	Winter Palace second floor 155, 156, 188–198, 204, 271, 282, 289 & 304–307
Treasure Galleries	Winter Palace first floor 42 & Large Hermitage first floor off room 121

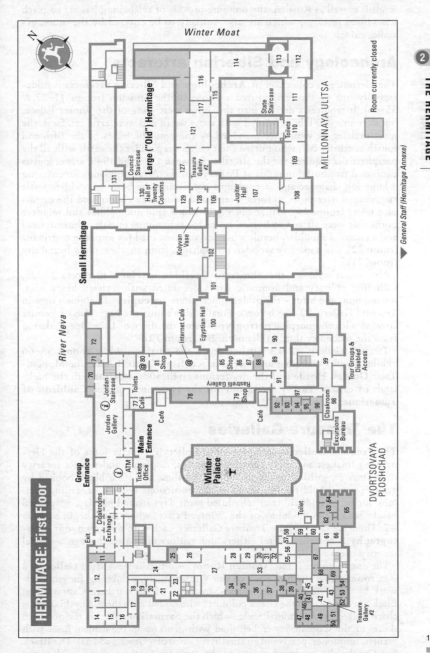

HERMITAGE: First Floor

N

Room currently closed

Winter Moat

MILLIONNAYA ULITSA

Large ("Old") Hermitage

State Staircase

Council Staircase

131

130 Hall of Twenty Columns

Treasure Gallery #2

127

128
129

106

Jupiter Hall

107

Kolyvan Vase

102

101

108
109
110
111
112
113
114
115
116
117
121

Toilets

Small Hermitage

River Neva

100

Egyptian Hall

Internet Café

@ 80

81 Shop

@

72

71

70

Jordan Staircase

Toilets

77 Café

78

79 Shop

Rastrelli Gallery

85 Shop

86
87
88
89
90

91

92
93
94
95

96

97

99

Cloakroom

98

Tour Groups & Disabled Access

General Staff (Hermitage Annexe)

Café

Café

Jordan Gallery

Main Entrance

Excursions Bureau

Winter Palace

DVORTSOVAYA PLOSHCHAD

Group Entrance

Exit

Exchange

Cloakrooms

ATM

Tickets Office

Toilet

60
59
58
57
56
55

61
66
67
68
69

62
63
64
65

11
12
13
14
15
16
17
18
19
20
21
22
23
24
25
26
27
28
29
30
31
32
33
34
35
36
37
38
39
40
41
42
43
44
45
46
47
48
49
50
51
52
53
54

Treasure Gallery #2

above the inside of the doorway. While most paintings are now captioned in English as well as Russian, the ongoing process of relabelling has yet to reach less-visited sections, which are also unlikely to be covered by the museum's audio-guides.

Archeology and Siberian artefacts

The Hermitage's collection of **Archeology and Siberian artefacts** is undeservedly one of the least-visited sections of the museum (rooms 11–27 & 55–66). It requires a detour into the dingy west wing of the Winter Palace, but in return you'll be rewarded with some weird and wonderful artefacts, the most exciting of which are provided by the nomadic tribes of the fifth and fourth centuries BC, who buried their chiefs deep under the earth with all the paraphernalia required for the afterlife. Between 1929 and 1949, archeologists excavated five burial mounds at **Pazyryk** in the Altay highlands, uncovering a huge log chamber and sarcophagus containing the body of a chief, a felt rug, draped over poles to form a tent, and a funerary chariot and the carcass of a horse (**room 26**). Other objects included appliqué saddles and reindeer horns that were affixed to horses' heads for ceremonial burials, a human head and a tattooed shoulder, beside a brazier and tent used for smoking marijuana (**room 22**), and a massive wooden sarcophagus from another, older burial site (**room 21**).

Also remarkable are the numerous **Scythian artefacts** in rooms 16–20, including military and domestic items decorated with stylized bears, elks, horses, lions and birds – the gilded objects here are **copies** of originals now in Treasure Gallery #2 (see below). Finally, don't miss the huge slab of granite covered with zoomorphic **petroglyphs** from the shore of Lake Onega, dating from the second or third millennium BC (**room 12**).

Treasure Gallery #2 lies further down the corridor, while **rooms 55–66** exhibit an ever-changing array of artefacts from **Central Asia**, the Mongol-Tatar **Golden Horde** and the mysterious civilization of **Uratu**, in the highlands of eastern Turkey. Look out for the two-tonne bronze **Cauldron of Tamerlane**, the fearsome Mongol ruler.

The Treasure Galleries

The **Treasure Galleries** (Dragotsenosti Galleryii) contain some of the Hermitage's smallest and most valuable treasures, displayed under strict security to visitors on **guided tours** (R300). Since these are often block-booked by groups, you should reserve ahead at the excursions bureau, or, failing that, look for an individuals' tour scheduled most days around midday, advertised beside *kassa* #3 in the lobby of the Winter Palace, where tours begin by *kassa* #2. There are two separate Treasure Galleries, each with their own tour. **Photography** is not allowed on either, and visitors must pass through a special security check.

The one to go for is the "**Golden Room**" – officially designated **Gallery #2** – in **room 42** on the first floor of the Winter Palace, exhibiting ancient goldwork by the nomadic Scythians and Sarmatians of the northern Caucasus and Black Sea littoral, and the Greek colonists who traded with them. **Scythian** art is characterized by the Animal Style, which the **Sarmatian** tribes on the northern shores of the Caspian Sea embellished with gems (as in the diadem inset with garnets, turquoises, pearls and an amethyst cameo of a Greek goddess). The **Black Sea Greeks** also produced objects in this style for Scythian clients, such as the electrum goblet discovered in a tumulus near Kerch – that could also be found in western Siberia, as evinced by belt buckles depicting a boar hunt and dragons beside the Tree of Life. Here, too, you'll find a few gem-encrusted tables, jugs and plates from the gifts sent by the **Mogul** emperor Shah Nadir to Empress Elizabeth (see p.136).

The "**Diamond Room**" or **Gallery #1**, off **room 121** in the Old Hermitage, exhibits bejewelled swords, horse-cloths and bridles, ecclesiastical vestments, chalices and icons of the sixteenth to nineteenth century, amassed by tsars from Peter the Great onwards, plus a smattering of Scythian goldwork.

The antiquities

Even if your interest in this collection is limited, a stroll through the first-floor **antiquities** rooms (100–131) is highly recommended. One of the less crowded parts of the Hermitage, the rooms are perfectly in keeping with their contents, marvellously decorated with a variety of Antique features and motifs, one of the best examples being the Hall of Twenty Columns.

The **Assyrian and Mesopotamian antiquities** in **rooms 89–90** were acquired by the Hermitage between 1860 and 1914. Stone reliefs from the palaces of Sargon II and Assurnasirpal II, and a huge inscribed slab from the main square of Palmyra, are juxtaposed with delightful Sumerian charm seals engraved with episodes from the *Epic of Gilgamesh*. However, most visitors head for the Egyptian Hall (**room 100**) and its **Egyptian antiquities**, consisting mainly of funerary artefacts taken from the Middle Kingdom tombs of four Pharaonic officials, whose painted sarcophagi and shrivelled mummies occupy centre stage. In the hall's display cases are amulets and heart scarabs intended to ensure the officials' safe passage into the afterlife, *shabti* (funerary) figures to perform menial tasks on their behalf, and texts from the *Book of the Dead* showing the judgement of Osiris. Sadly, there are no captions in English here.

Classical antiquities

The more extensive **Classical antiquities** (Greek and Roman) section begins with displays of Roman bas-reliefs in the corridor (**room 102**). From room 106 in the Large Hermitage you can go either left or right, but you'll have to retrace your steps at some point if you want to see the whole section.

Heading left, into **room 128**, you're confronted by the colossal **Kolyvan Vase**, whose elliptical bowl is over 5m long and 3m wide. Carved from Altay jasper over eleven years, the nineteen-tonne vase required 154 horses to drag it to Barnaul, whence it was hauled across frozen rivers to St Petersburg, to be kept in a shed while the walls of the New Hermitage were built around it. In **room 129** you'll find a gold funerary wreath inset with carnelian and some amusing little bronze mice nibbling nuts. Next door is the **Hall of Twenty Columns** (**room 130**), painted with Greco-Egyptian motifs and filled with Apulian amphorae and breastplates, Campanian vases and Etruscan bronzes from the third or fourth century BC. **Room 131** displays busts of the emperors Titus and Vespasian, and exits near the **Council Staircase**, whose orange and pink marble walls and wine-red pillars presage the European art on the floor above (see p.127).

Alternatively, head right from room 106 into the green marble **Jupiter Hall** (**room 107**), devoted to Classical statues, of which Venus disrobing, a vast seated Jupiter, and a club-wielding Muse of Tragedy are the most eye-catching. There are more fine statues in the rooms beyond, particularly **room 109**, where you'll

▲ Atlantes supporting the facade

find the lovely **Tauride Venus** acquired by Peter the Great from Pope Clement XI. From room 110, overlooking the muscular atlantes supporting the facade on Millionnaya ulitsa, you can reach the second floor via the **State Staircase**, its three flights flanked by tawny marble walls and grey columns.

Staying on the first floor, in **rooms 111–114** you can see superb Attic vases decorated with fine red-and-black figurative designs, and some rather dry Roman copies of Greek sculptures. However, the real incentive to carry on is to view Catherine the Great's collection of antique cameos and intaglios (**room 121**). The lapidary **Gonzaga Cameo** is one of the largest in the world – a triple-layered sardonyx bearing the profiles of Ptolemy Philadelphus and Queen

HERMITAGE: Second Floor

Winter Moat

Room currently closed

N

226 Raphael Loggia 227

228

229

244

224 225

216

215

222

221

214

213

212

211

210

209

208

207

206

217 Venetian Gallery

Council Staircase

253

254

Large ("Old") Hermitage

230

237

231

232 233 234 235 236

238 Large Skylight Room

239

240

252

251

250

249 Tent Room

248

247

246

245

241

242

243 Knights Hall

MILLIONNAYA ULITSA

Small Hermitage

205

204 Pavilion Hall

203

202

Peter's 255 Gallery

256

Peter's 257 Gallery

Hanging Garden

258

Romanov 262 Gallery

261

Romanov 262 Gallery

260

River Neva

201 Trophy Art

200

198 Hall of St. George

271

272 273 274 275

263 264 265 266 267 268

276 277 278 279 280 281

197 1812 Gallery

194 Peter's Throne Room

193 Field Marshal's Hall

i Jordan Staircase

195 Armorial Hall

196

282 Alexander Hall

290 291 292 293 294 295 296 297

192 Forehall

191 Nicholas Hall

190 Concert Hall

151

152 Tsars' Gallery

153 Staircase

283

284

285

286

287

288

289 White Hall

Winter Palace

DVORTSOVAYA PLOSHCHAD

189 Malachite Room

188

187 186

185

184

183 182

181 180 179

178

177 176

175

174 173 172 171 170 169 168 167

157 158 159 160 161 162 163 164 165 166

155

156 Rotunda

303 Dark Corridor

307

308

306 305 304

Raspberry Boudoir

Gold Drawing Room

298 299 300 301 302

Arsinoe, carved in Alexandria during the third century BC. Another superb example of Alexandrian craftsmanship is the head of Zeus, from the same era.

The State Rooms

The second-floor **State Rooms of the Winter Palace** are as memorable as anything on display in the Hermitage, and best seen while you've still got plenty of energy. Glittering with gold leaf and crystal chandeliers, and boasting acres of marble (mostly artificial), parquet, frescoes and mouldings, they attest to the opulence of the Imperial court. Having witnessed gala balls and thanksgiving services, investitures and declarations of war, the State Rooms then provided a stage for the posturing of the Provisional Government. For reasons that will make sense once you're embarked on the tour, certain rooms (nos. 155, 156, 175–187, 271 & 282) are covered on p.125 and the rest (nos. 204, 289 & 304–307) on p.127.

The most direct route from the Hermitage's lobby is by the **Jordan Staircase**, whose twin flights are overlooked by caryatids, *trompe l'oeil* atlantes and a fresco of the gods on Mount Olympus by Gaspar Diziani. The walls and balustrades drip with decoration – a typically effusive design by Bartolomeo Rastrelli, who created similar stairways for the Imperial summer palaces at Peterhof and Tsarskoe Selo. What you see, however, owes as much to Vasily Stasov, who restored the State Rooms after a devastating fire in 1837 and toned down some of the wilder excesses of his predecessors.

From the top of the staircase, you can strike out on two separate excursions into the State Rooms, one culminating in the Alexander Hall, the other leading to the Malachite Room. We've described the former route first – the amount of backtracking involved to cover both is about the same.

To the Alexander Hall

This series of rooms in the east wing of the palace is known as the **Great Enfilade**. Passing through the door on the left of the landing, you enter the **Field Marshals' Hall (room 193)**, so called because of the portraits of Russian military leaders that hung here before the Revolution; three have now been returned and others may follow. The hall was originally designed by Montferrand, whose careless juxtaposition of heating flues and flammable materials may have caused the great fire of 1837, which started in this room. Its current form reflects Stasov's Neoclassicism: pearly white, festooned with outsized vases and statuary, and dominated by a massive bronze chandelier.

The next stop is **Peter's Throne Room (room 194)**. Its title is purely honorific, since Peter the Great died over a century before Montferrand designed the room, but the atmosphere is palpably reverential. The walls are covered with burgundy velvet embroidered with Romanov eagles, while an oak and silver throne commissioned by Empress Anna from London occupies a dais below scores of gilded birds converging on the chamber's vault.

Stasov's Neoclassical decoration ran riot in the adjacent **Armorial Hall (room 195)**. Stucco warriors and battle standards flank the doors at either end, while gilded columns, giant lampstands and a jasper vase vie for your attention. The **1812 Gallery (room 197)** was modelled by Rossi on the Waterloo Chamber at Windsor Castle (also built to commemorate the victory over Napoleon). An Englishman, George Dawe, was commissioned to paint the portraits of Russian military leaders that line the barrel-vaulted gallery (some died before the portraits were completed and the gaps remain unfilled). Alexander I and his allies, Frederick Wilhelm III of Prussia and Franz I of Austria, merit life-sized equestrian portraits at one end.

Alongside the 1812 Gallery lies the eight-hundred-square-metre **Hall of St George (room 198)** – the main throne room. Built by Quarenghi, with lavish use of Carrara marble, the hall was inaugurated on St George's day in 1795 and became associated with solemn acts of state. Here, Alexander I swore that he would never make peace until Napoleon had been driven from Russia, and Nicholas II similarly vowed to defeat Germany at the outbreak of World War I. The emperor's throne is the only piece of furniture in the hall, its parquet floor consisting of sixteen kinds of wood.

To the left of room 270 is the **Cathedral (room 271)**, used originally as the private court chapel and not as large as its name suggests. Rastrelli's gilded Baroque interior was hardly touched by the fire of 1837, and the proportions are such that the ceiling seems to soar into the heavens, despite the small scale. Walk back through room 270, left into 280 and then turn right through 281 to emerge in the magnificent **Alexander Hall (room 282)**, designed by Alexander Bryullov in 1837 to commemorate the Napoleonic Wars. The military theme is reflected in the sky-blue and white bas-reliefs that cover the walls. Also notable are the stucco palm "umbrellas" that sprout from the vaulting and the intricate parquet floor. The hall is used for temporary exhibitions (closing half an hour before the rest of the museum) and interrupts a series of rooms devoted to French art (see p.132). At this point, you'll need to retrace your steps to the Jordan Staircase to see the rest of the state rooms.

To the Malachite Drawing Room and beyond

The river-facing **Neva Enfilade** contains some of the most famous rooms in the Winter Palace, chiefly associated with Nicholas II and the Provisional Government. Immediately ahead of the Jordan Staircase is a **Forehall (room 192)**, centred on a malachite and bronze pavilion that was used for champagne buffets whenever balls took place in the adjacent **Nicholas Hall (room 191)**. Named after the portrait of Nicholas I installed here in 1856, the hall can accommodate five thousand people and is used, along with the Forehall and the Concert Hall, to stage prestigious temporary exhibitions.

At this point, it's worth a detour into the corridor (**rooms 151 & 153**), known as the **Gallery of Russian Tsars**, hung with portraits of the same. Of particular interest are two of Catherine the Great, painted fourteen years apart; and one of her luckless son Paul, his snub nose flatteringly filled out. The nearby **Concert Hall (room 190)** affords a fine view of the Rostral Columns, across the Neva. By the far wall stands the enormous Baroque **sarcophagus** of St Alexander Nevsky, resembling a giant pen-and-ink stand and consisting of 1.5 tonnes of silver covering a wooden armature.

The **Malachite Drawing Room (room 189)**, beyond the Concert Hall, was created by Bryullov in 1839 for Nicholas I's wife, Alexandra Fyodorovna, its pilasters, fireplace, tables and knick-knacks fashioned from over two tonnes of the lustrous green stone (from the Urals) that gives the room its name. Kerensky's Provisional Government met here from July 1917 until their arrest by the Bolsheviks three months later, and it's easy to imagine the despondent ministers slumping on the divan before adjourning to the adjacent **White Dining Room (room 188)**, hung with allegorical tapestries of Africa, Asia and America. Here they were arrested (Kerensky had already fled) and obliged to sign a protocol dissolving the Provisional Government – the mantelpiece clock was stopped at that moment (2.10am).

From here you enter the barrel-vaulted **Moorish Dining Room (room 155)**, named after the black ceremonial guards costumed as Moors, who stood outside in Tsarist times. Beyond lies the **Rotunda (room 156)**, a lofty circular room with a coffered dome encircled by a balcony. From here you can continue southwards into the section on Russian art and culture (see below), or go back through the Malachite Drawing Room to visit the exhibition of Russian palace interiors.

Russian palace interiors

Opened in the 1980s as a temporary exhibition, the **nineteenth-century Russian palace interiors** proved so popular that they have remained in place ever since. The exhibition (closed for lunch 12.30–1.30pm) consists of a series of rooms (**175–187**), each arranged with furniture and objects of applied art re-creating the interior styles of each decade from the early 1800s to the Revolution. From the Empire-style Music Room, with its exquisite instruments by Hambs, you progress to the late nineteenth-century **Oriental Smoking Room**, Nicholas II's **Gothic Library**, the Style Moderne nursery with its luxurious child-sized furniture (used by Nicholas and Alexandra's children), and finally a neo-Russian room by Malyutin. Much of the furniture was designed by the architects who were working on the building at the time; in the Gothic Study, which represents the 1890s, even the waste bin forms an integral part of the ensemble.

Russian art and culture

The section on **Russian art and culture** nominally starts with the Gallery of Russian Tsars (see p.125) and the adjacent **room 152**, containing a mosaic copy of Kneller's famous portrait of the young Peter the Great, by the scientist Lomonosov. It resumes beyond the Rotunda, and includes rooms containing a miscellany of objects including Peter's dentistry equipment, death mask and a wax bust by Rastrelli (**room 157**); and the turnery on which he crafted objects such as an impressive multi-tiered ivory chandelier (**room 161**). In 1880, Alexander II narrowly escaped death when a bomb exploded below the latter room, killing eleven soldiers at lunchtime. Don't miss the gilded carnival sledge in the form of St George slaying a dragon, from the reign of the fun-loving Empress Elizabeth (**room 167**).

Rooms 168–173 exhibit an array of items, the result of Peter bringing in foreign craftsmen and the subsequent boom in painting and the applied arts during Catherine the Great's reign. Look out for the lizard-armed chair designed by Catherine's favourite architect, the Scotsman Charles Cameron, in room 171. Paul's throne as Grand Master of the Knights of Malta (see p.272) is in room 172, followed by incredible filigree ivory vases and the uniquely Russian steel dressing-table and desk sets in room 173 – a specialty of Tula craftsmen. From here you can continue on to the White Hall and Gold Drawing Room (see below) or return to the Field Marshals' Hall (see p.124) and head for the Western European art section in the Large Hermitage (see p.127).

The White Hall and Gold Drawing Room

Running round the southwest corner of the Winter Palace are several further state rooms that were revamped after the fire of 1837 for the wedding of the future Alexander II and Maria of Hessen-Darmstadt. The only significant interior to survive in its original restored state, however, is Bryullov's **White Hall** (room 289), its lightness and airiness in contrast to the surrounding apartments. It now houses some exquisite furniture along with eight large Romantic landscapes by **Hubert Robert**, a French artist who found fame in Russia while remaining largely unknown in Western Europe.

From here you emerge into one of the palace's most vulgar state rooms, the **Gold Drawing Room** (room 304), redecorated by Bryullov in the 1850s. Inspired by the interiors of Moscow's Kremlin, its patterned walls and vaulted ceiling are gilded all over. The room contains French and Italian cameos displayed in hexagonal cases. Photography is not allowed here.

The next room along, the **State Corner Study** (room 305), contains Sèvres porcelain and pieces from the Josiah Wedgwood "**Green Frog Service**" made for Catherine the Great – the frog being the whimsical coat of arms that she chose for her Chesma Palace. Beyond lies the 1850s **Raspberry Boudoir** (room 306) – the former private room of Alexander II's wife, Maria Alexandrovna – decorated in "Second Baroque" style, with rich crimson brocatelle hangings by Cartier, plus gold and mirrors galore – a decor designed by Gerald Bosset.

Bringing this sequence of rooms to an end with a flourish, **room 307** features temporary exhibitions of **jewellery** – sometimes objects by **Fabergé** from the collections of the Hermitage, other museums in St Petersburg and the Imperial palaces.

French paintings from the nineteenth and twentieth centuries

In 1993, the Hermitage became the first museum in Russia to admit possession of stores of "**trophy art**", appropriated from Germany at the end of World War II – some of it had previously been stolen by the Nazis in occupied Europe. As Russian legislators are at one with public opinion in opposing the return of any artworks until Russian claims for treasures despoiled by the Nazis are settled, the exhibition in **rooms 143–146** (which closes at 5pm, 4pm on Sun) is likely to remain for the foreseeable future – although mindful of its sensitive status, the Hermitage coyly omits all of the artworks therein from its website, and photograhpy is not allowed here.

The exhibition includes ten **Renoirs**, ranging from *Woman Brushing her Hair* to the light-filled *Low Tide at Yport*; four **Van Goghs**, notably the *White House at Night*; **Monet**'s lush *Garden in Bordighera*; **Gauguin**'s *Late Afternoon* and *Two Sisters* from his Tahitian period; and six **Cézannes**, including a *Mont Sainte-Victoire* and *Bathers*. Also look out for the *Road to Castel Gondolfo*, by **Derain**, the *Place de la Concorde* by **Degas**, and **Manet**'s *Portrait of Mme Isabelle Lemonnier*. **Daumier**'s *The Burden*, with its toiling laundress and child, is a rare exception to the prevailing mood of sunny optimism.

Italian art: thirteenth to eighteenth century

Spread through a score of small rooms (207–238) in the Large Hermitage, **Italian art** is well represented, with works by Leonardo, Botticelli, Michelangelo, Raphael and Titian, although there is a poor showing of works by the stars of the early Renaissance.

The most direct approach is via the Council Staircase (from Antiquities on the first floor), which emerges at the start of the section. Alternatively, if you are coming from the Field Marshals' Hall (room 193), head along the corridor (rooms 200 & 201) and over the covered bridge into another state room, the **Pavilion Hall** (room 204). Built by Stackenschneider in 1856, this dazzlingly light room combines elements of Classical, Islamic and Renaissance architecture, with a gilded balcony overlooking a mosaic based on one discovered in a Roman bathhouse. Taking centre stage is the **Peacock Clock**, a miracle of craftsman-

▲ The Pavilion Hall

ship by the English jeweller James Coxe, which once belonged to Catherine's lover Potemkin. On the rare occasions that the peacock "performs", it spreads its tail as a cockerel crows and a mushroom rotates in surreal accompaniment.

Simone Martini to Leonardo da Vinci

Room 207 boasts a small, graceful *Madonna* by the thirteenth-century Sienese painter **Simone Martini** and an opulent *Five Apostles* by the circle of **Gentile da Fabriano**. A tiny polygonal chamber leads to room 209, containing the radiant *St Augustus's Vision* by **Fra Filippo Lippi**, and work by the Dominican **Fra Angelico**, whose fresco *Madonna and Child, St Dominic and St Thomas Aquinas* is the largest painting in the room. Della Robbia terracottas and superb bas-reliefs by Rossellino fill the next few rooms. **Room 213** holds two small paintings by **Botticelli**, an enraptured St Sebastian by **Pietro Perugino** (who worked on the Sistine Chapel and was Raphael's teacher), and some gentle works by **Filippino Lippi**.

The high coffered ceiling and ornate decor of **room 214** rather upstage the only two works by **Leonardo da Vinci** in Russia. The earlier one – a lively piece with a youthful Mary dandling Jesus on her knee – is known as the *Benois Madonna*, after the family who sold it to Nicholas II in 1914. The other is the *Madonna Litta*, a later, more accomplished work depicting the Virgin suckling the infant Jesus.

Room 215 focuses on Leonardo's successors: *Portrait of a Woman* (also known as *Colombine* or *Flora*) is by his most faithful pupil, **Francesco Melzi**, in whose arms he died. From room 216, you can approach the Venetian Gallery or the Raphael Loggia, as described in the following sections.

Veronese, Titian and Giorgione

From 216, a corridor leads to **room 222**, containing a confident *Self-portrait* and a superb *Pietà* by **Veronese**. This leads into the **Venetian Gallery**, where **room 221** displays paintings by **Titian**, the most famous being the *Danäe* – one of five versions of the same subject which Titian made (the best known is in the Prado) – in which a nude languishes on a bed while Zeus appears as a shower of golden coins, though some regard the powerful *Saint Sebastian* and sensuous *Penitent Magdalene* of his final years as finer works. His *Portrait of a Young Woman* wearing a man's cloak, with one arm drawn across her breast, hangs in room 219. In between, you can admire **Giorgione**'s *Judith*, one of the few paintings in the world that is firmly attributed to him (in **room 217**).

The Raphael Loggia, Caravaggio and Michelangelo

Alternatively, you can head through room 216 into the **Raphael Loggia** (**rooms 226 & 227**), a long gallery lit by large windows overlooking the Winter Moat and the Hermitage Theatre. Commissioned by Catherine the Great, it was created between 1783 and 1792 by Quarenghi as a copy of Raphael's famous gallery in the Vatican Palace. Every surface, wall and vault is covered with copies on canvas of Raphael's frescoes, made by a team of artists under Christopher Unterberger. Notice how the Romanov double-headed eagle has been substituted for the papal coat of arms.

Off the loggia, **room 229** displays Italian and Russian majolica and faïence and works by **Raphael**. His *Madonna Constabile* was completed at the age of seventeen; the slightly later *Holy Family* depicts a beardless yet aged Joseph, besides which hangs an uncertain *Madonna and Child*. From there you can pass into **room 237** to find the famous *Lute Player* by **Caravaggio** and vast canvases by **Tintoretto** (*The Birth of St John the Baptist*) and **Veronese** (*The Conversion of Saul*), and then into **room 230** to see the sculpture *Crouching Youth* by **Michelangelo**, his chisel marks evident on its taut musculature.

Room 237 is one of three lofty halls illuminated by skylights, the largest leading to a gallery (**room 241**) displaying eighteenth-century sculpture, including the *Three Graces*, *Repentant Magdalene* and *Kiss of Cupid and Psyche* by **Canova**. Beyond this, the **Knights' Hall** (**room 243**) is full of highly decorated European weapons and armour from the Imperial arsenal; the four cavalry horses were stuffed by Klodt, who sculpted the ones on Anichkov most. Temporary exhibitions are mounted in the adjacent **Twelve-Column Hall** (**room 244**).

Spanish art: fifteenth to eighteenth century

The Hermitage's collection of **Spanish art** is the largest in the world outside Spain. Among the earlier works in **room 240** are a superb late fifteenth-century Gothic *Entombment of Christ* by an unknown master, and **El Greco**'s painterly depiction of *SS Peter and Paul* – according to legend, it was St Paul who converted the painter's native Greek island of Crete to Christianity.

Room 239 displays examples of the flowering of Spanish art during the seventeenth century – large religious works created for churches and monasteries, as well as more intimate pieces. Among them are *St Jerome and the Angel* by **Ribera**, and **Zurbarán**'s *St Laurentio* altarpiece, painted for the Monastery of St Joseph in Seville, which shows the grid on which the saint was roasted to death. **Murillo**'s *Immaculate Conception* differs from the usual presentation of the Virgin with her feet on the moon and stars overhead by taking the Assumption as its leitmotif – hence the picture's other title, *The Assumption of the Madonna*. His sugary *Adoration of Christ* is accompanied by the cheeky *Boy with a Dog*, equally typical of his sentimental style.

While religious themes were esteemed, **Velázquez** was equally willing to paint what were scornfully called *bodegón* (tavern) scenes, such as *Luncheon* – the figure on the right is supposedly Velázquez himself, who was only 18 at the·time. In later life he concentrated largely on portrayals of the Spanish royal family: his *Portrait of Count Olivarez* depicts the *éminence grise* and power behind the throne, who was also a friend of the artist. Another penetrating work is **Goya**'s portrait of the actress Antonia Zaráte, who died of consumption shortly after the completion of this picture, which betrays her inner anxiety.

Dutch, Flemish and Netherlandish art: fifteenth to eighteenth century

One of the Hermitage's great glories is its **Dutch, Flemish and Netherlandish art** collection. As well as one of the largest gatherings of works by Rembrandt outside the Netherlands, you'll also find one of the world's finest collections of paintings by Rubens and Van Dyck, many of which came from the Walpole Collection of Houghton Hall in Norfolk, bought by Catherine the Great in 1779 (see "English art", p.133). If you've come from the Italian art section, you'll start with the Rembrandts in room 254. Be warned that these are amongst the most crowded rooms in the Hermitage.

Rembrandt

In **room 254**, the twenty or so paintings by **Rembrandt** include some of the finest works from his early period of success in the 1630s, including light, optimistic canvases such as *Flora*, a portrait of his wife Saskia, completed shortly after their marriage. *The Sacrifice of Isaac* is from the same period, though more serious in content, while the *Descent from the Cross* is set at night to allow a dramatic use of light which focuses attention on the body of Christ and the grief-stricken Mary, prematurely aged and on the verge of collapse.

Rembrandt's *Danäe*, slashed by a deranged visitor in 1985, is back on show after twelve years of restoration. The picture was one of Rembrandt's personal favourites, and he parted with it only when he was forced to declare himself bankrupt in 1656.

Bankruptcy was not the only misfortune that Rembrandt suffered in later life: Saskia had died in 1642, shortly after giving birth to their fourth child, but Rembrandt married again in 1645, the same year he painted the calm domestic scene in *The Holy Family*, set in a Dutch carpenter's shop. The heavenly reward of the penitent is the theme of *The Return of the Prodigal Son*, bathed in scarlet and gold, one of Rembrandt's last canvases. Others include *The Adoration of the Magi, David's Parting from Jonathan*, and works by followers such as Ferdinand Bol.

To the Tent Room and beyond

If you're coming from the Skylight Rooms displaying Italian art (see p.129), you'll pass through **room 250**, displaying a huge pen-and-ink drawing of *Bacchus, Venus and Ceres*, by Hendrik Goltzius, an engraver who had to change mediums after he burnt his hand in a fire. Beyond lies the vast **Tent Room** (**room 249**), so called because of its unusual pitched roof and beautiful coffered ceiling painted in pastel shades, and which is stuffed with seventeenth-century Dutch genre paintings by **Frans Hals**, Jan Steen, Salomon van Ruisdael, and others. Beyond, **room 248** is also lavishly decorated, with artificial marble columns supporting a finely patterned ceiling. Among the many paintings here are several small canvases by **Jan Brueghel**, son of the great Pieter Brueghel the Elder (none of whose works appears in the Hermitage). Jan was an accomplished artist in his own right, a specialist in landscapes and still lifes.

Rubens, Van Dyck and Breughel

Works by **Rubens** at the height of his career (1610–20) fill **room 247**, including *Descent from the Cross*, a famous altarpiece painted for the Capuchin monastery at Lierre, near Antwerp. In Rembrandt's version, the reality of human suffering and the use of light were paramount, whereas Rubens stressed the contrast between the clothes of the figures and the pallid body of Christ. Beside it hangs *Bacchus*, whom Rubens depicted as a fat, jovial slob rather than a youthful partygoer, as traditionally portrayed.

As was usual when commissions poured in, students in Rubens' studio worked on the master's paintings, amongst them the young **Van Dyck**, who contributed to the *Feast at the House of Simon the Pharisee*, a resolutely secular treatment of a biblical theme. Later, he was court painter to (and knighted by) Charles I of England, producing some of his finest portraits, including those of the architect Inigo Jones, Thomas Wharton, Charles I and Queen Henrietta Maria, all on display in **room 246**, together with earlier works, such as a wonderful self-portrait.

Retracing your steps through room 248 brings you to a corridor (**room 258**) lined with Flemish landscapes and winter scenes, including **Pieter Breughel the Younger**'s *Robbers Attacking Peasants*. Another, more festive work by Breughel hangs in **room 262**, beside Lucas van Leyden's *Healing of the Blind Man*, en route to which you'll pass Dirk Jacobsz's group portrait of the Amsterdam Shooting Corporation and the Hieronymus Bosch-like *Legend of St Christopher*, by Jan Mandijn. This room forms part of an enfilade called the **Romanov Gallery**, which runs alongside Catherine's **Hanging Garden**, flanked by another enfilade named **Peter's Gallery** (rooms 255–257), leading to a **Study** (room 205) designed by Quarenghi – the only room in the Winter Palace to retain its original eighteenth-century decor: strawberry-coloured walls, a gold and white ceiling and yellow *faux marbre* columns.

German art: fifteenth to eighteenth century

The Hermitage's collection of **German art** from the fifteenth to eighteenth century is conveniently approached from the Dutch, Flemish and Netherlandish art section by continuing along the corridor (room 258) through to **room 263**. Unfortunately, this section is usually closed in summer, but if you are here at other times, you'll be able to see a few paintings by well-known names, including Lucas **Cranach the Elder**'s *Portrait of a Woman* and the first of his series of *Venus and Cupid* paintings, which dates from 1509. Ambrosius **Holbein**, older brother of Hans, lived a short life – his *Portrait of a Young Man* was completed at the age of 23, shortly before he died.

French art: fifteenth to eighteenth century

Thanks to an obsession with all things French during Catherine's reign, the Hermitage features an impressive collection of **French art**, particularly from the seventeenth and eighteenth centuries. The Romanovs employed many French artists, starting with Caravaque, who was engaged by Peter the Great and remained in Russia until his death. Nevertheless, this art has lost its appeal for many, bound up as it is with the cloyingly frivolous tastes of the French and Russian aristocracy, and these rooms (272–281 & 283–288) are among the least visited in the Hermitage.

The collection begins in room 272 with French fifteenth- and sixteenth-century metalwork, blue Limoges enamel tiles and carved furniture. The earliest French paintings, from the fifteenth and sixteenth centuries, are in room 274, while **room 275** displays **Simon Vouet**'s allegorical portraits.

From Poussin to Greuze

The Hermitage is particularly renowned for its collection of paintings by **Nicolas Poussin**, the founder of French Neoclassicism, whose artistic philosophy of order, reason and design was the antithesis of Rubens' more painterly style – the few drops of blood visible on Poussin's frenetic *Victory of Joshua over the Amalekites* are purely symbolic. Also in **room 279** is his best-known work in the Hermitage, the colourful *Landscape with Polyphemus*, whose orderly symbolism encapsulates Poussin's rational philosophy of painting.

The other great French artist of the day was **Claude Lorrain**, who began his career as a pastry cook to an Italian painter. **Room 280** exhibits tranquil pastoral scenes of the lost Golden Age of Antiquity, and his use of light – as in *The Four Times of Day* cycle – greatly influenced English artists such as Turner. But the primary role of art during the Golden Age of the "Sun King" was the glorification of absolute monarchy, as depicted in Pierre Mignard's gigantic *Magnanimity of Alexander the Great* in **room 283**, beyond the Alexander Hall (see p.125).

Room 284 exhibits works by **Antoine Watteau**. Best known for his cameos of socialites frozen in attitudes of pleasure, Watteau's paintings seem frivolous to contemporary eyes but his technique of "divisionism" (juxtaposing pure colours on the canvas, rather than mixing them on the palette) was a major influence on Seurat and the Pointillist school.

Room 285 has a few works by Watteau's followers **Nicolas Lancret** and **Jean-Baptiste Pater**, but the most powerful piece is **François Lemoyne**'s voluptuous *Jupiter and Io* – thought to be a copy of a lost painting by Correggio – in which Jupiter disguises himself as a cloud in order to seduce the young maid. The room also contains paintings by **François Boucher**, whose talents were considered by many to be wasted on the production of profitable pictures of frolicking goddesses and cherubs.

The intellectual atmosphere of Enlightenment France implicit in the paintings in **room 287** contrasts with the more corporeal works in previous rooms. **Char-**

din's *Still Life with the Attributes of the Arts*, commissioned by the St Petersburg Academy of Art, was sold by the Hermitage in 1849 under orders from Nicholas I, and only re-acquired by the museum during the Soviet period. The statue of the aged philosopher Voltaire by **Houdon** escaped a similar fate when, instead of following Nicholas's order to "get rid of this old monkey", a far-sighted curator locked it out of sight in the Hermitage library.

Critics have accused **Jean-Baptiste Greuze**, whom Catherine the Great greatly admired, of "insincerity, artificiality and misplaced voluptuousness". Judging by the works in **room 288**, it's difficult to disagree, yet he was originally popular precisely because "morality paintings" such as *Spoilt Child* and *The Paralytic* represented a move away from the frivolity of the Rococo. Here you'll also find *The Stolen Kiss* by **Jean Honoré Fragonard**, which once belonged to King Stanislaus Poniatowski of Poland, Catherine's former lover.

English art: seventeenth to nineteenth century

When the Hermitage opened to the public in 1852, it was the only gallery in Europe with a collection of **English art (rooms 298–300)**. Its core consists of the famous **Houghton Hall Collection** of Sir Robert Walpole, which Catherine the Great purchased from his dissolute grandson for a paltry £40,000 – thereby achieving posthumous revenge on Walpole, who had called her the "philosophizing tyrant". To rub it in, her buyer left a portrait of the empress on the bare walls of Houghton Hall. The majority of the works were Italian or Flemish, but there were enough English paintings from the sixteenth to the eighteenth century to kick-start a collection.

In 1790, the Hermitage acquired three large canvases by **Joshua Reynolds**, including *The Infant Hercules Strangling Serpents*, one of the last paintings he completed before he went blind. Commissioned by Catherine, it is meant to symbolize Russia besting her foes, but also features several of Reynolds' English contemporaries (including Dr Johnson as Tiresias). Two other masterpieces are **Thomas Gainsborough**'s *Portrait of a Lady in Blue*, and *The Forge* by **Joseph Wright** of Derby. Also in the collection is part of the unique 944-piece "Green Frog Service" made by **Josiah Wedgwood** for Catherine's Chesma Palace (another part of which is on display in room 305; see p.127).

Modern European art

After the State Rooms, the **third floor** of the Winter Palace is the most popular section of the Hermitage, covering **modern European art** in the nineteenth and twentieth centuries (**rooms 314–350**). To get there, take the staircase leading off from room 269 on the second floor, which brings you out at the beginning of the collection. Its breadth is impressively wide, but the highlight is undoubtedly the unique collection of works by **Matisse** and **Picasso**, which was assembled largely by two Moscow philanthropists, Sergei Shchukin and Ivan Morozov. Between them, they bought nearly fifty paintings by each artist in the five years before World War I, and they were largely responsible for collecting the fine spread of Impressionist and Post-Impressionist paintings also on display in this section.

In few other places in the world did such brilliant collections exist, and the works influenced a whole generation of Russian artists. Following the October Revolution, both collections were confiscated by the state, and in 1948

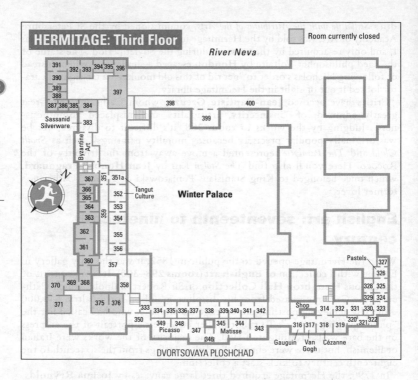

were divided between the Hermitage and Moscow's Pushkin Museum of Fine Arts. However, whereas Morozov was coerced into assigning his pictures to the state, Shchukin never did, and when one of the Matisses was sent to Italy in 2000, his grandson filed a lawsuit for its recovery, obliging the Hermitage to order its immediate return to Russia.

Though it's intended eventually to move the Impressionist and Post-Impressionist art from the Hermitage into the General Staff building, the ongoing refurbishment of the latter means that they are likely to remain in the Hermitage for some years to come.

From Gros to Gauguin

The earliest works on show are in **room 314**, which features early nineteenth-century portraits by **Roland Lefevre** and a swashbuckling picture of Napoleon by **Antoine-Jean Gros**, a pupil of David, but one whose fiery palette displays his admiration for Rubens. Next door in **room 332** you'll find some early nineteenth-century paintings by **Prud'hon** and **Guerin**, and **David**'s *Sappho and Phaon*. In **room 331**, beyond, **Ingres'** portrait of *Count Nikolai Guryev* provides a contrast to the Romanticism epitomized by two small canvases by **Eugène Delacroix**, *Moroccan Saddling a Horse* and *Lion Hunt in Morocco*, both inspired by his visit to that country in 1832.

At the far end of this section, it's worth a detour to see the **pastels** by **Degas**, **Picasso** and others in **room 326**, before retracing your steps and turning the corner into **rooms 321–322**, which are devoted to the forerunners of Impressionism: the artists of the Barbizon School. Small pearly landscapes by **Camille Corot** and gentle works by **Charles-François Daubigny** contrast with **Constant Troyon**'s large *Departure for the Market*, filled with early morning light.

From here, **room 320** takes you straight into the world of the Impressionists with **Renoir**'s full-length, richly clothed *Portrait of Jeanne Samary*. Aside from three landscapes by **Sisley**, **room 319** is dominated by **Monet**, ranging from early works such as the bright, direct *Lady in a Garden* (1867) to the atmospheric, fogbound *Waterloo Bridge* (1903). **Room 318** contains a good sample of **Cézanne**'s work, including *Lady in Blue* and one of the *Mont Sainte-Victoire* series, whose chromatic blocks provided a point of departure for Cubism. The only one of the older generation of Impressionists to appreciate Cézanne in his lifetime was **Pissarro**, represented here by *Boulevard Montmartre* and *French Theatre Square*.

Room 317 features several landscapes by **Van Gogh** and his little-known *Arena at Arles*, plus a few small canvases by the self-taught **Henri Rousseau** and Pointillist works by **Paul Signac** and **Henri-Edmond Cross**.

Room 316 is entirely devoted to paintings by **Gauguin** inspired by his sojourn in Tahiti, including the enigmatic *Idol* and *Woman Holding a Fruit*, thought to depict his Tahitian wife Tehura.

For the rest of the collection, head across the balcony above the Alexander Hall to **room 343**, which marks the beginning of the later, mostly twentieth-century collection, with landscapes by **Louis Vaitat** and some neo-Impressionist still lifes and *Le Jardin du Luxembourg* by Matisse.

Matisse, Picasso and the Fauvists

The **Matisse** collection begins in earnest in **room 344**, which displays three famous paintings commissioned by his patron Shchukin, whom he visited in Russia several times between 1908 and 1913. *Music* and *The Dance* marked a turning point in Matisse's career, the pink flesh of his earlier versions being replaced with red-hot primitive figures on a deep green-and-blue background. When first exhibited at the Salon d'Automne in Paris they were panned by critics and Shchukin cancelled the commission, but changed his mind on the train back to Russia. After the pictures were hung on the staircase of his Moscow mansion, Shchukin feared that the nude flautist would disturb his female guests, and personally painted out the musician's genitals. No such anxiety was aroused by *The Red Room*, which was designed for the dining room, fulfilling Matisse's stated objective to create art "as relaxing as a comfortable armchair".

Room 345 exhibits several Moorish scenes and a *Family Portrait* from 1912–1913, while **room 346** displays French landscapes influenced by Cézanne, painted between 1905 and 1908. In **room 347** you'll find works by Matisse's fellow Fauvists, the Dutch artist **Kees van Dongen**, the racing cyclist and violinist **Maurice de Vlamnick** (who boasted that he'd never set foot in the Louvre), and **André Derain**.

The **Picasso** collection begins in **room 348** with his best-loved early periods. The earliest work is *The Absinthe Drinker* of 1901, and there are two paintings from his Blue Period (1901–04) – the larger, *Sisters*, features gaunt, emaciated figures typical of his style at the time. Among the slew of Cubist pictures are *Dance with Veils*, *Dryad*, *Friendship* and *Three Women*, with more nudes and Cubist still lifes in room 349, along with some of his ceramics from Antibes.

This section concludes in **room 350**, exhibiting *Postcard* and an abstract *Composition* by the card-carrying Communist **Fernand Léger**, plus landscapes by lesser known contemporaries such as **Albert Marquet** and **Henri Le Fauconnier**.

Oriental art and culture and the Numismatic Collection

②

The **western wing** of the third floor is devoted to **Oriental art and culture**, but many sections are indefinitely closed for reorganization, making it hard to give specific directions. Depending on how things go, you may be able to reach some via the rooms beyond the Post-Impressionist section, or only from the floor below using the stairs that ascend to the third floor near the **Byzantine collection**, which ranges from Coptic textiles and carvings (**room 381**) to medieval icons (**room 382**).

Adjacent to this in **room 383** is a superb collection of **Sassanid silverware**, made in Iran between the third and seventh centuries and used as trade goods by merchants buying furs in Siberia, where the indigenous peoples venerated them as sacred totems.

Also look out for artefacts from the **Tangut culture** of Mongolia that was laid waste by Genghis Khan in 1227, leaving only the city of Khara-Khoto to be excavated by Kozlov in 1907–9, whence came statues of the Buddha and fantastical beasts (**room 351a**) and Bodhisattva scrolls (**room 352**) from the Cave of a Thousand Buddhas monastery. The **Chinese** collection includes Ming Dynasty porcelain and figurines (**room 355**), bamboo and rhino-horn carvings (**room 356**), and a nineteenth-century lacquer screen with twelve panels (**room 357**).

In the un-numbered rooms devoted to Indian art you'll find ornate **Mogul** armour and furniture, and watercolours of the ceremonial procession of Shah Akhbar II. Some of the pieces were made for Shah Jehan (builder of the Taj Mahal) and plundered during Nadir Shah's invasion of Dehli in 1739, before being sent as gifts to Empress Elizabeth; by the time they reached Russia by elephant, Catherine the Great was on the throne.

The **northern wing** is accessible via a staircase from the Rotunda (room 156) on the second floor and harbours a **Numismatic Collection (rooms 398–400)**, including Russian medals and Classical intaglios in gold mounts; only a selection is on view at any one time in temporary exhibitions (open Tues & Thurs).

The Russian Museum

The origins of the **Russian Museum** (Russkiy muzey; Русский музей) date back to the reign of Alexander III, who began to buy Russian art at the end of the nineteenth century with a view to establishing a national museum. His plans were realized by his son Nicholas II, who purchased the Mikhailovskiy Palace and opened it in 1898 as the nation's first public museum of Russian art, named after Alexander III. After the Revolution it was renamed the Russian Museum and acquired thousands of artworks confiscated from private collections. During the 1930s, the museum expanded into the palace's Rossi Wing and, later, into the Benois Wing beside the Griboedov Canal, named after its architect, Leonti Benois.

Along with the Tretyakov Gallery in Moscow, the museum contains the finest collection of **Russian art** in the world – some 400,000 works in total – ranging from medieval icons to the latest in conceptual art. The works neatly mirror Russia's history, tracing the development of the nation's art from Peter the Great's insistence on a break with old Muscovite traditions to the officially approved style of the latter-day Romanovs; from the soul-searching of the Wanderers and the explosion of Symbolism and Futurism to the Stalinist art form known as Socialist Realism and, most recently, Western-inspired multimedia.

As the museum earns money by sending some of its Futurist works for exhibition abroad, and often uses the rooms nominally displaying Socialist Realist art for temporary exhibitions of other kinds, you may find differences between what's described here and what's on show. In addition, the museum now has three other buildings – the **Marble Palace** (see p.85), the **Engineers' Castle** (see p.88) and the **Stroganov Palace** (see p.73) – used to show more of its eighteenth-century art collection and some of the thousands of works of applied art formerly relegated to the stores for lack of space. It's possible to buy a **combined ticket** (R600) covering all four museums, but you'll have to race around to use it, as it's only valid for 24 hours from the time of purchase.

Visiting the Russian Museum

The museum is located on ploshchad Iskusstv, off Nevskiy prospekt, less than ten minutes' walk from Gostiniy Dvor or Nevskiy Prospekt metro stations. During **opening hours** (10am–5pm, Mon till 4pm, closed Tues), you may have to wait outside for a bit if the building gets too crowded. Once through the main gates, head right across the courtyard to the eastern side of the main portico and go downstairs into the basement, where **tickets** (R300; students/children R150) and **photo permits** (R100) are sold. Cloakrooms, **toilets** and a **café** (closing one hour before the museum) are also situated in the basement. **Disabled access** must be arranged in advance (☏314 64 24).

▲ The Russian Museum

Upstairs in the main entrance hall of the Mikhailovskiy Palace you'll find two **information** points that usually have someone who speaks English on duty, though they're not particularly helpful. In theory, **guided tours** in foreign languages can be arranged in advance (☎314 34 48) for R300 per person up to a maximum of ten people, but qualified staff may not be available. Most visitors are content to rent an **audio-guide** (R300; ID required as deposit), or do without. The museum **shop** sells reproductions, souvenirs and all kinds of glossy books, videos and CD-ROMs, but its standard **guidebook** gives almost no information about the artists or where to find specific works. The museum's **website** (Ⓦwww.rusmuseum.ru) is less user-friendly than the Hermitage's, though it does list **temporary exhibitions**. Those in the **Benois Wing** require a **separate ticket** (R500), sold at the Benois Wing's entrance on the Griboedov Canal.

This chapter covers the permanent exhibition, whose art **collection** is arranged more or less chronologically, from top to bottom, starting on the second floor of the palace, continuing downstairs, then in the Rossi Wing and finally upstairs on the second floor of the Benois Wing. If that sounds confusing, well, it is.

Mikhailovskiy Palace (second floor)

To view the works on the **second floor** chronologically, start in room 1 and walk anticlockwise round the building – an approach that emphasizes the giant leap from early icon painting to the art of the eighteenth and nineteenth centuries. If you're here solely for the modern stuff, you could skip this floor of the palace entirely, but it would be a shame to miss the icons in rooms 1–4, or such extravaganzas as *The Last Day of Pompeii* or *The Wave*, in room 14.

Russian icons

For many centuries Russian art was exclusively religious in theme, and limited to mosaics, frescoes and **icons**, the holy images venerated in Orthodox

churches and households. The early icon painters were medieval monks for whom painting was a spiritual devotion, to be accompanied by fasting and prayer. Icons were repainted when their colours dulled and were often overlaid with golden, gem-encrusted frames. Their style and content were dictated by the canons of Byzantine art, faithfully preserved by the schools of Vladimir and Suzdal. However, a bolder and brighter Russian style emerged at Novgorod from the twelfth century onwards, which was to influence strongly the development of Russian art as a whole, and even the work of such "foreign" artists as Theophanes the Greek.

Icon painting reached a crossroads in the seventeenth century, when Russia's Orthodox Church was split between supporters of the reformist Patriarch Nikon and the arch-conservative Avvakum, both of whom opposed any innovations in painting. Nikon poked out the eyes of icons that offended him, while Avvakum fulminated against those who depicted saints "like a German, fat-bellied and corpulent". Ironically, the result was a gradual secularization of art, as Tsar Mikhail Romanov encouraged a new form known as the *parsuna*, or the representation of an ordinary human being – in fact, somewhere between an icon and realistic portraiture. Artists also began to paint on canvas as well as the traditional wooden panel, and although icon painting continued right up to the 1917 Revolution, its glory days had long passed, as Russia's leading painters concentrated on secular art.

One of the oldest works in **room 1** is the small, early twelfth-century icon, *The Archangel with the Golden Hair*, originally part of a deesis – the third and most important tier of an iconostasis, with Christ in Majesty occupying the central position. Another notable icon, *Boris and Gleb*, depicts the young princes of Kiev murdered by their pagan elder brother, Svyatopolk. Another historical subject is the *Battle of Novgorod and Suzdal*, depicting the former's triumph over the latter – a sixteenth-century icon of the Novgorod school, that hangs in **room 2**.

Room 3 showcases panels by known masters. The monk **Andrey Rublev** and his "fellow faster" **Daniil Cherny** collaborated on the two-metre-high

Apostle Peter and Apostle Paul, which originally formed part of the iconostasis of the Dormition Cathedral in Vladimir. Their spiritual successor in the second half of the fifteenth century was a Muscovite, **Dionysius**, whose *Archangel Gabriel*, *St John Chrystostomos* and *St Simeon the Stylite* hang here. The other great Moscow icon painter was **Simon Ushakov**, whose *Old Testament Trinity* can be seen in **room 4**.

Petrine art

Since many of the paintings of eighteenth-century Russia compare poorly with those of the West, the reasons for viewing them are as much historical as artistic. The reign of **Peter the Great** marked a turning point in Russian art. On his famous Grand Tour of Europe in 1697, the tsar began avidly buying pictures, initiating an activity that was to become an obsession with the later Romanovs. Then, in his determination to establish St Petersburg as the new artistic centre of Russia, Peter transferred the state icon workshop here from the Kremlin Armoury in Moscow, although he had no intention of building on that tradition, being intent on introducing Western art forms.

Encouraged by Peter, many foreign artists settled in St Petersburg, among them Gottfried Tannhauer, who may have painted the scene of Peter on his deathbed and the portrait of the young Elizabeth Petrovna in **room 5** – although the Russian Museum attributes the former to **Ivan Nikitin** (c.1680–1742), whose mastery of Western techniques is also manifest in his portraits of a Hetman (Cossack leader) and Tsarevna Praskovia Ivanova. Nikitin was one of several young Russian artists whom Peter sent abroad to be trained – a policy that had a great impact in the long term, though Nikitin himself fell victim to intrigues and was exiled to Tobolsk. Another promising artist trained abroad was **Andrey Matveev** (1701–39), whose unfinished *Self-portrait of the Artist and his Wife* is one of only a few of his canvases to have survived (in room 6).

Art under Elizabeth and Catherine

It wasn't until Elizabeth ascended the throne that Peter's plans to found a Russian **Academy of Arts** came to fruition. In 1757, an edict by the Senate established an academy in St Petersburg, although in its early years it remained an administrative department of Moscow University. **Room 6** features a medley of portraits by Elizabeth's court painter **Ivan Vishnyakov** (1699–1761), the Sheremetev family's serf-artist **Ivan Argunov** (1729–1802), and **Alexei Antropov** (1716–95), who served Catherine the Great. Antropov's best-known work is a *Portrait of Peter III*, Catherine's detested husband, whose elongated body and minuscule head are overwhelmed by an excess of background detail. Room 6 also contains mosaic portraits of Peter, Elizabeth and Catherine produced by the Imperial Glass Factory, and a bust of Prince Menshikov by Ivan Vitali.

The main reason to pause in **room 7** is to admire its gilded ceiling and a matronly bronze statue of Empress Anna, known as *Anna Ioannovna and an Arab Boy*, by the Italian sculptor Carlo Rastrelli, father of the famous architect. **Room 8** is largely given over to the talented **Fyodor Rokotov** (1736–1808), whose lively bust-length portraits put the emphasis firmly on the characters of the sitters. Also note the portrait by an unknown artist of the future tsar Peter III, wearing a red coat with a green sash.

Room 9 concentrates on the work of the Ukrainian **Anton Losenko** (1737–73), whose *Vladimir and Rogneda* was the first attempt by a native painter to depict a national historical subject on a large scale. His other canvases are concerned with more traditional biblical subjects, such as the *Wonderful Catch,* depicting Jesus doing a bit of proxy fishing, and a typically academic portrait of *Cain.* There's also a bronze *Prometheus* having his liver picked out, by Fyodor Gordeev.

The centrepiece of **room 10** is the life-sized statue, *Catherine, the Legislator,* by **Fyodor Shubin** (1740–1805), Russia's first great sculptor – Catherine and Potemkin were virtually the only enthusiastic patrons of his flowing Rococo style. On the walls hang paintings by **Dmitri Levitsky** (1735–1822), a Ukrainian Pole who, having never travelled abroad, could justifiably claim to be Russia's first truly homegrown talent. His best-known works are the series of light-hearted portraits of Catherine's favourite pupils from the Smolniy Institute for Young Noblewomen.

Apart from the main staircase, **room 11,** known as the **White Hall** (Beliy zal), is the finest example of the original white, gold and mauve-grey Neoclassical decor, designed – right down to the furniture – by the palace's architect, Carlo Rossi. Working with him on the *grisaille* decor was **Vladimir Borovikovsky** (1757–1825), the most sought-after portraitist of the late eighteenth century. **Room 12** displays his *Catherine the Great Promenading at Tsarskoe Selo* – a frank portrayal of the elderly empress exercising a dog – and one of Tsar Paul, dwarfed by sumptuous robes and drapery.

The Academy style

Napolcon's invasion of Russia in 1812 and the eventual triumphal entry of Russian forces into Paris were reflected in a marked shift towards Neoclassicism and patriotic themes, which became the hallmark of the **Academy style** for decades afterwards. In the applied arts, its counterpart was the Empire style, represented by a gigantic cut-glass and gilded crystal vase in **room 13.**

Room 14 is hung with monumental canvases, including two of the most famous – and theatrical – in the Russian Museum. *The Last Day of Pompeii* was painted by **Karl Bryullov** (1799–1852) while living in Rome, and won the Grand Prix at the Paris Salon in 1834. Sir Walter Scott reportedly sat for an hour in front of it before pronouncing that it was "not a painting but an epic" (though unkind commentators claim Scott's apparent devotion was due more to his great age and immobility).

While many Russians read *The Last Day* as an allegory of St Petersburg's fate (the city had been flooded some years earlier), another famous painting – *The Wave,* depicting a battered ship about to be sunk in a stormy sea – was said to prophesy the downfall of the Romanovs. Its creator, **Ivan Aivazovsky** (1817–1900), specialized in large seascapes and views of Constantinople and the Crimea. The seascapes were painted from memory in the studio rather than from life, as Aivazovsky believed that "the movements of the living elements elude the brush". He produced a staggering four to five thousand pictures and enjoyed an international reputation.

A third graduate to win renown abroad was **Alexander Ivanov** (1806–58), whose superb draughtsmanship won him a Gold Medal and a grant to study in Italy, where he spent most of his life. After being made an academician for *The Appearance of Christ before Mary Magdalene,* he wrote to his father, "You think that a lifelong salary of 6000–8000 rubles and a safe place in the Academy is a great blessing for an artist . . . but I think it is a curse." When not on loan elsewhere, his studies for such finished works are usually exhibited in **room 15** together with landscapes by other members of the semi-permanent Russian artists' colony in Rome, such as **Silvestr Shchedrin** (1791–1830), which line the corridor designated **room 16.** From 1820 onwards, many artists preferred to live abroad to escape the censorship imposed by Nicholas I or, in Ivanov's case, to safely indulge his passion for naked boys.

In **room 17** is a portrait of Empress Elizabeth's court painter J.F. Grooth, whose widow was persuaded to initiate Catherine's childlike husband Grand Duke Peter into the mysteries of sex after the Empress grew impatient at their failure to produce an heir.

Mikhailovskiy Palace (first floor)

On the **first floor** you can see how Russian art gradually escaped from its academic confines and came of age in the late nineteenth century. Rooms in the Mikhailovskiy Palace trace this development as far as the works of Repin and Vasnetsov, beyond which the story continues in the Rossi Wing (see p.145). If you wish to skip the lead up to Repin, you can go straight into room 38 at the bottom of the stairs instead of turning left into room 18, where the first-floor exhibition begins – though it would be a shame to miss the academic blockbusters in room 21.

Romanticism, genre and landscape painting

Romanticism in the pictorial arts was personified by **Orest Kiprensky** (1782–1836), the illegitimate child of a noble and a serf, who had tragic affairs, drank recklessly and died of tuberculosis in Rome. The finest of his early portraits in **room 18** is of Evgrav Davidov, a beefy Hussar officer who lost an arm and a leg in battle against Napoleon shortly after the picture was completed.

While state commissions usually went to artists who produced safe, monumental academic works, the late eighteenth- and nineteenth-century nobility and merchant class developed a taste for **genre painting** – scenes of rural or small-town life in particular. Its earliest practitioners were **Alexei Venetsianov** (1780–1847) and his pupil, **Grigori Soroka** (1823–64), whose work hangs in **room 19**. Venetsianov's *Cleaning Beetroot* strikes an authentic note of misery, but *In The Threshing Barn* resembles a stage set for figures in dreamlike poses; Soroka's river scenes carry more conviction. The work of **Pavel Fedotov** (1815–52) focused on artisans and bourgeois life, and was often infused with social criticism. *The Major's*

Mikhailovskiy Palace

Rossi Wing

Room currently closed

RUSSIAN MUSEUM: First Floor

▼ *ploshchad Iskusstv*

Courtship depicts a self-satisfied officer coming to inspect his unwilling young bride (**room 20**).

Antiquity continued to be the subject of major commissions – vast canvases such as *Christian Martyrs in the Colosseum* by **Konstantin Flavitsky** (1830–66), and *Nero's Death* by **Vasily Smirnov** (1858–90), titillated patrons with the thrill of blood, while **Genrikh Semiradsky** (1843–1902) specialized in erotic pagan scenes with titles like *Purina at the Posiedon Celebration in Elusium* (**room 21**).

Rooms 22 & 23 are largely devoted to the work of **Vasily Perov** (1834–82), the son of a baron exiled to Siberia, who began his career with satires against corruption; his *Monastery Refectory* – showing monks boozing and guzzling while the poor get short shrift – was banned by the authorities.

Others eschewed direct criticism in favour of **landscapes** in which discerning viewers might still detect social commentary. **Alexei Savrasov** (1830–97) is generally reckoned to be the "father of Russian landscape painting" and renowned as the teacher of Levitan (see p.145), who was to surpass his achievements. Though best known for *The Rooks Have Returned* in the Tretyakov Gallery, he is well represented here in **room 24** by *Rainbow, Ukranian Farmstead in an Oak Forest* and *Evening at a River*.

The Wanderers

In 1863, fourteen of the Academy's most talented pupils refused to paint the mythological subject set by their examiners, and left to set up an artists' co-operative that was the genesis of the Society for Travelling Art Exhibitions – known as the **Wanderers** (*peredvizhniki*) – which evaded censorship by showing their paintings at "wandering" exhibitions in the provinces. Most of these artists were in sympathy with the Populist movement and abided by Chernyshevsky's dictum that "Only content is able to refute the accusation that art is an empty diversion".

The Wanderers' leader, **Ivan Kramskoy** (1837–87), vowed to create a truly Russian school of art, and is best known for his Slavic *Christ in the Wilderness* (in the Tretyakov Gallery). His portraits in **room 25** are little different in style from those of his contemporaries in the West, but notable for their challenging stares. There's also a cute life-size statue of a child taking its first steps, by Fyodor Kamonssky.

Room 26 is devoted to the work of **Nicholas Ge** (1831–94), whose name is pronounced – and often spelled – "Gay". The grandson of a French émigré, Ge was torn between mathematics and painting until the award of the Academy's Gold Medal and a travel bursary decided the issue. One of the founder members of the Wanderers, he soon turned from landscapes to religious themes under the influence of Ivanov. Ge's *The Last Supper* horrified critics with its departure from traditional iconography, rendering the scene by candlelight, in a shabby setting. The painting for which he is best known to Russians is *Peter I Interrogating Tsarevich Alexei at Peterhof* – Peter later had his son killed.

During the Wanderers' meanderings, landscape painters were forging ahead on the path beaten by Savrasov. In **room 27** hang *Oak Trees*, *In the Thicket* and *Mast Pine Grove* by **Ivan Shishkin** (1832–98), lauded for their meticulous detail, but said by some critics to lack a sense of place – a charge that can't be levelled at the wintry Russian landscapes of **Fyodor Vasiliev** (1850–73) in **room 28**. His desolate *Thaw* was painted in the year that he became seriously ill with tuberculosis, whereas his Crimean *Mountains and Sea* exudes freshness and vitality.

Room 29 behind the main staircase contains two **computers** for accessing the museum's website, and leads into **room 30**, featuring Populist art, characterized by its strong social commentary. Titles like *Dividing the Family Property* by **Vasily Maximov** (1844–1911) and *Doss House* by **Vladimir Makovsky** (1846–1920), tell their own tale. Also notice *Before the Wedding*, by **Firs Zhuravlyev** (1836–1901), whose weeping bride and baffled parents invite speculation about a loveless match or shameful secret.

Other concerns are evident in **room 31**, which is dominated by *To the War* by **Karl Savitsky**, where conscripts are bid a tearful farewell at the station. While *Harvesting* by **Grigori Myasoyedov** (1834–1911), the so-called "father" of the Wanderers, exudes the bucolic optimism later associated with Socialist Realism, Chizkov's statue of an *Unfortunate Peasant* bespeaks poverty and desperation on the land.

A vulpine, white-marble Mephistopheles and statues of Spinoza and Nestor the Annalist by **Mikhail Antokolsky** (1842–1902) lead to a vast canvas by **Vasily Polenov** (1844–1927) that dominates **room 32**. In *Christ and the Adulteress*, Christ's humility is contrasted with the vicious piety of the priests, who incite the mob to stone a woman to death – an expression of sympathy for the sinner and contempt for the smug that resonated with Dostoyevsky's conception of Christianity.

The Repin rooms

Ilya Repin (1844–1930) was a late recruit to the Wanderers and subsequently became the foremost realist painter of his generation after training at the Academy following an apprenticeship at an icon workshop. **Room 33** displays *Leave-Taking of a Recruit*, in the sombre tradition of Savitsky's *To the War* (see above); a prize-winning student work, *Christ Raising the Daughter of Jairus*; and his famous *Barge-haulers on the Volga*, a study in human drudgery that became an icon for the Populist movement. In **room 34** are portraits of the composers Rubenstein and Glazunov, and a lively historical work, *The Zaporozhe Cossacks Writing a Mocking Letter to the Sultan*, in which swarthy warriors compose a reply to Sultan Mohammed IV's ultimatum.

In **room 35**, his portrait of Tolstoy, barefooted and dressed like a peasant, is juxtaposed with *October 17, 1905*, showing a crowd rejoicing at Nicholas II's assent to a constitution and parliament. Lastly, in **room 54** (off the Surikov section – see below) hangs Repin's *Ceremonial Meeting of the State Council, 7 May 1901*, a vast work that required scores of preliminary studies (some of which are on display). The councillors are painted like a still life, while Nicholas II is reduced to insignificance in the Grand Hall of the Mariinskiy Palace.

Surikov and Vasnetsov

During the 1880s, Russian historical painting adopted a form of Slavic mysticism, the leading exponent of which was Siberian-born **Vasily Surikov** (1846–1916), who studied at the Academy and was influenced by Ivanov. After his *Morning of the Execution of the Streltsy* (in Moscow), Surikov is best known for the huge canvases in **room 36**, particularly *Yermak's Conquest of Siberia*, which depicts the Cossacks storming across the River Irtysh to smash the Tatar hordes in 1595. After the death of his wife, Surikov retreated to Siberia, but in 1891 resumed his career with the festive *Taking the Snow Fortress by Storm*. Even cheerier is *Suvorov Crossing the Alps*, in which the army toboggans down the mountain like a group of excited schoolboys. In **room 37** hangs Surikov's colossal painting of the Cossack rebel leader Stepan Razin, brooding in a boat on the River Volga.

An Imperial city

The "Venice of the North", St Petersburg is every bit as grandiose, decrepit and vulnerable to flooding as its Italian counterpart. Rivers and canals make up one tenth of its area, with most parts of the city only 3m above sea level. The stucco facades of its palaces, painted in cool blues and yellows or rich hues of apricot or crimson, are reflected in the dark waters in a symphony of architectural styles – some European, others Russian – embodying the city's past as capital of the vast, multi-ethnic Tsarist Empire.

The interior of Peterhof, inspired by Versailles ▲

The Winter Palace, St Petersburg's finest example of Russian Baroque ▼

Petrine

When founding St Petersburg, Peter the Great hired foreign architects to realise his vision of an ideal city, an amalgam of Amsterdam, London and other European cities he had visited. You can still see the hut – **Peter's Cabin** – from which he oversaw the construction of the **Peter and Paul Fortress**, whose ravelins and needle-spired **Peter and Paul Cathedral** aped the "scientific" fortifications and Protestant churches of Königsberg and Rīga – the antithesis of Moscow's Kremlin and onion-domed skyline.

Dutch design had a big influence on Petrine architecture – gabled or hipped roofs are characteristic of the **Twelve Colleges** and **Menshikov Palace** on Vasilevskiy Island, Peter's **Summer Palace** by the River Fontanka and his **Wooden Palace** at Strelna. Versailles was the inspiration for **Peterhof** – a country palace with fountains, seaside pavilions and formal gardens – emulated by Peter's crony Menshikov at **Oranienbaum**. Although Vasilevskiy Island never became the city centre as he had envisaged, and Nevskiy prospekt ended up with a kink in it despite him supervising its progress with a spyglass from the Admiralty, Peter's regulations dictating the design of housing for each class became the template for urban planning in the city.

Russian Baroque

Peter's granddaughter Elizabeth let others worry about paving streets, focusing instead on extravagances. Her favourite architect Bartholomeo Rastrelli created the **Winter Palace**, the **Great Palace** at Peterhof, the **Catherine Palace** at Tsarskoe Selo with its famous **Amber Room**, and the **Smolniy Cathedral**. Rastrelli's style of Baroque – fluid mouldings and theatrical statuary offset against bright or pastel coloured stucco – was continued by his pupil Chevakinsky, who built the **Sheremetev Palace** on the Fontanka and the **St Nicholas Cathedral**. The palace interiors featured gilded tracery, floor-length mirrors, and huge tiled stoves, providing a suitable setting for Elizabeth's beloved cross-dressing balls.

Chinoiserie and Classicism

Elizabeth's heir Peter III dabbled in Chinoiserie, adorning the **Chinese Palace** at Oranienbaum with lacquer, oriental vases and landscapes mixed in with Rococo. Having deposed him, **Catherine the Great** preferred the **Classical** aesthetic of her Scottish architect Charles Cameron, who redesigned the interior of the Catherine Palace, attached the **Agate Room** and **Cameron Gallery**, and landscaped its grounds in the naturalistic English style. Her reign also saw the construction of hospitals and the embankment of the **Griboedov Canal**, nicknamed "Catherine's Gutter" by the populace, who compared its expense to that of her lovers, for whom she built the **Marble Palace** and **Tauride Palace**.

Her son "Mad" Paul rejected her taste by hiring another architect to finish his **Pavlovsk** estate and build the **Engineers' Castle** (where he was murdered). Catherine's grandson Alexander I re-embraced Classicism with the aid of an architect of genius, Carlo Rossi, who created the **General Staff building** facing the Winter Palace and other ensembles that still define the centre. Their stately proportions and martial bas-reliefs echo those of Imperial Rome – the "Russian Empire" style also typified by Rossi's **Yelagin Palace**.

▲ St Nicholas Cathedral

▲ Engineers' Castle
▼ The General Staff building

Neo-Russian and Style Moderne

Following the assassination of his father by revolutionaries, Alexander III built the **Church of the Saviour on the Blood** to mark the spot – a pseudo-medieval Muscovite edifice in deliberate opposition to St Petersburg's European heritage. **Neo-Russian** interiors – heavy "peasant" furniture and sombre colours – can be seen in the **Alexander Palace** at Tsarskoe Selo, and in certain rooms at the Winter Palace and at **Gatchina**. In the 1900s the Russian form of Art Nouveau – **Style Moderne** – flourished. The ornate **railings** beside the Church of the Saviour on the Blood, **Yeliseyev's** shop, **Vitebsk Station** and the Kshesinskaya mansion are fine examples.

Style Moderne railings by the Church of the Saviour on the Blood ▲

The Catherine Palace, Tsarskoe Selo ▼

Top five palaces

▶ **Winter Palace** (p.77) Fabulous state rooms and the vast art collection of the Hermitage make this top of the list.
▶ **Yusupov Palace** (p.108) Dazzlingly diverse décor – from Moorish to Rococo – and the cellar where Rasputin was murdered.
▶ **Tsarskoe Selo** (p.254) The Amber Room and romantic grounds of the Catherine Palace are only two of its many attractions, which can take a whole day to cover.
▶ **Peterhof** (p.237) Majestic fountains, the Great Palace, Monplaisir and the Gothic Cottage Palace embody the ultimate Tsarist theme park.
▶ **Pavlovsk** (p.265) More intimate than other Imperial palaces, with a park full of moribund follies.

Viktor Vasnetsov (1846–1926) was a priest's son who quit the seminary to apprentice himself to a lithographer and later won a place at the Academy. His penchant was for ancient Russian prehistory, myths and legends, which inspired such big dramatic compositions as *Scythians and Slavs Fighting* and *A Russian Knight at the Crossway* – though Vasnetsov also tackled contemporary subjects such as *A Festival on the Outskirts of Paris*, which likewise hangs in **room 38**.

The Rossi Wing

The exhibition continues on the first floor of the **Rossi Wing** (fligel Rossi), beyond the Surikov section and Repin's *Meeting of the State Council*. **Temporary exhibitions** of prints or textiles in the corridor (room 49) parallel to the enfilade and an array of **busts**, **casts** and **models** for statues in rooms 56–58 might tempt you off the trail, but it's worth sticking with the permanent exhibition of paintings.

Room 39 attests to the fashion for Orientalism, which for Russian artists encompassed not just the Holy Land, but also Central Asia, the Caucasus and the Balkans. The genre's leading exponent, **Vasily Vereshchagin**, was renowned for scenes such as *At the Entrance to the Mosque* and *In Jerusalem, The Royal Tombs*, and also for his anti-war pictures, typified by *Skobelev at Shipka*, where a vainglorious Russian general taking the salute is mocked by piles of dead soldiers in the foreground.

Rooms 40 and **41** focus on the work of **Arkhip Kuindzhi** (1841–1910), who grew apart from the Wanderers as he made ever greater use of colour as a symbolic element in stunning Caucasian landscapes – a tendency taken to its extreme by his pupil Roerich (see p147).

Exotic scenes of seventeenth-century Moscow by **Apollinary Vasnetsov** (brother of Viktor), Clavdy Lebeedeev and other artists fascinated by Old Russia – before the Westernizing and, as they saw it, corrupting influence of Peter the Great – are the leitmotif of **rooms 43** and **45**. The latter focuses on **Andrey Ryabushkin** (1861–1904), whose famous painting *They Are Coming* shows Muscovites nervously awaiting the arrival of the first Europeans. His *Moscow Street* revels in the mud of the wooden city and its Kremlin, while *Seventeenth-century Merchant Family* has characteristics of the archaic *parsuna* form (see p.139).

Sandwiched between Slav historicists, **room 44** is devoted to **Isaak Levitan** (1860–1900), widely regarded as the greatest Russian landscapist of the nineteenth century. His *Silence*, *The Lake* and *Moonlit Night* are characterized by their limpid rivers and soft light, and devoid of any hint of social criticism. For this you need to visit **room 46**, where the hardships of the poor are depicted in *Gleaning Coal in an Abandoned Pit* and *A Woman Spinner*, by **Nikolai Kasatkin** (1850–1930).

The final artist covered in the Rossi Wing is **Filip Malyavin** (1869–1940), a lay brother at the Russian monastery on Mount Athos in Greece before he took up painting. Most of the pictures in **room 47** are impressionistic portraits of actors, singers and critics, but his brilliant later, freer compositions, suggestive of Gauguin or Klimt, are represented by *Two Girls* and *Peasant Women Dancing*.

Room 48, featuring a seated statue of Ivan the Terrible by **Marc Antokolsky** (1842–1962), marks a divergence of ways. At this point you either turn right along a corridor past a larger-than-life **statue of Yermak** with a battleaxe, and **upstairs into the Benois Wing** to continue the tour of the art collection – or investigate the folk art section in the Rossi Wing, straight ahead.

Folk art

Though not all ten rooms may be open, this section offers an overview of traditional **Russian folk art** and handicrafts. Most of the exhibits were part of everyday life in Russian villages and many had a mystical significance. The first room displays *naboyki*, or block-printed indigo textiles and glazed tiles of the type often used to decorate seventeenth- and eighteenth-century buildings. Wood was used for making dwellings and all kinds of tools and objects from washboards to butter churns, often carved with geometric patterns and pagan symbols – especially the pediments of cottages. The rooms that follow are filled with the sort of things still produced by contemporary craftsmen, such as toys, lace, ceramics and lacquerware, plus a huge display of painted wooden cups and plates from Khokloma.

The Benois Wing

The **Benois Wing** (korpus Benoua) holds the museum's collection of late nineteenth- and twentieth-century Russian art – the permanent collection is housed on the second floor, while the first floor is given over entirely to **temporary exhibitions** of contemporary Russian and world art. Bear in mind that some of the avant-garde works in the permanent collection may be on loan to foreign museums and thus not be on show when you visit.

To reach the second floor from the main building, head along the corridor from room 48 on the first floor of the Rossi Wing and upstairs to room 66; the first floor is accessible only via the Benois Wing's own entrance on the Griboedov embankment, where separate tickets for temporary exhibitions are sold – opening hours are the same as for the main exhibition in the Russian Museum (tickets for which are also sold there).

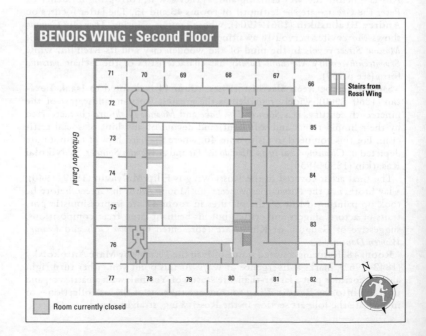

Abramtsevo artists and the World of Art

Room 66 is devoted to **Mikhail Nesterov** (1862–1942), whose religious paintings fell from favour in Soviet times, obliging him to concentrate on portraiture. Nesterov was a member of the **Abramtsevo artists' colony** at the country estate of the Moscow millionaire Mamontov, which was as influential as the Wanderers had been a generation earlier. Another kindred spirit, **Nikolai Roerich** (1874–1947), was fascinated by archeology and the Orient. His use of saturated colour was first applied to subjects from Russian history and later to Oriental mysticism, particularly after he went to live in India and Tibet (**room 67**).

While they shared the Abramtsevo artists' love of Russian folk art and myths, the **World of Art** (Mir Iskusstva) movement in St Petersburg (see p.194) was equally inspired by French and eighteenth-century court life – typified by works in **room 68** such as *Harlequin and Lady* by **Konstantin Somov** (1869–1939), and the *Commedia dell'arte* by **Alexander Benois** (1870–1960). Benois and **Léon Bakst** (1866–1924) designed costumes and stage sets for Diaghilev's Ballets Russes, and Bakst's dramatic tastes are given full rein in an apocalyptic vision of flooded temples and mega lightning-bolts, called *Terror Antiques*.

Valentin Serov (1865–1911) was brought up at Abramtsevo. While most of his work in **room 69** consists of society portraits (Count Felix and Princess Yusupov, the parents of Rasputin's assassin, among them), you may also find stark depictions of troops charging demonstrators, and opera set designs.

Konstantin Yuon (1875–1958) didn't belong to either circle, but his bright, panoramic folk scenes likewise emphasized decorative elements, a tendency taken even further by **Boris Kustodiev** (1878–1927). **Room 70** exhibits three of Kustodiev's best-known works: a fleshy *Merchant's Wife at Tea*; a snowy landscape with troikas, *At Shrovetide*; and a copy of his portrait of Chaliapin (see p.183). After the Revolution, both artists found favour with the new regime by producing panoramic views of proletarian festivals and Communist utopias.

Another Abramtsevo member, **Konstantin Korovin** (1861–1939), was the first Russian artist to turn to Impressionism in the 1880s, and was later invited by Diaghilev to design the cover of the first issue of the journal *World of Art*. **Room 72** juxtaposes his artistic journey from boulevard scenes of Paris and Yalta to decorative still lifes with pictures by his fellow Impressionist **Igor Grabar** (1871–1960).

Symbolism and the Blue Rose group

The Russian **Symbolist movement** involved artists both inside and outside Abramtsevo and the World of Art. In **room 73** you'll find works by **Viktor Borisov-Musatov** (1870–1905), whose *Self-portrait with His Sister* hints at the sexual tension between them, veiled with symbolism in the pictures of young women espied in gardens, which made up most of his oeuvre. The Symbolist movement was founded by **Mikhail Vrubel** (1856–1910), whose febrile, lushly textured paintings had a huge impact in Russia, not least the cabalistic "Demon" series that precipitated his mental breakdown – one may be found in **room 74**.

Musatov's followers at the Moscow School of Painting, Sculpture and Architecture became known as the **Blue Rose** group after the name of their first exhibition in 1907. Sharing a love of blue (symbolizing spirituality), dreams, and simplification of forms, they each sought a world of their own. **Pavel Kuznetsov** (1878–1968) found his ideal life with the Kirghiz nomads, portrayed in *Evening* *in the Steppes* and other works where soft blues and yellows predominate, whereas **Martiros Sariyan** (1880–1968) rendered the Near East in hues of red, yellow and indigo. Both are represented in **room 75**, along with others in the group.

Petrov-Vodkin and the Jack of Diamonds

Kuzma Petrov-Vodkin (1878–1939) was initially a Symbolist but remained independent of many of the groups that came and went in the 1900s. His theories on composition and spatial construction of the picture surface were highly influential on Soviet painters well into the 1970s, while his pre-revolutionary paintings made him popular with the authorities, at least until the rise of Socialist Realism. **Room 76** highlights his early works, such as *Youth*, *Dream*, an intense self-portrait and an iconic *Mother*.

The next two rooms feature artists from the **Jack of Diamonds** society that existed from 1910 to 1916. Cézanne was the main influence on **Aristarkh Lentulov** (1882–1943) and **Robert Falk** (1886–1958), whose *Landscape with Lavra*, still lifes and portraits hang in **room 78**, together with the bizarre *Lady with Pheasants* by **Ilya Mashkov** (1881–1944) and a famous portrait of the poetess Akhmatova by **Nathan Altman** (1889–1970), whose semi-Cubist *Sunflowers* is also on display.

Kandinsky, Goncharova and Larionov

Room 79 features a changing array of works by three major artists. **Vasily Kandinsky** (1866–1944) spent much of his career in Munich, where with Franz Marc he launched the Blaue Reiter (Blue Rider) group, which dealt a deathblow to European naturalism. Kandinsky believed in abstraction from nature and the spiritualization of art; each colour was thought to have a "corresponding vibration of the human soul". Although his theories greatly influenced many artists, in 1920 the Institute of Artistic Culture rejected them as too "subjective" and Kandinsky left Russia to take up a post at the Weimar Bauhaus. However, the Russian Museum retains many works from three series designated *Impressions, Improvisations* and *Compositions,* plus individually titled paintings such as *Dusk* and *Picture with Edges*.

In the years before the outbreak of war in 1914, Russian art was in ferment with movements akin to the Blaue Reiter and Cubism. The leading exponents of what became known as **Primitivism** were **Natalya Goncharova** (1881–1962) and **Mikhail Larionov** (1881–1964), both of whom quit the Jack of Diamonds in 1911 to form a new group, the Donkey's Tail. Goncharova asserted that all art was dead or decadent, except in Russia; that Picasso was a fraud and Cubism was old hat. Works such as *Four Evangelists*, *Whitening Linen* and *Sunflowers and Peasants* drew on folk art and icons for inspiration, while Larionov depicted drunks and whores and daubed his canvases with obscenities. Later, he launched a new style called **Rayonism**, whose manifesto declared that the genius of the age consisted of "trousers, jackets, shoes, tramways, buses, aeroplanes, railways, magnificent ships . . .". In Rayonist pictures rays of light break the object up, scatter it across the picture surface, creating a sense of movement, progression and disintegration. You may also find something by the Georgian artist **Niko Pirosmanashvili** (1863–1918), who pursued his own style of Primitivism and was so poor that he often painted on scraps of wood or tarpaulin.

Futurism

Some people visit the museum simply to see the art in **rooms 80–82**. As with room 79, paintings get rotated or sent abroad, but you can be sure of finding something by all of the big names in Russian **Futurism** – a catch-all term for the explosion of artistic styles and theories between 1910 and 1920. Early Futurists, such as the Burlyuk brothers and Mayakovsky, were out to shock – the Futurist manifesto was entitled *A Slap in the Face of Public Taste*. More cerebral was **Kazimir Malevich** (1878–1935), whose Cubo-Futurism – influenced by the bold lines of icons and peasant woodcuts – evolved into what he termed **Suprematism**, the "art of pure sensation". The Russian Museum has 136 works by Malevich, ranging from geometric canvases like *Black Circle* and *Suprematism: Yellow and Black* to the figurative *Red Cavalry*. Also look out for *Abstract Compositions* by **Olga Rozanova** (1886–1918), whose minimalism was later applied to ceramics and fabrics for the masses (now collectors' items).

Malevich's rival for ascendancy over the avant-garde movement was **Vladimir Tatlin** (1885–1953), whose early paintings, such as *The Sailor* (a self-portrait), gave little hint of what was to come. Having anticipated Dadaism with his junk collages, Tatlin experimented with theatre design and the "Culture of Materials". What came to be called **Constructivism** owed much to his collaboration with the theatre director Meyerhold and the painters **Lyubov Popova** (1889–1924) and **Nadezhda Udaltsova** (1885–1961). Much of their conceptual work was never realized: Tatlin's glider, *Letatlin*, never left the ground, while his *Monument to the Third International* – intended to be over 396m high and revolve on its axis, near the Peter and Paul Fortress – got a dusty response from Lenin.

Pavel Filonov (1883–1943) developed a system of "analytical art" to reflect the atomic nature of reality, layering detail upon detail to create such kaleidoscopic masterpieces as *Live Head*, *The Regeneration of Man*, *King's Feast* and *Formula of the Petrograd Proletariat*. Also look out for the vibrant red *Colour Composition* by **Boris Ender** (1893–1960) – an early pioneer of what would later be termed Abstract Expressionism – and work by **Alexander Rodchenko** (1891–1956), best known for his designs for ceramics, clothing and furniture, and for his photomontages, an art form that he invented.

Agitprop and Socialist Realism

Many of these artists threw themselves into the Revolution and produced what became known as **agitprop**, or "agitational propaganda". Posters became the new medium, brilliantly exploited by Mayakovsky (see p.205), Rodchenko and Vladimir Lebedev, and often aimed at promoting public health, literacy and recruitment for the Red Army. Although many Futurists derided easel painting, it too served for agitprop, from Malevich's *Red Cavalry* (see above) to Petrov-Vodkin's *Death of a Commissar* or the horrific *Disabled Veterans* by **Yuri Pimenov** (1903–77), in **room 83**.

By the late 1920s the avant-garde movement was divided between those who saw art as a spiritual activity, which, by becoming useful, ceased to exist, and those who insisted that artists must become technicians to bring "art into life" for the benefit of the masses. **Room 84** showcases work on themes such as sport, labour and collectivization, treated with freshness and vigour by artists who came of age at this time. **Alexander Deineka** (1899–1969) depicted steel- and textile-workers in stark tones and dramatic compositions, and later produced World War II masterpieces such as *Downed Flier*. Also full of energy are *Militarized Komsomol* and a tough, sexy *Metro Worker* with her steam-drill, by **Alexander Samokhvalov** (1894–1971).

The debate raged on until Stalin put an end to it all by making **Socialist Realism** obligatory in 1932. Its principles, as articulated by his mouthpiece Zhdanov, were *partiinost*, *ideinost* and *narodnost* (Party character, socialist content and national roots). While this still allowed some room for stylistic variation – as in Pimenov's bleak *Front Line Road* or Konchalovsky's folksy portrait of the writer Andrey Tolstoy in **room 85** – the prevailing style was a Stalinist take on nineteenth-century academicism. Works in this genre are legion, but rarely on display in the Russian Museum, except for major thematic exhibitions on the first floor of the Benois Wing. Its chief exponents were **Isaak Brodsky** (1884–1939), responsible for such works as *Lenin in the Smolniy*, and **Alexander Gerasimov** (1881–1963), to whom the world is indebted for *Stalin at the XVIth Congress of the Communist Party*.

Vasilevskiy Island

V asilevskiy Island (Vasilevskiy ostrov) cleaves the River Neva into its Bolshaya and Malaya branches, forming a strategic wedge whose eastern tip – or **Strelka** – is as much a part of St Petersburg's waterfront as the Winter Palace or Admiralty. The Strelka's **Rostral Columns** and former Stock Exchange (now the **Naval Museum**) are reminders that the city's port and commercial centre were once located here, while another, more enduring aspect of Vasilevskiy's erstwhile importance is the intellectual heritage bequeathed by St Petersburg's **University**, bolstered by a clutch of museums, including Peter the Great's infamous **Kunstkammer**, or "chamber of curiosities".

Originally, Peter envisaged making the island the centre of his capital. The first governor of St Petersburg, Alexander Menshikov, was an early resident (his **Menshikov Palace** is now the oldest building on the island) and Peter compelled other rich landowners and merchants to settle here. By 1726 the island had ten streets and over a thousand inhabitants, but wilderness still predominated and wolves remained a menace for decades to come. Living there also entailed hazardous crossings by sailing boat, as Peter had banned the use of rowing boats in order to instill a love of sailing, but unfortunately the ex-ferrymen made poor sailors. Moreover, Vasilevskiy Island became isolated from the mainland whenever a storm blew up or the Neva was choked with ice, dooming any hope of the island becoming the centre of St Petersburg.

Although Peter's plan for a network of canals was thwarted by Menshikov, who had them built so narrow as to be useless, their layout determined the grid of **avenues** and **lines** (see box p.154) within which subsequent development occurred. Politically, the proximity of factories and workers' slums to the university's student quarter fostered local militancy during the revolutions of 1905 and 1917. Moored beside the Neva and the Gulf of Finland are the Soviet **icebreaker Krasin** and a diesel **submarine** that are now both fascinating museums. The latter is located near **LenExpo** and the **Sea Terminal**, south of **Primorskiy district** that embodies the leaden giganticism of the Brezhnev era, while at the heart of the island lies the **Smolensk Cemetery** and St Petersburg's **Doll Museum**.

Around the Strelka

You can reach the **Strelka** by minibus (#7, #128, #141, #147, #187, #228) or trolleybus (#1, #7 & #10) from Nevskiy prospekt, or by walking across **Dvortsoviy most** (Palace Bridge), which offers fabulous views of both banks of the Neva. Built between 1908 and 1914 and reconstructed in the 1970s,

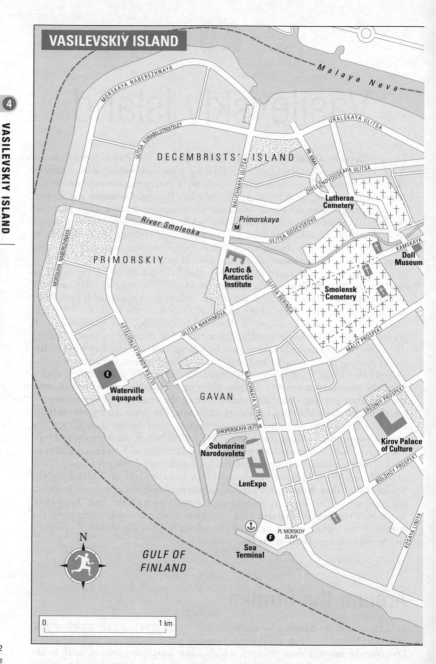

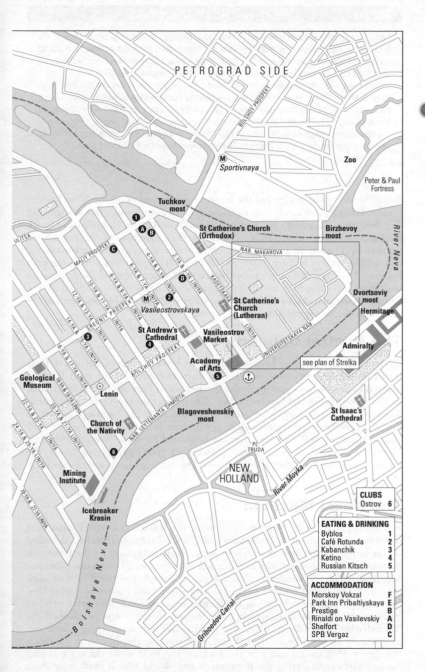

PETROGRAD SIDE

BOLSHOY PROSPEKT

M *Sportivnaya*

Zoo

Peter & Paul
Fortress

River Neva

**Tuchkov
most**

ULITSA

①

Ⓐ Ⓑ

MALIY PROSPEKT

Ⓒ

4-YA & 5-YA LINIYA

2-YA & 3-YA LINIYA

**St Catherine's Church
(Orthodox)**

**Birzhevoy
most**

NAB. MAKAROVA

Ⓓ

6-YA & 7-YA LINIYA

8-YA & 9-YA LINIYA

KADETSKAYA

**Dvortsoviy
most**

10-YA & 11-YA LINIYA

M

Vasileostrovskaya

②

12-YA & 13-YA LINIYA

SREDNIY PROSPEKT

**St Catherine's
Church
(Lutheran)**

Hermitage

14-YA & 15-YA LINIYA

③

**St Andrew's
Cathedral**

④

**Vasileostrov
Market**

UNIVERSITETSKAYA NAB.

Admiralty

16-YA & 17-YA LINIYA

BOLSHOY PROSPEKT

**Academy
of Arts**

⑤

see plan of Strelka

**Geological
Museum**

18-YA & 19-YA LINIYA

⊙
Lenin

⚓

20-YA & 21-YA LINIYA

22-YA & 23-YA LINIYA

**Blagoveshenskiy
most**

NAB. LEYTENANTA SHMIDTA

**St Isaac's
Cathedral**

24-YA & 25-YA LINIYA

**Church of
the Nativity**

⑥

PL.
TRUDA

**NEW
HOLLAND**

River Moyka

26-YA & 27-YA LINIYA

**Mining
Institute**

**Icebreaker
Krasin**

Bolshaya Neva

CLUBS	
Ostrov	**6**

EATING & DRINKING	
Byblos	**1**
Café Rotunda	**2**
Kabanchik	**3**
Ketino	**4**
Russian Kitsch	**5**

ACCOMMODATION	
Morskoy Vokzal	**F**
Park Inn Pribaltiyskaya	**E**
Prestige	**B**
Rinaldi on Vasilevskiy	**A**
Shelfort	**D**
SPB Vergaz	**C**

Griboedov Canal

the 250-metre-long bridge has the largest liftable span of all the Neva bridges – an amazing sight when it rises to allow ships to pass through late at night. By day, however, the Strelka steals the show with its Rostral Columns and Stock Exchange building, an ensemble created at the beginning of the nineteenth century by Thomas de Thomon, who also designed the granite embankments and cobbled ramps leading down to the Neva. This area was a working port between 1733 and 1885 – it's now the favoured place for newlyweds to come and toast their nuptials with champagne after being photographed at the Bronze Horseman. Many make further stops at Peter's Cabin and the cruiser *Aurora* on the Petrograd Side.

The Rostral Columns

Designed as navigational beacons, the twin brick-and-stucco **Rostral Columns** (Rostralnye kolonny) stand 32m high and once blazed with burning hemp oil at night; now gas-fired, the torches are lit only during festivals, such as Navy Day on the last Sunday in July. Their form derives from the Imperial Roman custom of erecting columns decorated with the sawn-off prows, or *rostrae* (beaks), of Carthaginian galleys captured in battle – although it is of course Russian naval victories that are honoured by these Rostral Columns. Figures at the base of each column personify Russia's great trade rivers: the Dnieper and Volga (on the column nearest Dvortsoviy most), and the Volkhov and Neva.

The Naval Museum

A sculptural tableau of Neptune harnessing the Baltic's tributaries surmounts the columned facade of St Petersburg's old Stock Exchange (Birzha), modelled on the temple of Paestum in southern Italy. Made redundant by the Bolshevik Revolution, the building was later turned into the **Naval Museum** (Voenno-Morskoy muzey; 11am–6pm, closed Mon & Tues & the last Thurs of each month; R320). Head upstairs past a ballistic missile and statues of Red sailors, to see the host of model ships in the former exchange hall. The prize exhibits here are the *botik* (boat) in which Peter learned to sail – a vessel dubbed the "Grandfather of the Russian Navy" – and Russia's oldest surviving submarine, designed by Dzhevetsky in 1881. Exhibits recounting the disaster at Tsushima Bay (see p.399) are relegated to the back of the hall, while the surrounding rooms chart events during the Revolution and World War II (with mug shots

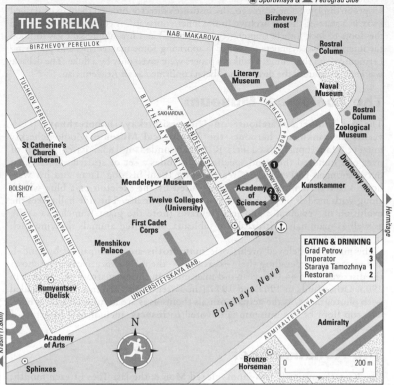

of the *Potemkin* mutineers and Kronstadt sailors) and conclude with the navy's postwar expansion. A collection of carved figureheads from eighteenth-century vessels fills the staircase up to the top floor, which is used for temporary exhibitions. Additionally, the Naval Museum runs two historic vessels as museums – the cruiser *Aurora* (p.178) and the submarine *Narodovolets* (p.162). At some point in the future, the Naval Museum is supposed to **move** to a site near New Holland (see p.106) and its current premises become an oil exchange – details should appear on the museum's Russian-only **website** (Ⓦwww.museum.navy.ru) in due course.

The Literary Museum

Early last century the Strelka's warehouses and customs building were all converted to academic use, with the Northern Warehouse becoming an institute for soil sciences, while the Customs House on naberezhnaya Makarova was taken over by the Institute of Russian Literature. Familiarly known as the **"Pushkin House"** (Pushkinskiy dom), it's home to a fusty **Literary Museum** (Mon–Fri 11am–5pm; Ⓦwww.pushkinhouse.spb.ru) with four rooms of furniture such as Gogol's armchair and Blok's desk, and portraits and personal effects including the poet Lermontov's cavalry sabre and Tolstoy's shirt and boots. You can only visit on a pre-booked **tour** (☎328 05 02; R450) and bibliophiles are likely to be disappointed by the lack of manuscripts on display. Some years ago, the institute's director ordered them to be stashed away in a state-of-the-art **archive** in the inner courtyard. A computer glitch caused the doors to lock (nearly trapping two archivists) and fire-suppressant gas to flood the interior. Two cylinders exploded, vaporizing some manuscripts and plastering Lermontov's on the ceiling; Pushkin's papers were saved only by a fluke. The debacle was kept secret until the director had been confirmed as an Academician.

The Zoological Museum

The old Southern Warehouse on **Universitetskaya naberezhnaya** (University Embankment) harbours the **Zoological Museum** (Zoologicheskiy muzey; 11am–6pm, closed Fri; R150). Founded in 1832, its collection of over one hundred thousand specimens includes a set of stuffed animals that once belonged to Peter the Great (among them his dog Titan and his warhorse Lizetta). Upstairs, you're confronted by the skeleton of a blue whale, along with models of polar bears and other Arctic life. The side hall traces the evolution of vertebrates and invertebrates (note the giant Kamchatka crab), as well as mammals, with realistic tableaux of stuffed animals showing each in its habitat.

The museum's beloved prehistoric **mammoths** are accompanied by models and photographs detailing their excavation – the most evocative display shows the discovery of a 44,000-year-old mammoth in the permafrost of Yakutsia in 1903. Other finds in 1961 and 1977 (the latter a baby mammoth) are recalled with photographs, as the actual animals themselves are in museums elsewhere. The top floor of the museum is devoted to **insects**, including a selection of live ones.

The Kunstkammer

The **Kunstkammer** (11am–6pm, closed Mon & the last Tues of each month; R200; ⓦwww.kunstkamera.ru), next door, is almost as popular as the Hermitage; expect to queue for half an hour at the entrance around the side of the sea-green building with its distinctive polygonal tower. Founded by Peter in 1714, its aim was to explain the mysteries of nature. The nucleus of its collection consisted of two thousand preparations by the Dutch embalmer Frederik Ruysch and an ethnographic "chamber of curios", also purchased in Holland. In Russia, Peter offered rewards for "human monsters", unknown birds and animals. Specimens had to be preserved in vinegar or spirits, while, to attract visitors, each received a glass of vodka. Originally, the Kunstkammer even had live exhibits, such as a man with only two digits on each limb, and a hermaphrodite (who escaped).

The **curios** are in a hall on the second floor, where photography is prohibited. While modern science can account for the two-headed calf and malformed foetuses, it's almost impossible for us to share the eighteenth-century taste for adorning dead babies' limbs with ruffles or baubles to emphasize their pathos, and the Kunstkammer no longer exhibits the skeleton of Peter's favourite giant, "Bourgeois" (whose penis is also in the storerooms). Case #1 holds surgical and dental instruments and teeth pulled by the tsar himself, a keen amateur dentist who kept records of his victims, among them "a person who made tablecloths" and "a fast-walking messenger".

On the same floor you'll find the Indian, Chinese, Mongolian and Arab sections of the **Museum of Anthropology and Ethnography** (Muzey Antropologii i Etnografii). Captions in English are so far limited to the

African section on the floor below, where you'll also find exhibits on the indigenous peoples of the Americas and the Aleutians. The diversity and virtuoso craftsmanship of the exhibits and dioramas makes this a wonderful museum.

In the tower is a **museum** recreating the study-laboratory of the "Russian Leonardo", **Mikhail Lomonosov** (1711–65), a fisherman's son from Archangel who codified Russian grammar, studied minerals and the heavens, and anticipated Dalton's theory of the atomic structure of matter in his *Elementa Chymiae Mathematica* (1741). On the two floors above this are a reconstruction of the first **Observatory** of the Academy of Sciences, and the **Great Gottorp Globe**, a kind of eighteenth-century planetarium designed by Lomonosov. Spectators sit inside the globe, which rotates on its axis, causing the planets and stars painted on the inner surface to revolve. Both can only be seen on a **guided tour** (R1200 for up to four people), which must be booked in advance (℡328 14 12).

The Twelve Colleges and the University

The next building along the embankment houses the **Academy of Sciences** (Akademiya nauk), the idea for which, like so many Russian institutions, was first mooted by Peter (who asked the German scientist and philosopher Leibnitz to devise a constitution), but only formally established after his death. Its austerely Neoclassical headquarters – built by Quarenghi between 1784 and 1787 – feature a **mosaic** of the Battle of Poltava by Lomonosov on the upper landing of the grand staircase, which can be glimpsed from the lobby (you probably won't be allowed any further). A **statue of Lomonosov** stands on Mendeleevskaya & 1-ya liniya, just beyond the academy.

Across the way you'll see the second-oldest building on the island, the **Twelve Colleges** (Dvenadtsat kollegii), its 400-metre-long facade painted sienna red with white facings, as in Petrine times. Executed by Trezzini, the building was designed to epitomize Peter's idea of a modern, efficient bureaucracy: the separate doors to the dozen different departments signified their autonomy and the uniform facade their common purpose. He was later enraged to discover that Menshikov had tampered with the plans, reducing the size of the buildings so as not to intrude on his own estates.

The *kollegii* were eventually replaced by ministries across the river, and in 1819 the building was given to **St Petersburg University** (Universitet Sankt-Peterburga). A bastion of freethinking and radicalism in Tsarist times, it educated many famous names in science, literature and politics. It was here that **Dmitri Mendeleyev** (1834–1907) worked out the Periodic Table of Elements having dreamt of the solution that had eluded him for months in 1869; his study has become a small **museum** (Mon–Fri 11am–3.30pm; R100) preserving his laboratory equipment and personal effects. The rector's house was the childhood home of the Symbolist poet Alexander Blok (who married Mendeleyev's daughter), while Alexander Popov sent what was arguably the world's first radio signal from the university labs (see p.106). Other alumni include Nikolai Chernyshevsky, author of the Utopian revolutionary novel *What is to be Done?*; Alexander Ulyanov, hanged for plotting to kill Alexander III; his brother Vladimir – better known as Lenin – who graduated with honours in law in 1891; Hitler's ideologue, Alfred Rosenberg; and Russia's president, Vladimir Putin, who joined the KGB after completing his law degree in 1975.

To the Menshikov Palace

Continuing west along Universitetskaya naberezhnaya, you'll come to the pale-yellow former barracks of the **First Cadet Corps**, which trained the sons of the aristocracy for a military career from as young as ten. In July 1917 the barracks hosted the First Congress of Workers' and Soldiers' Deputies, in which only ten percent of the deputies were Bolsheviks. When a speaker claimed that there wasn't a party willing to take control, Lenin shouted from the floor, "There is! No party has the right to refuse power and our party does not refuse it. It is ready to assume power at any time." On the embankment is a **monument** like a giant open book, inscribed with an ode by Pushkin, which was erected for the city's three hundredth anniversary.

The Menshikov Palace

Just beyond you'll see the gabled, golden-yellow **Menshikov Palace** (Menshikovskiy dvorets; 10.30am–4.30pm, closed Mon; R200). When built in the early eighteenth century, it was the first residence on Vasilevskiy Island and the finest in the city, surpassing even Peter's Summer Palace – the tsar didn't mind as he preferred to entertain at Menshikov's. By renting an audio-guide (R100, with R500 deposit) you need not join the guided tour in Russian (every half-hour), and admission to the palace is free with a combined ticket from the Hermitage (see p.117).

Though not as sumptuous as the later Imperial palaces, its Petrine-era decor is nonetheless striking. On the first floor is the **kitchen** and a **dining room** hung with tapestries. Objects on display include period costumes, plus a lathe and tools belonging to Peter. The statues in the Italianate hallway were imported from Europe by Menshikov in his desire to emulate Peter, and the stairway bears their entwined monograms. The rooms upstairs commence with the **secretary's quarters**, featuring plans of Kraków, Leyden and Utrecht, followed by two rooms faced with white and blue Dutch tiles. Family portraits and seascapes hang on silk ribbons, as was the fashion at that time.

The room containing the German four-poster bed and brass foot-warmer served as a bedroom for the sister of Menshikov's wife, while Menshikov's sumptuous **Walnut Study** is decorated with gilded pilasters and a portrait of Peter. Still more alien to Russian traditions was the **Grand Hall**, with its full-length mirrors that reflected couples dancing together (prior to Peter's time, mirrors were anathematized by the Orthodox Church and men and women rarely socialized together at all). Notice the cherubs holding the candelabras and the unique organ-clock, made in England. In Menshikov's day, the hall once hosted a "Dwarves' Wedding" for Peter's entertainment, with little tables in the centre set with miniature cutlery. Though the dwarves' drunken cavorting provoked hilarity, Menshikov regretted that they couldn't fire a tiny cannon specially cast for the occasion, for fear of disturbing his only son, lying ill elsewhere in the palace. The boy expired that night (which didn't stop Menshikov from celebrating his own name day soon afterwards) and the dwarf bride later died in childbirth – marriages between dwarves were subsequently forbidden.

Across the landing are the re-created rooms of his wife Dariya, filled with statues and Oriental porcelain – a prelude to the magnificent dining room and **master bedroom** decorated with Chinese silk wall hangings (not original to the palace), and Menshikov's **Blue Study**, with its ceiling fresco of Peter as Mars.

Of all the adventurers that staked their fortunes on Peter the Great, none was closer to the tsar than **Alexander Menshikov** (1673–1729). Humbly born (it was rumoured that he sold pies on the streets of Moscow as a child), Menshikov accompanied Peter on his Grand Tour of Europe in 1697. The tsar liked his enthusiasm for shipbuilding and carousing, and his artful blend of servility, familiarity and impertinence: soon they were inseparable.

After helping to crush the Streltsy Mutiny, Menshikov was showered with favours and responsibilities, becoming commandant of Shlisselburg and the first governor of St Petersburg. In 1703 he acquired a mistress whom Peter subsequently took a fancy to, married in secret and later crowned as Catherine I. The tsar addressed Menshikov as *Mein Herz* (My Heart), causing speculation that their relationship went "beyond honourable affection". In any event, Peter tolerated Menshikov's vanity (exemplified by the latter's palace at Oranienbaum, which was grander than the tsar's) and persistent corruption, forgiving speculations that others would have paid for with their lives.

As Peter lay dying, Menshikov engineered Catherine's succession as empress, then had all charges pending against himself annulled. He continued to flourish until Catherine's demise in 1727 when – accused of treason and fined 500,000 rubles – he was exiled to his Ukrainian estates by the boy-tsar Peter II, but allowed to depart with sixty wagonloads of valuables. Less than a year later, however, Menshikov and his family were stripped of all their possessions and exiled to the remote Siberian village of Berezovka, where they died in poverty. A famous painting by Repin depicts Menshikov brooding over his fate in a hut, with his family huddled together for warmth.

On the **embankment** outside the palace you can see the granite abutments of the old St Isaac's Bridge of 1729 – the first bridge across the Neva. The abutments supported a wooden pontoon bridge that had to be dismantled annually before the river froze and rebuilt after it thawed; it finally burned down in 1916.

On to the Krasin

Beyond the Menshikov Palace the sights are fewer and further apart, so you might wish to ride bus #1 or minibus #359 all the way to the **Krasin** (1.2km); other transport turns inland at 8-ya & 9-ya liniya. But it's tempting to walk the initial stretch anyway, as there are several sights within a few blocks. Beyond Kadetskaya ulitsa is a shady park centred on the **Rumyantsev Obelisk**, commemorating the victories of Marshal Rumyantsev in the Russo-Turkish War of 1768–74. Hewn from black granite and surmounted by a gilded orb and eagle, it was erected on Marsovo pole in 1799 and transferred to its present site in 1818.

The Academy of Arts and Pavlov Museum

Beyond the park stands the **Academy of Arts** (Akademiya khudozhestv), a huge mustard-coloured edifice built between 1764 and 1788 by Vallin de la Mothe and Alexander Kokoroniv. Set up by Empress Elizabeth and Catherine the Great, the academy trained artists, commissioned art that extolled the state and censored work deemed to be subversive. Students joined at the age of 6 and graduated at 21. Its roll call of graduates includes the architects Zakharov and Voronikhin; Pyotr Klodt, sculptor of the horses on Anichkov most; and the painters Karl Bryullov and Ilya Repin. A **museum** (11am–6pm, closed Mon & Tues; R200; ⓦwww.nimrah.com.ru) displays student work by such masters and architectural models and drawings of buildings in St Petersburg and abroad, including Sir Charles Barry's original designs for the Houses of Parliament in London. Diploma work by today's students is exhibited each September in the grandiose Parade Hall.

Two serene-faced Egyptian **sphinxes** ennoble the embankment outside. Carved from Aswan granite and weighing 32 tonnes apiece, they were found at Luxor in the 1820s and brought to Russia in 1832. A hieroglyphic inscription identifies them with Pharaoh Amunhotep III (1417–1379 BC), "Son of Ra, ruler of Thebes, the builder of monuments rising to the sky like four pillars holding up the vault of the heavens".

Further along the embankment, the **Academicians' House** (Dom akademikov), on the corner of 6–7-ya liniya, has provided accommodation for numerous scientists and linguists, as attested by the plaques on its facade. The Nobel Prize-winning physiologist Ivan Pavlov lived from 1918 until his death in 1936 in apartment #11. Now the **Pavlov Memorial Museum** (Mon–Fri 11am–5pm; free), it features a laboratory where the aged scientist could work without going to the Institute of Experimental Medicine (p.184), and a study filled with personal effects. To learn about Pavlov's life and work, come on Tuesday, when English-speaking Mr Lapovok can conduct a **tour** (ⓣ323 72 34; free, but donations welcome; best to ring in advance).

Along naberezhnaya Leytenanta Shmidta

The first permanent stone bridge across the Neva was erected near the Academicians' House between 1842 and 1850. Rebuilt and widened in the 1930s, it is universally known as **most Leytenanta Shmidta**, despite recently reverting to its Tsarist title, **Blagoveshenskiy most**. Its old namesake, Lieutenant Pyotr Schmidt, famously led a mutiny aboard the cruiser *Ochakov* during the 1905 Revolution, signalling to the tsar, "I assume command of the Southern Fleet. Schmidt."

In 1918 his name was also bestowed on the embankment beyond – naberezhnaya Leytenanta Shmidta – where he attended the **Higher Naval College** at no. 17. The oldest in Russia, the college boasts of having trained Rimsky-Korsakov (before he decided to study music) and several admirals. Whereas tributes are also paid to Nakhimov (the defender of Sebastopol), Lazarev (co-leader of the 1820 Antarctic expedition) and Krusenstern (who circumnavigated the globe in 1803–6), a veil is drawn over Rozhestvensky (who led the Baltic Fleet to disaster at Tsushima Bay) and Kolchak (a White Army leader during the Civil War). A plaque recalls that Lenin delivered a lecture here in May 1917 entitled "War and Revolution". Two hundred metres further west is the Neo-Russian-style **Church of the Nativity**, whose gilded domes lend a dash of glamour to the waterfront, lined with freighters piled high with timber. From there it's another 500m to the Mining Institute and the icebreaker *Krasin*, at 21-ya liniya.

The **Mining Institute** was founded by Peter the Great to locate new sources of minerals throughout the empire – particularly in the Urals – and train mining engineers and industrialists; graduates were ranked alongside officers and civil servants in the Petrine table of ranks. Even today, students and staff wear a black uniform with badges of rank, like the military and naval colleges. Statues of Pluto abducting Proserpine and Hercules struggling with Antaeus flank the institute's Classical portico, while Peter's boast that "Our Russian state abounds in riches more than many other lands and is blessed with metals and minerals" is borne out by the Geological Museum on Sredniy prospekt (see p.163).

The Krasin

Moored across the road from the Mining Institute is the **icebreaker Krasin**, a veteran of the Soviet "Conquest of the North" granted honourable retirement as a floating museum (April–Nov 10am–6pm, Dec–March 11am–5pm, closed Tues & the last Wed of each month; R200). The ship was built for the tsar's navy at Newcastle-upon-Tyne in England, but impounded after the Revolution until Trade Commissar Krasin ransomed it back in 1921. Renamed in his honour, the icebreaker was at the forefront of the international mission to rescue Nobile's trans-polar airship expedition of 1928, and saved a passenger steamer on its way back to Norway. In World War II, it was the only Soviet ship in the historic PQ-15 convoy to Murmansk, which ran the gauntlet of Nazi U-boats in order to deliver vital war materials to the USSR. Picking up Gagarin on his splashdown from orbit was another highpoint before the *Krasin* was relegated to other duties by the advent of nuclear-powered icebreakers in the 1960s. Its spacious bridge contains both antique and modern instruments, and the lifeboats and machinery on deck are likewise a mix of old and new. The extreme environment in which it operated obliged the *Krasin* to carry two giant spanners weighing 300 kilos, for replacing the propeller shaft.

Bolshoy prospekt and the Sea Terminal

Vasilevskiy Island's main axis is the broad **Bolshoy prospekt**, running 3.5km from Kadetskaya ulitsa southwest to the Sea Terminal. Lined with a mixture of Art Nouveau town houses and 1960s apartment buildings, the nicest stretch is around the Vasileostrov Market, within walking distance of Vasileostrovskaya metro station – or you can get there by trolleybus #10, which runs the length of Bolshoy prospekt to the Sea Terminal.

At its Kadetskaya end, the Neoclassical Lutheran **Church of St Catherine** (Tserkov Svyatoy Yekateriny) once catered to the island's German community before being turned into a recording studio for the Soviet music company Melodiya. One block west, the apartment building at Bolshoy prospekt 6 was the scene of a well-known tragedy of the Blockade. Between December 1941 and May 1942, 11-year-old **Tanya Savicheva** recorded in her diary the deaths of her sister, grandmother, brother, uncles and mother – all from starvation. Tanya herself was evacuated, but died the following year. Her diary is now in the Rumyantsev Mansion (see p.107).

Further on stands the eighteenth-century **Andreevskiy dvor**, a smaller version of the Gostiniy dvor on Nevskiy prospekt, adjacent to the **Vasileostrovskiy Market** (see p.374). On the other side of the prospekt, the elegant pink-and-white **Cathedral of St Andrew** (Andreevskiy sobor) – containing a gilded Baroque iconostasis – graces a pedestrianized stretch of **6-ya & 7-ya liniya**, where rollerbladers glide past street furniture. Beyond this, the only sights are a modest **Lenin statue** in the park near 16-ya & 17-ya liniya, and an old **fire station** whose tower was used for fire spotting before the advent of telephones.

▲ Streetlife on 6-ya & 7-ya liniya

The Sea Terminal and the submarine

Flanked by decaying factories, the prospekt culminates in the **Sea Terminal** on ploshchad Morskoy slavy (Marine Glory Square). This long moribund locality is awaiting its resurrection with the completion of a vast new Sea Terminal to harbour the gigantic cruise ships that currently moor further up the Neva, and meanwhile depends on trade fairs at **LenExpo**, whose blue-glass exhibition halls are flanked by a range of prefabricated *kottedzhi* for Russians seeking to buy a new holiday home outside the city.

Just beyond LenExpo a mothballed **submarine**, the *D-2 Narodovolets* (11am–5pm; closed Mon, Tues & the last Thurs of each month; R300), is surreally perched above an inlet. The only survivor of six "Dekabrist" class diesel submarines constructed at the Leningrad Baltic shipyards in the late 1920s, it saw active service with the Northern Fleet in the Bering and White seas and with the Baltic Fleet during World War II, before its retirement in 1956, and its eventual opening as a branch of the Naval Museum. The mandatory guided **tour** in Russian is conducted by an ex-nuclear submariner who – if the Cold War had turned hot – might have been instrumental in wiping your hometown off the map.

The sub is divided into seven sections by watertight doors, each with a brass plaque showing the alphabet in Morse code, so that crewmen could communicate by knocking if the intercom system failed. The **interior** is cramped, but much less than it would have been for the 53-man crew, as many of the bunk beds have been removed. You can't help marvelling at the minuscule size of the captain's cabin, the cook's galley, and the toilet cubicle – not to mention the torpedo room, where crewmen slept alongside the torpedoes. In the event of an emergency, they were obliged to escape by swimming out through the torpedo tubes.

Another, later submarine of the S-189 class is set to open as a private museum in 2008, somewhere on Vasilevskiy Island.

Sredniy prospekt

The island's "Middle Avenue", **Sredniy prospekt**, runs parallel to, and 500m north of, Bolshoy prospekt. Starting from Vasileostrovskaya metro on the corner of 6-ya & 7-ya liniya, you can walk a few blocks northeast to find the Orthodox **Church of St Catherine**, whose lofty dome and belfry are a local landmark. In the other direction, a shabby apartment block (no. 64) on the corner of 16-ya & 17-ya liniya was where **Stalin** lived after returning from his Siberian exile in 1917. Though other comrades cold-shouldered him, an old friend from the Caucasus, Sergei Alliluev, offered him lodgings; he later married Alliluev's daughter, Nadezhda, who committed suicide in 1932.

Just past 18-ya & 19-ya liniya, the **Geological Museum** (Geologicheskiy muzey; Mon–Fri 10am–5pm; free), at no. 74, exhibits a dazzling variety of minerals including a 1.5-metre-long crystal from the Altay Mountains, a chunk of Urals malachite weighing 1054kg, a copper nugget from Kazakhstan weighing 842kg, and an iron meteorite that landed in Siberia. The show is stolen by a vast **mosaic map** of the Soviet Union studded with diamonds, rubies and other gems from 500 sites, which required the work of over 700 people and won a prize at the Paris Exposition in 1937; it later stood in the St George's Hall of the Hermitage for 34 years. Two Soviet crests made of gems glitter below, while the **fossils** section features the skulls of a prehistoric mammoth and rhinoceros, and a dinosaur skeleton.

From here, it's possible to catch minibus #41 or #42 further down the prospekt to view the **Kirov Palace of Culture**. Intended to be the largest institution of its kind in the USSR when it was built in the 1930s, this colossal, crumbling edifice epitomizes the ugly side of Soviet Constructivism. It was designed by Noy Trotsky, who also built the Bolshoy dom HQ of the secret police and the postwar House of Soviets; had he been related to his famous namesake, he might have ended up inside the Bolshoy dom instead of building it.

Vasilevskiy Island

Streets and squares

Birzhevaya liniya	Биржевая линия
Bolshoy prospekt	Большой проспект
Kamskaya ul.	Камская ул.
ul. Korablestroiteley	ул. Кораблестроителей
nab. Leytenanta Shmidta	наб. Лейтенанта Шмидта
nab. Makarova	наб. Макарова
Maliy prospekt	Малый проспект
Mendeleevskaya liniya	Менделеевская линия
Nalichnaya ul.	Наличная ул.
Sezdovskaya liniya	Съездовская линия
Sredniy prospekt	Средний проспект
Universitetskaya nab.	Университетская наб.

Metro stations

Primorskaya	Приморская
Vasileostrovskaya	Василеостровская

Buildings and museums

Academy of Arts	Академия художеств
Academy of Sciences	Академия наук
Doll Museum	Кукол музей
Geological Museum	Геологический музей
Literary Museum	Литературный музей
Menshikov Palace	Меншиковский дворец
Museum of Anthropology and Ethnography	музей Антропологии и тнографии
Naval Museum	Военно-Морской музей
St Petersburg University	Университет Санкт-Петербурга
Submarine D-2 Narodovolets	Подводная лодка Д-2 Народоволец
Zoological Museum	Зоологический музей

The Primorskiy district

Beyond the factories north of Sredniy is **Maliy prospekt**, or "Small Avenue" – in fact it's just as long, but grimmer in parts, and the only real reason to visit is the Doll Museum and the Smolensk cemeteries on the banks of the River Smolenka. Beyond them, the vast "New Maritime" or **Primorskiy** district sprawls as far as **Decembrists' Island** (ostrov Dekabristov), the burial place of the executed participants of the Decembrist uprising. Gigantic blocks of high-rises and avenues that become gale-strength wind tunnels in winter make this area a shock for guests at the *Park Inn Pribaltiyskaya Hotel*, but residents cherish their view over the Gulf of Finland, and the sea wall is an impressive sight, especially when it catches the sun around dusk. Decaying shipyards, streets named after shipbuilders (Korablestroiteley), skippers (Shkiperskiy), bosuns (Botsmanskaya) and midshipmen (Michmanskaya), and the presence of the Arctic and Antarctic Institute, are all reminders of the district's maritime heritage.

The Doll Museum and Smolensk cemeteries

From Vasileostrovskaya metro, minibus #249A runs to the **Doll Museum** (muzey Kukol; Ⓦhttp://russiandolls.ru; Tues–Sun 11am–6pm; R100), entered via the garden behind Kamskaya ulitsa 8. The museum is a retail outlet for contemporary doll-makers, who can be seen working upstairs. The 1500-odd specimens on display mostly represent royalty, characters from fairy tales or figures in folk costumes from around the world, but there are also some contemporary archetypes – punks, drunks and fashion victims – and a roomful of (fairly innocuous) erotic dolls. On Sundays visitors have a chance to make a doll for themselves.

Minibuses terminate just beyond the museum, in sight of the gates of the **Smolensk Orthodox Cemetery** (Smolenskoe pravoslavnoe kladbishche), named after the Smolensk Field where the revolutionary Karakizov was hanged in 1866 for his attempt on the life of Alexander II, and another unsuccessful assassin, Solovyov, was executed in 1879. Many of the graves are smothered with vegetation, but the church inside the walls, and the **Chapel of Kseniya Peterburgskaya** (the city's favourite saint) – where believers kiss the walls – are both carefully tended. Since the cemetery was reserved for Orthodox believers, the dead of other denominations (mainly foreigners) were relegated to the smaller **Smolensk Lutheran Cemetery** (Smolenskoe lyuteranskoe kladbishche), north of the River Smolenka. The graves of a few British families are here, including those of the Scot Charles Baird, owner of a St Petersburg iron foundry, which made the neo-Gothic memorials on his family graves. Admiral Samuel Greig, the hero of Chesma, and his son, Admiral Alexis Greig, who led the defence of Sebastopol against the British during the Crimean War, are both buried in a family plot beside the central alley. To reach the Lutheran Cemetery, cross the bridge diagonally across the road from the minibus terminus.

5

The Peter and Paul Fortress, Petrograd Side and the Kirov Islands

Across the Neva from the Winter Palace, on the small Zayachiy (Hare) Island, lies the **Peter and Paul Fortress** – the historic kernel of St Petersburg, dating from 1703. This doughty fortress-cum-prison has had many of its buildings converted into museums and features a splendid cathedral containing the tombs of the Romanov monarchs. From the fortress, you can walk across to the urban mass of the **Petrograd Side** (Petrogradskaya storona), a mainly residential area crammed with Style Moderne buildings, which owes its character to a housing boom that started in the 1890s: by 1913 its population had risen from 75,000 to 250,000, after the newly completed Troitskiy most (Trinity Bridge) made the Petrograd Side accessible from the city centre. Most visitors make a beeline for the landmark **Mosque** and the **Museum of Russian Political History**, before heading east along the embankment to the legendary cruiser **Aurora**, which fired the opening shots of the Bolshevik Revolution. Inland, statues and **memorial apartments** commemorate famous people who lived or worked on the Petrograd Side, such as the opera singer Chaliapin and the Party leader Kirov.

More appealing still are the wooded **Kirov Islands**, northwest of the Petrograd Side, bounded by the Malaya, Srednaya and Bolshaya Nevka rivers. Long favoured as recreational areas, **Kamenniy** and **Yelagin** islands feature a host of picturesque *dachas* and official residences, as well as two summer **palaces**, while **Krestovskiy** Island is a popular place to relax at weekends in the summer.

Approaches

Many of the prime sights – including the fortress – are within five to ten minutes' walk of **Gorkovskaya metro** station (on the Moskovsko–Petrogradskaya line). A slower but more scenic way of getting to the fortress from the centre is by **tram #3** across Troitskiy most, from the northeast corner of Marsovo pole. Coming **on foot** from Vasilevskiy Island takes fifteen minutes – en route you'll cross **Birzhevoy most** (Exchange Bridge), from where there are fine views of the fortress. Walking across the handsome, but busy, 526-metre-long **Troitskiy most** isn't especially enjoyable on account of the traffic and (in summer) the heat, although it does provide a superb view of the Strelka. For a week or so each spring, when the fish are rising, the bridge is packed with fishermen day and night.

The Peter and Paul Fortress

Built to secure Russia's hold on the Neva delta, the **Peter and Paul Fortress** (Petropavlovskaya krepost) anticipated the foundation of St Petersburg by a year – and may even have suggested to Peter the Great the idea of building a city here. During 1703, forced labourers (who perished in their thousands) toiled from dawn to dusk on Zayachiy Island, constructing the fortress in just seven months. The crude earthworks were subsequently replaced by brick walls under the direction of Trezzini and later faced with granite slabs.

The fortress's role as a **prison** dates back to 1718, when Peter the Great's son, Alexei, was tortured to death within its walls. The "Secret House", built to contain Empress Anna's opponents, was subsequently used by Nicholas I to hold the Decembrists; later generations of revolutionaries were incarcerated in the Trubetskoy Bastion. The fortress was known as the "Russian Bastille", its grim reputation surpassed only by that of the Shlisselburg fortress on Lake Ladoga (see p.294), until the Soviet era made other prisons synonymous with even greater terror.

Incongruously, the island on which the fortress is sited is now a magnet for sunbathers, who pack its grassy spaces and pebbly **beaches** in summer, and for the hardy folk known as *morzhi* (walruses), who break holes in the ice in winter to swim in temperatures of -20°C. You can even take a **helicopter** ride over the fortress and the Neva basin; it takes off and lands on the grass behind the Golovkin Bastion (see p.42 for details).

While the island is permanently accessible and admission to the fortress is free, the Peter and Vasilevskiy gates are closed at 10pm and the museums within keep regular **opening hours** (11am–6pm, Tues till 5pm; closed Wed & the last Tues of each month), other than the cathedral (May–Sept daily 10am–7pm). You can buy an individual **ticket** for each at the ticket offices in the Ioannovskiy ravelin (daily 10am–6pm) or the Boat House (daily 10am–7.45pm), but if you're planning to visit more than just a few it's cheaper to buy a combined ticket (R250). The former office doubles as an **information** centre where you can get a free map and booklet or an **audio-guide** (R250, with ID as security) – though the latter is hardly necessary since they've improved the captioning in English.

Gates, ramparts and bastions

Approached by a footbridge on the east side of the fortress, the grey-and-white **Ivan Gate** (Ioannovskie vorota) penetrates an outlying rampart, the **Ioannovskiy ravelin**, which was added to in 1740 and once separated from the fortress by a moat. It's the last place you'd associate with space travel, but

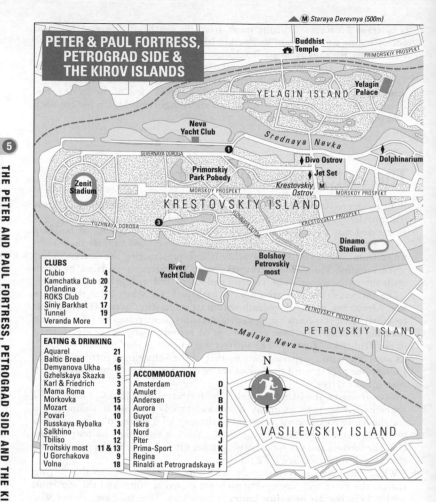

Staraya Derevnya (500m)

PETER & PAUL FORTRESS, PETROGRAD SIDE & THE KIROV ISLANDS

Buddhist Temple

PRIMORSKIY PROSPEKT

YELAGIN ISLAND

Yelagin Palace

Neva Yacht Club

Srednaya Nevka

SEVERNAYA DOROGA

Divo Ostrov

Dolphinarium

Primorskiy Park Pobedy

Jet Set

Zenit Stadium

MORSKOY PROSPEKT

Krestovskiy Ostrov

MORSKOY PROSPEKT

KRESTOVSKIY ISLAND

YUZHNAYA DOROGA

YUZHNAYA ULITSA

KRESTOVSKIY PROSPEKT

Dinamo Stadium

Bolshoy Petrovskiy most

River Yacht Club

CLUBS

Clubio	4
Kamchatka Club	20
Orlandina	2
ROKS Club	7
Siniy Barkhat	17
Tunnel	19
Veranda More	1

PETROVSKIY PROSPEKT

Malaya Neva

PETROVSKIY ISLAND

EATING & DRINKING

Aquarel	21
Baltic Bread	6
Demyanova Ukha	16
Gzhelskaya Skazka	5
Karl & Friedrich	3
Mama Roma	8
Morkovka	15
Mozart	14
Povari	10
Russkaya Rybalka	3
Salkhino	14
Tbiliso	12
Troitskiy most	11 & 13
U Gorchakova	9
Volna	18

ACCOMMODATION

Amsterdam	D
Amulet	I
Andersen	B
Aurora	H
Guyot	C
Iskra	G
Nord	A
Piter	J
Prima-Sport	K
Regina	E
Rinaldi at Petrogradskaya	F

N

VASILEVSKIY ISLAND

once accommodated a research lab where the first Soviet liquid-fuelled rocket was developed in 1932–33. Today, the **Cosmonautics Museum** – off to the right as you come through the Ivan Gate – traces the history of the Soviet space programme from *Sputnik* to the *Mir* orbital station, paying homage to the visionary scientist Konstantin Tsiolkovsky. Decades before the first satellite was put into orbit, he suggested multistage rockets to overcome the adverse mass/fuel ratio. The exhibits include rocket engines, spacesuits and a Soyuz-16 re-entry capsule of the kind that Soviet cosmonauts returned to Earth in.

Straight ahead is the main entrance to the fortress proper, the **Peter Gate** (Petrovskie vorota). Designed by Trezzini as a triumphal arch, the gate sports the double-headed eagle of the Romanovs and a wooden bas-relief depicting St Peter casting down the evil magus Simon. Lest anyone should miss the allegory of his defeat of Charles XII of Sweden, Tsar Peter appears among the onlookers, wearing a laurel wreath, while his martial and legislative vir-

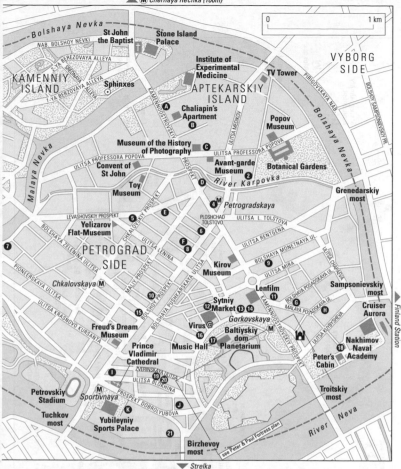

tues are personified by statues of Minerva (left) and Bellona (right), in niches flanking the gate.

Each of the six fortress bastions is named after the individual responsible for its construction, namely the *Gosudar* (Sovereign) and his cohorts Menshikov, Naryshkin, Zotov, Golovkin and Trubetskoy. The **Gosudarev Bastion** was the site of Tsarevich Alexei's death (see box, p.171) and contains a **Secret Passage** (10am–7pm, Tues till 5pm) which brings you out near a glass-encased **Rolls Royce** Silver Ghost of the kind that the Bolshevik leadership used in the 1920s, and a ramp up to a rooftop walkway with a **panoramic view of the Neva basin** (daily 10am–10pm; Oct–April till 8pm; R60), which runs from the Gosudarev to the **Naryshkin Bastion**. Beside the latter are two **cannons** which fire a single shot every day at noon (a custom originating in the eighteenth century, when few people had clocks), and a 24-gun salute at 8pm on January 27 to mark the anniversary of the breaking of the Siege of Leningrad; a shot fired at any other time signifies a flood warning. In 1917, the Bolsheviks agreed that a red lamp

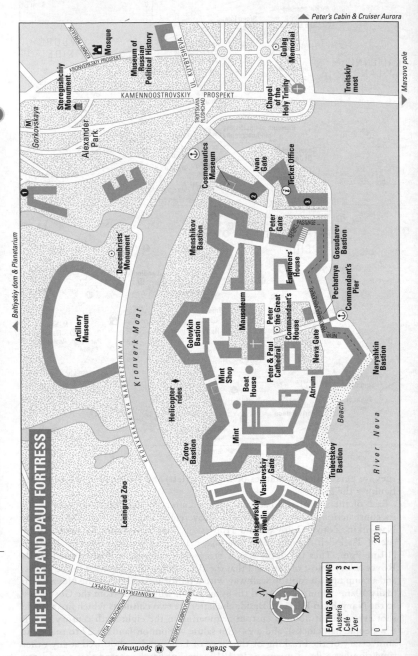

THE PETER AND PAUL FORTRESS

▲ Peter's Cabin & Cruiser Aurora

▲ Baltiyskiy dom & Planetarium

KONNY PEREULOK

Mosque

Sieregushchiy Monument

KRONVERKSKIY PROSPEKT

Museum of Russian Political History

Gulag Memorial

KAMENNOOSTROVSKIY PROSPEKT

UL. KUYBYSHEVA

Chapel of the Holy Trinity

Troitskiy most

M Gorkovskaya

Alexander Park

TROITSKAYA PLOSHCHAD

▲ Marsovo pole

Cosmonautics Museum

Ivan Gate

Ticket Office

Decembrists' Monument

Menshikov Bastion

Peter Gate

SECRET PASSAGE

Engineers' House

Gosudarev Bastion

Artillery Museum

Kronverk Moat

Golovkin Bastion

Mausoleum

Peter the Great

Commandant's House

Pechatnya

Commandant's Pier

KRONVERKSKAYA NABEREZHNAYA

Helicopter rides

Mint Shop

Boat House

Peter & Paul Cathedral

Neva Gate

Atrium

PAN
KRONNAYA

Naryshkin Bastion

Leningrad Zoo

Mint

Zotov Bastion

Beach

River Neva

Vasilevskiy Gate

Trubetskov Bastion

Alekseevskiy ravelin

200 m

N

KRONVERKSKIY PROSPEKT

PROSPEKT DOBROLYUBOVA

ULITSA YABLOCHKOVA

0

EATING & DRINKING

Austeria	3
Café	2
Zver	1

M Sportivnaya

Strelka ▼

M Sportivnaya

5

The death of Tsarevich Alexei

The life and death of **Tsarevich Alexei** (1690–1718) is a shameful indictment of his father, Peter the Great. Since childhood, the timid Alexei took after his mother, Evdokiya, whom Peter got rid of by confining her to a convent when Alexei was eight. His pious temperament was the antithesis of Peter's; his hostility to foreign innovations another cause of paternal contempt and filial bitterness. Ordered to live abroad, he communicated with clerics opposed to Peter's policies, promising to repeal them once he became tsar. When Peter told him to mend his ways or be "cut off like a gangrenous growth", Alexei offered to renounce the succession and become a monk, but then claimed sanctuary in Austria. Inveigled back home, he foolishly disclosed accomplice "conspirators" who, under torture, identified others. The tsar then confined Alexei in the Gosudarev Bastion and ordered his **interrogation** to begin with 25 lashes.

Although subsequent "confessions" convinced Peter that Alexei's death was essential to preserve his own security, he tried to shift the decision on to the clergy (who equivocated) and a secular court (which endorsed the verdict). Two days later the tsarevich was dead – officially from apoplexy, though rumour suggested that Peter himself beat Alexei to death. Ironically, the demise of the tsar's younger son, Peter Petrovich, a year later left Alexei's infant (also called Peter) the only surviving male of the Romanov line.

hung on the bastion's flagpole would be the signal for the *Aurora* to open fire on the Winter Palace, but when the moment arrived, the only lantern available wasn't red and couldn't be attached to the flagpole – so they had to wave it instead.

Between these two bastions is the **Neva Gate**, whose arch lists the "catastrophic" floods that have befallen St Petersburg (less serious ones being too numerous to count). The glorious view across the Neva would have afforded little consolation to prisoners leaving from the **Commandant's Pier**, bound for the gallows at Shlisselburg. Today it's used by **boats** making tours of the city's rivers and canals (40–90min; R200–350), while the **beach** between the Naryshkin and Trubetskoy bastions hosts a **festival of sand sculptures** and a **volleyball tournament** in the summer months (see p.47).

The Neva Curtain Wall beside the gate contains an exhibition on the **History of the Peter and Paul Fortress**, with models and plans detailing the evolution of its fortifications, and the **Pechatnya**, which demonstrates the art of printing with the help of working vintage presses and displays finds from excavations within the fortress, including the remains of an original cell.

The Engineers' House and the Commandant's House

Behind the Neva Curtain Wall, the **Engineers' House** (Inzhenerniy dom) contains a child-friendly exhibition called the **Street of Time**, where kids can peer into replica domestic interiors from the eighteenth to the twentieth centuries, try writing with nib-ink pens, and smell the scent that women wore in the 1950s.

For a grown-up exposition of the **History of St Petersburg**, don't miss the **Commandant's House** (Ober-Komendantskiy dom), whose occupant's responsibilities included the security of the prisoners in the fortress, and informing the tsar when the Neva became navigable by bringing him a goblet of river water.

The lower floor displays prehistoric and medieval artefacts from the vicinity of St Petersburg, whose subsequent social history is covered upstairs. Among the highlights are a reconstruction of the room where the Decembrists were interrogated in the presence of Nicholas I (who personally dictated their sentences); an animated video of the erection of the Alexander Column (see p.76); and a doll's-house-style model of a 1900s apartment block, with its upstairs-downstairs stratification of luxury and poverty.

In the park between the two buildings is a **statue of Peter the Great that only slightly** exaggerates his extraordinary physique. His spidery legs and fingers, massive torso and rounded shoulders are offset by a tiny head that uncannily resembles that of Marlon Brando as Don Corleone in *The Godfather*. Its sculptor, Mikhail Shemiakin, was exiled to America in the 1970s and presented the statue as a gift to the country of his birth in 1990.

The Peter and Paul Cathedral

The golden spire of the **Peter and Paul Cathedral** (Petropavlovskiy sobor) signals defiance from the heart of the fortress. "A hundred cannon, impregnable bastions and a garrison of 3000 men defend the place, which can be desecrated only when all St Petersburg lies in ruins", asserted *Murray's Handbook* in 1849. As a token of Peter's intent, a wooden church was erected on this site as soon as the fortress had been founded, replaced by a stone cathedral once the defences were upgraded. Looking far more Protestant than Orthodox, the cathedral's soaring spire was a visible assertion of Peter's wish that the skyline of St Petersburg be the antithesis of Moscow's.

The **belfry** was erected first and the ground was allowed time to settle beneath its weight before work commenced on the remainder of the cathedral, which was completed by Trezzini in 1733, long after Peter had died. At the nearby Boat House you can buy a ticket (R100) for a scheduled **tour** (daily May–Sept, as advertised) to the belfry's third level to inspect its carillon of 15 bells and **view** the city from a height of 43 metres – roughly one third of the way to the top of its gilded **spire**, which was deliberately made higher than the Ivan the Great Bell Tower in the Kremlin and remained the tallest structure in the city until the construction of the Television Tower. When the angel on top was blown askew in 1830, a roofer volunteered to climb up and fix it, using only a rope and hook, a feat later repeated by professional alpinists who camouflaged the spire to save it from the Luftwaffe in World War II and have restored it twice since then. During the last **restoration**, they found a note left to "future climbers" by those who restored it forty years earlier, complaining of low pay and time pressures. Continuing the tradition, the restorers of 1997 left their own message in a bottle for the next team to scale the spire.

The cathedral's **interior** is painted in tutti-frutti colours, with marbled columns ascending to a canopy of gilded acanthus leaves. Within the nave are the **tombs of the Romanov monarchs** from Peter the Great onwards (excluding Peter II and Ivan VI), whose coffins repose in vaults beneath the sarcophagi. All have marble slabs (designed in 1865, when the cathedral underwent major restoration) except for those of Alexander II and his wife, whose sarcophagi of Altay jasper and Urals rhodonite took seventeen years to carve and polish. The tombs of Peter (the only one sporting a bust of its occupant) and Catherine the Great are situated to the right of the iconostasis. Alexei is said to have been interred under the aisle, where "he would always be trampled on", but was actually buried in the family vault below Peter's sarcophagus.

On July 17, 1998, the remains of Russia's last royal family were finally laid to rest here, exactly eighty years after they were killed by the Bolsheviks in

Yekaterinburg. Located in the separate chapel of St Catherine the Martyr, off to the right as you enter the nave, the tomb officially contains the remains of Nicholas II, Alexandra and three of their five children, plus four servants who were shot with the family – although the Church remains sufficiently doubtful of their authenticity that, despite canonizing them as Orthodox martyrs, it has not declared the remains to be holy relics.

As a devout Slavophile, Nicholas would have probably preferred to end up in Moscow's Cathedral of the Archangel (where rulers before Peter the Great were buried) rather than in St Petersburg – which he detested – in a cathedral that looks more Protestant than Orthodox. The only icons to be found are on the **iconostasis**, dominated by the archangels Gabriel and Michael and framed by what look like stage curtains, with tassels and cords, all in wood. This lovely piece of work was designed by Ivan Zarudny and carved by Moscow craftsmen in the early eighteenth century. Nearby stand a pulpit (unusual in an Orthodox church) and a dais where the tsar's throne once stood.

In late June and early August, you can hear the cathedral's carillon during the **Soul of the Bells festival** (tickets R250; details on Ⓦwww.spbmuseum.ru).

The Grand Ducal Mausoleum

A side door leads from the nave into a corridor on the left lined with plans of the fortress and photos showing how it was protected in wartime and restored afterwards. In a room off the corridor is an exhibition on the **History of the Mint**, containing Tsarist and Soviet coins and medals. Look out for the medallion bearing Stalin's head and the replicas of the plaques that were sent to the Moon, Mars and Venus by Soviet spacecraft, all of which were manufactured in the fortress mint. You may also encounter a man dressed as Peter the Great, operating the hand-turned lathe with which he crafted many objects now exhibited in the Hermitage.

At the end of the corridor is the lofty **Grand Ducal Mausoleum** (Usypalnitsa), built for Nicholas II's cousins in the early twentieth century as the cathedral itself became too crowded for the burial of any but the closest relatives. The principal tomb belongs to Archduke Vladimir, the heir to the Romanov dynasty, who was born in Belgium after the Revolution and died in Miami – his remains were returned to Russia in 1992.

The Boat House and Mint

Opposite the cathedral exit stands a **Boat House** (Botniy dom) topped by a nymph with an oar, symbolizing navigation. The Neoclassical pavilion was erected in the 1760s to preserve the small boat in which Peter made his first sailing trips on the River Yauza, outside Moscow. That original boat now reposes in the Naval Museum (see p.154), while the Boat House contains an exact replica.

In the surrounding courtyard in January 1919, the Bolsheviks shot four grand dukes and other hostages taken at the start of the Red Terror the previous year, and whom they had sentenced to death in retaliation for the murders of Rosa Luxemburg and Karl Liebknicht in Berlin. When Maxim Gorky pleaded for the life of Grand Duke – and liberal historian – Nikolai Mikhailovich, Lenin replied: "The Revolution does not need historians."

Across the courtyard looms the **Mint** (Monetniy dvor), a yellow-and-white edifice dating from the 1790s, before which time coins were minted in the Naryshkin and Trubetskoy bastions. The world's first lever press for coining money was devised here in 1811 and the Mint continued to produce coins till the end of the Soviet era; its output is now limited to military medals and commemorative medallions, copies of which are sold in a **shop** (daily 10am–6pm) across the yard. The Mint itself is closed to the public.

The Trubetskoy Bastion

The **Trubetskoy Bastion** at the southwestern corner of the fortress was converted into a jail under the supposedly liberal Alexander II, and soon became the regime's main interrogation centre and a prison for generations of revolutionaries. First to be confined here were members of the Zemlya i Volya (Land and Liberty) and Narodnaya Volya (People's Will) organizations – the latter group responsible for killing Alexander himself. Next came would-be assassins such as Lenin's brother, Alexander Ulyanov; Socialist Revolutionary bombers such as Vera Figner; and Gorky and Trotsky in 1905. After the February Revolution, Tsarist ministers were imprisoned here, to be followed by members of the Provisional Government once the Bolsheviks took over. In a final turn of the wheel of repression, radical Kronstadt sailors were kept here before being shot or sent to the Gulag in 1921. The following year the prison became a museum to the infamies of Tsarism, omitting any mention of its role after the Revolution, a period that is still glossed over by tour guides.

The Prison Museum

Selective coverage aside, the **Prison Museum** fails to convey the full horror of conditions in Tsarist times. The accessible **cells** are stark and gloomy, but far worse ones existed within the ramparts, where the perpetual damp and cold made tuberculosis inevitable. Prisoners were never allowed to see each other - and rarely glimpsed their jailers. Some were denied visitors and reading material for decades; many went mad after a few years and several committed suicide. The **corridors** were carpeted to deaden sound, enabling the "Specials" to creep up and spy through the door slits without warning. This green-cloaked elite were the only guards allowed to see the prisoners' faces or give them orders (conversations were forbidden), but they were never told the prisoners' names in order to prevent word of their identity reaching the outside world. Inmates managed to communicate amongst themselves by knocking out messages in the "prisoners' alphabet" – a kind of Morse code – but anyone caught doing so risked being confined to an unlit punishment cell and fed on bread and water. Once a fortnight, each inmate was escorted to the **bathhouse** in the courtyard for a solitary scrub and exercise, but the corridor windows were painted over so that none might see who was exercising. A monument and a quotation from the anarchist Prince Kropotkin (a former prisoner) commemorate the prisoners' sufferings.

The Alekseevskiy ravelin

Leaving the fortress by its western **Vasilevskiy Gate**, you'll notice a U-shaped outbuilding marking the site of the now-demolished **Alekseevskiy ravelin**. Built by Empress Anna in the 1730s, this bastion contained the first long-term prison in the fortress, its maximum security "**Secret House**" reserved for those who fell foul of the intrigues of Anna's favourite, Count Biron. Here, too, Catherine the Great confined Alexander Radishchev for criticizing Russia's backwardness in his *Journey from St Petersburg to Moscow* (1780); and Alexander I imprisoned Ivan Pososhkov, author of *On Poverty and On Wealth*, who died in captivity in 1826. Under Nicholas I, the prison held many of the Decembrists and the Petrashevsky Circle (including Dostoyevsky); Bakunin (whose grovelling *Confessions* saved him from the gallows); and Chernyshevsky (who wrote *What is to be Done?* whilst in prison). The fortress commandant used to approach the critic Belinsky on the street and ask, "What's taking you so long? We've got a nice warm cell waiting for you."

Around the Kronverk

Apart from its own ramparts and bastions, the Peter and Paul Fortress was further protected by a system of outlying ramparts called the **Kronverk** – a name later given both to the moat separating Zayachiy Island from the "mainland" Petrograd Side and to the avenue encircling a park containing the zoo and the Artillery Museum. Over summer the waterway is busy with **motorboats** doing a 90-minute tour of the Neva and city canals (R300) and sometimes even powerboat races.

The zoo

Northwest of the fortress across the moat and entered from Kronverkskiy prospekt, the **Leningrad Zoo** (May–Oct daily 10am–7pm; Nov–April Tues–Sun 10am–5pm; R250), as it is still named, dates back to 1865 – and looks its age. Long starved of funds, it has had to send its elephants and hippopotamuses to other zoos, and the modernization of its enclosures has been endlessly delayed. The zoo is proud, though, of having bred polar bears and giraffes since the 1930s, and of the fact that none of the animals was eaten during the Blockade. It currently holds nearly 2000 animals and birds; those from warm climes spend the winter in heated quarters and can be seen only when they move into summer enclosures. Winter is the time to see polar foxes, sables, martens, elk and deer with their fur at its thickest. **Information** on events appears on ⓦwww.spbzoo.ru (in Russian only).

The Artillery Museum

Across the Kronverk Moat from the fortress's Golovkin Bastion stands a vast horseshoe-shaped arsenal, fronted by tanks and missile launchers. Inside, the **Artillery Museum** (Voenno-Istoricheskiy muzey Artillerii; 11am–5pm; closed Mon & Tues & last Thurs of each month; R300) has displays of artillery from medieval times until 1812, along with the pike that Peter carried as a foot soldier, an ornate coach from which Kutuzov harangued his troops at Borodino, and regimental banners (one depicting the Last Judgement, with foreigners writhing in hell).

Amongst the World War II exhibits upstairs are a "Katyusha" multiple-rocket launcher, a huge mural of trench warfare at Stalingrad and a diorama of Kursk, where the biggest tank battle in history took place. Next comes a corridor devoted to Signals, climaxing with a model of the ruined Reichstag and a gleeful painting of Hitler committing suicide.

Back downstairs in Hall 10 you'll find **Lenin's armoured car**, *Enemy of Capital*, on which he rode in triumph from Finland Station on April 3, 1917, making speeches from its gun turret. Nearby is a model of a dog with a mine strapped to its back; the Soviets trained them to run underneath Nazi tanks. Also notice the snazzy Red Army **uniforms** of the Civil War era, designed by a Futurist artist later killed in the purges.

On a grassy knoll just to the east of the arsenal, the **Decembrists' Monument** marks the spot where five leaders of the revolt were executed in July 1826. The gallows were erected in front of the condemned officers, who were ritually degraded by having their epaulettes torn off and their swords broken before hoods and nooses were slipped over their heads. The ropes broke for three of the men, but rather than being reprieved (as was customary in such cases), fresh ropes were brought and the hangings were repeated. The obelisk is inscribed with a poem by Pushkin, dedicated to a friend sentenced to a term of hard labour in Siberia for his part in the revolt.

The Alexander Park and Kronverkskiy prospekt

The **Alexander Park** (Aleksandrovskiy park) is a playground for Petersburgers of all ages. Laid out in 1845, it starts near the fortress as a shady romantic meander past a grotto and the **Steregushchiy Monument**, which commemorates the sailors who scuttled their torpedo boat rather than let it be captured at Tsushima Bay in 1904. Gorkovskaya metro station marks an abrupt change of mood, with teenagers hanging out drinking and playing guitars, and families heading for the **funfair** deeper into the park (see p.380). Behind this rises an enfilade of Stalinist edifices, composed of the **Baltiyskiy dom** venue for arts festivals (p.367), a **Planetarium** (p.380) and **Music Hall** (p.368). Nearby are several **all-night bars** where you can eat *shashlyk*, drink and people-watch.

Its perimeter is marked by **Kronverkskiy prospekt**, an arc that intersects with Kamennoostrovskiy prospekt near Gorkovskaya metro and ends at Troitskaya ploshchad (see the following sections). **Tram #40** runs along it en route to and from Krestovskiy Island. Until 1993 Kronverkskiy prospekt bore the name of the writer **Maxim Gorky**, who lived at no. 23 from 1914 to 1921. The dropping of his name reflects Gorky's diminished status in the post-Communist era, although Gorkovskaya metro station isn't likely to change its name.

Around Troitskaya ploshchad

A leafy expanse framed by main roads, **Troitskaya ploshchad** is named after the Trinity Cathedral (Troitskiy sobor) that once formed the nucleus of the Petrograd Side's merchants' quarter. In 1905, the square was the scene of one of the worst massacres of "Bloody Sunday", when 48 people were killed and scores wounded after soldiers opened fire on demonstrators approaching Troitskiy most to the south. In 1917, Trotsky harangued crowds here before the October Revolution, and in Soviet times it was called Revolution Square. Its present appearance dates from the mid-1930s, when the cathedral was demolished to make way for a gigantic Stalinist administrative building and the square was turned into a park. More recently it was solemnized by a bell-shaped **Chapel of the Holy Trinity**, faced with red and brown granite, and a **memorial to victims of the Gulag** made of a boulder from the Solovetskiy penal colony. Dozens gather here to remember the dead on the Day of Victims of the Repression (October 30).

The Museum of Russian Political History

Behind the park on ulitsa Kuybysheva stands the former **house of Mathilda Kshesinskaya** (1872–1971), Russia's prima ballerina before the Revolution, whose affair with Crown Prince Nicholas (later Nicholas II) was once the talk of St Petersburg. Gorky sniffed that she earned it "with leg-shaking and arm-swinging", but it was probably a gift from Nicholas. The house is the epitome of Style Moderne elegance, trimmed with tiles and floral tracery. In March 1917 the Bolsheviks commandeered it as their headquarters: Lenin came here straight from the Finland Station, addressed crowds from its balcony and mapped out Party strategy here until July 1917, when a Provisional Government clampdown sent the Bolsheviks into hiding and the house was wrecked by loyalist troops.

After restoration, it was an obvious home for the Museum of the Great October Socialist Revolution, which moved here from the Winter Palace in 1957. In 1991 this was recast as the **Museum of Russian Political History** (10am–6pm; closed Thurs; R150). If you're interested in the subject or in Kshesinskaya (to whom a section is devoted), it's worth booking a **tour** in English (T233 70 52; R700 for up to seven people). However, you don't need any knowledge of Russian to enjoy the snazzy Soviet porcelain decorated with slogans, and caricatures of Lenin from newspapers that would be shut down once the Bolsheviks seized power – nor to feel a frisson in the second-floor quarters used by the Central Committee in July 1917, including the room occupied by Lenin. For those who do speak Russian, information on lectures and other events appears on Ⓦwww.polithistory.ru.

The Mosque

Further north looms St Peterburg's **Mosque** (Mechet; daily 10am–7pm), an exotic feature of the skyline. Its ovoid cupola (copied from the Gur Emir Mausoleum of Tamerlane in Samarkand) and the fluted finials of its twin minarets are faced with brilliant azure tiles, greatly enlivening the severe facade, whose Islamic identity is otherwise apparent only from the arabesques around its portals. Constructed between 1910 and 1914 at the behest of the last emir of Bukhara to serve the city's Sunni Muslim community, the mosque has finally emerged from over a decade's restoration, and its interior looks stunning. However, the *jamat* (congregation) is wary of strangers – understandably, given racist attacks and FSB surveillance – so admission is by no means certain. Women must wear a headscarf and long, baggy clothing; men long trousers and a collared shirt; removing shoes (and having clean feet) are mandatory.

East along the embankment

Walking east from Troitskaya ploshchad along the Neva embankment, it's hard to imagine this area as the bustling port it was in Petersburg's infancy until you encounter **Peter's Cabin** (Domik Petra; 10am–5pm; closed Tues & the last Mon of each month; R200) in a park halfway along. Encased in a brick structure and preserved as a museum, it was built by army carpenters in May 1703 to enable the tsar to keep a close eye on the construction of the Peter and Paul Fortress over that summer. Its rough-hewn pine logs are painted to resemble bricks and there are only three rooms. Peter slept on a cot in what doubles as the hallway; the dining room and study look ready for his return. The museum includes his frock coat and pipe and a rowing boat that he made himself, as well as engravings of St Petersburg, Kronstadt and the battles of Hangö and Poltava.

On the embankment opposite the cabin are two **Shih Tza** (lion) statues of the kind that flank temples in China and Mongolia, brought here in 1907 from Kirin in Manchuria, where the Tsarist Empire was contending with Japan for control of the region's mineral resources.

Further along stands the imposing **residential block** of the Nakhimov Academy, a mustard-coloured building topped by Red Guard and Sailor statues and decorated with Futurist panels featuring tractors, banners and ships' prows. At the far end of the embankment, the large fountain outside the peacock-blue, Baroque-style **Nakhimov Naval Academy** is yet another popular spot for newlyweds to be photographed. As a college for aspiring naval officers, the academy's title and setting could hardly be more inspirational: named after the "hero of Sebastopol" in the Crimean War, the academy is bang opposite the warship whose cannon heralded the October Revolution.

The Aurora

The cruiser **Aurora** (kreyser *Avrora;* 10.30am–4pm; closed Mon & Fri; free; Ⓦwww.aurora.org.ru) looks comically miscast for its dramatic role in history, resembling an outsized model battleship complete with smart paint job and gleaming brasswork. Having long been an icon of the Revolution, it is now mocked by some as "the world's deadliest weapon – with one shot, it ruined the country for 75 years". Yet few would wish to see the *Aurora* removed, or credit the rumour that the original was secretly replaced by a less decrepit sister ship when it went for a refit in the 1970s. As a historical relic, it inspires affection across the political spectrum.

The 6731-tonne cruiser experienced a baptism of fire at Tsushima Bay, when it was one of the few ships in the Baltic Fleet that avoided being sunk by the Japanese. Docked in Petrograd for an overhaul just before the February Revolution, the *Aurora* was the first ship in the fleet to side with the Bolsheviks. On the night of October 25 it moved downriver and dropped anchor by what is now Blagoveshenskiy most. At 9.40pm its forward cannon fired the historic blank shot at the Winter Palace – the first in a sporadic barrage that accompanied the "storming" of the building (see p.75). After the palace had fallen, the ship's radio was used to broadcast Lenin's address, "To the Citizens of Russia!", proclaiming the victory of the proletarian revolution.

In the early 1920s the *Aurora* was converted into a training ship. With the advent of war in 1941, its heavy guns were removed for use on the Leningrad front, and the outmoded vessel was holed by the Luftwaffe and scuttled near Oranienbaum. Raised in peacetime, it was moored in its present location and declared a national monument in 1948, later opening as a museum – though it still belongs to the Russian navy and has a crew of eighty, fifty of whom live aboard the ship.

During **visiting** hours you can wander round on deck and tour a historical exhibition in four wardrooms below. One preserves hammocks, tables and ration lists for the crew in Tsarist times (though the room would have been far more crowded then). Elsewhere, note the portrait of the ship's captain framed by armoured plate with a hole left by the shell that killed him at Tsushima; and a model of the schooner *Granma* (dubbed "the little sister of the *Aurora*"), which landed Fidel Castro and his *compañeros* in Cuba, in the room full of "fraternal gifts" from the days when international socialism meant something.

To see more, book an English-language **tour** (☎230 84 40; R200) of the engine rooms and ammunition magazines on the lower armoured deck. Before the Revolution sailors held subversive meetings in the engine room since officers seldom went there, as it was noisy and dirty. Its three steam engines still work. Disappointingly, you barely glimpse the officers' wardroom where the whole crew now eats, never mind the captain's cabin, containing a piano from the Imperial yacht *Shtandart*.

Kamennoostrovskiy prospekt

Architecturally and socially, Petrograd Side takes its tone from **Kamennoostrovskiy prospekt** (Stone Island Avenue), an urban canyon that peters out as it approaches its namesake island. Many Petersburgers feel this avenue is at least as elegant as Nevskiy prospekt, with as much to offer in the way of shops, cinemas, restaurants and fine architecture – especially around **Avstriyskaya ploshchad** (Austrian Square), at the intersection with ulitsa Mira. The initial stretch from the Neva to the intersection is flanked by imposing villas and apartment buildings, built early last century when the avenue suddenly became a fashionable place to live. The area beyond Petrogradskaya metro station is less notable from an architectural viewpoint, but Aptekarskiy Island, at the prospekt's northern end, has several attractions. As the avenue is 2.5km long and it's 1km between metro stations, **minibus** #46 can save you a lot of footslogging between sights.

Around Gorkovskaya metro

Across the road from the Gorky statue at the lower end of the avenue stands a U-shaped **Style Moderne apartment building** (nos. 1–3) designed by Fyodor Lidval in 1902. The upper storeys are decorated with stucco shingles and fairy-tale beasts, while bizarre fish flank the main entrance, whose lobby contains stained-glass panels. At no. 5 is the beige-and-white former **villa of Count Sergei Witte**, the great industrialist of Tsarist Russia, who started as a railway clerk and rose through the civil service to become Finance Minister. Though successful in unleashing capitalist energies within Russia, his hopes for political liberalization were dashed by Nicholas II, who also ignored his advice on foreign affairs: after Witte was assassinated by an ultra-rightist in 1915, Nicholas remarked that his death was "a great relief" and "a sign from God".

Lenfilm Studios

Another token of talent spurned lies 100m up the avenue, in a Doric-porticoed, yellow building (nos. 10–12), set back behind a garden on the left. Founded in 1918 on the site of the Akvarium Summer Theatre (where the Lumière brothers had presented the first motion picture in Russia on May 4, 1896), the **Lenfilm Studios** were once the glory of the Soviet cinema industry, producing up to fifteen movies a year. During its golden era, between the wars, most of the films, such as the Vasilev brothers' *Chapaev*, focused on ordinary people making history. In the postwar period, Lenfilm gained international kudos with Kozintsev's adaptations of the works of Shakespeare, but many directors had their best work suppressed for years, until perestroika changed everything. The subsequent release of over two hundred banned films, followed by a new wave of *chernukha*, or "black" movies, dealing with Stalin and the camps, rapidly sated the public who had discovered the delights of home videos and Hollywood in the meantime.

The loss of its audience and state subsidies caused a crisis of confidence within Lenfilm, which was eventually broken up into smaller studios. These continue to produce highly acclaimed films such as Andrei Balabanov's *The Castle*, *Brother*, and *Of Freaks and Men*, but more income is now generated by Lenfilm studio crews working on foreign productions such as the romantic drama *Onegin*, or producing TV soaps and cop shows for the home market. Lenfilm's **website** (Ⓦwww.lenfilm.ru) features news of ongoing projects, press releases and a cine-bibliography of all the films ever made there, in Russian and English.

The Kirov Museum

Of more tangible historic interest is the hulking building at nos. 26–28, built shortly before World War I by the fashionable architect Leonty Benois. After the Revolution its luxury apartments were assigned to Bolshevik officials, including the head of the Leningrad Party organization, **Sergei Kirov**, who lived in a flat on the fourth floor until his murder in 1934. The **Kirov Museum** (muzey S.M. Kirova; 11am–6pm; closed Wed & the last Tues of each month; R70) presents him as an intellectual with a library of over 20,000 volumes; a man of the people who loved hunting and fishing (his rods and shotgun are displayed); and a leader whose study had a hotline to the Kremlin and a polar bearskin rug. Behind the desk hangs a picture of Stalin, who almost certainly organized Kirov's assassination as a pretext for unleashing the Great Terror (see p.201). In the hall you can see the uniform Kirov was wearing when he was shot at the Smolniy; the cap has a bloodstained hole at the back and the tunic is torn where medics tried to re-start his heart.

Tickets sold on the fifth floor include admission to a **Museum of Childhood** during Stalin's time, exhibiting posters, uniforms, banners and other artefacts related to the Komsomol and Young Pioneers – organizations to which every Soviet child belonged until the demise of Communism – accompanied by recordings of Komsomol songs and other patriotic ditties. Don't miss it.

From ploshchad Tolstovo to the River Karpovka

A couple of blocks further north, the avenue meets Bolshoy prospekt at **ploshchad Tolstovo** (Tolstoy Square), flanked by a building known as the **Tower House**, encrusted with balconies and crenellations copied from English, Scottish and Andalusian castles. Shortly afterwards you'll see the Soviet-era **Dom Mod** (Fashion House) beside **Petrogradskaya** metro station, opposite the **Lensoviet Palace of Culture**, which is now home to an array of slot machines, but also offers film screenings and jazz and pop gigs (see "Clubs and live venues", p.359). Further on is a large house (nos. 44–46), with central arches, built just before World War I for the last emir of Bukhara who, in 1920, fled from the Red Army to Afghanistan, "dropping favourite dancing boy after favourite dancing boy" to impede his pursuers.

▲ The Tower House

Beyond the house, the **River Karpovka** flows westwards from the Bolshaya to the Malaya Nevka, separating "mainland" Petrograd Side from Aptekarskiy Island, which is reached by the Pioneers' Bridge. Before crossing over, consider a detour along the shabby "mainland" side to see the Convent of St John or visit the Toy Museum on ulitsa Vsevoloda.

The six-room **Toy Museum** (muzey Igrushky; 11am–6pm; closed Mon & the last Tues of each month; R250) is a private venture, aimed at aficionados and collectors rather than kids seeking a hands-on experience. Their contemporary art-toys made of papier-mâché, logs or ceramics, wouldn't survive a day in a playroom. Vintage items include a Wilhelmine doll's house and a Bauhaus model from the 1950s made in Germany; an Edwardian tea service; and Russian, Asian and African rag dolls in folk costumes. Some Nigerian toys made from recycled tin cans, and work by contemporary local toy-makers such as Olga Gepp and Irina Sulmeneva, bring the exhibition up to date.

Round the corner, a red-granite plaque on the wall of naberezhnaya reki Karpovki 32 commemorates a crucial **meeting of the Central Committee**, on October 10, 1917. Held in the apartment of a Menshevik whose Bolshevik wife knew that he would be out for the night, its members arrived in disguise (Lenin shaved off his beard and wore a wig which kept slipping off his head), and only twelve out of twenty-one came. Lenin persuaded everyone but Zinoviev and Kamenev to endorse his proposal that preparations for a coup should begin (though no firm date was set). Thus the most momentous decision in the history of the Party was reached by a minority of the Central Committee, and recorded by Lenin in pencil on sheets torn from a child's notebook.

Of more interest to Lenin buffs is the **Yelizarov Flat-Museum** (muzey-kvartira Yelizarovykh; 10am–6pm, closed Tues & Sat; R200), in the former home of Lenin's sister, Anna, and her husband, Mark Yelizarov. The apartment (#24) is in a Style Moderne building shaped like a cruise liner and embodies the height of bourgeois comfort in 1913. You can see the bathtub and telephone that Lenin used during his clandestine stays there; it shows the laxity of the Tsarist police that the Yelizarovs were never punished for hiding him, whereas the Bolsheviks arrested relatives of "enemies of the people" as a matter of course. The flat is on the corner of ulitsa Lenina and Gazovaya ulitsa, 10–15 minutes' walk from the Toy Museum or Chkalovskaya metro.

Aptekarskiy Island

A leafier extension of the Petrograd Side, the Apothecary's or **Aptekarskiy Island** takes its name from the medicinal kitchen gardens established beside the Karpovka in 1713. Directly across the river from the Toy Museum, the **Convent of St John** (Ioannovskiy monastir) is an unmistakable landmark, crowned by Byzantine domes and gilded crosses. It was built to house the tomb of Father John of Kronstadt (1829–1908) – a famous preacher, anti-Semite and friend of the Imperial family – but in the 1920s the convent's nuns were sent to the Gulag, and it was seventy years before it was re-established. Its church is open for public services, but the rest of the complex is closed to outsiders. Elsewhere, the island is a mix of leafy suburbia and post-industrial dereliction, with a clutch of museums attesting to its former popularity with scientists, artists and other members of the intelligentsia.

Ulitsa Professora Popova

At ulitsa Professora Popova 10, you'll find a charming wooden house that was once the home of the painters Mikhail Matyushin and his wife Elena Guro, and is now the **Avant-garde Museum** (muzey Avantgard; 11am–5pm, closed Wed; R70), enshrining their friendship with Futurists such as Mayakovsky and Malevich, personal effects and Primitivist artworks. In a park across the road, the **Museum of the History of Photography** (muzey Istorii Fotografii; 11am–5pm, closed Sun & Mon & throughout July & Aug; R70) focuses on the work of Karl Bulla, who roamed St Petersburg capturing scenes from everyday life in the decade before the Revolution (see p.69).

The street itself is named after the scientist Alexander Popov whom Russians credit with inventing the radio (see p.106). Popov spent his final years refining his invention and exploring the electromagnetic spectrum at the **Electro-Technical Institute** at no. 5, where his abode-cum-laboratory is preserved as the **Popov Museum** (muzey A.S. Popova; Mon–Fri 11am–4pm; free). Dr Who would feel at home amongst its Edwardian jumble, but the scientific import of its contents and Popov's work will be lost on visitors who can't speak Russian.

Across the road lies the erstwhile Imperial **Botanical Gardens** (Botanicheskiy sad; daily 10am–9pm; R30), an institution that was so deeply Sovietized in Communist times that it remains mired in the Era of Stagnation even today. It's a shame, for the **greenhouses** (11am–5pm; closed Fri) contain over 6500 species and cultivated varieties, from as far away as Brazil and Ethiopia – but rather than being able to wander freely you must join a forty-minute **tour** (R70) of either the tropical (open year-round), subtropical (mid-Sept to June) or water plants (mid-May to Sept) sections – buy a ticket at the main entrance. The tropical bit is notable for its huge banana plant – one of several specimens sporting a medal ribbon for having survived the Blockade – and a torch-thistle cactus dubbed the "Queen of the Night", which flowers for one night in June (the place stays open till 4am for the event). While the greenhouses are falling apart, the rest of the gardens are a mess of bulldozer tracks and prefab shacks, as a refurbishment plan that nobody seems to understand limps on year after year.

The Television Tower

A few blocks up Aptekarskiy prospekt, St Petersburg's red-and-white **Television Tower** (Telebashnya; 10am–6pm; closed Mon) was the first in the Soviet Union – built by an all-female construction crew in 1962 – and is the city's tallest structure, surpassing the spire of the Peter and Paul Cathedral. Originally 316m in height, it stood one metre higher than the Eiffel Tower until 1985, when a new, shorter antenna was installed, reducing its height by six metres. On windy days the tower sways almost two metres. Unless access is suspended for security reasons, you can enjoy a fabulous **view of the city** from its observation platform, 191m up. Individual or group tours can be arranged at any time (☎234 78 87), or you can just turn up for the tour at 2pm on Saturday. Tours cost R150 per person if you're in a group of ten or more.

Chaliapin's apartment

The penultimate side street off Kamennoostrovskiy prospekt once resounded to the legendary bass-baritone of opera singer **Fyodor Chaliapin** (1873–1938), who settled at ul. Graftio 2b in 1914, having made his fortune in classic rags-to-riches fashion. Born in Kazan, he worked as a stevedore before joining a dance troupe at the age of 17. He made his operatic debut in the provinces and eventually landed a job at the Mariinskiy Theatre, but won renown in Moscow, first at the Private Opera and then as a soloist at the Bolshoy, notably in the title roles of *Boris Godunov* and *Ivan the Terrible*. Together with Nijinsky, he was the star of Diaghilev's Ballets Russes, which took Paris by storm in 1909. Initially enthused by the Revolution, Chaliapin was later branded an "enemy of the people" after he refused to return from a tour and settled in Paris (where Diaghilev already lived). It was over fifty years before his old apartment (by then a communal flat shared by thirteen families) became a museum, and even then it was coyly called the "Opera Section" of the Theatre

Museum until Raisa Gorbacheva had Chaliapin's Soviet citizenship posthumously restored.

The **memorial apartment** (noon–6pm; closed Mon & Tues & the last Fri of each month; R100) is stuffed with antique furniture safeguarded by Chaliapin's chef (to whom he left the flat), and possessions donated by his daughters. A famous life-size portrait by Kustodiev portrays Chaliapin as the personification of Russian folk culture (represented by a winter fair), while another full-length picture of him as an ancient demigod cracked two hours before his daughter Martha heard of his death in Paris. As befits a sybarite, his dining room is vast, with a table that could expand to seat thirty, and a divan to match; the antique weapons on the walls were used by Chaliapin during stage performances, while the amazing dragon-chair was a gift from Gorky. You can hear extracts from his most popular songs in what used to be the kitchen; chamber music **concerts** are held there from October to mid-April (Sat & Sun 4pm; ☏234 10 56 for details and bookings).

Pavlov and the Institute of Experimental Medicine

The name of the last street on the right – Akademika Pavlova – honours the scientist **Ivan Pavlov** (1849–1936), who worked for almost five decades at the **Institute of Experimental Medicine**. The son of a village priest, Pavlov was educated at a seminary, then studied science at St Petersburg University and medicine at the Military Academy, before becoming director of the institute in 1891. From investigating blood circulation he turned to digestion, developing the theory of conditioned reflexes through his experiments on **dogs**. Awarded the Nobel Prize for medicine in 1904, he continued his research after the Revolution with the support of Lenin, who considered Pavlov's work a major contribution to materialist philosophy. Ironically, Pavlov was a devout Christian, but the regime turned a blind eye to his role as a church elder, awarding him a pension of twenty thousand rubles on his 85th birthday, when Pavlov had a statue of a dog erected in the institute's forecourt.

Bolshoy prospekt

The Petrograd Side's other main axis is **Bolshoy prospekt**, an apartment-lined thoroughfare that meets Kamennoostrovskiy prospekt at ploshchad Tolstovo. Overground public **transport** follows a one-way system – down Bolshoy prospekt towards Vasilevskiy Island, and up Bolshaya Pushkarskaya ulitsa to Kamennoostrovskiy prospekt – but most places of interest are within walking distance of Sportivnaya metro.

The moated **Petrovskiy Stadium** (formerly the Lenin Stadium) has been the home ground of St Petersburg's premier football club **Zenit** for over a decade but now faces relegation (see box on p.188), while the nearby **Yubileyniy Sports Palace** hosts ice hockey and volleyball matches, and pop concerts. An iconic plaque on the wall facing the stadium recalls the 1991 killing of pop singer **Igor Talkov** by the bodyguard of another performer after a row over who should play first – Talkov's fans blamed a "Jewish conspiracy" and the far right adopted him as a martyr to their cause.

Further inland rise the proud belfry and onion domes of the **Prince Vladimir Cathedral** (Knyaz Vladimirskiy sobor; daily 9am–8pm), an eighteenth-century fusion of Baroque and Classical styles by Trezzini and Rinaldi. One of the icons in its possession has been identified as the miraculous *Our Lady of Kazan* that disappeared from the Kazan Cathedral ninety years earlier (see p.72). In pre-revolutionary times, the cathedral lent its name to the Vladimir Military Academy, whose cadets resisted the Bolshevik takeover until the building was bombarded. It subsequently became an academy for "Red Cadets", after whom the street on which it stood was renamed ulitsa Krasnovo Kursanty.

Freud's Dream Museum

In the Institute of Psychoanalysis at Bolshoy pr. 18a, **Freud's Dream Museum** (Tues & Sun noon–5pm; R30; ⊛www.freud.ru) is a brave attempt to represent ten of the dreams on which Freud based his theory of the unconscious mind, using spectrally lit images and objects such as suitcases or antique figurines. This voyage into Freud's psyche is the brainchild of Viktor Mazin, who has forged links with Freud museums and psychoanalytical circles in Vienna, London, Helsinki and Los Angeles, and collaborated on exhibitions with local artists such as Olga Torebluts and Andrei Khlobistyn. Mazin is keen to stress the contribution made to psychoanalysis by Russian émigrés, and that – contrary to Western belief – the subject was never banned in the Soviet Union, but merely pushed to the margins of psychiatry. If Lenin had been succeeded by Trotsky rather than Stalin, psychoanalysis might have become an aspect of Soviet ideology, for Trotsky saw it as a new dimension of dialectical materialism – unlike the paranoid Georgian, who would surely have liquidated anyone who tried to get him on the couch.

The Kirov Islands

The verdant archipelago lying off the northern flank of Petrograd Side is officially known as the **Kirov Islands** (Kirovskie ostrova), but everyone in St Petersburg uses the islands' traditional individual names: **Kamenniy**, **Yelagin** and **Krestovskiy**. Originally bestowed upon Imperial favourites, the islands soon became a summer residence for the wealthy and a place of enjoyment for all. This is still the case, except that most of the villas now belong to either institutions or foreigners, with telltale Mercedes parked along the quiet avenues and birch groves. Kamenniy and Yelagin islands harbour elegant palaces – one of which you can go inside – while Krestovskiy Island is a popular hang-out in the summer.

The only drawback is the size of the archipelago: seeing it all entails more walking around than is pleasant unless you use what limited **public transport** is available.

Approaches

The eastern end of **Kamenniy Island** is accessible by bus #46 from Kamennoostrovskiy prospekt or a ten-minute walk from Chernaya Rechka metro on the Vyborg Side. To reach Krestovskiy Island, ride the metro to Krestovskiy Ostrov station or tram #17 or #40 from Chkalovskaya metro. **Yelagin Island** can be reached on foot from Primorskiy prospekt, 2.5km west of Chernaya Rechka metro (bus #211 along the embankment), taking in the Buddhist Temple en route (see p.228).

Kamenniy Island

Reached from Aptekarskiy Island by the handsome Kamennoostrovskiy most, adorned with bronze reliefs and granite obelisks, Stone or **Kamenniy Island** lends its name to the Petrograd Side's main avenue, as well as the palace on the island's eastern tip. Built in 1776 by Catherine the Great for her son Paul, the **Stone Island Palace** (Kamennoostrovskiy dvorets) was inherited by Alexander I, who oversaw the war against Napoleon from here. Appropriately, it is now a military sanatorium, so you'll have to peer through the fence to see the columned portico with steps leading down to the water, or the English-style garden, but you can get a good view of the ornate frontage from the north. Nearer the main road stands the **Church of St John the Baptist**, a Gothic edifice by Yuri Felten, who probably also supervised the construction of the palace. Turned into a sports hall after World War II, it was re-established as a church in 1990 and recently restored as an exhibition hall.

Kamenniy Island was originally owned by Peter the Great's chancellor, Gavril Golovkin, and later passed into the hands of Alexei Bestuzhev-Ryumin, who brought thousands of serfs from Ukraine to drain the land and build embankments. By the end of the eighteenth century several aristocrats had built summer homes here, and in 1832 Russia's oldest noble family commissioned the architect Shustov to build the **Dolgorukov mansion** at naberezhnaya Maloy Nevki 11, 200m west of Kamennoostrovskiy most. A little further along the embankment are two green-and-gold Grecian **sphinxes** – the leafy area around them makes a nice spot to sit and rest a while. For a longer walk, carry on to **Peter's oak** at the crossroads near the bridge to Krestovskiy Island – reputedly planted by Peter the Great, and now a stump protected by bollards – and follow the road on towards Yelagin Island to see the wooden **Kamenniy Island Theatre**, dating back to the 1820s. Elsewhere, you'll see many new luxury condo blocks belonging to rich locals.

Yelagin Island

Known before the Revolution as the "Garden of Joy", on account of the orgiastic revels which took place here during the White Nights, **Yelagin Island** (daily: summer 6am–11pm; winter 10am–8pm) is nowadays designated a "Central Park of Culture and Rest", with traffic banned from its roads, and access from the archipelago and the mainland limited to wooden footbridges. Though largely deserted on working days, its serpentine lakes and shady clearings attract families at weekends and hordes of revellers on public holidays. During summer, people go **swimming** in the sedge-lake beside the main path, rent **rowing boats** or take a **cruise on the Gulf of Finland** from the landing stage on the southern side of the island. If a two-kilometre walk doesn't faze you, there's the lure of watching the sun set over the Gulf of Finland from a spit of land at the extreme west of the island dignified by granite lions. Alternatively, you can visit the Yelagin Palace, stroll across the island and cross a bridge to reach the Buddhist Temple on the Vyborg Side (see p.228).

The Yelagin Palace

The island's chief attraction is the **Yelagin Palace** (Yelaginskiy dvorets; 10am–5pm; closed Mon & Tues; R200; ⓦwww.elaginpark.spb.ru, in Russian only), commissioned by Alexander I for his mother, Maria Fyodorovna, in 1817. Eyebrows must have been raised when the job was given to Carlo Rossi, as rumour had it that he was fathered by Tsar Paul, Maria Fyodorovna's late husband, and

Alexander I embraced his destiny with reluctance, being fated to spend his reign (1801–25) dealing with Napoleon when all he really wanted to do was live quietly in Switzerland as a private citizen. Though his armies would make Russia a major European power, Alexander learned to detest the military during childhood, when he was made to drill in all weathers by his father, Paul – accounting for his morbid horror of rain. Shy, short-sighted, and partially lame and deaf, he felt happier in the company of his grandmother, Catherine the Great, who shared his interest in free-thinking.

When Alexander consented to a coup against his father, he didn't anticipate that Paul would be murdered (p.89). Upon hearing the news, Alexander burst into tears, until one of the conspirators snapped, "Stop playing the child and go rule!" As tsar, his sense of guilt possibly inclined him to propose a utopian European confederation at the Congress of Vienna, whose failure turned him towards religion. In the winter of 1825, he reportedly died whilst on holiday in the Crimea, but wild rumours of trickery impelled his mother to travel to Moscow and privately view the body in its coffin (which, against normal practice, had already been sealed). Despite a positive identification, tales persisted that she had lied and Alexander had faked his own death to become a hermit and atone for Paul's murder. Many legends identified him with a holy man called Dmitri of Siberia, and it is also said that a curious descendant opened Alexander's coffin, to find only sand and medals inside.

thus was Alexander's half-brother. Whatever the truth, Rossi proved equal to his first major commission, creating an ensemble of graceful Neoclassical buildings, decorated with the utmost refinement.

The palace has half a dozen exquisite **state rooms** linked by bronze-inlaid mahogany doors. Their superb parquet floors and moulded friezes are offset by motifs in *grisaille* – a technique using different shades of one or two colours to suggest bas-relief – while the **Grand Hall** boasts a plethora of statuary and *trompe l'oeil*. A sumptuous walnut study-ensemble on loan from the *Grand Hotel Europe* is the highlight of the palace's collection of antique furniture, besides which there are permanent exhibitions of Style Moderne **samovars** and **artistic glass** from the Soviet era. Temporary art exhibitions on the upper floor require a separate ticket.

Krestovskiy Island

The 420-hectare **Krestovskiy Island** was the last of the Kirov Islands to be developed, since its swampy terrain and proximity to the slums of the Petrograd Side deterred the wealthy from building here. Before the Imperial Yacht Club based itself on the island, Krestovskiy was "peculiarly the resort of the lower classes", as *Murray's Handbook* observed in 1849. Following the Revolution, entertainments became organized and sports facilities were developed, starting in 1925 with the **Dinamo Stadium** beside the Malaya Nevka and culminating in the Kirov Stadium – a Stalinist super-bowl now being replaced by the new Zenit Stadium. Aside from football, people come to enjoy the **Divo Ostrov Amusement Park** (Tues–Fri 11am–8pm, Sat & Sun 11am–9pm; ⓦwww.divo-ostrov.ru) near Krestovskiy Ostrov metro, or to eat, drink and flirt at the lakeside *Russkaya rybalka* and *Karl & Friedrich* **restaurants** (see p.352) on Friday and Saturday nights in summer, when a miniature "**tram**" conveys customers from Krestovskiy Ostrov metro to the restaurants.

Primorskiy Park Pobedy and the Zenit Stadium

The **Primorskiy Park Pobedy** (Seaside Park of Victory) recalls the autumn of 1945, when one hundred thousand malnourished citizens honoured the dead of the Blockade and celebrated their own survival by creating two large Victory Parks – one in the south of the city, the other on Krestovskiy Island. Soon afterwards work resumed on the **Kirov Stadium**, which had begun in 1932 but was halted by the war. This was built like a giant sand castle using mud scooped from the Gulf bed to form a ring-shaped mound, whose "crater" became the sports arena, its exterior embellished with colonnades. Alas, the architects didn't take account of the weather on the Gulf, which made the pitch unusable for six months of the year, to the detriment of its home team (see box).

Few fans mourn its demolition to build the new **Zenit Stadium**, designed by the late Japanese architect Kisho Kurokawa; a 60,000-seater "spacecraft" with a sliding roof, set for completion by 2009. Hopefully they'll find a place for V.B. Pinchuk's **statue of Kirov** in ticket-collecting mode, which stood outside the old stadium. The stadium is around fifteen minutes' walk from Krestovskiy Ostrov metro.

Across the Malaya Nevka

On the south side of Krestovskiy Island, the Malaya Nevka is spanned by several bridges including **Bolshoy Petrovskiy most**, from which **Rasputin's body** was dumped after he was shot at the Yusupov Palace. As an autopsy revealed, Rasputin was still alive, and the freezing water shocked him out of unconsciousness, for he apparently managed to free one hand and cross himself before drowning. The body was found washed up downriver after someone spotted one of his boots lying on the ice. The bridge connects with a detached sliver of the Petrograd Side known as **Petrovskiy Island**. Its western tip – Petrovskaya Kosa – harbours the **River Yacht Club**, which offers sailing trips around the Gulf; to get there, take trolleybus #7 from Sportivnaya metro to the end of the line, then walk the remaining 600m.

The Peter and Paul Fortress, Petrograd Side and the Kirov Islands

Streets and squares

ul. Akademika Pavlova	ул. Академика Павлова
Avstriyskaya ploshchad	Австрийская площадь
Bolshoy prospekt	Большой проспект
ul. Graftio	ул. Графтио
Kamennoostrovskiy prospekt	Каменноостровский проспект
Kronverkskiy prospekt	Кронверкский проспект
ul. Kuybysheva	ул. Куйбышева
Maliy prospekt	Малый проспект
ul. Professora Popova	ул. профессора Попова
nab. reki Karpovki	наб. реки Карповки
ploshchad Tolstovo	площадь Толстого
Troitskaya ploshchad	Троицкая площадь

Metro stations

Chkalovskaya	Чкаловская
Gorkovskaya	Горьковская
Krestovskiy Ostrov	Крестовский Остров
Petrogradskaya	Петроградская
Sportivnaya	Спортивная

Museums

Artillery Museum	Военно-Исторический музей Артиллерии
Chaliapin memorial apartment	мемориальная квартира Ф.И. Шаляпина
Freud's Dream Museum	музей Сновидений Зигмунда Фрейда
Kirov Museum	музей С.М. Кирова
Museum of Russian Political History	музей политической истории России
Peter's Cabin	домик Петра
Popov Museum	музей Попова
Toy Museum	музей Игрушки
Yelagin Palace	Елагинский дворец
Yelizarov Flat-Musem	музей-квартира Елизаровых

5

6

Liteyniy, Smolniy and Vladimirskaya

T he areas of **Liteyniy**, **Smolniy** and **Vladimirskaya** make up the remainder of central "mainland" St Petersburg and provide the chief points of interest between the River Fontanka and the Obvodniy Canal. Predominantly residential, the districts largely developed in the latter half of the nineteenth century, and to natives of the city each has a specific resonance. **Liteyniy prospekt** has been a centre of the arts, shopping and – with the secret police headquarters at its northern end – repression since the late nineteenth century. A couple of kilometres to the east lies the **Smolniy** district, whose focal point, Rastrelli's rocket-like **Smolniy Convent**, is a must on anyone's itinerary, as is the **Smolniy Institute**, from where the Bolsheviks launched the October Revolution.

Further south, the cemeteries at the **Alexander Nevsky Monastery** are the resting place for some of the city's most notable personalities, while back nearer the city centre the bustling market quarter of **Vladimirskaya** boasts a cluster of museums, including Dostoyevsky's apartment. Running southwest from Vladimirskaya is **Zagorodniy prospekt**, home of a musical tradition particularly associated with the Rimsky-Korsakov Museum, while further south is the blue-domed **Trinity Cathedral**.

Liteyniy prospekt

Liteyniy prospekt – running due north from Nevskiy prospekt to the Neva – is one of the oldest streets in the city, taking its name from the Liteyniy dvor, or "Smelting House", a cannon foundry established on the left bank of the Neva in 1711. It quickly became a major shopping street and the next most important avenue on the south bank after Nevskiy. While Liteyniy has fewer grand edifices, several eye-catching churches and museums can be seen on the side streets, and window-shopping and streetlife are diverting. The following account meanders back and forth, on and off the prospekt, more than you're likely to. Note that buildings on Liteyniy are **numbered** starting from the Neva, rather than Nevskiy prospekt, as you might expect.

The Sheremetev Palace and the Beloselskiy-Belozerskiy Palace on the Fontanka (see below) can be visited en route to Liteyniy. To reach the Bolshoy dom or other sights around the northern end of Liteyniy, catch a bus (#9) or trolleybus (#3, #8) near the junction with Nevskiy.

The Beloselskiy-Belozerskiy Palace

A Rococo throwback built by Andrey Stakenschneider in the mid-nineteenth-century heyday of Neoclassicism, the **Beloselskiy-Belozerskiy Palace** upstages the Anichkov Palace across the river (see Chapter 1), its muscled atlantes and sinuous window surrounds aping the Winter Palace's. Its last residents were Grand Duke Sergei and Elizabeth of Hesse, who founded a convent and became its abbess after Sergei was killed by Nihilists in 1905 – thirteen years before she herself was thrown down a mineshaft by Bolsheviks. Today, its state rooms house the **Sobchak Museum of the Formation of Democracy in Modern Russia** (noon–3pm, closed Wed; R100), a tribute to St Petersburg's first elected Mayor, Anatoly Sobchak, pictured rallying crowds against the 1991 putsch. Its message is that Sobchak's work is being furthered by his former protégé, Putin: democracy is in safe hands. The palace's **concert hall** has splendid oak panelling, filigree work and a ceiling with pendentive flowers and stucco traceries in the Eclectic style of the 1880s.

The Sheremetev Palace on the Fontanka

Along the Fontana embankment, north of Anichkov most, stands an array of ex-palaces founded in the eighteenth century and rebuilt a century later, many becoming institutes or hospitals even before the Revolution. Among them is the **Sheremetev Palace** at no. 34, whose golden-yellow facade set back behind majestic wrought-iron gates is one of the glories of the embankment. Named after one of Peter the Great's marshals, who built a palace here in 1712, the existing building was erected in the mid-eighteenth century and known as the **Fountain House** (Fontanniy dom) because of the many fountains, fed by the river, which once played in its grounds – a nickname still used today.

The Sheremetevs were great patrons of music and drama, and this was one of the capital's main venues for performing arts in the eighteenth century. Today, its restored upstairs rooms house a **Museum of Music** (noon–6pm, closed Mon, Tues & the last Fri of each month; R170) with three thousand instruments from Baroque harps to replica ancient Etrurian horns (recordings of which can be heard), set amongst furniture and paintings that evoke the Sheremetevs' lifestyle, but never belonged to them. Their own collection of fine art was expropriated after the Bolshevik Revolution, when the palace was turned into communal flats for scholars, artists and writers.

Among those lodged in a rear annexe (entered via Liteyniy pr. 53) was the great poet of Russia's "Silver Age", Anna Akhmatova, who stayed through forty-six years of turmoil, terror and famine (see box on p.194). The **Akhmatova Museum** (10.30am–6.30pm, Wed 1–9pm; closed Mon & the last Wed of each month; R100; ⓦwww.akhmatova.spb.ru) has six rooms of exhibits relating to her life; she lived, worked and slept in three of them, one of which she exchanged with the ex-wife of her third husband, after she left him in 1938. Here you'll find her desk, beneath a pen-portrait by Modigliani, the only surviving one of a series drawn during her stay in Paris. You can also see the secret police file on the poet Mandelstam, who was murdered in the Great Terror, and letters from Boris Pasternak, who loved her. In old age, Akhmatova was a muse for the poet **Joseph Brodsky**, who was later exiled, settling in Massachusetts. In 2003 Brodsky's widow donated the contents of his **"American Study"** to the museum; visitors can hear interviews with the Nobel laureate and read a transcript of his Kafkaesque trial for "social parasitism". A **video room** in the garden screens documentaries about Akhmatova, Gumilev, Pasternak and Tsvetaeva (in Russian and English)

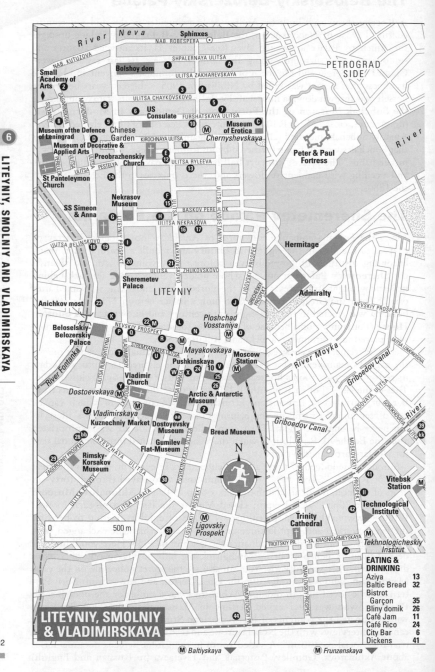

River **Neva**

Sphinxes

NAB. ROBESPERA

PETROGRAD SIDE

NAB. KUTUZOVA

SHPALERNAYA ULITSA

Small Academy of Arts ②

Bolshoy dom ①

A

ULITSA ZAKHAREVSKAYA

B

③ ④

ULITSA CHAYKOVSKOVO

⑤

⑥ **US Consulate**

⑦

FURSHATSKAYA ULITSA

⑧

⑨

⑩

M

Museum of Erotica C

Museum of the Defence of Leningrad D

Chinese Garden

KIROCHNAYA ULITSA

Chernyshevskaya

Museum of Decorative & Applied Arts

Preobrazhenskiy Church

⑪

E

⑫

ULITSA RYLEEVA

St Panteleymon Church

⑭

⑬

Nekrasov Museum

F ⑮

BASKOV PEREULOK

SS Simeon & Anna

G

H

ULITSA NEKRASOVA

⑯ ⑰

⑱ ⑲

ULITSA BELINSKOVO

⑳

㉑

ULITSA ZHUKOVSKOVO

Hermitage

Sheremetev Palace

LITEYNIY

Admiralty

NEVSKIY PROSPEKT

Anichkov most ㉓

K

J

Ploshchad Vosstaniya

Beloselskiy-Belozerskiy Palace

㉒ M

L

NEVSKIY PROSPEKT

P Q

M O

R S

T

Mayakovskaya

U

Moscow Station

River Moyka

Pushkinskaya

V

10

㉔

㉕

M

River Fontanka

W X

㉖

Y

Vladimir Church

M

Arctic & Antarctic Museum ②

Dostoevskaya

M

Griboedov Canal

㉗ *Vladimirskaya*

Kuznechniy Market

aa

Dostoyevsky Museum

Bread Museum

㉘ bb

Gumilev Flat-Museum

㉙

Rimsky-Korsakov Museum

N

RAZEZZHAYA ULITSA

ZAGRODNIY PROSPEKT

ULITSA PRAVDY

㉚

Vitebsk Station M

ULITSA MARATA

M *Ligovskiy Prospekt*

㉛

Trinity Cathedral

Technological Institute

M

Tekhnologicheskiy Institut

0 — 500 m

TROITSKIY PR.

1-YA KRASNOARMEYSKAYA

㊸

M *Baltiyskaya* ▼

M *Frunzenskaya* ▼

LITEYNIY, SMOLNIY & VLADIMIRSKAYA

EATING & DRINKING	
Aziya	13
Baltic Bread	32
Bistrot Garçon	35
Bliny domik	26
Café Jam	11
Café Rico	24
City Bar	6
Dickens	41

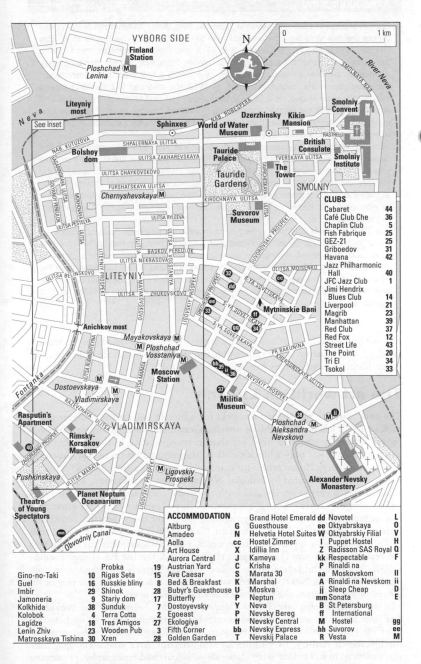

VYBORG SIDE

Finland Station

Ploshchad Lenina Ⓜ

Neva

Liteyniy most

See Inset

Bolshoy dom

Sphinxes

Dzerzhinsky

World of Water Museum

Kikin Mansion

Smolniy Convent

PL. RASTRELLI

SMOLNAYA NAB.

River Neva

N

0   1 km

NAB. ROBESPERA

SHPALERNAYA ULITSA

ULITSA ZAKHAREVSKAYA

Tauride Palace

British Consulate

TVERSKAYA ULITSA

Smolniy Institute

NAB. KUTUZOVA

GAGARINSKAYA ULITSA

SOLYANOY PEREULOK

MOKHOVAYA ULITSA

ULITSA CHAYKOVSKOVO

FURSHATSKAYA ULITSA

Chernyshevskaya Ⓜ

Tauride Gardens

TAVRICHESKAYA ULITSA

The Tower

SMOLNIY

KIROCHNAYA ULITSA

ULITSA RYLEEVA

Suvorov Museum

SUVOROVSKIY PROSPEKT

ULITSA PESTELYA

ULITSA

ULITSA

BASKOV PEREULOK

ULITSA NEKRASOVA

LITEYNIY

MAYAKOVSKAYA ULITSA

LIGOVSKIY PROSPEKT

ULITSA BELINSKOVO

LITEYNIY PROSPEKT

ULITSA ZHUKOVSKOVO

GRECHESKIY PROSPEKT

32

dd

cc

ULITSA MOISENKO

8-YA SOVETSKAYA

Mytninskie Bani

ee

33

ff

7-YA SOVETSKAYA

Anichkov most

Mayakovskaya Ⓜ

Ⓜ *Ploshchad Vosstaniya*

Ⓜ

gg

34

3-YA SOVETSKAYA

PR BAKUNINA

KHERSONSKAYA ULITSA

ULITSA RUBINSHTEYNA

Fontanka

hh 35 ii 36

Moscow Station

NEVSKIY PROSPEKT

Dostoevskaya Ⓜ

Ⓜ *Vladimirskaya*

RAZEZZHAYA ULITSA

37

Militia Museum

Rasputin's Apartment

ZAGORODNIY PROSPEKT

40

VLADIMIRSKAYA

Ploshchad Aleksandra Nevskovo

38

Ⓜ

jj

Ⓜ

Rimsky-Korsakov Museum

ULITSA MARATA

Pushkinskaya Ⓜ

Ⓜ *Ligovskiy Prospekt*

LIGOVSKIY PROSPEKT

Alexander Nevsky Monastery

Theatre of Young Spectators

mm

Planet Neptum Oceanarium

Obvodniy Canal

CLUBS

Cabaret	44
Café Club Che	36
Chaplin Club	5
Fish Fabrique	25
GEZ-21	25
Griboedov	31
Havana	42
Jazz Philharmonic Hall	40
JFC Jazz Club	1
Jimi Hendrix Blues Club	14
Liverpool	21
Magrib	23
Manhattan	39
Red Club	37
Red Fox	12
Street Life	43
The Point	20
Tri El	34
Tsokol	33

Gino-no-Taki	10	Probka	19
Guel	16	Rigas Seta	15
Imbir	29	Russkie bliny	8
Jamoneria	9	Shinok	28
Kolkhida	38	Stariy dom	17
Kolobok	4	Sunduk	7
Lagidze	18	Terra Cotta	2
Lenin Zhiv	23	Tres Amigos	27
Matrosskaya Tishina	30	Wooden Pub	3
		Xren	28

ACCOMMODATION

Altburg	G	Grand Hotel Emerald	dd	Novotel	L
Amadeo	N	Guesthouse	ee	Oktyabrskaya	O
Aolla	cc	Helvetia Hotel Suites	W	Oktyabrskiy Filial	V
Art House	X	Hostel Zimmer	I	Puppet Hostel	H
Aurora Central	C	Idillia Inn	Z	Radisson SAS Royal	Q
Austrian Yard	C	Kameya	kk	Respectable	F
Ave Caesar	S	Krisha	P	Rinaldi na	
Bed & Breakfast	K	Marata 30	aa	Moskovskom	ll
Buby's Guesthouse	U	Marshal	A	Rinaldi na Nevskom	ii
Butterfly	P	Moskva	jj	Sleep Cheap	D
Dostoyevsky	Y	Neptun	mm	Sonata	E
Egoeast	P	Neva	B	St Petersburg	
Ekologiya	ff	Nevsky Bereg	ff	International	
Fifth Corner	bb	Nevsky Central	M	Hostel	gg
Golden Garden	T	Nevsky Express	hh	Suvorov	ee
		Nevskij Palace	R	Vesta	M

193

Born in Odessa in 1889 and raised in Tsarskoe Selo, **Anna Akhmatova** lived in Paris (where she met Modigliani) before settling in St Petersburg with her husband, Nikolay Gumilev, an Assyriologist and explorer. In 1913, with Osip Mandelstam, they founded the Acmeist movement, espousing poetic clarity, freshness and emotional honesty. Akhmatova became a literary sensation – yet within a few years her poetry would seem archaic, in the revolutionary era. In 1918 she divorced Gumilev and moved into the Fountain House; as a "former bourgeois" she had to sweep the streets and share rations with her second husband, a Hermitage curator. In 1921 Gumilev was executed for treason and the stigma kept Akhmatova silent for a decade, not least to safeguard their young son, Lev.

In 1935 both Lev and Akhmatova's third husband, Nikolay Punin, were sent to the Gulag – inspiring her to secretly write her *Requiem* cycle, the finest poetry to have emerged from that terrible era. Following the Nazi invasion, she threw herself into the patriotic cause, writing a famous war poem, *Courage*, published in *Pravda*. Having experienced the first winter of the Blockade before being evacuated to Tashkent, she re-established her career as a poet, while Lev was released from the Gulag to fight in the Red Army.

In 1946, however, she was vilified once more in an infamous "cultural report" by Party Secretary Zhdanov as "a nun and a whore, who combines harlotry with prayer". After Lev's third arrest, Akhmatova gave in and wrote a series of poems glorifying Stalin. Lev was freed after Stalin's death, when Akhmatova also benefited from the "thaw". Her works were published again, she was allowed to travel abroad for the first time in fifty years and, until her death in 1966, enjoyed the acclaim so long denied her.

and exhibits audio-installations by local artists such as Luda Belova on Wednesday evenings. The museum is also responsible for preserving the abode of her son, the ethno-historian Lev Gumilev (see p.209).

The art world on Liteyniy

The middle stretch of Liteyniy prospekt has a literary and artistic pedigree going back to 1837, when the would-be novelist Goncharov rented a "modest official's room" at no. 52, where he lived for sixteen years, writing in the evenings after work. At least it was only a block's walk to the editorial offices of **Sovremennik** (*The Contemporary*), Russia's most influential literary journal from the 1840s till the 1870s. This was co-edited by **Nikolai Nekrasov** and **Ivan Panaev**, who lived in adjacent apartments at no. 36 and both enjoyed a cosy *ménage à trois* with Ivan's wife, Avdotya Panaeva – herself a writer. All three campaigned for the emancipation of women – but it was for highlighting the plight of the peasants before and after the Emancipation Act in 1861 that Nekrasov fell foul of the censors, thus earning posthumous approval in Soviet times, when his apartment was turned into the **Nekrasov Museum** (11am–5pm; closed Tues & the last Fri of each month; R100). It was an unlikely editorial office: the comfortably furnished suite even includes a ballroom. Nekrasov's bedroom is laid out as it was in the last year of his life, reconstructed from the sickbed scene which hangs *in situ*.

In the decades before the Revolution, the standard-bearer was the **World of Art** (Mir iskusstva) movement and magazine, whose influence long outlasted its brief life (1898–1904). Partly in reaction to the didactic artistic movements of the nineteenth century, its philosophy was "Art for Art's sake". The magazine was produced in full colour with elaborate woodcuts and typography, promoting

Style Moderne (the local version of Art Nouveau) and neglected aspects of Russian culture. Artists Alexandre Benois, Léon Bakst and Nikolai Roerich provided most of its material, but the magazine owed much to **Sergei Diaghilev**, the impresario known for his Russian ballet seasons in Paris, who edited it from his apartment at no. 45, near the corner of ulitsa Belinskovo (named after the critic Vissarion Belinsky).

Diaghilev lived conveniently near the literary salon run by the "decadent Madonna" **Zinaida Gippius** and her husband **Dmitri Merezhkovsky**, whose Symbolist soirees were only eclipsed by the advent of "Wednesdays" at The Tower (p.198). Gossip columns drooled over Gippius's pagan sensuality in an era when "Destruction was considered good taste, neurasthenia a sign of sophistication ... People made up vices and perversions for themselves so as not to seem insipid". After they emigrated in 1919, the grand apartments in the **Muruzi House** (no. 24) were divided into communal flats. Nobel Prize-winning poet **Joseph Brodsky** spent his childhood in a "room and a half" of flat #28, shared with three other families. The Muruzi House is on the corner of ulitsa Pestelya, and its Moorish facade was renowned as the grandest of any apartment building in St Petersburg when it opened in 1874.

The Preobrazhenskiy Church

A short way down ulitsa Pestelya, off Liteyniy, an oval wrought-iron grille enclosing captured Turkish cannon surrounds the Cathedral of the Transfiguration, better known as the **Preobrazhenskiy Church**. The original regimental church, which burnt down in 1825, was erected by **Empress Elizabeth**, the daughter of Peter the Great, as a token of gratitude to the Preobrazhenskiy Guards, whom she won over in her bid for power in 1741 with the immortal rallying cry: "Lads! You know whose daughter I am. Follow me." The present five-domed, Neoclassical structure was designed by Stasov in the late 1820s. Its **choir** is one of the best in the city (most of its members also sing in the Kapella Choir) and can be heard at daily services at 10am and 6pm.

Returning to Liteyniy and continuing north towards the Bolshoy dom, you'll see the pagoda roofs and gateways of a small **Chinese Garden**, providing a much needed splash of colour on the prospekt – a gift from the People's Republic of China, for St Petersburg's three hundredth birthday.

Solyanoy pereulok

West of Liteyniy is a quiet residential enclave whose spacious apartments were subdivided into communal flats for street cleaners and artists in Soviet times; many have now reverted to being swanky residences. Apart from being a nice area to stroll through, there are several sights on **Solyanoy pereulok** (Salt Lane), running parallel to the Fontanka, starting with the terracotta-and-white Baroque **Church of St Panteleymon** on the corner of ulitsa Pestelya.

The Mukhina College, next door, has been Russia's leading school of applied arts since its foundation by the banker Baron Steiglitz in 1876. He believed in inspiring students by surrounding them with fine art and design, and donated his own collection of tapestries, furniture and paintings. After the Revolution the best was taken for the Hermitage and the Steiglitzes were cast as "feudal exploiters", while the magnificent interior – designed by its first director, Max Messmacher – was crudely painted over. Further damage was sustained in World War II, when a shell holed the gigantic glass roof of the Medici Hall, only repaired in 2002. Students had a hand in the original decor and have been helping to restore the decorations without any funding. Its **Museum of Decorative and Applied Arts** (daily 11am–4.30pm; closed Aug; R400) has a fab collection of tiled stoves, Russian dolls, porcelain and furniture, while each hall is in a different style – Renaissance, Baroque, Flemish and medieval Russian. Note the antique lampstand in front of the building whose base features four cherubs practising the decorative arts, sometimes joined by contemporary outdoor sculptures.

Further up the street, anti-aircraft cannons flank the entrance to the **Museum of the Defence of Leningrad** (10am–5pm, Tues till 4pm; closed Wed & the last Thurs of each month; R100), devoted to "the Blockade" – the three-year siege of the city during World War II. The museum consists of one large exhibition hall on the second floor, with a fine array of wartime posters, including Todize's iconic *Rodina-Mat zovyot!* (The Motherland calls!). The centrepiece is a reconstruction of a typical apartment during the Blockade, complete with boarded-up windows, sooty walls and a few pieces of furniture – the rest having been used as fuel on the tiny stove. Around the edges of the hall are exhibits on artistic life during the siege. Several theatres and concert halls functioned throughout the Blockade, and even during the dreadful winter of 1941–42, starving citizens continued to attend exhibitions and concerts. The museum opened just three months after the Blockade was lifted and citizens donated many of its 37,000 exhibits – a sign of the collective pride which Stalin so feared that he purged Leningrad's Party cadres and intelligentsia yet again in 1948, when the museum's director was shot.

For light relief, stroll around the corner to ulitsa Chaykovskovo and through the gap between two blocks at no. 2/7 and a series of yards to find the **Small Academy of Arts**. Established by Academician Gubenko, this offers children over 5 years old free master classes by restorers from the Hermitage and Russian Museum, in painting, sculpture, ceramics and other arts. Over the years, they've transformed the **courtyard** where the academy is located into a riot of mosaics and creatures, like a scaled-down version of one of Gaudi's parks in Barcelona.

The Bolshoy dom

The city's record of heroism is even more poignant given that it owed so much of its suffering not to Russia's enemies, but to its own government – above all, to the Stalinist purges following the assassination of the Leningrad Party secretary, Sergei Kirov, in 1934. This purge was implemented from the headquarters of the secret police, universally known as the **Bolshoy dom** (Big House), from whose roof – it was said – "you can see Kolyma" (a labour camp in the Arctic Circle).

With chilling consistency, the Bolshoy dom – at Liteyniy pr. 4 – stands on the site of the old St Petersburg Regional Court, the scene of some of the most famous political trials in Tsarist times. The Nihilist assassins of Alexander II were condemned to death here, as was Lenin's brother for his attempt on the life of Alexander III; and Trotsky and other leaders of the 1905 Revolution.

After the court was torched in the 1917 February Revolution, a new building was custom-built for the Soviet secret police. Designed in 1931–32 by a trio of architects led by Noy Trotsky (no relation), it was one of the few large buildings erected in the centre between the wars. Ironically, during the Blockade it was one of the most comfortable places in Leningrad: heated (for the benefit of the jailers), shellproof and with a reliable supply of food – although political prisoners had to share cells with cannibals arrested for eating or selling human flesh.

In a similar vein, round the corner at Shpalernaya ulitsa 25, the Tsarist **House of Detention** – rebuilt after it was torched in the February Revolution – once held almost every notable revolutionary, including Lenin, who spent fourteen months here before being exiled to Siberia in 1897. According to those who experienced both Tsarist and Soviet prisons, conditions were far better in the former, which tolerated visits by prisoners' wives, gifts of food at Easter and inspections by the Political Red Cross (a charity shut down by the Bolsheviks).

As a sombre finale to this side of history, you can walk to the riverside and east along the embankment to see Mikhail Shemiakin's 1996 memorial to the victims of repression. It consists of two **sphinxes**, whose serene countenances are half eaten away to reveal their skulls beneath, and a miniature cell window mounted on the embankment wall, through which you can peer across the river towards Kresty Prison, where so many victims of the purges were incarcerated (see p.223). Appositely, this stretch of the embankment is named after Robespierre, the instigator of the Terror during the French Revolution.

The Smolniy district

Tucked into a bend in the River Neva, the **Smolniy district** is a quiet, slightly remote quarter. Most tourists are drawn here by the **Smolniy Convent**, while Petersburgers come to visit the **Tauride Gardens**. In Tsarist times the district was called Rozhdestvenskiy, after the regiment which had its barracks in the area, but with the establishment of the State Duma and, later, the Petrograd Soviet in the Tauride Palace, the district evolved into the country's main centre of power. The Smolniy Institute was the Bolsheviks' principal base during and after the October Revolution; it subsequently became the Leningrad Party headquarters, and now houses the Governor's office.

Although it's possible to walk two kilometres from Chernyshevskaya metro, through the Tauride Gardens and on to the Smolniy, it's wise to save your energy by riding some of the way. **Minibuses** to the Smolniy can be boarded anywhere along Suvorovskiy prospekt (#74, #147), or at Gorkovskaya or Petrogradskaya metro stations on the Petrograd Side (#46).

Along Furshtadtskaya ulitsa

If you're bent on walking, head east from Chernyshevskaya metro along **Furshtadtskaya ulitsa**, a leafy avenue lined with mansions once home to the Duma politicians Rodzyanko and Guchkov, where you'll now find the US, Austrian and German **consulates** and a neo-Baroque pile with a covered bridge, serving as a **Palace of Weddings** (registry office) – hence the white stretch-limos often seen nearby.

This is barely a block from the **Museum of Erotica** (muzey Erotiki; daily 8am–8pm; R15), in a basement proctology clinic at no. 47/11, entered from Tavricheskaya ulitsa. Having received a pop-up penile "Passport to Potency" as an admission ticket, visitors must squeeze past patients awaiting treatment, to see lots of hokey plastic "erotica" and what is supposedly Rasputin's penis, preserved after it was removed at his autopsy. Lacking the wart that was reputedly the secret of his sexual renown, the distended organ is exhibited with three of the handguns used to kill him (so the museum claims).

The Tauride Gardens and around

For some fresh air, enter the **Tauride Gardens** (Tavricheskiy sad; daily 7am–10pm; free) behind the Tauride Palace, with an antiquated **fairground**, ponds,

Prince Potemkin

Born into poverty in the Smolensk region, **Grigori Potemkin** (1739–91) – pronounced "Pot*yom*kin" – joined the army and swiftly rose through the ranks due to his energy and courage. Physically imposing but far from beautiful (he got rid of an infected eye by deliberately lancing it in a fit of impatience), he was soon noticed by Catherine and became her lover. Between campaigns her "Lion of the Jungle" would arrive unannounced at the Winter Palace, unshaven and clad only in his dressing gown and slippers. Even after she took other lovers – some of whom he selected – Potemkin remained her foremost friend and courtier. His enemies spread rumours belittling his achievements even before Catherine's inspection tour of Crimea in 1787, when it was said that he erected fake villages along her route to fool her into thinking that the newly colonized region was prospering. Though his biographer Sebag Montefiore (see p.420) refutes this, the slur stuck: "Potemkin villages" went down in history, and were raised to a fine art in Soviet times.

sunbathers, drinkers and courting couples. Cut across towards the southern part to reach the **Suvorov Museum** (10am–6pm; closed Tues, Wed & the first Mon of each month; R200; Ⓦwww.suvorovmuseum.ru), a quasi-fortified building erected in 1902 to commemorate the eighteenth-century generalissimo, Alexander Suvorov. "The harder the training, the easier the battle", was one of his maxims; it's said that Napoleon waited to invade Russia until Suvorov was dead. The museum displays Suvorov's personal effects, period militaria and antique model soldiers; its exterior is distinguished by colourful mosaics depicting his departure for the Italian campaign of 1799, and Russian troops crossing the Alps.

Among the *fin-de-siècle* residential blocks on **Tavricheskaya ulitsa**, the one on the corner of Tverskaya ulitsa once hosted a salon known as **"The Tower"**, frequented by Akhmatova, Blok and Mandelstam, where the mystic poet Vyacheslav Ivanov presided over his "Wednesdays" – intellectual free-for-alls that often lasted for days. The salon died out after Ivanov emigrated in 1912, but urban legend has it that a cabal of tower-dwelling mystics still watches over the city.

The Tauride Palace

The **Tauride Palace** (Tavricheskiy dvorets) was built by Catherine the Great for her lover, Prince Potemkin, the brains behind the annexation of Crimea (then known as Tauris or Tavriya, hence the palace's name). Completed by Stasov in 1789, it is one of the city's earliest examples of austere Neoclassicism; its main facade facing Shpalernaya ulitsa has a six-columned portico almost entirely devoid of decoration, and once had a clear view across the Neva. Potemkin occupied the palace for just over a year before his death in 1791, and threw the greatest New Year's Eve Ball the city had ever seen in a final effort to revive Catherine's love for him. Over three thousand guests filled the rooms, which were lit by fourteen thousand multicoloured lamps and twenty thousand candles. An elephant covered in gems and ridden by a Persian, a theatrical performance and fireworks were some of the entertainments. After Catherine's death, her son Paul deliberately ruined the interior by making it a stables and barracks for the Horseguards.

The palace is now in the hands of local authorities and closed to the public, but has a vital place in the city's history. In 1905, it was chosen as the venue for the **State Duma**, which – following the first parliamentary elections in Russian history – was inaugurated in May 1906. On February 27, 1917, in the final throes of the Tsarist autocracy, mutinous troops and demonstrators converged on the palace; inside a Provisional Committee was formed, which later became the Provisional Government, while in another wing of the palace, the Petrograd Soviet was re-established, thus creating a state of "dual power" that persisted until the October Revolution.

On January 5, 1918, the long-awaited **Constituent Assembly** met here for the first and last time. The first ever Russian parliament elected by universal suffrage, it was regarded by Lenin as "an old fairytale which there is no reason to carry on further". Having received only a quarter of the vote, the Bolsheviks surrounded the palace the next day and dismissed the Assembly.

Along Shpalernaya ulitsa

Shpalernaya ulitsa is a ley-line of past and present centres of power, linking the Bolshoy dom and the Smolniy, the Tauride Palace and a slew of barracks. When planning their seizure of power, the Bolsheviks included an objective on their doorstep – the eight-storey **Water Tower** near the Neva, which was the nerve centre of the city's water and sewage system, and an ideal observation point. The tower was built in 1861, in an attempt to end cholera epidemics by delivering filtered river water. After the 1908 epidemic the City Duma commissioned a larger plant from Siemens but the tower remained the water company's headquarters and is still in the hands of Vodakanal. As the city's tap water is notoriously contaminated with giardia and heavy metals, it seems cheeky of Vodakanal to brag of its achievements, but the **World of Water Museum** (muzey "Mir Vody"; 10am–5pm; closed Mon, Tues & the last Fri of each month; R50) is a slick effort, abetted by the British Council. Children will like the cascade of lights in the atrium and the antique toilets among the exhibits upstairs. These include a wooden water pipe from Petrine times; early fire engines; photos of luxurious *banyas* like Yegorov's – with doormen, ferns and a bridge above its pool; and a re-creation of a room during the Blockade, with its life-giving stove and mandatory portrait of Stalin. Captions are in Russian only, so most foreigners will emerge unaware of Vodakanal's pledge to ensure proper drinking water and that only treated sewage will be pumped into the Gulf of Finland, by – wait for it – 2015. However, the **view** from the tower's observation deck is great, and the garden and the statue of an old water carrier and his dog in the grounds are delightful.

A block or so beyond, you'll find a **statue of Felix Dzerzhinsky**, the "steel-eyed, spade-bearded" Polish-Lithuanian founder of the Soviet secret police, the Cheka. Erected in 1981, the statue resembles a leather fetishist's dream, clad in jackboots, greatcoat and peaked cap. Just beyond is the orange **Kikin Mansion**, one of the oldest surviving buildings in the city, erected in 1714 for Alexander Kikin, the head of the Admiralty and one of Peter the Great's companions on his Grand Tour of Europe. Later, however, Kikin was a prime mover in the conspiracy against Peter, which involved the tsar's son, Alexei – both he and Kikin were tortured to death as a result. Peter used the mansion to house his Kunstkammer collection. Damaged by shellfire in World War II, the house was later restored and now serves as a children's music school.

The Smolniy Complex

From the Kikin Mansion, it's impossible to miss the glorious ice-blue cathedral towering on the eastern horizon, which is the focal point and architectural masterpiece of the **Smolniy Complex**. Prosaically, its name derives from the Smolyanoy dvor, or "tar yard", sited here in the eighteenth century to caulk Peter the Great's warships. Later, Empress Elizabeth founded a convent on the site and Catherine the Great also started a boarding school for the daughters of the nobility – the Smolniy Institute for Young Noblewomen – which later became the headquarters of the Bolsheviks during the October Revolution.

The Smolniy Convent

Rastrelli's grandiose plans for the **Smolniy Convent** (Smolniy monastyr; summer: 10am–6pm, winter: 11am–6pm; closed Wed; R150) were never completed, not least because Empress Elizabeth's personal extravagance almost bankrupted the Imperial coffers. Had the original plans been realized, the building would have

▲ The Smolniy Cathedral

been the tallest structure in the city with a 140-metre-high bell tower. As it turned out, the empress ran out of money and the building was finished by Stasov only in 1835, in a more restrained Neoclassical fashion and with a bell tower less than half of the proposed height.

Nevertheless, the view of the **exterior** from ploshchad Rastrelli is superb: the soaring **cathedral** offset by four matching domes rising in perfect symmetry from the surrounding outbuildings. The austere white **interior** is disappointingly severe and suffered from neglect in the Soviet era, so it's not worth paying to go inside unless you're interested in seeing whatever temporary exhibition is showing on the first floor, or feeling energetic enough to climb up the 63-metre-high bell tower for a stupendous **view** of the Smolniy district. In addition to services held here on weekends and religious holidays, the cathedral also hosts **concerts** from early September until late June (℡271 95 43 for details and bookings).

The Smolniy Institute

The **Smolniy Institute** – now the Governor's office – was built in 1806–8 to house the Institute for Young Noblewomen, but gained its notoriety after the Bolshevik-dominated Petrograd Soviet moved here from the Tauride Palace in August 1917. Soon, the Smolniy was "deep in autumn mud chomped from thousands of pairs of boots", with Red Guards sleeping in its dormitories and armoured cars parked in the courtyard. Here, too, the **Military Revolutionary Committee** was established, which the Bolsheviks used as a legal means of arming their supporters in preparation for a coup. On the evening of October 25, the second **All-Russian Congress of Soviets** met at the Smolniy to the sound of shellfire. The Bolsheviks, who had a sizeable majority, tried to present the coup as a *fait accompli*, though fighting was still going on and the Provisional Government had yet to be arrested in the Winter Palace. When the Menshevik opposition called for an immediate ceasefire, Trotsky retorted: "You are miserable bankrupts, your role is played out. Go where you ought to be: into the dustbin of history."

Later, as the headquarters of the Leningrad Party organization, the Smolniy Institute witnessed the **assassination of Kirov**, the local Party boss, by Leonid Nikolaev on December 1, 1934. Stalin (who is thought to have masterminded the plot) rushed to Leningrad and interrogated Nikolaev, before passing an illegal decree enabling capital sentences to be carried out immediately – whereupon Nikolaev and 37 others were executed. This marked the beginning of a mass purge of Leningrad during which as many as one quarter of the city's population may have been arrested, the majority of them destined for the Gulag.

Though the Smolniy isn't open to casual visitors, nobody minds if you stroll around the **monuments** in the gardens out front. In 1923–24 two simple commemorative propylaea were built, with the inscriptions "Workers of All Countries Unite!" and "The First Soviet of the Proletarian Dictatorship". The busts of Marx and Engels still face each other across the gravel paths, while Lenin himself stands before the porticoed entrance. The square in front of the propylaea is also the site of the **British Consulate**, which rejoices in the address 5 ploshchad Proletarskoy dikatatury (Dictatorship of the Proletariat Square).

To Stariy Nevskiy and back

More than half of **Nevskiy prospekt** – some 2.5km – lies to the east of the River Fontanka, but for much of its length holds little of interest. Its chief attraction is the **Alexander Nevsky Monastery**, in the grounds of which are buried the city's most illustrious artists. At some point you may also find yourself in **ploshchad Vosstaniya**, halfway along the prospekt, a major road and metro junction and home to Moscow Station. Beyond the station, the avenue is traditionally known as **Stariy Nevskiy** – or "Old Nevskiy" – though it's not marked on maps as such. Designer shops and restaurants are bringing some chic to this once drab section of the prospekt, but it still doesn't reward strolling in the way that downtown Nevskiy does. This account starts at the monastery and works back towards the centre. It's best to use the metro to reach the monastery, and then Ploshchad Vosstaniya/Mayakovskaya stations, within walking distance of everything else; or travel back above ground to name-check the shops, by bus (#27) or trolleybus (#16, #22) – though not if you're in a hurry, as the traffic can be awful.

Alexander Nevsky Monastery

Nevskiy prospekt ends as it begins, beside the Neva – at a spot where an ancient Russian hero is honoured by the **Alexander Nevsky Monastery** (Aleksandro-Nevskaya lavra; daily 10am–7pm; free) and a lance-wielding equestrian statue. This was once believed to be the site of the thirteenth-century battle in which Prince Alexander of Novgorod defeated the Swedes, thus earning himself the sobriquet "Alexander Nevsky" ("Nevsky" being derived from the River Neva). Having thrashed the Swedes himself at Poltava, Peter the Great felt secure enough

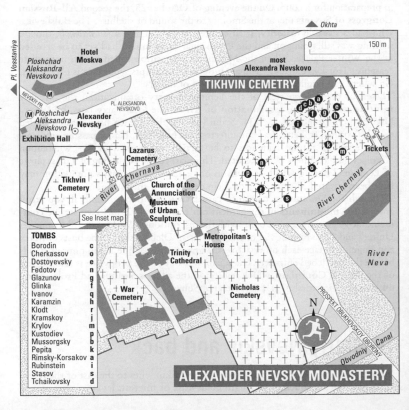

to found a monastery in St Petersburg, ten years after he began the city, and in 1724 he ensured its holiness by having the remains of the canonized prince transferred from Vladimir to the monastery. In 1797 it became one of only four in the Russian Empire to be given the title of *lavra*, the highest rank in Orthodox monasticism. As at all Orthodox monasteries, you won't be allowed inside wearing shorts or skimpy clothing, and smoking or photographing the monks is prohibited. Services and feast days are posted on Ⓦwww.lavra.spb.ru (in Russian only).

The Tikhvin and Lazarus cemeteries

Many tourists come simply to see the two cemeteries just inside the monastery's precincts. Both are covered by a single ticket (R140) sold at the entrance to the **Tikhvin Cemetery** (Tikhvinskoe kladbishche; daily 10am–7pm). Established in 1823, its list of luminaries runs the gamut of Russian culture. **Dostoyevsky**'s grave is off to the right, his name difficult to decipher from the ornate Cyrillic script. **Rimsky-Korsakov**'s bears a medieval Russian cross inset with icons; **Mussorgsky**'s a phrase from one of his works; **Borodin**'s a snippet from *Prince Igor* in a gilded mosaic behind his bust. **Tchaikovsky** has a grander, monumental tomb, while **Glinka**, **Glazunov** and **Rubinstein** lie nearer the main étoile. Elsewhere you can find the painters **Fedotov**, **Ivanov**, **Kramskoy**, **Kustodiev** and **Serov**; the sculptor **Klodt**; the choreographer **Pepita**; the fabulist **Krylov**, the historian **Karamzin**; the critic **Stasov** (sculpted in peasant dress) and the actor **Cherkassov** (who played *Ivan the Terrible* in Eisenstein's trilogy of films).

The diminutive **Lazarus Cemetery** (Lazarovskoe kladbishche; 11am–5pm, Fri–Sun till 7pm) is the oldest in the city, established by Peter the Great, whose sister Natalya was buried here in 1716. Its densely packed graves include those of the polymath **Lomonosov**, the architects **Rossi**, **Quarenghi**, **Voronikhin** and **Starov** (who built the nearby Trinity Cathedral), and Pushkin's wife, **Natalya Goncharova**, who is buried under the name of her second husband, Lanskaya. In the tiny **Church of St Lazarus** (daily 11am–4.30pm; R30) are buried Boris Sheremetev and other military figures from Petrine times.

The monastery and Trinity Cathedral

Beyond the narrow River Chernaya, the monastery proper forms a raspberry-red, two-storey enclosure around a tree-filled quadrant that incongruously serves as a cemetery for Communist activists and heroes of World War II. Trotsky's driver is buried in the grave beneath the curious ensemble of chains and wheels, facing the cathedral. En route you'll pass Trezzini's **Church of the Annunciation**, containing the **tombs** of Regent Anna Leopoldovna; Empress Elizabeth's lover, Razumovsky; Catherine the Great's illegitimate son, Prince Bobrinsky; Tsar Paul's mistress, Anna Lupukhina; Count Miloradovich, who was shot for leading the Decembrists' revolt; several Georgian crown princesses; and generalissimo Suvorov. The Soviets got round its Tsarist antecedents by renaming it the **Museum of Urban Sculpture** (11am–5pm; closed Mon & Thurs; R70). Upstairs is a large collection of **models** and designs for the city's monuments and sculptures, from Tsarist to Soviet times.

Trezzini also drew up a design for the monastery's **Trinity Cathedral** (not to be confused with the Trinity Cathedral beyond Zagorodniy prospekt), but failed to orient it towards the east, as Orthodox custom required, so the plans were scrapped. The job was left to Ivan Starov, who completed a more modest building in a Neoclassical style that sits awkwardly with the rest of the complex. The **interior**, however, is worth seeing, but bear in mind that this is a working church, not a museum: on Sundays it is pungent with incense and packed with worshippers genuflecting, kissing icons and lighting candles, while its choir is one of St Petersburg's best. The red agate and white marble **iconostasis** contains copies of works by Van Dyck and Rubens (among others), and the relics of St Alexander Nevsky are enshrined in a silver **sarcophagus** (a modest copy of the original, in the Hermitage), that draws hundreds of worshippers on his name day (September 12).

Behind the cathedral are the overgrown **Nicholas Cemetery** (daily: summer 9am–9pm; winter 9am–6pm; free), where the monastery's scholars and priests are buried, and the eighteenth-century **Metropolitan's House**, the home of St Petersburg's senior Orthodox cleric. Beyond the monastery's walls, on a side street off ploshchad Aleksandra Nevskovo, an **Exhibition Hall** (11am–5pm; closed Thurs & Fri; R70) features art shows.

The Militia Museum

The little-known **Militia Museum** is primarily intended for the Militia (police) themselves. Its discretion is matched by its location, in the yard of Poltavskaya ulitsa 12, running off Nevskiy prospekt midway between the monastery and ploshchad Vosstaniya. There's no sign as such, but Militia roster-boards give the game away. You can **visit** only by arrangement (Mon–Fri 10am–5pm; individual price negotiable; ☎717 95 36) and must take a guided tour in Russian, which is interesting if you're able to understand the language or can bring an interpreter along.

Five halls trace the **history of the Militia** since its establishment in 1917 until the 1970s, starting during the Civil War and the NEP era, when racketeering and fraud were as rife as they are today. During World War II, the Militia were responsible for civil defence in Leningrad and active as partisans behind enemy lines; other material documents social work amongst gangs of orphans, and crimes including gruesome photos of dismembered bodies from the Rosenblat and "Head in a Bucket" **cases** of the 1940s. Dioramas of muggings and the stuffed police tracker dog Sultan provide a light interlude. The main hall with its crimson banners is used for swearing in new recruits and another room (not open to visitors) contains mocked-up crime scenes on which trainee officers get to practise their forensic techniques.

One of the most notorious crimes in recent history happened only five minutes' drive from the museum, in 1997, when St Petersburg's Vice-Governor, **Mikhail Manevich**, was killed by a rooftop sniper as his car turned off Nevskiy onto ulitsa Marata. Nobody has ever been arrested for the crime, but it's thought that the motive was to halt his investigation of fraudulent city property deals.

Around ploshchad Vosstaniya

At the only bend in Nevskiy prospekt, the traffic-clogged intersection of **ploshchad Vosstaniya** (Uprising Square) is dominated by **Moscow Station** (Moskovskiy vokzal), whose peach-and-white facade looks more like a palace than a rail terminal; the architect built an identical one at the other end of the line in Moscow. Today, the facade is all that remains of the original station, which has been totally modernized inside.

The square was previously called Znamenskaya ploshchad, after a church that was demolished in 1940 and replaced by the spired rotunda of Ploshchad Vosstaniya metro station. It saw some of the bloodiest clashes between police and demonstrators during the February Revolution: here on February 25, Cossacks first turned on the police. The central **obelisk** was erected in 1985, on the site of a much ridiculed statue of Alexander III, which was removed in 1937 and can now be seen in the courtyard of the Marble Palace (p.85). The *Oktyabrskaya Hotel*, across the square from the station, has a **rooftop sign** that proclaims in Russian: "Leningrad – Hero City". Almost a dozen towns and cities were so designated, to honour their heroism during World War II.

Pushkinskaya 10

From Vosstaniya, turn south along Ligovskiy prospekt and pass through the arch of no. 53 to reach the artists' colony known as **Pushkinskaya 10** (Pushkinskaya desyat). Squatted in the 1980s, it remains a feature of the city's cultural scene though the building itself has largely been sold off to wealthy buyers – this is why visitors can no longer use the gated entrance on Pushkinskaya ulitsa, but must enter from Ligovskiy prospekt instead.

Entering the yard you'll find the Underground Bookshop and *Fish Fabrique Café* – low-key meeting places for musicians and artists. Photos of gigs and events line the stairs to the **Museum of the New Academy of Fine Arts** (3–7pm; closed Mon & Tues; ⓦwww.new.academy.ru) on the fourth floor of block B, celebrating two decades of work by diverse artists sharing an aesthetic known as Neo-Academism, which subverts both classicism and postmodernism. In block C, above the **John Lennon Temple** (where the anniversary of his birth is commemorated) and the **FOTOimage** gallery (Sat 4–7pm) on the second floor, the work of the New

Vladimir Mayakovsky

Vladimir Mayakovsky was born in Georgia in 1893. An enthusiastic supporter of the Bolshevik cause from an early age (he was elected to the Moscow committee when only 14 years old), Mayakovsky was arrested several times and given a six-month prison sentence in 1909. On his release, he enrolled at the Moscow Institute of Painting, Sculpture and Architecture and became friends with the Futurist painter, David Burlyuk. Together with other **Futurists**, they published a manifesto entitled *A Slap in the Face of Public Taste* and embarked on a publicity tour across Russia. Mayakovsky wore earrings and a yellow waistcoat with radishes in the buttonholes, scrawled obscenities on his face and recited avant-garde verses.

He threw himself into the October Revolution: as a friend remarked, "Mayakovsky entered the Revolution as he would his own home. He went right in and began opening windows." Though his reputation as a poet rests on his romantic, pre-revolutionary work, he is best known for his later propagandist writing, such as the poem "150,000,000". One of the founders of the **Left Front of Art (LEF)**, whose members included Osip Brik and Alexander Rodchenko, Mayakovsky also produced graphic art during the 1920s, including over six hundred giant cartoon advertisements for the Russian Telegraph Agency.

In 1930, five years after condemning the poet Yesenin for his "unrevolutionary" **suicide**, Mayakovsky killed himself in Moscow at the age of 37, with a revolver which he had once used as a prop in a film called *Not for Money Born*. His last unfinished poem lay beside him. Various motives have been advanced, ranging from despair over his love for Lili Brik to disillusionment with Soviet life, the philistinism of its censors, and hostile reviews of his most recent work. Whatever the truth, thousands filed past his open coffin at the Writers' Union, while a few years later Stalin decreed that "Mayakovsky was and remains the most talented poet of our Soviet epoch. Indifference to his memory and to his work is a crime." From then on, in the words of Pasternak, "Mayakovsky was sold to the people much as Catherine the Great had sold potatoes to the peasants".

Academy's founder Timur Novikov and colleagues are showcased in the **Museum of Nonconformist Art** (Wed–Sun 3–7pm) on the fourth floor. Check out what's on at the **Techno-Art Centre** (Mon–Fri 5–11.30pm, Sat & Sun 3–11pm) on the first floor of block D, and the **Gallery of Experimental Sound** on the third floor, hosting concerts (Mon & Tues from 8pm).

Around Mayakovskaya metro

Bohemian traditions run deep in the surrounding neighbourhood. The poet Mayakovsky (see box on p.205) lends his name to the nearby **Mayakovskaya** metro station – whose crimson mosaic platform walls are adorned with his visage – and to **ulitsa Mayakovskovo** on the other side of the prospekt, where he lived at no. 52 during 1915–17 to be close to Lili Brik, who lived nearby with her husband. On the same street, the absurdist writer **Daniil Kharms** resided for much of his life at no. 11, being known for his affected English plus fours and pipe, and for bowing to antique lampposts. His fate was even crueller than Mayakovsky's: arrested by the secret police and declared insane, he died in prison. In a Kharms-like twist, his wife – who was long thought to have died in the Blockade – was found to be living in Brazil in 1999. She hardly remembered him and wondered what all the fuss was about. The **plaque** on the facade of the building consists of a ledge bearing a shoe, cutlery and other objects, in absurdist juxtaposition.

Vladimirskaya

Vladimirskaya metro station, south of Nevskiy prospekt, forms the nucleus of the vibrant, slightly seedy **Vladimirskaya** area, whose sights include Kuznechniy Market, Dostoyevsky's apartment, the Arctic and Antarctic Museum, and the Bread Museum. All these are on, or just off, ulitsa Marata and Vladimirskiy prospekt; a continuation of the latter, **Zagorodniy prospekt,** cuts through a tract of inner suburbs associated with Dostoyevsky and Rasputin, to the Technological Institute – the birthplace of the Petrograd Soviet – and the Trinity Cathedral.

Around Kuznechniy pereulok

Coming by **metro**, you'll either arrive at Dostoevskaya metro, with its elegantly simple marble platforms, or at the older Vladimirskaya metro (to which Dostoevskaya is linked by an underground passage), with ornate lamps and a mosaic of prosperous peasants – before emerging near Kuznechniy Market, on the southern side of **Kuznechniy pereulok**. Just around the corner to the left from Vladimirskaya, a bronze **statue of Dostoyevsky** sits pensively, while peddlers and beggars vie for custom by the **Vladimir Church** on the corner of Kuznechniy pereulok, as in his time. A yellow Baroque beauty with five bronze onion domes and a Neoclassical bell tower, the church has now been restored, having served as an ambulance station until 1989. Its upstairs nave has a beguiling raspberry, pistachio and vanilla colour scheme.

The indoor **Kuznechniy Market** (Kuznechniy rynok; Mon–Sat 11am–8pm) is the best-stocked, most expensive market in the city. Most of the fruit and veg now come from Western Europe rather than Georgia or Kazakhstan, but there is a cornucopia of locally produced farmhouse honey, sour cream, hams, sausages, gherkins and pickled garlic – with herbs, mushrooms and berries on sale outside the market.

Born in Moscow in 1821, one of seven children fathered by a depressive, alcoholic physician, **Fyodor Dostoyevsky** lost his mother when he was 16 and his father (who was probably murdered by the family's serfs) two years later. A brief flirtation with socialist politics ended in Dostoyevsky's arrest and a death sentence, commuted at the last moment to four years' hard labour, plus further service as an ordinary soldier. In prison, he recanted socialism and became an ardent supporter of autocracy and Orthodoxy, but was regarded by the police as a subversive for many years afterwards. "How many lawbreakers they close their eyes to, while me they watch with suspicion and an eagle eye, a man who is devoted to the Tsar and the fatherland with all his heart and soul. It is an insult!" he raged. His first marriage and subsequent affairs were all dismal failures; gambling drained his meagre resources and he suffered from epilepsy. In 1866, to meet a tough deadline, he hired a 20-year-old stenographer, **Anna Snitkina**, to whom he dictated *The Gambler* in less than a month. Soon afterwards they married and she became his permanent secretary, gradually cured him of gambling, and made him a solid family man for the last quarter of his life.

While Dostoyevsky is renowned abroad as one of the greatest writers of the nineteenth century, his **reputation** inside Russia was long denigrated by the Left, which condemned him for engaging in polemics against the Nihilists. Between the 1930s and 1950s he wasn't even mentioned in Soviet textbooks, although he was eventually rehabilitated as a realist whose flaws embodied the contradictions of his era. None of his descendants dared reveal their identities until the early 1990s, when his great-grandson Andrey emerged from obscurity and undertook a tour of foreign literary societies, whom he disconcerted by his obsession with acquiring a Mercedes – with this, he scrapes a living as an unregistered taxi driver. A decade later, his sister Tatyana appealed for help in an open letter to a newspaper, bitterly comparing her life as a pensioner struggling to survive on $33 a month to the poor of *Crime and Punishment*.

The Dostoyevsky Museum

At Kuznechniy per. 5, beyond the market, the **Dostoyevsky Museum** (11am–5pm; closed Mon & the last Wed of each month; R120; ⓦwww.md.spb.ru) occupies the apartment into which Dostoyevsky and his wife moved in 1878, to escape the memory of their previous flat, where their son Alexei died. Reconstructed on the centenary of the writer's demise, using photos and drawings, the flat is surprisingly bright and cheerful: thanks to Anna, he enjoyed a cosy domestic life while creating his brooding masterpieces – the children would push notes under his door, reading "Papa, we love you". Dostoyevsky died of a throat haemorrhage while writing his diary; the clock in the study where he wrote *The Brothers Karamazov* is stopped at the exact time of his death: 8.38pm, on January 28, 1881. Also on display is a printed announcement of Dostoyevsky's exile and a set of prison leg-irons, such as he wore en route to Siberia. All the rooms are captioned in English, so you don't really need an audio-guide. At noon on Sundays, Russian **films** of his novels are screened downstairs; videos of the same, Dostoyevsky T-shirts and mugs are sold in the lobby.

The Arctic and Antarctic Museum

Across the intersection of Kuznechniy pereulok with ulitsa Marata is the former Old Believers' Church of St Nicholas, which was closed down by the Bolsheviks and reopened in 1937 as the **Arctic and Antarctic Museum** (10am–6pm, Sun till 4pm; closed Mon, Tues & the last Fri of each month; R100; ⓦwww.polarmuseum.sp.ru). Its history is entwined with the "Conquest of the North", an era when

▲ Kuznechniy Market

Polar exploration and aviation were as prestigious as space travel thirty years later. Not only did the Soviet Union create oil towns, research bases and fishing stations, supplied over thousands of miles, it boasted towns beyond the Arctic Circle that grew vegetables, enjoyed symphony orchestras and had sunlamps in their kindergartens. Whilst some have literally fallen apart since the end of Communism, the oil and nickel towns are now enjoying a new lease of life.

The museum's marble-columned hall is filled with stuffed polar wildlife, a mammoth's skull and tusk and the skiplane in which V.B. Shabrov flew from Leningrad to the Arctic in 1930. Off to the sides, at the back, are the leather tent used in the 1937–38 Soviet North Pole expedition and a model of a roomier hut with bunk beds and a portrait of Lenin, used by another group in 1954 – look out for the surgical tools that one explorer used to operate on himself. The dioramas of base camps and logistics are self-explanatory and uncontentious, unlike the exhibits upstairs, which purport to show how Soviet rule improved the lives of the Arctic peoples – the nuclear contamination of Novaya Zemlya and the Kola Peninsula are barely mentioned.

The Bread Museum

Carry on to the end of Kuznechniy pereulok and turn right onto Ligovskiy prospekt to find the **Bread Museum** (muzey khleba; Tues–Sat 10am–5pm; R100) at no. 73. Located on the fourth floor (take a lift from the foyer), it traces the history of a commodity dear to Russian hearts. Weddings, funerals, births and holy days each had their own special loaves, some as large as pillows. Peter the Great brought Germans over to run the city's first bakeries and outraged the populace by imposing a bread tax. Baking remained a male profession until World War I, when women were employed to alleviate the labour shortage and bread queues that were a major cause of the February Revolution. There are horrific photos from the famine of the early 1920s, and a moving section on the Blockade, when the daily bread ration was little larger than a pack of cigarettes and contained ingredients such as sunflower husks and oak bark.

The Gumilev Flat-Museum

A few blocks away, a drab building at Kolomenskaya ulitsa 1/15 harbours the **Gumilev Flat-Museum** (Tues–Sat 10.30am–6pm; R100; ⓦwww.akhmatova. spb.ru). As the son of an executed "traitor" and the poet Akhmatova (see box on p.194), Lev Gumilev spent three terms in the Gulag, "Once for my father, once for my mother and once for myself", interrupted by a spell in the Red Army when he helped capture Berlin. A brilliant scholar, he attributed the rise and fall of "ethnoses" (cultures) on the Eurasian steppe to sunspots, and saw the Mongol invasion as no bad thing – unlike Jews, whom he termed a parasitic ethnos (which admirers excuse as an aberration of his final years, afflicted by Alzheimer's). His Eurasian philosophy won many adherents in the perestroika era and is still esteemed by Kazakhstan's president. The museum displays Gumilev's flat as it was at his death in 1992, complete with a pack of the Belomor cigarettes (named after the White Sea Canal where he worked as a slave labourer) that he smoked incessantly. There is also a room devoted to his father, Nikolay, who dismissed warnings not to return to Russia by saying that he had survived savage tribes and wild animals in Africa, so needn't fear the Cheka – a fatal miscalculation.

Along Zagorodniy prospekt

The area around present-day **Zagorodniy prospekt** ("avenue beyond the city") was virgin forest until the middle of the eighteenth century when, in an effort to develop the area, Empress Anna divided it between two regiments of the Imperial Guard: the Semyonovskiy and the Izmailovskiy. Their paths through the woods paved the way for future streets and their massive parade ground (twice the size of Marsovo pole) became the site of St Petersburg's Hippodrome and the Vitebsk Station.

By the latter half of the nineteenth century, Zagorodniy prospekt had developed into a fashionable residential area associated with the city's musical elite. The director of the Conservatory, Rubinstein, lived for a while at no. 9 and Tchaikovsky spent a couple of years at no. 14. Just south of the intersection of streets known as **Five Corners**, which witnessed violent clashes during three revolutions, is the **Rimsky-Korsakov Museum** (11am–6pm; closed Mon, Tues & the last Fri of each month; R75), located in the composer's former apartment on the third floor of the building in no. 28's courtyard. It contains over 250 items kept by his widow and descendants after his death, in anticipation of just such a museum: among them two of his conductor's batons and a costume from his opera *The Snow Maiden*, designed by the artist Vrubel. The walls of the study are hung with portraits of composers whom Rimsky-Korsakov admired. At weekly soirees in the sitting room, Chaliapin sang and Rachmaninov, Scriabin and Stravinsky played the piano – **concerts** still take place here from August onwards (☎713 32 08 for details and bookings).

Pionerskaya ploshchad

Between the Rimsky-Korsakov Museum and Pushkinskaya metro is the ex-stamping ground of the **Semyonovskiy Guards**, the second of the elite regiments founded by Peter the Great. Their parade ground was the scene of the **mock execution of Dostoyevsky** and other members of the Petrashevsky Circle, a sadistic drama devised by Nicholas I. On December 22, 1849, after eight months in the Peter and Paul Fortress, the 21 men were brought here to face a firing squad. The first three were tied to a post (Dostoyevsky was in the next batch), hoods were pulled over their faces and the guards took aim, when an aide rode up with a proclamation and the general in charge read out the commutation of their sentences to hard labour. Two days later, fettered at the ankles, they began their 3000-kilometre trek to Omsk prison in Siberia.

In Soviet times the parade ground was renamed Pionerskaya ploshchad after the Communist youth organization, the Pioneers, and became the site of the **Theatre of Young Spectators** (TYuZ). At the park entrance stands a larger-than-life statue of **Alexander Griboedov** (1795–1829), a soldier and diplomat turned playwright who got into trouble with the censors for his *Woe from Wit* and was arrested for his Decembrist connections, but later rehabilitated and made an envoy to Persia. Alas, on their arrival in Tehran, he and his party were murdered by a mob which sacked the Russian Embassy after an Armenian eunuch had taken refuge there. During Soviet times, his name was bestowed upon the city's loveliest canal, which had previously been named after Catherine the Great.

Rasputin on Gorokhovaya ulitsa

Heading from Zagorodniy prospekt northwest up Gorokhovaya ulitsa (Street of Peas) for 100m brings you to the gloomy residential building at no. 64 that once housed **Rasputin's apartment** – on the third floor at the rear of the courtyard (now a communal flat and not open to visitors). The apartment was kept under permanent surveillance by the Tsarist Okhrana and, as noted by their agents, was visited regularly by Rasputin's aristocratic devotees and a host of other women hoping to win favours at court. Rasputin took his pleasure on a broken sofa, before he arose muttering, "Now, now, Mother. Everything is in order."

The street is also mentioned in Russian literature. The denouement of Dostoyevsky's *The Idiot* takes place in Rogozhin's house on Gorokhovaya ulitsa, "not far from Sadovaya ulitsa", while the Rasputin-like Stavrogin in *The Possessed* commits his crime on the street. Another fictional resident was the famously indolent Oblomov, in Goncharov's novel of the same name.

Vitebsk Station and Tekhnologicheskiy Institut

It's worth taking the metro to Pushkinskaya purely to see **Vitebsk Station** (Vitebskiy vokzal), which was the first train terminal in Russia when it opened in 1837, connecting St Petersburg with the palaces at Tsarskoe Selo and Pavlovsk. The existing station, built in 1904, is the finest **Style Moderne** edifice in St Petersburg, restored for the city's tercentenary. Its facade, halls and waiting rooms are a feast of Art Nouveau ironwork and stucco, tiles and stained-glass windows, with a grand stairway to the ex-Imperial Waiting Room, decorated with murals of the palatial destinations. Near the platforms serving the palaces stands a replica of a nineteenth-century steam train that once operated on the route.

One stop further by metro, the interchange station and the square called **Tekhnologicheskiy Institut** take their name from the Technological Institute, whose lecture theatre hosted the first meeting of the short-lived St Petersburg Soviet of Workers' and Soldiers' Deputies, created during the 1905 Revolution. Under the leadership of Trotsky, Gorky and others, its executive committee assumed the responsibilities of government, issuing a spate of decrees from the Free Economic Society building across the square (no. 33), now called the **Plekhanov House**.

Streets and squares

ploshchad Aleksandra Nevskovo	площадь Александра Невского
Bolshoy Kazechniy pereulok	Большой Казечный переулок
Furshtadtskaya ul.	Фурштадская ул.
Kirochnaya ul.	Кирочная ул.
1-ya Krasnoarmeyskaya ulitsa	1-я Красноармейская ул.
Kuznechniy pereulok	Кузнечный переулок
Ligovskiy prospekt	Лиговский проспект
Liteyniy prospekt	Литейный проспект
ul. Marata	ул. Марата
ul. Mayakovskovo	ул. Маяковского
ul. Pestelya	ул. Пестеля
ploshchad Rastrelli	площадь Растрелли
Shpalernaya ul.	Шпалерная ул.
Solyanoy pereulok	Соляной переулок
Tavricheskaya ul.	Таврическая ул.
Vladimirskiy prospekt	Владимирский проспект
ploshchad Vosstaniya	площадь Восстания
Zagorodniy prospekt	Загородный проспект

Metro stations

Ploshchad Aleksandra Nevskovo	Площадь Александра Невского
Chernyshevskaya	Чернышевская
Dostoevskaya	Достоевская
Ligovskiy Prospekt	Лиговский Проспект
Mayakovskaya	Маяковская
Pushkinskaya	Пушкинская
Tekhnologicheskiy Institut	Технологический Институт
Vladimirskaya	Владимирская
Ploshchad Vosstaniya	Площадь Восстания

Museums

Anna Akhmatova Museum	музей Анны Ахматовой
Arctic and Antarctic Museum	музей Арктики и Антарктики
Bread Museum	музей хлеба
Museum of Decorative and Applied Arts	музей Декоративно-прикладного искусства
Museum of the Defence of Leningrad	музей Обороны Ленинграда
Dostoyevsky Museum	музей-квартира Ф.М. Достоевского
Gumilev Flat-Museum	музей-квартира Льва Гумилёва
Militia Museum	музей истории Милиции
Museum of Music	музей Музыки
Nekrasov Museum	музей-квартира Н.А. Некрасова
Rimsky-Korsakov Museum	музей-квартира Н.А. Римского-Корсакова
Sobchak Museum of the Foundation of Democracy in Modern Russia	музей становления демократии в современной России им. А. Собчака
Suvorov Museum	музей А.В. Суворова
World of Water Museum	музей "Мир Воды"

6

LITEYNIY, SMOLNIY AND VLADIMIRSKAYA | Vladimirskaya

The Trinity Cathedral

The **Trinity Cathedral** (Troitskiy sobor) was originally the garrison church of the Izmailovskiy Guards – hence the enormous **Victory Column** made of captured Turkish cannons outside, removed in Soviet times and only recently reinstated. The cathedral itself is a severe Neoclassical design (1828–35) by Stasov, whose only **external** decoration consists of a frieze of seraphim beneath the cornice and a bas-relief above the portico. Its five ink-blue domes were as much a feature of the skyline as St Isaac's until a fire destroyed the central cupola in 2006, trebling the cost of restoring the cathedral, whose interior was gutted by the Soviets in 1938. It was here that Dostoyevsky married Anna Snitkina in 1867, four months after hiring her as his secretary (see p.207).

The cathedral is ten minutes' walk from Tekhnologicheskiy Institut metro, along 1-ya Krasnoarmeyskaya ulitsa (or you can take tram #16 from Sadovaya ploshchad, or bus #10 down Voznesenskiy prospekt). Krasnoarmeyskaya ulitsa is one of a grid of numbered streets where the Izmailovskiy Guards once lived with their families, renamed in honour of the Red Army in Soviet times.

7

The Southern Suburbs

The **Southern Suburbs**, largely open countryside until the mid-nineteenth century, cover a vast area beyond the Obvodniy Canal. The first buildings here were factories – some of the largest in the Tsarist Empire – and the slum housing that grew up around them became home to a militant working class, which was instrumental in the revolutions of 1905 and 1917. Following the October Revolution, numerous housing projects were undertaken to replace the slum dwellings, while during the 1930s Stalin planned (and partially completed) a new city centre in these suburbs in an attempt to replace the old one, so closely associated with the *ancien régime*. Later on, during the Blockade, the front line ran close to the working-class Narva and Avtovo districts.

While it lacks the beauty of the city centre and the distances involved preclude casual sightseeing, it would be a shame to miss the dramatic **Victory Monument** and the **House of Soviets** on Moskovskiy prospekt, or the charming **Chesma Church**. Another lure is the **Literatorskie mostki** graveyard in the Volkov Cemetery, where many famous Russians are buried. If you're looking for Soviet icons and monuments, check out the Constructivist buildings and elaborate **metro** stations of the Kirov district or the Futurist designs in the **Museum of Porcelain**, while trainspotters should head for the **Outdoor Railway Museum**. With the exception of the cemetery and Museum of Porcelain, everywhere described is within walking distance of a metro station on the Moskovsko–Petrogradskaya or Kirovsko–Vyborgkaya lines, which intersect at Tekhnologicheskiy Institut I and II.

Moskovskiy prospekt

Moskovskiy prospekt is the city's longest avenue, a six-lane boulevard running 9km from Sennaya ploshchad in the centre out to the Victory Monument on ploshchad Pobedy. Envisaged by Stalin as the central axis of postwar Leningrad, it is laid out on a Cyclopean scale and makes an awesome introduction to the city as you drive in from the airport. While no one would suggest walking more than a block or two along the prospekt, it's worth viewing some of the vast edifices and richly appointed metro stations that once betokened a Soviet Leningrad, meant to outshine the pre-revolutionary city centre.

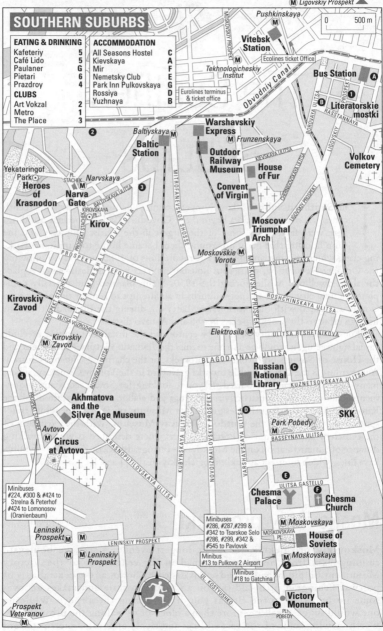

SOUTHERN SUBURBS

EATING & DRINKING		ACCOMMODATION	
Kafeteriy	5	All Seasons Hostel	C
Café Lido	5	Kievskaya	A
Paulaner		Mir	F
Pietari	6	Nemetsky Club	E
Prazdroy	4	Park Inn Pulkovskaya	G
CLUBS		Rossiya	D
Art Vokzal	2	Yuzhnaya	B
Metro	1		
The Place	3		

M Ligovskiy Prospekt ▲

Pushkinskaya

M

Vitebsk Station

Ecolines ticket Office

Tekhnologicheskiy Institut

0   500 m

Bus Station

A

1

Literatorskie mostki

B

RASSTANNAYA

Eurolines terminus & ticket office

Obvodniy Canal

MOSKOVSKIY PROSPEKT

BOROVAYA ULITSA

LIGOVSKIY PROSPEKT

2

Baltiyskaya

M

Warshavskiy Express

M Frunzenskaya

Volkov Cemetery

Baltic Station

Outdoor Railway Museum

House of Fur

KIEVSKAYA ULITSA

Yekateringof Park

PL STACHEK

Narvskaya

Convent of Virgin

M

Heroes of Krasnodon

Narva Gate

3

Moscow Triumphal Arch

CHERNIGOVSKAYA ULITSA

LIGOVSKIY PROSPEKT

BALTIYSKAYA ULITSA

KIROVSKAYA PL

Kirov

MITROFANEVSKOE SHOSSE

PROSPEKT STACHEK

ULITSA MARSHALA GOVOROVA

Moskovskie Vorota

M

UL KOLI TOMCHAKA

PROSPEKT STACHEK

ULITSA MARSHALA TREFOLEVA

MOSKOVSKIY PROSPEKT

ROSHCHINSKAYA ULITSA

VITEBSKIY PROSPEKT

Kirovskiy Zavod

ULITSA VOZROZHDENIYA

Elektrosila M

ULITSA RESHETNIKOVA

Kirovskiy Zavod

M

AVTOLSKAYA ULITSA

BLAGODATNAYA ULITSA

Russian National Library

C

KUZNETSOVSKAYA ULITSA

4

Akhmatova and the Silver Age Museum

KUBINSKAYA ULITSA

NOVOIZMAILOVSKIY PROSPEKT

VARSHAVSKAYA ULITSA

D

SKK

Avtovo

M

Park Pobedy

M

Circus at Avtovo

KRASNOPUTILOVSKAYA ULITSA

BASSEYNAYA ULITSA

Minibuses #224, #300 & #424 to Strelna & Peterhof #424 to Lomonosov (Oranienbaum)

E

ULITSA GASTELLO

F

Chesma Palace

Chesma Church

Leninskiy Prospekt M

M Leninskiy Prospekt

LENINSKIY PROSPEKT

Minibuses #286, #287, #299 & #342 to Tsarskoe Selo #286, #299, #342 & #545 to Pavlovsk

M Moskovskaya

MOSKOVSKAYA PL

House of Soviets

M Moskovskaya

Minibus #13 to Pulkovo 2 Airport

5

N

Minibus #18 to Gatchina

6

G

Victory Monument

PL. POBEDY

Prospekt Veteranov

M

As its name suggests, Moskovskiy prospekt has long been the main road to Moscow – though it didn't acquire this name until 1956. Before that it was called Stalin Avenue, which replaced International Avenue, bestowed after the Revolution; this in its turn replaced Trans-Balkan Avenue, commemorating the Russian troops who had marched down it in 1877 to fight the Turks in Bulgaria. While the Bolsheviks renamed several streets in the city centre after the revolutionary assassins of the 1870s, they chose to ignore a dramatic assassination carried out by the Socialist Revolutionary (SR) Party, their rivals on the left. On July 15, 1904, on the bridge that carries the avenue across the Obvodniy Canal, the SR Fighting Section succeeded in its third attempt on the life of the hated interior minister, Plehve, when an assassin disguised as a railway worker threw a bomb at Plehve's car, blowing him to smithereens.

The following highlights the best and minimizes the boring bits of the avenue. Starting from Frunzenskaya metro, you should alternate between **tram** #29 on the surface, and the Moskovsko–Petrogradskaya **metro** line beneath the avenue, which has several decorative stations to admire. The only impediment to this is the unwieldy system of "horizontal lifts" at some stations, whereby instead of having open platforms, passengers are separated from the tunnel by a wall with sliding doors, synchronized with the doors on the train.

From Frunzenskaya to Park Pobedy

Exiting at **Frunzenskaya** metro, with its aluminum and smalt portrait of the Civil War commander Mikhail Frunze, catch a tram south along the prospekt. On your left, notice the **House of Fur** at no. 98, where fur buyers from around the world gather for auctions three times a year, followed by the decrepit yet still lovely **Convent of the Virgin**, with its yellow-and-white facade, sweeping arcades and beetling bell tower.

Further on you'll sight the dourly imposing **Moscow Triumphal Arch** (Moskovskie vorota), a cast-iron monument modelled on Berlin's Brandenburg Gate. Built by Stasov in the late 1830s to commemorate victories against the Persians, Turks and Poles during the reign of Nicholas I, the arch was dismantled and put into storage in 1936 on Stalin's orders; during the Blockade its iron plates served as anti-tank obstacles. The arch was finally restored in 1961 – allegedly on the spot where all travellers entering the city once had to show that they brought bricks or stones with them, in obedience to a decree by Peter the Great, meant to improve the supply of building materials.

Enter Moskovskie Vorota station and ride on to the next stop, **Elektrosila**, to see a mosaic exalting the electrification of the Soviet Union, which the Elektrosila factory (founded in 1911 by the German company, Siemens-Schuckert) did much to further with its generators, turbines and alloys.

Surfacing again at **Park Pobedy**, you can stroll in a victory park laid out by volunteers in 1945. Its central "Heroes' Alley" flanked by busts of Leningraders twice named "Hero of the Soviet Union" or "Hero of Socialist Labour", leads to the **SKK** (Sportivno-kontsertniy kompleks), a circular sports and leisure complex hosting concerts as well as sports events. On the other side of the avenue stands the **Russian National Library**, built to supersede the venerable institution on Nevskiy prospekt. Returning to the metro, ride on to Moskovskaya station, on Moskovskaya ploshchad.

Moskovskaya ploshchad

Although plans for a giant ring road were never completed, the intended focus of the new centre was realized in the gargantuan **Moskovskaya ploshchad**,

▲ Lenin's Statue by Mikhail Anikushin

a fascinating legacy of Stalinist urban planning. The square is dominated by the **House of Soviets** (Dom Sovetov), begun by Noy Trotsky in 1936, but not completed until after the war. This administrative monolith is 220 metres long and fifty metres high, topped by a frieze portraying Soviet achievements; similar friezes appear on the surrounding buildings. A wartime machine-gun **pillbox** has been preserved as a memorial in front of the building, and in 1970 a bronze **statue of Lenin** (by Mikhail Anikushin) was unveiled in the centre of the square, recently made less austere by rows of fountains.

The Chesma Church and Palace

Within easy walking distance of Moskovskaya ploshchad are a couple of more alluring sights. The first is the **Chesma Church** (daily 9am–7pm), a stunning salmon-pink-and-white striped structure, built by Felten in 1777–80; it's situated just off ulitsa Gastello, behind the *Mir Hotel*. The traditional configuration of five Orthodox domes is almost lost in the feast of lanterns and zigzag crenellations that crown this bizarre "pastry Gothick" building. The church's name derives from the Turkish port of Çesme, where, in 1770, the Russians enjoyed one of their greatest naval victories. The building used to house a museum devoted to the battle but it has now reverted to the Church.

The whiteish **Chesma Palace** (Chesmenskiy dvorets), within sight of the church, was built for Catherine the Great as an Imperial staging post en route to Tsarskoe Selo and Pavlovsk. This was likewise designed by Felten in a kind of Turkish-Gothic style and whimsically known as the "Frog Swamp Palace", for which Catherine commissioned a special dinner service (see p.127). During the palace's conversion into a hospital for war veterans in the 1830s, it was substantially altered by the addition of three wings and the removal of much of its original decoration. Rasputin's body lay in state here after his murder; today the palace is a home for the elderly and closed to the public.

The Victory Monument

South of Moskovskaya ploshchad, it's a short walk past the district's main department stores to the **Victory Monument** (officially entitled the "Monument to the Defenders of Leningrad"), which commemorates the hardship that Leningrad's citizens endured during the Blockade. Paid for by public donations, it was unveiled in 1975 as the centrepiece of ploshchad Pobedy. The bowels of the monument consist of a vast broken ring of steel (symbolizing the breaking of the siege) lined with giant medals and flickering flames, where you can hear the strains of Shostakovich's Seventh Symphony, which was composed and performed during the Blockade. Off this lies a subterranean **memorial hall** (10am–6pm, Tues & Fri till 5pm; closed Wed & the last Tues of the month; free) with bronze caskets displaying relics from the siege, including a violin that was used to perform the symphony. The metronomic beat that you hear was broadcast over the radio throughout the Blockade, to symbolize the starving city's heartbeat.

Above the ground rises a 48-metre-high red granite obelisk, fronted by statues of a soldier and a worker. Most striking of all are the larger-than-life blackened bronze tableaux of partisans, salvage workers, nurses and other citizens, facing south towards the enemy. Constructed on a truly grand scale, it was designed to be viewed from a distance or from a passing vehicle on the main road to and from the airport, to remind foreign visitors of the price that the city paid to defeat the Nazis.

The Kirov district

In the latter half of the nineteenth century, the aristocratic *dacha* colony of Narva, on the road to Peterhof (and Narva, on the Estonian border) was transformed into a sea of hovels, factories and docks, and the whole district became one of the breeding grounds of the revolutionary movement. As such, it was one of the first areas to be redeveloped after the Revolution, when it was renamed the **Kirov district** and endowed with some of the best interwar architecture in the city. While the industrial giants that were its lifeblood have now been carved up and privatized, public space still reflects the collectivist spirit of those times, and the **metro** provides easy access to the district and many of its attractions. The first section of the Kirovsko–Vyborgkaya line, opened in 1955, ran from working-class Avtovo to downtown ploshchad Vosstaniya, and its lavish decor was meant to show the proletariat that they, too, could have palaces. For visitors, they rank alongside the architecture above ground as symbols of Soviet culture from an era when anything seemed possible.

The Outdoor Railway Museum

The **Outdoor Railway Museum** (Zheleznaya Doroga muzey; 11am–6pm; R150) celebrates the heritage of the world's largest rail network. If you're around at the time, come on Railway Workers' Day (August 5), when locomotives puff steam, staff wear dress uniforms and a band entertains their families. Amongst the postwar rolling stock in fetching colours, look out for the last ever steam locomotive manufactured in the Soviet Union (in 1956), emblazoned with the profiles of Lenin and Stalin, two rows to the right of a TM-3-12 artillery train (used in the Winter War and again in 1941), and a rail-based SS-24 intercontinental nuclear missile launcher. The museum lurks behind the former **Warsaw Station** on the Obvodniy Canal, now the **Warshavskiy Express** mall (10am–10pm daily), incorporating a cinema, bowling alley, exclusive restaurant and strip club.

Both are five minutes' walk from the **Baltic Station**, fronted by a square from which minibuses run to Peterhof, and Eurolines coaches depart for abroad (see p.28). The station is adjacent to **Baltiyskaya metro**, whose maritime-themed decor features grey marble walls, vaults resembling billowing sails, bronze anchors and a mosaic depicting the *Volley from the Cruiser Aurora*, at the end of the platform.

Ploshchad Stachek and Yekateringof Park

Narvskaya, the next station, is equally striking, lauding the achievements of local workers in peace, revolution and war. Notice the victory motifs in the cupola and a bas-relief of Lenin orating at the top of the escalator; underground are ivory-hued marble walls and 48 columns sculpted with miners, metallurgists, sailors and teachers at work, lit by crystal arcs flowing from the torches of crimson mosaic friezes.

You'll emerge on **ploshchad Stachek** (Strike Square), scene of the first of the many fatal clashes on "Bloody Sunday" (January 9, 1905). Tsarist troops fired without warning on the column of peaceful demonstrators heading for the Winter Palace, carrying portraits of the tsar and a white flag. In 1941, as the Nazis encircled Leningrad, a German motorcycle patrol managed to get as far as ploshchad Stachek, before it was annihilated.

At the centre of the square is the copper-plated **Narva Gate** (Narvskoe vorota), a diminutive triumphal arch erected to commemorate the Napoleonic Wars. The original arch was hastily designed by Quarenghi in wood, in order to greet the victorious Imperial armies returning from the west, but was later replaced by Stasov's present structure, crowned by a statue of Victory astride her six-horse chariot, painted a fetching sea-green.

Most of the surrounding architecture dates from a redevelopment of the late 1920s, when Constructivism was still in vogue. Examples include the **Gorky Palace of Culture** beside the metro, with its convex facade; a heroic **mural** on the building just beyond; and the department store on the other side of the square.

Crossing over via an underpass, it's a short walk to **Yekateringof Park**, where a palace founded by Peter the Great for his wife, Catherine, was given to the League of Young Communists, or Komsomol – who promptly burnt it down during a party. Just inside the park stand the **Heroes of Krasnodon**, honouring a Komsomol partisan detachment – perhaps the only monument left in St Petersburg to feature Stalin, on the banner held aloft by the partisans. Further in you'll find a lake with pedaloes, a fairground, a riding club and pensioners playing chess.

Kirovskaya ploshchad to Avtovo

To see how the reconstruction plan continued, walk 300m down prospekt Stachek, to the expanse of **Kirovskaya ploshchad**, a Stalinist set piece centred on a vast **statue of Kirov**, the assassinated Party boss (see p.201). On the right as you approach the square is the first **school** to be built in the city after the Revolution, with a ground plan in the shape of a hammer and sickle – a motif that also appears on the tower of another Constructivist edifice that houses the district administration, directly behind Kirov's statue.

There's more worth seeing at the two metro stations after Narvskaya. **Kirovskiy Zavod** is named after a heavy engineering plant; its marble pillars are surmounted by silver-plated symbols of oil extraction, steel and power production, watched by a saturnine red-granite Lenin at the end of the platform. The factory was founded in 1801 as the Putilov Works, and soon became Russia's largest enterprise (employing over 40,000 people) and the cradle of the working-class movement. It was the dismissal of four *Putilovtsiy* that sparked the 1905 Revolution, while a lockout primed the overthrow of Tsarism in 1917. During the Blockade it was battered by Nazi artillery but production never ceased, though workers had to tie themselves to their benches to avoid fainting from hunger. After the war, the factory produced submarine turbines and other high-tech military items – a specialization that brought it to the verge of bankruptcy when the defence budget was slashed in the 1990s. Today, its finances are healthier thanks to arms sales to India, China, Iran and Syria.

The proximity of the frontline to **Avtovo** during the war might explain the lavishness of its metro station – and certainly the martial motifs in the ticket hall. The platform's coffered roof is upheld by 46 columns, thirty clad in white marble, and sixteen in cut, patterned glass, mirrored inside to conceal the concrete shafts that bear the weight. Avtovo is an unlikely setting for the **Akhmatova and the Silver Age Museum** (Mon–Fri 10am–6pm; R70), founded by admirers of the poetess Akhmatova (see p.194). Its display traces the lives and relationships of such luminaries as Blok, Mandelstam, Roerich and Bakst. To get there, turn right outside the metro, keep going till you see the **Circus on Avtovo** (p.368) and head up Avtovskaya ulitsa, where the museum is identifiable by purple signs outside no.14.

The Literatorskie mostki

Although Dostoyevsky feared that he would be buried there "beside all my enemies", few luminaries of pre-revolutionary Russian culture would have spurned a plot in the **Literatorskie mostki** (April–Oct 11am–7pm; Nov–March 11am–5pm; closed Thurs), an elite enclosure within the Volkov Cemetery. Among the better-known personalities interred here are the writers **Turgenev** and **Andreyev**, the poet **Blok**, the painter **Petrov-Vodkin** and the scientists **Mendeleyev**, **Popov** and **Pavlov**, not to mention the "Father of Russian Marxism", **Plekhanov**. At the entrance is a **memorial hall** (11am–5pm; closed Thurs; free) with busts and exhibits devoted to many of the above, and a **plan** of the cemetery (in Russian only). Lenin's mother, two sisters and brother-in-law are buried in a specially landscaped section near the northern wall, and should **Lenin** himself ever be removed from his mausoleum on Red Square, he might end up beside them, as he is said to have requested (though no written evidence has been found to back up this claim).

To get there from the city centre, take the metro to Ligovskiy Prospekt station and then a **minibus** (#10, #25, #44 or #49) to the end of Rasstannaya ulitsa.

The Museum of Porcelain

During the eighteenth century, porcelain was highly prized and the secrets of its manufacture jealously guarded, obliging Peter the Great to buy his dinner services abroad. In 1744 Empress Elizabeth hired a Swede, Christoph Hunger, to found a Russian porcelain industry using clay deposits at Gzhel, outside Moscow. Under his assistant, Dmitri Vinogradov, the Imperial Porcelain Factory in St Petersburg began producing dinner services for the Court and nobility, while the Gardner, Batenin and Popov factories later appeared to cater to a wider market – all of which were nationalized after the October Revolution.

The **Museum of Porcelain** (muzey Farfora; daily 10.30am–6pm, Sun till 5pm; closed Mon; R200) is a branch of the Hermitage whose collection ranges from the 973-piece Arabesque Service of Catherine the Great to Style Moderne and Soviet glassware. Of particular interest are Constructivist pieces of the 1920s, including an impractical teapot designed by Malevich, plates decorated by Petrov-Vodkin and other Futurists, and cups from the Stalin and Brezhnev eras, celebrating the construction of the metro and the conquest of space.

To get there, take the metro to Lomonosovskaya station, cross the main road and head towards the Neva embankment, where you'll find the museum at prospekt Obukhovskoy Oborony 151. If you happen to have bought a combined ticket to the Hermitage (see p.117), this includes admission to the Museum of Porcelain.

The Southern Suburbs

Streets and squares

ul. Gastello	ул. Гастелло
Kirovskaya ploshchad	Кировская площадь
Ligovskiy prospekt	Лиговский проспект
Moskovskaya ploshchad	Московская площадь
Moskovskiy prospekt	Московский проспект
ploshchad Pobedy	площадь Победы
ul. Rasstannaya	ул. Расстанная
ploshchad Stachek	площадь Стачек

Metro stations

Avtovo	Автово
Baltiyskaya	Балтийская
Elektrosila	лектросила
Frunzenskaya	Фрунзенская
Kirovskiy Zavod	Кировский завод
Moskovskaya	Московская
Moskovskie Vorota	Московские Ворота
Narvskaya	Нарвская
Obukhovo	Обухово
Park Pobedy	Парк Победы

Museums and sights

Akhmatova and the Silver Age Museum	музей Ахматова Серебхряный век
Chesma Church	Чесменская церковь
Literatorskie mostki graveyard	Литераторские мостки некрополь
Museum of Porcelain	музей Фарфора
Outdoor Railway Museum	Железеная Дорога музей

8

Vyborg Side

The industrialized sprawl of the **Vyborg Side** (Vyborgkaya storona) holds little appeal compared to other parts of St Petersburg, but its contribution to the city's history is undeniable. As factories burgeoned along the Bolshaya Nevka embankment and slums spread northwards, the district became a hotbed of working-class militancy. Despite the forbidding presence of the Moscow Guards regiment and **Kresty Prison**, the locals erupted in 1905 and again in 1917, battling troops at the barricades. Lenin was welcomed back from exile at the **Finland Station** and subsequently hid out in the quarter before the October Revolution. Further north, **St Samson's Cathedral** remains a picturesque relic of eighteenth-century St Petersburg, while the sombre **Piskarov Memorial Cemetery** contains the remains of 470,000 victims of the Siege of Leningrad. Further west, the Staraya Derevnya district contains a delightful **Buddhist Temple**, across the river from Yelagin Island, and the **Hermitage Depository** (only accessible by arrangement). Future visitors may be awed or horrified by the **Gazprom Tower**, to be built across the river from the Smolniy (see box on p.227).

Given the distances between the sights, **getting around** involves using two or three separate **metro** lines that oblige you to return to the centre and change trains to switch from one line to another. Better options are to walk, if possible, or you can usually catch a **minibus** from Ploshchad Lenina, Chernaya Rechka or Staraya Derevnya metro stations to each sight, as detailed in the text.

Finland Station

The **Finland Station** (Finlyandskiy vokzal) seems an unlikely spot for a momentous, curtain-raising piece of history. Despite efforts to make the square outside – **ploshchad Lenina** – look imposing, the concrete shed that replaced the old station in the 1950s only looks impressive at night, floodlit gold and blue.

Nevertheless, it's possible to imagine the scene when the train carrying the exiles pulled into the station at 11.30pm on April 3, 1917. Alighting from the train, Lenin seemed stunned by his reception: the platform was decked with red-and-gold arches and lined with Kronstadt sailors and cheering Bolsheviks, while the square was packed with tens of thousands of spectators. Aboard an armoured car, he forged his way through the crowd, shouting, "Long live the Socialist Revolution!" and giving prizefighter's salutes from its turret.

You'll need a platform ticket to see the station's landmarks. The exit by which Lenin left is still preserved alongside platform 1, as is the adjacent waiting room where Chkheidze, Menshevik president of the Petrograd Soviet, welcomed him with cautious platitudes. Three months later, having provoked the Provi-

221

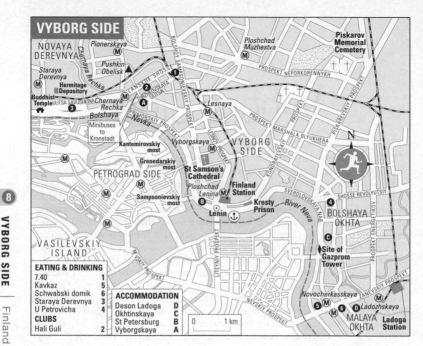

VYBORG SIDE

NOVAYA DEREVNYA
Pionerskaya
Pushkin Obelisk
Staraya Derevnya
Hermitage Depository
Buddhist Temple
ULITSA SAVUSHKINA
Chernaya Rechka
Bolshaya Nevka
Minibuses to Kronstadt
Kantemirovskiy most
Grenedarskiy most
PETROGRAD SIDE
Sampsonievskiy most
VASILEVSKIY ISLAND

Chernaya Rechka
PRIMORSKIY PROSPEKT
Vyborgskaya
Lesnaya
St Samson's Cathedral
Ploshchad Lenina
Lenin
Finland Station
Kresty Prison

BOLSHOY SAMPSONIEVSKIY PROSPEKT
FINLYANDSKAYA ULITSA
LENISA PROSPEKT
VYBORG SIDE
PROSPEKT MARSHALA BLYUKHERA
KONDRATEVSKIY

Ploshchad Muzhestva
PROSPEKT NEPOKORENNYKH
Piskarov Memorial Cemetery
PISKAREVSKIY PROSPEKT

N

SVERDLOVSKAYA NAB
SHOSSE REVOLYUTSIY
River Neva
BOLSHAYA OKHTA
Site of Gazprom Tower
PROSPEKT ENERGETIKOV

Novocherkasskaya
Ladozhskaya
MALAYA OKHTA
Ladoga Station
ZANEVSKIY PROSPEKT

EATING & DRINKING
7.40   1
Kavkaz   5
Schwabski domik 6
Staraya Derevnya 3
U Petrovicha   4
CLUBS
Hali Guli   2

ACCOMMODATION
Deson Ladoga   D
Okhtinskaya   C
St Petersburg B
Vyborgskaya   A

0   1 km

sional Government into cracking down on the Bolsheviks, Lenin was forced to flee, disguised in a wig and labourer's clothes. After hiding out near Razliv (see p.286), he was smuggled into Finland by train, disguised as a fireman. In the autumn he returned by the same train (with the help of its Finnish Communist driver, Hugo Jalava) to persuade his colleagues that the time was ripe for a coup (see p.225). The train's steam engine, **Locomotive #293**, stands in a glass pavilion near platform 10, having been presented by the Finnish government as a gift in 1957. Also notice the sculpted hammer and wrench beside platform 6/7, commemorating the **Road of Life** convoys that arrived here during the Blockade (see p.296).

The Lenin statue

At the riverside end of ploshchad Lenina stands the first ever **Lenin statue** to be unveiled in the Soviet Union (on November 7, 1926), setting the tone for the thousands that followed. Lenin has one thumb hooked into his waistcoat and gestures imperiously with his other hand; an oft-repeated pose which inspired the joke "Where did you get that waistcoat?" – "Over there." In time, the city acquired seven major statues of Lenin, each the butt of some witticism. One relates how a statue's arm broke off and the foundry cast its replacement holding a worker's cap, not realizing that the figure already wore one.

Ironically, Lenin abhorred the idea of statues in his honour, believing that "they only gather bird shit". His Last Testament forbade them and, it is said, stipulated a modest burial alongside his mother in the Volkov Cemetery; but Stalin enshrined Lenin's body on Moscow's Red Square. In the post-Communist era, St Petersburg considered a purge of its Soviet monuments but all the

Vladimir Ilyich Ulyanov (1870–1924) was born in Simbirsk on the Volga. His father was a schools inspector of Kalmyk ancestry, his ethnic-German mother a strict Lutheran. In 1887, his elder brother, Alexander, was arrested and hanged for his part in a student plot to kill the tsar. Vladimir never forgot this, or the ostracism of the Ulyanovs by their liberal friends – the source of his enduring scorn for "bourgeois radicals". Reading Chernyshevsky's *What Is to be Done?* (a title he would later use for one of his own works) and Marx's *Das Kapital* confirmed him into the faith of **revolutionary socialism**. His later alias, **Lenin**, referred to a cause célèbre (the strike of the Lena River gold-miners), but Party comrades nicknamed him *Starik* (old man), because of his premature baldness.

Exiled to Siberia for Marxist agitation in 1897, he was joined there by **Nadezhda Krupskaya**, whom he probably married in church to satisfy the authorities and keep her mother happy. In 1900, after his term of exile, Lenin left Russia to set up the Communist paper *Iskra* (*The Spark*) in Munich: the start of a seventeen-year odyssey around Europe, encompassing genteel poverty in Brussels, Paris, London and Zurich, where Lenin engaged in bitter sectarian battles with fellow exiled Marxists. In 1903 the Russian Social Democratic Labour Party – of which Lenin was a leading member – split into hardline **Bolsheviks** (majority) and moderate Mensheviks (minority), leaving Lenin with a group of radicals to forge into an instrument of his will. Whilst in Paris in 1910, he began a lasting political and romantic relationship with the vibrant French radical, **Inessa Armand**, who spent the war years with Lenin and Krupskaya in Switzerland.

Caught napping by the February Revolution of 1917 in Russia, Lenin hastened to return home. A deal was struck with the German government, which hoped to weaken Russia with "the bacillus of Bolshevism", to convey Lenin and his companions across Europe. Thirty exiles boarded the famous "sealed train" for Stockholm, crossed into Finland on sleighs and eventually transferred to an ordinary Russian train. Lenin stayed up all night quizzing soldiers about the military situation in Petrograd, as the train sped towards the city. He had already decided to take over the Petrograd Soviet and overthrow the Provisional Government: all that mattered was how and when.

See p.225 and p.402 for more about Lenin's seizure of power.

8

major Lenin statues were spared – a few have since succumbed to developers. Besides this one, the most striking statue still standing is at Moskovskya ploshschad, in the southern suburbs (see Chapter 7).

Kresty Prison

From the embankment beside ploshchad Lenina you can survey a bleak arc of the Neva between the most infamous buildings in the city. Across the river looms the headquarters of the secret police, the Bolshoy dom (p.196), while beyond the Arsenal on the Vyborg Side is Kresty Prison. During the 1930s and 1940s, the two "processed" scores of thousands of people, whose relatives traipsed between the buildings day after day, trying to discover the victims' fate. While the Bolshoy dom has lost its terrible grip on the population, ending up in Kresty is still to be feared by anyone arrested and charged by the Militia.

When **Kresty Prison** (ⓦwww.kresty.ru, in Russian only) was first built in the reign of Catherine the Great, it was considered a model of its kind, taking its name – "Crosses" – from its double cross-shaped configuration. Here, Trotsky and other revolutionaries awaited trial in 1905, and the Bolsheviks incarcer-

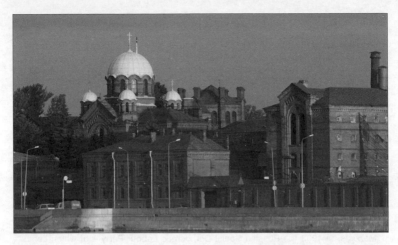

▲ Kresty Prison

ated the Provisional Government in October 1917. During the mass **purges** of 1934–36, the poet Akhmatova queued for 18 months outside Kresty, with a host of other women, all seeking news. One day, she was recognized by a stranger, who sidled up and whispered, "Can you describe this?" Akhmatova obliged with *Requiem*, a series of prose poems that opens with an account of the episode and concludes:

And from my motionless bronze-lidded sockets,

May the melting snow like teardrops slowly trickle.

And a prison dove coo somewhere over and over

As the ships sail softly down the flowing Neva.

Nowadays, it is a remand prison for "non-politicals" who spend up to eighteen months awaiting trial. Kresty was built to hold 3000 prisoners but until 2002 held twelve thousand, crammed ten or fifteen into a cell: today, thanks to efforts by NGOs, the Ministry of Justice and the European Union, the number is down to four prisoners per cell and the daily food budget (R50 per head) compares favourably with that of army conscripts. Nonetheless, tuberculosis is rife within the Russian penal system, where 90,000 prisoners are thought to be infected, one fifth of them with multi-drug-resistant TB.

That's something to bear in mind if you're tempted to join the voyeuristic one-hour **tour** offered by the administration (Sat & Sun at 10.30am, noon, 1.30pm & 3pm; R250), that's also available with an English-speaking guide from VB Excursions (Ⓦwww.vb-excursions) for R1050 per person. Tickets are sold at the lawyers' office at Arsenalnaya naberezhnaya 7 before the start of each tour; groups of ten or more may book an excursion on weekdays by calling ☏542 68 61. In any case, be sure to bring your passport along.

Visitors get to see a cell, the **chapel** – previously turned into a warders' club with a portrait of "Iron Felix" and the motto "Do as Dzerzhinsky would have done!" where the altar used to be – and Kresty's **museum**, with exhibits on famous prisoners and items crafted by others, such as a cops 'n' robbers chess set made from bits of chewed, dried, glazed bread.

St Samson's Cathedral

Behind the prison and the station is a hinterland of freight yards and factories. One of the earliest plants on the Vyborg Side was the Russian Diesel Factory, founded in 1824 by the Swedish immigrant **Emmanuel Nobel**, whose son, Ludwig, began producing pig iron here in 1862. Ludwig's son, Alfred, famously went on to invent dynamite and expiate his guilt by founding the Nobel prizes. Though most factories were nationalized soon after the Revolution, the economic demands of the Civil War meant that few benefits accrued to the proletariat until the early 1930s, when a Constructivist **workers' club** was built on the corner of Bolshoy Sampsonievskiy prospekt and Grenedarskaya ulitsa, a few minutes' walk frrom Vyborgkaya metro.

Across the road, **St Samson's Cathedral** (Sampsonievskiy sobor; 10am–8pm, closed Wed; R200) is an anachronism amid the smokestacks. One of the oldest churches in the city, it was built of wood in 1727, beside St Petersburg's first cemetery, where people of all faiths were buried (including the architects Trezzini and Le Blond and the sculptor Carlo Rastrelli), and dedicated to the saint whose feast day coincided with the date of the Battle of Poltava (July 10 by today's calendar). The existing stone edifice was completed in 1740 and possibly designed by Bartolomeo Rastrelli. Its magnificent 13-metre-high **iconostasis** is painted to resemble malachite and carved with cherubs and saints, and the side chapels are likewise a stylistic mix of Byzantine and Baroque. Notice the mural of Peter the Great after the Battle of Poltava in the vault, and the pictorial calendar that identifies each saint's feast day. The **secret wedding of Catherine the Great and Potemkin** is thought to have taken place here in 1774, attended only by three witnesses.

In the grounds is a gilded **monument** marking the graves of three courtiers beheaded on the orders of Empress Anna's lover, Count Biron, who was said to treat "Men like horses and horses like men". One of them, Artemi Volynskiy, was responsible for organizing the festivities at Anna's notorious Ice Palace on the Neva (see p.79). On the other side of the street stands a swashbuckling **statue of Peter the Great**.

Lenin's last secret address

A faded scarlet **mural** on the side of a tenement block is a mute reminder of **Lenin's last secret address**, Serdobolskaya ulitsa 1, where he stayed in the apartment of Party member Margarita Sofanova after returning from Finland. While the Central Committee procrastinated, Lenin feared that the moment for a coup would pass: on the night of October 24, he quit the flat, leaving a note reading, "I've gone where you didn't want me to go. Goodbye. Ilyich", and boarded a tram for the Smolniy. He and his companion, Eino Rahja, managed to bluff their way through several checkpoints to join their colleagues in the Smolniy. While the rest may be history, the idea that Lenin instantly assumed control of a well-planned coup owes much to Soviet propaganda. Though every textbook states that it occurred on October 25, 1917, the exact **date of the Bolshevik Revolution** is by no means certain. A 1962 conference of Soviet historians ended in violent disagreement – with one faction asserting the Revolution was on the morning of October 24, another, the afternoon of the same day, and a third, October 22. The implications are that the coup may have been well under way – if not virtually over – by the time that Lenin arrived, although the mural naturally emphasizes his central role and even features a map of his route to the Smolniy. Should you fancy seeing the mural, it's at the corner of Bolshoy Sampsonievskiy prospekt and Serdobolskaya ulitsa; trolleybus #21 runs all the way there from Chernaya Rechka metro.

Piskarov Memorial Cemetery

Until 1990 the **Piskarov Memorial Cemetery** (Piskaryovskoe memorialnoe kladbishche; daily 10am–5/6pm; free) in the city's northern suburbs used to be the first stop on Intourist excursions – a pointed reminder to visitors of the city's sacrifices in the war against fascism. Today, few tour groups visit the cemetery, but the grounds are still tidily kept and wreaths are laid every May 9 – Victory Day. Should you wish to pay your respects to the 670,000 citizens who died during the Blockade, the cemetery lies way out along prospekt Nepokoryonnykh – the "Avenue of the Unconquered". Bus #100 runs there from ploshchad Iskusstv (outside the Russian Museum) in the centre, or you can take the metro to Lesnaya station, then bus #33 to the end of the line, cross the train tracks and catch a #138 to the cemetery; either way takes about an hour, depending on the traffic.

The cemetery's **origins** lie in the mass burials that took place near the village of Piskarovka from February 1942 onwards. As nobody had the strength to dig the frozen ground, sappers blasted pits into which the unidentified bodies were tipped; some 470,000 people were interred like this. After the war, it took five years of grisly labour to transform the burial ground into a memorial cemetery, which was solemnly opened in 1960. Some might find its poignancy diminished by the regimented layout and cheery flowerbeds, but its sad power is palpable on rainy days and, above all, in winter.

At the entrance are two **memorial halls** containing grim photo-montages and personal effects, such as a facsimile of the diary of 11-year-old Tanya Savicheva, whose entire family starved to death (she was later evacuated, but also died). On display, too, is the cemetery register, open at a page bearing the entries: "February, 1942: 18th – 3,241 bodies; 19th – 5,559; 20th – 10,043". Further into the cemetery, beyond the trees, an **eternal flame**, kindled by a torch lit from Marsovo pole, flickers on a terrace above the necropolis.

Life during the Blockade

The Blockade may not have lasted for the full nine hundred days of popular legend, but the agonies associated with it defy exaggeration. Between early September 1941 – when the Germans cut off rail links to the city and began bombarding it – and February 7, 1944, when the first trainload of food pulled into Finland Station, Leningrad was dependent on its own resources and whatever could be brought across Lake Ladoga on the icy "Road of Life" in winter. The result was slow **starvation**, as daily rations shrank to 500–600 calories per person. In November 1941, the bread ration was 250 grammes per day for factory workers and 125 grammes for the other two-thirds of the population; the "bread" constituted fifty percent rye flour, the rest being bran, sawdust or anything else to hand. People boiled leather or wallpaper to make broth, and ate cats and dogs. Some even resorted to cannibalism so that citizens feared to walk past alleyways, lest they be garrotted and butchered; if discovered, cannibals were generally executed on the spot.

Although **bombardments** killed seventeen thousand people, far more deaths were caused by starvation and the cold. In winter there was no heating, no water, no electricity and no public transport; amidst blizzards, Leningraders queued for bread, drew water from frozen canals, scavenged for firewood and dragged their dead on sledges to the cemeteries. Eventually, the living grew too weak and the dead too numerous for individual funerals, and corpses were left at designated spots to be collected for burial in mass graves.

Flanking its 300-metre-long central avenue are 186 low, grassy mounds, each with a granite slab that simply records the year of burial and whether the dead were soldiers (marked by a red star) or civilians (with a hammer and sickle). At the far end, a six-metre-tall, bronze **statue of Mother Russia** by Vera Isayeva and Robert Taurit holds a garland of oak and laurel leaves, as if to place it on the graves of the fallen. The **memorial wall** behind is inscribed with a poem by the Blockade survivor Olga Bergholts.

Chernaya rechka and Staraya Derevnya

Chernaya rechka – or "Black Stream" – is an appropriate name for what is now a high-rise, industrialized zone; its only claim to fame is that it was in a meadow in this locality that **Pushkin's duel** with D'Anthès took place, on January 27, 1837. On the centenary of Pushkin's death a granite **obelisk** was erected on the spot, in what is now a park alongside Kolomyazhskiy prospekt, and a statue of the poet was installed in Chernaya Rechka metro station. Lermontov, too, fought a duel here with the son of the French ambassador, de Barantes, but escaped alive, only to be killed in another duel the following year in the Caucasus (where, ironically, he had been exiled for fighting the duel with Barantes).

Further west, the residential **Staraya Derevnya** (Old Village) district harbours the **Hermitage Depository**, where historic costumes, state carriages and other artefacts are stored. It can only be visited on prearranged tours under strict security; contact the excursions bureau (☏571 84 46; 10.30am–4pm; closed Mon) in the Hermitage (see Chapter 2) if you're interested. The Depository is at Zausadebnaya ulitsa 37A, in a warehouse zone across the main road from Staraya Derevnya metro.

The Gazprom Tower

Since 2006, conservationists and civic activists have been fighting an unequal battle against Governor Matvienko and the energy giant Gazprom's decision to build the **Gazprom Tower**, a headquarters and executive residence for its oil subsidiary which will form part of the "Gazprom City" development. Local architects boycotted the competition and three international jurors resigned in protest at the skyscraper heights allowed. The winning design (by the British-based firm RMJM) was a tapering, twisting, five-sided glass pinnacle rising 396m (1300 feet) into the air, across the river from the Smolniy. Better to pierce the sky than prod it, said the lead architect when challenged that it would ruin the city's horizontal skyline and dwarf every monument (prompting UNESCO to threaten to remove St Petersburg's World Heritage status if the plan goes ahead). Moreover, the city is to invest $2.2 billion but will not own a stake in Gazprom City, supposedly recouping its costs from future tax revenues – a taxpayer-funded handout to Russia's richest corporation. When opponents managed to get a referendum on the issue, a "doppelganger" group filed its own motion to confuse voters; in 2007 a protest march was "policed" with paratroopers parked just off Nevskiy to deter people from participating. When asked for his opinion on the matter, Putin replied: "There is no need to pass the buck to me. I have a lot of problems to deal with as it is." If you're curious to see how the foundations are progressing, take the metro to Novocherkaskaya and then trolleybus #7 or #18 or any minibus north along Novocherkaskiy prospekt. The construction site is just beyond the Bolsheoktinskiy bridge.

Otherwise, the only reason to make it out this far is to visit the Buddhist Temple, on the embankment facing Yelagin Island.

The Buddhist Temple

St Petersburg's **Buddhist Temple** (Buddiyskiy khram; daily 11am–7pm; free; Ⓦwww.dazan.spb.ru) is smaller than the city's mosque, synagogue and cathedrals, yet expresses its cultural heritage no less vividly. It is actually a *datsan*, or Buddhist monastery, whose monks observe all the rituals of their faith and have painstakingly restored the building. After years behind scaffolding, its magnificent facade can now be admired, with Tibetan-style sloping walls and a lilac, red and gold portico surmounted by totemic statues and a pagoda spire. Besides daily **services** at 10am and 3pm, the sixteen-day New Year festival (late Feb/early March) and other Tibetan holy days are celebrated here.

Most of Russia's Buddhists are Mongols from the Buryat region of central Siberia that was taken into the Tsarist Empire centuries ago. Buddhism was recognized as a "traditional" religion of the empire like Orthodoxy, Islam and Judaism, and the Soviets treated it less harshly than the others until a Buryat revolt in 1929 led Stalin to kill 35,000 Mongols and shut all the monasteries and temples – this one became an entomology institute until it was handed back to the Buryat Republic in 1991.

The *datsan* belongs to the Gelugpa or Yellow Hat sect of Tibetan Buddhism whose spiritual leader is the Dalai Lama. It was constructed in 1900–15 by the Buryat scholar Agvan-Dorjiev, with the support of Nicholas II's Buddhist physician Pyotr Badmaev, who had long urged the annexation of Manchuria to bring

Vyborg Side

Streets and squares

Arsenalnaya nab.	Арсенальная наб.
Bolshoy Sampsonievskiy prospekt	Большой Сампсониевский пр.
Kolomyazhskiy prospekt	Коломяжский пр.
ul. Lebedeva	ул. Лебедева
Lesnoy prospekt	Лесной пр.
Lipova alleya	Липова аллея
prospekt Nepokoryonnykh	пр. Непокорённых
Primorskiy prospekt	Приморский пр.
Serdobolskaya ul.	Сердобольская ул.
Sverdlovskaya nab.	Свердловская наб.
Zausadebnaya ul.	Заусадебная ул.

Metro stations

Chernaya Rechka	Чёрная речка
Lesnaya	Лесная
Ploshchad Lenina	площадь Ленина
Ploshchad Muzhestva	площадь Мужества
Staraya Derevnya	Старая Деревня
Vyborgkaya	Выборгская

Sights and monuments

Buddhist Temple	Буддийский храм
Finland Station	Финляндский вокзал
Piskarov Memorial Cemetery	Пискарёвское мемориальное кладбище
St Samson's Cathedral	Сампсониевский собор

all Buddhist Mongols into the empire, and was thus partly responsible for the war with Japan in 1905. Agvan-Dorjiev later made a Faustian pact with the Communists to preserve some vestiges of Buddhism in the Soviet Union, but was eventually arrested and killed in 1938.

The *datsan* is located at Primorskiy prospekt 91, near the bridge over to Yelagin Island (see p.186). The easiest way of **getting there** is by bus #110 from Staraya Derevnya metro south along Lipovaya alleya as far as ulitsa Savushkina, one block north of the temple; or by bus #211 or tram #46 from Chernaya Rechkaya metro along ulitsa Savushkina, alighting at Lipovaya alleya.

Out of
the City

Out of the City

The Imperial palaces

he Russian Imperial court was the largest and most extravagant in Europe, and the **Imperial palaces**, established outside St Petersburg during the eighteenth century, are its most spectacular legacy. During the golden age of autocracy, these estates grew ever more ostentatious, demonstrating the might of the Romanov dynasty through the sheer luxuriance of its residences. Largely designed by foreign architects, but constructed by Russian craftsmen using the Empire's vast natural resources of gold, marble, malachite, porphyry, lapis lazuli and amber, the palaces now count among the most important cultural monuments in Russia.

The peripatetic nature of **court life** meant that each ruler divided his or her time between several palaces, remodelling them as they saw fit. Initially, the palaces functioned as magnificent stage sets, against which scenes of murder, passion and intrigue were played out, but as St Petersburg grew ever more politically volatile, they became a place of refuge for the country's rulers. After the Revolution, the palaces were opened and ordinary citizens were invited to feast their eyes on the awesome facades and opulent interiors – the fruits of centuries of exploitation.

During **World War II**, all of the palaces except Oranienbaum lay within Nazi-occupied territory. Peterhof and Strelna bore the brunt of artillery barrages from Soviet-held Kronstadt, and were systematically looted by the Germans, who dynamited, burned and booby-trapped the other palaces as they fell back before the Soviet advance in 1944. This "cultural destruction" was one of the charges brought against the Nazis at the Nuremburg Trials by Soviet prosecutors. It was years before any of the palaces were reopened to the public, and the fact that they were reconstructed at all seems even more incredible than their creation.

Peterhof and **Tsarskoe Selo** are the most elaborate and popular of the palaces, followed – roughly in order of merit – by **Pavlovsk**, **Gatchina**, **Oranienbaum** and **Strelna**. All the palaces (but not all the towns in which they stand) have reverted to their pre-revolutionary **names** (as used in this chapter), but the Soviet titles of three of them are still often used by Russians: Petrodvorets (Peterhof), Pushkin (Tsarskoe Selo) and Lomonosov (Oranienbaum). These replaced the original names, which were considered to be too reactionary or too Germanic, while Gatchina was once briefly called Trotsk (after Trotsky).

Visiting the palaces

Minibuses are the easiest way to reach the palaces: the points of departure for services to Strelna, Peterhof, Tsarskoe Selo, Pavlovsk, Oranienbaum and Gatchina are all located close to metro stations, and shown on our map of the Southern Suburbs (p.214). Services run every ten to twenty minutes, and since you buy a

THE IMPERIAL PALACES

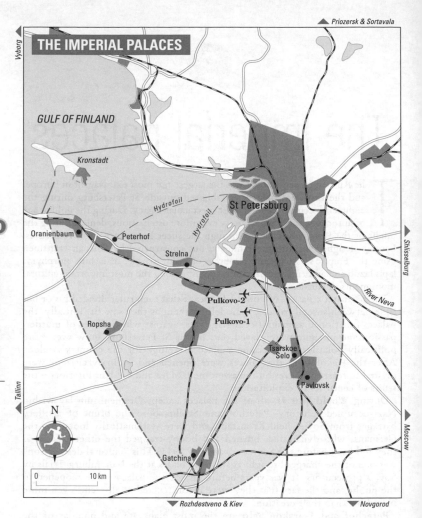

Priozersk & Sortavala

Vyborg

GULF OF FINLAND

Kronstadt

Hydrofoil

Hydrofoil

St Petersburg

Shlisselburg

Oranienbaum

Peterhof

Strelna

River Neva

Pulkovo-2

Pulkovo-1

Ropsha

Tsarskoe
Selo

Moscow

Pavlovsk

Tallinn

N

Gatchina

0   10 km

Rozhdestveno & Kiev

Novgorod

ticket on board, there's no need to queue or worry about finding the right ticket kiosk – which isn't the case with the **suburban train** system (*prigorodniy poezd* or *elektrichka*). Though trains are nearly as frequent as minibuses at weekends, they don't run at all between 10am and noon on weekdays, and foreigners are liable to be confused by the fact that tickets are only sold at certain kiosks (*prigorodniy kassy*). Last but not least are the **hydrofoils** that zoom across the Gulf to Peterhof and Strelna over summer – a highly scenic approach. Full transport details appear in the "Practicalities" boxes accompanying each account.

Several companies with kiosks outside Gostiniy dvor (see p.70) run **coach tours** to the palaces (except on days that they're closed) – scheduling two or three daily to Peterhof and Tsarskoe Selo, and three or four a week to Gatchina or Oranienbaum. The itinerary seldom covers all that there is to see at a site, and **commentary** is in Russian, except on Eclectica-Guide's 2pm **English**-language tours of Peterhof (R1880) and Tsarskoe Selo (R1880). Otherwise, rates vary between companies: Peterhof (R1200–1400); Oranienbaum (R650–850); Gatchina (R750–850); Tsarskoe Selo (R1200–1600); Pavlovsk (R800–1000); Tsarskoe Selo with Pavlovsk (R1600–1850).

These prices include entry charges to the park and main palace at the **ticket prices** for foreigners (**students** and **children** get a discount). Since a separate ticket is required for each palace or pavilion, the cost soon mounts up, particularly if you wish to take **photographs** or use a **video camera** indoors, which also requires a permit for each pavilion. The *kassa* will often be away from the palace itself, in a wooden booth or kiosk. On entry, many of the palaces require you to put on felt or plastic overshoes (*tapochki*) to protect their parquet floors.

Guided tours are on offer at most palaces, though invariably only in Russian; at some you're expected to join a group, but it's easy to slip away once past the ticket barrier, and sometimes possible to tack onto a foreign language group and listen to their guide. Keep an eye out, too, for various **temporary exhibitions**, featuring anything from Fabergé eggs to obscure aspects of Tsarist history.

Strelna

Only 23km from St Petersburg along the Gulf of Finland, **Strelna**, built on land wrested from Sweden during the Northern War, was the site of Peter the Great's original attempt to create a seaside palace to rival Versailles. In 1715, the **Wooden Palace** was built for Peter to live in while overseeing work on the great stone **Konstantin Palace** and its grounds, crisscrossed with canals and girdled by reservoirs. After five years' work, however, he realized that it was impossible to create the high-spurting fountains he desired without installing pumps, and that the palace's sea canal was prone to silt up – and therefore turned his attention to another site further west, which became Peterhof.

Thereafter, the Wooden Palace served as an overnight halt for journeys, while the stone palace remained unfinished until the reign of Empress Elizabeth. The home of grand dukes up until the Revolution, it later became a training school for the "Conquest of the North" and was pulverized during World War II. Whereas the Wooden Palace was restored under the aegis of the Peterhof Museum Reserve in the 1990s, fixing up the Konstantin Palace was

Practicalities

Strelna is easily reached from St Petersburg or Peterhof by **train** (alight at Strelna station and follow Frontovaya ulitsa to the Petersburg highway, then turn right and keep going till you cross the canal – the Wooden Palace lies across the road) or the **minibuses** (#224, #300, #424) that shuttle between Peterhof and Avtovo metro station in St Petersburg (ask to be dropped off at the Wooden Palace). Over summer, Russian Cruises operates **hydrofoils** (30min; R900), as scheduled at the Hermitage jetty in St Petersburg. These are partly for the benefit of guests **staying** at the *Baltic Star Hotel* (☎438 57 00, ⊛www.balticstar-hotel.ru; ➐) in the grounds of Putin's palace. Oligarchs in need of seclusion with the president are prepared to pay $5000 a day for an Elite Cottage, so R1100 for a VIP seat on the hydrofoil must seem like kopeks.

beyond anyone's budget until Putin decided to make it the Russian equivalent of Camp David and the venue for the G8 Summit of 2003. Its official title – the **Palace of Congresses** (Dvorets Kongressov) – evokes the former Soviet "parliament" and its interior is almost as lifeless – unlike the Wooden Palace, which is a genuine curiosity. In the future, however, the Konstantin Palace may display the late maestro **Rostopovich's art collection**, purchased for $50 million at Sotheby's by the billionaire Alisher Usmanov, and "donated to the nation" in 2007.

The Konstantin Palace

From the road, the **Konstantin Palace** (Konstantinovskiy dvorets; 10am–6pm; closed Wed) is an impressive sight: a vast buff chateau on a lofty terrace overlooking a park stretching to the shores of the Gulf, enclosed by a high fence topped with gilded eagles and security cameras. As a presidential palace whose creation was by financed by corporations, and whose running costs are met by Russian taxpayers while it rents luxury "Cottages" to oligarchs, it embodies the spirit of "Kremlin Inc" and isn't shy about making visitors pay either. An **excursions** bureau (☎438 5360) by the main entrance on Sankt-Peterburgsoe shosse offers various "themed" tours of the palace and/or park, of 90–120 minutes' duration. Each visitor requires an individual ticket (R170–280), plus which there's a charge for the guide (R1000), split between however many people are on the tour. A tour in any other language but Russian must be booked at least 24 hours (R3000) or further ahead (R2500), bearing in mind that the palace may be closed at short notice for state events, as posted on its **website** ⓦwww.konstantinpalace.ru (in Russian only). Be sure to bring your passport along.

Rigorous security checks and rude tour guides rub in the lacklustre interior, whose decor and furnishings hardly seem worth the $300 million spent on the palace. Visitors see the mirrored **ballroom** designed by Stackenschneider – used for the G8 Summit – and three **exhibitions** drawn from the collections of the Hermitage, Peterhof and the Naval Museum. A guide relates the history of the palace since Tsar Paul gave it to his second son, Konstantin, and its heyday under several grand dukes with similar forenames or patronymics – the last, Dmitri Konstantinovich, renounced the palace after the February Revolution, but was nonetheless shot by the Bolsheviks. Strelna is best known, however, for its association with his brother, **Konstantin Konstantinovich** (1858–1915), a poet, translator and playwright under the *nom de plume* of "K.R." (Konstantin Romanov), who fathered nine children but was also a secret homosexual, as his diaries posthumously revealed (and guides prefer to ignore).

Separate tours (R100–300) explore the manicured **Lower Park**. "Russian Versailles" (in the spring and summer) features the **terrace** from which Pavarotti serenaded Putin's guests, a **grotto**, great canal and island **Translators Pavilion** – but who could resist the chance to gawp at the interior of one of the **Elite Cottages** rented by oligarchs and world leaders, off towards the shore to the east in the "Consuls' Wood".

The Wooden Palace

Further west, on a ridge overlooking the Gulf, Peter's **Wooden Palace** (Derevyanniy dvorets; 10.30am–5pm; closed Mon & the last Tues of each month; R200) is a charming, two-storey building painted yellow and white.

While its decor is largely of the Petrine era – when wallpaper was a fashionable novelty – the palace's furnishings span almost two hundred years, since it was also used by later rulers. One of the finest exhibits is the weighty travel chest of Alexander III, incorporating a slide-out bed, folding desk, chairs, washstand, kitchen and homeopathic pharmacy, plus all kinds of implements including a device for stretching gloves.

Another room is devoted to pastimes: Peter loved chess and draughts, while his female successors preferred cards (playing for money was forbidden, so courtiers gambled for diamonds instead). In the **dining room**, with its beautiful tiled stove, notice the unique samovar with two taps belonging to Catherine the Great, who drank her tea with milk in the English fashion. Peter's **bedroom** has a four-poster curtained in green felt, with a patchwork quilt sewn by his wife, Catherine I, while his **study** contains a device for warming his feet while he worked at the desk. The final rooms are more formal, presaging the second-floor **Upper Hall**, adorned with Chinese vases, Japanese bronzes and European paintings.

Outside, the **garden** sports flowerbeds, glazed urns and fountains on its seaward side, and an apiary and vegetable plots to the rear which once supplied the palace with food. It was here, during the reign of Empress Anna, that potatoes were first grown in Russia – initially just for their flowers, which were worn at balls as a fashionable accessory. A little further on, a wooden cross and shrine mark the site of a church and bell tower, destroyed during the war. Sadly, nothing remains of Peter the Great's treehouse, where he used to enjoy smoking a pipe and watching ships on the Gulf in the evenings.

Peterhof (Petrodvorets)

As the first of the great Imperial palatial ensembles to be established outside St Petersburg, **Peterhof** embodies nearly three hundred years of Tsarist self-aggrandizement. As you'd expect from its name (meaning "Peter's Court" in German, and pronounced "Petergof" in Russian), its founder was **Peter the Great**. Flushed with triumph from the Northern War against Sweden, he decided to build a sumptuous palace beside the Gulf, following the construction of his island fortress of Kronstadt, which secured the seaborne approaches to the city.

After an abortive attempt at Strelna, Peterhof was selected as the site owing to its more favourable hydrography and coastline, which permitted the great fountains and access by water that Peter desired. Architects scrambled to keep up with the stream of projects issuing from his pen, while visiting ambassadors were often obliged to join the tsar in labouring on the site. Even so, Peterhof's existing Great Palace wasn't built until the reign of **Empress Elizabeth**, when court life became more opulent, reaching its apogee during the reign of **Catherine the Great**, whose acquaintance with Peterhof dated back to her loveless marriage to Peter III (see p.68). Although Catherine's immediate successors preferred other palaces, **Nicholas I** returned the court to Peterhof, building the Cottage Palace in the Alexandria Park, where the Imperial family lived with minimal pomp, reflecting the later Romanovs' creeping embourgeoisement.

In 1944, after Peterhof had been liberated from Nazi occupation, the authorities decided that its Germanic name was no longer appropriate and replaced it with its Russian equivalent, "Petrodvorets" (pronounced "Petrodvaryets").

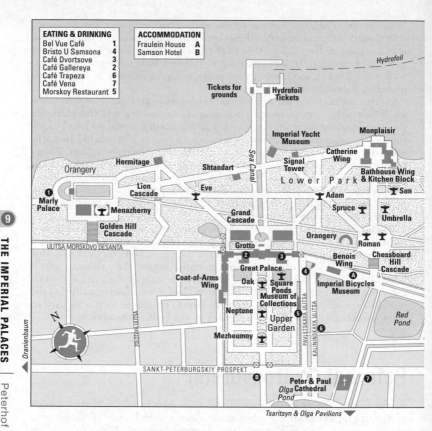

EATING & DRINKING
Bel Vue Café	1
Bristo U Samsona	4
Café Dvortsove	3
Café Gallereya	2
Café Trapeza	6
Café Vena	7
Morskoy Restaurant	5

ACCOMMODATION
Fraulein House	A
Samson Hotel	B

Tsaritsyn & Olga Pavilions ▼

In 1992, however, the palace officially reverted to its former name, Peterhof – although the **town** itself is still called **Petrodvorets**.

Unsurprisingly, the palace and park are the setting for several **festivals**, including the opening and closing of the "fountain season" (see p.244) and concerts and ballet in the grounds and the throne room of the palace during the White Nights in June. The latter are held under the aegis of the "Palaces of St Petersburg" festival, which also involves Tsarskoe Selo and Pavlovsk. For details, see the *St Petersburg Times* or *Where St Petersburg*. To whet your appetite for Peterhof, you can look at the pictures on the unofficial Peterhof **website** (Ⓦwww.peterhof.ru) – but you won't get much practical information from it, as it's in Russian only.

Approaching the Great Palace

Coming **by minibus** from St Petersburg (or Petergof train station), drivers announce "Fontany!" and drop you right outside the gates of the **Upper Garden**, entry to which is free. This way, you'll approach the Great Palace from the rear and must buy a ticket for the **Lower Park** (open daily 9am–7pm) at one of the kiosks by the gates on either side of the Great Palace. The usual entry charge is R300, but admission is free once the fountains are turned off at 5pm (6pm at weekends) or reduced to R200

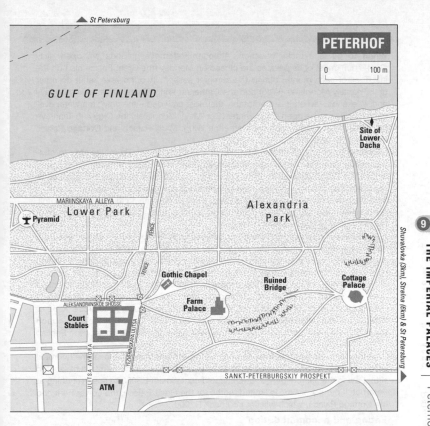

PETERHOF

0   100 m

GULF OF FINLAND

Site of
Lower
Dacha

MARIINSKAYA ALLEYA

Lower Park

**Alexandria
Park**

⊤ **Pyramid**

Gothic Chapel

**Ruined
Bridge**

**Cottage
Palace**

ALEKSANDRIINSKOE SHOSSE

**Farm
Palace**

**Court
Stables**

ULITSA AVRORA

YEZZHINSKAYA ULITSA

FENCE

FENCE

ATM

SANKT-PETERBURGSKIY PROSPEKT ▶

over winter, when they don't operate at all. If you come **by hydrofoil**, tickets for
the Lower Park are sold at the landing jetty, and you'll approach the palace via the
Sea Canal and **Grand Cascade**.

The Upper Garden

Entering the **Upper Garden** (Verkhniy sad) from the main road, the first thing
you see is the **Mezheumny Fountain**, whose name (meaning "a bit of this, a bit
of that") alludes to the many alterations it's undergone over the years, resulting
in a plump dragon and four dolphins; an alternative translation has it meaning
"neither here nor there", and refers to its location. The garden's focal point is
the **Neptune Fountain**, made in Nuremberg in 1650–58 to mark the end of the
Thirty Years War. The fountain turned out to require too much water to operate
and spent years in storage until it was snapped up by Tsarevich Paul for 30,000
rubles in 1782. Stolen by the Nazis, it was tracked down in Germany and rein-
stalled in 1956. Beyond this spouts the **Oak Fountain**, a complete misnomer for
a statue of Cupid donning a tragic mask in a circular pool ringed by allegorical
figures. Nearest to the palace are the so-called **Square Ponds**, sporting marble
statues of Venus and Apollo.

When to go is a tricky question. Although Peterhof's grounds are open daily (9am–7pm), most of its palaces are closed on Monday (the Great Palace also on the last Tues of each month) during the summer season. Two, however, shut on other days, namely Monplaisir (Wed) and the Catherine Wing (Thurs). This makes Fridays and weekends – when it is predictably the most crowded – the only time when everything is sure to be open. Over winter (Oct–May), Monplaisir, the Olga and Tsaritsyn pavilions are all closed, and the Catherine Wing, Marly Palace and Cottage Palace open only at weekends.

Getting there from St Petersburg is fairly straightforward. From late May to mid-September (weather permitting), **hydrofoils** (30–45min; R300–450 one way) speed across the Gulf of Finland to Peterhof, a trip that offers a splendid first glimpse of the Great Palace and a distant view of Kronstadt. Several firms firms run hydrofoils from the jetties by the Hermitage and Senate. If you're planning to return by hydrofoil, don't leave it too late to buy a ticket back, as long queues start forming from 4pm; the last hydrofoil leaves Peterhof at 6pm.

Alternatively, you can get there by public transport for about R50. **Minibuses** from outside the Baltic Station (#404) and Avtovo (#224, #300 & #424) and Prospekt Veteranov (#343) metro stations take 30–45 minutes if traffic isn't bad, and can drop you right outside Peterhof's Upper Garden. Some aren't numbered, but simply labelled ФОНТАНЫ (Fountains). **Suburban trains** from the Baltic Station (5.45am–midnight every 15–30min; 40min) aren't affected by traffic, but when you get off at Noviy Petergof station (not Stariy Petergof) you'll need to catch a local #350, #351, #352 or #356 bus to the palace grounds (10min). Or you can opt for one of the daily **coach tours** (R1200–1400) from outside Gostiniy dvor; Eclectica-Guide does one in English at 2pm (R1800).

Visitors need separate **tickets** to enter Peterhof's grounds (sold near the hydrofoil jetty, the Great Palace and the Court Stables) and each palace or museum (sold *in situ*). Paying the full foreigner's rate, it would cost almost R3000 to see everything at Peterhof; if money or time is limited, settle for the Great Palace, the Lower Park and the Cottage Palace, which will set you back R1000.

Eating and accommodation

The cheap *Bistro U Samsona* (daily 10am–10pm) near the Benois Wing serves soup, hot snacks and cakes, superior to the junk food on offer at the cafés scattered around the Lower Park. Foreign tour groups are usually fed at the *Café Dvortsove* (daily 10am–7pm) or *Café Gallereya* (daily 10am–8pm) on the first floor of the Great Palace, facing the Grand Cascade, or the dearer *Shtdandart* (daily 10am–6pm) near the Sea Canal, which all take credit cards. For a proper meal, head outside the palace grounds to the *Café Trapeza* (noon–10pm, closed Mon) on Kalininskaya ulitsa, the *Morskoy Restaurant* (daily 11am–10pm) by the Museum of Collections, or the *Café Vena* (daily 11am–11pm) on Sankt Peterburgskiy prospekt.

Given the regular transport between Peterhof and St Petersburg, there's no need **to stay** overnight unless you fancy hitting the sights before the day-trippers arrive. At the time of writing the *Samson Hotel* across the road from the Upper Garden was being refurbished, but the cosy three-star *Fraulein House* (☎450 54 03, ©peterhof-museum@mail.ru; ❹) beside the Benois Wing was open for business.

The Sea Canal and Grand Cascade

Approached by hydrofoil, the Great Palace rises like a golden curtain at the far end of the **Sea Canal** (Morskoy kanal), which flows through Peterhof's Lower Park and once formed an approach route for yachts. The granite-banked canal is flanked by 22 marble basins spurting water. By the shore, a small pavilion houses the **Imperial Yacht Museum** (June–Sept daily 10.30am–6pm; R110), featuring models and photos of, and objects from, the *Polar Star* and other vessels used by the latter-day Romanovs. A **Signal Tower**-cum-lighthouse stands by the shore.

Pressing on past a brass band dressed in Petrine-era costumes, you'll come to the **Voronikhin Colonnades**, named after the architect who designed this pair of Neoclassical pavilions that flank the huge circular basin below the **Grand Cascade** (Bolshoy kaskad). Here, the glittering muscular figure of Samson rends the jaws of a ferocious lion, symbolizing Russia's victory over Sweden in the Northern War: the lion is the heraldic beast of Sweden and the decisive Battle of Poltava occurred on St Samson's Day (June 27 by today's calendar) in 1709. The basin is filled by water cascading over blue-and-yellow ceramic steps and 142 jets spurting from 64 sources, including numerous other gilded **statues** and bas-reliefs.

If you're curious about Peterhof's waterworks it's worth visiting the split-level **Grotto** (Grot; 11am–5pm, Sat & Sun till 6pm; closed in winter; R110) beneath the Cascade. The uppermost grotto is lined with tufa rocks and was used for informal parties, while in the lower grotto jets of water are triggered to squirt anyone tempted by the fruit on the table. The giant pipes that feed the fountains were originally made of wood and were maintained by a special Fountain Corps of men and boys – the latter being employed to crawl through the pipes to repair them. Tickets are sold from a hatch in the side of the Great Palace, overlooking the cascade.

The Great Palace

The yellow, white and gold **Great Palace** (Bolshoy dvorets; 10.30am–5pm; closed Mon & the last Tues of each month; R500) is far removed from that originally designed for Peter by Le Blond in 1714–21. Peter's daughter, Empress Elizabeth, employed Bartolomeo Rastrelli to add a third storey and two wings terminating in pavilions with gilded cupolas, while much of the interior was later redesigned by Vallin de la Mothe and Yuri Felten, with further alterations made in the mid-nineteenth century. Yet there's a superb cohesion at work, a tribute both to the vision of the palace's original creators and to the skills of the experts who rebuilt Peterhof after World War II.

Though the ticket office for foreigners is inside the palace, you have to **queue** outside with Russian ticket holders to enter, before buying your own ticket from a *kassa* just beyond the cloakroom. The set **itinerary** leads from the "public" state rooms into the Imperial Suite, as if you were a courtier granted intimate access to the monarch, but your route might differ slightly from the one described below, depending on how crowded the palace gets.

The State Rooms

Visitors ascend to the **State Rooms** via Rastrelli's **Ceremonial Staircase**, aglow with gilded statues and vases, beneath a ceiling fresco of Aurora and Genius chasing away the night. Upstairs, you'll pass through an exhibition on the restoration of Peterhof to reach the watered-silk-papered **Blue Reception Room**, where the Imperial secretary once vetted visitors to the rooms beyond.

The **Chesma Room** takes its name from the Russian naval victory against the Turks at Chesma Bay in 1770, scenes from which decorate the walls. When Count Alexei Orlov, commander of the Russian squadron, saw Philippe Hackert's preliminary sketches, he criticized the depiction of a ship exploding in flames as unrealistic and arranged for a frigate to be blown up before the artist's eyes, as a model. Off to the right, you can gaze into (but not enter) the

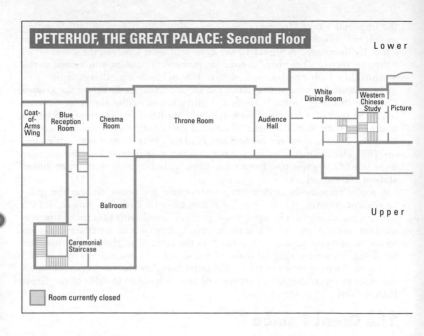

PETERHOF, THE GREAT PALACE: Second Floor

Lower

White Dining Room

Western Chinese Study

Picture

Coat-of-Arms Wing

Blue Reception Room

Chesma Room

Throne Room

Audience Hall

Ballroom

Upper

Ceremonial Staircase

Room currently closed

Ballroom, glittering with mirrors and gilded candelabras – Empress Elizabeth nicknamed it the Merchants' Hall because "they love gold", and had her favourite architect, Rastrelli, create a similar hall in the Catherine Palace at Tsarskoe Selo.

Next comes the **Throne Room**, the largest hall at Peterhof, once used for gala receptions and balls. Designed by Felten, its white-and-pistachio mouldings are offset by scarlet curtains, crystal chandeliers and a magnificent parquet floor. Amidst all this opulence, the throne at the far end is an almost humble addendum, overlooked by a portrait of Catherine the Great in the green uniform of the Preobrazhenskiy Guards, astride her horse, Brilliant.

Ladies-in-waiting once primped and preened in the mirrored **Audience Hall** (Audientszal) next door, where gilded cherubs and garlands festoon every frame and cornice. Bas-reliefs of wine jugs, wildfowl and musical instruments adorn the **White Dining Room** (Belaya stolovaya), with its mauve glass chandeliers, mint-green swags and a long table set with the 196-piece Catherine Dinner Service, made in Staffordshire, England.

Next comes the **Western Chinese Study**, one of a pair of rooms designed by de la Mothe in the 1760s, when chinoiserie was all the rage. Sumptuously decorated in red, green and gold lacquer, with a floor inlaid with thirteen kinds of wood, it contains a suitably Oriental tea service. From here, you pass into the **Picture Hall** (Kartinny zal) at the centre of the palace, overlooking the park and gardens. It is also dubbed the "Room of Fashion and Graces", and its walls are lined with 368 portraits of eight young court ladies wearing national costumes, by Elizabeth's court painter, Pietro Rotari.

The **Eastern Chinese Study** (Vostochniy Kitayskiy kabinet) originally looked quite different, its walls and furniture covered in white satin rather than the

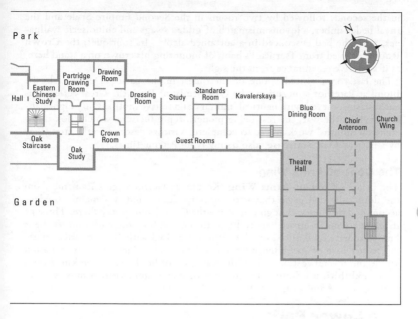

existing lacquer work (notice how the parquet clashes with the pseudo-Ming stove). Conversely, the **Partridge Drawing Room** (Kuropatochnaya gostinaya) next door is a meticulous re-creation: its partridge-spangled curtains and wall coverings use original fabric dating from the 1840s (itself patterned on eighteenth-century Lyons silk); there's also a harp and a Meissen porcelain figurine, typical features of noble Russian households of the period.

The Imperial Suite

The transition to the **Imperial Suite** is accomplished by an opulent Drawing Room (Divannaya) flaunting Chinese silk paintings and an outsized Ottoman divan. Notice the porcelain statue of Catherine's greyhound, Zemira, lying on a pillow. Her Dressing Room (Tualetnaya) and Study (Kabinet) are both tastefully furnished in French Empire style, with the latter containing portraits of Empress Elizabeth, the youthful Alexander I, Catherine and a bust of Voltaire, her favourite philosopher. From here you're channelled out of the Imperial Suite into the greenbrocade-papered **Standards Room**, where the Peterhof garrison formerly displayed its regimental banners, and the crimson **Equerries' Room** (Kavalerskaya), where aides-de-camp once reclined on the Chippendale chaises longues. The **Blue Dining Room** was commissioned by Nicholas I for banquets of 250 people, who dined from the "Cabbage Service" of 5550 pieces (most of which is on display), watched over by portraits of Maria Fyodorovna and Catherine the Great.

Although you can peer into the **Choir Anteroom**, the court Church of SS Peter and Paul is still under restoration, so the tour does a U-turn via the **Theatre Hall** into a suite of rooms occupied by **Nicholas I** when he was crown prince, and later by guests of the royal family. Portraits of Nicholas and his wife Alexandra Fyodorovna hang in the first room and their daughter Olga in the second; followed by two rooms in the Second Empire Style and the royal bedchamber, a joyous mismatch of gilded swags and chinoiserie wallpaper, with the bed ensconced in a curtained alcove. Its sobriquet, the **Crown Room**, derived from Tsar Paul's habit of mounting his crown on a stand here, as if to derive reassurance from the sight.

The last room visited is one of the oldest in the palace. Designed by Le Blond at Peterhof's inception, the **Oak Study** of Peter the Great reflects his enthusiasms, carved with nautical, military and festive motifs. Only eight panels survived the war, the rest being modern reproductions which took up to eighteen months' work apiece to complete. Visitors descend to the first floor by a narrow **Oak Staircase**, also dating from Petrine times.

The Coat-of-Arms Wing

The palace's **Coat-of-Arms Wing** (Korpus za Gerbom) gets its name from the double-headed eagle that surmounts its dome, and was mainly used to accommodate guests, though Catherine the Great liked to stay there. Three of its eight rooms re-create her study, bedroom and boudoir with objects she is known to have used, such as a silver samovar incised with playing cards, attesting to her love of gambling. Other items on display include her coronation saddle and several costumes from the wardrobe of her lover, Potemkin. Access to the **exhibition** is limited to fifteen people at a time; visitors must wait to join a group. Admission costs R400.

The Lower Park

Stretching down to the Gulf from the Great Palace, the 102-hectare **Lower Park** (Nizhniy park) is arranged around dozens of **fountains** that Alexandre Benois described as "the symbolic expression of the sea's dominion, the mist that rises from the waves as they surge towards its shore". In Catherine the Great's day the park was used for all-night festivities, illuminated by 10,000 candles. Today, the **fountain season** (late May to early October) is glorified by opening and closing ceremonies on the first Saturday or Sunday of June, and in the first or second week of October, with concerts, ballets and fireworks. The whole hydraulic system is gravity-fed by water from the Ropsha Hills, 22km away, via 50km of pipes, 22 locks and 18 lakes, discharging 100,000 cubic metres of water every day during summer. Over winter, the fountains are turned off and the statues encased in insulated boxes, to prevent them from cracking in the sub-zero temperatures.

The finest fountains are either clustered between the Chessboard Hill Cascade and Monplaisir, or ennoble the approaches to the Marly Palace. Keeping this in mind, it doesn't matter which of the many routes you take – the account below is one of many possibilities. The palaces themselves are covered afterwards.

East of the Grand Cascade's Samson statue stands the **Triton Fountain**, which honours the Russian naval victory over Sweden at Hangö, while further along the path is a piazza dominated by two **Roman Fountains**, like giant cake stands. The **Chessboard Hill Cascade** (Shakhmatnaya gorka) to the south boasts three dragons from which water spouts down a chequered chute flanked by statues of Greek and Roman deities. Between the Roman Fountains and Monplaisir are several more **joke fountains** (*shutikhi*), still primed to soak but too leaky to surprise. The **Umbrella Fountain** starts raining when you sit underneath it, as does the **Spruce Fountain**, disguised as a tree. To the east of the Umbrella is the **Pyramid Fountain**, whose 505 jets rise in seven tiers to form an apex.

▲ Peterhof's Chessboard Hill Cascade

Heading west towards the Marly Palace you'll first encounter the **Adam Fountain**, with Adam gazing soulfully over the rooftops of two Greco-Chinese pavilions, followed by the **Eve Fountain** – Eve with apple and fig leaf in hand – beyond the Sea Canal. From there you can detour northwards to the Hermitage or press on past the grey and white marble **Lion Cascade** (resembling a Greek temple) to the Marly Palace. The southern side of the park is flanked by the **Triton Bells Fountain**, named after the fish-tailed Triton boys who hold cups full of sculpted bells amidst clouds of spray. These precede the **Menazherny Fountains**, which use less water than their powerful jets suggest – their name derives from the French word *ménager,* meaning "to economize". Beyond rises the **Golden Hill Cascade** (Zolotaya gorka), a flight of waterfalls issuing from gilded orifices. Like the Chessboard Hill Cascade, it is flanked by allegorical statues and offers a ravishing view of the park.

Monplaisir

The seaside **Monplaisir** palace (June–Sept 10.30am–5pm; closed Wed, all winter and on rainy days; R300) was designed by Peter himself with the help of several architects. Its name (French for "my pleasure") reflects its purpose, for it was here that he relaxed while reviewing the construction of Peterhof or maneouvres by his fleet on the Gulf. Its decor is both homely and extravagant, reflecting the influence of Holland – where he learned shipbuilding – and his fondness for drunken revelry. It was also here that he interrogated his son Alexei before confining him to the Peter and Paul Fortress on suspicion of treason.

Starting with Peter's **art collection** (the first in Russia), you progress through the **Eastern Gallery**, with its sixteen glazed doors, into the extraordinary **Lacquered Study**. A feast of black, gold and red, its 94 lacquered panels were originally created by icon painters who spent months studying Chinese techniques but couldn't resist imparting a Russian flavour to their work. The originals were chopped up and used as firewood by the Nazis; what you see today was re-created from the evidence of three surviving panels.

In the **State Hall** beyond, the ceiling fresco of Apollo surrounded by figures from the *commedia dell'arte* must have swum before the eyes of those guests forced to drink from the dreaded Great Eagle Cup, holding 1.25 litres of fortified wine, which had to be drained in one gulp by anyone who broke Peter's rules. Envoys who passed out were roused next day and either issued with axes and ordered to join him in a bout of tree felling or taken for a bracing sail on the Gulf. Peter's wife, Catherine I, entered into the spirit of things by cooking meals in the Dutch-tiled **Pantry**, and inviting guests to help themselves to *zakuski* in the **Buffet**.

On the other side of the State Hall is Peter's **Naval Study**, with its tile-inlaid wainscotting and inspirational view of the Gulf. Their **Bedroom** is equally small and homely; his nightcap can be seen on the table beside the four-poster. The tour ends in the **Western Gallery**, decorated with an allegorical fresco and seascapes (including one of Zaandam, where Peter lived with a Dutch carpenter while working at the local shipyards).

Thirty years after Peter's death, Monplaisir was home to the future Empress Catherine the Great during her loveless marriage to Peter III. When he took a mistress, Catherine started an affair with Stanislaw Poniatowski (later to become the last king of Poland) and soon the royal couple were living apart: Peter at Oranienbaum and Catherine in a pavilion beside Monplaisir, called the Tea House. There, on July 28, 1762, she learned from Alexei Orlov that the coup against her husband was under way and hastened to Petersburg to rally her supporters. By nightfall she had become Empress of All the Russias.

The Catherine Wing

The **Catherine Wing** (Yekaterininskiy Korpus; June–Sept 10.30am–6pm; closed Thurs; Oct–May Sat & Sun 10.30am–5pm; R300) was added to Monplaisir by Empress Elizabeth in the 1740s to accommodate court balls and masquerades, and remodelled by Quarenghi for Catherine the Great in the 1780s. Its simple Baroque exterior defers to Monplaisir's, while the interior is plush but not overly opulent.

Tours begin in the **Blue Drawing Room**, which dates from the same period as Alexander I's **Study**. The latter is ornamented with knick-knacks relating to the 1812 Napoleonic invasion and a portrait of Alexander's murdered father, Paul. Next you enter Alexander's **Bedroom**, which contains a magnificent "boat" bed with candelabras mounted on the headboard; some ivory piquet cards belonging to Catherine the Great are preserved in a case by the far wall. Next door is the **Heating Room** – easily mistaken for a kitchen – where plates were kept warm during banquets. The blue-and-gold dinner service comes from Ropsha, where Catherine's husband, Peter III, was murdered. Proceeding through the **Green Drawing Room**, full of walnut furniture, and the stuccoed, mirrored **Blue Hall**, you enter the glittering **Yellow Hall**, its table set for a banquet of 45 guests. The red-and-gold Guryev Service comprises several thousand pieces and was made in St Petersburg early last century. Portraits of Alexander I and Catherine the Great are accompanied by a giant tapestry depicting Peter the Great at the helm of a storm-wracked dinghy, his companions cowering astern (based on a real event).

Other sights

Between the Catherine Wing and Monplaisir lies a **garden**, centred on the **Wheatsheaf Fountain**, whose 25 jets of water resemble heads of grain. A composition designed by Peter himself flanks the Wheatsheaf Fountain on four sides, consisting of gilded fountain-statues of Psyche, Apollo, Bacchus and a faun with a kid – collectively dubbed "the Bells". He also commissioned a **joke fountain** that squirts anybody who treads on a certain part of its gravel plot – always good for a laugh. The austere **Bathhouse Wing** (Baniy Korpus) and **Kitchen Block** that Catherine I added to Montplaisir give an idea of how royalty washed themselves and food was prepared, but aren't anything special (June–Sept 10.30am–6pm, closed Wed; Oct–May Sat & Sun 10.30am–4pm; R300).

The Hermitage and Marly Palace

En route between Monplaisir and the Marly Palace you can visit the **Hermitage** (Ermitazh; 10am–5.30pm; closed Mon; R110) near the shore, a moated, two-storey pavilion with round-headed windows and Corinthian pilasters gracing its sand-coloured facade. Designed for Peter the Great, but completed only after his death, it was intended for dining *sans* servants: guests ate upstairs, with a lovely view of Peterhof and the Gulf, and ordered dishes by placing notes on the table, which was lowered by pulleys to the kitchen below and then returned laden with delicacies. In 1797, the pulley chair by which guests were hoisted upstairs was replaced by a flight of stairs after a cable snapped, stranding Tsar Paul between floors. The upstairs **Dining Room** is hung with paintings, while the **Buffet** downstairs displays Japanese and Chinese porcelain and Russian crystal.

Nearby, a raised terrace shelters from the wind what used to be an **Orangery**, overlooking the Gulf, and the large pond that fronts the **Marly Palace** (June–Sept 10.30am–6pm, closed Mon; Oct–May Sat & Sun 10.30am–5pm; R130). Built around the same time as Monplaisir, this takes its name and inspiration from the French royal hunting lodge at Marly le Roi, which Peter saw during his Grand Tour of Europe. More of a cosy country house than a palace, it backs on to **fishponds** where Catherine fed her pet goldfish, nowadays stocked with sturgeon and trout, which visitors are invited to catch (rods available at the *Bel Vue Café*). A **guided tour** of the palace lasts about fifteen minutes.

In keeping with Peter's no-nonsense character, the Dutch-tiled **Kitchen** connects directly with the **Buffet**, so that dishes arrived hot at the table – an innovation that he was especially proud of. As usual, the four-poster in his **Bedroom** is far too short – Peter was 2.3 metres tall – and there's a small den where he drew plans and fiddled with instruments. Upstairs are guest rooms exhibiting Petrine memorabilia and a **Dining Room** with a superb view of the avenues converging on the palace.

The Alexandria Park

Landscaped in a naturalistic English style by Adam Menelaws, the **Alexandria Park** (daily 6am–10pm; free) surrounds the Cottage Palace of Nicholas I and Alexandra Fyodorovna (after whom the park is named). Finding Peterhof's Great Palace "unbearable", she pressed Nicholas to build a home suited to a cosier, bourgeois lifestyle, where they lived *en famille* with few servants and no protocol, but heavily guarded. The Cottage Palace is definitely worth a walk through the park, which can be entered via gates near the Court Stables, or from Sankt Peterburgskiy prospekt.

The **Court Stables** are a sprawling complex modelled by Leonty Benois on Hampton Court in England. The building now houses a sanatorium and can't be entered, but makes a fitting curtain-raiser for the Anglophile follies in the Alexandria Park. Just inside the gates is a **Gothic Chapel** (June–Sept daily except Mon 10.30am–5pm; R110) with rose windows and spiky pinnacles. Dedicated to St Alexander Nevsky, it was the Imperial family's private chapel from the reign of Nicholas I onwards.

Further east you'll pass the derelict **Farm Palace** (Fermerskiy dvorets), that was built as a combined stables, stud farm and hothouse for Alexander II, a keen weekend farmer. The path continues past a whimsical **Ruined Bridge** beside a gully that was once part of a waterway running down to the Gulf.

The Cottage Palace

The **Cottage Palace** (dvorets Kottedzh; June–Sept 10.30am–5pm, closed Mon; Oct–May Tues, Fri, Sat & Sun 10.30am–4pm; R200) is a two-storeyed gingerbread house designed in 1826–29 by Adam Menelaws in the then-fashionable pseudo-Gothic style. As you enter the lobby, notice the stone carved with Arabic script: a trophy from the fortress of Varna in Bulgaria, captured during the Russo-Turkish War of 1828–29. The **Tsaritsa's Study** has a stained-glass screen and a sensuous frieze around the window bay, while the adjacent **Grand Drawing Room** (Bolshaya gostinaya) boasts a starburst ceiling as intricate as lace, and a clock modelled on the facade of Rouen Cathedral. In the burgundy-coloured **Library** (Biblioteka) are a mother-of-pearl and ivory model of a castle near Potsdam and a screen decorated with German knights – reminders that Empress Alexandra was born Charlotte, princess of Prussia, while Nicholas I had a German mother. From the **Grand Reception Room**, you pass into a **Dining Room** (Stolovaya) bisected by Gothic pillars and flanked by pew-like chairs. Its long table is set with Alexandra's dinner service of 314 porcelain and 353 crystal pieces, specially commissioned for the cottage.

The **Staircase** is a triumph of *trompe l'oeil* by G.B. Scotti, who painted Gothic arches, vaults and windows all over the stairwell in subtle tones of grey and blue. On the floor above are the **family rooms**, modestly sized and decorated by Tsarist standards. First comes the suite of rooms belonging to Tsarevich Alexander, comprising a bathroom (Vannaya), classroom (Uchebnaya komnata) and a valet's room. In the tsar's **Dressing Room** scenes from the Russo-Turkish War hang alongside a marble-topped washstand and a screened-off shower. Next door is the **Tsar's Study**, followed by the **Blue Room** (Golubaya gostinaya), which belonged to Nicholas I's daughter, Maria

Nikolayevna. The room is furnished with Sèvres and Meissen porcelain and also contains a clock with 66 faces, one for each province of Russia (including "Russian America", as Alaska was known until 1867).

Entering the next room you skip a generation, for after Alexander II's assassination, the crown passed to his son, Alexander III, whose wife made this her **Drawing Room**. A sad tale lies behind the **Nursery** (Detskaya), beyond. Prepared decades earlier during Maria Nikolayevna's pregnancy, it was sealed up after she died in childbirth, its fabulous Doll's Tea Service left there for the baby that died with her.

Before leaving, nip upstairs to Nicholas I's **Naval Study**, a garret with a balcony overlooking the Gulf, from where he observed exercises off Kronstadt through a spyglass and gave orders to the fleet by telegraph or speaking trumpet.

On the anniversary of the 1918 massacre of the royal family at Yekaterinburg (July 17), admirers light candles and say prayers for them at the **site of the Lower Dacha** near the seashore. This was their favourite residence at Peterhof, where Nicholas II took two of the most fateful decisions of his reign, signing the October Manifesto of 1905 that granted a Duma (parliament), and mobilizing the Russian army in 1914. The *dacha* was totally destroyed during World War II and is unlikely to be rebuilt.

Other sights at Peterhof

For those who've got the stamina or cash to see more, there are other sights beyond the Lower and Alexandria parks. Closest to the Great Palace is the **Imperial Bicycles Museum** (June–Sept daily 10am–6pm; R110), exhibiting antique Penny-Farthings and other types ridden by the Romanovs. Across the way is the **Benois Wing** (Korpus Benoua), the former summer home of the Benois family, whose French ancestor, Louis, was Tsar Paul's chef. His son was "adopted" by Paul's widow and fathered six children, who became artists or architects; the actor Peter Ustinov was a descendant. The exhibition about the family was closed for refurbishment at the time of writing.

On Pavletskaya ulitsa, beside the Upper Garden, the **Museum of Collections** (10.30am–6pm; closed Mon & the last Tues of each month; R110) displays paintings by Roerich, Nesterov and other artists of the "Silver Age", and porcelain from Tsarist and Soviet times. Carrying on to the end of the street and crossing Sankt-Peterburgskiy prospekt, you'll see the **Peter and Paul Cathedral** (sobor Petra i Pavla). It looks nothing like its namesake in St Petersburg, resembling instead a medieval Russian church, embodying the Slavophilism of the 1890s.

Behind the cathedral lies the Olga Pond, where Nicholas I built summer residences for his wife and eldest daughter on two islands. The **Tsaritsyn Pavilion**, inspired by houses at Pompei, boasts fountains and Antique statues, while the **Olga Pavilion** resembles an Italian villa, with a belvedere and peacocks in its garden (both June–Sept daily 10.30am–5pm; R450).

Oranienbaum (Lomonosov)

Peter the Great's cohort, Prince Menshikov, began work at **Oranienbaum** in 1713, shortly after his master started Peterhof, 12km to the east. Typically, Menshikov set out to build a palace which would surpass Peterhof, planting orange trees in its Lower Garden ("Oranienbaum" is German for "orange tree") – the ultimate in

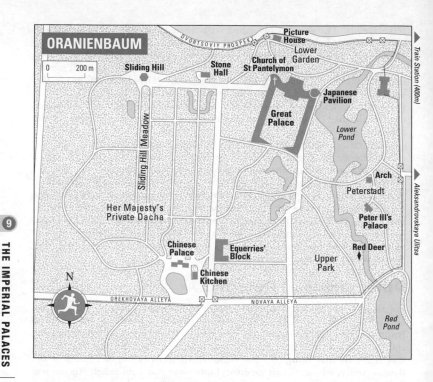

conspicuous consumption, given the local climate. The building of Oranienbaum bankrupted Menshikov and in 1728 the whole estate passed into the hands of the Crown, whereupon it was used as a naval hospital until Empress Elizabeth gave it to her nephew, the future Tsar Peter III and husband of Catherine the Great.

Catherine hated life at Oranienbaum – "I felt totally isolated, cried all day and spat blood", she wrote in her memoirs. Conversely, Peter had a wonderful time, putting his valets through military exercises or spending hours playing with lead soldiers on the dining tables. He was also fond of inflicting his violin-playing on those around him, although, according to Catherine, "He did not know a single note . . . for him the beauty of the music lay in the force and violence with which he played it."

Only after Peter's death did she return here, shunning the Great Palace for "Her Majesty's Privy Dacha", a series of pavilions in the grounds. In her last years she entirely lost interest, deeding the palace to the Naval Cadet Corps – an act revoked by her successor Paul, who gave it to his son Alexander. Its last private owners were the Grand Duke and Duchess of Mecklenburg-Strelitz, who fled the estate in 1917.

Although Oranienbaum never fell into the hands of the Germans during World War II, it suffered constant bombardment as a tiny enclave held by the Russians throughout the Blockade. After the war, both town and palace were renamed **Lomonosov**, after the famous Russian polymath who founded a glass factory in the area. Being designated as a local, not federal, monument, Oranienbaum was starved of funds and treated as a sinecure (one director blew its budget on buying Landcruisers for himself and his boyfriend) – a situation only now being

Aside from organized **excursions** (R650–850), Oranienbaum can be reached by **minibus** #424 or #424a from Avtovo metro in St Petersburg (1hr), or from Peterhof (15min), terminating at Lomonosov train station, itself accessible by suburban **train** from the city's Baltic Station, or Noviy Peterhof. Sit at the front of the train to be sure of seeing the platform sign. To reach the palace grounds, cut across a small park and bear right towards the grey-domed Church of Archangel Michael; the entrance to the Lower Garden is across the road beyond the church. There are **snack stands** near the station, and a **market** near the church sells fresh produce. Within the palace grounds there's a **café** in the Equerries' Block near the Chinese Palace.

Opening hours and events

Phone ☏422 47 96 or 422 80 16 to check that Oranienbaum is open; extensive drainage work and structural repairs are scheduled for 2008. Under normal circumstances, the park is **open** all year (daily 9am–9pm; R40), with no admission charge before 10am and after 6pm. Visitors need separate tickets for each building (sold on the spot), all of which are closed on Tuesday and the last Monday of each month; some are only open from May to September.

From June to September, **concerts** of classical music are held in the Stone Hall on Sundays at 2pm (R110).

remedied since it was placed under the wing of the Peterhof Museum Reserve.

Unlike other Imperial residences, its Great Palace is less decorative inside than its *faux* Oriental pavilions, and the park is quite wild and uncrowded.

The Great Palace

Entering the formal **Lower Garden** (Nizhniy sad) from Dvortsoviy prospekt and bearing right past the Lower Pond (with boats for rent for R100), you'll soon catch sight of the **Great Palace** (Bolshoy dvorets) on a lofty terrace overlooking the sea. Built in 1713 by the architect Schnadel, Menshikov had little over a decade to enjoy it before he was arrested for treason in 1727 and exiled to Siberia; the following year the Crown took possession of the estate, but not before his enemies, the Golitsyns, had stripped the colossal palace of all its valuables.

At the time of writing the palace was swathed in scaffolding, obscuring the drama of its double stairways ascending to a concave central block with massive domed pavilions at either end. Access is via the **Japanese Pavilion** (11am–5pm, Mon till 4pm; closed Mon & the last Tues of each month; R380 for both, R200 for the pavilion only) on the eastern side, named after the Japanese and Chinese vases, figurines and furniture displayed within. Notice the bas-relief of Grand Duchess Mecklenburg-Strelitz and the "dragon chair" on the lower floor.

Aside from its stuccoed **White Hall**, the palace's rooms are low-ceilinged and unadorned, though this may change after restoration. A melancholy array of **portraits** of Oranienbaum's owners includes Peter III, who abdicated here under duress shortly before he was murdered (see box p.254). The palace's lengthy side wings, screened by fences, have been occupied by the Navy ever since World War II.

The Upper Park

Beyond the Great Palace lies the **Upper Park** (Verkhniy park), whose network of minor paths is now lost in undergrowth, although the basic grid remains. It was Catherine's favourite part of the estate and is still by far the loveliest to wander through, with canals, bridges and ponds amidst firs, limes, oaks and silver birch.

After Peter's death, Catherine commissioned Rinaldi to build the two finest buildings at Oranienbaum here: the Sliding Hill and the Chinese Palace.

En route to the Sliding Hill you'll pass the **Stone Hall** (Kamenniy zal; 11am–5pm, Mon till 4pm; closed Tues & the last Mon of each month; R130) whence Catherine would sally forth in a chariot for costume balls, dressed as Minerva. Its turquoise and white pillared interior is used to display eighteenth-century busts of ancient and historical figures, and for summer concerts (see box on p.251).

▲ Oranienbaum's Sliding Hill pavillion

The Sliding Hill

A little way beyond stands the extraordinary **Sliding Hill** (Katalnaya gorka; 11am–5pm, Mon till 4pm; closed Tues & the last Mon of each month; R300), resembling an oversized slice of wedding cake. This sky-blue and white, three-storey pleasure pavilion is all that remains of a wooden **roller coaster** that once stretched for over 500m along the Upper Park. In winter, Catherine and her guests rode sledges; in summer, wheeled carts, offering a unique sensation of height and speed in a flat landscape, where nothing else moved faster than a horse could gallop. Such constructions were popular in eighteenth-century Russia and a regular feature in public fairgrounds, later spreading to Europe and America and giving rise to the mechanized versions seen today. When last seen, a **model** of the roller coaster was displayed in the Chinese Kitchen (see below), but should return to the Sliding Hill pavilion in the future.

The **Porcelain Room** (Farforoviy kabinet) features gilded stucco sprouting animalistic sconces that provide niches for some outrageously kitsch Meissen pottery, depicting "Chinese" and mythological scenes symbolizing Russia's victory over Turkey. The **White Room** (Beliy kabinet) – actually duck-egg blue and white – was Rinaldi's first venture into Neoclassicism after working in the Rococo style for many years. Its windows afford a distant view of Kronstadt Island: the curators claim they can forecast the weather from the visibility of Kronstadt's Naval Cathedral.

The Chinese Palace and Kitchen

At the far end of the Sliding Hill Meadow lies the area known as "Her Majesty's Private Dacha" – although Catherine spent only 48 days here in the course of her 34-year reign. Its highlight is the **Chinese Palace** (Kitayskiy dvorets; May–Sept 11am–5pm, Mon till 4pm; closed Tues & the last Mon of each month; R300), whose Baroque facade conceals a luxurious yet intimate **interior** in a fanciful Rococo style, with *faux marbre*, ceiling frescoes by Venetian painters and ornate parquet floors. The decor is completely European until the **Buglework Room** (Steklyarusniy kabinet) with its walls depicting peacocks, pheasants and other birds, fashioned from beads produced at the Lomonosov factory.

Despite the proximity of Russia to the East, "Chinese Rococo" reached St Petersburg via Europe. The first signs are in the **Small Chinese Room** (Maliy Kitayskiy kabinet), albeit confined to the wallpaper and some Oriental vases. The **Large Chinese Room** (Bolshoy Kitayskiy kabinet) shows no such restraint: its walls are covered with Chinese landscapes of wood and walrus-ivory marquetry, Chinese lanterns hang in two of its corners, and a fresco of the union of Europe and Asia (represented as a bride surrounded by warriors and mandarins) adorns the ceiling. The wonderfully carved full-sized billiard table was made in England.

East of the pond behind the palace lies a pavilion known as the **Chinese Kitchen** (11am–5pm, Mon till 4pm; closed Tues & the last Mon of each month; R130), quite bare inside, with a historical exhibition.

Peter III's Palace

From the Chinese Palace, you can navigate across the Upper Park past the **Equerries' Block** (Kavelerskiy korpus) and an outdoor enclosure of Siberian **red deer** to find the former haunt of Catherine's husband, Peter III. As heir to the throne, he was given Oranienbaum in 1743, two years before his marriage, which did not distract him from drilling his Holstein Guards in a mock military fortress called **Peterstadt**, of which nothing remains but a decrepit ceremonial archway.

Peter III

Peter III inherited his love of military affairs from his father, the Duke of Holstein. Happiest in the company of men, he couldn't cope with assertive, cultured women – least of all his wife, Catherine – and their marriage wasn't consummated for seven years. "When he left the room the dullest book was a delight", she recalled in her memoirs. In the first months of his reign, Peter managed to offend the clergy by his adherence to Lutheranism and the military by introducing Prussian uniforms and favouring his Holstein troops over the Imperial Guards. It became common knowledge at court that he was planning to send Catherine to a nunnery and enthrone his mistress, Countess Elizabeth Vorontsova.

In June 1762, just seven months into Peter's reign, Catherine launched a preemptive **coup**, marching on Oranienbaum with her lover, Grigori Orlov, and the Imperial Guards. Peter tried to flee to Kronstadt, but the garrison there had already defected and he was forced to return to Oranienbaum, where, in the words of his idol, Frederick the Great, he abdicated "like a child who is sent to bed". Stripped of his Prussian uniform, Peter fainted from shock and was carted off to the palace at Ropsha, where he soon met his **death**. The announcement blamed "apoplexy", but his demise was universally ascribed to the Orlov brothers, who reputedly strangled him after he refused to drink poisoned wine. As a final humiliation, Peter was interred at the Alexander Nevsky Monastery rather than the Peter and Paul Cathedral, until his son Paul became tsar and had him reburied with the other Romanov monarchs.

It was to spend more time with his soldiers – away from Catherine – that Peter commissioned Rinaldi to build him a residence within Peterstadt, completed the year he was murdered. **Peter III's Palace** (dvorets Petra III; 11am–5pm, Mon till 4pm; closed Tues & the last Mon of each month; R280) is a poignant memorial to his pretensions, underscored by his Holstein uniform dress coat, which looks the right size for a 12-year-old. His upstairs apartment includes a **Picture Hall** (Kartinniy zal) juxtaposing a patchwork of European paintings with chinoiserie hangings and lacquer work, while his **Boudoir** features scenes of military life at Peterstadt and a secret stairway of the kind that his son Paul installed in the Engineers' Castle in a vain attempt to avoid being murdered like his father.

Rather than tramping back through the park to the station, exit via the gates near Peter's Palace and catch a minibus back to St Petersburg from the far end of Aleksandrovskaya ulitsa.

Tsarskoe Selo (Pushkin)

Of all the Imperial palaces, none is more evocative of both the heyday and twilight years of the Romanovs than those at Tsarskoe Selo (Royal Village), 25km south of St Petersburg. This small town flanks two huge palaces, set amidst parkland: the glorious Catherine Palace, beloved of Catherine the Great, and the Alexander Palace, where the last tsar and tsaritsa dwelt. Tsarskoe Selo is also associated with the great poet Alexander Pushkin, who studied at the town's Lycée – and with Rasputin, a frequent visitor who was buried here for a short time. Lenin, too, came here several times before the Revolution, and once spent hours in the park, evading Tsarist agents.

Tsarskoe Selo was once a model town connected to Pavlovsk and St Petersburg by Russia's first train line (built for the Imperial family's convenience), and featuring electric lighting, piped water and sewage works. Its chessboard plan incorporates a scaled-down version of St Petersburg's Gostiniy dvor and numerous villas that were turned into orphanages after the Revolution, when the town was renamed Detskoe Selo – "Children's Village". In 1937, the name was changed to **Pushkin**, to commemorate the centenary of the poet's death; although the palace is now called Tsarskoe Selo again and the main streets bear their pre-revolutionary names, the **town** itself still bears the poet's name.

During the **Nazi occupation** (Sept 1941–Jan 1944), most of the population was deported to Gatchina where they lived in tents, while the Germans looted the palaces and left not a single house habitable. After liberation, the first window to be glazed was that of Pushkin's room in the Lycée. Following decades of **restoration** work, both palaces appear to be their old selves again (at least externally), but some pavilions are still unrestored, such is the effort and cost involved.

Visitors can enjoy two **festivals** in June: the one-day **Tsarskoe Selo Carnival** procession through the streets of town, and a series of operatic and chamber **concerts** in the throne room of the Catherine Palace – for the exact dates, see the *St Petersburg Times* or *Where St Petersburg*, or check out the municipal **website** Ⓦwww.pushkin-town.net. The Catherine Palace and Park are covered in detail on the Tsarskoe Selo Museum Reserve's site, Ⓦwww.tzar.ru.

The Catherine Palace

The existing **Catherine Palace** (Yekaterininskiy dvorets) owes everything to Empress Elizabeth, who made the village of Tsarskoe Selo her summer residence, had a palace built by three different architects and then decided to scrap it for another one, fit to rival Versailles. Her new Italian architect, Bartolomeo Rastrelli, rose to the challenge, creating a Baroque masterpiece that the delighted empress named after her mother, Catherine I. Despite being nearly a kilometre in circumference, its blue-and-white **facade** avoids monotony by using a profusion of atlantes, columns and pilasters, which were covered with gold leaf in Elizabeth's day, causing villagers to think that the roof itself was made of solid gold.

When Catherine the Great inherited the palace in 1762, she found the weathered gilding an eyesore and ordered it to be removed. She also objected to the **interior** – a continuous succession of interconnecting rooms – and engaged the Scottish architect Charles Cameron to make the alterations she desired. Thereafter, Catherine stayed every summer, living quite informally unless diplomatic protocol required otherwise.

After Catherine's death, her son Paul spurned Tsarskoe Selo and appropriated many items for his own palaces at Pavlovsk and Gatchina. Although the palace gained a new lease of life under her grandson, Alexander I, who celebrated Russia's victory over Napoleon by employing Viktor Stasov to redesign several rooms and repair fire damage after 1820, subsequent monarchs preferred Peterhof's Cottage Palace or the nearby Alexander Palace as summer residences.

The palace's grandest sweep faces the Alexander Park across a vast courtyard with gilded gates, through which courtiers and guests once entered. Nowadays, only large tour groups enter the palace from this direction; individual visitors approach from the opposite side, where the full glory of its 306-metre-long facade is apparent only if you step back a little into the Catherine Park.

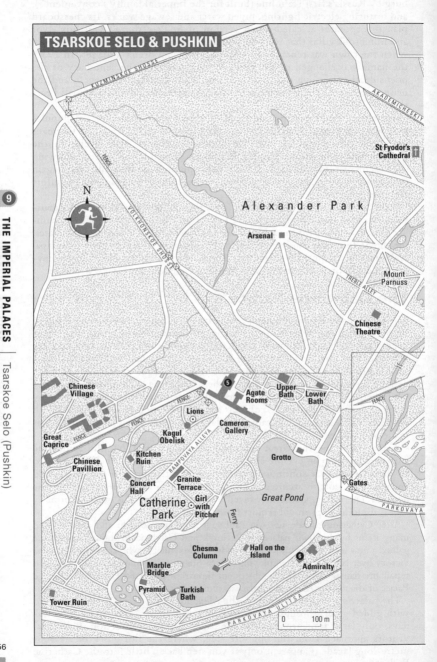

TSARSKOE SELO & PUSHKIN

KUZMINSKOE SHUSSE

AKADEMICHESKIY

St Fyodor's Cathedral

N

Alexander Park

Arsenal

Mount Parnuss

TREBLE ALLEY

Chinese Theatre

Chinese Village

Agate Rooms

Upper Bath

Lower Bath

FENCE

Lions

Cameron Gallery

Great Caprice

Kagul Obelisk

Chinese Pavillion

Kitchen Ruin

RAMPOVAYA ALLEYA

Grotto

Gates

FENCE

Concert Hall

Granite Terrace

Great Pond

PARKOVAYA

Catherine Park

Girl with Pitcher

Ferry

Chesma Column

Hall on the Island

Admiralty

Marble Bridge

Pyramid

Turkish Bath

Tower Ruin

PARKOVAYA ULITSA

0   100 m

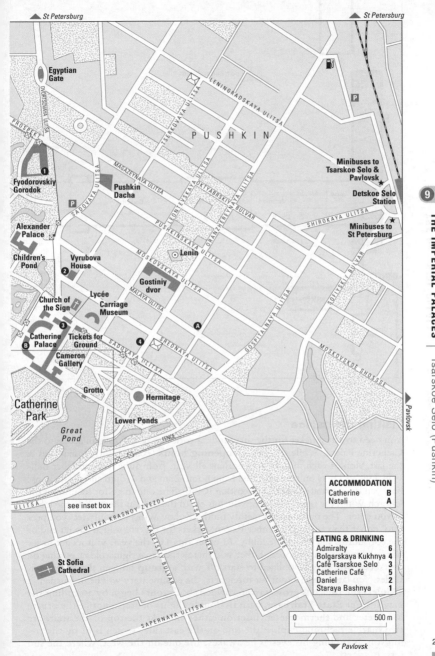

Egyptian Gate

LENINGRADSKAYA ULITSA

P U S H K I N

DVORTSKAYA ULITSA

PROSPEKT

1 Fyodorovskiy Gorodok

Minibuses to Tsarskoe Selo & Pavlovsk

Detskoe Selo Station

9

Magazeynaya Ulitsa

Pushkin Dacha

SHIROKAYA ULITSA

Minibuses to St Petersburg

Alexander Palace

SADOVAYA ULITSA

PUSHKINSKAYA ULITSA

Children's Pond

2 Vyrubova House

MOSKOVSKAYA ULITSA

⊙ Lenin

Gostiniy dvor

THE IMPERIAL PALACES | Tsarskoe Selo (Pushkin)

Lycée

MALAYA ULITSA

Church of the Sign

3 Carriage Museum

Catherine **B** Palace

Tickets for Ground

4

A SREDNAYA ULITSA

SADOVAYA ULITSA

GOSPITALNAYA ULITSA

MOSKOVSKOE SHOSSE

Cameron Gallery

Grotto

● Hermitage

Catherine Park

Lower Ponds

Great Pond

FENCE

▶ *Pavlovsk*

ULITSA

see inset box

ULITSA KRASNOY ZVEZDY

KADETSKIY BULVAR

ULITSA RADISHEVA

PAVLOVSKOE SHOSSE

ACCOMMODATION
| Catherine | **B** |
| Natali | **A** |

St Sofia Cathedral

EATING & DRINKING
Admiralty	6
Bolgarskaya Kukhnya	4
Café Tsarskoe Selo	3
Catherine Café	5
Daniel	2
Staraya Bashnya	1

0   500 m

SAPERNAYA ULITSA

▼ *Pavlovsk*

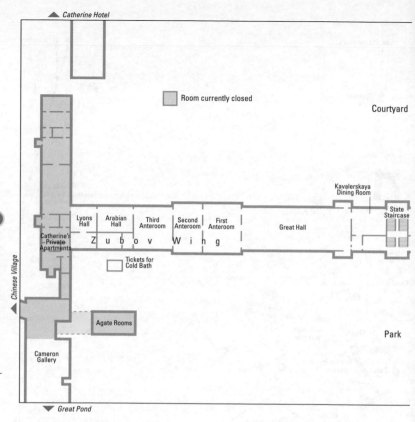

Catherine Hotel

Room currently closed

Courtyard

Kavalerskaya
Dining Room

State
Staircase

| Lyons Hall | Arabian Hall | Third Anteroom | Second Anteroom | First Anteroom | Great Hall |

Z u b o v   W i n g

Catherine's
Private
Apartments

Tickets for
Cold Bath

Chinese Village

Agate Rooms

Park

Cameron
Gallery

Great Pond

Visiting the palace

You need to buy a ticket for the surrounding park (see p.260) to gain access to the Catherine Palace. While the palace's **opening hours** (10am–5pm; closed Tues & the last Mon of each month) are constant all year, from June to September individual visitors may only be admitted from noon–2pm and 4–5pm and must choose between two separate **tours** (each costing R450). The one to go for focuses on the Church Wing, the ticket office for which is off to the right at the back of the lobby as you enter. The other dwells mainly on the Zubov Wing and only lets you peer into, rather than enter, the Amber Room; tickets for this are sold at the far end of the corridor to the left of the lobby. At other times of the year, visitors get to see all of the rooms that are open. Either way there's the usual rigmarole of putting on overshoes; you may be obliged to start off with a **group** but can slip away later. Unless you latch on to a tour for foreigners, the commentary will be in Russian.

Unless the palace is grossly overcrowded, both tours begin by ascending the magnificent **State Staircase**, with its double flights of steps; notice the ornate barometer and thermometer, inset on either side. At the top of the stairs are two marble reclining cupids; the one on the east side, which is lit by the rising sun, is rubbing his eyes as he awakes; the one on the west, where the sun sets, is asleep.

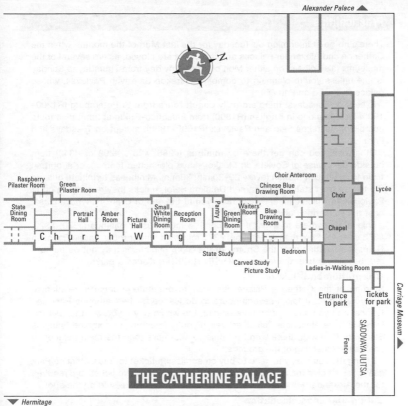

Raspberry Pilaster Room
Green Pilaster Room
State Dining Room
Portrait Hall
Amber Room
Picture Hall
Small White Dining Room
Reception Room
Pantry
Waiters' Room
Green Dining Room
Blue Drawing Room
Choir Anteroom
Chinese Blue Drawing Room
Choir
Lycée

C h u r c h   W i n g

State Study
Carved Study
Picture Study
Bedroom
Chapel
Ladies-in-Waiting Room

Entrance to park
Tickets for park

SADOVAYA ULITSA
Carriage Museum ▲
Fence

THE CATHERINE PALACE

▼ Hermitage

The Zubov Wing

Named after Catherine the Great's last lover, Platon Zubov, the palace's southern, **Zubov Wing** is still partly under restoration, and in any case visitors on both tours get to see the first two rooms off the State Staircase. The **Equerries' Dining Room** (Kavelerskaya stolovaya) is typical of Rastelli's work for Empress Elizabeth: a white salon with gilded mouldings and an ornate blue-and-white-tiled stove reaching almost to the ceiling. The adjacent **Great Hall** (Bolshoy zal) is 48m long and occupies the width of the palace; glittering with mirrors, gilded cherubs and garlands, its vast ceiling adorned with a fresco entitled *The Triumph of Russia*, glorifying the nation's achievements in the arts, sciences and war. This was used for costume balls, where Elizabeth loved to dress as a sailor or a Chevalier Guard and obliged male courtiers to wear women's clothing.

Beyond lie **Catherine's private apartments**, designed by Cameron. The only rooms open are the **Arabian Hall** with its arabesque motifs, and the **Lyons Hall**, swathed in yellow silk, but at some point in the future visitors may be able to view her Chinese Hall, Silver Room and Bedroom. A French envoy who saw her suite decades after her death reported that it also contained two small rooms full of erotic paintings of her lovers – but if these ever existed, they disappeared some time later.

There's no point in coming on Tuesday (or the last Mon of the month), when the Catherine and Alexander palaces and the Lycée are closed, as are several of the museums (also closed on either Mon or Wed). Any day from Thursday to Sunday is fine unless you're planning to combine Tsarskoe Selo with Pavlovsk, whose palace is closed on Friday.

Except on Tuesdays, there are daily **coach tours** from St Petersburg (R1200–1600) including one **in English** (R1800) from Eclectica-Guide at 2pm; plus tours combining Tsarskoe Selo and Pavlovsk (R1600–1850), except on Tuesdays and Fridays.

Otherwise, you can get there by **minibus** (#286, #287, #299 or #342) from outside the House of Soviets on Moskovskaya ploshchad (45min), or suburban **train** from Vitebsk Station (every 20–30min; 30min). Minibuses terminate outside the town's train station (still named Detskoe Selo), unless they're carrying on to Pavlovsk, in which case they can drop you at the end of Oranzhereynaya ulitsa, near the Catherine Palace.

This is also where to alight if you catch a local bus or minibus (#370, #372, #378 or #545) from the train station; #371 follows a longer route via the Egyptian Gates, terminating near the Church of the Sign. Minibuses may not be numbered, but simply bear the legend ДВОРЦЫ ПАРКИ (palaces & parks).

Orientation and tickets

Starting at the Catherine Palace, it's easy to orientate yourself in relation to everything else. It takes several hours to do justice to the Catherine Park and Palace, and you should plan on spending the whole day if you want to visit the Lycée and the Alexander Palace as well. If you're intending to combine Tsarskoe Selo with Pavlovsk, there won't be time to see more than the main palaces at each and something of the grounds.

During the summer, you need to buy an admission ticket for the Catherine Park as well as a ticket for the palace once inside the grounds. No tickets are required for the Alexander Park; tickets for the Alexander Palace are sold on the spot.

Eating and accommodation

Places to eat near the palace are poor value for money, whether you're talking takeaway pizzas from the *Café Tsarskoe Selo* (11am–midnight; closed Tues) opposite the Lycée; soup, pastries and beverages in the *Catherine Café* (noon–8pm) in the palace; or meals in the *Admiralty* (noon–11pm) by the Great Pond. It's better to track down the humble *Bolgarskaya Kukhnya* (11am–11pm) on Oranzhereynaya ulitsa, serving tasty Bulgarian dishes and wine. To splurge, try the ultra-stylish *Daniel* restaurant (☎466 91 16; noon–1am) on Srednaya ulitsa, with a Michelin-starred Swedish chef, or the less exorbitant *Staraya Bashnya* (☎466 66 98; noon–10pm) in a corner tower of the Fyodorovskiy Gorodok, on the edge of the Alexander Park.

Staying in town enables you to hit the sights before the crowds arrive. The *Natali* (☎466 29 13, ⓦwww.hotelnatali.rub; ❸) is a mini-hotel in an old house on Malaya ulitsa, ten minutes' walk from the Catherine Park, where the posh *Catherine Hotel* (☎466 80 42, ⓦwww.hotelkaterina.spb.ru; ❼) is ensconced in one of the palace's service wings. Both take credit cards.

The Church Wing

On the other side of the State Staircase is the **State Dining Room**, its walls hung with paintings of game and wildfowl, and its oval table is laid with Meissen china. The adjoining **Raspberry** and **Green Pilaster Rooms** are so-named after their gilt-edged pilasters, and precede a **Portrait Hall** hung with large portraits of empresses Elizabeth and Anna Ivanovna, and smaller ones of Catherine and Peter the Great.

THE IMPERIAL PALACES | Tsarskoe Selo (Pushkin)

Next comes the fabulous **Amber Room** (Yantarnaya komnata), whose honeyed hues complement the lapidary detail of four Florentine mosaics representing the five senses, composed of jasper, lapis lazuli, onyx, agate and quartz. It took twenty-four years to re-create the Amber Room that was stolen by the Nazis and disappeared (see box on p.262), and although the new one looks amazing, it needs a few years for the amber to mellow.

Beyond lies the **Picture Hall** (Kartinniy zal). Of the 130 canvases displayed here before the war, 114 were saved. Mostly Flemish, French and Italian religious works of the seventeenth and eighteenth centuries, they're offset by two huge wall-stoves and a parquet floor inlaid with pink and black palm wood.

Next comes a **Small White Dining Room** featuring a ceiling fresco of Venus bathing, and a **Reception Room** (Gostinaya Aleksandra I) belonging to Crown Prince Alexander, hung with Karl Robert portraits of Catherine and her predecessors. She doted on her grandson Alexander as much as she disliked her son, Paul. The **Pantry**, beyond, marks the end of the rooms decorated by Rastrelli.

The Cameron and Stasov Rooms

In the 1780s, Catherine commissioned Cameron to create a suite of rooms for Paul and his wife Maria Fyodorovna, whose Classicism is in striking contrast to Rastrelli's Baroque effusions – though it was Ivan Martos who actually sculpted the figures, garlands and cameos in the **Green Dining Room** (Zelionaya stolovaya), whose table is laid with the green-and-mauve Private Service, a wedding gift from Catherine.

While Rastrelli's rooms were heated by tiled stoves, Cameron's had European-style fireplaces, as in the **Waiters' Room** (Ofitsiantskaya), whose parquet floor is the only original one in the palace. Visitors who opted for a tour of the Zubov Wing are able to enter the **Blue Drawing Room** (Golubaya gostinaya), with its magnificent painted ceiling, floral-patterned wallpaper and blue-crystal floor lamps; the **Chinese Blue Drawing Room**, papered in silk hand-painted with Chinese landscapes; and Alexander's **Bedroom** (Opochivalnya), with its slender columns.

Conversely, those who signed up for the Church Wing tour are steered back through the Green Dining Room into Alexander I's **State Study**, an elegant confection of pink and blue *faux marbre*, with Karelian birch furniture. Like Alexander's other rooms in the palace, it was designed by Stasov after Russia's victory over Napoleon; a vase depicts Alexander entering Paris with his army in 1814.

The Agate Rooms and Cameron Gallery

Jutting out from the southeastern corner of the Catherine Palace, a whitewashed cloister leads to a nondescript two-storey building concealing Cameron's most fabulous creation: the **Agate Rooms** (Agatovye Komnaty; closed for restoration). Designed as a summer pavilion, these chambers flaunted all the mineral wealth of the Russian Empire, fashioned from agate, jasper, malachite, lapis lazuli, porphyry and alabaster. Catherine often held intimate dinner parties here, and the rooms connected directly to her private apartments on the upper floor of the palace. There's nothing left of the **Cold Bath** (Kholodnaya Banya; 10am–5pm; closed Thurs; free) on the lower level, now used for **temporary exhibitions**. Upstairs, the **Agate Room** proper sports a magnificent parquet floor from the palace that Catherine was building for her lover, Lanskoy, before his untimely death. The **Great Hall** beyond has malachite columns and a bronze coffered ceiling, and was originally lit by candelabras held by four marble maidens. A door leads directly to Catherine's private **Hanging Garden**, on a level with her private apartments and the upper storey of the Cameron Gallery.

The Amber Room

Amber – the fossilized resin of prehistoric pines – has been prized since Roman times, when a trading route from the Baltic to the Black Sea was established. In 1701 Frederick I of Prussia commissioned an **Amber Room** for Königsberg Castle, near the richest deposits on the Baltic coast. It took four years to gather enough amber to start work, and he died before its completion, whereupon his successor halted the project, and in 1716 gave the panels to Peter the Great in exchange for fifty giant guardsmen. In Russia they languished in crates for thirty years until Empress Elizabeth installed them in the Winter Palace, only to decide later that they'd look better in the Catherine Palace. There, Rastrelli supervised five master craftsmen fitting them into a larger room that entailed creating 48 square metres of mosaics composed of gemstones from the Urals and Caucasus, and filling the remaining space with mirrors and gilded sconces – a task completed in 1770. Legend has it that the room was exorcized on Elizabeth's orders, to expel the spirits of Prussian necromancers (Königsberg being an occult centre from medieval times until the fall of the Third Reich).

The room remained there until September 1941, when the Nazis captured Tsarskoe Selo. Staff had tried to disguise the room by wallpapering it, but the Germans weren't fooled and dismantled it in 36 hours. On Hitler's orders it was installed at Königsberg – a "return to its true home" according to Nazi propaganda – until RAF bombing raids compelled it to be crated up again. The crates were last recorded in the castle yard in January 1945, shortly before the departure of the liner *Wilhelm Gustloff*, crammed with German refugees, which was sunk by a Soviet submarine. Whether the Amber Room went down with the ship or was destroyed in the Red Army's bombardment of the castle, or remains hidden in the miles of tunnels beneath Königsberg, or elswhere, remains a mystery – treasure hunters were excavating a mine near the Czech border as this was written.

The **re-creation** of the Amber Room began in 1979 and ultimately cost over $12 million ($3.5 million donated by Ruhrgas). This involved techniques such as baking, or soaking bits of amber in wine or honey, to get the right shade, and backing panels with gold leaf to maximize their radiance. In 1997 the carvers were able to compare their own work with a fragment of panelling and a commode from the original room, seized by German police and returned to Russia – though neither features in the Amber Room that was inaugurated by Chancellor Schroeder and Putin in 2003. A conspiracy theory maintains that this is actually the *original* Amber Room, secretly salvaged from the seabed – its provenance disguised to avoid reminding public opinion of the 7700 refugees drowned aboard the *Wilhelm Gustloff*.

The **Cameron Gallery** (10am–5pm; closed Wed & the last Tues of each month; R220) is a perfect Neoclassical foil to the Baroque palace. Cameron reputedly doffed his hat to the Catherine Palace every time he passed it on the way to work, and continuously modified his own design of the gallery to harmonize with Rastrelli's creation. Among the antique statues installed beneath the arcades was a bust of Charles James Fox, arch enemy of British Prime Minister Pitt the Younger, whom the empress despised. Nowadays the gallery is used for **temporary exhibitions**, and accessible from the park by a grand flight of steps.

The Catherine Park

The 566-hectare **Catherine Park** (Yekaterininskiy park; daily 6am–10pm; R160; free admission after 5pm & during winter) is characterized by three styles of landscape gardening: French, English and Italian. Directly behind the Catherine Palace, the original nucleus of the park – commissioned by Elizabeth – was laid out geometrically in the French fashion, with pavilions and statues at the intersections. The **Upper Bath** was reserved for royalty and now hosts temporary exhibitions (10am–5pm; closed Wed; free); the **Lower Bath**, once used by courtiers, is still derelict. At the end of the avenue stands a **Hermitage** pavilion, whose Baroque facade echoes that of the Catherine Palace. Between the baths and the **Fish Canal** (which once supplied food for banquets) are marble statues of **Adam** and **Eve**, similar to those at Peterhof.

Around the Great Pond

One of the more alluring sights in the park is the **Great Pond**, the focal point of the romantic "English Park" below the Cameron Gallery. Here, the court floated on gilded boats, watching regattas of gondolas and sampans, or pyrotechnic battles between miniature warships. Its designer, John Bush, exploited the hilly terrain to create ravishing perspectives that Catherine's architects embellished with pavilions and follies. The island amid the lake is accessible by a **ferry** (R200) pulled by an underwater cable, for a guided tour of the **Hall on the Island**, where musicians once played, including a visit to the **Chesma Column**, which honours the Russian naval victory at Chesma Bay and is modelled on the Rostral Columns in St Petersburg.

A clockwise circuit of the pond takes about thirty minutes, starting with the so-called **Grotto** (10am–5pm; closed Thurs; R50), a blue and white pavilion whose ornately stuccoed hall was once decorated with 250,000 shells, and now hosts temporary exhibitions. Further on, you can wander off to the **Lower Ponds** and the marble **Column of Morea** (commemorating Russian victories in Greece in 1770), or head straight for the **Admiralty** – two Dutch-style boathouses flanking a tower (now a café). Further along are a former **Turkish Bath**, resembling an Ottoman mosque, the stone **Pyramid** where Catherine buried her favourite dogs, and Cameron's **Marble Bridge**, a copy of the Palladian bridge at Wilton House in England.

Towards the Chinese Village

West of the Great Pond lies the **"Italian Park"**, whose canals and hillocks are interlaced with paths meandering from one folly to another. Catherine liked to stroll here with her dogs, unaccompanied by courtiers; in *The Captain's Daughter*, Pushkin relates how the heroine of the tale, Maria Ivanovna, unknowingly encountered the empress and interceded for her betrothed. Even more fancifully, Catherine is supposed to have once told a sentry to stand watch over a violet that she wanted to pick, but then forgot about it. As the order was never revoked, a guard was posted on the spot for decades afterwards.

A zigzag trail taking in the park's highlights starts either at the **Granite Terrace** above the Great Pond, or the **Kagul Obelisk** beyond the Cameron Gallery. On an island further south are a small domed **Concert Hall** and **Kitchen Ruin**, the latter designed to look picturesque rather than for cooking purposes. On another islet, visible from the bridge, stands a **Chinese Pavilion** flying metal flags. Also known as the "Creaking Pavilion" because it was designed to creak whenever someone entered, it is now derelict and closed.

Across the water you'll spot the colourful **Chinese Village** (Kitayskaya derevnya), a series of Oriental pavilions beyond the Catherine Park's perimeter fence. Originally a whimsical folly, the village was later turned into a home for serfs who had run away from cruel masters. Ravaged during World War II, the pavilions have now been restored and turned into luxury apartments; the rental income is used to repay the restoration costs. Their upturned roofs are as gaudy as circus tents and crowned with dragons. From here, a path continues on to the **Great Caprice**, a massive humpback arch topped by a pagoda.

Beyond the Catherine Park

Leaving the Catherine Park by its main entrance on Sadovaya ulitsa, retain your ticket to qualify for free admission to the **Carriage Museum** (10am–5pm; closed Wed & the last Tues of each month in summer; open Sat & Sun only in winter; R100) in the former royal stables.

Sadovaya ulitsa is spanned by an arch linking the Catherine Palace to the Imperial **Lycée** (10.30am–5.30pm; closed Tues; R200) where **Alexander Pushkin** once studied. Established to provide a modern education for the sons of distinguished families, it proved more attractive to the poorer nobility than to great aristocrats. The 12-year-old Pushkin was a member of the first class presented to Alexander I at the inauguration ceremony in 1811. During his six years at the Lycée, he grew bold and lyrical, drank punch and wrote poetry, culminating in a bravura recital of his precocious *Recollections of Tsarskoe Selo* in the assembly hall in 1817.

Guided tours show you around the classrooms, music room and the physics laboratory – all equipped as in Pushkin's day. Upstairs in the dormitories, the cubbyhole labelled *No. 14. Alexander Pushkin* is reverentially preserved. If you understand Russian, you'll hear much about the influence of his favourite teacher, Kunitsyn (to whom he dedicated several poems), and his crafty valet, Sazanov, who secretly committed several murders and robberies in the two years that he was employed by Pushkin.

Passing under the arch you'll see the **Church of the Sign** (tserkov Znameniya), the oldest building in Tsarskoe Selo, dating back to 1734, followed by a **statue of Pushkin** daydreaming on a bench, created in 1900 by Robert Bach.

The Alexander Palace

Further north along Sadovaya ulitsa you'll pass the former **house of Anna Vyrubova** on Srednaya ulitsa. Empress Alexandra's closest friend, Vyrubova worshipped Rasputin and arranged meetings between them at her house. Rumoured to have had a lesbian relationship with Alexandra, or participated in his orgies, she had herself medically examined and declared a virgin after the February Revolution, before moving abroad. The plaque outside makes no mention of her, but notes that Pushkin's music teacher, Tepper De Ferguson, once lived there.

In Vyrubova's day, court life centred on the nearby **Alexander Palace** (Aleksandrovskiy dvorets; 10am–5pm; closed Tues & the last Wed of each month; R300), Nicholas II and Alexandra's principal residence. A Palladian pile that's regarded as Quarenghi's masterpiece, it was commissioned by Catherine the Great for her grandson, the future Alexander I, and later became the summer home of a succession of Imperial heirs. Following the end of the monarchy it became a museum of the Romanov dynasty, but the sympathetic impression it made on visitors irked the Bolsheviks, who sold off much of the contents in the late 1920s – although it remained a museum until the outbreak of war, when the Nazis looted the palace and turned it into an SS hospital. After the war the palace became a naval college; one wing has been restored and was opened to the public in 1997, with the support of the Alexander Palace Association, whose **website** (Ⓦwww.alexanderpalace. org) is a mine of information.

Though few of the rooms can compare with the Catherine Palace for magnificence, they have poignancy that other Imperial residences lack, due to the almost tangible presence of Nicholas, Alexandra and their children, some of whose **personal effects** are on display. Particularly moving are the uniforms that Tsarevich Alexei and his sisters wore in their capacity as honorary colonels of various regiments, and the fanciful headgear and harness of Alexei's pet donkey, accompanied by photos of him playing. The finest chambers are Nicholas's **New Study**, with its Art Nouveau columns, friezes and billiard table, and the **Reception Room**, with its oak ceiling, wainscotting and huge, hooded fireplace.

The Alexander Park and other sights

The adjacent **Alexander Park** (Aleksandrovskiy park; daily 10am–6pm; free) is wilder than the Catherine Park, with dank thickets, rickety bridges and algae-choked ponds. Southwest of the palace are such features as a **Chinese Theatre** and a wooded hillock dubbed **Mount Parnuss**; due north lies the **Fyodorovskiy Gorodok**, a barracks for the Imperial bodyguard built in 1913 to resemble a medieval Kremlin, that's now derelict aside from a restaurant in one of its towers. Visible above the trees to the west are the domes of **St Fyodor's Cathedral**, where Alexandra often prayed in the crypt, lamenting the murder of Rasputin. His grave was originally situated in the vicinity, but on the night of Nicholas's abdication the body was exhumed by soldiers, who stole the icon which Alexandra had placed in the coffin and burned the corpse to ashes (thus fulfilling one of Rasputin's own prophecies).

En route to the Gorodok, a brief detour along Kuzminskaya ulitsa will bring you to the **Pushkin dacha** (10am–4.30pm; closed Mon, Tues & the last Fri of each month; R50), a charming period residence where the poet and his wife spent the summer of 1831. One last sight is the incongruous **Egyptian Gate**, resembling the portico of a pharaonic temple, with reliefs of Isis and other deities – minibuses heading towards St Petersburg along the Peterburgskoe shosse run past it.

Pavlovsk

In 1777, in an unusually warm gesture, Catherine the Great gave 607 hectares of land along the River Slavyanka to her son, the future Tsar Paul, to reward him for the birth of a grandson who would continue the dynasty. The area – virgin forest used by the tsars for hunting – was named **Pavlovsk**, after Paul (*Pavel* in Russian), though the style of the Great Palace here is more a reflection of the tastes of his second wife, the German-born Maria Fyodorovna, who outlived him by 28 years and made many modifications after his death.

The Great Palace aside, Pavlovsk has nothing to compare with the splendid buildings to be seen at Peterhof or Tsarskoe Selo. Instead, it's the beauty of **Pavlovsk Park**, one of the largest landscaped parks in the world, which has drawn crowds for over a century. With the completion of Russia's first railway line, from St Petersburg to Pavlovsk, it became one of the most popular day-trips from the capital. Tolstoy came often, though as he confessed in his diary, he hated himself for it: "Went to Pavlovsk. Disgusting. Girls, silly music, girls, mechanical nightingale, girls, heat, cigarette smoke, girls, vodka, cheese, screams and shouts, girls, girls, girls!"

Pavlovsk's beauty was obliterated during the Nazi occupation, during which fifteen thousand locals were deported to labour camps in Germany and three

Practicalities

Pavlovsk is only 5km kilometres from Tsarskoe Selo and **getting there** from St Petersburg is the same: a 35-minute journey by **suburban train** (every 20–30min) from Vitebsk Station, or 45 minutes by minibus #286, #299, #342 or #545 from the House of Soviets on Moskovskaya ploshchad. The first three minibuses can drop you right outside the Great Palace; the #545 at the station opposite the park's Railway Gate. All four shuttle between Tsarskoe Selo and Pavlovsk, a 15-minute ride. Otherwise, you can visit Pavlovsk on a **guided tour** (R800–1000) from St Petersburg, together with Tsarskoe Selo (R1600–1850) if desired.

Orientation and tickets

With over 607 hectares of woodland and few signposts, it's easy to get lost in **Pavlovsk Park** once you stray beyond the Railway Gate or the Great Palace. The park is open daily from 7am–8pm, with a R100 entry charge from 8am–5pm, waived in wintertime (except during Christmas and Easter festivals). It's best to start with the palace and visit the park afterwards, but in any case you'll have to buy a park ticket at the outset. **Tickets** for the Great Palace are sold at a kiosk in the courtyard; if required for pavilions, you can buy them on the spot.

Eating

If you want to eat cheaply, it's best to bring your own picnic and head off into the park – or maybe grab a *shashlyk* and a beer at the outdoor *Café Snezhanka* (daily 11am–5pm) near Druzheskaya alleya. For more substantial fare, try *Podvorye* (daily noon–11pm; ℡466 85 44 to be sure of a table; ⓦwww.podvorye.ru) on Sadovaya ulitsa, a fancy restaurant in the style of an *izba* (wooden peasant cottage), 400m from the station (turn left as you come off the platform), which serves traditional Russian food with a flourish and includes Putin and Chirac among its satisfied customers. In the palace itself there's a posh self-service café (10am–6pm; closed Fri) in the Columned Hall in the south wing, serving expensive drinks, cakes and sandwiches.

years of vandalism concluded with a final orgy of destruction. Although Soviet sappers defused the mines left in the charred shell of the palace, its dome and roof had already been ruined, thousands of trees felled, and bridges and pavilions dynamited. It was five years before the park was reopened to the public and over a decade before any of the palace rooms could be visited.

The enormity of Pavlovsk's **restoration** is conveyed by the fact that over forty thousand fragments of plaster had to be salvaged and pieced together merely to re-create the sumptuous mouldings inside its central dome. All in all, the whole task of restoration took 26 years, an epic undertaking described in the book *Pavlovsk: The Life of a Russian Palace*. Besides the Museum Reserve's own **website** (ⓦwww.pavlovskmuseum.ru) you'll find a wealth of images and facts about Pavlovsk and other palaces at ⓦwww.alexanderpalace.org.

Should you happen to be here in **winter** the park is great fun for kids, with **sledging** on giant rubber tyres (*zadachki*) near the *Café Snezhanka*. In August, there are free **concerts** in the Round Hall at 2pm.

The Great Palace

The **Great Palace** (Bolshoy dvorets; May–Sept daily 10am–5pm; Oct–April closed Fri & the first Mon of each month; R200) has come a long way since its rather modest central building was erected in 1782–86 by Charles Cameron, who transformed Tsarskoe Selo's Catherine Palace. Cameron was one of the few architects to win Catherine the Great's lasting admiration, and she therefore foisted his talents upon her son as well. Pretty soon, however, his Palladian fixation and concern for minutiae began to clash with Paul's and Maria Fyodorovna's tastes, and he was eventually dismissed, his assistant, Vincenzo Brenna, being employed to extend the palace into a larger, more elaborate complex. Some of the best architects in St Petersburg were recruited to decorate its interior – Quarenghi, Rossi and Voronikhin among others – and the overall Neoclassical effect is surprisingly homogenous.

Life at Pavlovsk was conducted according to the whims of Paul and Maria. While he drilled his troops all day, she painted and embroidered. Guests found the social life extraordinarily dull; interminable gatherings where only banalities were exchanged. The palace was meant to be approached from the east, from where you get the best overall view off the great sweep of Brenna's semicircular wings. At the centre of the courtyard is a **statue of Paul** dressed in the Prussian military uniform he loved so much.

Pavlovsk is relatively uncrowded even during high season, and the separate entrances for individuals and tour groups mean that you shouldn't have to queue for more than a few minutes; tickets are sold inside the palace. The **itinerary** described below may not always be followed in practice, but most of the rooms are permanently open; some contain a photograph of their ruination during the war.

The State Rooms

Built during the era of the European Grand Tour and the first great archeological digs, the palace contains many motifs from antiquity, beginning with the **Egyptian Vestibule** (Yegipetskiy vestibyul) on the first floor, which is lined with pharaonic statues and zodiac medallions. From here, visitors are ushered upstairs to the second-floor **State Rooms** via the main **staircase**, designed by Brenna with martial motifs to pander to Paul's pretensions. The northern parade of rooms reflect his martial obsessions, the southern ones the more domesticated tastes of Maria Fyodorovna. The striking thing about all the rooms, though, is their relatively human scale – you could just about imagine living here – unlike those of the Great Palaces of Peterhof and Tsarskoe Selo.

At the top of the stairs, to the right, the domed **Italian Hall** (Italyanskiy zal) rises into the palace's central cupola. Its decor, intended by Cameron to evoke a Roman bathhouse, is uniformly Neoclassical, with rich helpings of *trompe l'oeil* and stucco and candelabras shaped like French horns.

Afterwards, cross the landing to pass through a small Valet's Room and Dressing Room, into **Paul's Study**, its huge desk crowned by a model Temple of Venus; the amber pen set was carved by Paul himself. His **Knights Study** is so-called for its tapestry of a soldier being knighted – by Paul in his dreams, judging by the **Hall of War** (Zal voyny), an explosion of gilded *objets de guerre*, where even the candelabras symbolize war spoils – although Paul himself never saw any military action. The bas-reliefs below the ceiling represent the Trojan Wars and *The Odyssey*.

The tsar's wing is connected to his wife's by Cameron's green-coloured **Grecian Hall** (Grecheskiy zal), meant to resemble the interior of a Greek temple. The most ornate room in the palace, it features exquisite jasper urns and eagle-winged divans; the fireplaces were taken from the Engineers' Castle after Paul's death. Maria's suite of rooms begins with the **Hall of Peace** (Zal mira), as gilt-ridden as Paul's Hall of War but garnished with floral motifs, musical instruments and symbols of fecundity.

Maria's Library is considered by many to be Voronikhin's masterpiece; not the least of whose treasures is the desk chair he designed for her, its back rest flanked by two fluted horns containing potted plants. The parquet flooring,

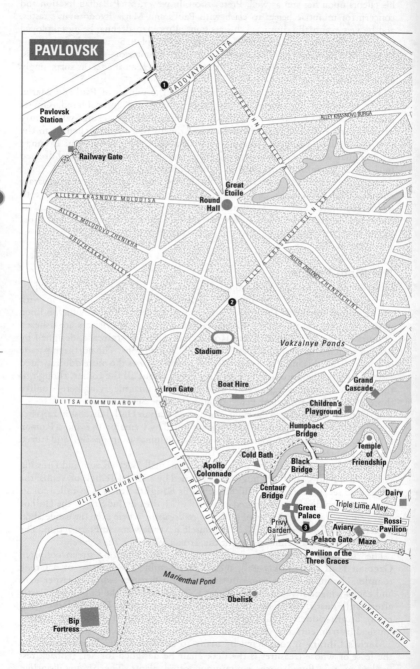

PAVLOVSK

Pavlovsk Station

Railway Gate

SADOVAYA ULISTA

ALLEY KRASNOVO BURGA

TIPPELENNAYA ALLEY

Great Étoile

Round Hall

ALLEYA KRASNOVO MOLODTSA

ALLEYA MOLODOVO ZHENIKHA

DRUZHESKAYA ALLEYA

ALLEYA KRASNOY SOLNTSA

ALLEYA ZHELENOY ZHENSHCHINY

Vokzalnye Ponds

Stadium

Iron Gate

Boat Hire

ULITSA KOMMUNAROV

Grand Cascade

Children's Playground

Humpback Bridge

Cold Bath

Apollo Colonnade

Black Bridge

Temple of Friendship

Centaur Bridge

Great Palace

Triple Lime Alley

Dairy

ULITSA MICHURINA

ULITSA REVOLYUTSII

Privy Garden

Aviary

Rossi Pavilion

Palace Gate

Maze

Pavilion of the Three Graces

Marienthal Pond

ULITSA LUNACHARSKOVO

Obelisk

Bip Fortress

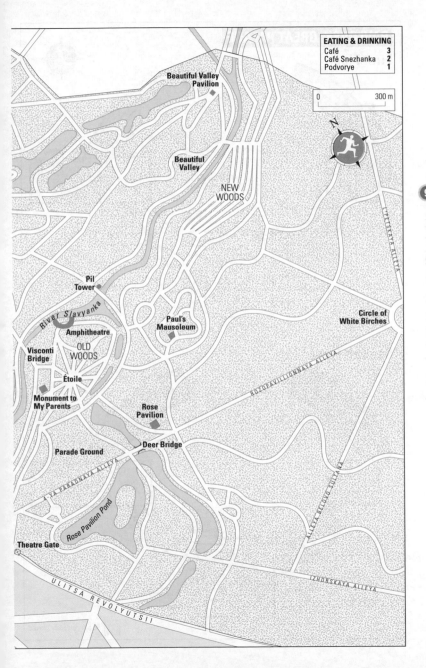

0   300 m

N

Beautiful Valley
Pavilion

Beautiful
Valley

NEW
WOODS

Pil
Tower

River *Slavyanka*

Paul's
Mausoleum

Circle of
White Birches

Amphitheatre

Visconti
Bridge

OLD
WOODS

Étoile

ROZOPAVILLIONNAYA ALLEYA

Monument to
My Parents

Rose
Pavilion

Deer Bridge

Parade Ground

4-YA PARADNAYA ALLEYA

Rose Pavilion Pond

ALLEYA BELOGO SULTANA

Theatre Gate

IZHORSKAYA ALLEYA

ULITSA REVOLYUTSII

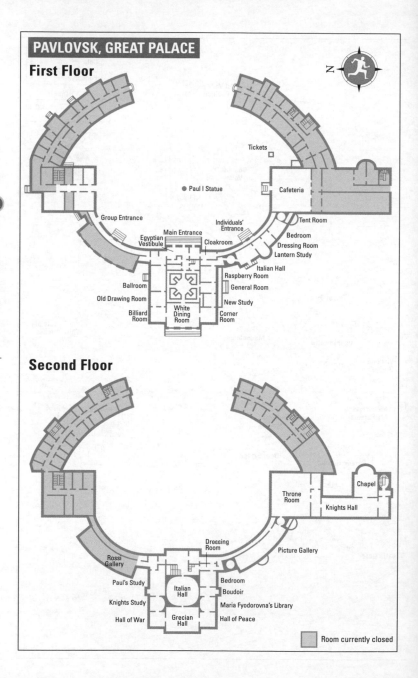

PAVLOVSK, GREAT PALACE

First Floor

N

Tickets

Paul I Statue

Cafeteria

Group Entrance

Individuals' Entrance

Tent Room

Egyptian Vestibule

Main Entrance

Cloakroom

Bedroom

Dressing Room

Lantern Study

Italian Hall

Raspberry Room

Ballroom

General Room

Old Drawing Room

New Study

Billiard Room

White Dining Room

Corner Room

Second Floor

Chapel

Throne Room

Knights Hall

Dressing Room

Picture Gallery

Rossi Gallery

Paul's Study

Italian Hall

Bedroom

Boudoir

Knights Study

Maria Fyodorovna's Library

Hall of War

Grecian Hall

Hall of Peace

Room currently closed

Given the oddities of many of the Romanovs, it's rather unfair that **Paul** (1754–1801) should be the only one tagged "the mad tsar". Rumours of illegitimacy plagued him throughout his life, though his boorish temperament and obsession with all things military were shared by his putative father, Peter III. However, his mother, Catherine, had already taken Sergei Saltykov as a lover when she became pregnant, so people drew the obvious conclusion.

Paul saw little of Catherine during **childhood**, and was just eight years old when his father was deposed with her consent. Although she immediately designated Paul as her successor, he never forgave her for his father's murder. As a child, Paul suffered from digestive problems, vomiting and diarrhoea, and in later life from insomnia, tantrums and paranoia. His first **marriage** was a disaster: his wife was seduced by his best friend and died in childbirth; but the second one proved happier, despite the fact that Maria Fyodorovna reputedly had an affair with her Scottish physician, Dr Wilson, who may have been the real father of Tsar Nicholas I (his face was strikingly like Wilson's and utterly unlike Paul's).

After Catherine's death, Paul sought to destroy everything she had stood for, sacking those who had enjoyed her favour and elevating those whom she had disgraced. Besides those embittered by their fall, he caused widespread resentment among the nobility by attempting to curtail their abuses of power. He abolished the 25 years' military service that oppressed the peasantry; planned to reform Russia's corrupt financial institutions; and almost acquired Malta as a Russian naval base – to the alarm of England, whose ambassador was involved in Paul's **assassination** (see p.89). After his death, Paul's worthy intentions were forgotten, and his faults and foibles emphasized. As he himself once remarked, "Anecdote pushes out History" – a view confirmed by Vitaly Melnikov's 2003 film, *Poor, Poor Pavel*.

inlaid with twelve different varieties of wood, is exceptional, while the bay study is surrounded by books on botany, her favourite hobby. Though you can't hear it in action, the table in her **Boudoir** plays melodies from Bach and Beethoven when its drawers are opened. In her **Bedroom**, with its murals of Antique gods and ruins, two golden putti stand at the end of the canopied gilt bed and a glass cabinet displays the 64-piece toilette set given to the tsaritsa by Marie Antoinette, with whom she got on famously while in Paris. Neither the bed nor the toilette set was ever used, their function being merely to impress visitors. Her **Dressing Room** (Tualetnaya) features an unusual steel dressing table with matching accessories all studded with "steel diamonds", produced by craftsmen from the state armouries at Tula, who could carry out private commissions in their spare time.

The southern wing

At this point, you leave the palace's original building and pass through tiny, ornate lobbies into the **southern wing**, designed by Brenna on a far grander scale. Its **Picture Gallery** (Kartinnaya galereya) is a case in point: a long, curving hall with white ruched curtains, it was built to display the seventeenth- and eighteenth-century paintings which Paul and his wife purchased on their Grand Tour of Europe. Whilst not outstanding, the collection includes works by Angelica Kauffmann, Tiepolo, Salvatore Rosa and a small sketch by Rubens.

Beyond lies the Great Dining Hall, also known as the **Throne Room** (Tronniy zal), whose most arresting feature is a giant ceiling fresco, designed by the Russo-

Italian set designer Pietro di Gottardo Gonzago, which struggles to achieve some sort of false perspective from the flat and rather low ceiling (the painting was in fact only executed during the postwar renovation, following the chance discovery of Gonzago's plans by Soviet restorers). The 606-piece **Gold Dinner Service**, made by the St Petersburg porcelain factory, is laid out on three large dining tables – otherwise the room is barely furnished. On special occasions, an orchestra used to play in the adjacent room which contains Classical sculptures representing two of Paul and Maria's daughters, who died during childhood.

After Napoleon seized Malta, the island's Order of Knights fled to Russia, where they promptly deposed the current Grand Master and elected Paul in his place. Paul was a wise choice in terms of position and wealth, but as an Orthodox believer, his election wasn't recognized by the pope. Nevertheless, he built the lime-green **Knights' Hall** (Kavalerskiy zal) to receive his charges. The hall displays a collection of Classical sculptures, but the only reference to the knights themselves is a small Maltese cross on the ceiling.

From here, you enter the **Imperial Chapel**, totally non-Orthodox in its design, with sculptural decoration and no iconostasis, but rather copies of European paintings in the Hermitage. Paul's throne stands in the corner of the gallery.

Retracing your steps through the Picture Gallery you'll find some backstairs to the **top floor**, once servants' quarters and now an interesting **exhibition of interiors** from the 1800s to the Revolution. Rooms typical of each period have been re-created to give a sense of how the urban and provincial gentry lived.

The private apartments

The same backstairs descend to the **first floor** of the north wing, where Paul and Maria had their **private apartments**, on a cosier scale than the State Rooms, but no less ornate. At this point, you can buy a separate ticket (R60) for Maria's rooms in the southern wing, or settle for seeing only their shared quarters.

First is the **Raspberry Room** (Malinoviy kabinet), so called for the colour of the upholstery and draperies, followed by the **General Room** (Obshchiy kabinet), where Paul and his family used to gather. Such gatherings were seldom happy for, as Chancellor Rostopchin observed, "Alexander hates his father, Konstantin fears him, the daughters, under their mother's influence, loathe him, and they all smile and would be glad to see him ground to powder."

Beyond lies Paul's formal **New Study** (Noviy kabinet), designed on simple, Neoclassical lines by Quarenghi and hung with a series of engraved copies of Raphael's frescoes for the papal chambers of the Vatican. Next comes the **Corner Room** (Uglovaya gostinaya), sporting lilac-tinted false marble walls and Karelian birch furniture. The room was designed by Carlo Rossi, who began his illustrious career here in 1803, redesigning fire-damaged rooms. The largest room on the first floor is the Cameron-designed **White Dining Room** (Belaya stolovaya), whose austerity was in keeping with Paul's liking for simple food – his favourite dish was cabbage.

Passing through the Billiard Room, whose table was destroyed during the war, you reach the **Old Drawing Room** (Staraya gostinaya), with pictures hung to replace the tapestries given to Paul by Louis XVI following his visit to Paris, recently returned to Gatchina (see p.274). More cheerful is the sky-blue and gold **Ballroom** (Tantsevalniy zal), restored to Cameron's original design after the war and dominated by two huge scenes of Rome by the French artist Hubert Robert.

Maria's private apartments overlooking the Privy Garden commence with an **Italian Hall** with curved walls of *faux marbre*, Empire-style motifs and furniture.

The Soviet heritage

The demise of the Soviet Union saw monuments toppled and streets and cities renamed – Leningrad became St Petersburg again. Where "Glory to the XXV Party Congress" once blazed from neon-signs, you now see brand names or movies. Yet seven decades of Soviet rule have left an indelible mark on the city – you needn't look far to find memorable relics of Communist times.

House of Soviets ▲

Dzerzhinsky, founder of the Bolshevik secret police ▼

Architecture

The **metro** once epitomized Soviet modernity. No expense was spared on the décor of stations under Stalin, though work halted during the war: most of the finest stations (see box opposite) are on the first section opened in 1955, between Avtovo and Ploshchad Vosstaniya. Design reached its nadir in the Brezhnev era but showed a return to form in the post-Soviet 1990s. Using the metro to explore beyond the centre you can check out **Constructivist** buildings from the 1920s like the hammer-and-sickle-shaped school on Kirovskaya ploshchad, or **Stalinist** monoliths such as the **House of Soviets** in the Southern Suburbs that were built with the intention of eclipsing the historic city centre.

Personality cults

Lenin statues were a feature of every town and city in the Soviet Union. The first ever, unveiled in 1926 outside Finland Station, portrays him orating atop an armoured car. A later example is the "taxi-hailing" Lenin in front of the House of Soviets. A smaller Vlad and busts of **Marx** and **Engels** lurk outside the Smolniy Institute, not far from a swaggering statue of **Dzerzhinsky**, founder of the secret police – whose peaked cap and jackboots could pass in a leather bar. While statues of the Bolshevik "martyr" **Kirov** bestride Krestovskiy Island and Kirovskaya ploshchad, the only remaining trace of **Stalin** is an obscure monument in Yekaterinof Park, where his face appears on the banner held by Young Communist partisans.

The cult of personality stretched to the preservation (or recreation) of their former abodes. Lenin stayed at what is now the

Yelizarov Flat-Museum, a *sarai* (barn) and *shalash* (hut) at **Razliv** and a cottage in **Vyborg** while evading arrest in 1917. His quarters in the Smolniy (not open to the public) were spartan compared with leaders under Stalin, judging by the **Kirov Flat-Museum**, with its polar-bearskin rug and servants' quarters. The **Museum of Childhood** evokes the Pioneers and Young Communists that generations of youth had to join with banners and rousing songs, while Stalin kitsch is juxtaposed with Gulag relics in the **Museum of Russian Political History**.

▲ Avtovo's High-Stalinist interior

▼ Narvskaya metro station

Top five metro stations

Our favourites are mostly on the Kirovsko-Vyborgskaya (red) line – see map at the back of this book. Sadly, nowadays photography is forbidden on the metro for security reasons.

▶ **Avtovo** (p.219) A wedding cake roof, gilded martial motifs and swirly columns of cut-glass or marble make this the most opulent of the city's metro stations.

▶ **Baltiyskaya** (p.218) Bas-reliefs of Tsarist admirals, sea-grey marble, vaults like sails and a mosaic depicting the *Volley from the Cruiser Aurora* evoke the Baltic.

▶ **Mayakovskaya** (p.206) Giant faces of the Soviet punk-poet Mayakovsky scowl at commuters from the crimson-enamelled walls of its sealed platform.

▶ **Narvskaya** (p.218) Workers and peasants imbibe Lenin's wisdom; the platform columns are sculpted with miners, metallurgists and teachers, lit by crystal arcs.

▶ **Ploshchad Vosstaniya** Bronze medallions of Lenin in hiding, leading the October Revolution and proclaiming Soviet power, on blood-red marble pylons.

A train featuring the profiles of Lenin and Stalin ▲

Kresty Prison ▲

Monument to the victims of repression, on the Neva embankment ▼

War memorials and hardware

The Bolsheviks saw war as the "locomotive of history". The Soviet state faced its supreme test with the Nazi invasion, when Leningrad endured nearly 900 days of siege. **Piskarov Memorial Cemetery** is a shrine to the 670,000 who died of cold, starvation or shelling. The front ran through the suburbs; war memorials range from **T-34 tanks** and the **Victory Monument** with its statues of soldiers, nurses, and salvage workers, to a **sign** on Nevskiy prospekt warning: "Citizens! In the event of artillery fire, this side of the street is the most dangerous!" Besides the iconic **Cruiser** *Aurora* that fired on the Winter Palace, and Lenin's armoured car *Enemy of Capital* in the **Artillery Museum**, you can see such hardware as the submarine *Narodovolets* and icebreaker *Krasin* on Vasilevskiy Island, or an SS-24 missile-train and a locomotive emblazoned with profiles of Lenin and Stalin in the **Outdoor Railway Museum**. Some of the many **bunkers** across the city now house nightclubs (see pp.257–258).

The Gulag

Two symbols of repression face each other across the Neva. **Kresty Prison** once held locals destined for the Gulag and is still a pre-trial prison; during the Great Terror, women traipsed between Kresty and the **Bolshoy dom** headquarters of the secret police seeking news of their men-folk. Today there are voyeuristic tours of Kresty (which has a museum of penal curios), but the Bolshoy dom is still off-limits (though highly visible). Between the two is a monument to the victims of repression, skull-faced **sphinxes** beside the river.

The decor becomes more intimate in her **Lantern Study**, with its bay window arch upheld by caryatids; letting its hair down in a gaudy **Dressing Room** and day **Bedroom** with a comfy couch and teaset to hand. The final, **Tent Room** has a U-shaped divan and French windows opening on to the Privy Garden – a delightful haven.

Pavlovsk Park

Pavlovsk Park (Pavlovskiy park; daily 7am–8pm; R100 8am–5pm) extends either side of the River Slavyanka. It was laid out by Cameron and Brenna, with help from the stage designer Gonzago; Voronikhin and Rossi also contributed, and some say that Capability Brown devised the original plan. The park's defining feature is its naturalistic landscaping, with undulating hills, meandering streams and hectares of wild forest – especially lovely in the autumn, with its richly hued foliage. Russians come to harvest mushrooms in June and August and berries in September, and to frolic in the winter snow.

"Each new step brings a new picture to the eyes", enthused the poet Vasily Zhukovskiy about the riverside gardens near the palace, where many of Cameron's and Rossi's **follies** stand; the rest are mainly in or around the Old Woods. You could cover a lot of these fairly comfortably in an afternoon, but are sure to get lost at some point: **signposting** is abysmal and locals may misdirect you inadvertently.

The **Privy Garden** (daily 11am–6pm; R80), behind the palace's southern wing, is separated from the rest of the park by a high iron railing. Laid out by Cameron in a formal Dutch style, with flowerbeds that explode with colour in summertime, it culminates in a Grecian **Pavilion of the Three Graces** named for its statues of Joy, Flowering and Brilliance.

Along the Slavyanka

From the terrace behind the Great Palace, you can survey the sweep of the Slavyanka Valley. High up on the far bank, Cameron's **Apollo Colonnade** was left a picturesque ruin after being struck by lightning and then damaged by a landslide during a storm. Down to the right, steps descend to the **Centaur Bridge**, guarded by four centaurs, leading to a derelict **Cold Bath** with a superb view uphill to the palace.

Downstream are the **Humpback Bridge** and the **Black Bridge** – with a monumental staircase running down from the palace to meet them. Beyond, by a sharp bend in the turgid river, stands the most eye-catching of Cameron's pavilions, the circular **Temple of Friendship** (Khram Druzhby), the first building in Russia to use the Doric order. Commissioned as a diplomatic gesture to cement the shaky relationship between Maria and Catherine the Great, it is studded with medallions illustrating the themes of platonic and romantic love.

At this point you can head straight for the Old Woods or by a roundabout route along the northern shore, crossing the **Visconti Bridge** or by the **Pil Tower**, a "ruined" fortification further downriver.

Around Triple Lime Alley

Another more-or-less direct route to the Old Woods is by the **Triple Lime Alley**, running 300m through a formal section of the park, its north side a parterre made up of two **Great Circles** with eighteenth-century statues of Peace and Justice at their centres. To the south, Cameron built an **Aviary** (Voler), used for small receptions and meals, now prettily strewn with vines and selling refreshments. On the other side of a low box-hedge **maze** stands the columned **Rossi Pavilion**, designed by him but erected only on the eve of World War I, which harbours a statue of Maria Fyodorovna. Behind this lies a common **grave** for the Soviet soldiers killed clearing Pavlovsk of mines.

In the opposite direction lies a **Dairy** (Molochnya) where Maria played at being a milkmaid like Marie Antoinette, while Paul drilled his regiments on a **Parade Ground** which she had reforested after his death. During Paul's reign, the police were ordered to scour the park, destroy any traditional round Russian hats and cut the lapels off coats and cloaks, to force people to dress like Germans.

The Old Woods and beyond

Covering a promontory at a fork in the river, the **Old Woods** are defined by twelve paths forming an **Étoile** centred on a statue of Apollo, patron of the Muses, with a ring of statues of Muses or mythological figure at the start of each path. The one to the right of Melephone (holding a grimacing mask) leads to the **Monument to My Parents**, a chunky pavilion erected by Maria in memory of her father and mother, the duke and duchess of Württemburg, whose profiles appear on the marble pyramid within.

Another path running off between two figures with lyres leads to a vandalized **Amphitheatre** with a view of the Slavyanka from the Visconti Bridge to the Pil Tower. Yet another runs northeast across a bridge into tall birch-woods surrounding **Paul's Mausoleum**, a gloomy, granite-columned pile built by Thomas de Thomon at Maria's instruction. Not that Paul is actually buried here – he lies with the other Romanovs in the Peter and Paul Cathedral.

From here you can turn south towards the **Rose Pavilion** (Rozoviy pavilon; May–Sept daily 10am–5pm; R100), with an ante-hall of models and engravings of historic structures, and a large hall used for occasional **concerts**, with feathered candelabras and garlands of waxed flowers suspended from a ceiling fresco of muses, gods and musical instruments.

Other sights

The wooded park between the river and the Railway Gate is crisscrossed by paths emanating from a **Great Étoile** and **Round Hall**, where **concerts** are held in August. To the south are another étoile that's a focus for **winter sports** (see p.384) and **boat** hire on the Railway Ponds (Vokzalnye prudy; R150 p/hr).

Leaving the park by its Palace Gate, you need only cross ulitsa Revolyutsii to find yourself beside the **Marienthal Pond**, in a hilly area once dubbed the "Russian Switzerland". The far shore has a granite **Obelisk** marking the foundation of Pavlovsk in 1782, but the near side has a finer view of the oddly named **Bip Fortress**. A mock-Gothic castle built by Brenna in 1795 to flatter Paul's military pretensions, its bronze helmet-tower and crenellated wings were being turned into a hotel when last seen.

Gatchina

In 1776, Catherine the Great gave **Gatchina** and its neighbouring villages to her lover, Grigori Orlov, as a reward for helping her to depose (and dispose of) her husband, Peter III. Its enormous palace wasn't completed by Rinaldi until 1781; by then Orlov – tormented by visions of Peter's ghost – was on the verge of insanity and had only two miserable years to enjoy it before he died, whereupon

GATCHINA

St Petersburg

N

NIKOLAEVSKAYA ULITSA

Pavlovskiy Cathedral

ULITSA RADISHEVA

ULITSA KHOLOVA

BULVARNAYA ULITSA

ULITSA DOSTOEVSKOVO

Lenin

SOBORNAYA ULITSA

KRASNAYA ULITSA

PROSPEKT 25 OKTYABRYA

Cathedral of the Assumption

ULITSA CHKALOVA

LEONOVA ULITSA

Black Lake

Priory Palace

Admiralty Gates

Birch Gates

Botanical Gardens

Water Labyrinth

Priory Park

Konnetable Column

Birch Cabin

Temple of Venus

Island of Love

White Lake

Silver Lake

Hunchback Bridge

Iron Gates

Chesma Column

Privy Garden

Great Palace

Tsar Paul

Submarine

Gatchina-Baltiyskaya Station

KRASNOARMEYSKIY PROSPEKT

Museum of Aviation History

ULITSA GRIGORINA

Menagerie Park

Metallic Gates

Black Gates

Silvia Park

Silvia Gates

Farm

Aviary

KRASNOARMEYSKIY PROSPEKT

St Petersburg

ACCOMMODATION	
Gaakel House	A
EATING & DRINKING	
Café Kare	5
Café Robinzon	3
Eurasia	1
Pyramida Pizzeria	2
Shanghai	4

0   200 m

Located about 50km south of St Petersburg, Gatchina is accessible by **minibus** #18 from Moskovskaya metro station, which takes about 45 minutes and runs past the palace en route to Gatchina-Baltiyskaya train station. Alternatively, catch a **suburban train** (every 40min; 6.30am–midnight) from St Petersburg's Baltic Station to the same destination – though beware that some stop instead at the Tatyanino and Gatchina-Varshavskaya stations on the other side of town from the palace, which entails a much longer walk. Or you can sign up for an organized **excursion** (R750–850) from St Petersburg.

In the unlikely event that you want **to stay**, there's the comfortable *Hotel Gaakel House* (☎944 84 77, ⊛www.gakkel.ru; ❹), whose *Pyotr Perviy* restaurant is the finest in town. Other places **to eat** include *Café Robinzon*, *Shanghai* and *Pyramida Pizzeria* on Sobornaya ulitsa; the *Eurasia* sushi-bar on prospekt 25 Oktyabrya; and *Café Kare* in the Great Palace, which has billiards and Russian pool and stays open till 2am.

Catherine promptly passed it on to her son, **Paul**, who thus inherited Gatchina from his own father's murderer. Paul had Vincenzo Brenna remodel the palace during the 1790s, raising the height of its semi-circular galleries and side blocks, and installing cannons and sentry boxes to make it look even more like a feudal castle or a barracks – which suited Paul's interests perfectly.

During its heyday, five thousand people were employed at Gatchina (most from families that had served the Romanovs for generations), while its kennels included every breed of dog from borzois to bulldogs (used for bear-hunting). Some thirty years after Paul's murder, Gatchina became the residence of Nicholas I, who had both side blocks reconstructed and his own living quarters installed on the first floor of the Arsenal Block, while the late eighteenth-century State Rooms in the central block were restored. The next monarch to spend much time at Gatchina was **Alexander III**, who fled here for security reasons immediately after his father's funeral. For almost two years Alexander lived in seclusion, dressing like a peasant, shovelling snow and cutting wood. When a visitor expressed surprise, he retorted: "Well, what else can I do till the Nihilists are stamped out?"

In October 1917, Gatchina witnessed the ignominious "last stand" of the Provisional Government, whose leader **Kerensky** fled here in an American embassy car on the morning of October 25, thus escaping arrest at the Winter Palace. After lunch he drove on to Pskov and persuaded a cavalry unit to return with him to Gatchina, whose curator lamented that "the prospect of lodging an entire Cossack division in the palace was not a happy one". In the event, Kerensky refused to accompany them into battle, remaining in his room "lying on the couch, swallowing tranquillizers", until he slipped away disguised as a sailor (*not* a female nurse, as alleged by the Soviets) on October 31.

His nemesis **Trotsky** was made of sterner stuff. In July 1919, Red Guards halted the final advance of White forces from Estonia (the "kennel of the dogs of the counter-revolution") at Gatchina, where Trotsky led them into battle waving a walking stick. To commemorate his heroism, the town was renamed Trotsk – but reverted to its old name after Trotsky became synonymous with "deviationism" in Stalin's Russia.

Like the other palaces, Gatchina was ravaged by the Nazis in World War II, though its staff managed to evacuate four trainloads of treasures before the Germans arrived. It was turned into a naval college after the war, and restoration work didn't begin

THE IMPERIAL PALACES | Gatchina

until 1985; even then it was accorded far lower priority than Peterhof or Tsarskoe Selo – hence the small number of rooms that have been restored and the fact that work is still continuing. Restorers have been helped, however, by a collection of 1870s watercolours by Edward Hau and Luigi Premazzi, which illustrated many rooms in meticulous detail.

The palace

The semicircular palace flanks a courtyard where regiments once drilled, fronted by a dry moat and a thigh-booted **statue of Paul**. His fervent militarism and admiration for German ways endeared him to Gatchina's Nazi occupiers, who posted a sentry to protect the statue from being vandalized – till 1944, when they tried to destroy the palace before retreating. Its two-metre-thick walls withstood the blast, but the interior was gutted.

Built of weathered limestone, the **Great Palace** (10am–6pm; closed Mon & the first Tues of each month; R220) is in stark contrast to its counterparts at Pavlovsk, Peterhof and Tsarskoe Selo, whose stucco facades are painted in bright colours. Restoration has been confined to the central section, and the interiors of the Arsenal and Kitchen blocks will probably never be renewed, since most paintings and photographs of their decor perished at the same time as the originals.

Having seen a one-room exhibition on the palace's history, you put on *tapochki* and are welcomed by staff in eighteenth-century livery at the foot of the **Grand Staircase**. Upstairs, you can turn left into the **Chesma Gallery**, whose ravaged stucco shows how the palace looked after World War II, and descend the backstairs to a circular **Church** (11am–6pm) with a skylight-cupola; at 1pm on Sunday, there's a tour (R50) of its belfry with a demonstration of bell-ringing.

However, most visitors head straight for the State Rooms, via an **Antechamber** decorated with armorial mouldings and a ceiling fresco of the Virgin and infant Jesus, illuminated by chandeliers in drum-like casings. Paul's love of the military is also echoed by the trumpet-shaped candelabras in the columned **Marble Dining Room**, which Nicholas I's wife later used as a bathroom. Beyond lies Paul's **Throne Hall**, with its red velvet and gilt throne and pistachio-coloured walls hung with Gobelin tapestries presented by Louis XVI of France – one represents Asia and depicts a leopard savaging a zebra; the other Africa, showing a tribal chieftain in a litter.

The **Crimson Drawing Room** was once adorned by three Gobelin tapestries illustrating scenes from *Don Quixote,* of which only one – showing Sancho Panza's arrival on the isle of Baratana – now hangs *in situ*, but the others may soon return from Pavlovsk, after a saga worthy of Gogol's satires. At one point, Gatchina's director wrote to the Ministry of Culture requesting the tapestries' return. Shortly afterwards he was appointed director of Pavlovsk, in which capacity he received his own request, and rejected it. In Paul's **State Bedroom**, gilded mirrors create the illusion of a corridor receding to infinity, while a disguised door beside his bed leads to the secret passage beneath the palace.

Finest of all is the **White Hall**, or ballroom. Its parquet floor is inlaid with nine kinds of rare wood and its ceiling festooned with stucco garlands. Notice the lion and the lobster above the two main doorways, representing the astrological symbols for the months of July and August, when the palace was used as an Imperial residence. Paul's wife had her own suite, with a pale-blue and sage-green **Dressing Room** adorned with marble medallions of Catherine and Roman emperors, and an **Oval Boudoir** in tutti-frutti colours and *trompe*

l'oeil, overlooking the park.

Rooms on the floor above exhibit **paintings** of historical rather than artistic merit; scenes of life at Gatchina during Nicholas I's reign; portraits of Catherine the Great as a young bride and an old woman; her lovers Potemkin and Zubov; and Paul's daughter Anna, who was wooed by Napoleon – whom Maria Fyodorovna dismissed as "that Corsican show-off" – and later married into the Greek royal family (making her an ancestor of Britain's current Prince of Wales).

Returning to the first floor to remove your *tapochki*, you'll be ushered into an **Exhibition of Weaponry**, either brought back as booty, received as gifts or purchased by the tsars, displaying extraordinary craftsmanship and a generous use of gold, silver, ivory and coral. This leads to Paul's private quarters, which haven't been restored yet but exhibit his thigh-boots and other possessions. From here, follow the sign to a dank **subterranean passage** (podzemniy khod) that runs from the palace to the Silver Lake – not, as you might imagine, a product of Paul's fear of assassination, but created during Orlov's time as a folly. Its acoustics are such that a word spoken at one end echoes back from the far end, 100m away.

The park and town

Behind the palace, Paul's formal **Privy Garden** (daily 11am–6pm; R70) pales beside the wild expanse of Gatchina's **park** (admission free), with paths wending across a chain of islands between the **White and Silver lakes**. The former never freezes over, and provided a testing ground for the first Russian submarine (see p.280). On its far side, a derelict **Temple of Venus** stands on the Island of Love, where pleasure boats once docked, while on the mainland is a postwar replica of another folly. The **Birch Cabin** (Berozavaya izba; May–Sept 11am–6.30pm; closed Mon; R60) resembles a stack of logs from the outside, but contains a palatial mirrored room (you can peer through the windows to save buying a ticket).

Besides the geometric **Silvia Park**, there are two ex-hunting grounds: to the north, **Menagerie Park** is where Alexander III took his children to fol-

Palaces and parks

Strelna	Стрельна
Konstantin Palace	Константиновский дворец
Shuvalovka	Шуваловка
Wooden Palace	Деревяный дворец
Peterhof	Петергоф
Petrodvorets	Петродворец
Alexandria Park	Парк Александрия
Bathhouse Wing	Банный корпус
Benois Wing	Корпус Бенуа
Catherine Wing	Екатерининский корпус
Cottage Palace	Коттедж
Great Palace	Большой дворец
Hermitage	рмитаж
Lower Park	Нижний парк
Marly Palace	Марли дворец
Monplaisir	Монплезир
Upper Garden	Верхний сад
Oranienbaum	Ораниенбаум
Lomonosov	Ломоносов
Chinese Palace	Китайский дворец
Great Palace	Большой дворец
Japanese Pavilion	Японский павильон
Lower Park	Нижний парк
Peter III's Palace	дворец Петра III
Sliding Hill	Катальная горка
Upper Park	Верхний парк
Tsarskoe Selo	Царское село
Pushkin	Пушкин
Alexander Palace	Александровский дворец
Alexander Park	Александровский парк
Catherine Palace	Екатерининский дворец
Catherine Park	Екатерининский парк
Pavlovsk	Павловск
Great Palace	Большой дворец
Pavlovsk Park	Павловский парк
Gatchina	Гатчина
Birch Cabin	Береовая изба
Great Palace	Большой дворец
Priory Palace	Приоратский дворец

low animal tracks in summer and dig paths through the snow during winter; in the other direction lies the **Priory Park**, named after the **Priory Palace** (10am–6pm; closed Mon & Tues; R50) overlooking the **Black Lake**. This Germanic-looking edifice was built for Prince Conday, Prior of the Maltese Knights of St John, who never actually lived there. Its architect, Nikolai Lvov, pioneered the use of rammed earth as a building material, which proved robust enough to withstand a bomb landing nearby during World War II. An exhibition upstairs features plans for many buildings in the German style, annotated by Paul with the order "Let it be!" – but they were never realized due to his murder.

The town itself boasts two imposing neo-Russian edifices: the yellow, green-domed **Pavlovskiy Cathedral** and the white, blue-spired **Cathedral of the Assumption**, plus some folksy **wooden houses** along ulitsa Chkalova. Named after the Soviet aviator who made the first trans-polar flight in 1937, this street was once the location of the Imperial Military Aviation School. In 1913, the world's first four-engined plane was designed here by Igor Sikorsky (who later emigrated to the US, where he perfected the helicopter), two years after Gleb Kotelnikov tested the first knapsack-parachute. These and other feats are celebrated in the **Museum of Aviation History** (Fri, Sat & Sun 11am–4pm; R70), between the palace and the station. Outside stands a scale model of the **submarine** that was tested before the royal family in 1879; designed by Stepan Dzhevetskiy, it had a crew of four, who pedalled to turn its propeller.

Kronstadt, the Gulf coast and Vyborg

The island fortress and naval base of **Kronstadt** was established soon after
St Petersburg was founded. Sited on Kotlin Island in the Gulf of Finland,
the fortress was the linchpin of the city's defences against seaborne invasion
and the home port of the Baltic Fleet, yet would later become the state's
Achilles heel when its forces revolted against tsar and commissar alike. Off-limits
to foreigners for decades, this weirdly time-warped town now welcomes tourists,
but is likely to appeal mainly to those keen on maritime history or bizarre urban
landscapes.

A more mainstream attraction is the **Karelian Isthmus** between the Gulf of Finland and Lake Ladoga, where Petersburgers relax at their *dachas* between bouts of
sunbathing, swimming and mushroom-picking. It's a soothing landscape of silver
birches and misty hollows, with spectacular sunsets reflected in limpid water, the
mosquitoes being the only drawback. You'll need a car, however, really to explore
the region. Relying on public transport, you're limited to the towns along the
Gulf coast: namely **Razliv**, where Lenin hid out in 1917; **Repino**, which houses
the delightful memorial house of the artist Repin; and historic **Vyborg**, with its
castle, Nordic houses and romantic Park Monrepos.

Historically, the Karelian Isthmus has been a bone of contention between Russia and its Baltic neighbours since medieval times. In 1812 it passed to the Grand
Duchy of Finland (then a semi-autonomous part of the Tsarist Empire), with the
frontier drawn to the east of Kronstadt. During the revolutionary turmoil of
1917, the Finns seized the opportunity to declare independence and the isthmus
remained Finnish territory until the Winter War of 1939–40, when Stalin annexed
Karelia to form a buffer zone to protect Leningrad. To regain Karelia, Finland
allied itself with Nazi Germany in World War II and the Red Army was driven
out; when it returned in 1944, Stalin claimed even more territory in the far north
(now the Karelian Republic), which Russia retains to this day, insisting that the
matter is non-negotiable.

Kronstadt and the sea forts

Peter the Great was quick to grasp the strategic value of Kotlin Island, 30km out in
the Gulf: the waters to the north of the island were too shallow for large ships to

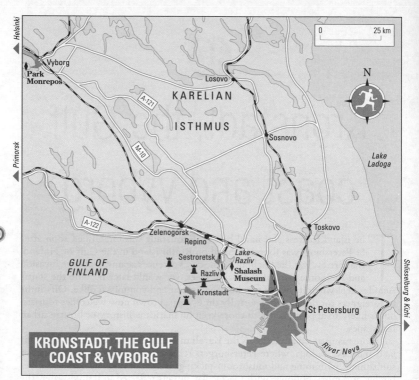

**KRONSTADT, THE GULF
COAST & VYBORG**

pass through, while a sandbank off the southern shore compelled vessels to sail close to the island. In the winter of 1703–4 Peter erected the offshore Kronschlot Fort, followed by a shipyard on Kotlin Island; the large colony that developed around them took the name Kronstadt (City of the Crown) in 1723. Its defences, floating batteries and naval harbour made this the strongest base in the Baltic, augmented by smaller *forty*, or sea forts, constructed on outlying man-made islands over the centuries, which repelled British and French fleets in 1854, and the Nazis in the 1940s.

Kronstadt's **revolutionary tradition** dates back to 1825, when a Kronstadt officer, Bestushev, led the Decembrist rebels; later, the military wing of the Narodnaya Volya (People's Will) was secretly headed by a sailor, Sukhanov. As the first revolutionary wave crashed over Russia, the Kronstadt sailors mutinied in 1905 and 1906, avenging years of maltreatment by throwing their officers into the ships' furnaces. After the fall of Tsarism in 1917, the sailors declared their own revolutionary Soviet and then an independent republic. The Bolsheviks could never have carried out the October Revolution, or survived the Civil War, without the Kronstadt sailors, whom they deployed as shock troops: "the pride and glory of the Revolution", Trotsky called them. The world was therefore stunned when they revolted yet again in 1921 – this time, against the Bolsheviks (see box opposite).

Kronstadt

Until 1992, foreigners could visit **Kronstadt** only by the risky expedient of being smuggled in disguised as a Russian. Today the island is freely accessible even to

The eighteen-day **Kronstadt sailors' revolt** of March 1921 went under the slogan "Soviets without Communism". Their manifesto demanded freedom of speech and assembly, the abolition of Bolshevik dictatorship and an end to War Communism. Only the ice-locked Gulf prevented the rebel cruisers *Sevastopol* and *Petropavlovsk* from steaming into the Neva basin and holding St Petersburg hostage. With a thaw imminent, Trotsky warned the rebels: "Only those who surrender unconditionally can count on the mercy of the Soviet Republic" – but few responded.

Two hours before dawn on March 8, 45,000 white-clad Red Army troops advanced on Kronstadt, across the frozen Gulf, unnoticed until they were within 500m of the fortress, when a third of them drowned after Kronstadt's cannons ruptured the ice. The next assault was spearheaded by volunteers from the Tenth Party Congress, who laid ladders between the ruptured ice floes and then swarmed across to establish a beachhead. The fortress was subsequently stormed on the night of March 16–17. Besides the thirty thousand killed on both sides in the battle, 2000 sailors were executed on the spot and many more sent to the Gulag (though 8000 managed to escape across the ice to Finland). The sailors were posthumously pardoned in 1994.

solo tourists, but you would still be unwise to **photograph** any warships or barracks, or to drink the local **water**, which is even more polluted than St Petersburg's owing to a **tidal barrage** that spans the neck of the Gulf. Intended to protect the city from flooding, its massive sluice gates loom above the road atop the barrage that connects Kronstadt to the northern shore of the mainland. It is planned eventually to build a road to the southern side of the Gulf as well – in the meantime, locals wishing to reach Oranienbaum during winter simply drive across the ice.

Anyone arriving by hydrofoil from St Petersburg or ferry from Oranienbaum will see warships of the Baltic Fleet in Kronstadt's Middle Harbour, before disembarking near Petrovskiy Park, centred on a swashbuckling **statue of Peter the Great**, inscribed: "To defend the fleet and its base to the last of one's strength is the highest duty." Sailors still stand guard over the sluice gates of the Petrovskiy Dock, the decrepit **Italian Palace** housing the Sailors' Club and the **Tidal Gauge** that measures the ever-fluctuating sea level in the Gulf of Finland. There are monuments to sailors or submariners in every park and square, juxtaposed with surreal installations such as the **sea-mine** used as a charity collection box on prospekt Lenina, the **submarine conning tower** on ploshchad Roshalya and the **gun turret** guarding the bridge to Yakornaya ploshchad (Anchor Square).

The square is dominated by the splendid **Naval Cathedral** – a massive neo-Byzantine edifice designed by Kosyakov in 1903–13, whose interior is being restored after decades of neglect. At the time of writing visitors could only enter a chapel just off the square and the **Museum of the Kronstadt Fortress** (11am–5pm; closed Mon, Tues & the last Thurs of each month; R300) beneath the cupola. Model warships, engravings and photos of sea battles and manoeuvres culminate in a diorama of Kronstadt under Nazi bombardment; the 1921 sailors' revolt is presented from a perspective unchanged since the 1970s, their "rehabilitation" ignored in the Russian-only text.

Transcending such awkward historical disputes, an **Eternal Flame** burns in honour of the fallen defenders of World War II, beyond a glorious Art Nouveau **monument to Admiral Makarov**, whose distinguished career was crowned by disaster with the sinking of the Baltic Fleet at Tsushima in 1905: notice the scenes of Polar exploration around its base. Another mariner commemorated by a statue on nearby Sovetskaya ulitsa is Faddei Bellinghausen, who explored Antarctica during 1820–21. Also worth seeing are the "**musical**

▲ Kronstadt's Naval Cathedral

fountain" in the park off ulitsa Karla Marksa – where locals socialize – and the rambling **Summer Garden**, with a ravine spanned by a footbridge, linking Yakornaya ploshchad to Krasnaya ulitsa.

The rest of the town consists of decaying factories, barracks and oily eighteenth-century canals and dock basins that crisscross the centre, their names redolent of faraway lands. In Petrine times these were lined with taverns and brothels where sailors caroused; long afterwards, the preacher Father **John of Kronstadt** made his name here by crusading for 53 years against drunkenness, vice and poverty – founding workshops, a refectory, pharmacy and primary school. After his death in 1908 he was buried in the St Petersburg convent that now bears his name (see p.182), mourned by a crowd of 60,000 and "sung out" by a weeping Imperial Choir.

Practicalities

Tour firms outside St Petersburg's Gostiniy dvor run daily coach **excursions** (4–5hr; R400–600) to Kronstadt; some visit Fort Konstantin as well as the town. In summer, Russian Cruises runs occasional trips by **hydrofoil** from the Hermitage dock to Kronstadt (4hr including a tour of town; R1400) or the sea forts (2hr; R600). Alternatively, it's an hour by **minibus** #510 (R40) from Chernaya Rechka metro (see map on p.222), reaching Kronstadt via the barrage from the northern mainland, and terminating near the local Gostiniy dvor on prospekt Lenina. Minibuses returning to St Petersburg leave from a side street across the road. There is also a **car ferry** (every 2–3hr; 45min) from Oranienbaum on the southern shore of the Gulf.

Prospekt Lenina has a few places **to eat and drink**. *Zolotoy Lev* does Chinese grub, *Café Skaza borsch* and *pelmeni*, and *Café Blues*, soup, salads and draught Czech Kozel beer – or you can down a beer beside the musical fountain.

The sea forts

Aficionados of maritime life or naval history might consider visiting some of the old *forty* – or **sea forts** – built on man-made islands in the Gulf, which last saw active service during World War II. The so-called **Numbered Northern Forts** were constructed in the 1800s and upgraded just in time for the Crimean War, when they repulsed an Anglo-French fleet under Admiral Napier, which lost two ships to sea mines (their first ever use in warfare) before withdrawing. Two forts are accessible on foot from the tidal barrage between Kronstadt and the mainland, but their crumbling casements are hardly worth the effort.

Fort Konstantin, on the southernmost tip of the island, is an accretion of armoured casements for a battery of 6-inch guns; silos for two 11-inch retractable cannons; rooftop bunkers and mountings for anti-aircraft guns; powder magazines and sleeping quarters for a thousand men. All the guns were stripped out in the 1960s, but the derelict complex is fun to explore. Two café-bars complete the amenities of its grandly named International Customs Terminal, where foreign cargo ships and yachts must register. You can reach Fort Konstantin by taxi (about R100), or on a ferry **cruise** (daily at 3.30pm & 5.30pm; R250) from Kronstadt, which passes **Fort Peter** and Fort Alexander en route.

A motorboat can take visitors from Fort Konstantin out to **Fort Alexander**, 600m offshore. Built with great difficulty by the military engineer Van der Veide (1838–45), this kidney-shaped bastion had four gun decks and 103 cannon ports, which Napier dared not engage. It developed a sinister reputation as the "**Plague Fort**" (*Chumnoy*), when research into a vaccine for bubonic plague was conducted here from 1897 to 1917. The fort had a laboratory, a menagerie, stables and lodgings for the scientists and their families, whose only link to St Petersburg was a steamship called *Microbe*. Those who died in lab accidents were cremated at the fort. Having reverted to a naval role after the Revolution, it was finally decommissioned in the 1960s; cannons, blast doors and fittings were removed and the shell was left to rot until rave organizers began staging **all-night parties** there, with a chartered boat to carry ticket-holders from St Petersburg and back (see p.359.

If you have the time and money, it's possible to hire a yacht with crew to reach **Obruchef** or **Totleben**, two large island forts with concrete casements and harbours built in the 1900s between Kotlin Island and Sestroretsk, that served as anti-aircraft gun platforms in World War II. Visits involve an overnight stay with a *shashlyk* barbecue. Compare quotes from Sunny Sailing and the River Yacht Club in St Petersburg (see p.384).

The Gulf coast

The **Gulf coast** of the Karelian Isthmus begins on the edge of St Petersburg, from where a ribbon of urban development extends northwest along the water as far as Zelenogorsk. Happily, for most of the way high-rise buildings are less in evidence than clapboard *dachas*, painted in bold colours and decorated with intricate fretwork gables. Zelenogorsk is the main area for **beaches** and **windsurfing**, but Russian holidaymakers are equally fond of the birch woods and lakes that lie inland, such as the **bathing lakes** near Dubki and Lisiy Nos, 30km from the city.

With a **car** you can stop wherever looks promising along the coast, or venture into the interior. Public transport is less flexible, but enables visitors to see a fair amount. *Elektrichka* **trains** from Finland Station (Ploshchad Lenina metro) run every thirty minutes. There are two lines, the direct, inland Vyborg line, and the Krugovoy or round-coast line (sometimes closed for repairs). Bear in mind that not all trains stop at all stations, and tickets for the express to Vyborg are sold at the international desk, *not* in the main booking hall, where you can expect to queue for half an hour to get a seat on a regular train.

Razliv and Repino are both accessible by **minibus** #400 from ploshchad Lenina outside Finland Station; the #417 and #425 from ulitsa Savushkina, near Chernaya Rechka metro, run only as far as Sestroretsk; while the **bus** service from Parnas metro to Vyborg follows the M-10, inland, rather than the coastal road.

Razliv

In Soviet times, tourists and schoolchildren were regularly bussed into **Razliv** to view two hideouts used by Lenin before the Revolution, both reverentially preserved as memorial museums. Now, only true believers and curiosity-seekers bother to come, and Razliv is otherwise just a residential satellite of Sestroretsk, further up the road. Of the two, the Shalash Museum is hard to reach without a car, though the Sarai Museum is easily accessible by public transport – minibuses and buses stop at several points along the road through Razliv, or you can come by *elektrichka* train, getting off at the Tarkhovka halt. Either way, the journey from St Petersburg takes about 45 minutes. It's wise to phone ahead to check that the Lenin museums are open – the numbers are given below.

The Sarai Museum

The **Sarai Museum** (11am–7pm; closed Wed; ☎434 61 45; R100) is at ulitsa Yemelyanova 2, a signposted ten-minute walk from the *elektrichka* stop. Lenin arrived here by train on the night of July 10, 1917, a fugitive from Petrograd, where the Provisional Government had begun cracking down on the Bolsheviks. His host was a local munitions worker and secret Party member, Nikolai Yemelyanov, whose family were then living in a small barn (*sarai*) while their house was being repaired. Lenin was installed in the loft, reached by a steep ladder, until he found other quarters (see below).

The year after Lenin's death in 1924, the barn was given concrete underpinning, impregnated with protective resins and later shielded from the elements by a glass screen, resulting in the surreal building that you see today. On the first floor are the family's possessions; in the loft above, copies of the chairs and samovar which Lenin used (the originals were formerly displayed in the main Lenin Museum in Leningrad). The **house** opposite the barn exhibits photographs of various Bolsheviks in disguise and copies of the articles that Lenin wrote while staying here.

The Shalash Museum

Four kilometres north of the main road through Razliv, the turn-off to the lakeside **Shalash Museum** (11am–7pm, closed Wed; ☎437 30 98; R100) is signposted by a large Soviet monument. In 1917, the far shore of Lake Razliv was accessible only by boat and offered greater concealment than the barn, where Lenin was liable to be spotted by government spies. Yemelyanov told his neighbours that he planned to raise a cow and had hired a Finn to cut the hay. Under this pretext, Lenin moved into a hut (*shalash*) made of branches and thatch, in a clearing by the lake: a "green study" where he wrote articles such as *On Slogans* and *The Answer*, and began *The State and Revolution*. After a fortnight, however, even this hideout seemed too risky, and on August 8 he was smuggled into Finland disguised as a steam-engine fireman (see p.222).

What used to be a meadow is now laid out with paths and features a granite **monument** with a stylized representation of the hut. Being made of perishable hay – and occasionally set alight by vandals – the **hut** itself is rebuilt every year. In the nearby glass-and-concrete **pavilion** you can see copies of the peasant's smock and scythe that Lenin used, a blue notebook containing his notes for *The State and Revolution*, and Vladimir Pinchuk's statue, *Lenin in Razliv*. Ironically, all the surrounding land has now been sold to rich Russians who have built **villas** around the lake and a Lenin-themed, country-club-style **restaurant**, *Shalash* (☎437 60 55; daily 1pm till the last customer leaves), with Euro-Russian cuisine, a kids' menu and a disco.

Repino

Repino, 47km northwest of St Petersburg, is what Russians call a *posyolok*, or small urban-type settlement, named after the eminent painter **Ilya Repin** (1844–1930), who built a house near what was then the village of Kuokkala and lived there permanently from 1900. He showed no inclination to leave even after Kuokkala became Finnish territory in 1917, but continued to receive visitors and honours from Soviet Russia until his death. Turned into a museum after the Soviet annexation of Karelia, the house was burned to the ground by the Nazis in 1944 and painstakingly re-created in the 1950s – when locals also took pride in Kuokaala-born **Mikhail Botvinnik** (1911–1995) winning the first postwar world chess championship while pursuing a parallel career as an electrical engineer.

If you arrive **by train**, head from the station down towards the sea and then, after 600m, turn left onto ulitsa Repina – the brightly coloured gates of Repin's estate are 500m further along. Coming **by minibus** #400 from St Petersburg, ask to get off at Penaty.

Repin's house: Penaty

Repin's house (May–Sept 10.30am–5pm; Oct–April 10.30am–4pm; closed Mon & Tues; but phone ☎323 64 96 to check first as the house sometimes closes for weeks on end for repairs; R200) is named **Penaty** after the household gods of ancient Rome, the Penates, a title that suits its highbrow domesticity. The picturesque wooden building has a steep glass roof and an abundance of windows, while the **interior** reflects the progressive views of Repin and his wife, Natalya Nordman. A sign in the cloakroom advises: "Take off your own coats. Don't wait for servants – there aren't any." On Wednesdays, when the Repins held open house, guests were expected to announce their own arrival by ringing a gong.

Only intimates were admitted to Repin's **study**, which contains a huge jasper paperweight and statues of Tolstoy and the critic Stasov. The drawing room is hung with autographed pictures of Gorky and Chaliapin, and there's a painting of the Repins' artist son, Yuri. Repin himself also dabbled in sculpture: his statue of Tolstoy occupies the glassed-over winter veranda. The dining room features a round table with a revolving centre. Guests had to serve themselves (without asking others to pass anything) and stow the dirty dishes in the drawers underneath; anyone who didn't was obliged to mount the lectern in the corner of the room and deliver an impromptu speech. Only vegetarian food was served.

The best room in the house is Repin's **studio**, upstairs, filled with light and cluttered with *objets* and sketches. Notice the metre-long brushes and the special palette-belt, which the ageing artist used to compensate for his long-sightedness and atrophying muscles. Beside the stove are various props used in his famous painting of *The Zaporodzhe Cossacks Writing a Mocking Letter to the Sultan*, and Repin's last self-portrait, painted at the age of 76. Finally, you go up to the top floor to view a touching home movie of Repin and his friends throwing snowballs in the grounds of Penaty.

The grounds behind the house contain two follies, the **Temple of Osiris and Isis** and the **Tower of Scheherazade**, both built of wood. **Repin's grave** is on top of a hillock by an oak tree, as stipulated in his will – follow the path leading off to the right to reach it.

Vyborg

After the Soviet Union imploded, the long-neglected town of **Vyborg**, 174km from St Petersburg and just 30km from the Finnish border, looked to Finland to revive its fortunes – an ironic reassertion of past leanings, given that the Finns regard Vyborg (which they call Viipuri) as theirs by right. Architecturally, at least, they have a point, as its old quarter consists of Baltic merchants' houses and Lutheran churches, while the centre is defined by Finnish Art Nouveau and Modernist architecture, interspersed with Soviet eyesores. Demographically, however, this town of 82,000 people is definitely Russian, not least because most of its Finnish population fled in 1944 (those that stayed were sent to the Gulag) – and Russians have lived here since the town's earliest days. In Soviet times, Vyborg's port, paper mills and optics factory employed half the town's population; today, its economy is heavily dependent on cross-border tourism, smuggling and prostitution, though it is hoped that the construction of a new **gas pipeline** to Germany will revive the town's fortunes.

With luck, your visit might coincide with one of Vyborg's annual **festivals**: the Sonorous Nightingale children's festival in May; the Knights' Tournament historical pageant in July (see p.290); the yacht regatta in July; or the "Window of Europe" film festival in August. A festival of techno music may also take place in June or July.

The Town

The town is spread out over the series of rocky peninsulas that enclose Vyborg Bay, on the Gulf of Finland. Ignoring the industrial suburbs, basic **orientation** is fairly simple; from the **train** and **bus stations** on the northern mainland, a grid of streets spreads around Park Lenina and west to the old quarter, huddled on the peninsula's cape. The castle, situated on an island off the end of the peninsula, is easily recognizable by its lofty tower, visible from all around the bay. Vyborg

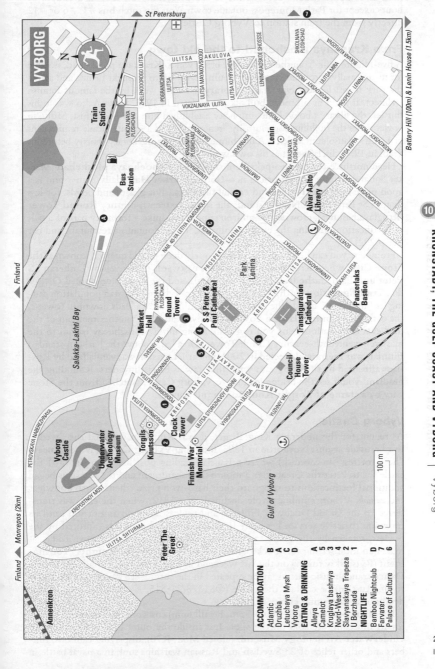

VYBORG

N

▲ St Petersburg

Train Station

Bus Station

Salakka-Lakhti Bay

▲ Finland

Finland ▲

Monrepos (2km) ▲

Gulf of Vyborg

Vyborg Castle

Underwater Archeology Museum

Torgils Knutsson

Market Hall

Round Tower

Clock Tower

Finnish War Memorial

S S Peter & Paul Cathedral

PROSPEKT LENINA

Park Lenina

Transfiguration Cathedral

Council House Tower

Panzerlaks Bastion

Alvar Aalto Library

Lenin

Peter The Great

ULITSA SHTURMA

Annenkron

Battery Hill (100m) & Lenin House (1.5km) ▶

KRASNOARMEYSKAYA ULITSA

KREPOSTNAYA ULITSA

100 m

0   100 m

ACCOMMODATION
Atlantic   B
Druzhba   A
Letuchaya Mysh   A
Vyborg   D

EATING & DRINKING
Alleya   A
Camelot   5
Kruglaya bashnya   3
Nord-West   4
Slavyanskaya Trapeza   2
U Borzhada   1

NIGHTLIFE
Bamboo Nightclub   D
Farvater   7
Palace of Culture   6

10

itself is compact enough for visitors to see everything on foot in a couple of hours except for Park Monrepos, outside town. You can catch **bus** #1, #6 or #12 directly from the train station to Vyborg Castle.

From Krasnaya ploshchad to the old town

A five-minute walk from the station will bring you to **Krasnaya ploshchad**, notable for its unusually corpulent **statue of Lenin**. Carry on to prospekt Lenina and across the park to reach the **Alvar Aalto Library**, an early work by the famous Finnish architect, fronted by a bronze bull elk. Completed in 1935, when Aalto was in his thirties, the library's boxy, light simplicity established him as a Modernist. Sadly, in Soviet times the building was clumsily "renovated" and a granite facade reminiscent of Lenin's mausoleum added – Aalto himself, revisiting the library shortly before his death in 1976, disclaimed it as his own work.

Head northwest along prospekt Lenina to reach **Rynochnaya ploshchad** (Market Square), whose orange-brick, neo-Gothic **Market Hall** (daily 8am–6pm) is a good place to buy **cut-glass** and crystal tumblers, shot glasses and bowls, for less than in St Petersburg. Nearby stands the squat, sixteenth-century **Round Tower** (Kruglaya bashnya), crowned by an iron cupola and spike – formerly part of a belt of fortifications girdling the entire peninsula, it now contains a restaurant and bar (see p.292).

From here you can head into the picturesquely decrepit old quarter, known as the **Stone City**, where Krepostnaya ulitsa leads eastwards to the yellow Lutheran **SS Peter and Paul Cathedral**, built in the 1790s, and the pink, blue-domed Orthodox **Transfiguration Cathedral** that catered to Vyborg's Russian population during its Finnish era. Beside the nearby cinema, ulitsa Titova leads downhill towards the octagonal **Council House Tower** (Bashnya Ratushi) – another remnant of the medieval fortifications – or you can walk along ulitsa Storozhevoy bashni to the massive seventeenth-century **Clock Tower**. On a ledge above the harbour stands a **Finnish war memorial** erected in 2001: an earlier version was vandalized by Russians affronted by this tribute to what they saw as Fascist invaders. Rounding the headland you'll see the bridge leading to Vyborg Castle, watched from the Stone City by a **statue of Torglis Knutsson** in full armour.

Vyborg Castle

As regent for the underage King Birger, it was Knutsson who led the Swedes' third crusade against Novgorod in 1293, founding **Vyborg Castle** (Wiborg means "holy fortress" in Swedish) where a Russian trading port had been. In 1701 the castle fell to Peter the Great after a month's bombardment and the Russians began additional fortifications to safeguard their hard-won prize – henceforth known as the *zamok*. Vyborg's military role declined after 1812, when the city was transferred to the Grand Duchy of Finland, and the castle served as a prison until its reversion to active service between 1939 and 1944, when it was captured by the Soviets, retaken by the Finns and recaptured again by the Red Army. Today, it makes an ideal setting for mock battles and sieges during the **Knights' Tournament** (Rytsarskiy turnir) on the last weekend in July, and 2007's smash-hit **Castle Dance** trance-music party may be repeated in the future; see Ⓦwww.castledance.ru (in Russian) or contact the castle (☎81378/21 515, ✉castle@vyborg.ru) for details of forthcoming events.

The **island-castle** (daily 11am–7pm, Fri till 6pm) costs only R5 to enter; tickets for its museums are sold on the spot. Just inside the outer gate is Russia's only **Underwater Archeology Museum** (closed Mon; R70), displaying cannons, timbers and other relics of 23 Swedish and Russian warships sunk in a naval battle in

1790, recovered from the Gulf by volunteer divers at depths of 9–34 metres. Finds from World War II subs and other wrecks may be exhibited in the future.

An inner yard of raw masonry wends uphill past a den used by medieval-enactment enthusiasts to display their costumes at weekends to a citadel whose **Historical Museum** (closed Mon; R80) of maps and weapons is less inviting than the 48-metre-high **St Olaf's Tower** (R50), which affords a stunning **view** of the whole town and far out into the Gulf of Finland.

Other fortifications – and the Lenin House

If you're into military history, there are a few other overgrown fortifications, including **Annenkron** (Anna's Crown), which guards the peninsula beyond Vyborg Castle. Named after its founder, Empress Anna Ioannovna, its coronet-shaped array of curtain walls and enfilading ravelins are typical of the Vauban-style fortifications of the eighteenth century. Near the docks below the Stone City, the three-storey **Panzerlaks** (Shield of the Lakes) **bastion** was once part of the Swedish "Horned Fortress" constructed at the end of the sixteenth century, and now contains a studio-gallery. Further east is **Battery Hill** (Batareynaya gora), whose sunken galleries were laid out in the 1860s by the military engineer Totleben; the front line ran across it at the end of the Winter War in 1940. For more on these and other fortifications in Karelia, visit Ⓦwww.nortfort.ru.

Out beyond Battery Hill, the drab suburb of Yuzhniy Posyolok makes an unlikely setting for a **Lenin Memorial House** (10am–6pm, closed Wed & Sat; free), until you recall his taste for out-of-the-way hide-outs. After escaping to Finland disguised as a train fireman, Lenin was enraged by the Central Committee's "parliamentary tactics" and returned to Russia in September 1917 to urge immediate revolution from the safety of Vyborg, before slipping back to Petrograd (see box on p.223). The timbered cottage was opened as a museum in 1958, after the Finnish gift of Locomotive #293 (see p.222). Phone Ⓣ81378/20110 to check the house is open before taking a taxi (R50) to Rubezhnaya ulitsa 15.

Park Monrepos

Arguably Vyborg's top attraction, the seaside **Park Monrepos** (daily 10am–8pm; R100; Ⓣ817378/20539, Ⓔpark_monrepo@vbg.ru) grafts the Classicism and Romantic landscaping of Pavlovsk to the wilder shores of Karelia. Situated 2–3km beyond the castle, it's accessible by bus #1, #6 or #17 to the village of Severniy Posyolok, a fifteen-minute walk away: it's easier, however, to take a taxi directly from Vyborg to the park (R60–70) and arrange for it to pick you up again later. Entered by a massive wooden neo-Gothic gateway, the park uses the mossy, red granite crags and boulders of the Karelian shoreline to stunning effect, enhanced by dwarf firs and spruces that give it something of the look of a Japanese garden, embellished by Classical pavilions and Gothic follies – though sadly it's rather run-down owing to lack of funds. Laid out in 1759 by Commandant Stupishin, the park attained its apotheosis under Baron Nikolai, whose family is buried in a mock castle on the rocky **Isle of the Dead** (accessible by rowing boat). The isle lies off to the left beyond the wooden **palace** of Count Wurtemburg – being restored by Finns – while further to the west, the **Narcissus Spring** gushes medicinal water. To learn more about the park's history, visit Ⓦwww.oblmuseums.spb.ru/eng/museums/20/info.html.

Practicalities

Aside from signing up for a coach **excursion** (Sat 9am; 9–10hr; R900) outside Gostiniy dvor, the easiest way of reaching Vyborg from St Petersburg is by **bus** #850 (every 30min 6am–7pm; 2hr; R150) from Parnas metro, the northernmost stop on the (blue) Moskovsko-Petrogradskaya line. No booking is required, unlike coming by **train** from Finland Station, where tickets for the 8am *Baltika Express* (2hr) and another fast train leaving at 1pm are sold in a separate hall, while pensioners queue in the main hall for unpadded seats on stopping trains which take a butt-numbing three hours to reach Vyborg. **Motorists** have a choice of three routes: the M-10 "Scandinavia" highway (notorious for crashes between Vyborg and the Finnish border), the coastal A-122, or the A-121, which runs furthest inland.

Vyborg doesn't have a tourist office but **information** can be obtained at the reception desk of local hotels, where someone usually speaks English. **Websites** are little help at present: Ⓦwww.vyborg.net is largely in Russian and Finnish; Ⓦwww.ru way out of date, and Ⓦwww.vbg.ru merely offers a live-cam view of the city and weather reports. However, **changing money** is no problem, with a 24-hour currency exchange in the *Druzhba* hotel, and ATMs in the train station and on prospekt Lenina.

Accommodation

Although prices compare favourably with St Petersburg, most hotels charge higher rates from Friday to Sunday, when coach-loads of carousing Finns make it wise to reserve a room – or stay during the week when Vyborg is quieter. Breakfast is included unless stated otherwise.

Atlantic Podgornaya ul. 9 ☎81378/24 776, ℮atlantik.viborg@mail.ru. Non-smoking rooms in the heart of the Stone City; the mansard (attic) ones are lovely and cost little more than regular ones, with or without private bathrooms. Takes Maestro, MC and Visa. ❷
Druzhba Zheleznodorozhnaya ul. 5 ☎ & ℉81378/25 744, ℮druzba@vbg.spb.ru. Overlooking the bay near the station, this ageing 1980s pyramid-shaped complex has en-suite rooms with satellite TV, video channel and minibar; a free sauna for guests (the suites have their own private saunas) and tennis courts. Amex, DC, MC, Visa. ❸

Letuchaya Mysh ul. Nikolaeva 3 ☎81378/34 537, Ⓦwww.bathotel.ru. The "Bat" is a very friendly, cosy mini-hotel in an old building in the centre, entered from the rear. All rooms en suite (some non-smoking) with cable TV. Café; Internet access. Breakfast R180. Maestro, MC, Visa. ❸
Vyborg Leningradskiy pr. 19 ☎81378/22 383, ℮booking@lens.spb.ru.
A refurbished three-star establishment on a busy road in the centre, featuring a restaurant, sauna and nightclub. ❸

Eating, drinking and nightlife

You can eat almost anywhere in Vyborg without worrying about the cost. Phone numbers are given where it might be necessary to book a table at weekends, or enquire what's happening at a club.

Alleya Druzhba Hotel. Frequented by Finnish tourists and businessmen, this grill-restaurant serves French and Russian cuisine. Amex, DC, MC, Visa. Daily 7.30am–midnight.
Bamboo Nightclub Vyborg Hotel. Full of hookers and stag-partying Finns at weekends (when there's a show), but otherwise quiet. Entry R150, free for hotel guests. Daily 9pm–4am.
Camelot Krasnoarmeyskaya ul.14 ☎81378/55 322. Medieval Russian and Scandinavian

dishes feature on the menu of this knightly themed café, with an outdoor dining tent in the summer. MC, Visa. Daily 11am–midnight.
Farvater Ulyanovskaya ul. 13 Ⓦwww.x-farvater.ru. A house/electro and hip-hop club in the suburbs to the east of the centre (R50–150 by taxi), with regular parties. Fri, Sat & Sun 10am–5am.
Kruglaya bashnya Rynochnaya pl. ☎81378/23 648. Atmospheric restaurant on the top floor of the Round Tower, with Russian and Finn-

ish dishes (menu in English), live music at weekends and a downstairs bar that's open till the small hours. MC, Union, Visa. Daily 9am–2am.

Nord-West Rynochnaya ul. 17 ☏81378/25 893. Just behind the Round Tower, this Finn-friendly bar-restaurant does great salmon cream soup and seafood entrées. MC, Visa. Daily 10am–midnight.

Palace of Culture Krepostnaya ul. ☏81378/20 560. Dance to house and pop in the club (Fri & Sat 10pm–6am; R100 cover), watch a movie (from R80), or scoff cheap European or "Japanese" food in this one-stop enter-tainments venue in the centre of town.

Slavyanskaya Trapeza ul. Yuzhniy val 4/2 ☏81378/93 299. This folksy cellar-restau-rant in the Stone City does hearty Russian soups, stews and fish dishes. No credit cards. Daily noon–2am.

U Borzhada Podgornaya ul. 10 ☏81378/34 007. A cosy beer-restaurant affiliated to the *Atlantic Hotel*, serving steaks and other Euro fare, draught Czech and Belgian beers. MC and Visa. Daily 24 hours.

Kronstadt, the Gulf Coast and Vyborg

Kronstadt	Кронштадт
Razliv	Разлив
Repino	Репино
Sestroretsk	Сестрорецк
Zelenogorsk	Зеленогорск
Vyborg	Выборг
Krasnaya ploshchad	Красная площадь
Krepostnaya ul.	Крепостная ул.
prospekt Lenina	пр. Ленина
Leningradskiy prospekt	Ленинградский проспект
Luzhskaya ul.	Лужская ул.
Podgornaya ul.	Подгорня ул.
ul. Nikolaeva	ул. Николаева
Rynochnaya ploshchad	Рыночная площадь
ul. Storozhevoy bashni	ул. Сторожевой б%ни
ul. Titova	ул. Титтова
Ulyanovskaya ul.	Уляновская ул.
ul. Yuzhniy val	ул. Южний вал
Zheleznodorozhnaya ul.	Железнодорожная ул.

11

Shlisselburg, Valaam and Kizhi

The eastern shore of the Karelian Isthmus is craggier than the Gulf coast, reflecting the stormy nature of **Lake Ladoga** (Ladozhskoe ozero). Covering 17,872 square kilometres, Ladoga is Europe's largest lake and the source of the River Neva. Frozen over for up to six months of the year, it became famous during World War II for the **"Road of Life"**, which enabled Leningrad to survive the Blockade. Whenever the ice was thick enough, convoys drove across the lake through the night, hoping to avoid the Luftwaffe. In this way, 1,500,000 tonnes of supplies and 450,000 troops reached the city, and 1,200,000 civilians were evacuated.

Near the lake's outflow into the Neva, the Tsarist prison fortress of **Shlisselburg** makes an interesting day-trip in summer (the fortress is closed from November to April). At the other end of Ladoga, the **Valaam** archipelago is renowned for its hermitages and natural beauty, and during the navigation season (May–Sept) is a popular destination for **day-trips** by hydrofoil and longer **cruises** by ship (see box on p.302). Some cruises continue further north to **Lake Onega** (Onezhskoe ozero) and the fabulous wooden churches of **Kizhi** island, within 100km of the infamous **White Sea Canal**. Valaam and Kizhi can also be reached independently, entailing a night's stay in Priozersk or Petrozavodsk. This will allow you more time to explore the islands and might even work out cheaper than the cost of a cruise during high season, but will inevitably take longer – say two days for either site and its associated town, or a week for both.

Shlisselburg (Schlüsselburg)

The island fortress of **Shlisselburg** was born of rivalry between the medieval rulers of Novgorod and Sweden, who realized that the River Neva's outflow from Lake Ladoga held the key to the lucrative trade route between Russia and the Baltic. First fortified in 1323 by Prince Yuri of Novgorod, the island known to the Russians as **Oreshek** ("little nut") and to the Swedes as Noteborg constantly changed hands until its definitive recapture in 1702 by Peter the Great, who renamed it Schlüsselburg (meaning "Key Fortress" in German).

Having lost its military significance after Peter's victory over Sweden in the Northern War, the fortress became a **prison** for anyone threatening autocracy, becoming synonymous with Tsarist oppression as the Lubyanka would be in Soviet times. In the February 1917 Revolution it fell without a shot being fired, and prisoners joyfully burnt their cell blocks. When asked if it should be preserved

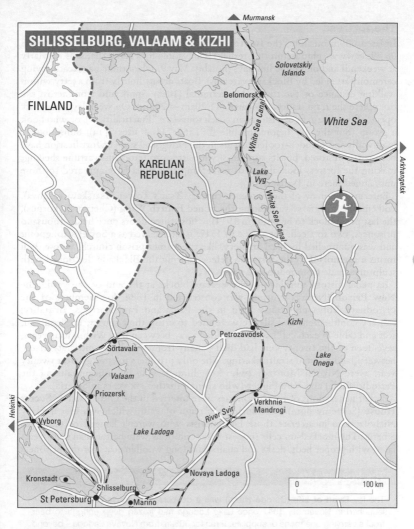

Murmansk

Solovetskiy
Islands

FINLAND

Belomorsk

White Sea

Arkhangelsk

KARELIAN
REPUBLIC

Lake
Vyg

White Sea Canal

White Sea Canal

N

11

SHLISSELBURG, VALAAM AND KIZHI

Kizhi

Petrozavodsk

Sortavala

Lake
Onega

Valaam

Priozersk

Verkhnie-
Mandrogi

River Svir

Helsinki

Vyborg

Lake Ladoga

Kronstadt

Novaya Ladoga

0   100 km

Shlisselburg

St Petersburg

Marino

as a monument to tyranny, they replied: "We have suffered enough, let the foul place crumble to ruin!"

Nonetheless, the Bolsheviks turned it into a **museum** devoted to the infamies of Tsarism a few years after Ladoga became the gateway to a chain of waterways and penal camps reaching to the Solovetskiy Islands within the Arctic Circle, where uncounted thousands perished building the White Sea Canal (see p.301). Although the town fell to the Nazis in 1941, the fortress held out for 500 days until the Blockade of Leningrad was broken. In honour of this feat, the town was renamed Petrokrepost (Peter's Fortress) – a name that's still used in everyday speech, notwithstanding its official reversion to Shlisselburg (a Russified form of the original name) in 1990.

The fortress

Isolated 600m offshore, the **fortress** (May–Oct daily 11am–6pm; R170; ☏498 06 79, ⓦwww.spbmuseum.ru/oreshek) is accessible by a **ferry** that sails regularly at weekends and on public holidays (notably May 9, when there's a wreath-laying ceremony attended by Blockade veterans). Boats depart hourly from a jetty within walking distance of the town's bus terminal (10am–5pm), and from across the bay where the train station is located (11.20am–4.20pm). On weekdays they only operate for the benefit of visitors on coach tours (see "Practicalities"), or who book a group tour the day before (mobile ☏81362/74104 after 7pm). Shlisselburg's high **walls** and wooden-roofed towers in the Novgorod style of fortification have been partly restored, but its ruinous skyline attests to ferocious wartime shelling, making the fortress look almost as forbidding as it must have appeared to those imprisoned there in Tsarist days.

Entering the maw of the sixteenth-century **Tsar's Tower** (Tsarskaya bashnya), you emerge in a grassy yard facing the ruined **Fourth Wing** (Chetvortiy korpus), the last penal block to be built (in 1911), whose three floors once held a thousand prisoners, two to a cell. Set ablaze in 1917, it later served as a Soviet strongpoint and was pummelled by Nazi artillery, like the former prison church, whose shell forms a **memorial** to the fortress's defence during the Blockade, festooned with sculptures made from redundant weaponry.

Its penal history unfolds in two separate blocks at the end of the yard. The **New Prison** (Novaya tyurma) was constructed in 1884, for members of the Narodnaya Volya previously held in the Peter and Paul Fortress. Brutality, solitary confinement and silence were used to crush their spirits; the iron bed, seat and table in each cell had to be folded away between use. Within four years, seventeen of the twenty-one had died – many from suicide, despite nets strung between landings and straitjacketing. The only prisoners to emerge after twenty years were Nikolai Morozov (who kept himself sane by conceptualizing the Periodic Table) and Vera Figner (who spent a further six years in Siberia).

Earlier generations of revolutionaries were interred in the Old Prison or **Secret House** (Sekretny dom) built during the reign of Paul, which was first used by Nicholas I to incarcerate those Decembrists who weren't hanged or exiled to Siberia. The mocked-up cells suggest that conditions were better than sixty years later, with proper beds, desks and chairs, and long woollen coats for the prisoners

The Road of Life

The icy **Road of Life** (Doroga zhizni) was a desperate response to the Blockade, launched in November 1941 once Lake Ladoga had frozen deep enough to bear trucks carrying one tonne of supplies. It ran for 308km from Novaya Ladoga – beyond the Nazi encirclement – through forests and swamps and across 30km of ice, to deliver the first supplies on the eighty-third day of the siege. By mid-December there were sixty trails across the ice, used by 3500 trucks, which allowed an increase in the bread ration when morale was at breaking point, preserving Leningrad through the first winter of the siege. During the second winter the Road was their only lifeline for supplies and the evacuation of tens of thousands of non-combatants. In January 1943 the Soviets counter-attacked round the southern shore of Ladoga, and on February 7 the first train from newly liberated Shlisselburg arrived at Finland Station on the 526th day of the siege – signifying that the Blockade had been broken, though it wasn't lifted until January 1944. The event is depicted by a diorama in the **Breakthrough of the Blockade Museum** (10am–6pm; closed Mon & the last Fri of each month; R100) at **Marino**, off a ramp of the Ladozhskiy bridge over the Neva en route to Shlisselburg – buses can drop you nearby on request.

to wear against the pervasive cold and damp. Yet some latter-day inmates spent only a few weeks here, before being hung in the yard; a **plaque** marks the spot where Lenin's brother, Alexander Ulyanov, was executed for attempted regicide in 1887.

Still earlier there was the (no longer extant) **Tower of Cells**, where VIPs were confined. Peter the Great's half-sister Maria was lucky to spend only three years there for "encouraging disaffection"; Prince Golitsyn languished until the overthrow of Count Biron – who ended up in Shlisselburg himself. The cruellest fate was that of Anna Leopoldovna's son, **Ivan VI**, who was deposed as a baby by Empress Elizabeth and as "Prisoner No. 1" denied any education or enjoyment so that he would grow up unfit to be a tsar, before being murdered in 1764 after trying to escape, according to standing orders maintained since Elizabeth's time by Catherine the Great. Catherine herself saw fit to imprison the publisher and Freemason Novikov and the Chechen rebel leader Sheikh Mansur, who died in prison in 1793.

To dispel the grim mood, exit by a portal near Ulyanov's execution place, to find a rocky **beach** where you can sunbathe and even swim in the lake – just beware of broken glass and the strong currents only 5m offshore.

Practicalities

From May to October, Baltia Tour and Davranov Travel outside Gostiniy dvor (see p.70) run daily **coach excursions** to Shlisselburg (6hr; R600–750), while from mid-May to mid-September Russian Cruises (see box on p.302) offers a **hydrofoil** trip from the Finland Station pier (Sat & Sun 1pm; 4hr 30min; R1200). Otherwise you can get there by taking the metro to Ulitsa Dybenko station and then **bus** #575 (R50), or an unofficial **taxi** (about R500) for the 40- to 60-minute drive down the highway. Shlisselburg's bus and taxi terminus is just across the sluice gates from the jetty for ferries to the fortress, which makes this a far more convenient approach than by **train** from Finland Station to the railway halt at Morozova, on the far side of Shlisselburg Bay.

A couple of beer and *shashlyk* dens by the town jetty and in the park near the bus terminal can satisfy your need for **food**, but there's nowhere to stay – nor any reason to. Buses back to St Petersburg are less frequent after 5pm; the last one leaves shortly before 11pm.

Valaam

The islands of the **Valaam** archipelago at the northern end of Ladoga have a unique history and society, shaped by mystics, exiles and nature. Despite being icebound for five months of the year, Valaam is blessed with a favourable microclimate, enjoying twice the sunshine of St Petersburg and abounding in berries, mushrooms, wild flowers, butterflies and songbirds. It remains almost as quiet as it was when Avram of Rostov – the founder of Valaam's hermetic tradition – arrived in 960, and heard a leaf fall in the forest.

For Orthodox believers, Valaam is a **holy isle** of saints and hermits, whose shrines echo Christ's Passion in the Holy Land; a "Jerusalem of the North", offering redemption to the sinful and miracles to the faithful. The monastery's own resurrection has been remarkable, for until six monks returned in 1989 there had been none on Valaam since 1940, when its brethren and treasures were evacuated to Finland as Stalin occupied Karelia. In the meantime, Valaam had served as a dumping ground for disfigured and disabled war veterans, isolated from Soviet society until 1967, when it became a tourist destination for Leningrad's intelligentsia, and both sides were shocked by the gulf in living standards and horizons.

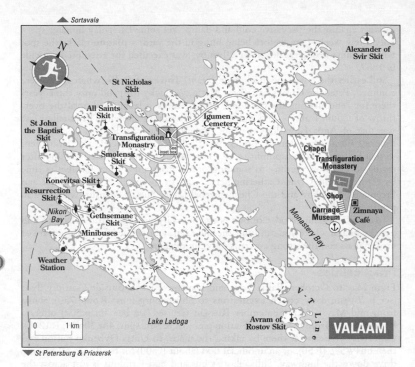

Over the last two decades the **monastery** has recovered its former de facto sovereignty over Valaam; its classification as a state museum-reserve (like Peterhof or Kizhi) masks the reality that the clergy call the shots. Restoration of the monastery is the only building work allowed on the island, whose six hundred inhabitants are disgruntled that their promised new housing hasn't materialized and would probably leave if the monastery banned liquor and tobacco, as in Tsarist times. Locals also complain of being excluded from moneymaking activities such as trout farming, and of the monks erecting roadblocks to impede traffic. The Patriarch of the Russian Orthodox Church (who was once a monk on Valaam) has even ensured that the local army garrison consists of true believers, with leave to fast and attend holy festivals.

The monastery

The origins of the **Monastery of the Transfiguration of the Saviour** (Spaso-Preobrazhenskiy Valaamskiy monastyr) are obscure, but there may have been a cloister here even before Avram's arrival. Legend attributes the conversion of the pagans of Valaam to none other than the Apostle Andrew, the "First Called", who is said to have smashed their sacrificial altars. It certainly existed by 1163, when the relics of saints Sergei and German were brought from Novgorod to Valaam. From the fourteenth century onwards the monastery was often sacked by the Swedes, and served as a fortress against them. Laid waste in 1611, it was rebuilt a century later with funds from Peter the Great, and reached its zenith in the 1880s and 1890s, when the existing cathedral and residential blocks were built, hermitages were rebuilt or founded, and there were nearly a thousand monks in residence. Although six hundred were conscripted and all but two hermitages closed during

▲ Monastery of the Transfiguration of the Saviour

World War I, the monastery had the good fortune to end up on Finnish territory and escape the scourging of the Church in Russia – while monks who fled Karelia in 1940 were able to establish the New Valaam Monastery in Finland, whose rejection of Moscow's Patriarchal authority during the Soviet era was reciprocated by the Russian Church. Although the Orthodox Church in exile rejoined the "mother" church in 2007, New Valaam declined to do so and still recognizes the Patriarch of Constantinople.

The Transfiguration Monastery's **website** (Ⓦwww.valaam.ru) is one of many devoted to Valaam and its saints – the movement is also strong in America, where eighteenth-century missionaries from Valaam made converts and founded churches and monasteries as far afield as Alaska. It features **chants** by Valaam's brethren and some evocative photos of the monastery in olden days, but no practical information; the site for the Valaam Museum-Reserve (Ⓦwww.museums.karelia.ru, in Russian only) is even less tourist friendly.

The two-hundred-odd monks on Valaam maintain their own **"time zone"**, synchronized to Jerusalem and the Holy Land rather than Moscow. Among the **monks** are an ex-Moscow DJ, a Socialist Realist artist turned icon painter and an actor who found God through a stage adaptation of Dostoyevsky's *The Possessed*. Rising at 5.30am, they spend up to ten hours a day praying in the **cathedral**, whose lower Church of SS Sergei and German contains their relics, and the icon *Our Lady of Valaam* (Mon–Fri 10am–5pm; free). The huge upper Church of the Transfiguration is still under repair, but its blue cupola and the red and white crosses that emblazon its facade are visible all around Monastery Bay.

Visitors are told not to photograph the monks and that entry to churches is conditional on men wearing long trousers and women full-length skirts and headscarves. Women in trousers may be offered a wraparound skirt to pass muster, but shouldn't count on it – the monks would prefer that only pilgrims disturbed their sanctuary.

Beyond the monastery's walls, a small **Carriage Museum** (Mon–Fri 10am–5pm; R50) near the landing stage on Monastery Bay displays buggies, *troikas* and other vehicles, used before cars came to the island. Today, bearded monks speed around its dirt roads in jeeps like an occupying army.

The skits

The **skit** (pronounced "skeet") or hermitage – the domicile of a few monks living under stricter vows than their monastic brethren, such as continual silence and prayer or a vegan diet – is a leitmotif of Valaam's landscape and religious life. The first skits were founded by Abbot Nazary in the 1790s, with rock-cut cells in emulation of bygone, solitary hermits such as Avram or Alexander of Svir, but these proved so harmful to the health that Abbot Damaskin (known for sleeping in a coffin) built brick living quarters, so that the larger skits came to resemble miniature monasteries.

The **Resurrection Skit**, overlooking Nikon Bay, was built during the 1890s where a hermit of the previous century had lived in a cave with snakes, and where St Andrew is said to have raised a stone cross only 28 years after the death of Christ. Its tidy quadrangle of brick dwellings could be mistaken for a private school, but for the monastery guides who greet visitors disembarking from cruise ships in the bay.

Ten minutes' walk inland, the **Gethsemane Skit** is a simple cream-coloured wooden church near a picturesquely dark lake, offset by the sky-blue roofs and the spires of surrounding cabins where the monks live. From here you can follow a path through the woods to the **Konevitsa Skit** – a wooden chapel, used only on holy days, in a wonderful location atop the sheer cliffs of a narrow bay. A trail with stretches of timber baulks circumvents **Lake Igumen** and the **Black Lake**, with one route returning to the main road between the Resurrection Skit and the monastery, and the other forging on towards Saints' Island.

The smallest of the three main islands in the archipelago, this has now been declared **off-limits** so that the five monks at the **All Saints' Skit** may adhere to their rule of continuous prayer, abjuring the sight of women and the consumption of flesh. This is the oldest, most romantic-looking of Valaam's hermitages, with a stone church and cells on the spot where St Alexander of Svir once lived, amid a sheltered clearing whose shallow soil is quickly warmed by the sun, enabling the monks to grow water melons as well as vegetables.

The other hermitages are accessible only by boat. Visitors who sign up for the organized trip from Nikon Bay to the monastery will get a distant view of the **John the Baptist Skit** – which is likewise **off-limits** – and a closer one of the **Nicholas Skit** at the mouth of Monastery Bay, whose monks formerly acted as customs officials, searching incoming vessels for booze and tobacco. But you'll need to charter your own boat to reach the remote mini-archipelagos where the **Alexander of Svir** and **Avram of Rostov** hermitages are sited. The latter also hosts an observation tower, a bunker with naval guns and other relics from the **V-T Line** of **fortifications** that the Finns built in 1942 to stop the Soviets from outflanking the Mannerheim Line. This outpost's garrison withdrew to avoid being cut off after the Red Army breached the V-T Line in June 1944. A boat trip and tour of the site takes about three hours.

Practicalities

Valaam is situated about 250km from St Petersburg. From May to September the easiest way of getting there is an **excursion by hydrofoil** from the Angliyskaya naberezhnaya pier west of the Admiralty. Alien Shipping (Angliyskaya nab. 4 ☏327 54 54, ⓦwww.alienshipping.ru, in Russian only) charges R2800 for a tour departing at 8am (daily except Mon); Neva Travel (ul. Professora Popova 28 ☏234 00 82, ⓦwww.neva-travel.ru) R4500 for a similarly scheduled service. Both entail eight hours travel and allow you six hours on Valaam. To stay longer means taking a **cruise** (see box overleaf), or travelling **via Priozersk**, two hours from St Petersburg by **train** #853 which leaves the Finland Station at 5.30pm. You'll have to stay the night in Priozersk before catching the 9.30am ferry (3hr; R250) or the 11am hydrofoil (1hr 30min; R500) to Valaam next day. You can book accommodation through **tour agencies** Valaam-Invest in St Petersburg (Moskovskiy pr. 120, office #405; ☏331 50 91, ⓦwww.valaam.twell.ru) or Alta in Priozersk (Krasnoarmeyskaya ul. 8/1 ☏81379/35 794, ⓦwww.alta.pl.ru). Both offer two-day excursions, or longer trips to the Lake Onega petroglyphs (see p.120) and other sites.

Over winter, when boats don't operate, it's possible to reach Valaam by **snowmobile from Sortavala** on the northern shore of Lake Ladoga (accessible from St Petersburg by train). Contact the North-West Travel Bureau in Petrozavodsk (ul. Titova 11, office 10 ☏8142/707 616, ⓔnwtb@onego.ru, ⓦwww.nwtb.ru, in Russian only) for details of their small-group snowmobile excursions.

Tourist accommodation on Valaam is limited to the all-year-round *Zimnaya Hotel* (☏81430/38 248; ❸) near the monastery, so reservations are essential. It has clean, spartan doubles (one en suite, the rest sharing hot-water facilities) and a café (breakfast not included). There are *shashlyk* dens at Nikon Bay and below

From May to September, **cruise boats** depart for Valaam and Kizhi every day or so from St Petersburg's River Terminal (Rechnoy vokzal) at prospekt Obukhovskoy obornony 95, near Proletarskaya metro. Whether you're booking a cruise from home or hoping to get a berth in Russia, always check the name of the ship, as some are far better than others. This is usually reflected in the cost of the cruise but not always; the larger, newer vessels may undercut their older rivals. Shop around.

Russian Cruises (Nevskiy pr. 51 ☏325 61 20, ⓦwww.russian-cruises.ru, in Russian) operates the triple-deck M/S *Svyataya Rus* ("Holy Russia"), used mainly for two-night cruises to Valaam, starting at R7500 per person sharing a standard cabin, with higher rates at weekends and throughout July and August. Its amenities are only surpassed by the four-star M/S *Kazan*, launched by **Alien Shipping** in 2007, which has satellite TV in each cabin, a sauna, gym and outdoor pool, with cruises to Valaam costing from R9500 per person. Bookings are through Alien Shipping (see p.41) or Inflot Travel in the *Morskoy Vokzal* hotel on Vasilevskiy Island (2nd floor ☏322 66 99).

Then there is a fleet of boats built in East Germany in the 1970s and 1980s; some are better than others, but all are past their prime. Prices are directly related to the standard of the vessel: M/S *Kuybishev* is cheapest, *Belinsky* and *Sankt-Peterburg* a step up, and *Suvorov* the dearest. These cruises are sold online by **Nordic Travel** (ⓦwww.nordictravel.ru; see p.306) in Petrozavodsk (purchasers get an email or faxed voucher in lieu of a ticket) and sometimes also by travel agencies in St Petersburg. A two-night cruise to Valaam costs from R8750 in the week, R10300 at weekends. You can pay even less (R5200–6000) for a cruise on the *Popov*, an older, Russian-built ship, run by **Turflot** (☏448 38 09, ⓦwww.turflot.ru).

While a two-night cruise gives you the best part of a day on **Valaam**, the price may or may not include a motorboat trip around the island to Monastery Bay and/or a guided walk. Check before buying a tour. Most cruises to **Kizhi** allow passengers only two or three hours on the island, and actually spend longer at Valaam and Verkhnie Mandrogi (see p.303). Four-night cruises (from R15,500) are available throughout the navigation season, and a three-night version only in July and August. Don't bother with an optional extra day in Petrozavodsk.

The long **journey** to Kizhi and back can pall unless you bring books or other entertainment. Packages include all **meals** except dinner the first night (which isn't served till 10pm) and breakfast on return to Petersburg (which isn't provided at all); vegetarians need to bring alternatives to the meaty, Soviet canteen-style fare. Passengers are assigned a shift (*smena*) for meals and excursions; announcements are in Russian only. **Alcohol**, soft drinks and cigarettes are dear by Russian standards, so you may wish to bring your own – not that this deters people from making merry at the **disco**. As there are no facilities for exchanging **money** or using credit cards, you should bring enough rubles to cover expenses.

the monastery; a **shop** near the latter sells tinned food, booze and cigarettes; or you can buy delicious smoked fish, berries, mushrooms and honey at **stalls** near the minibus stop above Nikon Bay. There are no exchange offices, but you might be able to change euros with cruise boat staff or locals.

Some cruise boats offer passengers a free **guided walk** from the Resurrection to the Konevitsa Skit to ensure that nobody gets lost, as well as a motorboat ride around the coast to visit the monastery. There's nothing to stop you exploring the island for yourself, however: local **minibuses** leaving from the stalls uphill from the landing stage run to and from the monastery (6.5km) 8–9am, 1–3pm and 6–8pm (R50 per person). Skippers offer private **boat trips** to beaches, lakes or

The White Sea Canal

The notion of linking the White Sea to the Baltic originated in Petrine times, but remained a pipe dream until 1930, when Stalin made it a goal of the First Five-Year Plan. To avoid importing costly machinery, the task was assigned to **Gulag** slave workers; the required specialists were simply arrested by the NKVD. For twenty months, up to 180,000 **prisoners** at a time toiled with shovels, picks and barrows to cut through 37km of solid granite. Perhaps 100,000 died hewing the first few kilometres of deep excavations; some put the total workforce at 300,000 and death toll as high as 200,000 – but nobody really knows, as the survivors were set to work on subsequent canal projects that were equally fatal.

Inaugurated in March 1933, the canal was extolled for "re-forging" criminals into honest citizens. A "brigade" of **writers** led by Gorky took a cruise on the waterway and produced a book entitled *A Canal Called Stalin* (as it was originally named). One author had a brother in the canal camps and kept silent to protect him, but it seems most of the others were fooled by the staged normality (as US senators would later be at other camps). Henceforth, forced labour became the norm for all major construction projects in Stalin's Russia.

The canal's human cost was underscored by its futility. Ice-bound for half the year and too small for maritime vessels, it fulfilled neither its economic nor strategic rationale. Only a few barges carrying timber or fuel pass through its locks each day. Yet as a feat of **engineering** it once had a place in the record books: its 227 kilometres feature seven locks that raise boats 70m to Lake Onega, and twelve along the River Vyg, rising 102m – not including the locks on the Svir that handle the 30m difference between Onega and Ladoga. Bizarrely, the canal is still commemorated by a brand of cigarettes, *Belomor* (short for *Belomorkanal*), whose packet bears a map of the waterway.

islands for about R1500 an hour (group rate), and minibus driver Dmitri Soshkin (mobile ☎7921/220 4802) will happily **charter** the *Maksim* for trips of several days exploring the remoter islands or **fishing**.

From Ladoga to Lake Onega

If you're cruising to Kizhi, you'll sail from Ladoga into Lake Onega up the **River Svir**. This 230-kilometre waterway is partly canalized, with two huge **locks** that form the final stage of the Baltic–White Sea Canal (see box above), but looks quite wild for much of its length, lined with pine and birch forests. In early May and September, its estuary on Ladoga supports vast numbers of **birds**: 200,000 ducks, 150,000 geese and up to 5000 swans, plus cranes, warblers, snipes and rarer species such as White-winged Black Terns. The isthmuses on either side of Ladoga are under the White Sea–Baltic Flyway, the route along which millions of birds from northern Russia migrate to and from their wintering grounds in Western Europe and Africa.

A decade ago, a St Petersburg entrepreneur capitalized on the river's tourist traffic by creating **Verkhnie Mandrogi** – a Disneyesque version of a "traditional" Russian village of the nineteenth century, where a community of Veps previously had a settlement called Mandrogi, meaning "Pine Trees on the Bog". Instead of decrepit cottages, muddy tracks and drunken peasants, there are extravagantly carved and painted houses, neat paths and a community of craftspeople that moves in over summer to produce handicrafts for sale. During a televised visit, Putin was shown painting a *matryoshka* and throwing a clay pot; as thanks for the publicity the village received, he was given a house there. The largest building in the settlement is full of **workshops** making dolls, carved figures, lace and ceramics. Other diversions include a **vodka museum** (with sampling), pony rides, and photo opportunities with a bear cub. Several *bliny* bars and rustic-style eateries feed up to 2000 visitors a day at the height of the season.

Kizhi

The northern half of **Lake Onega** is characterized by low-lying peninsulas and islands termed *Zaonezhe* ("Beyond the Onega"), that were the domain of the pagan Ves and Saami peoples of Karelia until their absorption by the kingdom of Novgorod in the twelfth century. At the heart of the archipelago lies the small island of **Kizhi**, whose name (pronounced "*Kee*-zhi") is thought to derive from the ritual games (*kizhat*) that were once held there. Kizhi remained the religious and commercial centre of the region under Russian rule: its domain numbered 130 villages by the sixteenth century and was rich in timber, furs and foodstuffs, though it was repeatedly invaded by Swedes, Poles and Lithuanians until Russia's victory in the Northern War brought peace, and an upsurge in construction across the region gave rise to some of the finest **wooden architecture** in Europe, exemplified by Kizhi's *pogost* complex.

Owing to Kizhi's remoteness, both the buildings and the folk culture that sustained them survived into the twentieth century, but were deteriorating as a result of the declining, ageing population (the custom that elder daughters had to marry first didn't help) and the impact of modernization. From 1948 onwards, Soviet ethnographers studied the villages, purchased outstanding buildings and began moving them to Kizhi to create what is now the **Open-air Museum of History, Architecture and Ethnography** (daily: June–May 9am–9pm; Sept to mid-Oct & late May 8am–8pm; mid-Oct to mid-May 10am–3pm; R500) – a folklore reservation of both indigenous and reconstructed villages. Their thirty-odd inhabitants have a lifestyle that isn't so different from their grandparents' but their aspirations are higher, influenced by Petrozavodsk and the summer influx of tour guides (who stay with local families). While tourism offers an economic lifeline, the number of visitors has been limited to 130,000 a year to minimize damage to the environment. There is **free entry for under-18s** on the first day of each month.

Disembarking tourists are filtered through the museum's entrance to buy a ticket that covers all the buildings designated as museums and to be assigned a **guide** speaking English, French or German – the entrance charge and guide fee (R75) may be included in the price of cruises or excursions from Petrozavodsk. It's worth staying with a guide since they are well informed, but there's nothing to stop you from wandering off. Sadly, cruise schedules limit visitors to a mere two hours on Kizhi, which is enough time to explore the *pogost* and the nearby village, but not the rest of the island – day-trippers from Petrozavodsk get longer (see p.306). Note that smoking is permitted only in designated areas of the island.

If you can, time your visit to catch one of the local **festivals**. The Festival of Kizhi Volost (Aug 23) features folk music, dancing and handicrafts, while other events are mainly religious, but still end in feasting and drinking – such as the Easter gatherings, the festivals of Christ's Transfiguration (Aug 19) and the Intercession of the Virgin (Oct 14) and the chapel feast of the Dormition at Vasilevo (Aug 28). For a preview of Kizhi, check out the museum's informative, nicely illustrated **website** ⓦhttp://kizhi.karelia.ru.

The pogost

Built over three centuries by local carpenters, the *pogost* comprises an extraordinary ensemble of disparate wooden structures enclosed by a dry-stone stockade. The

⑪

pogost was begun in 1714 with the 37-metre-high **Church of the Transfiguration** – a magnificent edifice twice as tall as St Basil's in Moscow, with 22 onion domes upon tiers of *bochka* (barrel) roofs, inset one above another to form a cascade of shingles reaching almost to the ground. Its dramatic silhouette is enhanced by the contrast between its dark fir timbers and the silvery shingles (called *cheshui* – or "fish scales" – in Russian) of its roofs and domes. Despite gutters to channel rainwater away, and an inner flush roof to catch any leaks and carry them into a drain, rot affected its beams over the centuries; the interior is now supported by a metal cage and off-limits to visitors, pending restoration by 2014.

Despite the legend that, after its completion, master carpenter Nestor cast his axe into the lake, vowing, "There has not been, nowhere is and never will be a church like this!", the inhabitants of Kizhi had another go fifty years later, erecting the **Church of the Intercession**, whose boxy, nine-domed silhouette offsets the pyramidal Church of the Transfiguration. Meant for winter use, it became the only place of worship after 1937, till services were banned entirely after World War II, when the open-air museum was established. They resumed in 1997 under Father Nikolai, a French-born priest who still runs the parish. Among the diverse icons from the Onega region is a splendid *Last Judgement* from the Chapel of St Nicholas Tomskiy. A tall, freestanding **bell tower** of 1874 completes the *pogost*. Its existence today is owed to a Finnish pilot, who was ordered to bomb the *pogost* as a "partisan centre" in 1944 but flew away without doing so.

The villages

Afterwards you can make a circuit of a reconstructed village nearby. There are two large farmsteads that once belonged to middling-affluent peasants, combining home and barn under one roof, with spacious, functional living quarters full of artefacts. The **Oshevnev house**, built in 1876, features a baby-walker and a faceless doll (for superstitious reasons), and is used for demonstrating weaving and pearl embroidery (locals used to collect pearls from the lake), while the **Yelizarov house** from Seredeka contains an array of boats and sleighs. The latter was inhabited until the 1950s, and its living room boasts a family tree going back to the seventeenth century. Further along are a rustic *banya* and an octagonal tent-roofed **Chapel of the Archangel Michael**, from Lelikozero in the Kizhi skerries, whose bells toll melodiously. Drying racks, a threshing barn and a windmill are followed by the **Church of the Resurrection of Lazarus** from the Muromskiy Monastery in northern Karelia. The oldest wooden church extant in Russia (1390), it was reputedly built by a monk, Lazarus, whom the pagans decided not to kill after he cured a child of blindness.

Walking anywhere else, you should be sure to stick to paths as there are poisonous **snakes** and blood-sucking **ticks** on the island. If time allows, head for the **Chapel of St Veronica's Veil** on Naryina Hill, whose picturesque witch's hat belfry adorns the highest point on Kizhi. From there, the trail diverges towards two villages indigenous to Kizhi (though some of the buildings in them have been transplanted from other sites) and still inhabited. **Vasilevo**, on the western side of the island, boasts the finest secular building on Kizhi: the enormous, rambling **Sergin house** that once accommodated a family of 22. Taken from the village of Munozero, it now shares the limelight with the **Sergeeva house** from Lipovitsy, the abode of the Vasilevs, one of the most prosperous local families a century ago. Nearby is the earliest native church on the island, the seventeenth-century **Assumption Church**, whose large octagonal bell tower originally doubled as a watchtower.

Across the island, **Yamka** lacks any outstanding houses but epitomizes the traditional Zaonezhne village, with dwellings running along the shore facing the lake, fields and kitchen gardens out back, barns and granaries nearby, and a windmill,

Shlisselburg, Valaam and Kizhi

Kizhi	Кижи
Marinovo	Мариново
Petrozavodsk	Петрозаводск
Shlisselburg	Шлиссельбург
Sortavala	Сортавала
Valaam	Валаам

threshing barn and wayside cross further on. As with all Kizhi's timber structures, the logs were felled in the late autumn after the final ring of the tree had hardened, and left on the ground until late spring. By using axes instead of saws, the grain of the wood was closed rather than left open to moisture; and nails were dispensed with in favour of notches or mortise and tenon joints, which are better suited to the climate.

Practicalities

As an alternative to cruising, you can **get to Kizhi via Petrozavodsk** on the Karelian mainland. Overnight **train** #657 from St Petersburg arrives at Petrozavodsk shortly before 7am, giving you time to get to the waterfront to catch the 9am **hydrofoil** that runs from June to August if enough people have booked tickets (☏8142/796 415), or the 1pm service (there's another at 6pm) that operates throughout the navigation season. The 66km crossing takes an hour and fifteen minutes; a return ticket costs R1000. As hydrofoils **leave** Kizhi at 3.30pm and 8.30pm, you may be able to stay there for up to ten hours – far longer than cruise passengers.

From mid-December to mid-April, when shipping is suspended, Nordic Travel (Kluchevskoe shosse 13 ☏8142/560 201, ⊕www.nordic-travel.ru) in Petrozavodsk offers an excursion (5–7hr) to Kizhi by **hovercraft** (R7350/R4375 per person for two/four people) if the ice-cover allows it, or you can get there by **helicopter** (☏8142/747 566 for information).

On Kizhi itself, a small lakeside **café** serves soup, smoked fish and *kalitkiya* (traditional pies made from rye-flour, filled with mashed potato). As the basic hotel next door is usually fully occupied by guides, there is **no accommodation** for tourists on Kizhi, and camping out is strictly forbidden.

This means catching a train back to St Petersburg that night (which needs pre-booking) or stay on in **Petrozavodsk**. Fortunately, the Karelian capital (pop. 280,000) offers a range of **accommodation**: central hotels include the *Maski* (pr. Marksa 3a ☏8142/761 478, ⊜mrteatr@karelia.ru; ●) and *Severnaya* (pr. Lenina 21/6 ☏8142/762 224, ⊜severnaja@onego.ru; ●), the latter with a sauna and Jacuzzi. For more **information** and a **map** of the city, see the online magazine *KomArt* (⊕http://komart.karelia.ru).

12

Novgorod

Centuries before St Petersburg was dreamt of, **Novgorod** was the lodestar of northern Russia, a beacon of civilization that some Russian historians have characterized as the first (or only) democracy in Russian history. Today, its medieval **Kremlin** and **churches** draw Russian tourists in droves, while the **Museum of Wooden Architecture** and **monasteries** outside town enshrine folk customs and religious faith. A beach and leafy promenades contribute to the mellow ambience of the city centre, where there are plenty of places to eat and drink cheaply, and folklore events and music **festivals** throughout the year. Although it's possible to see Novgorod on a long day excursion from St Petersburg, you'd do better to stay overnight; local accommodation is also good value, and there's even a tourist office that really knows its job and is keen to help.

Despite its name, meaning "New Town", Novgorod is Russia's oldest city, founded, according to popular belief, by the Varangian (Scandinavian) Prince Rurik in 862 AD. By the end of the tenth century it had developed into an important commercial centre thanks to its position on the River Volkhov, which flows north into Lake Ladoga and on to the Gulf of Finland – part of an ancient trade route in amber and furs, from Scandinavia to Greece. Originally ruled by the eldest son of the prince of Kiev, Novgorod was later governed by popular **assemblies** (*veche*) dominated by wealthy landlords whose attitude was "if the prince is no good, into the mud with him". As the only major city in Russia to withstand the Tatar invasion, and the seat of a principality that stretched to Poland and the White Sea, it became known as **Velikiy Novgorod** (Great Novgorod) – a title still used today to distinguish it from Nizhniy Novgorod on the Volga. Its wealth and status were reflected by over a hundred churches and a score of monasteries that formed their own school of icon painting, while the level of **literacy** amongst the population was unmatched by anywhere else in Russia, as attested by over 750 texts inscribed on birch bark that have been found during excavations since 1951.

Novgorod remained proudly independent until Ivan III brought it under the administrative control of Muscovy in 1478. Yet its free spirit was so persistent that **Ivan the Terrible** suspected the city of forging a secret deal with Poland. In 1570 he surrounded it with a high timber wall to prevent anyone from leaving. Every day for five weeks, hundreds of citizens were put to death in front of the tsar and his depraved son: stories tell of dozens being fried alive in a giant metal pan, and estimates of the number slaughtered range from 15,000 to 60,000. So many bodies were thrown into the Volkhov that "the river overflowed its banks", and for years afterwards, citizens were ordered to gather in the centre to conceal the extent of the depopulation from foreign visitors. After Ivan's death, the Kremlin was strengthened at Boris Godunov's bidding, but occupied by the Swedes from 1611 to 1617. After their eviction, Novgorod's inhabitants rebuilt it and restored the fortifications, which played a vital role in the defence against Swedish attack for decades afterwards.

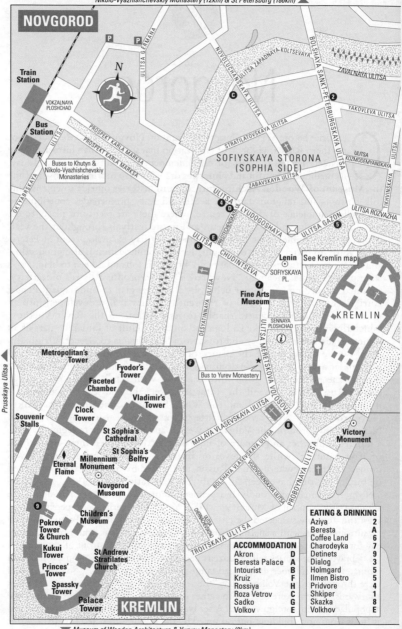

NOVGOROD

Nikolo-Vyazhishchevskiy Monastery (12km) & St Petersburg (186km)

Train Station

VOKZALNAYA PLOSHCHAD

Bus Station

Buses to Khutyn & Nikolo-Vyazhishchevskiy Monasteries

PROSPEKT KARLA MARKSA

PROSPEKT KARLA MARKSA

OKTYABRSKAYA

ULITSA GERMANA

NOVOLUCHANSKAYA ULITSA

ZAPADNAYA KOLTSEVAYA

BOLSHAYA SANKT-PETERBURGSKAYA ULITSA

ZAVALNAYA ULITSA

YAKOVLEVA ULITSA

STRATILATOVSKAYA ULITSA

SOFIYSKAYA STORONA
(SOPHIA SIDE)

ULITSA KOZMODEMYANSKAYA

ZABAVSKAYA ULITSA

ULITSA LYUDOGOSHAYA

ULITSA GAZON

ULITSA ROZVAZHA

ULITSA CHUDINTSEVA

PREOBRAZHENSKAYA UL.

DESYATINNAYA ULITSA

Lenin

SOFIYSKAYA PL.

Fine Arts Museum

SENNAYA PLOSHCHAD

See Kremlin map

KREMLIN

i

ULITSA MERETSKOVA-VOLOSOVA

MALAYA VLASEVSKAYA ULITSA

BOLSHAYA VLASEVSKAYA ULITSA

VOZDVIZHENSKAYA ULITSA

PROBOYNAYA ULITSA

Bus to Yurev Monastery

Victory Monument

TROITSKAYA ULITSA

Prusskaya Ulitsa

Metropolitan's Tower

Fyodor's Tower

Faceted Chamber

Vladimir's Tower

Clock Tower

St Sophia's Cathedral

Souvenir Stalls

St Sophia's Belfry

Millennium Monument

Eternal Flame

Novgorod Museum

Children's Museum

Pokrov Tower & Church

Kukui Tower

St Andrew Stratilates Church

Princes' Tower

Spassky Tower

Palace Tower

KREMLIN

ACCOMMODATION

Akron	D
Beresta Palace	A
Intourist	B
Kruiz	F
Rossiya	H
Roza Vetrov	C
Sadko	G
Volkov	E

EATING & DRINKING

Aziya	2
Beresta	A
Coffee Land	6
Charodeyka	7
Detinets	9
Dialog	3
Holmgard	5
Ilmen Bistro	5
Pridvore	4
Shkiper	1
Skazka	8
Volkhov	E

Museum of Wooden Architecture & Yuryev Monastery (3km)

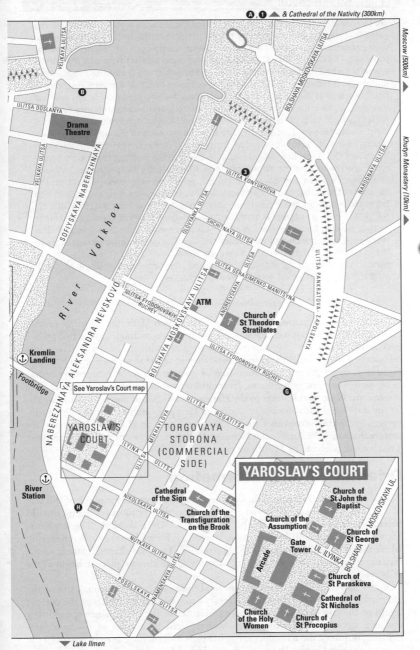

& Cathedral of the Nativity (300km)

Moscow (500km)

Khutyn Monastery (10km)

VELIKAYA ULITSA

ULITSA DOSLANYA

Drama Theatre

VELIKAYA ULITSA

SOFIYSKAYA NABEREZHNAYA

R i v e r   V o l k h o v

ALEKSANDRA NEVSKOVO

BOLSHAYA MOSKOVSKAYA ULITSA

NARODNAYA ULITSA

ULITSA KONYUKHOVA

OLOVYANA ULITSA

SHCHITNAYA ULITSA

ULITSA

ULITSA GERASIMENKO-MANITSYNA

ANDREEVSKAYA

ULITSA PANKRATOVA-ZAPOLSKAYA

ULITSA FYODOROVSKIY RUCHEY

ATM

Church of St Theodore Stratilates

ULITSA FYODOROVSKIY RUCHEY

Kremlin Landing

Footbridge

NABEREZHNAYA

See Yaroslav's Court map

MIKHAYLOVA

ULITSA ROGATITSA

BOLSHAYA MOSKOVSKAYA ULITSA

YAROSLAV'S COURT

ILYINA ULITSA

TORGOVAYA STORONA (COMMERCIAL SIDE)

River Station

Cathedral of the Sign

NIKOLSKAYA ULITSA

Church of the Transfiguration on the Brook

NUTKAYA ULITSA

ZNAMENSKAYA ULITSA

POSOLSKAYA ULITSA

▼ Lake Ilmen

YAROSLAV'S COURT

Church of St John the Baptist

BOLSHAYA MOSKOVSKAYA UL.

Church of the Assumption

Gate Tower

UL ILYINKA

Church of St George

Arcade

Church of St Paraskeva

Cathedral of St Nicholas

Church of the Holy Women

Church of St Procopius

12

NOVGOROD

309

Try to time your visit to coincide with one of the festivals staged throughout the year. Towards the end of February there's the Shrovetide festival of **Maslenitsa**, with pancakes galore and traditional entertainments such as "storming the ice fortress". The **Day of Slav Culture** (May 24) honours saints Kyril and Methodius – who brought Christianity to the Slavs and invented the Cyrillic alphabet – with liturgies and bell-ringing in the Kremlin, concerts and folklore performances in churches and at the Museum of Wooden Architecture (see p.316). On the first weekend in June the museum hosts the **Sadko international folklore festival**, featuring traditional games and sideshows and lots of handicrafts and musical instruments for sale, followed by **City Day**, on the second Sunday in June, with floats, concerts, sporting events, contests and fireworks, in the Kremlin and Yaroslav's Court, on Sofiyskaya ploshchad and at the beach. Novgorod's pagan roots are revived on the **Night of Ivana Kupala** (July 6), when merrymakers jump over bonfires and go swimming in Lake Ilmen. The party is held on the far shore of the lake, some 30km from town; buses collect revellers at 5pm and bring them back in the small hours (book one month ahead; ☎8162/730 227; R450). During the **autumn**, the city hosts a variety of sporting, musical and other cultural events, that vary from year to year (see the tourist office website). The festive calendar concludes with *troika* rides and other **winter** entertainments at the Museum of Wooden Architecture (Dec 7–9 & Dec 20–Feb 15), and a carnival featuring *Ded Moroz* (Grandfather Frost) and *Snegurochka* (the Snow Maiden), on Sofiyskaya ploshchad on **New Year**'s night (Dec 31).

⑫

NOVGOROD

Things remained relatively peaceful until **World War II**, during which 98 percent of Novgorod's buildings were ruined and its population decimated as the front rolled back and forth over the city. As a matter of patriotic pride the Soviets determinedly rebuilt the Kremlin walls, the churches and the rest of the town from scratch. Today, Novgorod seems genteel and crime-free by comparison to St Petersburg, despite being on a major smuggling route. Its administration has cultivated foreign ties and investment; Novgorod belongs to the **Hanseatic League** of northern European cities and is twinned with Strasbourg under the Tacis programme for encouraging convergence with the **European Union** – Novgorod won an EU award for exemplary performance in 1997 (unlike the Novgorod Region, notorious for its corruption). The city will celebrate its **1150th anniversary** in 2009.

Orientation and information

The factories and tower blocks that you see on arrival account for much of this city of 220,000, but are easily ignored once you cross the dry moat encircling the **old town**, divided neatly in two by the sweep of the River Volkhov. The left bank, known as the **Sophia Side** (Sofiyskaya storona), is focused on the walled Kremlin, where the prince and later the archbishop resided. This oval-shaped fortress, which predates its more famous namesake in Moscow, is the obvious place to begin a tour of Novgorod.

On the opposite bank is the **Commercial Side** (Torgovaya storona), site of the old marketplace and once home to the city's rich merchants. Much of the present layout of the city dates from the reign of Catherine the Great, when the existing medieval network of narrow streets was replaced by a series of thoroughfares radiating out from the Kremlin on the left bank and running at right angles to the river on the right bank. The two sides are linked by a pedestrian footbridge from the Kremlin and a road-bridge further north.

Arriving at the bus or station on the Sophia Side, walk 800m along prospekt Karla Marksa and ulitsa Chudintseva, until you reach the main square, Sofiyskaya ploshchad, with its landmark Lenin statue. One block south of there, on Sennaya ploshchad, you'll find Novgorod's **tourist office** (daily 10am–6pm; ☏8162/773 074, ⓦhttp://visitnovgorod.ru), named the "Red Izba" (cottage) after the design of its premises. Its friendly staff can tell you anything you might want to know and may phone around on your behalf if asked nicely; a lot of info is featured on their regularly updated **website**. Across the way is another office (☏8162/739 688), sign-posted in Russian, which sells tickets for local museums and a **bus tour** (Sat & Sun at 2pm; R170) that briefly visits the Kremlin, the Commercial Side, and the Yurev, Nikolo-Vyazhishchevskiy or Khutyn monasteries outside town (see p.316).

The Kremlin

Novgorod's **Kremlin** (known locally as the *Detinets* or citadel) looks almost as mighty as Moscow's. Indeed, Muscovite architects supervised the construction of its red-brick walls at the end of the fifteenth century to supersede the stone ones raised by the Novgorodians in 1302, which in their turn replaced the original wooden ramparts erected by Prince Vladimir in 1044. Most of the **towers** date from the 1480s; their steeply pitched wooden roofs show how Moscow's Kremlin might look without the spires that were added in the seventeenth century, while a wide, overgrown ditch that encircles the centre of Novgorod marks the course of its medieval outer ring of **earthworks** (called a *val* in Russian). In olden times, as many as eighteen churches and 150 houses were crammed inside the citadel, though much of the Kremlin now consists of open space. The **walls** are best seen from the east, along the river, being obscured by trees on the western side. **Access** to the territory of the Kremlin (6am–midnight; free) is unrestricted, though the museums within observe regular opening hours.

St Sophia's Cathedral (Sofiyskiy sobor; daily 8am–1pm & 2–6pm; free) is the earliest and by far the largest of all the churches in Novgorod and has been the Kremlin's main landmark since its completion in the mid-eleventh century. Commissioned by Yaroslav the Wise, this Byzantine edifice resembles its namesake in Kiev, which Yaroslav had erected a decade earlier – it may in fact have been constructed by the same Greek master builders. As such it represents the peak of princely power in Novgorod and afterwards became a symbol of great civic pride: "Where St Sophia is, there is Novgorod" mused Prince Mstislav as Novgorod held out against the Tatars.

The cathedral's five silver bulbous domes cluster around a slightly raised, golden helmet dome topped by a stone pigeon. Legend has it that if the pigeon ever falls, Novgorod will suffer a calamity; so far the worst fate to befall it was being hit by a bullet shortly before the town was occupied by the Germans in 1942. In Soviet times the cathedral was classified as a museum and worship forbidden; like many such buildings, it was returned to the Orthodox Church in 1991. Though the exterior has long been plastered and whitewashed, it was once bare brick, as can be seen on a small patch on the northern side. The only original decorative features that survive are on the western facade, which sports a faded fresco and the splendid bronze twelfth-century **Magdeburg Doors**, made in Germany and covered with little figures in high relief (the sculptors themselves are depicted in the bottom left-hand corner).

Inside, on the far side of the nave, a framed fragment of eleventh-century fresco survives – a portrait of the Byzantine emperor Constantine and his mother Helen. Here you can also see part of the original floor, nearly 2m below the level of the current one. Other minor patches of frescoes can be seen in the cupola and on the embrasures, but most of these date from the end of the nineteenth century. The well-preserved iconostasis is one of the oldest in Russia and includes works from the eleventh to seventeenth century; to the right of the altar, encased in a box, is the famous **Icon of the Sign**, with its damaged eye (see p.315). Note also the vast chandelier, which was a present from Tsar Boris Godunov, and the ornately carved wooden chapel where Ivan the Terrible used to pray before he ravaged Novgorod. **Services** are held at 10am and 6pm every day.

To the east of the cathedral stands **St Sophia's Belfry** (Sat & Sun 10am–1pm & 1.30–5.30pm; R50), constructed during the fifteenth to seventeenth century, but drastically altered in the nineteenth century. The giant bells which once tolled from its arched upper gallery are now displayed outside in their dismantled state, but a score of smaller ones are still working, and can be seen from the rooftop, which also affords a fine **view** of the river with the Cathedral of the Nativity visible to the north.

On the other side is an octagonal **Clock Tower**, erected by Archbishop Evfimii in the fifteenth century, whose famous bell, that summoned citizens to meetings of the *veche*, was carried off to Moscow by Ivan III after he revoked Novgorod's charter of self-government. Evfimii was also responsible for the **Faceted Chamber** (Granovitaya palata), whose nondescript exterior conceals a rib-vaulted, fifteenth-century reception hall, now a high-security exhibition of ecclesiastical treasures (labelled in English) within a **Museum of Applied, Decorative and Jewellers' Art** (10am–6pm, closed Wed & the last Fri of each month; R70), that includes life-sized embroidered "portrait shrouds" of Varlaam Khutynskiy, Anthony the Roman and other local saints.

From the Millennium Monument to the Kukui Tower

At the centre of the Kremlin stands the vast, bell-shaped **Millennium Monument**, cast in iron by an English company and unveiled in 1862 on the thousandth anniversary of Rurik's arrival in Novgorod. Figures representing Mother Russia and the Orthodox Church crown the monument's giant globe, while around it (clockwise from the south) stand Rurik, Prince Vladimir, the tsars Mikhail (the first Romanov), Peter the Great and Ivan III, and lastly Dmitri Donskoy trampling a Tatar. A frieze around the base of the monument contains more than a hundred smaller figures, including Catherine the Great, Alexander Nevsky, Pushkin, Lermontov and Glinka, as well as sundry other military and artistic personages. The Nazis dismantled the 65-tonne monument during World War II, intending to transport it to Germany, but never got around to doing so. West of the monument, an **eternal flame** commemorates those who died during the fight to liberate Novgorod from Nazi occupation. Like the Tomb of the Unknown Soldier by the Kremlin walls in Moscow, it is a traditional spot for newlyweds to lay flowers and have their photographs taken.

Behind the Millennium Monument is an E-shaped administrative block where the radical writer Alexander Herzen worked in the 1840s during one of his many periods of internal exile. Now home to the **Novgorod History Museum** (10am–6pm; closed Tues & the last Thurs of each month; R90), its first floor is devoted to historical artefacts, ranging from birch-bark texts and an original segment of tree-trunk pavement from the fifteenth century to a bullet-holed bust of Tolstoy that received its wounds during the Nazi occupation. On the upper floor you'll find a splendid collection of **icons** from the Novgorod school, including *The Battle Between Novgorod and Suzdal*, which dates from the 1560s – somewhat later than the version in the Russian Museum in St Petersburg.

Beyond this, a tiny **Children's Museum** (10am–6pm; closed Tues; R60) mounts temporary exhibitions aimed at kids – but they'll have more fun climbing the **Kukui Tower** (11am–2pm & 3–7pm; closed Mon & Thurs; R60), which has a splendid **panoramic view** of the Kremlin and the Sophia Side. The last of the Kremlin towers to be built (in the seventeenth century), it embodies the lessons that Muscovite fortress builders had learned from Italian experts two centuries previously.

Outside the Kremlin

On Sovetskaya ploshchad, outside the Kremlin, the **Fine Arts Museum** (10am–6pm; closed Mon & the first Thurs of each month; R60) musters a good showing by many of the artists featured in St Petersburg's Russian Museum. Paintings to look out for include Ge's Catherine the Great smirking over the coffin of Empress Elizabeth, and a copy of his famous *Peter the Great Interrogating Tsarevich Alexei at Peterhof*; nocturnal landscapes by Aivazovsky; Repin's *Last Supper*; an orgy scene by Svedomsky; set designs by Golovin and other luminaries of the World of Art, and a vibrant *Peasant Woman* by Malevin. The top floor is devoted to work by artists from the Soviet era, including Nepromyanashchy's illustrations for Gogol's tales and Zhuravlev's Cubist *Novgorod Kremlin*.

Numerous stalls by the path from the Kremlin to Sennaya ploshchad sell souvenirs and artworks. Besides the usual *matryoshka* dolls, icons and Palekh lacquer-ware, there are traditional local **handicrafts** as well as boxes and platters made from birch bark; linen tablecloths, blouses and dresses; "bears on a seesaw" and other amusing toys – all at far lower prices than in St Petersburg or Moscow.

In summertime, residents flock to the sandy **beach** beside the Kremlin to tan themselves and bathe in the River Volkhov. Ask at the Kremlin landing stage about one-hour **river cruises** (R70–200, depending on the vessel) to the lovely wetlands at the mouth of Lake Ilmen; there may also be a disco cruise aboard the *Moskva* (Fri, Sat & Sun at 9pm; R250).

The Commercial Side

From the river bank on the east side of the Kremlin, there's a great view of the **Commercial Side** (Torgovaya storona), site of Novgorod's medieval market. More than any other Russian city, Novgorod developed a middle class of artisans and merchants thanks to its unique access to trade routes with the rest of northern Europe. During the city's medieval heyday, numerous wooden and masonry churches were built on this side of the river, funded increasingly by the mercantile class, and the market once boasted 1500 stalls selling everything from silver and bone to honey and fur – though all that remains now is a long section of the old seventeenth-century **arcade**, and beyond it, from the same period, a tent-roofed **gate tower** (10am–6pm; closed Tues, Wed & the first Mon of each month; R60) containing an exhibition of ecclesiastical artefacts.

The foundation of St Petersburg in 1703 dealt a major blow to Novgorod's commercial prosperity, and the final straw came in 1851, when the new railway linking Moscow and St Petersburg bypassed the town entirely. By the mid-nineteenth century, an English traveller found "no life left in the bazaar; customers are so rare. The principal trade seems to be that of icons."

Yaroslav's Court

The densest cluster of surviving medieval buildings is to be found immediately behind the arcade, where the palace of Yaroslav the Wise once stood in a grassy area still known as **Yaroslav's Court** (Yaroslavovo dvorishche). Its most important surviving building is the **Cathedral of St Nicholas** (Nikolskiy sobor; 10am–noon & 1–6pm; closed Mon, Tues & the last Fri of each month; R50), which once enshrined an icon that reputedly cured Yaroslav of an illness. Built in 1113 in a Byzantine style that was a deliberate challenge to St Sophia's, it originally sported a full complement of five domes, which unfortunately received a bashing in World War II. The only interior feature worth mentioning is a graphically gruesome but severely damaged fresco of Job afflicted with boils.

The neighbouring **Church of St Paraskeva** (Tserkov Paraskevy Pyatnitsi; April–Sept 11am–6pm; closed Mon & Wed; R25) was commissioned a century later by the newly ascendant local merchants and dedicated to the patron saint of commerce. Its interior is lofty yet narrow, with massive pillars upholding a cupola with traces of saints and seraphims still visible.

Beyond this are two sixteenth-century *trapeznie* churches – churches that included a refectory (*trapezna*) at the west end – which heralded the beginning of a new period of building by the Muscovite merchants who controlled Novgorod following Ivan III's occupation. The wooden-roofed **Church of the Holy Women** (Tserkov Zhon-mironosits), built in 1510 by the merchant Ivan Syrkov, and now a children's centre, is a classic example, with an arcaded refectory and a series of *kokoshniki*, or decorative wooden gables. The smaller **Church of St Procopius** (Tserkov Prokopiya), begun by Syrkov's son in 1529, likewise departed from the austere norm of Novgorod, reflecting the more fanciful tastes of its Muscovite patron; it is currently closed for repairs.

North of St Paraskeva, check out the *Na Torgu* **crafts shop** (daily 10am–7pm), before crossing the road to the former **Church of St George**, housing an exhibition called "A Walk Around Old Novgorod", with sepia photos and merchants' wares from Tsarist times (10am–noon & 1.30–6pm; closed Wed, Thurs & the last Mon of each month; R60). The nearby **Church of St John the Baptist** and **Church of the Assumption** were begun by Prince Vsevolod some years before he and his family were hounded out of Novgorod by the local nobility in 1137. Neither is open.

Beyond Yaroslav's Court

One of Novgorod's finest creations stands 500m east of Yaroslav's Court, on ulitsa Ilyina. The **Church of the Transfiguration on the Brook** (Tserkov Spasa Preobrazheniya na Ilyine; 10am–5pm; closed Mon, Tues & the last Thurs of each month; R90) was built in 1374 by the *ulichani*, or street community, which kept its bank vault on the upper floor. A standard single-domed structure with a tall drum (the steeply pitched roof is modern), the church has a facade notable for a mix of pagan and Christian symbolism – sun signs and anthropomorphic crosses, either indented or in relief – while the interior contains fragmentary fourteenth-century **frescoes**, the only documented paintings in Novgorod by Theophanes the Greek, Andrei Rublev's teacher. The best preserved are on the upper levels, depicting the Trinity, the saints David, Daniel, Semyon the older and younger, and Olympus, all seated on pillars. During the war, Germans used the church as a machine-gun nest.

Across the road stands the **Cathedral of the Sign** (Znamenskiy sobor; April–Oct 10am–5pm; Nov–March 10am–4pm; closed Wed & the first Thurs of each month; R60), built in the seventeenth-century's state-approved Muscovite style, although its surrounding outbuildings make it look more like a monastic complex. Its refectory and nave feature wonderful frescoes in hues of russet, pink and blue. To the right of the doorway, between two windows, look out for the one of Peter the Great (in a green suit) awaiting judgement for his reforms of the Orthodox Church. The cathedral's predecessor on this site was built to house the famous **Icon of the Sign**, which was carried to the walls of Novgorod's Kremlin when the town was besieged by the Suzdalians in 1169. Legend has it that when one of the enemy's arrows pierced the icon's right eye, the Virgin turned her face away to weep and the Suzdalian soldiers went blind and started killing each other in a frenzy. It is now displayed in St Sophia's Cathedral (see p.312).

Both churches stand at the crossroads of ulitsa Ilyina and **Znamenskaya ulitsa**, which is lined with the sort of picturesque **wooden houses** that characterized the majority of towns and villages in Russia before 1917, though the ones that you see here were built shortly after World War II. There are too many other churches scattered around the Commercial Side to describe them all, but two deserve special mention. On the north side of ulitsa Fyodorovskiy ruchey stands the **Church of St Theodore Stratilates** (tserkov Fyodora Stratilata; 10am–5pm; closed Thurs, Fri & the last Wed of each month; R60), the prototype for the Church of the Transfiguration on Ilyina, built by the widow and son of a wealthy merchant. It's a classic example of fourteenth-century Novgorodian architecture, a single-domed cubic structure, modestly decorated on the outside and containing fourteenth-century frescoes within.

Last but not least is the **Cathedral of the Nativity** (Rozdenstvenskiy sobor; 10am–5pm; closed Wed & the first Thurs of each month; R60), located at the far northern end of Bolshaya Moskovskaya ulitsa, 500m beyond the *Beresta Palace* (bus #1, #4 or #5). This was once the centrepiece of the Antonov Monastery (whose buildings are now occupied by Novgorod University), founded in 1125 by St Anthony the Roman, who is said to have floated all the way from Rome to Novgorod on a rock. Most of the frescoes in the cathedral date from the nineteenth century; those in the refectory hall depict the life of Anthony, whom the Russians call Antonni Rimylani.

Outside town

If you want to explore further afield, it's only a three-kilometre journey south to the shores of **Lake Ilmen**. Here you'll find the **Yurev Monastery** – the largest surviving complex of its kind in Novgorod – and the wonderful **Museum of Wooden Architecture**, which is also the site of several festivals (see box on p310). Two **convents** to the north of town are worth visiting if you're around for longer. At all these religious establishments, visitors must **dress** appropriately: long trousers for men, and headscarves and full-length skirts for women.

The weekend **bus tour** (see p.311) features one of the three localities, and each is accessible by **public transport**. For the Yurev Monastery and Museum of Wooden Architecture, catch bus #7 or #7a, running every twenty minutes, across the road from the tourist office. Less frequent services to the convents leave from the bus station, as detailed under each.

The Yurev Monastery

Once there were over twenty monasteries and convents around Novgorod, some with hundreds of monks or nuns. Forcibly suppressed in Soviet times, a few have been revived since the early 1990s, starting with the **Yurev Monastery** (Yuryev monastyr; daily 10am–8pm; free) that was founded by Prince Vsevolod in 1117, and used as a barracks by the Spanish Fascist Blue

Division in World War II. Surrounded by massive white walls and with a 52-metre-high bell tower above the entrance, the complex has now been partially restored by monks.

At its heart is the majestic **Cathedral of St George** (Georgievskiy sobor; R60), built in 1119 by a "Master Peter" who is renowned as the first truly Russian architect. As one of the final great churches to be built by the Novgorod princes, it was a last-ditch attempt to surpass St Sophia, which was by then in the hands of the archbishop. During his rape of Novgorod, Ivan the Terrible personally wrenched the icons from its iconostasis. Although twelfth-century frescoes survive here and there, most date from the nineteenth century. On the west wall is a splendid *Last Judgement*, with the Devil seated on the Beast of the Apocalypse and the dead being raised from their graves; another fresco depicts a crocodile and an elephant from Noah's ark.

The Museum of Wooden Architecture

In the woods 500m back down the road to Novgorod, the **Museum of Wooden Architecture** (muzey Derevyannovo Zodchestva; daily: April–Oct 10am–6pm; Nov–March 10am–5pm; R90) was established on the site of the ancient village of Vitoslavlitsy in the 1960s to display old timber buildings from the Novgorod region. Wood was the most practicable and readily available building material in northern Russia – from the earliest times the Novgorodians were derided by others as mere "carpenters".

The oldest buildings here date from the sixteenth century, including a wonderful **Church of the Nativity from Peredeiki** encircled by a raised gallery where the villagers would gossip after services. Most of the houses feature large lean-to barns, although the actual living quarters were much smaller, with benches on opposite sides of the room for the adults to sleep on, men on one side and women on the other. As the children slept just below the roof and grandparents above the stove, opportunities for procreation were limited to the weekly visit to the *banya* (bathhouse).

The museum hosts an annual **folk festival** and **events** marking Maslenitsa, the Day of Slav Culture, City Day, and New Year (see box on p.310).

The Nikolo-Vyazhishchevskiy and Khutyn convents

Another architectural gem in a sylvan setting is the **Nikolo-Vyazhishchevskiy Monastery** (Nikolo-Vyazhishchevskiy monastyr; daily 8am–8pm; free). First recorded in 1391, it became one of the richest monasteries under the patronage of Archbishop Evfimii, who had once been a monk there. The existing complex epitomizes the florid Muscovite style of the late seventeenth century – particularly the **Church of St John the Baptist**, linked to its belfry by a long refectory with bands of polychrome **tiles** in high relief. Across the way stands the smaller **Church of St Nicholas**, built fourteen years earlier, in 1685, with an upper summer church reached by a two-storey gallery. Since being restored a decade ago, Nikolo-Vyazhishchevskiy has been a **convent**. Located 12km north of town, it can be reached by **bus** #123 from the city bus station (at 12.20pm and 5.40pm daily, plus 6.10am and 7.10am at weekends).

The **Khutyn Monastery of the Transfiguration of the Saviour** (Khutinskiy Spaso-Preobrazhenskiy monastyr; daily 10am–5pm; free) was reputedly founded in the twelfth century on a site controlled by evil spirits, which were exorcized by monks led by Varlaam Khutynskiy (whose portrait shroud is in the Faceted Palace museum). Although the monastery was patronized by the rulers of Muscovy from the fifteenth century, its **Cathedral of the Trans-**

▲ The Museum of Wooden Architecture

figuration – built in 1515 – is closer to the Novgorod style of the previous century, with rounded apses, blind arches and an austere white facade topped by clusters of green onion domes. Like Nikolo-Vyazhishchevskiy, it has been re-consecrated as a nunnery. **Bus** #121 from Novgorod's terminal (at 6.30am, 9am and 11.25am daily – plus 1.30pm at weekends and 2.30pm on weekdays) runs all the way to the convent, 10km east of town – the journey takes half an hour, and the bus heads back to town thirty minutes later.

Practicalities

Novgorod is 186km south of St Petersburg, a three-and-a-half-hour journey by road. If you don't mind the restrictions of an **organized tour**, it's probably easiest to take your pick of the rival companies whose kiosks stand outside Gostiniy dvor, offering day-trips by coach to Novgorod (12–13hr; R750–1000). The price includes admission to whichever museums and churches are featured on the tour, but commentary is in Russian only.

Buses from St Petersburg (R250) leave roughly every hour from the bus station by the Obvodniy Canal (see map on p.214). The first departs at 7.30am; the last bus back leaves Novgorod at 8pm. If you're intending a day-trip, buy a ticket for an early bus the day before, and the return journey as soon as you arrive. Buses are air-conditioned but lack toilets, with only one pit-stop en route. **Trains** from St Petersburg are comfier but less convenient, with a slow train (5hr) from Vitebsk Station at 8am on Mondays and Tuesdays, and a daily fast service (3hr) from Moscow Station at 5.15pm. Novgorod is also accessible **from Moscow** by overnight train (8hr; arriving at 6am), and **from Ríga** by bus (Wed & Sun; 11hr 30min)

You can change **money** at *Sberbank* on the corner on Prusskaya ulitsa, or use the **ATMs** outside the tourist office or in the Kremlin's souvenir shop. There's **Internet** access at the *Skazka* café (see p.320).

Accommodation

If you fancy staying with a local English-speaking family, very pleasant **B&B** in a quiet area of the inner city can be pre-booked in St Petersburg through HOFA (see p.323). Otherwise, you can take your pick of local **hotels**, which are unlikely to be all booked up whatever the time of year – though it's worth reserving a room if you're set on staying somewhere in particular:

Akron Predtechenskaya ul. 24 ☎8162/736 918, ✉topol@mail.natm.ru. Centrally located, it has homely rooms with bathrooms and TV; "lux" ones have a lounge with tea-making gear. ❷

Beresta Palace Studentcheskaya ul. 2 ☎8162/186 910, ✉beresta@fclnovgorod.ru, ⓦwww.fclnovgorod.ru. Located 1km north of the Commercial Side, this four-star hotel has disabled access, a swimming pool, sauna and tennis courts (free for guests), a restaurant, DHL office and ATM. Buffet breakfast included. Takes Amex, DC, MC and Visa. ❹

Intourist Velikaya ul. 16 ☎8162/774 410, ✉nov@intourist.natm.ru, ⓦwww.intourist.natm.ru. This 1970s behemoth overlooking the river has clean rooms with TV and basic bathrooms, one step up from – and slightly dearer than – the *Akron*. Amex, DC, MC, Visa. ❷

Kruiz Prusskaya ul. 11 ☎8162/772 283. The cheapest place in Novgorod, its swanky lobby belies the shabby triple-bed rooms; ones with private bathrooms cost a little extra. It looks like a block of flats, with no sign outside. ❶

Rossiya nab. Aleksandra Nevskovo 19/1 ☎8162/634 185, ⓕ8162/636 086. The next cheapest option, okay in summer but chilly in winter. Some rooms have a great view of the river. There's a 25 percent reservation fee for the first night. Breakfast included. ❶

Roza Vetrov Novoluchanskaya ul. 27a ☎8162/772 033, ⓕ8162/771 463. A shabby, clean hostel on a quiet backstreet beside the *val*; rooms with shared or private bathrooms – "lux" ones have a fridge, TV, sofa, and crockery. Each floor has a kitchen and an ironing board. ❷

Sadko ul. Fyodorovskiy ruchey 16 ☎8162/660 920, ✉sadko@novline.ru, ⓦwww.veliky-novgorod.ru. A decent two-star hotel on the Commercial Side. Rooms are carpeted, with tiny bathrooms. Buffet breakfast included. ❷

Volkhov Predtechenskaya ul. 24 ☎8162/335 505, ✉volkhov@novtour.ru, ⓦwww.novtour.ru. Only a tad dearer than *Sadko*, but more central and better value; its "half-lux" suites are superior to and cost less than a standard room at the *Beresta Palace*. Amex, EC, MC, Visa. ❸

Eating, drinking and nightlife

Phone numbers are given where it's advisable to reserve in the evening.

Aziya Yakovleva ul. 22/1 ☏ 8162/272 227.
Basement café on the Sophia Side, serving Uzbek, Russian and Japanese food; in the summer it has a *shashyk* grill on the square across the road. Daily noon–midnight.

Beresta Beresta Palace Hotel ☏ 8162/186 910.
Chintzy restaurant whose menu runs the gamut from bear medallions with cranberries to Wiener schnitzel, rounded off by a strawberry flambé dessert – but not so good as other, less expensive places. Accepts Amex, DC, MC and Visa. Daily 7–11am, noon–4pm & 6–11pm.

Coffee Land ul. Chudintseva 7. Freshly brewed coffee, herbal teas, ice-cream sundaes and cakes. All major cards. Daily 11am–11pm.

Charodeyka ul. Meretskova-Volosova 1/1. Chrome and glass, indoor-outdoor café with a Euro-oriented menu of pizzas, steaks, chicken dishes, salads and ice-cream sundaes. Maestro, MC, Visa. Daily 10am–11pm.

 Detinets In the Pokrovskaya Tower of the Kremlin ☏ 8162/774 624. Medieval-style restaurant specializing in ancient Russian recipes such as baked carp, beef-in-the-pot, and drinks like *medovukha* (honey mead) and *sbittern* (a herbal concoction, served warm). Tables outdoors in the summer; live music in the evenings, when reservations are recommended. Daily noon–5pm & 7–11pm.

Dialog Bolshaya Moskovskaya ul. 37/9 ☏ 8162/662 822. An inexpensive Chinese restaurant on the Commercial Side. Mon–Fri 11am–2.30am, Sat & Sun 2.30pm–6am.

 Holmgard ul. Gazon 2 ☏ 8162/777 192. This posh restaurant above the *Ilmen Bistro* offers Russian and Scandinavian dishes cooked over an open fire, and an extensive wine list. Daily noon–midnight.

Ilmen Bistro ul. Gazon 2. Popular with teenagers and families, this self-service place has salads, burgers, Russian dishes, ice cream and tables in the park. Daily 10am–10pm.

Pridvore Lyudogoshaya ul. 3 ☏ 8162/2774 343, ⓦ www.pridvore.ru. Excellent Russian food, but you'd do best to eat in the bar rather than the restaurant, where the service is

⑫

NOVGOROD

Novgorod	Новгород
Streets and squares	
Bolshaya Moskovskaya ul.	Большая Московски ул.
Bolshaya Vlasevskaya ul.	Большая Власьевская ул.
ul. Fyodorovskiy ruchey	ул. Фёдоровский ручей
ul. Gazon	ул. Газон
ul. Ilyina	ул. Ильина
Lyudogoshaya ul.	Людогошая ул.
ul. Meretskova-Volosova	ул. Мерецкова-Волосова
Novoluchanskaya ul.	Новолучанская ул.
Predtechenskaya ul.	Предтеченская ул.
prospekt Karla Marksa	проспект Карла Маркса
Sennaya ploshchad	Сенная площадь
Sofiyskaya ploshchad	Софийская площадь
Studencheskaya ul.	Студенческая ул.
Velikaya ul.	Великая ул.
Yakovleva ul.	Яковлева ул.
Znamenskaya ul.	Знаменская ул.
Sights	
Faceted Chamber	Грановитая палата
Khutyn Monastery	Хутынский монастырь
Museum of Wooden Architecture	музей Деревянного Зодчества
Nikolo-Vyazhishchevskiy Monastery	Николо-Вяжищевский монастырь
St Sophia's Cathedral	Софийский собор
Yurev Monastery	Юрьевский монастырь

a bit slapdash. Does a cut-price weekday lunch. Maestro, MC, Visa. Noon–midnight, closed Sun.

Shkiper Studencheskaya ul. 2a Regular guests at the *Beresta Palace* slip across the hotel car park to this inexpensive roadhouse, which has tasty *shashlyk*, live Georgian music some evenings, and dancing if customers are in the mood. Mon–Fri 1pm–1am, Sat & Sun 1pm–3am.

Skazka ul. Meretskova-Volosova 13. Cheery, kid-centred café with slot machines and Internet. Hosts summer barbecues and live music in the evenings. Children's menu. MC, Union, Visa. Daily noon–midnight.

Volkhov Volkhov Hotel ☎8162/335 509. Better value for money than the *Beresta* if you're going to splurge. Try the salmon appetizer, the veal medallions with mushroom sauce or stuffed pike-perch from Lake Ilmen, with a chocolate and coffee mousse to follow. Amex, EC, MC, Visa. Daily 7am–midnight.

Listings

Listings

13

Accommodation

A ccommodation is likely to be by far the largest chunk of your daily expenditure, with most half-decent hotels or mini-hotels charging over €60–80 for a double room in high season. In the past, the system was biased towards package tourists, but independent travellers can now compare rates on hotel websites with those being quoted by accommodation **agencies** (see overleaf), and the range of accommodation has opened up: many apartments are available for rent and well-run mini-hotels offer better value than the aged Soviet hotels that used to be the only option for those who couldn't afford deluxe establishments.

While the supply of accommodation has improved enormously, it still falls short of demand in June, July and August, making **reservations** essential at this time. Everywhere charges more in **high season** (June–Sept, Christmas, New Year and Easter); some charge mid-season rates in May; during October, November, February, March and April, **low-season** rates are 30–50 percent less than in high season.

Really cheap accommodation is hard to find in high season; **low-budget travellers** are limited to hostels and a few sub-average mini-hotels. If you can bear to miss the White Nights, you'll get far more for your money; stylish mini-hotels or luxury apartments can be excellent value in low season and even top-class hotels offer attractive rates.

The acceptability of **credit cards** in listings below is indicated by the abbreviations: Amex = American Express; DC = Diners Club; EC = Eurocard; JCB = Japanese Credit Bank; MC = MasterCard. Russia's central bank levies a small **surcharge** on card transactions initiated abroad, and some mini-hotels prefer bank transfers instead.

Visas and registration

While **visas and registration** (see p.28) are taken care of for package tourists, independent travellers require visa support and must be registered once in St Petersburg. Large **hotels** can register guests for the duration of their hotel stay, however they obtained their visa support – a few places have a sideline in registering "virtual" guests on behalf of mini-hotels that aren't legally able to. Depending on their legal status, some mini-hotels offer visa support for a fee per person; registration may cost extra, if handled by an agency. Visa support is also available online for tourists booking hotel rooms and maybe also **homestay** or **flat rental**. In the case of the last two, only the company that issued your visa invitation is legally allowed to register you, so it's vital that they have an office (or accredited partner) in St Petersburg. Similarly, **hostels** may only register guests who got their visa support from the hostel (or its partner). Beware of staying somewhere that can do neither, as this will leave you liable to a fine if you can't find somebody to register you. The Way to Russia website (ⓦ www. waytorussia.net) spells out the **current regulations** in all their Kafkaesque complexity.

The **cost of visa support** cited for accommodation agencies or individual hotels listed below refers to visa support for a single person for a regular tourist visa.

Accommodation agencies

Accommodation agencies and the Internet allow tourists to shop around for **discounts** at hotels. This applies equally to deluxe hotels such as the *Astoria*, old Soviet behemoths, and the many new mini-hotels that market themselves online while staying invisible at street level. As a rule, the prices in our listings refer to rack rates, and you should be able to save anything from €20 to €100 by booking through an agency rather than the hotel itself. Some of the agencies below have **walk-in offices** in St Petersburg that can arrange a room on the spot; others only do business **online** and may need several days' notice if visa support is required.

All Hotels of Russia ⓦ www.all-hotels.ru. One of Russia's leading online agencies, offering discounts at over twenty hotels in St Petersburg, apartments from R16000 a week in the centre, or R6000 in the suburbs. Their website has a currency converter.

Arent ☎ 715 03 26 (24hr), ⓦ www .apartment-rentals-russia.com. Economy (from R1250 per night), standard (from R1750) and elite (from R5000) apartments in the centre; visa support (R700) and registration (R350). Payment by MC or Visa.

B&B Rinaldi ☎ 325 41 88 (24hr), ⓦ www.rinaldi. ru. Operates mini-hotels on Vasilevskiy Island, the Petrograd Side and all over downtown, plus the *Antonio House* hostel. Visa support (R550), transfers and other services. Takes DC, EC, MC, Union and Visa.

Bed & Breakfast Nevskiy pr. 74 ☎ 325 65 36, ⓦ www.discount-travel-petersburg.ru; **10min walk from Mayakovskaya or Gostiniy Dvor metro.** The office in the yard does bookings at their hostels (see p.335) and comfortable (from R5000 a night) or deluxe (from R5600) apartments in the centre; visa support (R750), registration (R500) and airport transfers (R1000). Payment by bank transfer or in cash; no cards. Mon–Fri 10am–6pm.

Central Real Estate Agency Nevskiy pr. 107 ☎ 324 99 22, ⓦ www.allestate.ru/enrent. phb; 5min walk from Ploshchad Vosstaniya metro. Has a wide range of apartments for short- or long-term rental. Open Mon–Fri 10am–9pm, Sat & Sun 10am–7pm.

City Realty Muchnoy per. 2 ☎ 570 63 42, ⓦ www.cityrealtyrussia.com; 5min walk from Sadovaya/Sennaya Ploshchad metro. An American-owned firm with apartments for all budgets, which does visa support (R750) and registration (R1050). Mon–Fri 9.30am–6.30pm.

Flatmate.Ru ⓦ http:flatmate.ru. English/Russian language website for flat-sharers and landlords to get in contact, set up by Way to Russia (see below).

Host Families Accommodation (HOFA) ⓦ www. hofa.ru. Homestay B&B (from R665 per person) and apartment rental (from R1930 a night) in the centre; transfers, tours, excursions and language tuition in St Petersburg and other cities.

Hotels Reservation Centre ⓦ www.hotels.msk. ru. Online agency with a range of hotels in St Petersburg and throughout Russia, priced in euros or dollars.

Lodging.ru ⓦ www.lodging.ru. Russian agency offering discounts at a dozen or so hotels in St Petersburg and other cities in Russia, priced in euros or dollars.

Nevsky Hotels ☎ 703 38 60, ⓦ www.hon.ru. Owns six mini-hotels (see listings) on or just off Nevskiy, and several luxury apartments with saunas and/or Jacuzzis, sleeping three (R10500 nightly) or four (R15000). Visa support (R1050), transfers and other services.

Oksana's ⓦ www.oksanas.net. Agent for over 30 flats in the centre, starting at R4550 a night for a one-bedroom apartment with all mod cons. Visa support R700; registration R700.

Ost-West Kontaktservice Nevskiy pr. 105 ☏327 34 16, ⓦwww.ostwest.com; 5min walk from Ploshchad Vosstaniya metro. Their office in the yard near pl. Vosstaniya does bookings at mini-hotels and apartments (from R2700); visa support (R1680) and one month's registration (R600) are free if you book accommodation through the agency. Mon–Fri 10am–6pm.

Russian Guide Network ⓦwww .russianguidenetwork.com. This website offers local guides, links and warts-and-all reviews of hotels and guesthouses in St Petersburg; prices are out of date but most of the remarks still hold true.

Russian St Petersburg Tours Maliy pr. 87, Petrograd Side ☏974 03 73, ⓦwww.russian-st-petersburg.com; 5min walk from Petrogradskaya metro. Runs a language school

and arranges B&B (R875), hotel and hostel bookings, visa support and registration (R700 each).

St Petersburg Hotels Guide ⓦwww.hotels.spb. ru. Discount bookings at diverse hotels, and homestay from R1250. Visa support, registration and airport transfers.

Way to Russia ⓦwww.waytorussia.net. Russia-based travel portal offering apartments (from R1250 a night), visa support (R750) and registration (R500), Russian railway bookings and many other tourist services and links.

Windows on Nevsky ☏272 26 32, ⓦwww. w-o-n.ru. Local agency (daily 10am–6pm) that rents two-bed apartments on or just off Nevskiy (from R3375 per night in high season). Free visa support and registration for clients.

Hotels and guesthouses

St Petersburg now has a huge array of **hotels**, from multinational chains to chic mini-hotels or guesthouses with real character. While medium-sized and large hotels are highly visible, **mini-hotels** and **guesthouses** keep a low profile – and may not even be licensed. Many occupy former flats within apartment blocks, which are typically arranged round an inner **courtyard** (*dvor*), accessible from the street via an archway, with several public **stairways** to separate parts of the complex. These are often dirty and gloomy, but some fabulous places exist in run-down buildings. The **security** of these communal areas may be non-existent, or depend on a code being input into the outer door (see "Flat rental"); some *dvor* are gated, with a bell to ring for access and CCTV. Identifying the right entrance can be difficult; many have only a tiny **sign** or no sign at all. If any doubt exists

Accommodation prices

The accommodation lists below are divided into areas; within each section the lists are arranged alphabetically. All accommodation has been coded according to the price categories below (in rubles, with approximate euro equivalents):

❶ Under R1000   under €30
❷ R1000–2000   €30–60
❸ R2000–3000   €60–85
❹ R3000–4000   €85–115
❺ R4000–6000   €115–170
❻ R6000–8000   €170–230
❼ R8000–10000   €230–285
❽ R10000–15000   €285–430
❾ Over R15000   over €430

All prices are for the **cheapest double room available in high season** (which may mean without a private bath or shower in the very cheapest places). For a single room, expect to pay around two-thirds of the price. During low season, rates are usually 30–50 percent lower. The prices given in this guide include service and city taxes.

or you need to know the current door-code (some change at intervals), call ahead to obtain the exact details.

When selecting a hotel, consider its **location**. With lots of options within the Fontanka, off Liteyniy prospekt or the lower end of Nevskiy, and the "central" areas of Vasilevskiy Island and the Petrograd Side, there's no need to stay in the suburbs unless you're on an especially tight budget or leave finding somewhere till the last moment. Proximity to a **metro** station is certainly advantageous, but some places are relatively far from one while still being in **walking** distance of many sights, in atmospheric quarters of the inner city. Check our chapter maps for locations.

Rooms overlooking major roads will suffer from traffic **noise** unless they have sound-proofing or are at least four floors above street level, and from **air pollution** if you have to open the windows to cope with the sultry heat of summer. At this time of year, **mosquitoes** are a serious pest – especially near canals and rivers (which means much of the city centre) – making **air-conditioning** (a/c) a real plus. If it doesn't exist, the room's *fortochka* (small ventilation window) should be screened to keep mosquitoes out (if not, buy a Raptor device, see p.32).

The system of **rating** hotels with stars should be taken with a pinch of salt. When a hotel was built (or last refurbished) is more important. Whereas two-star hotels are always 1950s low-rises with matchbox rooms, often without en-suite facilities, three-star hotels may be refitted 1970s complexes with restaurants and nightclubs, or brand-new mini-hotels that can be as stylish as four- and five-star hotels, built and run to international standards. While the cheapest rooms at old hotels may lack en-suite **bathrooms**, these are generally mandatory for three-stars upwards. **Decor** is age-related, too; places basically unchanged since Soviet times (described in our reviews by the shorthand *sovok*, a slang term for Soviet that literally means "dustpan") have ugly wallpaper, stained carpets, shoddy furniture and beds that are too short. *Sovok* may also describe places that have been refurbished using the cheapest furnishings. Conversely, hotels or guesthouses may have antiques or artworks in the rooms.

At larger hotels you'll receive a **guest card** that enables you to pass the security guards and claim your room key – don't lose it. Top hotels have electronic card keys for improved security. Most big hotels have a **service bureau**, which can obtain theatre tickets and suchlike. In older hotels, each floor is monitored by a **concierge** or *dezhurnaya*, who will keep your key while you're away and can arrange to have your laundry done.

Within the Fontanka

If you're looking for a location near the major sights, this is it. Here are some of the city's premier hotels – but also a fair number of reasonably priced mini-hotels, many in the atmospheric quarters between St Isaac's Cathedral and the Fontanka. All the accommodation in this section is marked on the Within the Fontanka map on pp.62–63, unless otherwise stated.

Admiral nab. kanala Griboedova 33, apt. 7 ☎571 09 13, ⓦwww.admiralhotel.ru (in Russian); 15min walk from Nevskiy Prospekt/Gostiniy Dvor metro. See map on pp.64–65. Beside a canal not far off Nevskiy, this inexpensive

mini-hotel has rooms with or without showers. Press *280# at the gate, turn left inside the arch and input door-code *345#. No cards. ❸

Ambassador pr. Rimskovo-Korsakova 5–7 ☎331 88 44, ⓦwww.ambassador-hotel.ru; 10min walk from Sadovaya/Sennaya Ploshchad metro. Quite close to the Mariinskiy, this chic four-star hotel has excellent disabled facilities, a 16-metre pool, and large rooms with plasma TVs. Free visa support. All major cards. ❻

Andrey & Sasha Gorokhovaya ul. 3, sixth floor (see map on p.94); nab. kanala Griboedova 49, fifth floor ☎mobile 7921/409 6701, ⓔasamatuga@mail.ru; both 15min walk from Nevskiy Prospekt/Gostiniy Dvor metro. Two cosy arty B&Bs sleeping up to four; the

Gorokhovaya one is in the inner yard, with no lift. Andrey and Sasha are fantastic hosts who often cook for guests. No cards. ❸

Angleterre Malaya Morskaya ul. 24 ☎494 56 66, ⓦwww.angleterrehotel.com; 15min walk from Nevskiy Prospekt/Gostiniy Dvor metro. See map on p.94. A stone's throw from St Isaac's, this historic five-star annexe to the *Astoria* shares its facilities. Breakfast R1000. All major cards. ❽

Arkadia nab. reki Moyki 58A ☎571 61 73, ⓦwww.arkadiahotel.ru; 15min walk from Sadovaya/Sennaya Ploshchad metro. See map on p.94. On the Moyka, not far from St Isaac's, this small purpose-built hotel has a/c en-suite rooms (the attic suites are especially stylish), a sauna and plunge pool. Amex, Cirrus, Maestro, MC, Visa. ❺

Asteria nab. reki Fontanki 71 ☎337 24 04, ⓔinfo@asteriahotel.ru; 15min walk from Sadovaya or Pushkinskaya metro. Rooms with baths, hair-dryers and Internet access, over-looking the Fontanka. No cards. ❹

Astoria Bolshaya Morskaya ul. 39 ☎494 57 57, ⓦwww.thehotelastoria.com; 15min walk from Nevskiy Prospekt/Gostiniy Dvor metro. See map on p.94. Five-star big brother to the *Angleterre*, that's played host to Lenin and Thatcher. Rooms are light and airy but with-out a/c; the decor is a mix of Art Nouveau and Classical. Breakfast R1000. All major cards. ❾

Ave Caesar Bolshaya Konyushennaya ul. 25 ☎314 54 82, ⓦwww.cezar-hotel.ru; 5min from Nevskiy Prospekt/Gostiniy Dvor metro. See map on p.80. Dead central; all rooms with show-ers and Wi-Fi, some with Jacuzzis and one with a circular bed and mirrors. Amex, MC, Visa. ❺

B&B Randhouse Bolshaya Morskaya ul. 25, apt. 17 ☎314 63 63; Malaya Mor-skaya ul. 7, apt. 1 ☎570 45 97; per. Gritsova 11, apt. 83 ☎310 70 75, ⓦwww.randhouse.ru; the first two 15min walk from Nevskiy Prospekt/ Gostiniy Dvor metro, and marked on the map on p.94; the last right by Sadovaya/Sennaya Ploshchad metro. Three cool mini-hotels named after the St Petersburg-born libertar-ian philosopher Ayn Rand; some rooms with fireplaces, the cheapest sharing bathrooms. Visa support R900. No cards. ❷

Belveder-Nevsky Bolshaya Konyushennaya ul. 29 ☎571 83 38, ⓦwww.belveder-nevsky.spb. ru; 5min walk from Nevskiy prospekt/Gostiniy dvor metro. See map on p.80. Just off Nevskiy, this small business-hotel has a/c, Internet,

voicemail and a Swedish buffet breakfast. Amex, Maestro, MC, Union, Visa. ❺

Casa Leto Bolshaya Morskaya ul. 34 ☎314 66 22, ⓦwww.casaleto.com; 15min from Nevskiy Prospekt/Gostiniy Dvor metro. See map on p.94. Ultra-chic non-smok-ing boutique hotel reached by a shabby-grand stairwell. Complimentary fruit and refreshments. Visa support R550. Amex, MC, Visa; discount for cash payment. ❻

Columb Kazanskaya ul. 41☎315 70 93, ⓦwww. columbhotel.com; 10min walk from Sadovaya/ Sennaya Ploshchad metro. Three comfy a/c rooms near the Haymarket district. Internet. Ask for the door code. Major cards. ❹

Dolce Vita nab. kanala Griboedova 34 ☎310 50 72; 10min walk from Gostiniy Dvor metro. See map on pp.64–65. This canal-side mini-hotel has small, cosy en-suite rooms with fridges and TVs. No cards. ❹

Ermitage Millionnaya ul. 11 ☎571 54 97, ⓦwww.ermitage.spb.ru; 20min walk from Nevskiy Prospekt/Gostiniy Dvor metro. See map on p.80. An elegant, intimate nest in the former mansion of Tsar Paul's mistress, near the Hermitage. Major cards. ❺

Fortecia Millionnaya ul. 29 (in the yard) ☎315 08 28, ⓦwww.fortecia.ru (in Russian); 15min walk from Nevskiy Prospekt/ Gostiniy Dvor metro. See map on p.80. Quiet, comfy, rather small a/c rooms, right by the Hermitage. No cards. ❹

Grand Hotel Europe Mikhailovskaya ul. 1/7 ☎329 60 00, ⓦwww.grandhotel-europe.com; near Nevskiy Prospekt/Gostiniy Dvor metro. See map on pp.64–65. The best-situated five-star hotel in the city; Clinton, Kohl and Sharon

▼ The Grand Hotel Europe

Stone have enjoyed its marbled magnificence. All rooms have huge bathrooms and a/c; the fancier suites are virtual Art Nouveau museum pieces. Non-smoking floor. Sauna, solarium and gym. Amex, DC, MC, Visa. ❻

🏃 **Korona** Malaya Konyushennaya ul. 7, apt. 68 ☎571 00 86, ⓦwww.korona-spb.com; 5min walk from Nevskiy Prospekt metro. See map on p.80. Unmarked at street level (press the "call" button beside door #8), this mini-hotel's discretion is matched by its comfort. All rooms with a/c and satellite TV; suites with Jacuzzis; sauna. EC, Maestro, MC, Visa. ❺

Matisov Domik nab. reki Pryazhki 3/1 ☎495 02 42, ⓦwww.matisov.spb.ru; bus #22 from Gostiniy Dvor metro. A comfy villa-type hotel within walking distance of the Mariinskiy but little else. En-suite rooms with satellite TV; suites have kitchens. Secure parking. MC, Visa. ❻

🏃 **Moyka 5** nab. reki Moyki 5 ☎601 06 36, ⓦwww.hon.ru; 15min walk from Nevskiy Prospekt/Gostiniy Dvor metro. See map on p.80. One of the best Nevsky Hotels (see below), only 5mins from the Hermitage. Some rooms have Jacuzzis or saunas. Major cards. ❻

Na Muchnom Sadovaya ul. 25 (entrance on Muchnoy per.) ☎310 04 12, ⓦwww.namuchnom.ru; 10min walk from Sadovaya/Sennaya Ploshchad metro. A cheap sovok hotel in *Crime and Punishment* territory; most rooms share bathrooms. DC, JCB, MC, Visa. ❷

Na Sadovy Sadovaya ul. 53 ☎314 45 10, ⓦwww.nasadovy.spb.ru (in Russian); 10min walk from Sadovaya/Sennaya Ploshchad metro. Similar to Na Muchnom: clean, cheap and *sovok*; enter the yard and turn right to find it. No cards. ❷

Nevsky Aster Bolshaya Konyushennaya ul. 25 ☎336 65 85, ⓦwww.hon.ru; 5min walk from Nevskiy prospekt/Gostiniy dvor metro. See map on p.80. Just off Nevskiy, this place is less stylish than other Nevsky Hotels but comfy enough. Major cards. ❺

Nevsky Deluxe Bolshaya Konyushennaya ul. 14 ☎312 31 31, ⓦwww.hon.ru; directions as above. See map on p.80. Another Nevsky Hotel on the same street, with seven large a/c rooms (two with Jacuzzis) and free Wi-Fi. Major cards. ❻

Nevsky Grand Bolshaya Konyushennaya ul. 10 ☎336 65 60; directions as above. See map on p.80. The third and largest Nevsky Hotel on

the street has a range of rooms, some with saunas or Jacuzzis. Major cards. ❻

Nevsky Inn Kirpiichniy per. 2, apt. 19 ☎972 68 73, ⓦwww.nevskyinn.ru; 10min walk from Nevskiy Prospekt metro. See map on pp.64–65. Airy en-suite rooms sharing a kitchen and bar area with free Internet access, just off Nevskiy. The door-code is 19B. Visa support R900. No cards. ❹

🏃 **Petro Palace** Malaya Morskaya ul. 14 ☎571 28 80, ⓦwww.petropalacehotel.com; 15min walk from Nevskiy Prospket metro. See map on p.94. Besides its central location, this smart new four-star has a pool, fitness centre and sauna, and fine views from its seventh floor. Free visa support. Breakfast R500. All major credit (not debit) cards. ❼

Polikoff Nevskiy pr. 64/11, apt. 24–26 ☎955 34 88, ⓦwww.polikoff.net; 10min walk from Gostiniy Dvor metro. See map on pp.64–65. Enter the door on Karavanaya ulitsa, then punch code #26 to access this non-smoking mini-hotel on the fourth floor (no lift), with quiet, comfy rooms, free Wi-Fi and a Swedish buffet breakfast. Visa support R1230. No cards. ❹

Premiere ul. Soyuz Pechatnikov 4 ☎714 18 77, ⓦwww.spbhotel.com; 20min walk from Sadovaya metro. A low-key mini-hotel near the Mariinskiy and the Synagogue, reached by a communal stairway. No cards. ❹

🏃 **Pushka Inn** nab. reki Moyki 14 ☎312 09 13, ⓦwww.pushkainn.ru; 15min walk from Nevskiy Prospekt metro. See map on p.80. Chic rooms and apartments with Wi-Fi and satellite TV, on a lovely canal beside Pushkin's apartment. Breakfast R350. All cards except Amex. ❻

🏃 **Rachmaninov** Kazanskaya ul. 5, ☎571 74 66, ⓦwww.hotelrachmaninov.com; 5min walk from Nevskiy Prospekt/Gostiniy Dvor metro. See map on pp.64–65. A boutique hotel in the composer's former home near the Kazan Cathedral, with an art gallery, antiques and Wi-Fi. Visa support R350. All cards except Amex. ❺

Renaissance St Petersburg Baltic Pochtamtskaya ul. 4 ☎380 40 00, ⓦwww.marriott.com/ledbr; 20min walk from Gostiniy Dvor or Sadovaya metro. See map on p.94. Smaller than the other five-stars but no less grand, with a stunning lobby and atrium; boutique rooms (some for wheelchair users, others on two levels); gym, sauna and solarium. All major cards. ❽

Residence Gorokhovaya ul. 8, third floor ☎312 73 77, ⓦwww.residencehotels.ru; 15min walk from Nevskiy Prospekt/Gostiniy Dvor metro. See map on p.94. One of several mini-hotels on this street between St Isaac's and the Hermitage, it has large, high-ceilinged a/c rooms with proper baths. Free visa support. No cards. ❺

Solo Gorokhovaya ul. 3, apt. 17 ☎315 93 00, ⓦwww.solo-hotel.ru (in Russian); 15min walk from Nevskiy Prospekt metro. See map on p.94. This second-floor mini-hotel near St Isaac's has a/c rooms with Wi-Fi. All cards except Amex. ❸

Sonata Gorokhovaya ul. 3, apt. 20 ☎315 51 12, ⓦwww.hotel-sonata.com; directions as above. See map on p.94. Two floors above the Solo, this slightly inferior place has some rooms with baths. All cards except Amex. ❺

Staraya Vena (Old Vienna) Gorokhovaya ul. 8, second floor ☎312 93 39, ⓦwww.vena.old-spb.ru; directions as above. See map on p.94. In the same building as the Residence, this stylish Freud-themed mini-hotel has Wi-Fi, spacious a/c doubles and a lovely breakfast room. Amex, MC, Visa. ❺

St Petersburg City Guide nab. kanala Griboedova 29, ☎312 69 28, ⓦwww.petersburg-hotel.com; 5min walk from Nevskiy Prospekt metro. See map on pp.64–65. By a lovely bridge on the Griboedov Canal, on the left as you enter the yard; look for the door of flat #9 – there's no sign to identify this Swiss-owned mini-hotel. ❸

Swiss Star nab. reki Fontanki 93/26 ☎929 2793, ⓦwww.swiss-star.ru. 5min walk from Sennaya Ploshchad/Sadovaya metro. Clean Swiss-run mini-hotel on the Fontanka; the cheapest rooms share bathrooms. Visa support R1250. No cards. ❸

Turgenev Bolshaya Konyushennaya ul. 13 ☎314 45 29; 5min walk from Nevskiy prospekt/Gostiniy dvor metro. See map on p.80. Near the Church of the Saviour on the Blood, this family guesthouse is furnished with antiques, and will meet guests at the airport for free. No cards. ❺

Vasilevskiy Island

Location is everything on Vasilevskiy. The low-numbered *linii* (see p.154) are within walking distance of a metro, whereas Gavan and Primorskiy are bleak high-rise zones, where you have to rely on minibuses to reach Primorskaya metro or "mainland" St Petersburg. The nicest hotels are in the vicinity of Vasileostrovskaya metro station (which gets ridiculously crowded in rush hour) or Sportivnaya metro on the Petrograd Side (which doesn't). All the accommodation below is marked on the map on pp.152–153.

Morskoy Vokzal pl. Morskoy Slavy 1 ☎322 60 40. ⓦwww.mvhotel.ru; minibus #128 or #129 from Nevskiy pr. A 1970s monstrosity above the Sea Terminal, far from anything except the D-2 submarine, it has decent rooms and a Swedish buffet breakfast. Amex, DC, JCB, MC. ❻

Park Inn Pribaltiyskaya ul. Korablestroiteley 14 ☎329 26 26, ⓦwww.parkinn.com.ru; minibus #128 or #129 from Nevskiy pr., or #162 from Primorskaya metro. This colossal hotel beside the Gulf features an amazing aqua park, a bowling alley and a ballroom. Rooms are on the small size, but have a/c, TV and fridge. Free visa support. Major cards. ❻

Prestige 3-ya liniya 52, block 4H ☎328 50 11, ⓦwww.prestigehotel.spb.ru; 10min walk from Vasileostrovskaya or Sportivnaya metro. Groovy Austin Powers-style pad with comfy en-suite rooms with satellite TV; it's worth paying R600 extra for a suite with a Jacuzzi. Free visa support. All major cards. ❺

Rinaldi on Vasilevskiy Maliy pr. 6 ☎323 21 55, ⓦwww.rinaldi.ru; 10min walk from Vasileostrovskaya metro. Cramped, clean mini-hotel facing a yard; turn left once through the arch. Four en-suite rooms with a budget feel, plus a small kitchen. Major cards. ❹

Shelfort 3-ya liniya 26 ☎323 36 26, ⓦwww.shelfort.ru; 10min walk from Vasileostrovskaya metro. Occupying two floors of an ornate 1900s building, this mini-hotel boasts large rooms (two with antique fireplaces), Wi-Fi and a great breakfast (R150). Visa support R350. Major cards. ❺

SPB Vergaz 7-ya liniya 70 ☎327 88 83, ⓔhotel@vergaz.spb.ru; 5min walk from Vasileostrovskaya metro. An excellent choice, with a smart lobby, en-suite rooms with cable TV, an apartment with a kitchen, and a bar/café and sauna. Breakfast R250. No cards. ❹

Petrograd Side and the Kirov Islands

Petrograd Side is an interesting location, with a reasonable range of accommodation. All the hotels listed below are marked on the map on pp.168–169.

Amsterdam nab. reki Karpovki 14 ☏347 56 55, ⓦwww.eurasia-hotel.spb. ru; 5min walk from Petrogradskaya metro. A dinky Dutch-themed place with satellite TV, bathrobes, hairdryers and Wi-Fi in its rooms – ask for one at the back. Maestro, MC, Visa. ❸

Amulet Bolshoy pr. 5, apt. 12 ☏235 82 32, ⓦwww.amulet-hotels.ru; 5min walk from Sportivnaya metro. Simple, clean, en-suite rooms with TV and fridges, near Freud's Dream Museum. Non-smoking throughout. No cards. ❸

Andersen ul. Chapygina 4 ☏740 51 40, ⓦwww. andersenhotel.ru; 5min walk from Petrogradskaya metro. A new, anodyne business hotel where a room with a Jacuzzi is affordable, with lower rates at weekends. Visa support (R670). Amex, DC, JCB, MC, Visa. ❺

Aurora Malaya Posadskaya ul. 15 ☏233 36 41, ⓦwww.hotel-aurora.ru; 10min walk from Gorkovskaya metro. In the block behind the one facing the street, this cosy mini-hotel has rooms with TVs, and fridges, with showers or sharing facilities. Visa support (R700). No cards. ❸

Guyot ul. Professora Popova 23 ☏347 56 28, ⓦwww.guyot.spb.ru; 15min walk from Petrogradskaya metro. A boutique business hotel with a pool, sauna, *banya* and gym, behind a business centre on Apetarskiy Island. Free visa support and registration. DC, EC, MC, Visa. ❼

Iskra Malaya Posadskaya ul. 10/1 ☏230 60 27, ⓦwww.iskrahotel.ru; 5min walk from Gorkovskaya metro. Named after the Bolshevik newspaper, this quiet ground-floor mini-hotel has en-suite rooms with TV and fridges. Internet. Visa support (R1050). No cards. ❸

Nord Kamennoostrovskiy pr. 73/75 (access via ul. Akademika Pavlova, through the yard), seventh floor ☏234 39 30, ⓦwww.hotelnord.spb.ru; 15min walk from Petrogradskaya metro. A stylish attic minihotel with ten spacious, sun-drenched rooms, a bar and communal zone. Swedish buffet breakfast. Under-12s stay for free. No cards. ❹

Piter pr. Dobrolyubova 5/1 ☏325 15 18; 10min walk from Sportivnaya metro. Its tiny rooms mar what might otherwise be a good option, within walking range of the Peter and Paul Fortress and the Strelka, with a sauna and billiards. No cards. ❸

Regina ul. Podrezova 21 ☏230 35 65, ⓦwww. eurasia-hotel.spb.ru; 10min walk from Petrogradskaya metro. Sister hotel to the *Amsterdam*, in a modern building with underground parking, on a quiet backstreet. Maestro, MC, Visa. ❹

Rinaldi at Petrogradskaya Bolshoy pr. 74 (entrance via ul. Podrezova) ☏232 15 12, ⓦwww.rinaldi.ru; 10min walk from Petrogradskaya metro. Small IKEA-ish rooms with bathroom, TV and sound-proofed windows. MC, Visa. ❸

Liteniy, Smolniy and Vladimirskaya

There are many mini-hotels on, or just off, Nevskiy, which complement the three-star megaliths that have been around since the 1970s and luxury piles catering to business travellers. All the accommodation below is marked on the map on pp.192–193.

Altburg Liteyniy pr. 35, third floor ☏327 00 99, ⓦwww.altburg.ru; 15min walk from Mayakovskaya or Chernyshevskaya metro. Cosy en-suite rooms, a large a/c suite and a minikitchen. No cards. ❹

Amadeo Nevskiy pr. 108 ☏579 69 96, ⓦwww. amadeo-hotel.ru (in Russian); near Mayakovskaya/Ploshchad Vosstaniya metro. A quiet mini-hotel in a rear yard off Nevskiy, with a cheery decor and a/c throughout. MC, Visa. ❹

Aolla 10-ya Sovetskaya ul. 11 ☏271 31 05, ⓦwww.hotelaolla.ru (in Russian); trolleybus #5 or #7 from Ploshchad Vosstaniya metro. Small, clean *sovok* rooms at the back of a yard in an out-of-the-way location. Registration R400. No cards. ❸

Art House ul. Marata 10-6, third floor ☏572 37 26, ⓦwww.arthousehotel. ru; 5min walk from Mayakovskaya/Ploshchad Vosstaniya metro. Press #6B at street level to reach this funky mini-hotel with variously styled rooms (Moroccan, medieval, etc) and a kitchen. Visa support R750; registration R300.No cards. ❸

Aurora Central Ligovskiy pr. 21 ☏275 12 50, ⓦwww.hotel-aurora.ru; 5min walk from

Ploshchad Vosstaniya metro. A dozen elegant rooms with baths, a/c and cable TV, not far off Nevskiy. Visa support R350. All major cards. **❺**

Austrian Yard Furshtatskaya ul. 45 ☏279 82 35, ⓦwww.austrianyard.com; 5min walk from Chernyshevskaya metro. In a gated yard near the Tauride Garden. Rooms with satellite TV and bathrooms decorated with Egyptian hieroglyphs; sauna, billiards and secure parking. No cards. **❹**

Ave Caesar Stremyannaya ul. 14 ☏764 29 15, ⓦwww.cezar-hotel.ru; 5min walk from Ploshchad Vosstaniya/Mayakovskaya metro. Similar to their other hotel on Bolshaya Konyushennaya, with a/c, Wi-Fi and slightly *sovok* decor. Amex, MC, Visa. **❺**

🏃 **Bubyr's Guesthouse** Stremyannaya ul. 11, apt. #10 ☏mobile: 79046021340, ⓦwww.bubyrs.com; directions as above. A lovely sixth-floor flat furnished with antiques, *Japanoiserie* and contemporary art, with a bar, kitchen, library and free fruit. The owners have another at ul. Marata 22–24, near the Arctic and Antarctic Museum. **❹**

🏃 **Butterfly** Vladimirskiy pr. 1, third floor ☏982 11 77, ⓦwww.butterfly-hotel.ru; 5min walk from Mayakovskaya metro. In the same building as two other mini-hotels, just off Nevskiy. Pleasant a/c rooms with fridges (some sharing bathrooms) and an apartment with a kitchen. MC, Visa. **❹**

Dostoyevsky Vladimirskiy pr. 19 ☏331 32 00, ⓦwww.dostoyevsky-hotel.ru; by Dostoyevskaya metro. Near Dostoyevsky's last residence, this plush hotel above the Vladimirskiy Passage mall has a/c sound-insulated rooms, some for disabled guests. Amex, MC, Visa. **❼**

Egoeast Vladimirskiy pr. 1, second floor ☏982 11 77, ⓦwww.tourworld.ru/index_eng.htm; 5min walk from Mayakovskaya metro. Four business-class rooms, one floor below the *Butterfly*. Free visa support and registration. Maestro, MC, Visa. **❺**

Ekologiya Degtyarnaya ul. 15 ☏271 52 02, ⓔymcekolog@peterstar.ru; minibus #147 from Ploshchad Vosstaniya metro. Clean *sovok* rooms in a remote location. Little English spoken. Registration R500. No cards. **❹**

Fifth Corner Zagorodniy pr. 13 ☏380 81 81, ⓦwww.5ugol.ru (in Russian); 5min walk from Vladimirskaya/Dostoevskaya metro. Overlooking "Five Corners" (see p.209), it combines minimalist chic with 1950s retro and Wi-Fi. Major cards. **❺**

Golden Garden Vladimirskiy pr. 9 ☏572 22 33, ⓦwww.hotel.goldengarden.ru; 10min walk from Mayakovskaya or Dostoyevskaya metro. Opulent boutique hotel with Italian and Russian restaurants and a casino. Visa support R800. All major cards. **❽**

Grand Hotel Emerald Suvorovskiy pr. 18 ☏740 50 00; minibus #147 from Mayakovskaya metro. This five-star hotel has a sauna, Turkish bath and fitness centre. All major cards. **❽**

Guesthouse Grechiskiy pr. 13 ☏271 30 89, ⓦwww.ghspb.ru; 10min walk from Ploshchad Vosstaniya metro. Small, clean rooms with TV and showers. Visa support R1000. Maestro, MC, Visa. **❸**

Helvetia Hotel Suites ul. Marata 11 ☏326 53 53, ⓦwww.helvetia-suites.ru; 5min walk from Ploshchad Vosstaniya/Mayakovskaya metro. A smart apartment-hotel in a gated yard beside the Swiss consulate. All rooms with fans and kitchens; some have washing machines and a/c. MC, Visa. **❽**

Idillia Inn Kuznechniy per. 18, second floor ☏713 18 19, ⓦwww.idilliainn.ru; 10min walk from Ploshchad Vosstaniya or Dostoevskaya/Vladimirskaya metro. Cheesy-looking en-suite rooms near the Dostoyevsky Museum, with a kitchen and free Internet. Visa support R300. Maestro, MC, Visa. **❸**

Kameya (Cameo) nab. reki Fontanki 90 ☏312 08 58, ⓦwww.cameohotel.ru; 10min walk from Pushkinskaya or Sennaya Ploshchad metro. Very quiet a/c rooms in a small park off the Fontanka. Swedish buffet breakfast. Major cards. **❺**

🏃 **Krisha (Roof)** Vladimirskiy pr. 1, sixth floor ☏570 37 28, ⓦwww.krisha-spb.ru; 5min walk from Mayakovskaya metro. Just off Nevskiy in the same building as the *Butterly* and *Egoeast*, this comfy mini-hotel has a retro decor, and its "lux" rooms come with four-poster beds. No cards. **❹**

Marata 30 ul. Marata 30, second floor ☏713 19 91, ⓦwww.marata30.spb.ru (in Russian); 10min walk from Vladimirskaya/Dostoevskaya metro. Simple high-ceilinged a/c rooms with Internet, near the Dostoyevsky Museum. No cards. **❺**

Marshal Shpalernaya ul. 41 ☏579 99 55, ⓦwww.marshal-hotel.ru; 15min walk from Chernyshevskaya metro. Pleasant a/c rooms (one with a waterbed), a sauna, bar and restaurant, in a former cavalry barracks where the wartime Finnish president, Field Marshal Mannerheim, was once an ensign. DC, MC, Visa. **❻**

Moskva (Moscow) pl. Alexandra Nevskovo 2 ☎333 24 44, ⓦwww.hotel-moscow.ru; by Ploshchad Alexandra Nevskovo I metro. Enormous, refurbished 1970s hotel with some rooms overlooking the Alexander Nevsky Monastery; there's billiards and a sauna, and a first-night reservation fee of 25 percent. Major cards. ⑤

Neptun nab. Obvodnovo kanala 93A ☎324 46 10, ⓦwww.neptun.spb.ru; 15min walk from Pushkinskaya metro. A 1990s business-class hotel with a pool, bowling and billiards, in a grim location by the Obvodniy Canal. Cheaper at weekends. DC, EC, JCB, MC, Visa. ⑤

Neva ul. Chaykovskovo 17 ☎578 05 35, ⓦwww.nevahotel.spb.ru; 5min walk from Chernyshevskaya metro. An old Soviet hotel in a town house that was once a brothel, 15min walk from the Summer Garden. Refurbished rooms R1000 extra. Sauna; billiards. MC, Visa. ⑤

Nevsky Bereg Nevskiy pr. 122, third floor ☎441 39 43, ⓦwww.nevsky-bereg.ru; 5min walk from Ploshchad Vosstaniya metro. Smallish a/c rooms with flat-screen TVs and large "lux" ones with saunas and Jacuzzis. ⑤

Nevsky Central Nevskiy pr. 90–92, third floor ☎273 73 14, ⓦwww.hon.ru; near Mayakovskaya metro. Part of the Nevsky Hotels chain, this comfy, modern place is in the block behind *Café Max*; enter the yard and bear left. ⑤

Nevsky Express Nevskiy pr. 91–93 ☎717 18 88, ⓦwww.hon.ru; near Mayakovskaya metro. Another hotel in the same chain; the entrance is hard to find, but it has all mod cons including a sauna. ⑤

Nevskij Palace Nevskiy pr. 57 ☎380 20 01, ⓦwww.corinthia.ru; 5min walk from Mayakovskaya metro. This five-star Corinthia hotel has an award-winning restaurant; sauna, solarium and secure parking. Free visa support. Breakfast R1000. All major cards. ⑧

Novotel ul. Mayakovskovo 3A ☎335 11 88, ⓦwww.novotel.spb.ru; near Ploshchad Vosstaniya/Mayakovskaya metro. Just off Nevskiy, this post-modern tower of Pisa has all mod-cons, a fitness centre and disabled access. Free visa support. Breakfast R600. All major cards. ⑥

Oktyabrskaya Ligovskiy pr. 10 ☎578 18 22, ⓦwww.hoteloktiabrskaya.ru; near Ploshchad Vosstaniya/Mayakovskaya metro. A refurbished Soviet warren facing on busy junction by Moscow Station, it is popular with budget tour groups but overpriced for independ-ent travellers. Bar, billiards, Internet. Major cards. ⑥

Oktyabrskiy Filial (aka Ligovskiy Block) Ligovskiy pr. 43/45 ☎718 15 15, ⓦwww.hoteloktiabrskaya.ru; as above. This cheaper offshoot of the *Oktyabrskaya* nearer Moscow Station has decent rooms of all shapes and sizes. ⑤

Radisson SAS Royal Nevskiy pr. 49/2 ☎322 50 00, ⓦwww.stpetersburg.radissonsas.com; 10min walk from Mayakovskaya or Gostiniy Dvor metro. An anodyne five-star with a sauna, solarium and Jacuzzi. Breakfast R900. Free visa support. Major cards. ⑧

Respectable ul. Mayakovskovo 36–38, second floor ☎275 40 11, ⓦwww.respectale.ru; 15min walk from Chernyshevskaya metro. Quiet, high-ceilinged rooms, some sharing showers; one has an antique stove, another, a bay window nook. Kitchen; free soft drinks. No cards. ③

Rinaldi na Moskovskom Moskovskiy pr. 20 ☎316 05 79, ⓦwww.rinaldi.ru; 5min walk from Tekhnologicheskiy Institut metro. A quiet a/c mini-hotel in the Rinaldi chain, reached via the arch on the right in the yard. Major cards. ④

Rinaldi na Nevskom Nevskiy pr. 103 ☎717 44 18, ⓦwww.rinaldi.ru; 5min walk from Ploshchad Vosstaniya metro. A grander, roomier Rinaldi mini-hotel near Moscow Station. Major cards. ⑤

🏃 **Sonata** ul. Mayakovskovo 50 ☎380 40 90, ⓦwww.hotel-sonata.com; 10min walk from Chernyshevskaya metro. A pleasant mini-hotel with a café and bar, above the *Red Fox* jazz club (see p.361). ④

Suvorov 5-ya Sovetskaya ul. 3/13 ☎271 08 59, ⓦwww.suvorov hotel.spb.ru; 5min walk from Mayakovskaya metro. This comfortable mini-hotel round the corner from the *Guesthouse* also has an apartment to rent nearby. Visa support R700. Amex, Maestro, MC, Visa. ④

🏃 **Vesta** Nevskiy pr. 90/92 ☎272 13 22, ⓦwww.vestahotel.spb.ru; 5min walk from Mayakovskaya metro. In the same block as *Nevsky Central* but further back in the yard (which has a nice kids' playground), it is attractively furnished, with an intimate ambience. Free visa support. Breakfast R200. Major cards. ⑤

The Southern Suburbs

The Southern Suburbs are far from attractive as a rule, but some parts are well served by metro, making it more convenient than you'd think. Park Pobedy and Moskovskaya ploshchad are a fifteen to twenty-minute ride from the centre; both localities are quite leafy, with a mixture of high-ceilinged Stalinist apartments and later matchbox low-rises. See the map on p.214 for locations.

Kievskaya Dnepropetrovskaya ul. 49 ☎706 04 56, **15min walk from Ligovskiy Prospekt metro.** Near the intercity bus station but nothing else, this sovok hotel has small, clean rooms (some en suite) and billiards. No cards. ❷

Mir ul. Gastello 17 ☎708 51 66, Ⓦwww.hotel-mir.spb.ru; **15min walk from Park Pobedy metro.** This refurbished 1960s hotel off Moskovskiy pr. has clean matchbox rooms; the cheapest (without showers) overlook the Chesma Church. MC, Visa. ❷

🏃 **Nemetsky Club ul. Gastello 20** ☎371 51 04, Ⓦwww.hotelgermanclub.com; **10min walk from Moskovskaya metro.** Go through the arch at Moskovskiy pr. 202–204 to find this quirky, comfy hotel in the third block along, whose credo "Russian hospitality, German order" is reflected in its helpful staff and good security. Sauna; Wi-Fi. DC, JCB, MC, Visa. ❸

Park Inn Pulkovskaya pl. Pobedy 1 ☎740 39 00, Ⓦwww.parkinn.com.ru; **10min walk from Moskovskaya metro.** Spacious a/c rooms overlooking the Victory Monument; amenities include a sauna, gym, tennis courts and brewery restaurant. Free visa support. All major cards. ❼

Rossiya pl. Chernyshevskovo 11 ☎329 39 09, Ⓦwww.rossiya-hotel.ru; **5min walk from Park Pobedy metro.** A refurbished Stalinist three-star with a sauna; all rooms en suite, with TV. Major cards. ❹

Yuzhnaya Rasstannaya ul. 2 ☎766 10 88, Ⓦwww.southern.ru (in Russian only); **bus #3 from Ploshchad Vosstaniya or Ligovskiy Prospekt metro.** Clean sovok rooms (the cheapest without showers), far from everywhere but the Volkov Cemetery. No cards. ❷

Vyborg Side

Vyborg Side is the district with the least going for it in terms of ambience, although the *St Petersburg Hotel* has the saving grace of being near the cruiser *Aurora*, with great views of the Neva. The high-rise Okhta district east of the Neva could become the city's financial centre if the Gazprom Tower goes ahead, but metro stations are few and far between. All accommodation here is marked on the map on p.222.

Deson Ladoga pr. Shaumyana 26 ☎528 53 93; **10min walk from Novocherkasskaya metro.** A pleasant, modest hotel with English-speaking staff and a restaurant serving European and Chinese cuisine. A morning sauna and Swedish breakfast included in the price. All major cards. ❹

Okhtinskaya Bolsheokhtinskiy pr. 4 ☎227 26 18, Ⓦwww.okhtinskaya.spb.ru; **bus #105 from Ploshchad Vosstaniya metro.** Awkward to reach but otherwise decent, with a fine view of the Smolniy Convent across the Neva, a/c rooms with satellite TV and showers, and a sauna. Buffet breakfast. Major cards. ❹

🏃 **St Petersburg Pirogovskaya nab. 5/2** ☎380 19 19, Ⓦwww.hotel-spb.ru; **15min walk from Ploshchad Lenina metro.** If you're going to stay at this 1970s behemoth, it's worth paying a bit extra for a renovated room with a superb view of the Neva. All rooms en suite with TV and phone; sauna and business centre. Major cards. ❹

Vyborgskaya Torzhovskaya ul. 3 ☎740 58 13, Ⓔvyb@mail.linkey.ru; **5min walk from Chernaya Rechka metro.** Accessible 1960s hotel, clean but overpriced for what you get. *Sovok* rooms with washbasins; renovated en-suite ones cost nearly three times more. No cards. ❷

Homestay accommodation

Some agencies in St Petersburg and abroad can arrange homestay accommodation in the city. HOFA (see p.324) is especially recommended, as many of its hosts are academics, who speak foreign languages. **Staying with a Russian family**, you'll be well looked after and experience the cosy domesticity that is the obverse of brusque public life. Your introduction to this homely world will be a pair of *tapochki* – the slippers which Russians wear indoors to avoid tramping in mud – followed by a cup of tea or a shot of vodka. Your room will be clean and comfortable, though it can be disconcerting to discover, in small apartments, that it belongs to one of the family, who will sleep elsewhere for the duration of your stay.

Another, more disagreeable, surprise might be that the district **hot water** supply has been cut off, as happens for up to two weeks during the summer, so that the utilities company can clean the water mains. Don't blame your hosts should this happen – it's not their fault. All you can do is put up with it, or move to another district of the city that isn't affected at the time. The water company gives only a week's notice that supplies will be cut off, so a flat with its own boiler is highly desirable.

If you book through an agency that also provides visa support, your **registration** should be handled automatically – but be sure to verify that this is so. There have been instances where agencies failed to follow through with the paperwork, landing their clients in a bureaucratic nightmare.

Flat rental

If you're going to be in town longer than a week, or are coming as a group of friends or a family, you should consider renting a self-contained **apartment** (*kvartira*) to save money and enjoy more privacy than a hotel or B&B allows. This can be done before you arrive through agencies such as Arent, HOFA, Ost-West Kontaktservice, Bed & Breakfast, City Realty and others (see p.324), or directly through certain landlords. Some charge on a per person basis, others according to the size and quality of the apartment. If you're staying for a long time and would like to economize by **sharing** a flat, visit Flatmate.Ru (http://flatmate.ru), where prospective flat-sharers and landlords can make contact.

Broadly speaking, flats come with Soviet fittings, or **refurbished** to "Russian" (a new kitchen and bathroom) or "Euro Standard" (using imported fixtures), but in either category there are some places that are superlative and others that are disappointing. You can get a really cool deluxe pad with a Jacuzzi and plasma TV – the author once had a flat with a columned ballroom. Unsurprisingly, flats in high-rise blocks outside the centre are significantly cheaper.

Aside from the price, location and decor, the things to look for are a **boiler** (*kolonka*), so you won't be deprived of hot water if the district supply is cut off, a **bed** that's long enough to be comfortable, and a **door** that provides good security. Most apartments have a sturdy (often steel-plated) door with two or even three locks, while the door from the building (or yard) onto the street may be locked by a device which requires you to punch in a code. **Door codes** usually consist of three digits (sometimes including Cyrillic letters, or the # and ★ signs); you have to push all three buttons simultaneously to make it work.

Hostels

Ever since the Russian Youth Hostel Association (RYHA) and the first international hostel were set up by a Californian and his Russian partners in 1992, St Petersburg's **hostels** have faced the dilemma that not enough backpackers visit the city outside summer to balance their books without raising prices so high that their clientele decides that cheapo hotels offer better value for money. Another constraint is that, by law, hostels may register only guests who've obtained their visa support through the hostel or its partner agency – which means that guests who didn't and stay longer than three days risk being in breach of registration rules. Yet new hostels open each year and the general standard is improving. Hot water in the bathrooms is standard, and some places have mosquito-screens or coils in the rooms, Internet access, a café or other facilities. There are no age or membership restrictions, but a Hostelling International (HI), RYHA or ISIC student card may get you R30–50 discount. RYHA cards are also valid for discounts at hostels in Moscow and Latvia.

The **prices** quoted here are for high season, and include breakfast unless stated otherwise.

All Seasons Yakovlevskiy per. 11 ☎327 10 70, ⓦwww.hostel.ru; 10min walk from Park Pobedy metro. See map on p.214. In the southern suburbs, 15min by metro from the centre, and handy for reaching the Imperial palaces, this simple hostel has single (R1400), double (R1400), triple (R1650) and quadruple (R1920) rooms, sharing facilities.

Antonio House nab. reki Fontanki 53 ☎320 99 96, ⓦwww.antoniohouse.ru; 10min walk from Nevskiy Prospekt/Gostiniy Dvor metro. See map on pp.64–65. Not far from Nevskiy, by the Fontanka, this large hostel is plain but clean, with a laundry, kitchen and library. Rooms sleep from three to ten people; a bed costs R600 to R300 accordingly. Visa support (R550) and bookings through B&B Rinaldi (p.324).

🏃 **Bed & Breakfast** Kazanskaya ul. 11, second floor ☎320 66 52; directions as above. Nevskiy pr. 106 ☎ 325 65 36; near Mayakovskaya/Ploshchad Vosstaniya metro. ⓦwww.discount-travel-petersburg.ru. The first (marked on the map on pp.64–65) is just past the *Cuba Hostel*, the second (marked on the map on pp.192–193) beyond the Fontanka. Both hostels have simple rooms sleeping one (R800) to five people (R500 each), sharing bathrooms, a kitchen and laundry.

🏃 **Cuba Hostel** Kazanskaya ul. 5, fourth floor ☎921 71 15, ⓦwww.cubahostel. ru; 5min walk from Nevskiy Prospekt/Gostiniy Dvor metro. See map on pp.64–65. Near the Kazan Cathedral, it has decent rooms sleeping four to ten people (R650 to R500 each), a kitchen, Internet, lockers and laundry.

Herzen University Hostel Kazanskaya ul. 6 ☎314 74 72, ⓔhotel@herzen.spb.ru; 5min walk from Nevskiy Prospekt/Gostiniy Dvor metro. See map on pp.64–65. Just 100m behind the Kazan Cathedral, this trainee teachers' hostel has good security and clean rooms with showers or baths; a café,

karaoke-bar and Internet. On the downside, they can't provide visa support or register guests, and a single/ double room costs R1700/R2400.

Hostel Zimmer Liteyniy pr. 46, second floor ☎973 37 57; 15min walk from Mayakovskaya metro. See map on pp.192–193. Within walking distance of many sights, this place is shabby but friendly, with a kitchen, washing machine and Internet, double rooms (R600) and single-sex dorms sleeping six (R475 a bed). In the summer they also have a hard-to-find overflow hostel in a residential block at ul. Pestelya 7. No breakfast. Visa support R1050.

🏃 **Nord Hostel** Bolshaya Morskaya ul. 10 ☎571 03 42, ⓦwww.nordhostel.ru; 10min walk from Nevskiy Prospekt/Gostiniy Dvor metro. See map on pp.64–65. Almost next door to the General Staff building and a minute's walk from the Hermitage, this hostel has dorm beds (R840), doubles (R1160), Internet and umbrella rental.

Prima-Sport Hostel pr. Dobrolyubova 14 ☎324 70 77, ⓦwww.prima-numerov.net; 5min walk from Sportivnaya metro. See map on pp.168–169. Within walking distance of the Peter and Paul Fortress, this hostel has en-suite a/c rooms with/without windows, sleeping one (R1000/R1500), two (R2000/R1200) or three (R3900/R2300) in bunk beds. Amex, DC, Maestro, MC, Visa.

Puppet Hostel ul. Nekrasova 12, fourth floor ☎272 54 01, ⓦhttp://hostel-puppet.ru; 15min walk from Chernyshevskaya metro. See map on pp.192–193. Just off Liteyniy pr., within walking distance of the Engineers' Castle; reached via the trade entrance of a puppet theatre. Security is OK but the premises are a bit shabby, with doubles (R1740) and dorms (R690 per bed) sharing washrooms. Free tickets to the puppet theatre. Visa support and registration R875.

🏃 **St Petersburg International Hostel** 3-ya Sovetskaya ul. 28 ☎329 80 18, ⓦwww.

ryh.ru; 10min walk from Ploshchad Vosstaniya metro. See map on pp.192–193. On a quiet street north of Moscow Station, this long-established, clean and friendly hostel has Internet, laundry service, salubrious washrooms and tight security. You can pay R690 for a bed in a 3- to 5-bed dorm, or R1680 for a double room. Visa support R750. No cards.

Sleep Cheap Mokhovaya ul. 18, apt. 32 ☎715 13 04, ⓦwww.sleepcheap.ru; 15min walk from Chernyshevskaya metro. See map on pp.192–193. In a quiet neighbourhood within walking distance of the Summer Garden, this friendly hostel has two eight-bunk dorms with spotless facilities; a bed costs R670. Airport transfer R700 per person. No cards.

14

Eating and drinking

St Petersburg is a city whose oldest citizens have experienced famine during the Siege of Leningrad; their children, decades of food shortages, queuing and *sovok* restaurants; and their grandchildren, a diversity of food only the well-to-do enjoyed before the Revolution. Many have never had it so good and any Russian with the means delights in dining out as adventurously or extravagantly as possible. **Cafés** and **restaurants** offer all kinds of cuisine and surroundings, aimed at anyone with a disposable income – from mega-rich oligarchs and expense-account expatriates to fashion-conscious teenagers. While some places at the top end of the market can rightfully boast of their *haute cuisine*, there are lots whose decor and pretensions surpass their cooking, where the clientele's main aim seems to be to flash their money around.

While all bars, cafés and restaurants take **payment** in rubles a few tourist-oriented places still list prices in dollars, euros or so-called "standard units" (using the Cyrillic abbreviation УЕ [Тщеу Снкшдддшс]), which amounts to the same thing (see p.55). In that case, the total is converted into rubles at the current central bank rate or the rate of exchange advertised on the premises (which may be less favourable). It's often (though not always) true that a menu in foreign currency or standard units is an indication that the establishment is overpriced.

Credit cards are accepted by many restaurants – we've indicated in our listings which ones are accepted using the relevant abbreviations (Amex = American Express, DC = Diners Club, MC = MasterCard, EC = Eurocard, JCB = Japanese Credit Bank) – but you shouldn't take it for granted.

Breakfast, bakeries and snacks

At home, most Russians take **breakfast** (*zavtrak*) very seriously, tucking into calorific dishes such as pancakes (*bliny*) or buckwheat porridge (*kasha*), with curd cheese (*tvorog*) and sour cream (*smetana*), although some settle simply for a cup of tea and a slice of bread. Hotels serve an approximation of the "Continental" breakfast, probably just a fried egg, bread, butter and jam; the flashier joints, however, provide a *Shvedskiy stol*, or "Swedish table", a sort of smorgasbord. Anyone hankering for a Full English breakfast should head for the *Dickens pub* on the Fontanka (p.348), which even has baked beans.

If you're not staying in a hotel, the best options for breakfast are coffee or fast-food chains, cafés or bakeries serving *bliny*, **pastries** (*pirozhnoe*) and **pies** (*pirozhki*), filled with cabbage, curd cheese or rice. Meat ones should be treated with caution (never buy from street kiosks or at train stations), but can be trusted at chains such as *Coffee House*, *Idealnaya Chashka* or the wonderful pie outlet *Stolle* (see p.347).

Bread (*khleb*), available from bakeries (*bulochnaya*), is one of the country's culinary strong points. "Black" bread (known as *chorniy* or *rzhanoy*) is the traditional variety: a dense rye bread with a distinctive sourdough flavour and amazing longevity. *Karelskiy* is similar but with fruit; *surozhniy* is a lighter version, made with a mixture of wheat and rye. French-style baguettes (*baton*) – white, mixed-grain or plaited with poppy seeds – are also popular. For wholegrain, focaccia or fruit breads, check out the *Baltic Bread* chain.

Russians are very fond of **cakes** (*tort*). The *Sladoezhka* chain of patisseries sells all kinds of freshly made fruit or chocolate gateaux, while supermarkets stock cakes whose main ingredients are sponge dough, honey, a spice such as cinnamon or ginger or lots of cream and jam. Whatever the season, Russians are always happy to eat **ice cream** (*morozhenoe*), available from kiosks all over town. Much of the locally produced ice cream is cheaper and of better quality than the imported brands; try the popular crème-brûlée or Eskimo, a sort of choc-ice.

Department stores, theatres and major museums feature a stand-up *bufet*, offering open **sandwiches** with salami, salmon, pickled herring, caviar, boiled egg, or other nibbles. Less appealing buffets can be found in train and bus stations, and around metro stations and markets.

Zakuski

Despite the popularity of sushi and Western fast food, Russian culinary traditions are still strong, especially with regard to *bliny* (pancakes), one of the best-loved of Russian **zakuski** – small dishes or hors d'oeuvres, which are often a meal in themselves. *Zakuski* traditionally form the basis of the *Russkiy stol*, or "Russian table", which sags under the weight of the numerous dishes while the samovar steams away. Among the upper classes in Tsarist times, *zakuski* were merely the prelude to the main meal, as foreign guests would discover to their dismay after gorging themselves on these delights. Salted fish, like sprats or herrings, are a firm favourite, as are gherkins, smoked or pickled mushrooms, spiced feta, assorted cold meats and salads. Hard-boiled eggs and *bliny* are often served with **caviar** (*ikra*), which comes in two basic varieties. Red caviar (*krasnaya ikra*) is salmon roe and has larger eggs than the costlier black caviar (*chornaya ikra*), which comes from sturgeon.

Meals

Russians usually eat their main meal at lunchtime (*obed*), between 1 and 4pm, and traditionally have only *zakuski* or salad and tea for supper (*uzhin*). Restaurants, on the other hand, make much more of the evening, though many now offer a set-price business lunch to attract extra customers.

Menus are usually written in Russian only, although more and more places now also offer a short English version. However, the Russian menu is usually typed up every day, whereas the English version will give only a general idea of what might be available. In such cases, you're probably better off asking what they recommend (*shto-by vy po rekomendovali?*), which can elicit some surprisingly frank replies.

If your main concern is price, you'll need to stick to **fast-food** outlets or **cafés**, the latter providing some of the best **ethnic food** in the city, including Armenian (*Armyanskiy*), Georgian (*Gruzinskiy*), and Korean (*Koreyskiy*), as well as traditional Russian cooking.

Russian cuisine owes many debts to Jewish, Ukrainian and Caucasian cooking, but remains firmly tied to its peasant origins. In former times, the staple diet of black bread, potatoes, cabbages, cucumber and onions made for bland eating – *Shchi da kasha, pishcha nasha* ("cabbage soup and porridge are our food") as one saying goes – with flavourings limited to sour cream, garlic, vinegar, honey, dill and a few other fresh herbs. These tastes – salty, sweet, sour, pickled – remained the norm, even among the aristocracy, until Peter the Great introduced French chefs to his court in the early eighteenth century. Since the 1990s, foreign and local chefs have created a **nouvelle** cuisine of lighter dishes based on traditional recipes with an Asian or Mediterranean twist – as at restaurants such as *Fasol* and *Imbir* – but the old-style, heavier cuisine still predominates.

Most menus start with a choice of soup or *zakuski*. **Soup** (*sup*) has long played an important role in Russian cuisine (the spoon appeared on the Russian table over four hundred years before the fork). Cabbage soup, or *shchi*, has been the principal dish for the last millennium, served with a generous dollop of sour cream; beetroot soup, or *borsch*, originally from Ukraine, is equally ubiquitous. While older Russians don't consider even large meaty soups to be a meal and expect guests to consume a main course as well, the under-40s are more weight-conscious. Chilled soups (*okroshki*) are popular in summer, made from whatever fresh vegetables are available and flavoured with *kvas* or *kefir* (see pp.343–344).

Main courses are overwhelmingly based on **meat** (*myaso*), usually beef, mutton or pork, and sometimes accompanied by a simple sauce (mushroom or cheese). Meat may also make its way into *pelmeni*, a Russian version of ravioli, served in a broth, or a sour cream or tomato sauce. As far as regional meat dishes go, the most common are Georgian barbecued **kebabs** (*shashlyk*), or pilau-style Uzbek rice dishes called *plov*.

A wide variety of **fish and seafood** is available in St Petersburg. Pickled fish is a popular starter (try *selyodka pod shuby*, herring in a "fur coat" of beetroot, carrot, egg and mayonnaise), while fresh fish often appears as a main course – salmon, sturgeon and cod are the most common choices, though upmarket restaurants may boast sea bass, lobster and oysters as well.

Menus often list main dishes separately from the **vegetables** that accompany it – called *garnir* – which have to be ordered separately. Where the meat is accompanied by vegetables, you may see an entry on the menu along the lines of 100/25/100g, which refers to the respective weight in grams of the meat (or fish) portion, and its accompanying servings of rice/potatoes and vegetable *garnir*. In ethnic restaurants, meat is almost always served on its own.

Desserts (*sladkoe*) are not a strong feature of Russian cuisine. Ice cream, fruit, apple pie (*yablochniy pirog*) and jam pancakes (*blinchikiy s varenem*) are restaurant perennials (fancier places may also feature tiramisu), while in Caucasian restaurants you may get the flaky pastry and honey dessert, *pakhlava* (like Greek or Turkish baklava).

Ethnic food

The influence of diverse culinary traditions on Russian food is epitomized by *pelmeni* (ravioli). Originating as *dim sum* in pork-eating China, it spread as *manty* to the mutton-eating cultures along the Silk Road and westwards with the Tatars to Crimea, before being adopted by Russian peasants in Siberia – whence the recipe spread to European Russia. Closer to home, Jewish, Russian and Ukrainian cooking were so entwined that the only dishes not claimed by all three traditions are ones using pork. The cuisines of the Caucasus were also a lasting influence; most Russian restaurants have *shashlyk*, the Georgian kebab, or *tolma*, Armenian stuffed vine leaves, on the menu. Yet each ethnic cuisine is distinctive and deserves to be experienced in a proper "national" restaurant.

In Soviet times **Georgian** restaurants were the most esteemed, and Caucasian entrepreneurs supplied Russian cities with fruit, wine and flowers. Georgians have a legend that God took a meal break from Creation, tripped over the

Caucasus range and spilled his food onto the land below – their cuisine was "scraps from Heaven's table". Its distinctive ingredients include ground walnuts and walnut oil for cooking; condiments such as *khmeli-suneli* (dried coriander, chilli, garlic, pepper and marigold petals), *adzhika* (tomato, red pepper and chilli sauce) and *tkemali* (plum sauce); and lashings of fresh dill, coriander and parsley, which are also eaten raw, to cleanse the palate between courses, and used to garnish cheeses made from sheep's or goat's milk. Traditionally, dishes of aubergines, tomatoes, garlic and beans were the staple diet, but feast days were marked by banquets of meaty soups, stews and kebabs, with repeated toasts in wine or brandy, orchestrated by a *tamada* (toast master). Favourites include *satsivi*, a cold dish of chicken in walnut sauce; *chikhirtmi*, lemon-flavoured chicken soup; *kharcho*, spicy beef soup; and *khinkali*, dumplings stuffed with lamb or a mixture of pork and beef. *Khachapuri*, a delicious cheesy soft bread that's served hot, is a filling starter; the version from Adzhariya (*khachapuri po-Adzharskiy*) has an egg in the middle.

Armenian and **Azerbaijani** cuisine is closer to Middle Eastern cooking (with the addition of dried nuts, saffron and ginger), while **Uzbek** cuisine features *khinkali* (a kind of spicy *pelmeni*), sausages made from pony meat (*kazy*) and juicy samosa-type pastries filled with meat or greens (*chebureki*). Ginger and garlic also feature prominently in **Korean** food, originally introduced by Korean railway workers exiled to Kazakhstan in the 1930s. Marinated beef dishes such as *bulkogi* are fried at your table, accompanied by raw vegetables and hot pickled garlic relish (*kimichi*). One dish often found even in non-Korean eateries is spicy carrot salad (*morkov po-koreyskiy*). **Ukrainian** food is similar to Russian but even heavier; the classic starter is *salo* (salted, smoked pig fat), followed by pork, beef, rabbit or other meaty stews. **Jewish** dishes such as *farshmak* (chopped

pickled herring), *tschav* (sorrel soup) or gefilte fish are seldom found outside Jewish restaurants.

More recently, Russians have fallen in love with **Japanese** food to the extent that sushi is now a "national" dish like curry in Britain or couscous in France – though sushi and sashimi aren't far removed from smoked fish *zakuski*, or the salmon and crab diet of Russia's Far Northern peoples. **Indonesian** food is also currently chic, while a decade's exposure to **Indian** and **Chinese** cuisine has acclimatized sophisticated locals to curries and spicy dishes that were previously toned down to suit Russian tastes. Many restaurants feature several different cuisines on their menu (sushi, Russian and Mediterranean, for example), while others are into **fusion** (Russian or Mediterranean influenced by Japanese or Indonesian are currently popular).

Among the **other cuisines** represented by at least one restaurant in St Petersburg are Columbian, French, German, Italian, Latvian, Lebanese, Mexican, Peruvian and Scandinavian.

Vegetarian food

Although the situation for **vegetarians** has improved a lot with the spread of salad bars and health- (or at least weight-watching) awareness, meat still takes pride of place in the nation's cuisine. While fish eaters will find plenty to sustain them, strict vegetarians often have to fall back on *bliny* stuffed with mushrooms or cabbage, *griby s smetanoy* (mushrooms cooked with onions and sour cream), or the cold summer soup *okroshka*. You could also try asking for *postniy shchi* (meatless, literally "fasting", *shchi*, or cabbage soup) or *ovoschnoy plov* (vegetable pilaf). If you're obliged to spell things out, the crucial phrases are *ya vegetarianets/vegetarianka*, I'm a vegetarian (masculine/feminine), and *Kakiye u vas yest blyuda bez myasa ili ryby?* Is there anything without meat or fish? For emphasis you could add *ya ne yem myasnovo ili rybnovo* (I don't eat meat or fish).

In general, **ethnic restaurants** (Georgian, Lebanese, Korean, Indian, Indonesian or Chinese) have the most interesting vegetarian options, such as Korean carrot salad, Caucasian aubergine puree or the Georgian bean dish *lobio*, though many pizzerias run to veggie pizzas and salad bars. For those **self-catering**, vegetables are wide available in markets (see p.374) an on the streets, and many supermarkets sell beans, grains and pulses. Locally produced fruit and vegetables are available only from June to October; at other times of the year everything is imported.

Drinking

The story goes that the tenth-century Russian prince Vladimir, when pondering which religion to adopt for his state, rejected Judaism because its adherents were seen as weak and scattered; Catholicism because the pope claimed precedence over sovereigns; and Islam because "Drinking is the joy of the Russians. We cannot live without it."

A thousand years on, **alcohol** remains a central part of Russian life, and the prime cause of falling life expectancy of Russian males. It's a sobering experience to visit provincial towns where almost every man is stumbling drunk by midday, or villages where dozens have died from toxic hooch. In St Petersburg, virtually all cafés serve alcohol, and it seems as if every tenth pedestrian is swigging from a bottle of beer. As the cost of drinks in **cafés** and **bars** is more than you'd pay in **shops**, many Russians prefer to drink at home. Shops are now forbidden to sell drinks that contain over 15 percent alcohol (all spirits and some liquors) between 11pm and 8am, but beer and wine are sold 24 hours a day. It is **illegal** to drink spirits on the streets or in parks (though the law is flouted by alcoholics), but beer drinking is not an offence.

Drinking spirits in a bar, the usual **measures** are 50 or 100 grams (*pyatdesyat/sto gram*), which for those used to British pub measures seem extremely generous. If you're invited to eat with Russians, it can be difficult to avoid drinking a succession of **toasts** in vodka, each glass tossed back *do dna* – to the end – as refusal may cause offence. The only ironclad excuse is to pretend that you have a liver problem, or suffer from alcoholism. If you do submit to a drinking session, be sure to eat something after each shot – Russians say that even the smell of a crust of bread is better than nothing.

Vodka and other spirits

Vodka is the national drink – its name means something like "a little drop of water". It is produced from grain, usually wheat, but rye is also used in Russia. Normally served chilled, vodka is drunk neat in one gulp, followed by a mouthful of food, such as pickled herring, cucumber or mushrooms; many people inhale deeply before tossing the liquor down their throats. Drinking small amounts at a time, and eating as you go, it's possible to consume an awful lot without passing out – though you soon reach a plateau of inebriated exhilaration.

Taste isn't a prime consideration; what counts is that the vodka isn't **bootleg liquor** (*podelnaya, falshivaya* or *levnaya* in Russian). At best, this means that buyers find themselves drinking something weaker than they bargained for; at worst, they're imbibing diluted methanol, which can cause blindness or even death. As a rule of thumb, avoid anything costing under R100 for a half-litre.

Among the hundreds of local **brands** on the market, the best are produced by the St Petersburg distillery Liviz (Diplomat, Russkiy Standart and Five Star) and its Moscow rivals Kristall (Kristall

...ave a wealth of phrases and gestures to signify drinking vodka, the most ...e being to tap the side of your chin or windpipe. The story goes that there ... peasant who saved the life of Peter the Great and was rewarded with the ...ght to drink as much vodka as he liked from any distillery. Fearing that a written *ukaz* would be stolen while he was drunk, the man begged the tsar to stamp the Imperial seal on his throat – the origin of the tapping gesture.

Fittingly, the Russian word for drunk – *pyany* – comes from an incident where two columns of drunken soldiers advancing on either side of the Pyany River mistook each other for the enemy and opened fire. Given its long and disreputable role in Russian warfare, it's ironic that the Tsarist government's prohibition of vodka for the duration of World War I did more harm than good, by depriving the state of a third of its revenue and stoking class hatred of the aristocracy, whose consumption of cognac and champagne continued unabated. Stalin knew better during World War II, when soldiers received a large tot of vodka before going into battle.

In Soviet society, vodka was the preferred form of payment for any kind of work outside the official economy and the nexus for encounters between strangers needing to "go three" on a bottle – a half-litre bottle shared between three people was reckoned to be the cheapest and most companionable way to get a bit drunk. Whereas rationing vodka was the most unpopular thing that Gorbachev ever did, Yeltsin's budgets categorized it as an essential commodity like bread or milk. Despite Yeltsin's notorious fondness for vodka, one would rather not believe Shevardnadze's claim to have found him lying dead drunk in the White House during the 1991 putsch, though at the time Shevardnadze told the crowd outside that "I have met the President and he is standing firm in defence of democracy".

and Gzhelka) and Flagman (official vodka purveyors to the Kremlin), though many drinkers regard imported vodkas such as Absolut, Finlandia or Smirnoff as more prestigious.

In addition to standard vodka you'll also see **flavoured vodkas** such as *pertsovka* (hot pepper vodka), *limonaya* (lemon vodka), *okhotnichaya* (hunter's vodka with juniper berries, ginger and cloves), *starka* (apple and pear-leaf vodka) and *zubrovka* (bison-grass vodka). The Ukrainian brand Khortitsya produces honey-and-lemon, horseradish, and caramel-flavoured vodkas.

Other domestic liquors include **cognac** (*konyak*), which is pretty rough compared to French brandy, but easy enough to acquire a taste for. Traditionally, the best brands hailed from Armenia (Ararat) and Moldova (Beliy Aist), but most bottles now sold in Russia are actually raw spirit flavoured with caramel; Daghestani cognac is more likely to be made from grapes, at least.

Otherwise, you can find imported spirits such as whisky, gin and tequila in many bars and shops, along with Irish Cream, Amaretto and sickly Austrian fruit brandies.

Beer, wine and champagne

Beer is the preferred drink of younger Russians if only because it's widely available – and consumed – at any time of day or night, and hardly regarded as alcohol, but simply as a refreshing drink. Some of Russia's best-selling beers come from St Petersburg breweries. **Baltika** beers come in 50cl bottles, numbered from 1 to 12 (mainly in order of their strength). The most popular are #3, "Classic" lager (ask for Troika), #4, "Original" brown ale, and #5, "Porter" stout; #6 and #7 are often found on tap in pool bars and discos; #9 is the strongest; #10 has an aroma of almond and basil, and Medovoe supposedly tastes of honey. **Stepan Razin** (named after the peasant rebel hero) produces eleven different beers, including Spetsialnoe (only 3.6 percent alcohol), the light pilsner Admiralteyskoe, the potent Kalinkin (7 percent), and Zolotoe, with a fine aroma of malt and hops. The **Vena** brewery is best known for Nevskoe Originalnoe (which won second prize at a beer festival in Britain) and Porter (a gold medal-winner in Denmark); it also makes Svetloe, a light beer, and Kronverk, without alcohol. More recent newcomers are **Bochkarev**, whose Svetloe (light) and Tyomnoe (dark) are very popular, and **Tinkoff**, which bottles some of the unfiltered beers available on tap at its microbrewery near the Kazan Cathedral (see p.347). Other Russian brands include Afanasy, a mild ale brewed in Nizhniy Novgorod, and Sibirskaya Korona (Siberian Crown) lager. You're bound to find some of these **on tap** (*razlivnoe*) in bars, together with imports such as Carlsberg, Holsten, Staropramen, Pilsner Urquell or Guinness, which may also come in bottles or cans in shops.

The **wine** (*vino*) on sale in St Petersburg is mostly from the European Union, California or Chile. Traditionally, Russia imported wine from Crimea, Moldova and Georgia (the last two being made from varieties of grapes almost unknown abroad, a treat for foreign wine-lovers), but since Russia imposed a trade embargo on Georgia some years ago, Georgian wine has vanished from the shelves and is only rarely found in restaurants. If you get a chance, try the dry reds Mukuzani and Saperavi, or the sweeter full-bodied reds Kindzmarauli and Khvanchkara, drunk by Stalin. Crimea is better known for its **fortified wines** Portvini (port) and Masala, which are known in Russian as *baramatukha* or "babbling juice", the equivalent of Thunderbird in the States.

Despite notice from France that Russia's concession to use the word **champagne** has expired (it was granted after World War II in gratitude to the Soviet Union), not all local manufac-

turers have relabelled their product "Soviet Sparkling" (*Sovietskoe Igristoe*), and consumers still request "Soviet champagne" (*Sovetskoe shampanskoe*, or *shampanskoe* for short). Besides being far cheaper than the French variety, some of it is quite drinkable if properly chilled. The two types to go for are *sukhoe* and *bryut*, which are both reasonably dry; *polusukhoe* or "medium dry" is actually very sweet, and *sladkoe* is like connecting yourself to a glucose drip. It's indicative of Russian taste that the last two are the most popular.

Tea, coffee and soft drinks

Traditionally, Russian tea (*chay*), was brewed and stewed for hours, and topped up with boiling water from an ornate tea urn, or samovar, but nowadays almost everywhere uses teabags. Many cafés and some coffeehouse chains also offer herbal or fruit-flavoured teas, which were traditionally prepared at home using herbs and leaves from the forest (*travyanoy chay*), or ginseng and ginger from the east. Most Russians drink tea without milk and you need to ask for it in cafés. **Milk** (*moloko*) itself is sold in stores alongside **kefir**, a sour milk drink that's something of an acquired taste for foreigners. There are full cream and low-fat versions of both.

Coffee (*kofe*) is sold all over the place and varies enormously in quality. Kiosks and cheap cafés use vile powdered stuff; avoid places with automats and look for a proper coffee maker on the premises. Seattle-style coffee houses are all the rage in St Petersburg, with chains such as *Coffee House* and *Idealnaya Chaska* serving espresso, cappuccino, lattes, mocca, flavoured coffees and alcoholic coffee cocktails. A few old-fashioned cafés prepare Turkish or Arabic coffee by heating it in hot sand, a method used in Soviet times.

Pepsi and Coca-Cola jostle for sales with cheaper brands of **fizzy drinks** imported from Eastern Europe, or manufactured in Russia. Besides generic colas, lemonades and orangeades, you'll see such distinctly Russian drinks as **kvas**, an unusual but delicious thirst-quencher made from fermented rye bread; **myod**, or honey-mead, which is seen as a soft drink but contains alcohol; and **tarkhun**, a bright green, sickly sweet drink made from tarragon – all of which have made a comeback since they fell out of fashion with the demise of the Soviet Union.

The days when the only **mineral water** (*mineralnaya voda*) available was Narzan and Borzhomi from the Cau-casus (both now hard to find, due to the embargo on Georgia) are long over. Kiosks and shops are full of Evian, Vittel and Perrier, and diverse Russian brands of spring water, which may be carbon-ated (*gazirovanaya voda*) or without gas (*negazirovanaya*). There are several vari-eties of the brand Ariana, each from a different source and recommended for a specific ailment, while the brand Svyati Istochik (Sacred Spring) comes with a blessing from the Orthodox Patriarch.

Fast-food chains

Now taken for granted by younger Russians, **fast-food chains** are hugely popular in Moscow and St Petersburg, offering a variety of food and standards of hygiene

The chain gang

Chaynaya Lozhka (Teaspoon**)** Nevskiy pr. 44, Gostiniy Dvor metro; Nevskiy pr. 45, Mayakovskaya metro; ul. Vosstaniya 5, Ploshchad Vosstaniya metro; Kamennoos-trovskiy pr. 31, Petrogradskaya metro; Grazdanskiy pr. 41, Akademicheskaya metro; Zanevskiy pr. 71/1, Ladozhskaya metro (all daily 9am–11pm). Eye-wateringly colou-red decor, tasty *bliny* and salads, and a range of loose-leaf teas.

Coffee House Nevskiy pr. 7–9 & 43, Nevskiy Prospekt/Gostiniy Dvor metro; Vladi-mirskiy pr. 1, Mayakovskaya metro; Sadovaya ul. 8, Gostiniy Dvor metro; Malaya Sadovaya ul. 3, Gostinniy Dvor metro; ul. Lva Tolstovo 1–3, Petrogradskaya metro; and many other locations (most open 24hr). Russia's equivalent of *Starbucks*. No smoking. No cards.

Eurasia Nevskiy pr. 3, Nevskiy Prospekt metro (daily 24hr; see map on pp.64–65); Bolshaya Konyushennaya 10, Nevskiy Prospekt metro; Liteyniy pr. 28, Chernyshev-skaya metro; Bolshoy pr. 14, Sportivnaya metro (daily noon–5am); Kronverkskiy pr. 13/2, Gorkovskaya metro (daily noon–5am); Kamennoostrovskiy pr. 44, Petrograd-skaya metro (all daily noon–midnight unless stated otherwise). Cheap sushi, spring rolls, noodle dishes and miso soup. No cards.

Idealnaya Chashka (Ideal Cup). Nevskiy pr. 15, 112 & 130, Nevskiy Prospekt/Gostiniy Dvor, Mayakovskaya/Ploshchad Vosstaniya or Ploshchad Aleksandra Nev-skovo metros; Vladimirskiy pr. 1, Mayakovskaya metro; Sadovaya ul. 25, Sennaya Ploshchad or Gostiniy Dvor metros; Kirochnaya ul. 19, Chernyshevskaya metro; Moskovskiy pr. 6, Sadovaya/Sennaya Ploshchad metro; Kamennoostrovskiy pr. 2, Gorkovskaya metro; Bolshoy pr. 82, Petrogradskaya metro; Sredniy pr. 46, Vasile-ostrovskaya metro (all daily 7am–11pm). All kinds of coffees, coffee cocktails and desserts. No smoking. No cards.

Laima. Nab. kanala Griboedova 16, Nevskiy Prospekt/Gostiniy Dvor metro; Bolshoy pr. 88, Petrogradskaya metro (both daily 24hr). Salads, soups, stuffed peppers, chicken, fish, kebabs, fresh juices, milkshakes and beer. No smoking. No cards.

McDonald's Bolshaya Morskaya ul. 11/6, Nevskiy Prospekt metro; Kamennoos-trovskiy pr. 39, Petrogradskaya metro; Moskovskiy pr. 195a, Moskovskaya metro; Sennaya pl. 4/1, Sennaya Ploshchad/Sadovaya metro; Sredniy pr. 29a, Vasileos-

and service infinitely superior to the grimy *stolovaya* (canteens) that were widespread during Soviet times. Besides such worldwide giants as *McDonald's, Pizza Hut* and *Subway*, there are various national chains serving Russian food – *bliny* (pancakes), salads and kebabs – that's far tastier and healthier than the food of the burger chains. There are also some awful ones, dishing up half-defrosted *bliny* and other inedible junk. **Avoid** *Blin Donalds, Fiesta, Galeo, Hannover Bistro*, and anywhere named simply "Bistro". The outlets listed in the box below are reliable, but not reviewed under cafés or included on **maps** in this book (except for a few branches on the downtown stretch of Nevskiy prospekt, where there are few places to eat that aren't chains).

Cafés and bars

Cafés and **bars** in St Petersburg run the gamut from humble eateries to trendy watering holes, and since most places serve alcohol (beer, if not spirits and cocktails too) the distinction between them is often a fine one. With some exceptions (mostly places in top-class hotels) cafés are generally cheaper than fully fledged restaurants, making them popular with Russians who have some disposable income, but don't ride around in a Mercedes.

trovskaya metro (all daily 7am–11.30pm). No smoking. No cards.

Pizza Hut Gorokhovaya ul. 16, on the corner of the Moyka embankment, Sadovaya/Sennaya Ploshchad metro (daily 10am–11pm); Nevskiy pr. 96, Mayakovskaya/Ploshchad Vosstaniya metro (daily 11am–11pm).
Discounts before 4pm. Major cards

🏃 **Sladkoezhka** (Sweet Tooth) Malaya Morskaya ul. 9, Nevskiy Prospekt metro; Nevskiy pr. 88, Mayakovskaya metro; Gorokhovaya ul. 44, Sadovaya/Sennaya Ploshchad metro; Sadovya ul. 60, Sadovaya metro; ul. Marata 2, Mayakovskaya metro; Zakharevskaya ul. 25, Chernyshevskaya metro (all daily 10am–11pm). Patisserie chain with good coffee, cakes, sundaes, cocktails, wine and spirits. No smoking.

Sbarro Nevskiy pr. 40–42, Gostiniy Dvor metro; Sadovaya ul. 25a, Sadovaya metro; 7-ya liniya 34, Vasileostrovskaya metro (all daily 10am–11pm). Self-service pizza chain.

Subway Nevskiy pr. 20, Nevskiy Prospekt metro (Mon–Thurs 10am–10pm, Fri–Sun 10am–5am); Sennaya mall, Sennaya pl., Sadovaya metro (daily 10am–9pm). Sandwiches to eat in or take away.

🏃 **Teremok** Located on Manezhnaya pl., just off Sadovaya pl. and outside several mainline train and suburban metro stations (all daily 11am–11pm). Brown-and-yellow kiosks or cafés selling freshly made *bliny* with savoury or sweet fillings. No cards.

U Tyoshi na blinakh (At Mother-in-Law's for Pancakes) Malaya Morskaya ul. 4/1, Nevskiy Prospekt metro; Ligovskiy pr. 29, Ploshchad Vosstaniya metro; Gorokhovaya ul. 41/33, on the corner of Sadovaya ul., Sadovaya/Sennaya Ploshchad metro (all daily 24hr). Rustic-style Russian chain with salads, chicken Kiev, *bliny*, stuffed cabbage, soups and alcohol. No cards.

🏃 **Yolki Palki** (Fiddlesticks) Nevskiy pr. 88, Mayakovskaya metro; Malaya Konyushennaya ul. 9, Nevskiy Prospekt/Gostiniy Dvor metro (see map on p.80); 10-ya liniya 27, Vasileostrovskaya metro; Moskovskiy pr. 175, Park Pobedy metro (all daily 24hr). Another folksy chain serving traditional Russian dishes, *kvas*, beer and vodka; their all-you-can-eat buffet (R300) is a winner. MC, Visa.

Though all cafés are private ventures nowadays, some retain the surly habits of Soviet days, when customers counted themselves lucky if they were served at all, and even where they aim to please, you sometimes find inexplicable lapses in standards or decorum. However, you can also find some delicious meals and friendly watering holes if you know where to look, and the number of acceptable places is rising all the time.

Another phenomenon is **street cafés** (usually open from May to late Sept), where you can have a coffee, beer or hamburger, while watching the world go by. There are several on Malaya Sadovaya ulitsa, just off Nevskiy, and along the prospekt itself, outside the Lutheran Church at no. 24, by the Portico opposite the *Grand Hotel Europe* (no. 33) and the beer garden in the yard of no. 86 – but you'll find them all around the centre and in residential districts too.

The following selection is listed in alphabetical order under area headings corresponding to the chapters in the Guide section. We've provided phone numbers for bars and cafés where it's advisable to phone ahead and reserve a table, particularly if you are planning to eat.

Within the Fontanka

The cafés and bars below are marked on the map on pp.62–63, unless specified otherwise.

Aprikosov (Apricots) Nevskiy pr. 40; Gostiniy Dvor/Nevskiy Prospekt metro. See map on pp.64–65. This nineteenth-century *kofeynya* (coffee house) is one of the oldest still extant, with an elegant Chinoiserie decor. Full of tourists by day, it attracts a Russian crowd at night. Maestro, MC, Visa. Daily noon–2am.

Avocado Sennaya pl. 7; Sennaya Ploshchad/Sadovaya metro. A cut above other all-night eateries in this area, *Avocado* does sushi, miso soup and *shashlyk*. Business lunch R300. No cards. Daily 11am–6am.

Bier König (Beer King) Gorokhovaya ul. 40; Sennaya Ploshchad/Sadovaya metro. A bierkeller with vaulted ceilings, Wi-Fi and Turbo-folk music. It serves wurst, mashed potatoes and fried cabbage, as well as twenty different draught beers. Business lunch from R160. MC, Visa Mon–Fri 11am–1am, Sat & Sun 11am–5am.

Bochka (Barrel) Millionnaya ul. 27; Nevskiy Prospekt metro. See map on p.80. Humble basement café popular with staff at the Hermitage for its cheap *solyanka*, *pelmeni* and Russian salads. No cards. Daily 11am–11pm.

Dve Palochki (Two Chopsticks) Nevskiy pr. 22 (see map on pp.64–65) and Italyanskaya ul. 6 (see map on p.80); Nevskiy Prospekt/Gostiniy Dvor metro. Inexpensive Japanese food; the sushi and teriyaki aren't great but you can't fault their baked rolls – try the crab rolls with shitake mushroom sauce. Blankets provided

for diners on the terrace. Major cards. Daily 11am–6am.

Gastronom (Delicatessen) Marsovo pole 7 ☎314 38 49; Nevskiy Prospekt/Gostiniy Dvor metro. See map on p.80. A trendy hang-out with street tables in the summer, its menu features well-prepared Italian, Japanese and Russian dishes. No cards. Mon–Thurs & Sun noon–midnight, Fri & Sat noon–3am.

Idiot Café nab. reki Moyki 82; Sadovaya/Sennaya Ploshchad metro. Named after the Dostoyevsky novel, this cosy basement furnished with divans and period junk is popular with foreigners. Its (mainly) vegetarian menu is strongest on *borsch*, *pelmeni*, *bliny* and pickled nibbles. All orders come with a shot of vodka. No cards. Daily 11am–11pm.

Il Patio Nevskiy pr. 30 ☎314 82 15; Nevskiy Prospekt/Gostiniy Dvor metro. See map on pp.64–65. One of the best cheapish options on Nevskiy, this pizzeria is popular with tourists and locals alike, with tables outside. All cards. Sun–Thurs 8am–midnight, Fri & Sat 8am–6am; summer daily 8am–6am.

La Cucaracha (The Cockroach) nab. reki Fontanki 39 ☎710 40 46; Gostiniy Dvor metro. See map on pp.64–65. Tex-Mex cantina where the bill can be reasonable if you don't splurge on margaritas or aged tequila; 20 percent off meals on weekdays from noon–4pm; happy hour 6–8pm; live music Tues, Thurs & Fri. DC, JCB, Maestro, MC, Visa. Mon–Thurs & Sun noon–1am, Fri & Sat noon–5am.

Lyod (Ice) Kazanskaya ul. 2; Gostiniy Dvor/Nevskiy Prospekt metro. See map on pp.64–65. An ice bar, where customers are given mittens, cloaks and felt boots to cope with its –5C°

chill: the walls, chairs and glasses are all made from ice. Mon–Thurs from 1pm, Fri–Sun from 3pm until the last customer leaves. **Macco Club** Nevskiy pr. 27; **Gostiniy Dvor/Nevskiy Prospekt metro. See map on pp.64–65.** A coffee shop and patisserie that has been around forever, currently themed on Kalahari Bushmen in a bid to attract hip "urban warriors". Daily 9am–11pm.

Shatyor (Tent) Italyanskaya ul. 2 ⓦwww.shateropencafe.ru; **Nevskiy Prospekt/Gostiniy Dvor metro. See map p.80.** This silk-tent-roofed summer café is a popular chill-out spot for clubbers and fashionistas, serving hot snacks, salads, ice creams and cocktails. Live music from 8.30pm (see website for details). June–Sept daily 8am–6am.

Stolle Konyushennaya per. 2, **Nevskiy Prospekt/Gostiniy Dvor metro (see map on p.80); ul. Dekabristov 19 & 33, Sadovaya/Sennaya Ploshchad metro.** This mini-chain of cafés bakes wonderful sweet and savoury pies (from R50). The first branch is not far from the Church of the Saviour on the Blood, the other two in walking range of the Mariinskiy Theatre. Daily 8am–10pm.

Tinkoff Kazanskaya ul. 7; **Nevskiy Prospekt/Gostiniy Dvor metro. See map on pp.64–65.** Russia's oldest micro-brewery features ten varieties of freshly brewed beer (try the White Unfiltered), a sushi bar, restaurant with Euro cuisine, TV sports and live music (Wed–Sun). The sushi is good value but drinks are costly. MC, Visa. Daily noon–2am.

Zhili Byli (Once Upon a Time) Nevskiy pr. 50; **Gostiniy Dvor/Nevskiy Prospekt metro. See map on pp.64–65.** St Petersburg *Sex and the City* babes' hang-out with a terrace that's almost too close to streetlife for comfort. Wide range of salads, hot snacks, cakes and sundaes, at affordable prices. Daily 24hr.

Vasilevskiy Island

Café Rotunda 5-ya liniya 42; **Vasileostrovskaya metro. See map on pp.152–153.** If you can't stomach the fast-food joints near the metro station, this Russian take on a Parisian bistro does steaks, seafood, soups and salads, with wine as well as beer and vodka to drink. No cards. Daily 11am–11pm.

Petrograd Side

The listings in this section are marked on the map on pp.168–169, unless stated otherwise.

Baltic Bread on Bolshoy Bolshoy pr. 80; **Petrogradskaya metro.** Sells over 200 types of loaves, puff-pastry savouries, gateaux and pastries, to be enjoyed with coffee. Good for breakfast. No cards. Daily 9am–10pm.

Café in the Ioannevskiy ravelin of the Peter and Paul Fortress; **Gorkovskaya metro. See map on p.170.** The only cheapish place to eat within the fortress does omelettes, soups, pasta, meat dishes, draught beer and hot drinks. No cards. Daily 10am–6pm.

Gzhelskaya Skazka (Gzhel Fairytale) in the park at the corner of Levashovskiy pr. and Chkalovskiy pr.; **Petrogradskaya metro.** An indoor/outdoor bar decorated with Gzhel porcelain figures, near the Yelizarov Flat-Museum (see p.182). No cards. Daily 11am–11pm.

Mama Roma Bolshoy pr. 70/72; **Petrogradskaya metro.** Pizzas, pasta, salads and focaccia bread. Business lunch and take-outs. Free Wi-Fi. No cards. Daily 11am–1am.

Morkovka (Carrot) Bolshoy pr. 32 ⓦwww.morkovka.org; **Chkalovskaya metro.** Trendy veggie café serving everything from carrot patties to beetroot salad with prunes, plus fish dishes and desserts, with a complimentary glass of carrot juice. MC, Visa. Daily noon–midnight.

Mozart Kronverkskiy pr. 23; **Gorkovskaya metro.** Enjoy schnitzel, fried carp, Austrian beer, cocktails or flavoured coffees in this cosy non-smoking café near the Alexander Park. No cards. Daily 9am–11pm.

Tbiliso Sytninskaya ul. 10 ☎232 93 91; **Gorkovskaya metro.** One of the oldest Georgian cafés in the city, its decor has greatly improved while its home-made cheese, *khachapuri* and stews remain as good as ever. Live music 8–11pm. No cards. Daily noon–1am.

Troitskiy most Malaya Posadskaya ul. 2 and Kronverkskiy pr. 31; **Gorkovskaya metro.** Two good-value vegetarian cafés near the Peter and Paul Fortress, serving salads, hot dishes, cakes, juices and herbal teas, with whale noises and chill-out music to relax customers. No smoking. No cards. Daily 9am–11pm.

Liteniy, Smolniy and Vladimirskaya

The listings in this section are marked on the map on pp.192–193.

Aziya (Asia) ul. Ryleeva 23 ☎272 01 68; **Chernyshevskaya metro.** Tasty Uzbek and Russian cuisine at amazingly low prices.

Try the spicy vegetable or lamb *cheburek*, and a soup or a kebab and you'll be stuffed. No cards. Daily 11am–11pm.

Baltic Bread Grechiskiy pr. 25; tram #5 or #7 from Ploshchad Vosstaniya metro. All kinds of bread, pastries and savouries, with a few tables, six blocks from the *St Petersburg International Hostel*. No cards. Daily 10am–9pm.

Bliny domik (Pancake Cottage) Kolokolnaya ul. 8; Dostoevskaya metro. This busy place not only serves *bliny* with all kinds of fillings, but spicy aubergine salad, cheese or meat fondue, herbal teas and a full breakfast menu – all very tasty and affordable. No cards. Daily 8am–11pm.

Café Club Che Poltavskaya ul. 3 ☏717 76 00; Ploshchad Vosstaniya metro. A funky café-bar serving coffee, soup and hot snacks, which turns into an all-night club with live jazz or blues (see p.360). No cards. Daily 9am–7am.

Café Jam ul. Ryleeva 12 ☏719 69 33; Chernyshevskaya metro. Tasty Scandinavian, Russian and Korean food under one roof, with a stylish interior, art exhibitions, and live jazz on Wed & Fri. Business lunch R170. No cards. Daily noon–11pm.

Café Rico Pushkinskaya ul. 1/3; Mayakovskaya/Ploshchad Vosstaniya metro. Ethno-funk café with Arabic coffee, coffee cocktails, cakes, ice cream, fresh juices, and a fountain. No smoking. No cards. Mon–Fri 9am–midnight, Sat & Sun 10am–midnight.

City Bar Furshtatskaya ul. 20; Chernyshevskaya metro ☏448 58 37, ⓦwww.citybar.ru St Petersburg's *Cheers*: an expat-friendly, split-level venue with sofas, Wi-Fi, all-day breakfasts and delicious burgers, plus DJs and comedians on Fri & Sat evenings. Daily 8am till the last guest leaves.

Dickens nab. reki Fontanki 108; Sadovaya or Pushkinskaya metro. Dickens theme-pub with a summer terrace and an upstairs restaurant with an open fireplace; cask ales, fine whiskies, Sky Sports, and a full English breakfast (R250) served from 8am–5pm. Major cards. Tues–Thurs 8am–2pm, Mon & Sun 8am–1am, Fri & Sat 8am–3pm.

Guel ul. Nekrasova 15; Chernyshevskaya metro. Cakes, pies, ice creams and bread, to eat in or take away; cakes are 20 percent cheaper after 8pm. Daily 8.30am–10pm.

Kolobok ul. Chaykovskovo 40 marked on Zakhare; Chernyshevskaya metro. Named after the roly-poly doughy hero of

Russian folklore, this self-service place has tasty sweet and savoury *pirozhki* (pies), hot meals and salads. No cards. Daily 7.30am–9pm.

Lagidze ul. Belinskovo 3; Gostiniy Dvor metro. One of the oldest Georgian cafés in town, its decor and service are casual but its *khachapuri*, *tsatsivi* and other dishes are all spot-on, and cheap. No cards. Daily 11am–midnight.

Lenin Zhiv (Lenin Lives) nab. reki Fontanki 40; Mayakovskaya or Gostiniy Dvor metro. Worth a drink purely for its decor – a hybrid of Constructivist chic and Soviet High Command bunker, with Meccano-style furniture and toilets like airlocks. Belgian beer; business lunch R180. No cards. Daily 24hr.

Russkie bliny (Russian Pancakes) ul. Gagarinskaya 13; 15–20min from Nevskiy Prospekt metro. Very popular, cheap lunchtime spot. The *bliny* with red caviar or the *blinchiki* (folded deep-fried *bliny*) with mushrooms or pureed salt fish are great. Come before 1pm or after 2.30pm to avoid the queues. No cards. Mon–Fri 11am–6pm.

Stariy dom (Old House) ul. Nekrasova 27; Chernyshevskaya metro. Basement café serving authentic Azerbaijani cuisine. Go for the marinated nibbles with vodka, then a meatball and chervil soup or a kebab – there's even ram's balls if you fancy them – before finishing up with a pot of smoked black tea. No cards. Daily 11am–midnight.

Sunduk (The Chest) Furshtatskaya ul. 42 ☏272 31 00, ⓦwww.cafésunduk.ru; Chernyshevskaya metro. Funky art café with Euro/Russian food and Spanish, blues or jazz music (8.30–11pm). No cards. Mon–Fri 10am–midnight, Sat & Sun 11am–midnight.

Wooden Pub ul. Chaykovskovo 36; Chernyshevskaya metro. Friendly basement bar with tables outside in summer, featuring imported draught beers, spirits and French wines, seafood snacks, and a saxophonist and fiddler (Fri & Sat night). No cards. Daily 11am–2am.

The Southern Suburbs

The listings in this section are marked on the map on p.214.

Café Lido Moskovskiy pr. 216; Moskovskaya metro. Cakes, ice creams and coffee accompanied by MTV. Daily 24hr.

Kafeteriy address as above. Spacious confectioner's with a big choice of cakes, ices, savouries, soups and coffee – good if you feel hungry after coming back from Gatchina (the minibus stops outside). No cards. Daily 10am–10pm.

Prazdroy pr. Stachek 57; Kirovskiy Zavod metro. Cosy pub with traditional Czech cuisine

(vegetarians needn't bother), beers, an extended set busin (Mon–Fri 11am–5pm) and bi cards. Daily 11am–1am (Fri

Restaurants

St Petersburg's restaurants are as diverse as the food they serve. At the top end of the scale, you'll probably feel uncomfortable if you're not dressed to the hilt – though not many places impose a formal dress code (a jacket and tie for men, a skirt or dress for women). A service charge is rarely included on the bill, so you can tip (or not) as you like. Some places feature floorshows consisting of folk music, belly dancing or maybe a striptease act (which Russians regard with equanimity), for which there may or may not be a surcharge. At most restaurants it's customary to consign your coat to the cloakroom on arrival; if you are helped to put it back on later, a small tip is warranted.

From noon to 4pm on weekdays, many places offer a set **business lunch** of three or four courses at lower prices than you'd pay dining à la carte, though the quality and quantity may not be as good. Look for signboards outside with the Cyrillic words бизнеС ланьч (pronounced *biznes lanch*), and in the local foreign-language press, where you can also find details of all-you-can eat **Sunday brunches** at the *Nevskij Palace* and *Grand Hotel Europe* as well as **food festivals** held at these and other deluxe hotels.

You can read **reviews** of local restaurants in English on Ⓦwww.eng.peterout. ru/eda and Ⓦwww.restoran.ru; if you understand Russian, visit Ⓦwww.menu.ru or the archive of *Time Out Petersburg*'s reviews on Ⓦwww.timeout.ru.

We've given **telephone numbers** for all the restaurants listed, as reserving in advance is always a good idea, particularly if you want to eat after 9pm. Most places have at least one member of staff with a rudimentary grasp of English. If not, a useful phrase to get your tongue around is *Ya khochu zakazat stol na . . . cheloveka sevodnya na . . . chasov* (I want to reserve a table for . . . people for . . . o'clock today).

The restaurant listings are divided into geographical areas that correspond to the chapters, and into price categories, too – inexpensive, moderate, expensive and very expensive. You should be able to get a soup, a main course, a dessert plus a couple of beers in the price bracket indicated:

Inexpensive under R1000
Moderate R1000–1500
Expensive R1500–2500
Very expensive over R2500

These categorizations refer to dining à la carte, but many restaurants offer a business lunch or Sunday brunch that costs a lot less than this. Generally, beer and vodka are cheap enough to **drink** a lot without hugely increasing the final bill – but wine or imported liquors are another matter, especially in restaurants with deluxe cellars. Never order wine without verifying the price.

The listings in this section are marked on the map on pp.62–63, unless specified otherwise.

Inexpensive

Da Albertone Millionnaya ul. 23 ☎315 86 73, ⊛www.daalbertone.ru; Gostiniy Dvor/Nevskiy Prospekt metro. See map on p.80. Close to the Hermitage, this above-average pizzeria is child-friendly, with a 20 percent discount on meals from 11am–2pm and a 5–7pm happy hour. Major cards. Daily 11am–11pm.

Baku Sadovaya ul. 12/23 ☎941 37 56; Gostiniy Dvor metro. See map on pp.64–65. An ornate shrine to Azerbaijani cuisine, with lots of baked vegetable options, kebabs and pilafs, and meat or fish served on hot coals (saj). Live music and belly dancing most nights. Major cards. Daily noon–2am.

Fasol (Beans) Gorokhovaya ul. 17 ☎571 09 07, ⊛www.fasolcafe.ru (in Russian); Nevskiy Prospekt metro. Minimalist, laid-back and fashionable, its menu features Russian, Italian and Asian dishes. Try the cabbage and duck soup, or the forshmak (chopped herring salad) with potato pancakes as a starter. No cards. Daily noon–midnight.

Ket u Mimino Karavannaya ul. 24 ☎315 38 00; Gostiniy Dvor metro. See map on pp.64–65. Unpretentious, cosy basement den specializing in Georgian and European cooking; Its owner is descended from Georgian princes. No cards. Daily noon–11pm.

La Strada Bolshaya Konyushennaya ul. 27 ☎312 47 00; Gostiniy Dvor/Nevskiy Prospekt metro. See map on pp.64–65. Designed to resemble a pavement café, this child-friendly place has a wood-fired pizza oven and salad bar. Try the antipasto with baked potatoes. MC, Union, Visa. Daily from noon till the last customer leaves.

Ne Goryuy (Don't Worry) Kirpichniy per. 3 ☎571 69 50; Nevskiy Prospekt metro. See map on pp.64–65. Another excellent-value Georgian restaurant, named after a Soviet comedy film; its menu features eight different types of khatchapuri for starters. Major cards. Daily noon–midnight.

Moderate

1001 Nights Millionnaya ul. 21/6 ☎570 17 03; Nevskiy Prospekt metro. See map on p.80. Delicious Uzbek food, with plenty of salads

if you don't fancy specialities such as kazy (horse sausage). Waitresses in silk gowns, Uzbek musicians and belly dancers (Fri–Sun 8.30pm & 10pm). Business lunch R190. MC, Union, Visa. Daily 11am–11pm.

Karavan (Caravan) Voznesenskiy pr. 46 ☎571 28 00; Sadovaya/Sennaya Ploshchad metro. Azerbaijani, Georgian and Uzbek cuisine, with bread baked in a clay oven. Their shashlyk and chebureki are fantastic. No cards. Daily noon–2am.

Lehaim Lermentovskiy pr. 2 ☎572 56 16; bus #22 from Nevskiy Prospekt metro. A fancy kosher restaurant tucked away beneath the Great Synagogue (see p.113), serving generous portions of traditional Jewish cooking. No cards. Daily noon–11.30pm.

Olivia Bolshaya Morskaya ul. 11 ☎314 65 63; Nevskiy Prospekt metro. See map on p.94. Capacious Greek restaurant with a kids' menu and playroom, authentic dishes, retsina and ouzo, a varied salad bar, live music (Tues–Thurs) and lessons in Greek dancing (Fri & Sat). Major cards. Daily noon–midnight.

Sukawati Kazanskaya ul. 8 ☎312 05 40; Nevskiy Prospekt metro. See map on pp.64–65). Great for vegetarians, but meat eaters will also enjoy this decorative Indonesian restaurant. Try the spring rolls (lumpia) and rice platters (nasi goreng). Major cards. Daily noon–5am.

Tandoor Voznesenkiy pr. 2 ☎312 38 86; Nevskiy Prospekt metro. See map on p.94. The city's oldest Indian restaurant, near St Isaac's, has a nice ambience and vegetarians will be heartened by the choice of dishes. Business lunch R320; set dinner R800. Major cards. Daily noon–11pm.

Tandoori Nights Voznesenkiy pr. 4 ☎312 87 72; Nevskiy Prospekt metro. See map on p.94. Just around the corner from Tandoor, this new, upscale Indian restaurant does mouth-watering Tandoori dishes cooked in a clay oven. Major cards. Daily 11am–midnight.

Yerivan nab. Treki Fontanki 51 ☎703 38 20; Gostiniy Dvor metro. See map on pp.64–65. Traditional Armenian cooking, heavy on mutton and veal, complemented by Armenian rugs and brightly patterned tablecloths in the Rustic Room. No cards. Daily noon–11pm.

Expensive

1913 Vosnesenskiy pr. 13/2 ☎315 51 48; bus #22 from Nevskiy pr. Its name refers to Russia's "best ever year", before the outbreak of war and revolutions. Generous portions of simple rural dishes like potato pancakes with bacon and sour cream (*draniky*), and richer options such as lobster fricassée. Guitar, accordion and violin music 8–11pm. MC, Visa. Daily noon–1am.

Caviar Bar Grand Hotel Europe, Mikhailovskaya ul. 1–7 ☎329 66 22; Gostiniy Dvor/Nevskiy Prospekt metro. See map on pp.64–65. An aristocratic haunt before the Revolution, serving Kamchatka crab, Siberian *pelmeni* in champagne sauce, sturgeon and salmon mousse, accompanied by champagne or deluxe vodkas. Major cards. Daily 5.30pm–1am.

Europe Grand Hotel Europe, Mikhailovskaya ul. 1–7 ☎329 60 00; as above. Heavily sauced European and Russian dishes, impeccably served in a sumptuous Art Nouveau setting. Jacket and tie required. Come for the Sunday champagne jazz brunch (12.30–4pm; R3000). DC, MC, Visa. Open for breakfast (daily 7–10.30am) and dinner (Mon–Sat 7–11pm).

Shyolk (Silk) Malaya Konyushennaya ul. 4/2 ☎571 50 78; Nevskiy Prospekt/ Gostiniy Dvor metro. See map on p.80. Gauzy drapes, silk-upholstered sofas, soft lighting and Italian and Japanese cuisine make this a favourite for business lunches and romantic dinners. DJ and dancing at weekends. Major cards. Mon–Thurs & Sun 1pm–1am, Fri & Sat 1pm–3am.

Stroganoff Steak House Konnogvardeyskiy bul. 4 ☎314 55 14; Nevskiy Prospekt metro. See map on p.94. Steaks are flown in from around the world to appear on the tables at this spacious, bare-brick and dark leather den in the former Horseguards' stables. Major cards. Daily noon–1am.

Very expensive

Dvoryanskoe Gnezdo (The Noble Nest) ul. Dekabristov 21 ☎312 32 05; Sadovaya/Sennaya Ploshchad metro. Housed in the summer pavilion of the Yusupov Palace, near the Mariinskiy Theatre, it draws on European, Russian and Asian traditions for its *haute cuisine*, with live classical music from 8pm. Formal dress and reservations required. Major cards. Daily noon–midnight.

Graf Suvorov ul. Lomonosova 6 ☎315 43 26, Ⓦwww.grafsuvorov.ru; Gostiniy Dvor metro. See map on pp.64–65. Gourmet Russian and European food served in surroundings of lashings of gilt, fake marble and repro

antiques. Try the bear fillet or deer carpaccio. Musical evenings from Gypsy to jazz or Soviet retro. Major cards. Daily from noon till the last customer leaves.

Taleon Club nab. reki Moyki 59 ☎324 99 11, Ⓦwww.taleon.ru; Nevskiy Prospekt metro. See map on pp.64–65. Housed in the splendid mansion of the merchant Yeliseev (p.73), latterly the Institute of Marxism Leninism, this is the place to go if you've money to burn. Its menu runs from Escoffier classics to tilapia with rock lobsters and chanterelle mushrooms. Major cards. Daily 7.30am–11pm.

Vasilevskiy Island

The listings in this section are marked on the map on pp.152–153, unless stated otherwise. Some places are nearer to Sportivnaya metro on the Petrograd Side than to Vasileostrovskaya metro on Vasilevskiy Island; others are best reached by minibus from the city centre.

Inexpensive

Imperator (Emperor) Tamozhniy per. 2 ☎323 30 31; minibus #47, #128 or #129 from Nevskiy pr. See map on p.155. The cheapest place to eat on the Strelka, whether you go for its filling but unexciting business lunch (R150), or Russian, Caucasian or Mexican dishes à la carte (with chanson music some evenings). No cards. Daily 10am–1am.

Kabanchik (Little Boar) Sredniy pr. 54 ☎322 21 11; Vasileostrovskaya metro. It's worth a few blocks' walk from the metro to reach this peaceful, wood-panelled Georgian restaurant, whose food is almost as good as at *Ketino* (see below) but much cheaper. No cards. Daily 10am–11pm.

Moderate

Byblos Maliy pr. 5 ☎325 85 64; Sportivnaya metro. This Lebanese restaurant serves tasty *kibbe*, *tabuli*, humus, stuffed vine leaves and yogurt-rich salads. Lebanese wines, hookahs with flavoured tobaccos, as well as live music with belly dancing (Fri & Sat). Maestro, MC, Visa. Daily 11am–11pm.

Grad Petrov Universitetskaya nab. 5 ☎326 0137, Ⓦwww.die-kneipe.ru; minibus #47, #128 or #129 from Nevskiy pr. See map on p.155. All bare brickwork and brass kettles, this brewery-restaurant specializes in contemporary German cuisine. No cards. Daily noon till the last person leaves.

🏃 **Ketino** 9-ya liniya 20 ☎ 326 01 96, ✉ ketino@mail.ru; Vasileostrovskaya metro. While the atmosphere is less intimate than at its Petrograd Side sister restaurant, *Salkhino* (p.352), the Georgian food is even better. Try a few starters before ordering any main courses – you may not need them. Wine is expensive. No cards. Daily 11am–11pm.

Expensive

Restoran (The Restaurant) Tamozhniy per. 2 ☎ 327 89 79; minibus #47, #128 or #129 from Nevskiy pr. See map on p.155. Located opposite the Kunstkammer, its decor is so minimalist that the owners asked the designer "Is that it?" The food is traditional Russian and made from the finest ingredients, but it takes ages to arrive. All major cards. Daily noon–midnight.

Russian Kitsch Universitetskaya nab. 25 ☎ 325 11 22; Vasileostrovskaya metro. Perestroika-themed luxury café with lurid images of Brezhnev and menus disguised as tracts by Lenin or Stalin. Come to gawp and have a drink, even if you can't afford to try its fusion cuisine or sushi. No cards. Daily noon–4am.

Staraya Tamozhnya (Old Customs House) Tamozhniy per. 1 ☎ 327 89 90; minibus #47, #128 or #129 from Nevskiy pr. See map p.155. Also near the Kunstkammer, this classy cellar conversion has an open kitchen with a French-oriented menu of dishes such as lobster, steak and caviar *bliny*. MC, Visa. Daily 1pm–1am.

Petrograd Side

The listings in this section are marked on the map on pp.168–169, unless stated otherwise.

Inexpensive

Demyanova Ukha (Demyan's Ukha) Kronverkskiy pr. 53 ☎ 232 80 90; Gorkovskaya metro. *Ukha* is the local equivalent of *bouillabaisse*, and this Soviet-style place features every kind of fish dish in the Russian culinary lexicon. Business lunch R150. Live music Sat & Sun 9.30–11pm. Major cards. Daily noon–midnight.

Povari Bolshoy pr. 38/40 ☎ 233 70 42; Chakalovskaya metro. This Italian restaurant doesn't do pizzas, but its freshly made pasta dishes are fantastic. In warm weather, you can sit outside and watch the streetlife. No smoking. No cards. Daily 10am–1am.

Moderate

Karl & Friedrich Yuzhnaya Doroga 11 ☎ 320 79 78; Krestovskiy Ostrov metro. Ironically named after Marx and Engels, this Bavarian brewery-restaurant has a French chef, an outdoor *shashlyk* grill, and a child-minder (Mon–Fri 7–10pm, Sat & Sun 2–10pm). At weekends over summer, an open "train" shuttles between the restaurant and the metro. No cards. Daily noon–2am.

🏃 **Salkhino** Kronverkskiy pr. 25 ☎ 232 78 91, ✉ katino@mail.ru; Gorkovskaya metro. This cosy café hung with paintings by local artists serves some of the best Georgian food on the Petrograd Side – booking is advisable at any time. No cards. Daily 11am–11pm.

U Gorchakova (At Gorchakov's) Bolshaya Monetnaya ul. 19 ☎ 233 93 72; Petrogradskaya metro. Russian and Ukrainian *haute cuisine* (try the roast veal with cherries), a lavish wine cellar, flavoured vodkas, *medovukha* (mead) and *sbiten* (a herbal liquor) complemented by a theatrical decor and nostalgic piano music. Major cards. Daily noon–midnight.

Volna (Wave) Petrovskaya nab. 4 ☎ 322 53 83; Gorkovskaya metro. Just behind Peter the Great's Cabin (see p.177), its Japanese minimalist decor befits its Asian-accented fusion cooking. No cards. Daily noon–midnight.

Zver (Wild Animal) Alexander Park 5 ☎ 232 20 62, 🌐 www.restoran-zver.spb.ru; Gorkovskaya metro. See map on p.170. This steakhouse-style hall does wild boar, deer and salmon served on skewers, and a less intimidating children's menu. DC, MC, Visa. Daily noon until the last customer leaves.

Expensive

Austeria in the Ioanavskiy ravelin of the Peter and Paul Fortress ☎ 230 03 69, 🌐 www.restaurant-austeria.spb.ru; Gorkovskaya metro. See map on p.170. Recipes from the time of Peter the Great, with sauce combinations such as cranberry and horseradish, and all sorts of flavoured vodkas. Billiard room and horn band. No cards. Daily noon–midnight.

Russkaya rybalka (Russian Fishing) Yuzhnaya Doroga 11 ☎ 323 98 13; Krestovskiy Ostrov metro. Under the same management as *Karl & Friedrich* (see above), this nearby pond-side theme-restaurant lets diners hook their own trout, sturgeon or sterlet, and watch it being grilled. No cards. Daily noon–9am.

Very expensive

Aquarel (Watercolour) pr. Dobrolyubova 14a, first floor ⊤320 86 00; Sportivnaya metro. A high-tech, glass-walled fusion restaurant-boat with stunning views of the Neva, live lobster tanks, a bar, leather armchairs and circular sofas. Upstairs is a less expensive Italian bistro, *Aquarellisimo*. Major cards. Daily noon until the last guest leaves.

Liteniy, Smolniy and Vladimirskaya

The listings in this section are marked on the map on pp.192–193.

Inexpensive

Gino-no-Taki pr. Chernyshevskovo 17 ⊤272 09 58; Chernyshevskaya metro. Stylish, traditionally designed Japanese restaurant with 180 dishes on its menu, plus sake, and attentive service. All major cards except Amex. Daily 11am–6am.

Jamoneria Liteyniy pr. 11 ⊤327 34 77; Mayakovskaya metro. Move over Almodóvar – almost every dish here is made from *jamón*, with Spanish wines and *finos* to wash them down. Tapas R250, paella for two R400. Maestro, MC, Visa. Daily 11.30am–11pm.

Rigas Seta (Riga Courtyard) ul. Mayakovskovo 34/4 ⊤273 11 49, ⓦwww.rigasseta.ru; 15min walk from Mayakovskaya or Chernyshevskaya metro. A cosy Latvian restaurant serving such native specialties as mutton on the bone with prunes and apricots. No cards. Daily noon–11pm.

▼ Austeria in the Peter and Paul Fortress

Moderate

Imbir (Ginger) Zagorodniy pr. 15 T713 32 15, ⓦwww.imbircafe.ru (in Russian); Doestoevskaya metro. Sister-restaurant to *Fasol* (see p.350), its menu is a mix of sushi, noodles, fish dishes and nouvelle Russian cuisine – try the Imbir salad with prawns and chicken, or the poached salmon. No cards. Daily noon–2am.

Imperial Nevskij Palace Hotel, Nevskiy pr. 57 ⊤380 20 01; Mayakovskaya metro. Enjoy a wonderful view of Nevskiy as you tuck into the buffet of Japanese, Mexican, Thai and Indian appetizers (noon–4pm) or the caviar bar, or choose from the Continental menu. Jazz brunch Sun noon–4pm. Children's menu and playroom. All major cards. Mon–Sat 7–11pm.

Kolkhida (Colchis) Nevskiy pr. 176 ⊤274 25 14; Ploshchad Aleksandra Nevskovo metro. Its name refers to the ancient land (now Georgia) where Jason sought the Golden Fleece. Being close to the Alexander Nevsky Monastery and Moskva Hotel it mainly caters to tour groups, but its Georgian food is tasty. Major cards. Daily noon–midnight.

Matrosskaya Tishina (Sailors' Silence) ul. Marata 54/34 ⊤764 44 13, ⓦwww.tishina.ru; Ligovskiy Prospekt metro. A "fish fashion restaurant" with portholes, oysters on ice and aquariums brimming with giant perch, crab and lobsters. MC, Visa. Daily noon–midnight.

Shinok (Puppy) Zagorodniy pr. 13 ⊤571 82 62; Dostoevskaya/Vladimirskaya metro. Jolly Ukrainian basement tavern with folk music after 9pm. Try one of the two kinds of *borsch* or four varieties of *vareniki* (dumplings) as starters, with suckling pig, chicken or rabbit to follow, accompanied by *gorilka* (Ukrainian vodka). Major cards. Daily 11am–5am, Mon till 2am.

Terra Cotta Gagarinskaya ul. 6/1 ⊤336 30 14, ⓦwww.terracotta. ru; Chernyshevskaya metro. "Drink, dine and dance" restaurant whose menu includes sea bass, saté chicken and Belgian waffles, with DJs and regular themed party nights. No cards. Sun–Wed noon–1am, Thurs–Sat noon–3am.

Tres Amigos ul. Rubinshteyna 25 ⊤572 26 85; Dostoevskaya/Vladimirskaya metro. An Aztec beer hall serving zesty Columbian, Ecuadorian, Mexican and Peruvian dishes, with a children's menu and playroom, supervised at weekends; Latin dance show Fri & Sun nights. MC, Visa. Daily noon until the last customer leaves.

Xren Zagorodniy pr. 13, second floor ☎347 88 50; Dostoevskaya/Vladimirskaya metro. Three differently styled rooms overlooking "Five Corners", where you can enjoy two-colour gazpacho, duck and couscous, and other nouvelle Continental dishes. Major cards. Daily noon–1am.

Expensive

Bistrot Garçon Nevskiy pr. 95 ☎717 24 67; Ploshchad Vosstaniya metro. An intimate French restaurant with a wonderful seasonal menu, enlivened by a chanteuse or accordionist some nights. Major cards. Daily 9am–1am.

Landskrona Nevskij Palace Hotel, Nevskiy pr. 57 ☎380 20 01; Mayakovskaya metro. Top-floor restaurant with superb views of the city skyline, a summer terrace, gourmet Mediterranean specialties and silver service; it serves a wonderful brunch (Sun 12.30–5pm) and has live music at night. Major cards. Daily 6.30pm–midnight.

Probka (Cork) ul. Belinskovo 5 ☎273 49 04, ⓦwww.probka.ru; Gostiniy Dvor metro. This chic wine restaurant serves the best Italian cuisine in the city; the downstairs wine-bar is more affordable, and there's also a shop selling fresh Italian products and ingredients. Major cards. Daily 1–4pm & 7pm–midnight.

The Southern Suburbs

The listings in this section are marked on the map on p.214.

Moderate

Paulaner Park Inn Pulkovskaya Hotel, pl. Pobedy 1 ☎740 39 32; Moskovskaya metro. This large brewery-restaurant serving hearty Bavarian and Swiss dishes is aimed at tour groups, but good for a meal or a drink if you're visiting the Victory Monument. Major cards. Daily noon–1am.

Pietari Moskovskiy pr. 222; Moskovskaya metro. Finnish-style venture with pasta dishes, reindeer steaks, tiger-prawn salad and sturgeon *solyanka*. There's no need to reserve for the

restaurant (live music 8–11pm) or beer hall. Major cards. Daily 11am–midnight.

Vyborg Side

The listings in this section are marked on the map on p.222.

Inexpensive

Schwabski domik (Swabian Cottage) Novocherkasskiy pr. 28/19 ☎528 89 85, ⓦwww.schwabski.ru; Novocherkasskaya metro. A wood-panelled bar-restaurant-bistro serving German and Czech fare; each section has a different menu. Major cards. Daily 11am–1am; pub till 11pm.

Moderate

7.40 Bolshoy Samsonievskiy pr. 108 ☎492 34 44; tram #21 from Chernaya Rechka metro. Jewish home cooking (not all kosher) amid photos and ephemera of the Jewish heritage in Russia, with live music at night. Don't miss the nearby Lenin mural (p.225). Maestro, MC, Visa. Mon 3–11pm, Tues–Sun noon–10pm.

Kavkaz (Caucasus) ul. Stakhanovistov 5 ☎444 43 09; Novocherkasskaya metro. Good for Georgian specialities such as *khachapuri*, *shashlyk*, marinated meat *basturma* and *khash* (tripe soup, supposedly a cure for hangovers). Major cards except Amex. Daily noon–midnight.

Staraya Derevnya (Old Village) ul. Savushkina 72 ☎431 00 00; tram #2 or #31 from Chernaya Rechka metro. Family-run restaurant serving Russian home-cooking, accompanied by piano and accordion music (Sun–Thurs) or Gypsy, Russian and Jewish songs (Fri & Sat). The beef with plum and nut sauce is a winner. Be sure to reserve. No cards. Daily 1–10pm.

Expensive

U Petrovicha (At Petrovich's) Sredneokhtinskiy pr. 44 ☎227 21 35; tram #7 or bus #174 from Novocherkasskaya metro. The crummy neighbourhood is forgotten once you're settled in this cosy den, with its eighteenth-century decor and Russian festive dishes, such as elk, wild boar, rabbit or suckling pig. Musical duets 7–11pm. Reservations required. No cards. Daily noon–11pm.

Clubs and live venues

S t Petersburg isn't a city that goes to bed early. With alcohol on sale 24 hours, Russian youths wander the streets from one *tsusovka* (event) to another, playing guitars in parks or the subways. During the White Nights, even families with young children come to watch the bridges rise along the Neva embankments and enjoy the music and party atmosphere. Winter may force parties indoors, but there's no let-up on the club scene. Whether it's jazz-fusion, trance, grunge, S&M or gender bending, there are **clubs** for all tastes. Local DJs and foreign guests perform at most of these, and there are lots of one-off theme parties. Many double as **live music venues** for acts spanning the range of tastes from home-grown ska to thrash, plus alternative and world music bands from abroad – big-name acts are likely to stage concerts in one of the city's sports palaces or stadiums.

The term *klub* can cover anything from an arthouse café with a spot of live music to a dance warehouse, or a fancy nightclub with a restaurant and casino. Most cater to a certain crowd, whether it's creative professionals, students, shell-suited flatheads or designer-draped models. While formal dress codes are rare, **face control** (*feys kontrol*) is widespread. Russians distinguish between "democratic" face control (aimed at keeping out hooligans and bandits), and the kind that favours the rich (never mind how they behave). It's unwise to rile club security staff, however rude they might be. If you end up in a club full of shaven-headed **gangsters**, be careful not to flash your money around but don't be too nervous; they are out for a good time and unlikely to be looking for trouble. Men should be aware that most of the tourist-oriented or top-end clubs are full of **prostitutes**, for whom dancing with guys is just a prelude to business – though there are also lots of girls simply out for a good time, which can lead to misunderstandings. Striptease or pole-dancing acts are a feature of quite a few clubs and generally not regarded as sleazy by Russians – and cabaret shows can be even raunchier.

Admission charges and **drinks** prices are modest in most places, but a few clubs are pricey on both counts – see the reviews below. To find out the latest on up-and-coming events, check the **listings** sections in the Friday edition of the *St Petersburg Times* or the current month's issue of *Pulse*, or drop into any Titanik music store (see "Shopping", p.376) to browse through the flyers for gigs and parties. If you can understand Russian, another source of information about parties and events is the **website** Ⓦ www.club.ru, where you can also **buy tickets** for pop concerts and dance events. These can also be purchased at the Titanik music store at Nevskiy prospekt 63, open 24hr (Ⓦ www.titanik.spb.ru).

Many clubs in the centre are in the "polygon" of streets surrounding Gostiniy dvor, making it easy to wander from one to another. In the case of clubs or events on Vasilevskiy Island, the Petrograd or Vyborg Side, be careful not to find yourself stranded on the wrong side of the Neva when the **bridges** are raised in the small hours (see p.40).

⑮

Pop, dance, rock and world music

Russian pop is something of a joke to foreigners, but there's more to it than the faux-lesbian duo T.A.T.U. or the syrupy pop primadonna Alla Pugachova. Sergei Shnurov (who did the soundtrack for the gangster movie *Boomer*) and Lube (the only Russian group whose concerts have been attended by Putin) are the big names in Lyuberstsy music – a home-grown fusion of gangsta rap and Russian thieves' songs that shares the airwaves with the boy bands and girl groups churned out by *Fabrika* (the Russian equivalent of *Pop Idol*). Zemfira, Glyucosa and Varvara (known for the Celtic and Arabic influences on her music) are the divas of techno, while Blestyashchie and Nochniy Snaipery do plaintive folk-rock. Mumiy Troll from Vladivostok (led by the androgynous, intellectual Ilya Lagushenko) is the best known indie band, while St Petersburg is the home of the ska group Dva Samolota and vintage rockers DDT, who still play occasionally.

You can hear all kinds of music in the local clubs, especially during **SKIF** (ⓦwww.kuryokhin.ru/skif), a three-day **festival** of DJs, performance artists and bands from all over Russia and abroad, in April. Local **DJs** Sasha Kaktus, Raf, Banderas (house), Pushkin (progressive house, trance), Manifesto, Soul Sister (funk, R&B), Pushkarev, Yuka (electro) and Britz (post-punk, indie) are joined by foreign celebrities like Leeroy Thornhill, Lottie and Judge Jules during the annual **FortDance party** (see box on p.359).

Art Vokzal nab. Obvodnovo kanala 138 ☎495 90 04, ⓦwww.artvokzal.ru (in Russian only); minibus #67 or #267 from Baltiyskaya metro. See map on p.214. Incongruously installed in the "Red Triangle" factory, this art club hosts puppet shows for adults, tango, cult indie bands and other events (entry charge R200–400). Daily 11am–6am.

Buddha Bar Bolshaya Morskaya ul. 46 ☎314 70 17; Nevskiy Prospekt metro. See map on p.94. Deep house rules at this basement club with a Hindu-meets-cyberpunk decor and go-go girls, frequented by gangsters and fashionistas. Daily 6pm till the last customer leaves.

City Club Apraksin dvor, korpus 13 (access via Sadovaya ul.) ☎310 05 49; Nevskiy Prospekt/ Gostiniy Dvor metro. See map on pp.62–63. Above *Money Honey* (see opposite), this laid-back disco with pool tables hosts occasional gigs, for which it charges R100–300 entry. Daily 11am–5am.

Clubio Dom Mod, Kamennoostrovskiy pr. 37, first floor ☎329 30 91, ⓦwww.clubio.ru (in Russian only); Petrogradskaya metro. See map on pp168–169. DJ parties, bikini nights, firemen's evenings and other themed events, in what is by day a café serving breakfast and lunch. Admission R100–200 after 8pm. Sun–Thurs 11am–2am, Fri & Sat 11am–4am.

🏃 **Dacha** Dumskaya ul. 9; Nevskiy Prospekt/Gostiniy Dvor metro. See map

on pp.64–65. This tiny, fun bar gets packed out long before DJs start playing rock, soul and ska at 10pm, and the crowd spills onto the street – you must pay a deposit to take your drink outside. Admission Fri & Sat R100. Daily 6pm–6am.

Fidel Dumskaya ul. 9 ☎ mobile 8691/809 6103, ⓦwww.barfidel.ru (in Russian); Nevskiy Prospekt/Gostiniy Dvor metro. See map on p.64–65. Next door to Dacha, this Castro-themed DJ bar founded by Dva Samolota's bassist plays ska, Latino and Balkanbeat music after 10pm. Daily 8pm–6am.

Fish Fabriqué Ligovskiy pr. 53, third floor ☎764 48 57, ⓦwww.fishfabrique.spb.ru (in Russian); Ploshchad Vosstaniya metro. See map on pp.192–193. A legendary alternative café for artists and musicians at Pushkinskaya 10, featuring table football, cheap food and cult movies, with a cover charge (R150–200) for concerts from 11pm. Daily 5pm–6am (with a break from 8.30–9pm Fri & Sat).

GEZ–21 Ligovskiy pr. 53, block Б, third floor ☎764 52 58, ⓦwww.tac.spb.ru (in Russian only); Ploshchad Vosstaniya metro. See map on pp.192–193. In the same complex as Fish *Fabriqué*, the Gallery of Experimental Sound (GEZ) features electronic, jazz and rock concerts (from 9pm) and films (Wed & Sun at 8pm). Entry to concerts R70. Daily 5–11.30pm, Sat 3–11.30pm.

🏃 **Griboedov Club** Voronezhskaya ul. 2a ☎164 43 55, ⓦwww.griboedovclub.ru (in

Russian); Ligovskiy Prospekt metro. See map on pp.192–193. Run by the band Dva Samolota, this club in a deep bomb shelter also has an above-ground café with a Wi-Fi zone, Griboedov on the Hill. Gigs (from jazz-hop to Goth rock) start at 10pm, rave and house parties at midnight; Wed is Soviet retro disco night. Free entry before 8pm, then R100–400. Mon, Tues & Thurs noon–6am, Wed, Fri & Sat 6pm–7am.

Havana Club Moskovskiy pr. 24 ☎575 04 88, Ⓦwww.havana-club.ru (in Russian only); Tekhnologicheskiy Institut metro. See map on pp.192–193. Ricky Martin rules in this sizzling Cuban-themed club with a beer evening (Mon), student party (Tues), R&B and Latino party (Wed) and ladies' night (Sun). Admission Mon–Wed & Sun R90–120, Fri & Sat R150–250. Daily 6pm–6am.

Kamchatka ul. Blokhina 15 ☎498 08 87; Sportivnaya metro. See map on pp.168–169. In the same neck of the woods as Tunnel (see p.358), this club plays house and techno, with occasional gigs. Cover R100–200. Daily 7–11pm.

Konyushenniy dvor (aka Marstall) nab. kanala Griboedova 5 ☎315 76 07, Ⓦwww.kondvor.ru (in Russian only); Nevskiy Prospekt/Gostiniy Dvor metro. See map on p.80. A hassle-free disco and strip joint (after 11pm) thronged with foreigners, fun-loving local girls and hookers. Free entry with foreign passport, otherwise R200. Daily 1pm–6am.

Lyod Limon (Lemon Ice) nab. kanala Griboedova 6 ☎438 14 50, Ⓦwww.ledlimon.ru (in Russian); Nevskiy Prospekt/Gostiniy Dvor metro. See map on p.80. Not far from the above, this popular dance club plays house music and has a revolving bar. Entry with a club card (available free, 8–10pm); Wed & Thurs R150, Fri & Sat R250. Wed–Sat 10pm–6am.

Magrib (Maghreb) Nevskiy pr. 84 ☎275 12 55; Mayakovskaya metro. See map on pp.192–193. Fashionable Moroccan-themed restaurant-club with divans, hookahs (and hookers), Oriental, Japanese and European cuisine, and DJs playing house and trance. Maestro, MC, Visa. Cover Wed–Thurs & Sun R200, Fri & Sat R300–400. Daily except Mon 6pm–6am.

Manhattan nab. reki Fontank 90 ☎713 19 45, Ⓦwww.manhattan.ru (in Russian); Sadovaya metro. See map on pp.192–193. Laidback music club with acoustic, indie, rock or blues concerts most nights from 8pm (entry free–R250). Mon–Thurs & Sun 1pm–2am, Fri & Sat 1pm–5am.

Metro Ligovskiy pr. 174 ☎766 02 04, Ⓦwww.metro.club.ru; Ligovskiy Prospekt metro, then any minibus south. See map on p.214. Huge, mainstream club with Russian and Eurodance music on the first floor, techno and house on the second, and parties on the third level (which has a laid-back saloon bar). No chewing gum allowed. Cover R180–400. Daily 10pm–6am.

Money Honey Apraksin dvor, korpus 13 (enter via Sadovaya ul.) ☎310 05 49, Ⓦwww.moneyhoney.ru; Nevskiy Prospekt/Gostiniy Dvor metro. See map on pp.62–63. A sprawling saloon for local rockabillies to strut their stuff, that's rowdy but relaxed. Nightly live music at 8pm & 12.30am; free entry before 7pm; afterwards R100, Fri & Sat R200. Daily 10am–5.30am.

Obekt (Object) nab. reki Moyki 82 ☎312 11 34; Sennaya Ploshchad metro. See map on pp.62–63. Almost next door to the *Idiot Café* (see p.346), this cool basement bar has sofas, DJs and a genre rota. Wed: Fiesta Latin party; Thurs: drum 'n' bass; Sat: trip-hop, nu-jazz and bossa nova. Takes Maestro, MC and Visa. Cover R100–200. Mon–Thurs noon–6am, Fri & Sat 5pm–6am, Sun 7pm–6am.

Orlandina nab. reki Karpovki 5/2 ☎234 80 46, Ⓦwww.orlandina.ru (in Russian); Petrogradskaya metro. See map on pp.168–169. Owned by the local music label Caravan Records, this art-rock club features DJs and concerts of alternative, folk-rock, reggae or Brit pop, from 7pm. Entry R150–400 after 5.30pm; discount with club card. Mon–Fri 10am–11pm, Sat 10am–6am, Sun 6–11pm.

Ostrov (Island) nab. Leytenanta Shmidta 37 ☎328 46 49, Ⓦwww.ostrovspb.ru (in Russian); minibus #128 from Nevskiy pr. to 17-ya liniya, then walk to the Neva embankment. See map on pp.152–153. Fun rules, with a revolving dance floor with artificial rain and snow and erotic shows, plus a chill-out room with hammocks. Food and drinks are expensive. R300 entry until 11pm, then R400. Fri–Sat 10pm–6am.

Purga (Blizzard) nab. reki Fontanki 11 (☎570 51 23) and 13 (☎571 23 10), Ⓦwww.purga-club.ru (in Russian); Gostiniy Dvor metro. See map on p.80. At no. 11 they celebrate New Year every midnight with champagne, the Soviet anthem and

Brezhnev on TV, before the disco. No. 13 resembles the sperm bank in *Everything You Always Wanted to Know about Sex* and stages mock weddings between clubbers. Free entry if you book a table (Wed–Thurs R500, Fri–Sun from R1200), otherwise R100, Fri–Sun R200. No. 11: daily 4pm–6am; no. 13: Wed–Sun 8pm till the last customer leaves.

Red Club Poltavskaya ul. 7 ☎717 00 00, ⓦwww.clubred.ru (in Russian); Ploshchad Vosstaniya metro. See map on pp.192–193. A warehouse-style club in the backstreets near Moscow Station, with DJs playing house and techno, and R&B, rock, folk, jazz, soul or blues. Entry R150–650. Thurs–Sun 7pm–6am.

Revolution Sadovaya ul. 28 ☎571 59 15, ⓦwww.revolutionclub.ru (in Russian); Gostiniy Dvor metro. See map on pp.64–65. Popular with students, this dance club has two floors, four bars, a video chill-out room and regular party nights. Cover Mon–Fri R150, Sat & Sun up to R250. Daily 11am–6am.

ROKS Club nab. Admirala Lazareva ☎931 76 79, ⓦwww.roksclub.com (in Russian); Chkalovskaya metro. See map on pp.168–169. Co-owned by Radio ROKS and a bikers' club, this club has an awesome sound system, a vast dance floor, DJs playing rock or drum 'n' bass, and gigs by indie or punk bands Tues–Sun from 8pm. Cover R100–300. Daily 5pm–midnight (or later).

Rossi's Club ul. Zodchestvo Rossi 1/3 ☎710 40 16, ⓦwww.rossis.ru (in Russian); Gostiniy Dvor metro. See map on pp.64–65. Fun dance and karaoke club with James Bond nights, beer parties, strip shows or stand-up comedy from 9pm onwards – you may have to queue to get in. Entry for men R50–400; women free–R300, depending on the time and day of the week. Daily 7pm–6am.

The Place ul. Marshala Govorova 47 ☎252 46 83, ⓦwww.placeclub.ru (in Russian); Narvskaya or Baltiyskaya metro. See map on p.214. Why not start out in the Southern Suburbs, at this stylish evening club with plush sofas and a swing, hosting concerts (Sat from 8pm), DJs, parties and art events (R150–400)? Daily 10am–10pm.

The Point Liteyniy pr. 52 ☎719 76 34, ⓦwww.pointclub.ru (in Russian); Mayakovskaya metro. See map on pp.192–193. A cosy grunge-style basement where bands alternate with DJs from 8pm onwards (R100–200 cover). Daily 1pm–6am.

Tsinik (Cynic) per. Antonenko 4 ☎312 95 26, ⓦwww.cinic.spb.ru; Sennaya Ploshchad metro. See map on p.94. A boho basement "trash café" near St Isaac's Cathedral, featuring table football, DJs, Wi-Fi, garlic bread and occasional gigs. Mon–Thurs & Sun 10am–3am, Fri & Sat 10am–7am.

Tsokol (aka Zoccolo) 3-ya Sovetskaya ul. 2/3 ☎274 94 67, ⓦwww.zoccolo.ru (in Russian); Ploshchad Vosstaniya metro. See map on pp.192–193. Small, friendly club with rock and indie concerts from 8pm (cover from R100) and cheap drinks. Mon–Thurs & Sun 7pm–midnight, Fri & Sat 7pm–6am.

Tunnel corner of Zverinskaya ul. and Lyubyan-skiy per. ☎8901/305 48 62, ⓦwww.tunnelclub.ru (in Russian); Sportivnaya or Gorkovskaya metro. See map on pp.168–169. Russia's oldest techno club, in a former nuclear bunker with full-on lasers and a stoned under-20s crowd. Entry Thurs R100, Fri from R170, Sat from R230. Thurs–Sat midnight–8am.

Veranda More Severnaya doroga 74 ☎922 39 02, ⓦwww.verandamore.ru (in Russian); Krestovskiy Ostrov metro. See map on pp.168–169. Open from mid-May to early Sept, this terrace club-café overlooking a canal has DJs from 3pm and occasional concerts, when there's an entry charge of R600. Daily noon till 1am (or later).

Occasional live venues

The following places are sometimes used for **concerts** by major Russian pop stars or foreign bands – look out for flyers in music shops, or in the *St Petersburg Times* or *Pulse* magazine for details. Artists such as Paul McCartney, Elton John and the Rolling Stones have been allowed to play on **Dvortsovaya ploshchad**, outside the Hermitage – to the fury of its director, who fears that the decibels will damage the building and its artworks.

FortDance

If you were looking for somewhere to stage a rave, an abandoned plague laboratory and naval fort way out in the Gulf of Finland wouldn't spring to mind – unless you were from the inventive crowd that held "pool parties" at St Petersburg swimming baths in the 1990s. While these ended after someone drowned, **FortDance** has grown since 2000 into Russia's top dance party, attended by celebrity DJs and guests (arriving by helicopter or yacht), as well as clubbers from across the world. The main action is at **Fort Alexander**, off the coast of Kronstadt, which has two arenas, with a third one onshore at Fort Konstantin (see p.285). Besides amazing sound and lighting, there's a rooftop mojito bar, a secret VIP lounge and S&M dungeons with topless dancers for rent. Lottie, Mark Spoon, Judge Jules, Touche and Annie Mac have all DJed at FortDance. The one-day event takes place towards the end of July, as detailed on ⓦwww.fortdance.com and ⓦwww.club.ru (in Russian only). **Tickets** are available from Titanik stores or online at ⓦwww.concert.ru, for R2900 if bought more than three weeks ahead, up to R4500 on the day. A shuttle-bus for ticket-holders runs from Chernaya Rechka metro to Fort Konstantin from 3pm onwards.

In 2007 another, purely techno party, **Castle Dance**, was staged at **Vyborg** castle (see p.290). Check ⓦwww.castledance.ru (in Russian) to see if proves to be more than a one-off event.

Bolshoy Concert Hall Oktyabrskiy (Bolshoy kontsertniy zal, or BKZ) Ligovskiy pr. 6 ☏275 12 73, ⓦwww.bkz.sp.ru; Ploshchad Vosstaniya metro. Used by Russian pop stars, the Eifman and Male Ballet companies, plus visiting foreign acts. Box office Mon–Fri 11am–8pm, Sat & Sun 11am–7pm.
Ice Palace (Ledovy dvorets) pr. Pyatiletok 1 ☏718 66 20, ⓦwww.newarena.spb.ru; Prospekt Bolshevikov metro. With seating for 14,000, and the finest lighting, sound and televisual facilities in the city, the Ice Palace hosts concerts by the likes of Bjork.

Lensoviet Palace of Culture Kamennoostrovskiy pr. 42 ☏346 04 38; Petrogradskaya metro. A popular venue for veteran Russian bands such as Akvarium. Box office daily 11am–3pm & 4–8pm.
SKK pr. Yuriya Gagarina 8 ☏378 17 10; Park Pobedy metro. Used for concerts by big-name bands. Box office daily 10am–6.30pm.
Yubileyniy Sports Palace pr. Dobrolyubova 18 ☏323 93 22, ⓦwww.yubi.ru; Sportivnaya metro. An occasional venue for big-name bands or DJ marathons during summer, not to mention all-night ice-skating discos. The box office is open daily noon–7pm.

Cabaret and comedy clubs

Chaplin Club ul. Chaykovskovo 59, ☏272 66 49; Chernyshevskaya metro. See map on pp.192–193. A cosy comedy club founded by the clown-mime troupe Litsedei, with evening shows that can be enjoyed with no knowledge of Russian (R80–300; table reservations essential). Otherwise it's just a place to eat and drink. Accepts Maestro, MC, Visa. Daily noon–11pm.
Hali Guli Lanskoe shosse 23 ☏246 99 10; Vyborgskaya metro. See map on p.222. Notorious bad-taste club aimed at rich Russians with no inhibitions: waitresses are encouraged to swear and smoke; patrons, to

engage in drinking contests, dancing on tables and lewd acts. You need to understand Russian to get the smutty cabaret. Arrive before the show starts at 10pm or they may not let you in. Entry R500–700; accepts MC, Visa. Daily 4pm–4am.
Siniy Barkhat (Blue Velvet) Music Hall, Alexander Park ☏232 81 73; Gorkovskaya metro. See map on pp.168–169. Interaction with the performers is also encouraged at this two-floor venue hosting cabaret, transvestite shows, miniature theatre or clown shows from 9pm. Entry R100–200. Fri–Sun 8pm–midnight.

Gay and lesbian clubs

Two of the clubs below – *Central Station* and *Greshniki* – are close to the city's cruising ground, the ploschad Ostrovskovo (see p.68), within the main downtown clubbing zone.

Cabaret nab. Obvodnovo kanala 181 ☎575 45 12; Baltiyskaya metro. See map on p.214. Housed in a Soviet-style Palace of Culture, this club is famous for its transvestite shows with impersonations of Russian pop stars (from 2am). Entry R200–500 Fri & Sat, Sun free. Fri–Sun 11pm–6am; closed Mon–Thurs.

Central Station ul. Lomonosova 1/28 ☎312 36 00, ⓦ www.centralstation.ru (in Russian); Nevskiy Prospekt/Gostiniy Dvor metro. See map on pp.64–65. In the heart of clubland, just around the corner from its older rival *Greshniki*, this popular club has eight bars and two stages for shows, pajama parties, and DJs Soda, Velvet and Slutkey. Entry free–R300. Daily 6pm–6am, Fri & Sat till 7am.

Greshniki (Sinners) nab. kanala Griboedova 28/1 ☎570 42 91, ⓦ www.greshniki.ru; Nevskiy Prospekt/Gostiniy Dvor metro. See map on pp.64–65. S&M dungeon decor, staff dressed as angels or demons, leather-clad strippers and door-less toilets, plus a roof for cooling off with a view of the canal. Entry for men free or R150; women R300–500. Daily 10pm–6am.

Tri El 5-ya Sovetskaya ul. 45 ☎710 20 16, ⓦ www.triel.spb.ru; Ploshchad Vosstaniya metro. See map on pp.192–193. Russia's only fully lesbian club (all the others are gay clubs with lesbian nights) features striptease and transvestite shows (Fri & Sat), concerts (Thurs at 7pm), dance parties, and pool on other days. Women only except on Thurs & Fri. Free entry Tues & Wed; other days R50–150. Tues 5pm–midnight, Wed 9pm–6am, Thurs 7pm–6am, Fri–Sun 10pm–6am; closed Mon.

Jazz and blues

St Petersburg has an indigenous jazz tradition going back to the 1930s, and its clubs lure talent from across Russia and the Baltic States, plus musicians from elsewhere during the **Jazz Guitar** (early March), **White Nights Swing** (early July) and **Autumn Rhythms** (mid-November) festivals. Besides the clubs listed below, there are **jazz cruises** on the River Neva from June to September, sailing from the Hermitage jetty every Saturday at 6pm. There's swing and trad jazz on one deck, free-form on the other. Tickets are available from theatre ticket kiosks around the city. **Blues**, Cuban, flamenco and *fado* music also have their admirers. Two useful **websites** with audio links are "Jazz in Russia" (ⓦ www.jazz.ru) – whose text in English includes a section on festivals – and "Blues" (ⓦ www.blues.ru), in Russian only.

Café-Club Che Poltavskaya ul. 3 ☎277 76 00; Ploshchad Ploshchad Vosstaniya metro. See map on pp.192–193. A mellow café by day, its nighttime vibe is sultry with cocktails and cigars, with live blues or jazz from 10pm–3am, and free entry. Daily 9am–7am.

Jazz Philharmonic Hall Zagorodniy pr. 27 ☎764 85 65, ⓦ www.jazz-hall.spb.ru; Vladimirskaya/Dostoevskaya metro. See map on pp.192–193. A formal venue founded by jazz violinist David Goloshchokin. The Bolshoy zal is used for mainstream and Dixieland jazz, the smaller Ellington Hall for intimate, candlelit concerts. Advance tickets from the box office (2–8pm) R100–200; student discount for the Bolshoy zal. Tues–Sun 7–11pm; Ellington Hall Tues, Fri & Sat 8–11pm.

JFC Jazz Club Shpalernaya ul. 33 ☎272 98 50, ⓦ www.jfc.spb.ru; Chernyshevskaya metro. See map on pp.192–193. Run by award-winning jazz musician Andrei Kondakov, this is a relaxed venue for all styles of jazz, art rock and fusion. Table reservations for gigs is essential, as the club is tiny. Entry from R100. Daily 7–10.30pm.

Jimi Hendrix Blues Club Liteyniy pr. 33 ☎570 88 13; Chernyshevskaya metro.

See map on pp.192–193. One of the best venues for jazz, blues, rock and country; gigs start at 8.30pm and cost R100–200. Mon–Sat 11am–1am.

Red Fox ul. Mayakovskovo 50 ☎275 42 14, ⓦwww.rfjc.ru; Chernyshevskaya metro. See map on pp.192–193. Agreeable jazz/blues café with live music of the 1930s and 1940s daily except Mon from 8–10pm (R60–100 entry). Café opens 10.30am on weekdays, 2pm on Sat & Sun.

Street Life 2-ya Krasnoarmeyskaya ul. 6, ☎575 05 45, ⓦwww.street-life.spb.ru (in Russian); Tekhnologicheskiy Institut metro. See map on pp.192–193. A jazz-restaurant with fusion cooking where you might also hear reggae, swing or blues from 9pm (entry from R200); call ahead to book tickets and a table. Maestro, MC, Visa. Daily midnight–2am.

The Arts

For well over a century, St Petersburg has been one of the world's great centres of **classical music and ballet**, most famously represented by the Mariinskiy opera and ballet company – formerly called the Kirov, the name by which it's still marketed abroad – and also by its fine orchestras and choirs. Although many suffered from the withdrawal of state funding and the exodus of talented artists in the early 1990s, the Mariinskiy has retained its world-class reputation for classical ballet, and acquired new laurels as an opera house.

Despite small drama troupes springing up all over, **theatre** has had a harder time, largely because of the language barrier, which prevents it from attracting richer, foreign audiences. Nevertheless, there are performances that don't require much (if any) knowledge of Russian, such as **mime** and **puppetry**. The revival of Russia's **film** industry since directors abandoned the slow tempo of Soviet cinematography in favour of action movies like the supernatural thrillers *Night Watch* and *Day Watch* has favoured Moscow's studios rather than St Petersburg's. However, the **visual arts** are thriving, with dozens of exhibitions, multimedia and performance events every month – though they're not always widely advertised.

If you're lucky (or you've planned ahead), you'll be able to catch specific **festivals** or annual events – see pp.45–47 for a full rundown.

Tickets and information

For most concerts and theatrical performances, you can buy **tickets** from the venue's box office (*kassa*), the many theatre-ticket kiosks (*teatralnaya kassa*) on the streets and in metro stations, or from the **central box office** at Nevskiy pr. 42 (℡571 31 83; Mon–Fri 10am–9pm, Sat & Sun 10am–8pm). The Mariinskiy has its own **online booking** (Ⓦwww.mariinsky.ru, which also gives news and performance schedules); tickets for other venues are obtainable from Ⓦwww.kassir.ru (℡703 40 40) or Ⓦwww.bilet.ru (℡380 80 50), which both accept payment by Master-Card or Visa, or in cash (when picking up the tickets or if delivered), but add a hefty mark-up and sometimes fail to deliver on time; the first website is bilingual, the second in Russian only. The booking site Ⓦwww.balletandopera.com is good for checking what's on but charges the steepest mark up. Buying tickets from **touts** outside venues is fraught with risks – if you do buy a ticket this way, check the date and the seats specified on the ticket. In Russian, the stalls are *parter*; the first or second tier of balconies are the *beletazh* and all the rest are *balkon* seats; *ryad* means row, and *mesto*, seat. Be sure to keep your ticket if you leave the auditorium during the intermission; some places won't let you back in without it.

Unfortunately for visitors, a **two-tier price system** whereby foreigners are charged far more than Russians applies at the Mariinskiy, Maliy Opera and Ballet,

theatre	театр
cinema	кино-театр
theatre-ticket kiosk	театральная касса
box office	касса
balcony	балкон
beletazh	белэтаж
stalls	партер
seat	место
row	ряд

Hermitage and Maliy theatres, as well as the State Circus. While a local acquaintance can obtain you tickets at the Russian price, it's almost impossible to get past the vigilant *babushki* at the Mariinskiy, who send foreigners back to pay the premium charge – though at other venues you might manage to sneak through if you speak Russian or really look the part.

Music lovers planning to be in town for some time might buy **abonimenty**, batches of tickets to about ten concerts – by a specific composer, or in a genre such as chamber music – performed at one concert hall or different venues over the course of a month or two. There are various *abonimenty* available, and besides saving you money they can also save you the hassle of queuing for popular concerts if you choose them carefully beforehand.

The *St Petersburg Times* (Fri edition), *Pulse* and *Where St Petersburg* carry **English-language listings** of events at the main concert halls and theatres, although the listings in Russian-language newspapers such as *Chas Pik* (especially its weekly supplement, *Pyatnitsa*) or magazines such as *Time Out Peterburg* or *Vash Dosug* are more comprehensive. Gala concerts at the Mariinskiy, Hermitage and Aleksandrinskiy theatres and the Imperial palaces are also advertised on the website Ⓦwww.balletandopera.com. Bear in mind that some (though by no means all) theatres and concert halls are **closed in July or August**.

Ballet, opera and classical music

Due to the demand by visitors, tickets for **ballet** at the Mariinskiy can be hard to obtain, but don't despair if you have no luck, as there are several other respected venues for ballet and opera, and the Mariinskiy isn't the only star act in town. The Eifman Company has won rave reviews for its modern gloss on classical ballet styles and even performs at the Mariinskiy during the August break, though it's now so popular that getting tickets can be difficult. Another well-known company is Valery Mikhailovsky's Male Ballet, which performs *Swan Lake* and other classics with more than a *soupçon* of irony. Conversely, the Stars of the St Petersburg Ballet festival at the Hermitage Theatre in June and July purports to feature leading dancers at the Mariinskiy, but tends to be performed by little-known understudies.

Under director Valery Gergiev the Mariinskiy has not only nurtured a new generation of great dancers, but has inaugurated a new golden age of **opera**, unseen since the era of Chaliapin. Besides inviting the film director Konchalovsky to stage Prokofiev's *War and Peace*, he has risked disapproval by introducing Wagner to the Mariinskiy's repertoire – a composer never liked in Russia, whose works now take precedence over the Italian and French operas traditionally beloved of Russians. The only negative aspect to this success is that Gergiev, along with star singers such as Olga Borodina and Nikolai Putilin,

Folklore shows

A spectacle that might appeal to some are **folklore shows**, featuring Russian folk songs and high-kicking Cossack dancers, with a bit of ballet for good measure. The "Feel Yourself Russian" bash in the ballroom of the Nikolaevskiy Palace on pl. Truda (☏312 55 00, ⓦwww.folkshow.ru; R1200) includes vodka, champagne and *zakuski*, and is held daily at 6.30 and 9pm. Or there's the show in the concert hall of the Anichkov Palace on Nevskiy pr. (☏310 99 88), which starts at 7.30pm daily (R800).

▼ Russian folklore show

are often abroad – which is great for attracting sponsorship to the Mariinskiy, but means that they're not in St Petersburg as often as their fans – and visiting tourists – would like.

Classical music concerts take place throughout the year, with the largest number during the Stars of the White Nights Festival at the Mariinskiy. In addition to the main venues listed below, there are also concerts in churches and palaces – including Peterhof, Tsarskoe Selo and Pavlovsk, outside St Petersburg. Details of gala concerts throughout the year appear on ⓦwww.balletandopera.com; websites dedicated to specific festivals include ⓦwww.palacefest.ru (Palaces of St Petersburg Festival), ⓦwww.earlymusic.ru (Early Music Festival) and ⓦwww.musicalolympus.ru (Musical Olympus Festival).

You should definitely try to hear some **Russian Orthodox Church music**, which is solely choral and wonderfully in keeping with the rituals of the faith. Splendid choirs perform at the Preobrazhenskiy Church off Liteyniy prospekt (daily 10am & 6pm), the Alexander Nevsky Monastery's Trinity Cathedral (daily 10am & 6pm), and the Kazan Cathedral (daily 9am & 7.30pm). Over the summer, Orthodox choral music is also performed by Vadim Afanasiev's Male Choir of St Petersburg at the Atrium in the Peter and Paul Fortress, where a **bell-ringing** festival is also held in the cathedral.

Military bands are also worth hearing: they often play in the Alexander Garden at lunchtime on Sundays during summer, and come out in force on Victory Day, Navy Day and the Defenders of the Motherland Day.

Concert halls, opera houses and other venues

Aleksandriinskiy Theatre pl. Ostrovskovo 2 ☏312 15 45, ⓦwww.alexandrinsky.ru; Gostiniy Dvor metro; box office daily 11am–3pm & 4–8pm. A beautiful Neoclassical theatre designed by Rossi, used for opera and ballet as well as drama. Besides favourites such as *The Nutcracker* and *Swan Lake*, staged by the St Petersburg Theatre of Classical Ballet, you may find the Eifman Ballet performing here.

Atrium in the Peter and Paul Fortress ☏933 30 94; Gorkovskaya metro. The place to hear concerts by the Male Choir of St Petersburg at 7pm on Mon & Fri in summer.

Beloselskiy-Belozerskiy Palace Nevskiy pr. 41 ☏315 52 36; Gostiniy Dvor metro; box office Mon, Tues & Thurs–Sun 1–5pm. The palace's mirrored ballroom hosts performances by the St Petersburg City Concert Orchestra, and folklore shows.

Bolshoy Concert Hall Oktyabrskiy (Bolshoy kontsertniy zal, or BKZ) Ligovskiy pr. 6 ☏275 12 73, ⓦwww.bkz.sp.ru; Ploshchad Vosstaniya metro; box office Mon–Fri 11am–8pm, Sat & Sun 11am–7pm. One of the city's largest concert halls, with comfy seating and unobstructed views. Used by Russian pop stars, the Eifman and Male Ballet companies as well as visiting international acts. Ballet performances are to recorded music.

Conservatory Opera and Ballet Theatre (Teatr Opery i Baleta Konservatorii) Teatralnaya pl. 3 ☏312 25 19, ⓦwww.conservatory.ru; bus #22 from Nevskiy prospekt; box office daily 11am–7pm. The Conservatory's own company of students and teachers stages some fine opera and ballet performances, but the lack of star performers means that tickets are fairly easy to come by. Their website lists events in Russian only; the English version is solely for musicians wishing to study there.

Eifman Ballet Theatre ul. Liza Chaykinoy 2 ☏230 78 45; Sportivnaya metro. When not appearing at the Mariinskiy, the BKZ or abroad, this world-renowned company may perform at their own studio-theatre. Boris Eifman's reinterpretations of classical ballets are superb, but his own choreography can sometimes be embarrassingly self-obsessed, so be careful to check what's on the bill.

Hermitage Theatre Dvortsovaya nab. 34 ☏571 90 25; Nevskiy Prospekt/Gostiniy Dvor metro.

Between May and October, Catherine the Great's private theatre is an exquisite venue for evening concerts by chamber groups from the Philharmonia, and gala performances by Mariinskiy soloists and dancers. It also has its own resident orchestra, the St Petersburg Kamerata. Tickets (sold at kiosks and hotels only) aren't numbered, so be sure to arrive early to claim a decent seat.

Kapella nab. reki Moyki 20 ☏314 10 58; Nevskiy Prospekt/Gostiniy Dvor metro; box office daily noon–3pm & 4–7pm. The oldest concert hall in St Petersburg, with its own renowned choir and State Kapella Orchestra, drawn from students at the Conservatory, who join forces to perform music of varying styles and ages, from Baroque to twentieth century. The Kapella hosts the international Prokofiev Young Violinists contest (early March) and an Early Music festival (late Sept till mid-Oct).

Kannon Dance ul. Dekabristov 34 ☏714 20 27, ⓦwww.kannondance.ru; bus #22 from Nevskiy pr. Modern jazz-dance school near the Mariinskiy, whose *Stansiya* theatre is used by local contemporary dance troupes. The school organizes the Open Look international festival of modern dance in June or July – staged at the Music Hall and other venues.

Male Ballet (Muzhskoy balet) Gorokhovaya ul. 71 ⓦwww.maleballet.spb.ru; Pushkinskaya metro. Valery Mikhailovsky was principal dancer for the Eifman company before founding his acclaimed all-male ballet company in 1992. It performs "Classical Transformations" of Tchaikovsky ballets, and modern compositions such as *Ecce Homo*, with music by Vangelis, Sinck and Albinoni. When not abroad, it appears at venues such as the BKZ, as advertised in the local press and by posters outside their rehearsal studio.

Maliy Opera and Ballet Theatre (Maliy operniy teatr, aka the Mussorgsky or Mikhailovskiy Theatre) pl. Iskusstv 1 ☏595 43 05, ⓦwww.mikhailovsky.ru; Nevskiy Prospekt/Gostiniy Dvor metro; box office daily 11am–3pm & 4–8pm. Though the ballet and opera at the Maliy aren't as good as at the Mariinskiy, its apricot-and-silver auditorium is no less beautiful and its repertoire includes ballets such as *Giselle*, *Les Sylphides* and *Swan Lake*, and Russian operas like *Prince Igor* and *Khovanshchina*. A small museum on the third floor displays designs for the first productions of Prokofiev's *War and Peace* and Shostakovich's *The Nose*. Tickets are easy to come by, except in August when the Mariinskiy is closed and tour groups come here instead. **Mariinskiy Theatre (Mariinskiy teatr) Teatralnaya pl. 2 ☎714 12 11; Concert Hall ul. Pisareva 20 ☎326 41 41; ⓦwww.mariinsky.ru; bus #22 from Nevskiy prospekt, or tram #5 from Sennaya Ploshchad/Sadovaya metro; box office daily 11am–7pm**. The sumptuous nineteenth-century ballet and opera house now has a separate Concert Hall three blocks away, and a second stage underway near the old building. The Mariinskiy ballet company is on tour for much of the year, leaving lesser dancers behind; the best time to catch it is during winter, when ballerinas such as Yuliana Lopatkina, Diana Vishneva and Altinai Asilmuratova are around. At this time of the year the Mariinskiy also stages *The Golden Cockerel* for kids, performed by junior members of the Vaganova ballet school. As for opera, Wagner rules at present, but Verdi, Bizet, Mozart and Rossini are still staged. Look out for the baritones Victor Chernomortsev and Nikolai Putilin, or even a rare appearance by Olga Borodina, who's more of a fixture at La Scala, the Met or Covent Garden nowadays. At the Mariinskiy, Russian operas are staged with English subtitles, and foreign operas with Russian ones. The company doesn't perform in August. Tickets sell out fast, so it's worth booking before you arrive in Russia. This can be done on the Mariinskiy's website up to sixty days in advance. You can pay by MasterCard or Visa and get an email voucher to exchange for tickets at the *kassa* just before the performance, or pay cash upon collection, in which case the tickets must be collected within 72 hours of booking. If you leave things till the last moment, you should see what (if anything) is available at the theatre's downtown box office on the mezzanine level of the Haute Coutre Gallery on Dumskaya ulitsa, or the central ticket office at Nevskiy pr. 42, before trying hotel service bureaux or hoping to get a cheap standby seat at 6pm on the night of the performance. You may want to dress up to the nines, quaff champagne and promenade with your companion around the Great Hall during the intermission – since that's what everyone else does.

Peter and Paul Cathedral in the Peter and Paul Fortress ☎238 05 03, ⓦwww.spbmuseum.ru; Gorkovskaya metro. Hosts concerts of choral music (religious and secular) and bell-ringing during the summer months.

Philharmonia (Filarmoniya) Mikhaylovskaya ul. 2 ☎710 40 85, ⓦwww.philharmonia.spb. ru; Nevskiy Prospekt/Gostiniy Dvor metro; box office daily 11am–3pm & 4–8pm. The grand Bolshoy zal, named after Shostakovich, is home to the St Petersburg Philharmonic Orchestra, whose concerts vary depending on the conductor; Mariss Jansons or Yuri Temirkanov are sure to sell out fast. The hall is also used by visiting foreign artists and an orchestra called Klassika that specializes in Strauss waltzes and other lowbrow favourites. The smaller Maliy zal (named after Glinka) has better acoustics and a separate entrance (at Nevskiy pr. 30) and phone number (☎311 15 31). It's used for solo and chamber recitals, which are usually excellent.

Rimsky-Korsakov Museum Zagorodniy pr. 28 ☎713 32 08; Vladimirskaya/Dostoevskaya metro. Chamber music performances and recitals in the composer's former apartment (see p.209), from Aug till May. Book ahead as seating is limited.

Smolniy Cathedral pl. Rastrelli 3 ☎271 95 43, ⓦwww.cathedral.ru; minibus #74 or #147 from Suvorovskiy prospekt. Performances of orchestral and choral music in what is outwardly one of the most striking buildings in St Petersburg (see p.201). Its bare interior is a let-down, but the acoustics are wonderful.

St Petersburg Opera Galernaya ul. 33 ☎314 09 55; trolleybus #5 or #22 from Nevskiy prospekt. Ensconced in a former baronial mansion, the company is known for Yuri Alexandrov's staging of the Pushkin-based operatic trilogy *The Queen of Spades*, *Eugene Onegin* and *Boris Godunov*. Its repertoire also includes Offenbach's operetta *La Belle Hélène*.

Yubileyniy Sports Palace pl. Dobrolyubova 18 ☎323 93 22, ⓦwww.yubi.ru; Sportivnaya metro. Sports complex on the Petrograd Side with an ice rink that stages "ballet on ice" shows during the winter.

Theatre

St Petersburg prides itself on its dramatic tradition and boasts several sumptuously appointed **theatres**, but at present can't honestly claim superiority over Moscow – unlike with ballet and opera – although a couple of companies are deservedly acclaimed. Though the fact that shows are invariably in Russian limits its appeal to foreigners, you don't need to understand much to appreciate some of the more experimental productions, puppetry, musicals, mime or the circus. The main events in the theatrical calendar are the **Festival of Russian Theatres**, with performers from all the CIS countries (mid-April), the **Baltic House Festival** of drama from northern Russia and the Baltic States (Oct), and the **Aleksandriinksiy Festival** (mid-Sept till late Oct), attracting companies from around the world. The first two events are held at the Baltiyskiy dom, the last at the Aleksandriinskiy Theatre.

Drama theatres

Akimov Comedy Theatre Nevskiy pr. 56 ☎312 45 55; Nevskiy Prospekt/Gostiniy Dvor metro; box office daily noon–3pm & 4–8pm. If your Russian is up to it, this is the place to catch such comic classics as *The Importance of Being Earnest*, Bulgakov's adaptation of Molière's works, or an acclaimed production of Shakespeare's *Twelfth Night*.

Aleksandriinskiy Theatre pl. Ostrovskovo 2 ☎312 15 45, ⊛www.alexandrinsky.ru; Gostiniy Dvor metro; box office daily 11am–3pm & 4–8pm. Most of the forty-odd plays in its repertoire are by the nineteenth-century dramatist Alexander Ostrovsky, but you can also see Gogol's *The Marriage* and Wilde's *Lady Windermere's Fan*. Since 2006 it has hosted an international drama festival (see above).

Baltiyskiy dom (Baltic House) Alexander Park 4 ☎232 35 39, ⊛www.baltichouse.spb.ru; Gorkovskaya metro; box office daily noon–3pm & 4–7pm. The Baltiyskiy dom's Farce Theatre is the main crowd-puller, while the Small Stage puts on romances and comedies. However, the real attraction is the wealth of talent at the two international drama festivals held here (see above).

BDT (Bolshoy dramaticheskiy teatr) nab. reki Fontanki 65 ☎310 92 42, ⊛www.bdt.spb.ru; Gostiniy Dvor metro; box office daily 11am–3pm & 4–7pm. The city's most heavyweight theatre, its repertoire includes Chekhov, Gogol and other Russian classics, Stoppard's *Arcadia* and Strindberg's *The Father*. At the *malaya stena* (studio theatre) you can see works in progress, drama competitions and festival shows. In July and August, the main auditorium often hosts performances of *Swan Lake* and *Giselle* by soloists from the Mariinskiy.

Interior Theatre (Interierniy teatr) Nevskiy pr. 104 ☎273 14 54; Mayakovskaya metro. Stories and legends from the history of St Petersburg imaginatively enacted for audiences of 5- to 12-year-olds, plus plays for adults, such as *Hamlet*. Worth visiting just to see the costumes and models, like Madame Tussaud's redone in the style of *Frankenstein*. Closed mid-July to mid-Sept.

Komissarzhevskiy Drama Theatre (Teatr imeni V.F. Komissarzhevskoy, or KDF), Italyanskaya ul. 19 ☎571 31 02; Nevskiy Prospekt/Gostiniy Dvor metro; box office daily 11am–3pm & 4–7pm. Known for intense realist dramas that are particularly inaccessible to non-Russian speakers, the KDF has tried to widen its appeal by staging farces such as Woody Allen's *A Midsummer Night's Sex Comedy*. Closed Mon & Tues.

Lensoviet Theatre Vladimirskiy pr. 12 ☎713 21 91, ⊛www.lensov-theatre.spb.ru; Vladimirskaya/Dostoyevskaya metro; online booking and tickets sold at a discount 11am–noon. The performances on its second, smaller stage are especially good. Their repertoire includes *Waiting for Godot*, Pinter's *The Lover*, Bruckner's *Voychek*, and Nabokov's *King, Queen, Knave*.

Maliy Dramatic Theatre (Maliy dramaticheskiy teatr or MDT, aka Teatr Yevropy), ul. Rubinshteyna 18 ☎713 20 78, ⊛www.mdt-dodin.ru; Mayakovskaya metro; box office daily noon–7.30pm. Under Lev Dodin this troupe has won numerous prizes for its coruscating productions of the classics – its repertoire includes *The Seagull*, *Uncle Vanya*, *Play Without a Name*, *Gaudeamus*, *The Master and Margarita* and a nine-and-a-half-hour version of Dostoyevsky's *The Possessed*.

Priyut komedianta (Comedians' Refuge) Sadovaya ul. 27 ☎310 33 14; Sadovaya/Sen-

Mime

Many **mime groups** have no permanent home, so look out for performances at Baltiyskiy dom. One of the best-known groups is **Derevo**, who produce fascinating shows using influences from Japanese Butto to traditional clowning and mime. The most popular clowns perform with **Litsedei**, who organize mime festivals in St Petersburg, and sometimes appear at the *Chaplin Club* (see p.359) – while another clown-mime troupe, **Mimigranty**, have their own theatre (see below). Also watch out for **DaNet**, whose use of masks has won them prizes all over Europe.

naya Ploshchad metro. Renowned for Yuri Tomoshevsky's adaptations of prose and poetry readings from the "Silver Age" of Russian literature, but also stages the alcoholic epic known abroad as *Moscow Stations*, and Wilde's Lady Windermere's Fan. Closed June 25–Aug 1.

Theatre on Liteyniy (Dramaticheskiy teatr na Liteynom), Liteyniy pr. 51 ☎273 53 35; Mayakovskaya/Ploshchad Vosstaniya metro; box office daily 11am–3pm & 4–7pm. This company features some of St Petersburg's best actors, with a repertoire including Shakespeare, Molière, Tolstoy and Sophocles. The only theatre in the city with wheelchair access. Closed during July.

Yusupov Palace Theatre nab. reki Moyki 94 ☎314 98 83. This gorgeous private theatre occasionally hosts concerts and light opera.

Puppetry, musicals and circus

Bolshoy Puppet Theatre (Bolshoy teatr kukol), ul. Nekrasova 10 ☎273 66 72; Mayakovskaya metro; box office Mon–Fri 10.30am–3pm & 4–7pm, Sat & Sun 10.30am–6pm. Programmes aimed at kids aged 3–10, which don't always involve puppets. Its repertoire includes *Snow White*, *Little Red Riding Hood* and *The Tale of Yemelya*.

Children's Ice Theatre (Detskiy Ledoviy teatr) Ligovskiy pr. 148 ☎712 86 25; Ligovskiy Prospekt metro. Dramas and spectacles on ice, appealing to children of all ages.

Circus at Avtovo (Tsirk na Avtovo) Avtovskaya ul. 1 ☎784 97 42; Avtovo metro; box office daily 10am–7pm. Traditional circus performances and spectacles on specific themes, including a "Rhapsody on Ice" show with all the performers on iceboards or skates. Tickets R100–400.

Demmi Marionette Theatre (Teatr marionetok imeni Demmeni) Nevskiy pr. 52 ☎571 21 56; Nevskiy Prospekt/Gostiniy Dvor metro; box

office daily 10.30am–2.15pm & 3.15–6pm. Founded in 1918, this marionette (stringed puppet) theatre has won a bunch of awards at international puppet festivals.

Fairytale Puppet Theatre (Kukolniy teatr skazki) Moskovskiy pr. 121 ☎388 22 63; Moskovskie Vorota metro; box office Tues–Sun 10.30am–noon & 1.30–4pm. Performances aimed at children aged 5 and over, including *Pinocchio*, *Thumbelina*, *The Nutcracker and the Mouse King* and *The Tale of Lazy Ivan*. Closed Mon.

Mimigranty Clown-Mime Theatre Rizhskiy pr. 23, Block 2 ☎251 63 28; Baltiyskaya metro; box office Mon–Fri 11am–7pm, Sat 1–7pm, Sun 11am–4pm. When they're not clowning around on the streets, Mimigranty can be found in their theatre on the seedy side of the Fontanka. Their repertoire includes *The Circus of Shardam-S*, by the cult writer Daniil Kharms, Pinter's *The Caretaker* and an improvisation for clowns entitled *Comedy with Murder*.

Music Hall (Myuzik Holl) Alexander Park 4 ☎232 92 01, ⓦwww.musichall.spb.ru; Gorkovskaya metro; box office daily noon–3pm & 4–7pm. In the same complex as the Baltiyskiy dom and the Planetarium, it stages *Dr Dolittle from Zverinskaya Street* for children, and a Busby Berkley-style musical, *St Petersburg Crescendo*, besides hosting visiting circus troupes from abroad, and the Open Look dance festival in June.

State Circus (Tsirk) nab. reki Fontanki 3 ☎314 84 78, ⓦwww.circus.spb.ru; Nevskiy Prospekt/Gostiniy Dvor metro; box office daily 11am–7pm. Russia's oldest circus, based here since 1877. Trapeze artists, acrobats, illusionists, performing bears and seals – a real old-style show that you'll either love or hate. Tickets (R100–600) can usually be bought on the spot; children under 3 enter for free. Closed mid-July to mid-Sept. Performances start at 3pm & 7pm.

Theatre of Young Spectators (Teatr yunykh zriteley, or TYuZ) Pionerskaya pl. 1 ☎712

41 02; Pushkinskaya metro; box office daily 11am–2pm & 3–6pm. Musicals and dance shows aimed at children and teenagers, including Saint-Exupéry's *The Little Prince*. Performances start at 11am & 6pm. Also hosts the international festival of modern dance in July.

Zazerkalye (Through the Looking Glass) ul. Rubinshteyna 13 ☎712 51 35; Vladimirskaya/Dostoevskaya metro; box office daily noon–3pm & 4–7pm. Colourful opera and ballet for children that's also enjoyable for adults, with productions such as an opera-musical based on *The Hobbit*, and Puccini's *La Bohème*.

Film

Although Russian action movies are extremely popular, the majority of **films** screened in St Petersburg are Hollywood blockbusters or Euro B-movies, dubbed into Russian with varying degrees of sophistication. Many long-neglected local cinemas have been refurbished with comfy seating, Dolby Digital sound and air-conditioning, and there are several new multiplexes. All cinemas are non-smoking; none takes credit cards or phone bookings.

To find out **what's showing**, see the Friday edition of the *St Petersburg Times*. If you understand Russian you can peruse a weekly list posted outside the Avrora Cinema on Nevskiy prospekt or obtain film schedules at any cinema by calling ☎064, 050 or 089.

The **Festival of Festivals** (Ⓦwww.filmfest.ru) in June and the **Open Cinema** (Ⓦwww.opencinema.afisha.ru) festival of short films and animation in August are the best time to catch new Russian and foreign movies. Venues include the Dom kino and Rodina cinemas, and the Strelka and Peter and Paul Fortress for outdoor screenings during the Open Cinema. There is also a film festival in Vyborg, in May.

Avrora (Aurora) Nevskiy pr. 60 ☎050, 064 or 089 Ⓦwww.avrora.spb.ru; Gostiniy Dvor metro. The city's oldest cinema (founded in 1913), now fully modernized, may show films in its café besides the main feature in the auditorium.

Dom kino Karavannaya ul. 12 ☎314 56 14, Ⓦwww.domkino.spb.ru; Nevskiy Prospekt/Gostiniy Dvor metro. A clubhouse for the city's filmmakers, with a bar and restaurant, it shows Russian and foreign arthouse movies and hosts film festivals.

Jam Hall Kamennoostrovskiy pr. 42 ☎346 40 82; Petrogradskaya metro; and Leninskiy pr. 160 ☎370 72; Leninskiy Prospekt metro. These two luxury cinemas have separate tables seating 2–7 people, with individual lighting and bar service. The one on the Petrograd Side is easier to reach.

Kolizey Nevskiy pr. 100 ☎272 87 75; Mayakovskaya metro. Very comfortable two-screen cinema whose amenities include VIP boxes

and divans for partying or horizontal viewing, and three bars.

Kristall Palace Nevskiy pr. 72 ☎272 23 82; Mayakovskaya metro. Mostly screens blockbusters – Russian or Hollywood.

Mirazh (Mirage) Bolshoy pr. 35 ☎498 05 63; Sportivnaya metro; and Gulliver mall, Torfyanaya doroga 7 ☎441 22 33; Staraya Derevnya metro. Two four-screen cinemas that sometimes show undubbed foreign films – on the Petrograd Side and the Vyborg Side, respectively. Both have several bars, billiards, Internet and a fusion restaurant.

Pik (Peak) in the Pik mall on Sennaya pl. ☎449 24 32; Sadovaya/Sennaya Ploshchad metro. A fourth-floor multiplex screening mainstream Russian and foreign movies.

Rodina (Motherland) Karavannaya ul. 12 ☎571 61 31; Nevskiy Prospekt/Gostiniy Dvor metro. Next door to the Dom kino, this modernized cinema features a bar, billiards and a DVD store, and is also a venue for film festivals.

The visual arts

St Petersburg has dozens of **private galleries** and **exhibition halls**, in addition to the temporary displays which can be seen in its museums and state galleries. Many of the private galleries cater for the tourist market with picture-postcard paintings of the city, alongside *matryoshka* dolls, balalaikas and other handicrafts, but there's often more exciting art on display, too. At the city's best-known exhibition spaces you're guaranteed to find something interesting – look out especially for temporary exhibitions at the Benois Wing of the Russian Museum (p.138), the Marble Palace (p.85) or in the Engineers' Castle (p.88). In addition, there are countless **street artists** showing off their talents along Nevskiy prospekt and outside the major tourist attractions.

Albom 5-ya liniya 36 ⊗323 57 15, ⓦ www.
album-gallery.ru; **Vasileostrovskaya metro.**
Multimedia projects, paintings, drawings and photos by contemporary Russian artists. Visits by prior arrangement. Tues–Sun noon–7pm.

Centre of National Cultures Nevskiy pr. 166
T717 12 16; **Ploshchad Vosstaniya metro.** Solo exhibitions by independent artists, ranging from batiks to handmade toys or plastic carvings. Accepts Visa, MC. Tues–Sat 11am–7pm.

Golubaya gostinaya (Blue Hall) Bolshaya
Morskaya ul. 38, second floor ⊗315 74 14;
Nevskiy Prospekt/Gostiniy Dvor metro. Outlet for members of the St Petersburg Artists' Union, that also deals in Socialist Realist artworks (export documentation and a framing service available). All major cards. Daily noon–7pm.

KGallery nab. reki Fontanki 24 ⊗273 00 56;
Gostiniy Dvor metro. Works by Soviet artists and a unique collection of propaganda porcelain from the 1920s and 1930s (not for export). Daily 11am–8pm.

Manège (Manezh) Isaakievskaya pl. 1 ⊗314
88 59; **Nevskiy Prospekt metro.** Used for temporary exhibitions by the Artists' Union and others, including an annual showcase of contemporary art in August, and an international Biennale in late July. Daily 11am–7pm, except Thurs.

Marina Gisich Gallery nab. reki Fontanki 121,
apt. 13 ⊗314 43 80, ⓦ www.gisich.com;
Sadovaya metro. Individual exhibitions by contemporary artists in a private flat-gallery, viewable by arrangement only; check the website to see what's on. Mon–Fri 11am–7pm.

Masters' Guild Nevskiy pr. 82 ⊗579 09 79;
Mayakovskaya metro. High-quality, long-established gallery specializing in well-

known artists formerly involved in the Stergovlitsi and LOSKh movements. Export documentation available. Daily 11am–7pm.

Pechatnya (Printing Press) in the Peter and
Paul Fortress ⊗238 07 42; **Gorkovskaya metro.**
Woodcuts, etchings and linocuts by some of St Petersburg's best graphic artists, in a refurbished Petrine-era printers. Major cards. Daily 11am–6pm.

Pushkinskaya 10 entry through arch of Ligov-
skiy pr. 53; Ploshchad Vosstaniya metro. A longstanding artists' squat that's become part of the mainstream art world (see p.205). Diverse exhibitions at the KINO-FOT film gallery (Wed–Sun 3–7pm) on the seventh floor of block A; FOTOimage gallery (Sat 4–7pm) on the second floor of block C; and the Techno-Art Centre (Mon–Fri 5–11pm, Sat & Sun 3–11.30pm) and Gallery of Experimental Sound (see GEZ-21 on p.356) on the first and third floors of block D.

Pylos Embassy nab. reki Moyki 35 ⊗315 43 63;
Nevskiy Prospekt metro. Just around the corner from the Hermitage, this gallery focuses on realist painting, graphic art and photography. Major cards. Daily 11am–7pm.

Rachmaninov Dvorik Kazanskaya ul. 5 ⊗312
95 58; **Nevskiy Prospekt/Gostiniy Dvor metro.** A photo-gallery attached to the Rachmaninov cultural centre, reached by going through the second arch beside the *Rachmaninov Hotel* (see p.328). Major cards. Daily 11am–7pm.

Sol-Art Stolyanoy per. 15 ⊗327 30 82; **Mayako-**
vskaya metro. Gallery dealing in contemporary St Petersburg artists, whose paintings and prints are stacked alongside Palekh boxes and other souvenirs, in the lobby of the Museum of Decorative and Applied Arts (see p.196). Amex, DC, Visa. Daily 10am–6pm.

Shopping

Whilst older Russians, conditioned by decades of queuing and carrying an *avoska* ("just in case" bag), find the notion of **shopping** for pleasure strange, those with money revel in the diversity of products and today's teenagers are as label-conscious and shopping-happy as any in Europe. Shopping malls have sprung up all over the city, often combined with bowling alleys or cinemas. For visitors, it's never been easier to buy foodstuffs, souvenirs and gifts; the main bargains are CDs, porcelain, lacquer-ware, Soviet memorabilia, caviar and vodka. If you're visiting Novgorod, you'll find traditional handicrafts far cheaper there than in St Petersburg. Shop assistants in Soviet times were famously rude, and it's still unusual to be treated courteously unless you're a big-spender in a ritzy salon. Most shops now use the one-stop system, though a few infuriating stores still insist on customers paying at the *kassa* before collecting their goods, which entails queuing at least twice.

Antiques and icons

Antiques are loosely defined in Russia; anything pre-1960 can be deemed part of the national heritage and needs an **export licence** from the Ministry of Culture (see p.31). Lovely as they are, bronze and silver **samovars** (tea urns) are probably not worth the hassle of exporting legally (you can find them in flea markets abroad), and impossible to get past the scanners at the airport. The same goes for **icons** – although contemporary icons which can look as fine as antiques, yet aren't subject to controls, are sold at the *lavka* (church shop) in the Alexander Nevsky Monastery and various churches in the city. However, the samovars made today aren't worth buying at all.

La Russe Stremyannaya ul. 3, ⓦ www.larusse. ru.com; Mayakovskaya metro. Peasant wood-carvings, textiles, hand-painted furniture, samovars and Soviet knick-knacks – some antiques, some repro. Major cards. Daily 11am–8pm.

Peterburg Nevskiy pr. 54; Gostiniy Dvor metro. A salon to window-shop antique furniture, statuettes, icons and porcelain, even if you can't afford their prices. Major cards. Daily 10am–8pm.

Rapsodiya (Rhapsody) Bolshaya Konyushen-naya ul. 13; Nevskiy Prospekt metro. Furniture, silverware, bronzes and ceramics. Maestro, MC, Visa. Mon–Sat 11am–7pm, Sun noon–7pm.

Russkie Traditsii (Russian Traditions) nab reki Fontanki 88, ⓦ www.antiqspb.ru; Pushkinskaya metro. Antique icons, bronzes, porcelain and glass. No cards. Mon–Sat 10am–8pm, Sun 11am–7pm.

Sekunda Liteyniy pr. 61, Mayakovskaya metro. Enter the yard to find this shop selling old photos, antique icons, porcelain, jewellery and Soviet memorabilia. No cards. Mon–Sat 11am–7pm, Sun 11am–6pm.

Staraya Kniga (Old Book) Kamennoostrovskiy pr. 17; Gorkovskaya metro. Icons, old books, furniture, bronzes, porcelain and antique Soviet memorabilia. No cards. Mon–Fri 10am–7pm, Sat 11am–6pm.

Books, maps and prints

Books about the Hermitage, the Russian Museum and the Imperial palaces are widely available in English and other languages (the Russian version of the same book is usually cheaper). If you can read Russian, bookshops offer a feast of literature and non-fiction at low prices (hardbacks especially), whereas the selection of imported books in other languages (on Russian history and society, or foreign fiction) is inevitably limited. The same is true of **maps**; locally produced ones in Cyrillic script are far more up to date than foreign maps. Glossy **calendars** featuring views of the city or the Imperial palaces, Russian icons or Old Masters, and reproduction posters and **prints** (on Soviet themes or historic lithographs of the city) are good buys. Legally, a **licence** is required to take books or prints more than twenty years old out of the country.

Angliya (England) nab. reki Fontanki 40, Ⓦ**www.anglophile.ru; Gostiniy Dvor metro.** Stocks all kinds of books in English, with a good selection on Russia and the city's widest range of English-language bestsellers. It has a relaxed, anglophile ambience, and hosts art exhibitions. Major cards. Mon–Fri 10am–8pm, Sat & Sun 11am–7pm.

Britannia ul. Marata 10, Mayakovskaya metro. Another English-language bookstore, which specializes in literature. No cards. Mon–Fri 10am–7pm, Sat 11am–pm.

Bukvoed (Pedant) Ligovskiy pr. 10/118, Oktyabrskaya Hotel, Ploshchad Vosstaniya metro. This megastore has tons of art books, a good selection of history and fiction in foreign languages, posters, calendars, repro prints and helpful staff. All major cards. Daily 24hr.

Dom knigi (House of Books) Nevskiy pr. 28, Nevskiy Prospekt/Gostiniy Dvor metro; and Nevskiy pr. 62, Mayakovskaya metro. The historic bookstore in the Singer building stocks maps, art books, posters and calendars,

but for anything else you need to visit the new branch opposite the Anichkov Palace. All major cards. Both daily 9am–midnight.

Dom knigi na Liteynom (House of Books on Liteyniy) Liteyniy pr. 30; Chernyshevskaya metro. Russian and secondhand foreign books; prints, maps, calendars and stationery. No cards. Mon–Sat 10am–9pm, Sun 11am–7pm.

Dom voennoy knigi (House of Military Books) Nevskiy pr. 20, Nevskiy Prospekt metro. Despite its name it stocks everything from romances and blockbusters to art books, posters, CD-ROMs and model kits. Major cards. Daily 24hr.

Pechatnya (Printing Press) in the Peter and Paul Fortress; Gorkovskaya metro. A Petrine-era printing house that sells a fantastic range of woodcuts, etchings and linocuts – some repro antiques, others limited editions by contemporary artists. All major cards. Daily 11am–6pm.

Clothing and accessories

While the city is awash with stores selling Italian, French and US designer clothing, prices are higher than abroad, and Russians with money to travel often restock their wardrobes in Paris or London. For visitors, the only bargains are Russian **linen** and **fur** hats and coats (if you've no moral scruples about fur). Fake fur **hats** are a popular souvenir, but if you're going to wear a real fur *ushanka* here, avoid cheap rabbit-fur versions, as Russians look down on people wearing "road kill". If you've money to burn or an interest in fashion you should check out some of the boutiques devoted to Russian designers (see below). Their work is showcased in mid-October during St Petersburg's **fashion week**, Defile on the Neva.

Boutique nab. kanala Griboedova 27, Gostiniy Dvor metro. Irina Ashkinadze organizes fashion week, and exclusively sells clothes by designers from Russia, Ukraine, Belarus,

the Caucuses and Central Asia. No cards. Mon–Sat 11am–8pm, Sun noon–7pm.

Lilla Kisselenko Kirochnaya ul. 47, Ⓦ**www. kisselenko.ru; Chernyshevskaya metro.** One of

St Petersburg's home-grown talents, Kisse-lenko is known for her intricate ethnographic designs and accessories. No cards. Mon–Fri 11am–6pm.

Slavyanskiy Stil (Slav Style) Pushkinskaya ul. 5, Ⓦwww.linorusso.ru; Ploshchad Vosstaniya metro. Fine linen products – blouses, skirts, shirts, tablecloths, sheets and duvet covers. The clothes are updates of traditional Rus-sian designs: waist-less shirts buttoned at the collar and ankle-length sleeveless *sara-fan* dresses (with or without embroidery). Maestro, Union, Visa. Mon–Fri 11am–8pm, Sat & Sun 11am–7pm.

Tatyana Parfionova Nevskiy pr. 51, Ⓦwww. parfionova.ru; Mayakovskaya metro. The first St Petersburg designer to start her own fashion house; her salon also sells *haute couture* by other designers. Amex, DC, Maestro, MC, Visa. Mon–Fri noon–8pm.

Tovar dlya Voennikh Sadovaya ul. 26, Sadovaya metro. A store catering to the armed forces, police and security guards, that stocks peaked caps, fake fur hats, stripy Airborne Forces vests, parade uniforms, combat fatigues, badges and insignia (Soviet repro or contemporary). Most items are sold to anyone who asks. No cards. Mon–Sat 10am–7pm.

Underground Shop Ligovskiy pr. 53, Ploshchad Vosstaniya metro. In the courtyard of the Pushkinskaya 10 artists' colony (see p.205), this shop sells club wear and parapher-nalia, CDs and posters of Russian indie and underground bands. No cards. Daily 11am–8pm.

Yelena Tsvetkova Nevskiy pr. 53, Mayakovskaya metro. Office wear, evening gowns, furs and shoes for Alpha businesswomen. No cards. Daily 11am–11pm.

Department stores and malls

The city's **department stores** face stiff competition from a new generation of **shopping malls** (known in Russian as *torgovye kompleksy*, abbreviated to *T/K*), incorporating shops, eateries and entertainment under one roof. Many are in the high-rise suburbs or on the outskirts of the city (accessible by special minibuses from the nearest metro station), though, with one exception, we have only listed below those that are all in the centre.

Gostiniy dvor Nevskiy pr. 35 Ⓦwww.bgd.ru, Gostiniy Dvor/Nevskiy Prospekt metro. A his-toric landmark (see p.70), each of its three floors is 1km in circumference and honey-combed with stores selling shoes, lingerie, jewellery, cosmetics and souvenirs. Some take credit cards. Daily 10am–10pm, Wed & Thurs till 10.30pm.

Grand Palace Nevskiy pr. 44; Gostiniy Dvor/ Nevskiy Prospekt metro. A four-floor mall devoted to fashion and fripperies, featur-ing Sonia Rykiel, Swarovski, Missoni, Christian Dior and others, plus a chocolate boutique and jeweller's. Major cards. Daily 11am–9pm.

Moskovskiy univermag Moskovskiy pr. 205–207 & 220–222; Moskovskaya metro. On both sides of the prospekt en route to the airport, these ex-Soviet mega-stores sell souvenirs, fur hats, clothes, porcelain, chocolates, caviar, booze, software and much else. MC, Visa. Mon–Sat 10am–9pm, Sun 11am–9pm.

Passazh Nevskiy pr. 48; Gostiniy Dvor/Nevskiy

Prospekt metro. Near the Grand Palace, this stately nineteenth-century arcade has shops selling repro antiques, porcelain, glassware, shoes and cosmetics, with a supermarket in the basement. Maestro, MC, Visa. Mon–Sat 10am–9pm, Sun 11am–9pm; supermarket till 10pm.

Pik Sennaya pl. 2, Sadovaya/Sennaya Plosh-chad metro. Looming over the square where Raskolnikov once knelt in atonement, this mirror-glass mall with its cinema (see p.369) would have surely outraged Dostoyevsky. Major cards. Daily 10am–10pm.

Sennaya ul. Yefimova 3, Sadovaya/Sennaya Ploshchad metro. Directly behind Pik, this mall contains a bowling alley (see p.384) and backs onto the Sennoy market (p.374). Major cards. Daily 10am–9pm.

Vladimirskiy Passage Vladimirkiy pr. 19; Vladimirskaya /Dostoevskaya metro. A swanky mall with a great bakery, patisserie and coffee shop on the first floor and a well-stocked supermarket in the basement (p.375). Major cards. Daily 11am–9pm.

Lacquered boxes and tableware

After *matryoshka* dolls (see "Toys") the commonest souvenirs are **lacquered boxes** made from papier-mâché, varying in size and shape from pillboxes to jewellery caskets. Traditionally they were produced by four villages where the poor soil made handicrafts a better source of income than agriculture, each of which developed their own style, but nowadays imitations are widely produced and only connoisseurs know the differences between the Palekh, Fedosino, Khuly and Mstyora styles – which most people would lump together as lush, minutely detailed depictions of Russian fairy tales, medieval cities or rural scenes. Other "folk" products sold all over the city are birch-wood **bowls**, **spoons** and **platters** from Khokloma, painted with floral patterns in red, black and gold. Finally there are objects made from supple **birch bark** – purses, handbags, slippers, lampshades, tablemats, coasters and fruit baskets – manufactured in Novgorod (and much cheaper to buy there). All are widely available at wildly differing prices – shop around.

Lakir (Lacquer) Muchnoy per. 2; Sennaya Ploshchad metro. This shop on a side street near the Economics University sells nothing but lacquered boxes of all shapes, sizes and designs. No cards. Mon–Fri noon–5pm.
Vernissazh nab. kanala Griboedova; Nevskiy Prospekt metro. The city's main outdoor

tourist market, beside the Church of the Saviour on the Blood, has an infinite variety of boxes, *matryoshky*, Khokloma bowls, fur hats and watches. Some stalls take credit cards; haggling is acceptable at most of them. Daily 9am–9pm.

Markets and food and drink stores

While local groceries and supermarkets stock a range of Russian and foreign products, the freshest produce is found at **markets** (*rynok*), where vendors tempt buyers with nibbles of fruit, cheese, sour cream, ham, pickles and other homemade delights. Although the larger stores may accept credit cards, at smaller shops and markets you'll need to pay cash. Shopping for gifts, the best buys are **caviar** and **vodka**. Caviar should be bought in a delicatessen or supermarket rather than a market, where the stuff on sale is almost certainly of illicit origin and may be unsafe to eat. Vodka and other spirits are best purchased in a *firmeny magazin* such as Liviz or Dagvino.

Markets

Kuznechniy Kuznechniy per. 3; Vladimirskaya/Dostoevskaya metro. The best-stocked, most expensive market hall in the city, up the road from Dostoyevsky's last apartment (see p.207). Worth a visit just for the atmosphere. Mon–Sat 8am–8pm, Sun 8am–7pm.
Maltsevskiy ul. Nekrasova 52; Ploshchad Vosstaniya. Still better known by its former name, Nekrasovskiy, this is good for beans, fruit 'n' veg and oriental spices, though the "fresh" butter and cream can be rancid. Mon–Sat 8am–7pm, Sun 8am–4pm.
Sennoy Moskovskiy pr. 4–6; Sennaya Ploshchad metro. The cheapest food market in the centre, behind the Pik and Sennaya malls. Mon–Sat 8am–7pm, Sun 8am–4pm.

Sytniy Sytninskaya pl. 3–5; Gorkovskaya metro. Another rewarding market for Caucasian food produce, where the chefs of some of the best Georgian restaurants in town do their shopping. Mon–Sat 8am–7pm, Sun 8am–4pm.
Vasileostrovskiy Bolshoy pr. 14/16; Vasileostrovskaya metro. Also known as the Andreevskiy, after the Church of St Andrew across the road, this renovated eighteenth-century market hall has several kiosks outside selling *lavash* bread and other Armenian specialities. Mon–Sat 8am–7pm, Sun 8am–4pm.

Specialist food and drink stores

Baltic Bread Vladimirskiy pr. 19 (first floor of the Vladimirskiy Passage mall), Dostoevskaya metro;

Grechiskiy pr. 25, tram #5 or #7 from Ploshchad Vosstaniya metro; Bolshoy pr. 80, Petrogradskaya metro. These three outlets sell over 200 types of freshly baked loaves, rolls, sweet and savoury pastries and gateaux, and serve tea and coffee. Daily 9am–10pm; the Vladimirskiy Passage branch closes at 9pm.

Chocolate Museum Nevskiy pr. 62, Mayakovskaya metro; ul. Zhukovskovo 18, Ploshchad Vosstaniya metro. Handmade dark and milk chocolates – liquors and other soft-centres sold by weight, plus individually moulded pieces; a bust of Lenin costs R560, a chess set, R600. Major cards. Daily 11am–9pm.

Dagvino Nevskiy pr. 172, Ploshchad Aleksandra Nevskovo metro; Ligovskiy pr. 82, Ligovskiy Prospekt metro. Specializes in Dagestani cognacs (some extremely costly, in cut-glass presentation bottles), plus vodka, French wines and liquors. MC, Visa. Nevskiy branch: Mon–Sat 9am–9pm, Sun 9am–7pm; Ligovskiy: daily 9am–8pm.

Himalaya 1-ya Sovetskaya 10, Ploshchad Vosstaniya metro. An Indian corner shop selling curry spices, Thai, Chinese and Japanese food products, sauces, snacks and Bollywood videos. No cards. Daily 24hr.

Lend Vladimirskiy pr. 19, Dostoevskaya metro. This lavishly stocked supermarket in the basement of the Vladimirskiy Passage mall runs to tofu, Japanese buckwheat noodles, Thai sauces and Mediterranean delicacies. Major cards. Daily 24hr.

Liviz Nevskiy pr. 43, Ploshchad Vosstaniya metro; ul. Zhukovskovo 27, Mayakovskaya metro; Sinoptskaya nab. 56, Ploshchad Aleksandra Nevskovo metro. A chain of outlets for Liviz vodkas, Moldavian, Georgian and French wines and other alcohol, all guaranteed not to be bootlegs. No cards. Daily 9am–8pm.

Pchelovodstvo (Bee-Keeping) Liteyniy pr. 42; Mayakovskaya metro. All kinds of fresh honey from the Rostov region, plus creams and remedies made from bee pollen and royal jelly, as well as honey-flavoured herbal teas. No cards. Mon–Sat 10am–8pm.

▼ The interior of Yeliseyev's food store

Yeliseyev's Nevskiy pr. 56; Gostiniy Dvor metro. A famous food store (see p.69), known for its gorgeous Style Moderne decor and above-average range of caviar, smoked fish, alcohol and chocolates. It was closed for "refurbishment" at the time of writing, and some fear it may never re-open, but become offices instead.

Krupskaya Fabrika pr. ul. Vosstaniya 15, Ploshchad Vosstaniya metro. A retail outlet for the Krupskaya Confectionery Factory (named after Lenin's wife), a well-known Soviet manufacturer that's still going strong. No cards. Mon–Fri 10.30am–6.30pm.

Music, videos and CD-ROMs

Hollywood and Microsoft may fume, but Russia remains the world's largest market for **pirate** CDs, DVDs, videos, cassettes, CD-ROMs, computer games and software. While bootlegs are now rare in chain stores, kiosks at metro stations and in markets stock them alongside licensed products and will happily tell you which is which. The quality of pirated products varies from abysmal to indistinguishable from the real thing, though it's said that three out of four pirated computer programmes have some kind of defect or virus. You can also buy the latest electronic gadgets such as iPhones weeks before they go on sale in Western Europe, complete with hacked software to get around tied-provider deals.

Aisberg (Iceberg) Liteyniy pr. 63, Mayakovskaya metro; Zagorodniy pr. 10, Vladimirskaya metro; Kamennoostrovskiy pr. 38, Petrogradskaya metro. Music and video chain with thousands of CDs, DVDs and CD-ROMs. No cards. Daily 24hr.

505 Nevskiy pr. 72, Mayakovskaya metro; Moskovskiy pr. 197, Moskovskaya metro; ul. Komsomola 35, Ploshchad Lenina metro. Another chain with an excellent range of games, CDs and DVDs at very reasonable prices. No cards. Mon–Sat 10am–11pm, Sun 11am–11pm.

Klassica Mikhaylovskaya ul. 2; Nevskiy Prospekt metro. The city's oldest music shop is still one of the best places to buy classical, opera, folk and church music on CDs, tapes and vinyl; it also sells books and videos about music, and scores. Major cards. Daily 11am–3pm & 4–7.30pm.

Otkryty Mir (Open World) Malaya Morskaya ul. 11; Nevskiy Prospekt metro. Stocks a wide range of classical, jazz and ethnic music on CD, DVD, cassettes and vinyl. No cards. Daily 10am–10pm.

Titanik Nevskiy pr. 158, Ploshchad Aleksandra Nevskovo metro; Nevskiy pr. 63, Mayakovskaya metro; Kirochnaya ul. 17, Chernyshevskaya metro; Zagorodniy pr. 10, Vladimirskaya/Dostoevskaya metro; ⓦ www.titanik-spb.ru. Chain with a vast array of music CDs, Hollywood and Soviet movies and cartoons (some in English), and CD-ROM games. They also sell tickets to pop concerts, dance events and Zenit football matches. No cards. Daily 24hr.

Severnaya Lira (Northern Lyre) Nevskiy pr. 26; Nevskiy Prospekt/Gostiniy Dvor metro. Sheet music, CDs, music books and musical instruments. Major cards. Mon–Fri 10am–8pm, Sat & Sun 11am–7pm.

Porcelain, glass and crystal

St Petersburg has a long tradition of manufacturing **porcelain** (*farfor*), glass and crystal ware; most of the factories producing them today were founded to supply the court and nobility with settings for their banquets. Russian Futurists leapt at the chance to turn these status symbols into utensils for the masses – the first Soviet ceramics bore the Romanov seal, over-painted with revolutionary imagery. Today, such porcelain is highly prized and requires an export licence (as does anything pre-revolutionary), but high-quality reproductions are easily found and freely exportable. Among the most popular are Empire Style blue, gold and white patterns from Tver and Novgorod, Constructivist motifs from the 1920s, and sets celebrating the Moscow metro or Soviet feats in space. Blue and white Gzhel ceramic figurines are also widely available, though much of what's on offer is overpriced rubbish. Cut **glass** (*steklo*) or **crystal** (*khrustal*) glasses, bowls, ornamental vases and knick-knacks are a feature of most Russian homes, though the designs tend to be very 1970s.

Imperial Porcelain Nevskiy pr. 160, Ploshchad Aleksandra Nevskovo metro; pr. Obukhovskoy Oboroniy 151, Lomonosovskaya metro; ⓦ www.lomonosovporcelain.ru. Europe's third-oldest porcelain factory (see p.220) has over 500 items in its catalogue. The Nevskiy branch (daily 10am–8pm) is easier to reach than the factory showroom (Mon–Fri 10am–7pm, Sat & Sun 11am–5pm); to get to the latter from Lomonosovskaya metro, head towards the Neva embankment and turn left (north). Packing and export service available. Amex, DC, JCB, Maestro, MC, Visa.

Russian Museum Inzhenernaya ul. 4; Gostiniy Dvor/Nevskiy Prospekt metro. The museum shop sells reproductions of some of the Futurist crockery in its storerooms, with designs by Malevich, Rodchenko, Popova and El Lissitsky. Major cards. Mon 10am–5pm, Wed–Sun 10am–6pm.

World of Crystal ul. Sedova 69; Lomonosovskaya metro. The showroom of the Gus Khrustalniy factory is in the same district as the Lomonosov factory, and offers a big choice of crystal tableware, vases and curios. No cards. Mon–Sat 10am–8pm, Sun 11am–6pm.

Soviet memorabilia

Soviet memorabilia is as popular with tourists as it was when the USSR still existed, but most of the posters, uniforms and watches on sale today are **reproductions** rather than originals. About the only genuine items that are ubiquitous are **lapel pins** (*znachki*). In Soviet times, every sports club, factory or hobby society had its own and collectors traded them – *Pravda* once rebuked the Plumbers' Union for producing a badge shaped like a toilet. Nowadays, *znachki* made of semi-precious metals, or featuring Trotsky or Beria, are rare enough to be valuable – but there are millions of enamelled alloy or plastic badges around. Repro **posters** are sold in many bookshops besides the one below and are currently popular with Russians who never experienced Soviet life – whereas military fur hats, peaked caps or pointy felt Budyonny hats (named after the Civil War cavalry commander) are strictly for tourists (or conscripts). They're sold at street stalls near the major tourist sites and at Tovar dlya Voennikh (see "Clothing and accessories"). For authentic vintage memorabilia, try Sekunda, Staraya Kniga or La Russe (see "Antiques and icons").

Main Post Office Pochamtskaya ul. 9; trolleybus #5 or #22 from Nevskiy pr. Cosmonauts, collective farms and Marxism-Leninism are among the themes celebrated by Soviet commemorative stamps, sold at the philately booth in the Main Post Office (see p.106). Many of the designs are exquisite, and stamps are cheap. No cards. Mon–Sat 9am–7pm, Sun 10am–4pm.

Mint Shop in the Peter and Paul Fortress; Gorkovskaya metro. Sells certified replicas of military, anniversary and commemorative medals bearing the visages of tsars, Lenin, Stalin, marshals or cosmonauts, issued by the Mint over three centuries. Major cards. Daily 10am–6pm.

Knizhniy Salon Nevskiy pr. 94, Mayakovskaya/Ploshchad Vosstaniya metro. Stocks cheap repro posters and fridge magnets extolling the Communist Party or agitating against alcoholism – the one of a guy refusing a glass of vodka adorns the ice box in many a Russian home. No cards. Mon–Fri 10am–11pm, Sat & Sun 10am–10pm.

Sports equipment

Hunting and fishing are widely popular in Russia (obliging every cabinet minister to claim that their summer vacation was spent doing one or the other), while the younger generation is into inline skating, skateboarding or martial arts. For visitors invited to go camping in the wilderness – or spend a weekend at someone's *dacha* – the following specialist stores may prove useful.

Frankardi nab. Bolshoy reki Nevki 24; Chernaya Rechka metro. Everything for skiing, snow-boarding, ice-skating and jet-skiing. No cards. Daily 10am–7pm.

Snaryazhenie (Gear) Stremyannaya ul. 3; Mayakovskaya metro. Rock-climbing, hiking, skiing and camping equipment. No cards. Mon–Sat 10am–8pm, Sun 10am–6pm.

Soldat Udachi (Soldier of Fortune) ul. Nekrasova 37, Cheryshevskaya metro; Bolshoy pr. 17, Vasileostrovskaya metro; ⦿ www.soldatudachi.ru. Two macho outlets for camping, hunting and fishing gear, Swiss Army knives, Maglite torches, GPS devices, martial arts equipment, reproduction antique weapons and modern military firearms. No cards. Mon–Sat 10am–6pm.

Sportmaster Moskovskiy pr. 10; Sadovaya metro. Skis and skiwear, swimwear, tennis racquets, trainers and camping equipment. Major cards. Daily 10am–10pm.

Techno Sport Centre Morskoy Vokzal Hotel, pl. Morskoy Slavy 1; minibus #129 from Primorskaya metro. Clothing and gear for yachting, surfing, scuba diving, fishing, bird-watching and other pursuits. Major cards. Daily 10am–10pm.

Toys

Nesting dolls or *matryoshky*, are a cliché souvenir and symbol of Russia. Invented in 1890 at the children's workshop of the Abramtsevo artists' colony, the original design of a headscarfed peasant woman was subverted during perestroika, when Gorby, Lenin et al appeared – since followed by Putin, Bush and Bin Laden (one version panders to Islamophobia with Bin Laden, Arafat, a Chechen suicide bomber and a miniature Koran). All these are sold at stalls, shops and museums throughout the centre. You may also see traditional wooden toys from Novgorod, such as **dancing bears** and **bears on a see-saw**, which are also produced in joke forms such as two bears taking it in turns to work on a computer, or one bear spanking the other with a broom.

Doll Museum Kamskaya ul. 8 ⓦhttp://russian-dolls.ru; minibus #249A from Vasileostrovskaya metro. Handmade dolls by local designers (some of whom can be seen working upstairs, better treated as art than consigned to the playroom. Come on Sunday, when children can make their own and the R100 admission charge doesn't seem unjust. MC, Visa. Tues–Sun 11am–6pm.

Toy Museum ul. Vsevoloda 22/32; Petrogradskaya metro. This private museum charges you R250 to look around, and sells artistic handmade toys at collectors' prices. Open 11am–6pm; closed Mon & the last Tues of each month.

Children's
St Petersburg

A lthough Russians dote on **children**, St Petersburg is not a child-friendly environment, especially for toddlers: parks and playgrounds are littered with broken glass or even syringes, and slides and swings are often unsafe. However, in compensation, there are many attractions for kids to see and enjoy. Circuses, puppet shows, musicals and spectacles on ice are detailed under "The Arts" (Chapter 16). Russians have high expectations of their children's attention span and behaviour; you'll see 6-year-olds sitting through three-hour ballets at the Mariinskiy or Maliy theatres (where the minimum age is 5 for matinees, 8 for evening performances). St Petersburg's aquaparks (see p.387) are readily accessible to visitors, and children are welcome to accompany adults to the *banya* (bathhouse), or to a football or ice hockey match (see Chapter 19, "Sports"). For toys and souvenirs, see "Shopping" (Chapter 17).

Children ride for free on public **transport** (except minibuses) up to the age of seven, and pay the adult fare thereafter. Outside summer, Russians **dress** their children in hats, scarves and layers of clothing – when foreign parents might simply pop a sweater on – and do their best to ensure that Russian kids never sit on the ground, for fear of catching cold or developing maladies in later life. Russian grannies (*babushki*) feel free to admonish strangers who allow their own kids to go "undressed", and breastfeeding in public is regarded as something that "only Gypsies do". Baby food and disposable nappies are available at most supermarkets and pharmacies, though you may wish to bring a small supply to tide you over.

Attractions

Museums that might interest children of all ages are the bizarre Kunstkammer and Museum of Anthropology (p.156), the Railway Museum (p.104) and the Arctic and Antarctic Museum (p.207). If they're unfazed by the language barrier, they can join Russian kids to try their hand at printmaking, weaving or pottery at the Children's Centre (Sat & Sun 11am–5pm) of the Russian Ethnographic Museum (see p.92). The World of Water Museum has a collection of antique toilets and a beguiling illuminated fountain in its atrium (see p.199). Children going through a bellicose phase might also enjoy the *Narodovolets* submarine (p.162), the cruiser *Aurora* (p.178), the Naval Museum (p.154) and the Artillery Museum (p.175). Young girls are more likely to enjoy the Doll Museum (p.166) or Toy Museum (p.181).

Of the **Imperial palaces** outside the city (see Chapter 9), Peterhof, Tsarskoe Selo and Pavlovsk are the most enjoyable for kids, with huge parks, truly fabulous interiors and the odd amusement park or boating lake. Peterhof is especially rewarding, as children love to try their luck with the "joke" fountains in Lower Park (see p.247). A trip to the woods and beaches of the **Karelian Isthmus** is also recommended in the summer; Zelenogorsk has the best beach for bathing (see Chapter 10).

St Petersburg's state-of-the-art **Planet Neptun Oceanarium** (ul. Marata 89 ☎ 448 00 77; Pushkinskaya metro; daily 10am–10pm, closed the last Mon of each month) is the largest in Russia, featuring fish from the Arctic to the Amazon and a 35-metre-long walk-through sea tunnel surrounded by sharks. Tickets cost R300–400 on weekdays, R400–500 at weekends; child rates are R150–300 and R250–350.

The ageing **Dolphinarium** on Krestovskiy Island (Konstantinovskiy pr. 19 ☎ 235 46 31, ⓦ www.dolphinarium.ru; Krestovskiy Ostrov metro) has an hour-long performance (Wed & Thurs 4pm & 6pm, Fri 2pm & 4pm, Sat noon, 4pm & 6pm, Sun noon, 2pm & 4pm; adults R160–250; children R70–150) by dolphins and a sea lion (with which kids can be photographed) – but the conditions they're kept in will dismay adults if not children, as is also the case with animals at the city's **Zoo** (p.175).

The latter is within walking distance of the city's **Planetarium** in the Alexander Park, whose rota of shows includes footage from the *Mir* space station besides the usual astronomical projections (Tues–Sun 10.30am–6pm).

Activities

Toddlers should enjoy **parks** such as the Tauride Gardens (p.197) which has an old-fashioned funfair and several play areas; the Yusupov Garden (p.105) on Sadovaya ulitsa, where you can paddle in the pool; and the Summer Garden, with its picturesque statues (though you can't touch them). Most of the city's **playgrounds** (often in the courtyards of residential blocks) are poorly maintained, but there are two excellent public facilities on the Petrograd Side: on Kamennoostrovskiy prospekt, 100m south of Petrogradskaya metro, and at the corner of Bolshaya Pushkarskaya and ulitsa Lenina. In the city centre, you could get away with using the playgrounds for residents in the gated block at Italyanskaya ul. 27 (leading through to Malaya Sadovaya ul. 4), or the block between Gagarinskaya ulitsa and the River Fontanka, where the Small Academy of Arts is located (see below).

Older kids should head for one of the city's **amusement parks. Alisa** (daily 11am–9pm; pay per ride) in the Alexander Park near Gorkovskaya metro is within walking distance of the Peter and Paul Fortress and the Planetarium, with bouncy castles, dodgems and carousels. On Krestovskiy Island, the larger **Divo Ostrov** (☎ 323 97 07, ⓦ www.divo-ostrov.ru; Tues–Fri 11am–8pm, Sat & Sun 11am–9pm) is divided into zones (kids, family, prizes and thrills), with rides in ascending order of scariness, up to Booster and Catapult in the thrills zone. You can pay per ride (R30–300) or buy a package valid for all rides in any one zone or all of them (R550–1700 per person). The park also holds "extreme nights", when DJs accompany rides in the thrills zone.

Krestovskiy Island is also great for **rollerblading** or **cycling** – a good way for kids to meet Russians their age – with a shop hiring all the gear not far from Divo Ostrov and the local metro station. Less energetically, you could pass an hour or so on a **boat trip** – either a guided tour of the city's river and canals, or hiring a motorboat (see p.41) – while a **hydrofoil** ride to Peterhof (p.240) is an unforgettable experience; children pay half the adult rate.

If you're settling in St Petersburg with children, they may like to join the **Small Academy of Arts** (Malaya Akademiya Iskusstv) in the courtyard of nab. reki Fontanki 2 ⓣ273 20 62 (see p.196), across the Fontanka from the Summer Garden. The academy takes children from 5 years upwards for twice-weekly crafts' days (ceramics, sculpture, murals, etc), and one day a week visiting museums to study under master restorers and curators. Adults are welcome to participate, too; all the teachers and helpers are volunteers, and the academy is free of charge. The only snag is, it's closed over summer.

Eating

Kids demanding to eat something familiar can be pacified with a visit to *McDonald's* or *Pizza Hut*, while the Russian chain *Laima* has tasty salads, burgers, chips and other childish favourites – for addresses see the box on pp.345–346. But it would be a shame not to give Russian food a try – in particular, the different-flavoured pies at *Stolle* (see p.347), or pancakes with condensed milk (*bliny so sgushchenkoy*), are often popular with children. You can get *bliny* at almost any café, but they are especially good at *Bliny domik* (p.348) and *Russkie bliny* (p.348), while the chains *U Tyoshi na blinakh* and *Yolki Palki* have fun decor. **Child-friendly restaurants** include *Da Albertone* (p.350), *La Strada* (p.350), *Olivia* (p.350) and *Tres Amigos* (p.353) in the centre, and *Karl & Friedrich* on Krestovskiy Island – the last three have play areas, and the last two, childminders. For a **special occasion**, there's the *Mary Poppins Café* (ul. Nekrasova 23 ⓣ275 51 44; Chernyshevskaya metro): themed around the children's classic of the same name, it can lay on clown shows, fireworks, live music and parties for children.

Street entertainment

There are often **buskers and street performers** along Nevskiy prospekt and outside major tourist spots. Don't miss the guy who plays tunes on a saw by the Church of the Saviour on the Blood. At the Peter and Paul Fortress and Peterhof, kids can be photographed with actors wearing eighteenth-century period costumes, and hire crinolines or frock coats to dress up for the shot.

Crossing the panoramic Neva Basin is fun, too: **trams** #2 and #54 from Sadovaya ulitsa cross the river within sight of the Peter and Paul Fortress, and in summer antique trams run from Finland Station into the centre, giving views of the cruiser *Aurora*. For those children who can keep awake until the early hours, the spectacle of the **bridges** on the Neva opening to let ships through is a memorable one (see p.40 for times).

Sports

n Soviet times, **sport** was accorded high status: a carefully nurtured elite of Olympic medal-winning athletes were heralded as proof of Communism's superiority, while ordinary citizens were exhorted to pursue sporting activities to make them "ready for labour and defence". Consequently, there's no shortage of sports facilities in St Petersburg, though many are for club members only; visitors can either try striking a deal with the staff, or settle for paying higher rates to use hotel facilities. If you're doing any outdoor activities, including sports such as horse riding and yachting, be sure that they're covered by your **insurance** policy.

For the slothful majority, however, the most popular activity remains visiting the **bathhouse**, or *banya*. Russian bathhouses are a world unto themselves and are the preferred cure for the malady known locally as "feeling heavy" – which encompasses everything from having flu to being depressed. For a truly Russian experience, a visit to the *banya* is an absolute must.

Bathhouses

The Russian **banya** is as much a national institution as the sauna in Finland. Traditionally, peasants stoked up the village bathhouse and washed away the week's grime on Fridays; Saturdays were for drinking and Sundays for church – "a *banya* for the soul". Townspeople were equally devoted to the *banya*: the wealthy had private ones, while others visited public bathhouses, favoured as much for their conviviality as the quality of their hot room. In Russia's favourite Soviet romantic comedy, *Irony of Fate*, the hero gets so drunk at the *banya* celebrating his stag night in Moscow that he ends up in Leningrad by mistake, and meets his true love there.

So here's the procedure when **visiting a banya**. Some have separate floors for men and women, while others operate on different days for each sex, but whatever the set-up, there's no mixed bathing, except in the section available for private rental (where anything goes). The only thing the *banya* will definitely provide (for a modest price) is a sheet in which to wrap yourself. You should **bring** a towel, shampoo, some plastic sandals and possibly a hat to protect your head (towels, flip-flops and weird mushroom-shaped felt hats can be rented at some *banyas*). At the entrance, you can buy a *venik* – a leafy bunch of birch twigs (or prickly juniper twigs for the really hardy) – with which bathers fan and flail themselves (and each other) in the steam room, to open up the skin's pores and enhance blood circulation. This isn't obligatory, but it feels great afterwards.

Hand your coat and valuables to the cloakroom attendant before going into the changing rooms. Beyond these lies a washroom with a **cold plunge pool** (*basseyn*); the metal basins are for soaking your *venik* to make it supple. Finally you enter the **hot room** – or *parilka* – with its tiers of wooden benches – the higher up you go, the hotter it gets. Unlike in a Finnish sauna, it's a damp heat, as from time to time water is thrown onto the stove to produce steam. Five to seven minutes is as long as novices should attempt in the *parilka*. After a dunk in the cold bath and a rest, you can return to the *parilka* for more heat torture, before cooling off again – a process repeated several times, with breaks for tea and conversation.

Two hours is the usual time allowed in the **communal baths** and the rental period for **private sections** (*individualnoe nomer*) – though you can reserve a *nomer* for longer if desired. **Prices** vary from place to place; expect to pay R50–350 an hour in the communal section or R600–2500 for an hour's rental of a *nomer*, depending on its size (from 4–10 people) and amenities. Some baths have both regular and "lux" communal and private sections; "erotic massage" is on offer at many, but not the public baths which locals take their children to.

Many *banya*-goers cover their heads with hats to protect them from the heat, while others take advantage of traditional health cures and beauty treatments: men rub salt over their bodies in order to sweat more copiously, and women coat themselves with honey, to make their skin softer – you can also throw beer on the stove for a wonderful yeasty aroma. As *banya*-going is a dehydrating experience, it's advisable not to go drunk, with a bad hangover or on a full stomach. Beer is usually on sale in the men's section, but women should bring their own drinks. The traditional farewell salutation to fellow *banya*-goers is "*S lyogkim parom*" – "May the steam be with you".

Lastly, a word of **warning**: Russian mobsters love partying at the *banya*. They usually rent a private section and bring their girlfriends or call girls along; drunken quarrels may occur, followed by murders the next day (so Militia detectives say). This tends to happen on Thursday nights, at baths that stay open late. By day, the clientele is far more respectable as a rule.

Hamam Zastavskaya ul. 19 ☎380 08 37; **Moskovskie Vorota metro.** A Turkish steam bath, Finnish sauna, wood-fired *banya* and swimming pool in one complex, with billiards, karaoke, Turkish, classical and erotic soap massage, plus apartments for rent by the hour. Daily 24hr.

Kazatchiy bani Bolshoy Kazatchiy per. 11 ☎712 50 79; **Pushkinskaya metro.** R100/hr in the communal section, R1000 for a *nomer* for up to ten people. Daily 24hr.

Kruglye bani ul. Karbesheva 29a ☎550 09 85; **Ploshchad Muzhestva metro.** Favoured by expatriates on Wednesday nights, it occupies a round building opposite the metro – hence its name, the "Round Baths". R75/ R320 an hour in the regular/lux communal section; R600–800 for a four-person *nomer*. Mon, Tues & Fri–Sun 8am–10pm.

Mytninskie Bani ul. Mytninskaya 17/19 ☎271 71 19; **trolleybus #10 from pl. Vosstaniya.** One of the few wood-stoked *banya*s still operating in town, its public section (R75/hr) is quite shabby, but the private sauna (R1000)

is fine, with a whirlpool plunge bath. Mon, Tues & Fri–Sun 8am–7pm.

Smolninskie bani ul. Krasnovo Tekstilshika 7 ☎710 0969; **Chernyshevskaya metro.** Has a swimming pool, bar and billiards room. R50/ hr in the communal section, R500–1000/hr for a *nomer* for 6–8 people. Wed–Sun 24hr.

Neptun 17-ya liniya 38 ☎321 81 54; **Vasileostrovskaya metro.** Sauna, *parilka* and private cubicles. Mon & Thurs–Sun 8am–10.30pm.

VIP Sauna Gavanskaya ul. 5 ☎325 55 64; minibus #129 from Gostiniy Dvor metro. Its amenities include a Russian *banya*, Finnish sauna, swimming pool and billiards. Thursday nights are best avoided, unless you want to mix with Goodfellas. Daily 24hr.

Yamskie bani ul. Dostoevskovo 9 ☎312 58 36; **Vladimirskaya metro.** Frequented by the *banya* cognoscenti and well kept by local standards. Thursday is cheap day for pensioners, so there are huge queues. Also has a "lux" section with private rooms (R1000/hr for up to 8 people) and a gym. Daily 9am–midnight.

Boating and yachting

A relaxing way to spend a couple of hours is to go **boating** on the serpentine lakes of Yelagin Island. Rowboats can be rented for about R250 an hour on the lake near the bridge to Vyborg Side, though it's best to avoid weekends and public holidays, when facilities are oversubscribed. More ambitiously, you could go **yachting** on the Gulf of Finland, where strong winds make for fast, exciting sailing, especially during the **St Petersburg Sailing Week** (mid-Aug) and **Vyborg regatta** (July). Charter trips range from a couple of hours to overnight expeditions to uninhabited islands or sea forts (see p.285) out in the Gulf. Most yachts sleep six to eight people, and prices depend on the firm or club and what you want to do, so it's definitely worth comparing quotes.

Neva Yacht Club Martynova nab. 94 ☎235 27 22; **Krestovskiy Ostrov metro.** Favoured by non-sailers who enjoy partying with babes and booze aboard a yacht or power-cruiser, but also used by real enthusiasts. Enquires to Tatyana Bykova ☎966 26 01. Daily 24hr.
River Yacht Club (aka Tsentralniy Yacht Club), Petrovskaya Kosa 9, Petrovskiy Island ☎235 66 36; trolleybus #7 from Nevskiy pr. to the end of the line. This club once produced teams for the Olympics and was founded as long ago as 1858. Mon–Fri 10am–6pm.
Sunny Sailing ul. Vosstaniya 55 ☎ 322 96 86, ⓦwww.sailing.spb.ru; **Ploshchad Vosstaniya metro.** An upmarket agency chartering all kinds of boats moored at Stelna, near Peterhof; for trips to Valaam they use yachts out of Priozersk. Mon–Fri 10am–8pm.

Bowling and billiards

The city has several well-equipped **bowling** alleys and hundreds of places with **billiards** or pool tables. The main difference between Russian billiards and the English game is that there are no cannons – you can score points only by straightforward pots.

AMF Warshavskiy Express mall, nab. Obvodnovo kanala 118 ☎333 11 43; **Baltiyskaya metro.** A well-equipped bowling alley in the same building as an exclusive restaurant and strip club, near the Outdoor Railway Museum. Daily 11am–6am.
Aquatoria Vyborgskaya nab. 61 ☎718 35 18, ⓦwww.aquatoria.ru; **Lesnaya metro.** Mega entertainment complex near Kantimirovskiy most, with nine "Brunswick" lanes, "Cosmic Bowling" and lanes for kids, Russian and American billiards, and a disco (Wed–Sun 10pm–6am) with go-go dancers and strippers. Daily noon–6am.
Bowling City ul. Yefimova 3, Sennaya mall, third floor ☎380 30 05, ⓦwww.bowlingcity.ru; **Sennaya Ploshchad/Sadovaya metro.** Boasts 36 lanes, a sports bar, restaurant, karaoke and children's zone. Daily 24hr.

Fartver pl. Morskoy Slavy 1, third floor ☎322 69 39, ⓦwww.bowling.spb.ru; minibus #K128 from **Nevskiy pr.** A well-equipped six-lane bowling club in the *Morskoy Vokzal Hotel* on Vasilevskiy Island. Maestro, MC, Visa. Mon–Fri noon–2am, Sat & Sun 10am–2am.
LDM Club ul. Professora Popova 47 ☎234 44 48; bus #10 from **Petrogradskaya metro.** Billiards, pool and darts, with live blues music and a bar, in the *LDM* entertainment centre on Petrograd Side. There's also a Q-Zar laser-gun labyrinth that can be rented in 15-minute blocks by groups of up to forty shooters. Daily 10am–6am.
M11 Moskovskiy pr. 111 ☎441 30 00, ⓦwww.m111.ru; **Moskovskie Vorota metro.** Sixteen bowling lanes, plus kids' lanes, Russian billiards and pool tables. Discounts for children under 14 Mon–Fri noon–8pm. Fri & Sat live music from 11pm, cabaret after midnight. Daily noon–6am.

Cycling, rollerblading and running

Cycling for pleasure is increasingly hip in St Petersburg, with cyclists asserting themselves in a mass bike ride every Friday night (see p.40). While cycling in the centre is daunting, residential backwaters and the leafy Kirov Islands are perfect, with fresh air and little or no traffic. You can either hire a bike from Velocity or Skat Prokat (see "Cycling" in Basics, p.40) in the city centre and pedal all the way to Yelagin or Krestovskiy Island, or take the metro to Krestovskiy Ostrov and hire a bike on the spot from Jet Set (☎973 21 45; Mon–Fri 11am–11pm, Sat & Sun 10am–11pm), near the station (see map on pp.168–169). Jet Set also rents rollerblades, helmets and other safety gear.

Rollerblading (inline skating) is hugely popular among local youth. The flat expanse of Dvortsovaya ploshchad and the bumpy granite embankments along the Neva are hot sites in the centre; traffic-free avenues and bags of space are just a metro ride away on Krestovskiy Island. Krestovskiy is also the best place for **running** and features on the itinerary of the city's **Marathon** at the end of June (see ⓦhttp://flaspb.narod.ru/wnwn.html for details).

Gyms

While most **gyms** in St Petersburg require membership, it's worth asking about introductory offers or discounts. Most of the top hotels have gyms open to non-residents for a fee.

Ambassador Ambassador Hotel, pr. Rimskovo-Korsakova 5–7 ☎609 09 75, ⓦwww.ambassador-hotel.ru; Sadovaya metro. Excellent facilities in luxurious surroundings, including a 16-metre swimming pool. All major cards. Daily 24hr.

Flying Dutchman Mytninskaya nab. 5, by Birzhevoy most ☎336 37 37; Sportivnaya metro. This upscale leisure centre aboard a replica eighteenth-century Dutch frigate has a wide range of equipment, sauna, solarium and three restaurants. Major cards. Daily 8am till the last client leaves.

Neptun Neptun Hotel, nab. Obvodnovo kanala 93a ☎320 26 12 or 324 46 96; Pushkinskaya metro. Gym, aerobics room, pool and sauna. Maestro, MC, Visa. Pool: daily 7am–11.30pm; gym: Mon–Fri 7am–11pm, Sat & Sun 10am–11pm.

Planet Fitness ⓦwww.spb.fitness.ru. A chain of gyms with various membership deals – check the website for special offers, addresses and opening hours.

World Class ul.Yefimova 4a ☎333 33 30, ⓦwww.worldclass.ru; Sadovaya metro. Also worth checking this gym for deals. Mon–Fri 7am–midnight, Sat & Sun 9am–11pm.

Ice hockey

Ice hockey (*khokkey*) runs soccer a close second as Russia's most popular sport, and SKA St Petersburg is one of the country's best teams, despite an exodus of top strikers to foreign clubs. Matches are fast and physical, cold yet compelling viewing – the season starts in September and culminates in the annual world championships the following summer, when the Russians strive to defeat Sweden, Canada and the US. The club trains and plays friendly matches at the SKA Palace of Sports, but league games are held at the Yubileyniy Sports Palace, while for internationals the action shifts to the high-tech Ice Palace. Matches are played throughout the year, as listed in *Chas Pik* and *Sport Ekspress*; the latter is the best source of information on all spectator sports, if you can understand Russian.

Ice Palace **(Ledovy dvorets) pr. Pyatiletok 1**
☎718 66 20, Ⓦwww.newarena.spb.ru; **Prospekt
Bolshevikov metro.** With seating for 14,000,
and the finest lighting, sound and televisual
facilities in the city, the Ice Palace hosts
championship matches as well as major
pop concerts.
SKA Palace of Sports **Zhdanovskaya nab. 2**
☎237 00 73; **Sportivnaya metro.** SKA's home
ground is smaller and old-fashioned compared to the other two venues. When not
being used for training it's a public skating
rink.
Yubileyniy Sports Palace **pr. Dobrolyubova
18** ☎323 93 22, Ⓦwww.yubi.ru; **Sportivnaya
metro.** The main venue for Russian league
games, it's also an indoor skating rink. The
box office is open daily noon–7pm.

Climbing, kayaking and skydiving

Given St Petersburg's flat topography, local **rock-climbing** enthusiasts are obliged
to go to the Karelian Isthmus, where participants of any nationality may attend
the "Climbing for Everybody" **festival** in the first half of May, held 150km north
of St Petersburg; trains from Finland Station run to Kuznechnoe, 15km from the
site. For details, check out the website Ⓦwww.climbing.spb.ru. Equipment can be
bought in St Petersburg at Snaryazhenie (see "Shopping", p.377).

The **rapids at Losovo**, 90km from St Petersburg towards Priozersk, offer some
of the best **kayaking** in Russia, with a "fall" of 1000m, flowing at 9m per second,
rated grade four in difficulty. Thousands of kayakers from Finland and Russia
come here to compete in the three-day "White Nights of Vuoksa" **festival** at the
end of June.

Alternatively, you could get your adrenalin flowing by **skydiving** with Baltic
Airlines (Nevskiy pr. 7/9 ☎104 16 76, Ⓦwww.balticairlines.ru) at Rzhevka
Airfield, east of the city. You jump strapped to an instructor so no experience
is needed. For more possibilities and contacts, visit Ⓦwww.risk.ru – an online
magazine for Russian hazardous sports enthusiasts.

Skating, skiing and snowboarding

During winter, Russians dig out their ice skates or skis and revel in the snow. If
you can borrow or buy a pair of skates, some picturesque places to go **ice-skating** are the frozen straits between the Peter and Paul Fortress and the Kronverk,
the Krasnaya Zarya open-air rink on Lesnoy prospekt, or the lake in the Tauride
Gardens. Alternatively, you can rent skates and use the indoor **rinks** at the Yubileyniy Sports Palace or the SKA Palace of Sports (see "Ice Hockey"); both are near
Sportivnaya metro. In addition, both the Tauride Gardens and the park behind
the Russian Museum are popular nursery slopes, where children learn to ski. The
local terrain dictates that cross-country rather than downhill **skiing** is the norm;
two popular destinations are Toskovo on the Karelian Isthmus (accessible by
train from Finland Station) and the park surrounding Pavlovsk Palace (see p.266).
Snowboarding enthusiasts make do with any steep bank or slope going. You can
buy skates, skiing and snowboarding gear at Frankardi or Sportmaster (see "Shopping", p.377).

Soccer

While the Russian oligarch Roman Abramovich is feted in Britain for owning
Chelsea football club and the tycoon Alisher Usmanov has tried to buy Arsenal,

Russian **soccer** (*futbol*) has only recently began to be funded on a scale to match its European counterparts. St Petersburg's **Zenit** (Ⓦwww.fc-zenit.ru; see box on p.188) won the Russian Championship in 2007 but faces stiff competition from premier league Muscovite rivals Spartak and TsKA.

There are two national competitions: the Russian **Championship** (premier league), running from spring to autumn, and the Russian **Cup**, which starts in the summer and ends in the summer of the next year. Games usually begin at 2pm; tickets can be obtained from local theatre-ticket kiosks or agencies (see p.362), Titanik music shops (see p.378) or the stadium box office. For a **schedule of the year's matches**, check Ⓦwww.russianfootball.com, or the Russian football union's Ⓦwww.rfs.ru.

Petrovskiy Stadium Petrovskiy Island ☎328 89 01, Ⓦwww.petrovsky.spb.ru; **Sportivnaya metro.** Currently the city's premier soccer venue – until the completion of the Zenit Stadium – it has seating for 30,000 and under-field heating, but no protection from rain or snow.
Zenit Stadium Krestovskiy Island; tram #17 or #40 from Chakalovskaya metro, or 15min walk from Krestovskiy Ostrov metro. Under con-

struction at the time of writing, this 60,000-seat successor to the Kirov Stadium (see p.188) should open in late 2008 or early 2009. It will have a sliding roof and meet UEFA standards; one city legislator proposed laying a beer pipeline to the stadium, seemingly unaware that selling alcohol at matches is prohibited.

Swimming

Locals take pride in the so-called "**walruses**" (*morzhi*), who swim in the polluted Neva by the Peter and Paul Fortress all year round, breaking holes in the ice during winter. This rugged tradition has produced some great Olympic swimmers, but unsurprisingly most people just swim in the summer, at Yelagin Island, the parks surrounding the Imperial palaces, or along the coast or inland on the Karelian Isthmus (see Chapter 10). Few people are deterred by algae in the water or broken glass on the shore; littering is appalling. Yet public **swimming pools** are only supposed to admit bathers with a health certificate (*spravka*) from a Russian doctor. They tend to limit bathers to only half an hour in the water and insist that **children** are accompanied to the changing room by an adult of the same sex (even if the adult isn't going to swim). And some close from July to September anyway. Hotel pools (see "Gyms") don't have the same restrictions, but it can be difficult for non-residents to gain access to them, as guests get priority. Anyone with children would do best to head for Waterville **aquapark**.

BMF Pool Sredniy pr. 87 ☎322 45 05; **Vasile-ostrovskaya metro.** Has children's pools, a sauna and training hall. Daily 7am–10pm.
LDM Water Centre ul. Professora Popova 47 ☎234 97 72; **bus #25 from Petrogradskaya metro.** Fun pool with slides and waterfalls, next to the LDM Club (see p.384). A certificate is required in theory, but seldom asked for in practice. There's also a solarium and hydro-massage. Daily 8am–11pm.
Petrogradets ul. Lva Tolstovo 8 ☎232 10 74; **Petrogradskaya metro.** Indoor pool, fitness club, sauna and solarium. Daily 7.30am–9.45pm.

Waterville ul. Korabelstroiteley 14 ☎324 47 00, Ⓦwww.waterville.ru; **minibus #128 or #129 from Primorskaya or Gostiniy Dvor metro.** Beside the *Park Inn Pribaltiyskaya* hotel, this is the largest, best-equipped aquapark in Russia, with extreme slides, competitions, play areas, bars, steam-room and massage. Adults R700/R990 weekdays/weekends & holidays; children R490/R690. Daily 9am–11pm.

Tennis

Disdained in Soviet times as an aristocratic sport, tennis was imbued with fame and glamour by Anna Kournikova and her successors, who have made Russia a world leader in the sport. Russia's premier international fixture is the Kremlin Cup, held in Moscow (though prizes aren't as lavish now as they were under tennis-loving president Yeltsin). St Petersburg's **Tennis Open** hasn't the cash to lure major foreign players, and is held indoors at the SKK in October. If you want to play yourself, **courts** can be rented at the following places for R200–500 an hour.

Dinamo pr. Dinamo 44 ☎235 00 55; Krestovskiy Ostrov metro. Clay, synthetic and indoor courts – booking essential. Daily 7am–11pm.

SKK (Sportivniy-Kulturniy Kompleks) pr. Yuriya Gagarina 8 ☎378 17 10; Park Pobedy metro.

Indoor venue for the Tennis Open championship in October. Daily 7am–11pm.

Yelagin Tennis Club near the palace on Yelagin Island ☎430 11 21; Staraya Derevnya metro. Indoor and outdoor courts, sauna and solarium. Daily 7am–11pm.

Windsurfing and scuba diving

Windsurfing is becoming a popular sport at resorts on the Gulf coast – particularly Zelenogorsk, whose Golden Beach hosts the annual **Baltic Cup** championship in the second half of July. There are no hire shops at resorts yet, but you can buy boards and wetsuits at the Techno Sport Centre on Vasilevskiy Island (see "Shopping", p.377).

Scuba diving in the murky waters of the Neva and the Gulf isn't so inviting, but there's a wealth of historical remains and sunken wrecks to explore around the sea forts of Kronstadt and the offshore waters of Vyborg (see Chapter 10). Excursions are organized by Red Shark Divers (5-ya Sovetskaya ul. 3 ☎110 27 95), which also runs PADI open water courses, ice diving, family trips, and rents and sells diving equipment.

Contexts

Contexts

A history of St Petersburg

For a city barely three hundred years old, St Petersburg has experienced more than its fair share of upheaval. Founded by Peter the Great as a "window on the West", and steeped in culture and bloodshed, it was admired and despised in equal measure as the Imperial capital of the Romanov dynasty and the most European of Russian cities. As the cradle of three revolutions, St Petersburg has a history inseparable from that of modern Russia, whose own travails are reflected in the city's changing names: from Tsarist St Petersburg to revolutionary Petrograd, and from Soviet Leningrad back to post-Communist St Petersburg. The city celebrated its tercentenary in 2003.

Peter the Great

The foundation of St Petersburg was the work of Tsar Peter I, a giant in body and spirit better known as **Peter the Great** (1682–1725), one of the "great despots" of Russian history. After a disturbed and violent childhood – at the age of 10 he witnessed the murder of many of his closest relatives by the Kremlin Guards – he became obsessed with all things military and nautical, drilling regiments during his early teens and learning the art of shipbuilding at first hand in Dutch shipyards during his famous "Great Embassy" to Western Europe in 1697.

Following his tour, where he had been gripped by what he saw, Peter embarked upon the forced **westernization** of his backward homeland. He changed the country's name from Muscovy to Russia and proceeded to violate many of the most cherished traditions of Old Muscovy and the Orthodox Church. His courtiers were ordered to wear Hungarian or German dress instead of their familiar kaftans, and the tsar personally cut off their flowing beards – a symbol of pride for Orthodox believers, whose religion held that only the unshorn had a chance

Names and dates

Slightly confusingly for those unfamiliar with Russian history, the city has been known by several names throughout its existence. In this book we have used whichever one is chronologically appropriate, namely:

Prior to August 31, 1914 – **St Petersburg**
August 31, 1914 to January 26, 1924 – **Petrograd**
January 26, 1924 to September 1991 – **Leningrad**
From September 1991 to present day – **St Petersburg**

Russia has been chronologically out of sync with other parts of Europe for much of this time. In 1700, Peter the Great forced Russians to adopt the **Julian calendar** that was then in use in Western Europe, in place of the old system dictated by the Orthodox Church. Ironically, Western Europe changed to the Gregorian calendar not long afterwards, but this time the Russians refused to follow suit. However, the Julian calendar was less accurate and by the twentieth century lagged behind the Gregorian by almost two weeks. The Soviet regime introduced the **Gregorian calendar** in February 1918 – in that year January 31 was followed by February 14 – which explains why they always celebrated the Great October Revolution on November 7. In this book we have kept to the old-style calendar for events that occurred before February 1918.

to enter heaven. When Peter extended the ban on beards throughout society and decreed the substitution of the Julian calendar for the Orthodox one, he was denounced as the Antichrist for imperilling Russians' salvation and perverting time itself. In response, he replaced the self-governing Patriarchate with a Holy Synod subordinate to the tsar, but permitted devout believers to keep their beards, providing they paid a "beard tax".

Of more lasting import was Peter's creation of the **Table of Ranks**, or *chin*. This abolished the hereditary nobility and recast a new aristocracy based on service to the state, extending across the civil service and the armed forces to include engineers and specialists at every level. In theory, promotion was based on merit rather than birth, and the system was meant to dissolve snobbish distinctions between those who served the greater good of the nation. It did see able men of humble origin elevated to the highest ranks of the state – such as Mikhail Shafirov, a Jew who became Peter's foreign secretary – but in practice, the *chin* soon became a self-interested bureaucracy. The *chinovnik*, or bureaucrat, would be a stock character in the plays of Gogol and Chekhov a century and a half later, and a byword for corruption, then as nowadays.

To impose his vision on Russia, Peter relied on repressive measures characteristic of Old Muscovy and introduced new ones that his Tsarist or Communist successors would exploit to the hilt. It was Peter who invented the internal passport system, and who organized forced labour gangs to build his great projects. War characterized much of Peter's reign and many of his reforms were fashioned simply to keep Russia's military machine running smoothly. The quest for a seaport dominated his thinking and in 1700 a peace treaty with Turkey left Peter free to pursue the foundation of a new capital with trading access to the West via the Baltic Sea.

The major Baltic power of the day was Sweden and the war between the Russians and Swedes, known as the **Great Northern War**, lasted from 1700 to 1721. In 1700, at **Narva**, 150km west of present-day St Petersburg, the 18-year-old Swedish king, Charles XII, put the Russians to flight but failed to follow up his victory with a march on Moscow, concentrating instead on subduing the rebellious Poles. Peter took advantage of the break in hostilities to strengthen his position around the Gulf of Finland.

The foundation of St Petersburg

Although popular legend has it that prior to the foundation of St Petersburg the Neva delta was an uninhabited wilderness, in fact there already existed a Swedish trading town, **Nyen**, in what is now the Okhta district, which had to be overrun before Peter could establish his new capital. Nonetheless, the site he chose was so exposed that it can fairly be termed a settlement in the wilderness – a fetid marshland chronically prone to flooding, with few natural or human resources nearby. On May 16, 1703, Peter is said to have snatched a halberd from one of his soldiers, cut two strips of turf, laid them across each other, and declared, "Here there shall be a town!"; though, of course, Pushkin's version of Peter's speech – "By nature we are fated here to cut a window through to Europe" – is more famous. Either way, **Sankt Pietr Burkh** (as it was originally called in the Dutch fashion) soon became known as the "city built on bones". Thousands of Swedish prisoners-of-war were joined by other non-Russians press-ganged from the far reaches of the Empire. Conditions were dire: there was a shortage of basic tools;

earth had to be carried in the workers' clothing; and thousands died of starvation, cold, disease and exhaustion.

Nevertheless, in less than five months, a wooden fortress had been built on a small island. Next a wooden church was erected, along with a modest wooden cottage, which served as Peter's residence, and an inn, the *Four Frigates*, which doubled as the town hall. Within a year, there were fifteen houses on nearby Petrograd Island, where Peter first intended to base his new city, and the beginnings of the Admiralty on the mainland, then little more than a shipyard.

In the summer of 1706, with St Petersburg barely on the map, Charles XII invaded Russia. Again, within an ace of victory, he made the fateful decision not to march on Moscow, but to concentrate on Ukraine. Charles's supply and baggage train was attacked and defeated en route from Estonia in 1708; the Russian winter inflicted yet more casualties; and on June 27, 1709, at the **Battle of Poltava**, Peter trounced Charles, forcing him to flee to Turkey. The Great Northern War dragged on for another twelve years, but, as Peter put it, "Now the final stone has been laid in the foundation of St Petersburg."

In 1710, the Imperial family moved to the new city, together with all government institutions, and in 1712, Peter declared St Petersburg the Russian capital. Owing to the shortage of masons, a decree was issued forbidding building in stone anywhere in the Empire outside St Petersburg; while small landowners and nobles were obliged to resettle in the city and finance the building of their own houses. Encampments larger than the city itself rose up to absorb the incoming labour force. Floods still plagued the islands – at one point Peter himself nearly drowned on Nevskiy prospekt – and wolves roamed the streets after dark, devouring anyone foolish enough to go outside.

Peter's successors

Having killed his only natural heir, Peter was forced to issue a decree claiming the right to nominate his successor, but when he died in 1725, he was so ill that he was unable to speak. Initially his wife, **Catherine I**, was hailed as tsaritsa but she died after a reign of less than two years. Peter's grandson, **Peter II**, then became tsar and moved the capital and the court back to Moscow in 1728, leaving St Petersburg in decline.

Peter II's sudden death from smallpox in 1730 left the throne wide open. In desperation, the Privy Council turned to a German-born niece of Peter the Great. Empress **Anna Ioannovna** (1730–40) re-established St Petersburg as the capital and brought with her an entourage of German courtiers. Her reign was characterized by cruelty and decadence. Affairs of state were handled by her favourite, Ernst-Johann Buhren, a Baltic German baron who executed or exiled thousands of alleged opponents – a reign of terror known as the *Bironovshchina*, after his Russified name, Biron.

Anna died childless in 1740, leaving the crown to her great-nephew, **Ivan VI**, who – because of his youth – was put under the regency of his mother, **Anna Leopoldovna**. However, real power remained in the hands of the hated Biron, until a coup, backed by the Preobrazhenskiy Guards and financed with French money, elevated Peter the Great's daughter Elizabeth Petrovna to the throne, whereupon Biron and Ivan were imprisoned at Shlisselburg (see p.297).

Elizabeth and Peter III

Like her father, Empress **Elizabeth** (1741–61) was stubborn, quick-tempered and devoted to Russia, but, unlike him, she detested serious occupations and "abandoned herself to every excess of intemperance and lubricity". Elizabeth was almost illiterate and her court favourite, Razumovsky (a Cossack shepherd turned chorister whom she secretly married), couldn't write at all. She liked dancing and hunting, often stayed up all night, spent hours preening herself and lived in chaotic apartments, the wardrobes stacked with over fifteen thousand dresses, the floors littered with unpaid bills. Her extravagances resulted in a budget deficit of eight million rubles by 1761.

Although Elizabeth hated the sight of blood, she would order torture at the slightest offence – or throw her slipper in the offender's face. Yet she abolished the death penalty and retained as one of her principal advisers the enlightened Count Shuvalov, who encouraged her in the foundation of Moscow University and the St Petersburg **Academy of Arts**. In foreign affairs, Elizabeth displayed a determined hostility towards Prussia, participating in both the War of Austrian Succession (1740–48) and the Seven Years' War (1756–63), during which Russian troops occupied Berlin.

On Elizabeth's death in 1761, the new tsar – her nephew, **Peter III** – adopted a strongly pro-Prussian policy, forcing the army into Prussian uniforms and offending the clergy by sticking to the Lutheran faith of his Holstein homeland. His concession to the nobility was the abolition of the compulsory 25-year state service. It was a decree of great consequence, for it created a large, privileged leisured class, hitherto unknown in Russia. Childish, moody and impotent, Peter was no match for his intelligent, sophisticated wife, Sophia of Anhalt-Zerbst, who ingratiated herself with her subjects by joining the Orthodox Church, changing her name to Catherine in the process. Their marriage was a sham, and in June 1762 she and her lover, Grigori Orlov, staged a **coup** with the backing of the Imperial Guards. Peter was imprisoned in the palace of Ropsha, and soon murdered by the Orlov brothers.

Catherine the Great

The long reign of **Catherine the Great** (1762–96) saw the emergence of Russia as a truly great European power. Catherine was a woman of considerable culture and learning and a great patron of the arts. Many of St Petersburg's greatest architectural masterpieces – including the Winter Palace, the Smolniy Cathedral and the Tauride Palace – were completed during her reign, while Catherine's art collection still forms the core of the Hermitage. Inevitably, however, she is best known for her private life; her most prominent favourite, Count Potemkin, oversaw the most important territorial gain of her reign – the annexation of Crimea in 1783, which secured the Black Sea coast for Russia.

After consolidating her position as an autocrat – after all, she had no legitimate claim to the throne – Catherine enjoyed a brief honeymoon as a liberal. French became the language of the court, and with it came the ideas of the **Enlightenment**. Catherine herself conducted a lengthy correspondence with Voltaire, but the lofty intentions of her reforms were watered down by her advisers to little more than a reassertion of "benevolent" despotism. When it came to the crucial question of the emancipation of the serfs, the issue was, not for the first or last time, swept under the carpet. And when writers like Radishchev began to take her at her word and publish critical works, she responded by exiling them to Siberia.

Catherine's liberal leanings were given a worse jolt by the **Pugachev Revolt**, which broke out east of the River Volga in 1773, under the leadership of a Don Cossack named Pugachev. Thousands of serfs responded to Pugachev's call for freedom from the landowners and division of their estates and for two years conducted a guerrilla campaign before being crushed by troops. The French Revolution killed off what was left of Catherine's benevolence and in her later years she relied ever more on unbridled autocracy.

Paul and Alexander I

On Catherine's death in 1796, her son **Paul** became tsar. Not without reason, he detested his mother, and immediately set about reversing most of her policies: his first act was to give his putative father, Peter III, a decent burial. Like Peter III, Paul was a moody, militarily obsessed man who worshipped everything Prussian. He offended the army by forcing the Guards back into Prussian uniform and the nobility by attempting to curtail some of the privileges they had enjoyed under Catherine, and reintroduced the idea of male hereditary succession that had been abandoned by Peter the Great.

Paul was strangled to death in March 1801 (see p.89), in a palace coup that had the tacit approval of his son, **Alexander I** (1801–25). Alexander shared Catherine's penchant for the ideas of the Enlightenment, but also exhibited a strong streak of religious conservatism. His reign was, in any case, dominated by foreign affairs and, in particular, the imminent conflict with Napoleon. His anti-Napoleonic alliance with Austria and Prussia proved a dismal failure, producing a series of Allied defeats that prompted Alexander to switch sides and join with Napoleon – an alliance sealed by the Treaty of Tilsit in 1807, but which proved to be only temporary.

The Patriotic War

In June 1812, Napoleon crossed the River Niemen and invaded Russia with his Grand Army of 600,000 men – twice the size of any force the Russians could muster. Progress was slow, with the Russians employing "scorched earth" tactics to great effect, while partisans harassed the French flanks. Patriotic fervour forced the Russian general, **Kutuzov**, into fighting a pitched battle with Napoleon, despite having only 100,000 men at his disposal. The **Battle of Borodino**, outside Moscow, resulted in horrific casualties on both sides, but produced no outright victor. Napoleon continued on his march, entering Moscow in September; the following day, the city was consumed in a fire. The popular Russian belief at the time was that the French were responsible, though the governor of Moscow – determined to avoid the capture of his city – was actually the culprit.

Despite sacrificing Moscow to the French, Alexander refused to leave St Petersburg and meet with Napoleon, leaving the latter no choice but to forget his conquest and begin the long retreat home. Harassed by Russian regulars and partisans, and unprepared for the ferocity of the Russian winter, the Napoleonic Grand Army was reduced to a mere 30,000 men when it finally re-crossed the Niemen. The Russians pursued Napoleon all the way back to Paris, which they occupied in 1814. At the Congress of Vienna, the following year, Russia was assured of its share of spoils in the carve-up of Europe.

The Decembrists

Another result of the war was that it exposed thousands of Russians to life in other countries. Aristocrats and gentry noted parliaments and constitutional monarchies, while peasant foot soldiers saw how much better their lot could be without serfdom. As the tsar and his chief minister, Count Akracheev, were sure that any reforms would endanger autocracy, opposition festered underground. Guards officers and liberal aristocrats formed innocuously named groups such as the "Southern Society" (led by Colonel Pavel Pestel), whose aim was to establish a classless utopia; and the "Northern Society", which favoured a constitutional monarchy. Both conducted secret propaganda and recruitment and planned to assassinate the tsar.

When Alexander died in November 1825, without leaving a male heir, the plotters sought to take advantage of the dynastic crisis by hurriedly devising a coup on December 14, when the Guards were to swear allegiance to Alexander's younger brother, Nicholas. For six hours, loyalist troops and rebel **Decembrists** (as they became known) faced one another across what is now ploshchad Dekabristov, with neither side prepared to fire the first shot. As dusk fell, Nicholas gave the order to clear the square: within two hours the revolt was crushed and hundreds of corpses were tipped into the River Neva.

Nicholas I

In the aftermath of the revolt, **Nicholas I** (1825–55) personally interrogated many of the plotters. Five ringleaders were executed and more than a hundred exiled to Siberia. Though no mention of this "horrible and extraordinary plot" (as he called it) was allowed in public, the fate of so many aristocrats inevitably resulted in gossip – especially when Countess Volkonskaya followed her husband into exile, inspiring other wives to do likewise. Although the Decembrists themselves failed, their example would be upheld by future generations of Russian revolutionaries.

Nicholas's credo was encapsulated in the slogan "Orthodoxy, Autocracy, Nationality". The status quo was to be maintained at all costs: censorship increased, as did police surveillance, carried out by the infamous **Third Section** of the tsar's personal Chancellery, which kept a close watch on potential subversives. The most intractable problem, as ever, was **serfdom**, "the powder-magazine under the state", as Nicholas's police chief put it. Serfs accounted for four-fifths of the population, and during the late 1820s there were several rebellions, though none so grave as the Pugachev revolt. The economic position of Russia's serfs remained more or less stagnant throughout Nicholas's reign, and hampered the industrialization of the country, which was mostly confined to developments in the cotton and beet-sugar industries.

Perhaps the greatest social change took place among the educated classes, where deferential admiration for the tsar was replaced by scorn and dissent. The writer Dostoyevsky was among those drawn to the clandestine **Petrashevsky Circle** of utopian socialists, who dreamt of a peasant rebellion. In 1849, over a hundred of them were arrested as Nicholas clamped down in the wake of revolutions in Poland and Hungary, which his armies suppressed, earning him the nickname the "Gendarme of Europe" abroad (at home, he was known as *Palkin*, or "The Stick" because of his fondness for using them for beatings).

In early 1854, the **Crimean War** broke out and Russia found itself at war with Britain, France and Turkey. The war went badly for the Russians and served to highlight the flaws and inadequacies inherent in the Tsarist Empire: Russian troops defending Sebastopol faced rifles with muskets; Russian sailing ships had to do battle with enemy steamers; and the lack of rail-lines meant that Russian soldiers were no better supplied than their Allied foes, who were thousands of miles from home. The Allied capture of Sebastopol in 1855 almost certainly helped to accelerate the death of the despondent Nicholas, whose last words of advice to his son and successor were "Hold on to everything!"

The Great Reforms

In fact, the new tsar, **Alexander II** (1855–81), had to sue for peace and initiate changes. The surviving Decembrists and Petrashevsky exiles were released, police surveillance eased and many of the censorship restrictions lifted. The most significant of the so-called **Great Reforms** was the **emancipation of the serfs**, which earned him the sobriquet of "Tsar Liberator". Although two-thirds of the land worked by serfs was handed over to village communes, the ex-serfs were saddled with "redemption payments" to the former landowners over 49 years, and neither side was happy with the deal. Other reforms were more successful. Obligatory military service for peasants was reduced from twenty-five years to six; appointed regional *zemstva* (assemblies) marked the beginning of limited local self-government; trial by jury and a trained judiciary were instituted; and Jews were allowed to live outside the Pale of Settlement.

Yet Alexander baulked at any major constitutional shift from autocracy, disappointing those who had hoped for a "revolution from above". The 1860s saw an upsurge in peasant unrest and a radicalization of the opposition movements coalescing among the educated elite. From the ranks of the disaffected intelligentsia came the amorphous **Populist** (Narodnik) movement, which gathered momentum throughout the late 1860s and early 1870s. Its chief ideologue, **Nikolai Chernyshevsky**, was committed to establishing a socialist society based on the peasant commune, without the intervening stage of capitalism – but there were differing views on how to do this. Initially, the **Nihilists** – as the writer Turgenev dubbed them in his novel *Fathers and Sons* – led the charge, most famously with the first attempt on the tsar's life, carried out in April 1866 by the clandestine organization, "Hell".

Another school of thought believed in taking the Populist message to the people, a proselytizing campaign that climaxed in the "**crazy summer**" of 1874, when thousands of students roamed the countryside attempting to convert the peasantry to their cause. Most exhortations fell on deaf ears, for although the peasants were fed up with their lot they distrusted townspeople and remained loyal to the tsar. The state nevertheless made mass arrests, which culminated in the notorious trials of "the 50" and "the 193", held in St Petersburg in 1877–78.

Following what was probably Russia's first political demonstration, outside St Petersburg's Kazan Cathedral in 1876, a new organization was founded, called

Land and Liberty, which soon split over the use of violence. Land redistribution was the major aim of the "Black Partition", one of whose leaders, Plekhanov, went on to found the first Russian Marxist political grouping; while the **People's Will** (Narodnaya Volya) believed that revolution could be hastened by spectacular terrorist acts – "propaganda of the deed" – culminating in the assassination of the tsar himself in March 1881 (see p.83).

Reaction and industrialization

But regicide failed to stir the masses to revolution, and the new tsar, **Alexander III** (1881–94), was even less inclined than his father to institute political change. Assisted by his ultra-reactionary chancellor, Pobedonostsev, the tsar shelved all constitutional reforms, increased police surveillance and cut back the powers of the *zemstva*. The police stood by during a wave of **pogroms** in 1881–82, Pobedonostsev subsequently promulgating anti-Semitic laws that reversed the emancipation of the Jews instituted by Alexander II. Though hated by Russian liberals, the regime succeeded in uprooting the terrorist underground, which wouldn't pose a danger until a decade hence.

Yet despite turning the clock back in many ways, social and economic change was inexorable. The emancipation of the serfs had led to ever more peasants seeking work in the cities. **Industrialization** increased with breakneck speed – Russia's rate of growth outstripped that of all the other European powers. In St Petersburg, huge factories sprang up in the suburbs, where the harsh conditions and exposure to new ideas and ways of life gradually forged an urban working class. Although it didn't begin to make an impact on politics until the late 1890s, this influx transformed St Petersburg into the fourth largest city in Europe, with all the desperate poverty, child beggars and prostitution described in *Crime and Punishment*. Ministers were keenly aware that the urban poor were a potential threat to the regime, but industrialization was essential if Russia was to compete with other European powers, and legislating factory conditions seemed a slippery slope to wider reforms.

One problem that nobody anticipated was the death of Alexander III, at the age of 49. Immensely strong (he used to bend steel pokers for fun), he had been expected to reign for at least another decade. His heir, Nicholas, had barely begun to be initiated into the business of government and was "nothing but a boy, whose judgements are childish" (as Alexander described him). Nobody was more shocked and unprepared than the tsarevich when Alexander died in 1894, worn out by overwork and nephritis (he loved vodka and defied his doctors' orders by swigging from flasks hidden in his thigh-boots).

The gathering storm

If ever there was a ruler unfit to reign at a critical time (1894–1917), it was **Nicholas II**. Obsessed by trivia, he hated delegating authority, yet was chronically indecisive, consulting "grandparents, aunts, mummy and anyone else" and adopting "the view of the last person to whom he talks". His wife, the German-born princess Alexandra of Hesse, was a fervent convert to Orthodoxy who shared his belief in divinely ordained autocracy and a mystic bond between tsar and peasantry. Painfully shy at receptions and appalled by the lax morals of high society, she was scorned by the aristocracy and urged Nicholas to "stand up" to his ministers. At their Moscow coronation in May 1896, 1300 people were killed in a stampede – an inauspicious start to a doomed reign.

By rejecting the constitutional reforms proposed by the *zemstvo* of Tver as "senseless dreams", Nicholas dismayed liberals and turned moderate Populists into militants. The late 1890s saw a resurgence of underground activity by the **Socialist Revolutionary Party**, or SRs, whose terrorist wing, the SR Fighting Section, assassinated the interior minister, Sipyagin, and the tsar's chief minister, Plehve, but still failed to attract the mass of the peasantry to its cause. Meanwhile, some of the intelligentsia had shifted its ideological stance towards **Marxism**, which pinned its hopes on the urban proletariat as the future agent of revolution. A Russian Marxist organization was founded as early as 1883 by exiles in Switzerland, but its membership was so tiny that, when out boating on Lake Geneva, its "father", **Georgy Plekhanov**, joked, "Be careful: if this boat sinks, it's the end of Russian Marxism."

Yet its ideas spread back home, disseminated by study groups and underground newspapers. In 1898, Plekhanov was joined by Vladimir Ilyich Ulyanov – better known as **Lenin** – and founded the Russian Social Democratic Labour Party (RSDLP). At its 1902 congress in Brussels, it split into two factions over the nature of the party and its membership. Lenin wanted it restricted to active militants, obeying orders from the leadership, while his rival Martov desired a looser, mass membership. Adroitly, Lenin provoked half of Martov's supporters to walk out, thereby claiming for his own faction the description **Bolsheviks** ("majority") and casting his opponents as **Mensheviks** ("minority").

In Russia, meanwhile, the tsar continued to ignore pleas from the *zemstvo* and business groups to legalize moderate parties and establish a parliamentary system and civil rights. This failure to broaden his base of support and bring new talent into government while Russia was relatively stable would leave the regime perilously isolated when events took a turn for the worse.

The 1905 Revolution

In 1900, Russia's economic boom ended. Unemployed workers streamed back to their villages, where land-hunger and poverty fuelled unrest. The interior minister, Plevhe, organized anti-Semitic pogroms to "drown the revolution in Jewish blood", and urged a "short victorious war" with Japan. But the **Russo-Japanese War** soon led to disaster at Port Arthur, sending shockwaves across Russia. In the capital, a strike broke out at the giant Putilov engineering plant and quickly spread to other factories that encircled the city.

On January 9, 1905 – **Bloody Sunday** – 150,000 strikers and their families converged on the Winter Palace to hand a petition to the tsar, demanding civil rights and labour laws. In a series of separate incidents, the Imperial Guards fired on the crowd to disperse the protesters, killing as many as one thousand demonstrators and wounding several thousand others. For the rest of his reign, the tsar would never quite shake off his reputation as "Bloody Nicholas".

When the first wave of strikes petered out, the tsar clung to the hope that a reversal of fortune in the Far East would ease his troubles. The Baltic Fleet sailed halfway round the world to confront the Japanese navy only to be destroyed at **Tsushima Bay**, triggering a mutiny in the Black Sea Fleet that forced the tsar to make peace with Japan and concede the establishment of a consultative assembly – the **Duma** (from the Russian word *dumat*, "to think"). However, this was insufficient to prevent a printers' strike in St Petersburg from developing into an all-out general strike. Further mutinies occurred among the troops and the countryside slid into anarchy.

By mid-October, Nicholas had little choice but to grant further concessions. In the **October Manifesto**, he gave a future Duma the power of veto over laws, promised basic civil liberties and appointed Count Witte as Russia's first prime minister. Meanwhile, in the capital, workers seized the initiative and created the **St Petersburg Soviet**, made up of some 500 delegates elected by over 200,000 workers (Soviet meaning "council" in Russian). Under the co-chairmanship of **Leon Trotsky** (who had yet to join the Bolsheviks), it pursued a moderate policy, criticizing the proposed Duma, but not calling for an armed uprising – but still the middle classes took fright.

With the opposition divided over the issue of participation in the Duma, Nicholas seized the chance to arrest the leaders of the Soviet in December, and crushed a belated Bolshevik-inspired uprising in Moscow. During 1906 there were further mutinies, and mayhem in the countryside, but the high point of the revolution had passed. Notwithstanding isolated terrorist successes by the SR Fighting Section, the workers' movement began to decline, while the revolutionary elite languished in prison or, like Lenin, was forced into an impotent exile in Europe.

The only joy for Nicholas and Alexandra during these years was the birth of a son, **Alexei** – and even this soon became a source of pain, for the tsarevich was afflicted by haemophilia, an incurable condition that put him at constant risk of death, a fact they dared not admit to the nation.

The Duma

Of the parties formed in the wake of the October Manifesto, the largest was the Constitutional Democratic, or Kadet, Party, founded by Professor Milyukov to represent Russia's liberal bourgeoisie, whose aims were shared by many of Nicholas's officials. Although the first nationwide elections in Russian history (on a broad-based franchise, though far from universal suffrage) propelled the Kadets to the forefront, the inauguration of the **First Duma** at the Tauride Palace (May 10, 1906) saw an unprecedented confrontation of courtiers and peasants' and workers' deputies, whose faces impressed the Dowager Empress with their "incomprehensible hatred". After ten weeks of debate, the issue of land distribution reared its head, prompting the tsar to surround the palace with troops and dissolve the Duma. The succeeding Second Duma suffered a similar fate.

Witte's successor as prime minister, **Pyotr Stolypin**, sent nearly 60,000 political detainees to Siberia or the gallows (nicknamed "Stolypin's necktie"), but knew that repression alone was not enough. The **Third Duma**, elected on a much narrower franchise, duly ratified a package of reforms that let peasants leave the village communes to farm privately. Stolypin envisaged a new class of rural entrepreneurs as a bulwark against revolution, so that the state could wager its security "not on the needy and the drunken, but on the sturdy and the strong". However, this new class grew far slower than he had hoped, and Stolypin was also frustrated by Nicholas and Alexandra's increasing dependence on the debauched "holy man", **Rasputin**, whom they believed held the key to the survival of their son, Alexei. Stolypin's assassination by a secret police double agent in 1911 deprived Nicholas of his ablest statesmen only a few years before the regime would face its sternest test.

The most positive post-revolutionary repercussions took place within **the arts**. From 1905 to 1914, St Petersburg and Moscow experienced an extraordinary outburst of artistic energy: Diaghilev's Ballets Russes dazzled Europe; Chekhov premiered his works in the capital; poets and writers held Symbolist seances in city salons; while Mayakovsky and other Futurists toured the country, shocking the general public with their statements on art.

World War I

By 1914, Europe's Great Powers were enmeshed in alliances that made war almost inevitable, once the fuse had been lit. The assassination of the Habsburg Archduke Ferdinand in Sarajevo, Austria-Hungary's ultimatum to Serbia and German mobilization left Russian public opinion baying for war in defence of its "Slav brothers". In the patriotic fervour accompanying the outbreak of **World War I**, the name of the capital, St Petersburg, was deemed too Germanic and replaced by the more Russian-sounding **Petrograd**. The first Russian offensive ended in defeat at Tannenberg in August 1914, with estimated casualties of 170,000. From then onwards, there was rarely any good news from the front; in the first year alone, around four million soldiers lost their lives. In an attempt to show his authority, the tsar assumed supreme command of the armed forces – a post for which he was totally unqualified – and left his wife in charge of the home front.

By 1916, even monarchists were angry. Empress Alexandra, the "German woman", was openly accused of treason, and Rasputin was assassinated by a group of aristocrats desperate to force a change of policy. Ensconced with his son in the General Staff headquarters at Mogilev, Nicholas refused to be moved. As inflation spiralled and food shortages worsened, strikes began to break out again in Petrograd. By the beginning of 1917, everyone from generals to peasants talked of an imminent uprising.

The February Revolution

On February 22, 1917, there was a lockout of workers at the Putilov works in Petrograd. Next day (International Women's Day), thousands of women and workers thronged the streets attacking bread shops, singing the *Marseillaise* and calling for the overthrow of the tsar. Soldiers and Cossacks fraternized with the demonstrators. On February 27, prisons were stormed and the Fourth Duma was surrounded by demonstrators and mutinous troops. It hastily approved the establishment of a Provisional Committee "for the re-establishment of order in the capital", while Trotsky and the Mensheviks quickly revived the Petrograd Soviet. On March 2, en route to the capital, the tsar was finally persuaded to abdicate in favour of his brother, Grand Duke Michael, who gave up his claim to the throne the following day: the Romanov dynasty had ended.

Out of the ferment arose what Russians called "**dual power**" (*dvovlastie*). The **Provisional Government**, under the liberal Count Lvov, tried to assert itself as the legitimate successor to Tsarist despotism. Freedom of speech and a political amnesty were immediately decreed; there were to be elections for a Constituent Assembly, but there was to be no end to the war. This last policy pacified the generals, but quickly eroded the Provisional Government's popularity. The other power base was the **Petrograd Soviet**, dominated by Mensheviks, which was prepared to give qualified support to the "bourgeois revolution" until the time was ripe for the establishment of socialism. The Soviet's chief achievement was the effecting of "Order No. 1", authorizing the formation of Soviets throughout the army, whose existence rapidly undermined military discipline.

After ditching some of its more right-wing elements, the Provisional Government cooperated more closely with the Petrograd Soviet. **Alexander Kerensky** became minister of war and toured the front calling for a fresh offensive against the Germans. It began well, but soon turned into a retreat, while discontent in Petrograd peaked again in a wave of violent protests known as the **July Days**. Soldiers and workers, egged on by local Anarchists and Bolsheviks, marched on the Soviet, calling for the overthrow of the Provisional Government. However, Lenin, who had returned from exile in April, felt that the time was not right for an armed uprising, and the Soviet was unwilling to act. In the end, troops loyal to the government arrived in Petrograd and restored order. Trotsky and others were arrested, Lenin was accused of being a German spy and forced once more into exile, and the Bolsheviks as a whole were branded as traitors.

Kerensky used the opportunity to tighten his grip on the Provisional Government, taking over as leader from Count Lvov and making the fateful decision to move into the Winter Palace. If the July Days were a blow to the Left, the abortive **Kornilov Revolt** was an even greater setback for the Right. In late August, the army's commander-in-chief attempted to march on Petrograd and crush Bolshevism once and for all. Whether he had been encouraged in this by Kerensky is uncertain, but in the event, Kerensky turned on Kornilov, urging the Bolsheviks and workers' militia to defend the capital. Kerensky duly appointed himself commander-in-chief, but it was the Left who were now in the ascendance.

The October Revolution

During September, the country slid into chaos: soldiers deserted the front in droves; the countryside was in turmoil; and the "Bolshevization" of the Soviets continued apace. By mid-month, Lenin, who was still in hiding in Finland, urged a coup against the Provisional Government, but didn't win over the Bolshevik leadership until mid-October, whereupon Trotsky used the Military Revolutionary Committee which had been established by the Petrograd Soviet to defend the city against the threat of counter-revolution, to ready the Bolshevik Red Guards for action, from their headquarters at the Smolniy Institute.

The **October Revolution** is thought to have begun in the early hours of the 25th, with the occupation of key points in Petrograd by Red Guards. Kerensky fled the city, ostensibly to rally support; it was in fact his final exit. Posters announcing the overthrow of the Provisional Government appeared on the streets at 10am, though it wasn't until 2am the following day that the government's ministers were formally arrested in the Winter Palace. It was an almost bloodless coup (in Petrograd at least), but it unleashed the most bloody civil war and regime in Russia's history.

It had been planned to coincide with the Second All-Russian Congress of Soviets, which convened at the Smolniy. At the congress, the Bolsheviks' majority was enhanced when the Mensheviks and right-wing SRs walked out in protest at the coup. Lenin delivered his two famous decrees, calling for an end to the war and approving the seizure of land by the peasants. An all-Bolshevik **Council of People's Commissars** was established, headed by Lenin, with Trotsky as Commissar for Foreign Affairs. A spate of decrees proclaimed an eight-hour working day, the abolition of social classes and the nationalization of all banks and financial organizations.

Conditions in Petrograd deteriorated further. Food was scarcer than ever; rumours of anti-Bolshevik plots abounded. As early as December 1917, Lenin created a new secret police, the "All-Russian Extraordinary Commission for Struggle against Counter-Revolution, Speculation and Sabotage", or **Cheka** (aptly meaning "linchpin" in Russian). Although the Bolsheviks had reluctantly agreed to abolish the death penalty in October, the Cheka, under "Iron" **Felix Dzerzhinsky**, reserved the right to "have recourse to a firing squad when it becomes obvious that there is no other way".

Following elections, the long-awaited **Constituent Assembly** met for the first and only time on January 5, 1918, in the Tauride Palace. Having received only a quarter of the vote, the Bolsheviks surrounded the palace next day; Red Guards eventually dismissing those inside with the words, "Push off. We want to go home."

Civil War

In February 1918 the Germans launched a fresh offensive, compelling Trotsky to sign the **Treaty of Brest-Litovsk**, which handed over Poland, Finland, Belarus, the Baltics and – most painfully of all – Ukraine, Russia's bread basket. Following the treaty, the Bolsheviks transferred the **capital** from Petrograd to **Moscow** – leaving the city more exposed than ever to foreign attack. Within two years, Petrograd's population had shrunk by 65 percent, to 799,000.

At the Seventh Party Congress, at which the RSDLP was renamed the **Communist Party**, the Left SRs walked out in protest at the treaty. On July 6, an SR member assassinated the German ambassador, and the next day the SRs staged an abortive coup in Moscow, followed by the assassination of the Petrograd Cheka chief, Uritsky, and an attempt on Lenin's life in August. The Bolsheviks responded with the **Red Terror**. Declaring "an end to clemency and slackness", the Cheka immediately shot 512 hostages in Petrograd and 500 at Kronstadt. Dzerzhinsky's deputy pronounced that one look at a suspect's hands would suffice to determine his class allegiance.

By this time a **Civil War** was raging across Russia, fuelled by **foreign intervention**. A Czech Legion seized control of much of the Trans-Siberian Railway; British troops landed in Murmansk and Baku; US, Japanese, French and Italian forces took over Vladivostok; while the Germans controlled the vast tracts of land given to them under the Brest-Litovsk treaty. Fearing that the **Imperial family** would be freed from captivity in Yekaterinburg, Lenin ordered their **execution**, carried out by local Bolsheviks on July 16–17.

With the end of World War I, foreign troops began to return home, leaving the Reds and the **Whites** (anti-Soviet forces) to fight it out. What the Reds lacked in military experience they made up for in ideological motivation and iron discipline. Conversely, the Whites represented every type of political movement from monarchists to SRs. The sides were evenly matched in numbers and rivalled each other in ferocity when it came to exacting revenge on collaborators. Ultimately, the Reds prevailed, though not without a few close calls: in the autumn of 1919 a White force of 20,000 was prevented from capturing Petrograd only by the personal intervention of Trotsky, who rallied the Red Army and turned the tide of the battle at Gatchina.

Besides costing the lives of millions, the Civil War promoted the militarization of Soviet society, under the rubric of "**War Communism**". Workers' control in the factories and the nationalization of land had plunged the economy into chaos just as the Civil War broke out. To cope, the Bolsheviks introduced stringent centralization and labour discipline. With currency almost worthless, the peasants had little incentive to sell their produce in the cities, so Red Guards were sent into the countryside to seize food, and "committees of the poor" were set up to stimulate class war against the richer peasantry, or *kulaks*.

The Kronstadt revolt and the NEP

By 1921, Russia was economically devastated. The Communists faced widespread workers' unrest and divisions within the Party. A **Workers' Opposition faction** demanded the separation of the trade unions from the Party and fewer wage differentials. In February, even the Kronstadt sailors – who had been among the Bolsheviks' staunchest supporters – turned against the Party. The **Kronstadt sailors' revolt** precipitated a general strike in Petrograd when troops once more refused to fire on the crowds. Rejecting calls for negotiations, the Bolsheviks accused the Kronstadt sailors of acting under the orders of a White general and, after a bloody battle, succeeded in crushing the rebellion (see p.283).

Whilst the revolt was under way, Lenin persuaded the **Tenth Party Congress** to ban factions and declare a virtual end to democratic debate. Those SRs still at large were rounded up and either exiled or subjected to the first Soviet show trial, in 1922. From now on, real power was in the hands of the emerging party bureaucracy, or **Secretariat**, whose first General Secretary was the Georgian Communist, **Iosif Stalin**.

At the congress, Lenin unveiled his **New Economic Policy** (NEP), whereby the state maintained control of the "commanding heights" of the economy, but restored a limited free market for agricultural produce and consumer goods, giving peasants an incentive to increase productivity, and stimulating trade. It was a formula that favoured the peasantry and speculators of all kinds (known as "Nepmen") rather than the urban working class, who dubbed the NEP the "New Exploitation of the Proletariat".

Stalin and Collectivization

Lenin's death on January 24, 1924 inaugurated an all-out power struggle. Trotsky, the hero of the Civil War, and Bukharin, the chief exponent of the NEP, were by far the most popular figures in the Party, but it was **Stalin**, as head of the Secretariat, who held the aces. Stalin organized Lenin's funeral and was the chief architect in his deification, which began with the renaming of Petrograd as **Leningrad**. Using classic divide-and-rule tactics, Stalin picked off his rivals one by one, beginning with the exile of Trotsky in 1925, followed by the neutralization of Zinoviev, the Leningrad Party boss, and Bukharin in 1929.

Abandoning the NEP, in the first Five-Year Plan (1928–32), Stalin ordered the forced **collectivization** of agriculture and industrialization on an unprecedented scale. Declaring its aim to be "the elimination of the *kulak* as a class", the Party waged open war on a peasantry who were overwhelmingly hostile to collectivization. This conflict has been called the "Third Revolution" – for it transformed Russian society more than any of the previous ones. Bolshevik brutality, the destruction of livestock and the ensuing chaos all contributed to the **famine of 1932–33**, which resulted in the death of as many as five million people.

Stalin ascribed the consequences to Party cadres "dizzy with success" and advocated more realistic goals for the second Five-Year Plan. In 1934, at the Seventeenth Party **"Congress of Victors"**, he declared that the Party had triumphed, pronouncing that "Life has become better, Comrades. Life has become gayer". While the 2000-plus delegates cheered, there were many who privately thought that, with Soviet power assured, Stalin should make way for a new General Secretary and a return to collegial decision-making. The likeliest candidate was the Leningrad Party boss, **Sergei Kirov**, who had popular appeal, yet lacked the urge to dominate his colleagues.

The Great Terror

Whether there was ever a chance of unseating Stalin is among the many "what ifs" of Russian history. In reality, **Kirov's assassination** at the Smolniy on December 1, 1934, gave Stalin the pretext for a **purge of Leningrad** that saw 30,000–40,000 citizens arrested in the spring of 1935 alone, and perhaps as many as a quarter of the city's population within a year – the majority destined for the **Gulag**, or "Corrective Labour Camps and Labour Settlements".

This was merely the prelude to a nationwide frenzy of fear and denunciation. At the first of the great Moscow **show trials** in the summer of 1936, Lenin's old comrades, Kamenev and Zinoviev, "confessed" to Kirov's murder and were shot along with fourteen others (Zinoviev begged, "For God's sake, tell Stalin … he'll say it's all a dreadful mistake!"). In early 1937, the head of the NKVD (secret police), Genrikh Yagoda, was arrested and succeeded by the dwarfish Nikolai Yezhov, who presided over the darkest period in Russian history, the *Yezhovshchina*, or **Great Terror**, of 1937–38. The total number of people arrested is thought to have been in the region of eight million, of whom at least a million were executed, while countless others died in the camps. Besides the lives lost or blighted, the loss of engineers, scientists and skilled workers wrought havoc on industry, research and the railways – there came a point beyond which terror was self-defeating, even for the most ruthless regime. So in December, 1938, Yezhov was replaced by Lavrenty Beria – a signal from Stalin that the worst was over, for the time being.

Few realized that purges within the Red Army had left it gravely weakened. From the defence minister Marshal Tukhackevsky downwards, the majority of senior officers had been either shot or sent to camps, and their hastily promoted successors were under-qualified and afraid to display any initiative. As Anglo-French appeasement allowed Nazi Germany to invade Austria and Czechoslova-kia, and to set its sights on Poland, Stalin feared that the USSR would be next on its *Drang nach Osten* (Drive to the East) and authorized Foreign Minister Molotov to negotiate with his Nazi counterpart. The Molotov-Ribbentrop pact of August 1939 bound both parties to non-aggression, and the Soviets to supply food and raw materials to the Nazis. It also contained secret clauses relating to the division of Poland and the Soviet occupation of the Baltic States, which was put into prac-tice in the first weeks of World War II. In October, Stalin demanded the moving of the Finnish frontier further from Leningrad, and in November, attacked the Karelian Isthmus. But the **Winter War** (1939–40) exposed the flaws of the Red Army, and although it eventually prevailed – taking Karelia – Stalin's act ensured that Finland would join the Nazi invasion to recover its lost territory.

The Great Patriotic War

On June 22, 1941, Hitler's forces invaded the Soviet Union, starting what Russians call the **Great Patriotic War**. Despite advance warnings from numerous sources, Stalin was taken by surprise and apparently suffered a nervous breakdown, while his subordinates attempted to grapple with the crisis. In the first days of the war, over a thousand Soviet aircraft were destroyed on the ground; whole armies were encircled and captured; and local Party officials fled from the advancing *Blitzkrieg*. In some regions the population welcomed the Germans as liberators – until Nazi brutality flung them back into the arms of Stalin.

The position of **Leningrad** soon became critical. By September 1941, it was virtually surrounded by German forces, whose operational directive read: "The Führer has decided to wipe the city of Petersburg off the face of the earth. It is proposed to tighten up the blockade of the city and level it to the ground by shelling and continuous bombing from the air." So began the terrible "900 Days" of starvation and bombardment, known to Russians as the **Blockade** (*blokada*). No preparations had been made for a siege: indeed, shortly before it began, food had actually been sent out of Leningrad to the forces at the front. The only supply line lay across Lake Ladoga, to the east of the city, where trucks could cross the icy **Road of Life** (see p.296) when the lake was frozen in winter. Yet, despite heroic improvisations, Leningrad came close to collapse in the winter of 1941–42, when 53,000 people died in December alone. By the second winter, supplies were better organized and the population had developed a powerful sense of solidarity, but

▲ Peterhof, as the Nazis left it

even so, 670,000 citizens died before the Blockade was finally broken in January 1944. In recognition of its sacrifices, Leningrad was proclaimed a "**Hero City**" of the Soviet Union; its shops were supplied with the best food in the country and every child born in the city received a special medal.

Stalin's final years

After the enormous sacrifices of the war – in which 27 million Soviet citizens had perished – people longed for a peaceful, freer life. But any liberalization was anathema to Stalin, whose suspicion of rivals and subversive trends was stronger than ever. It seems likely that he planned to purge the Politburo of all those who had served him since the 1930s, and install a new generation of lackeys. As ever, he used others to pick off his victims and script the show trials. Beria and Malenkov united against **Andrei Zhdanov**, who had been promoted to the Politburo for leading Leningrad through the Blockade. Criticized for a "lack of ideological vigilance" in his home city, Zhdanov responded with a crackdown on "anti-patriotic elements" among the intelligentsia, launching a vitriolic attack on two local journals and vilifying the city's beloved poet, Akhmatova, as "half-nun, half-whore".

When Zhdanov died (or was poisoned) in 1948, Beria fabricated the "**Leningrad Affair**", in which Zhdanov's closest allies were accused of trying to seize power and were executed. Thousands of Leningraders fell victim to the witch-hunt that followed and wound up in the Gulag. Stalin's final show trial was the notorious "**Doctors' Plot**", where eminent physicians "confessed" to murdering Zhdanov and plotting to kill others in the Politburo. It was "no coincidence" (a phrase beloved of Stalin) that the doctors were mostly Jewish, nor that the list of their intended victims omitted Beria. The stage was being set for a nationwide pogrom and the deportation of all Jews to a remote region of Siberia for "their own protection", while Beria would be cast as the villain in future show trials. Thankfully, two months into the charade, the **death of Stalin** (March 5, 1953) brought an end to proceedings and charges were dropped.

Khrushchev

Stalin's successors jockeyed for power. The odious Beria was the first to be arrested and executed, in July 1953; Malenkov lasted until 1955, before he was forced to resign; Molotov hung on until 1957. The man who emerged as the next Soviet leader was **Nikita Khrushchev**, who, in 1956, when his position was by no means unassailable, gave a "**Secret Speech**" to the Twentieth Party Congress, in which Stalin's name was for the first time officially linked with Kirov's murder and the sufferings of millions during the Great Terror. So traumatic was the revelation that many delegates fainted on the spot. In the same year, thousands were rehabilitated and returned from the camps. Yet for all its courage, Khrushchev's **de-Stalinization** was strictly limited in scope – after all, he himself had earned the nickname "Butcher of the Ukraine" during the *Yezhovshchina*.

The cultural **thaw** that followed Khrushchev's speech was equally selective, allowing the publication of Solzhenitsyn's account of the Gulag, *One Day in the Life of Ivan Denisovich*, but rejecting Pasternak's *Doctor Zhivago*. Khrushchev emptied the camps, only to send dissidents to psychiatric hospitals. In **foreign affairs**, he was not one to shy away from confrontation, either. Soviet tanks spilled blood on the streets of Budapest in 1956, while Khrushchev oversaw the building of the Berlin Wall and, in October 1962, took the world to the edge of the nuclear precipice during the Cuban Missile Crisis. He also boasted that the Soviet Union would surpass the West in the production of consumer goods within twenty years, and pinned the nation's hopes on developing the so-called "Virgin Lands" of Siberia and Kazakhstan.

By 1964, Khrushchev had managed to alienate all the main interest groups in the Soviet hierarchy. As the Virgin Lands turned into a dust bowl, his economic boasts rang hollow and the Soviet public was deeply embarrassed by his boorish behaviour at the United Nations, where Khrushchev interrupted a speech by banging on the table with his shoe. In October 1964, his enemies took advantage of his vacation at the Black Sea to mount a bloodless coup, and on his return to Moscow, Khrushchev was presented with his resignation "for reasons of health". It was a sign of the changes since Stalin's death that he was the first disgraced Soviet leader to be allowed to live on in obscurity, rather than being shot.

Brezhnev and the Era of Stagnation

Khrushchev's ultimate successor, **Leonid Brezhnev**, made an about-turn. Military expenditure rose, attacks on Stalin ceased and the subject of the Great Terror became taboo again. The show trial of the writers, Sinyavsky and Daniel, in 1966, marked the end of the thaw and was followed by a wave of repression in major cities, while the crushing of the Prague Spring in 1968 showed that the new Soviet leaders were as ruthless as their predecessors in stamping out dissent abroad. Owing to press censorship and public indifference, most Russians knew little of **Alexander Solzhenitsyn** when he was exiled to the West in 1974, and even less of **Andrei Sakharov**, the nuclear physicist sentenced to internal exile for his human-rights campaigns.

Despite Party and KGB control of society, the Brezhnev era is now remembered in Russia as a rare period of peace and stability. With many goods subsidized, citizens could bask in the knowledge that meat and bread cost the same as they had done in 1950 (even if you did have to queue for it), while those with money had recourse to the burgeoning black market. The newfound security of the Party cadres (subject to fewer purges than at any time since the Soviet system began) led to unprecedented corruption. As sclerosis set in across the board, industrial and agricultural output declined to new lows. By 1970, the average age of the Politburo was over 70 – embodying the geriatric nature of Soviet politics in what would later be called the **Era of Stagnation** (*zastoynoe vremya*).

Brezhnev died in 1982 and was succeeded by the former KGB chief **Yuri Andropov**, who had hardly begun an anti-corruption campaign when he too expired (February 1984). Brezhnev's clique took fright at the prospect of yet more change and elected the 73-year-old **Konstantin Chernenko** as General Secretary, but when he also died barely a year later, it was clear that the post required some new blood.

The Gorbachev years

Mikhail Gorbachev – at 53, the youngest of the Politburo – was chosen with a brief to "get things moving". The first of his policies to send shock waves through society – a campaign against alcohol – was the most unpopular, abortive initiative of his career, followed shortly afterwards by the coining of the two famous buzz words of the Gorbachev era: **glasnost** (openness) and **perestroika** (restructuring). The first took a battering when, in April 1986, the world's worst nuclear disaster – at **Chernobyl** – was hushed up for a full three days, before the Swedes forced an admission out of the Soviet authorities.

Regardless, Gorbachev pressed on, shaking up the bureaucracy and launching investigations into officials who had abused their positions in the Brezhnev era. One of the most energetic campaigners against corruption was the new Moscow Party chief, **Boris Yeltsin**, who openly attacked Gorbachev and the hardline ideologist, Yegor Ligachev before dramatically resigning from the Politburo and being sacked as Moscow Party leader soon afterwards.

As Gorbachev abandoned his balancing act and realigned himself with the hardliners, radicals within the Party formed the **Democratic Union**, the first organized opposition movement to emerge since 1921. Gorbachev promptly banned its meetings and created a new security force – the **OMON** – while in the Baltic republics, nationalist **Popular Fronts** emerged. Estonia was the first to make the break, declaring sovereignty in November 1988 and raising the national flag in place of the hammer and sickle the following year.

In the March 1989 **elections** for the Congress of People's Deputies, Soviet voters were, for the first time in decades, allowed to choose from more than one candidate, some of whom were even non-Party members. Despite the heavily rigged selection process, radicals – including Yeltsin and Sakharov – managed to get elected. At the congress in May, a Latvian deputy demanded an enquiry into events in Georgia, where Soviet troops had recently killed 21 protesters. When Sakharov urged an end to one-party rule, his microphone was switched off – a futile gesture, since the sessions were broadcast live on TV.

Gorbachev's next crisis came with the **miners' strike** in July, when thousands walked out in protest at shortages, safety standards and poor wages. Gorbachev managed to entice them back to work with various promises, but the myth of the Soviet Union as a workers' state had been shattered forever. The events which swept across Eastern Europe throughout 1989, culminating with the **fall of the Berlin Wall** and the Velvet Revolution in Czechoslovakia, were another blow to the old guard, but Gorbachev was more concerned with holding together the Soviet Union itself. That Communism now faced its greatest crisis at home was made plain by unprecedented counter-demonstrations during the October Revolution celebrations on November 7, 1989: one of the banners read: "Workers of the World – we're sorry."

1990 proved no better for Gorbachev or the Party. In January, Soviet tanks rolled into the Azerbaijani capital, Baku, to crush the independence movement there – more than a hundred people were killed. In February, Moscow witnessed the largest **demonstration** since the 1917 Revolution, calling for an end to one-party rule and protesting against rising anti-Semitic violence.

The voters registered their disgust with the Party at **local elections**. In the republics, nationalists swept the board and declarations of independence soon followed, while in Russia, the **Democratic Platform** gained majorities in the city councils of Leningrad and Moscow. Gavril Popov became chairman of the Moscow council, while an equally reformist law professor, **Anatoly Sobchak**, was elected to the post in Leningrad. In May, Yeltsin secured his election as chairman of the Russian parliament and, two weeks later, in imitation of the Baltic States, declared **Russian independence** from the Soviet Union (June 12, 1990).

In July, the Soviet Communist Party held its last ever congress. Yeltsin tore up his Party card in full view of the cameras – two million had done the same by the end of the year. The economic crisis, spiralling crime and chronic food shortages put Gorbachev under renewed pressure from hardliners. As winter set in, leadership reshuffles gave the Interior Ministry and control of the media back to the hardliners, and the liberal foreign minister, Edvard Shevardnadze, resigned, warning that "dictatorship is coming".

In January, 1991, thirteen Lithuanians were killed by Soviet troops as they defended the national TV centre. A week later in Latvia, the OMON stormed the Latvian Interior Ministry in Rīga, killing five people. In June, citizens of Leningrad narrowly voted in a referendum to rename the city **St Petersburg**, while both Moscow and St Petersburg voted in new radical mayors (Popov and Sobchak) to run the reorganized city administrations.

Popular disgust with Party rule was manifest in the huge majority of votes cast for Yeltsin in the **Russian presidential election** of June 12, 1991. As Russia's first ever democratically elected leader, he could claim a mandate for bold moves and soon issued a decree calling for the removal of Party "cells" from factories. In response, leading hardliners published an appeal for action "to lead the country to a dignified and sovereign future". Another indication of what might be in store came at the end of July, when seven Lithuanian border guards were shot dead in one of the continuing Soviet army attacks on Baltic customs posts.

The end of the USSR

On Monday August 19, 1991, the Soviet Union awoke to the soothing sounds of Chopin on the radio and *Swan Lake* on TV. A **state of emergency** had been declared, Gorbachev had resigned "for health reasons" and the country was now ruled by a "State Committee for the State of Emergency in the USSR", consisting of many of his recent appointees, under the nominal leadership of Gennady Yenayev. Gorbachev himself, then on holiday in Crimea, had been asked to back the coup but refused and was consequently under house arrest. So began what Russians call the **putsch**.

In **Moscow**, tanks stationed themselves at key points, including the Russian parliament building, known as the **White House**, where a small group of protesters gathered. When the first tank approached, Yeltsin leapt aboard, shook hands with its commander and appealed to the crowd (and accompanying TV crews): "You can erect a throne using bayonets, but you cannot sit on bayonets for long." News of the standoff – and Yeltsin's appeal to soldiers not to "let yourselves be turned into blind weapons" – was broadcast around the world and beamed back to millions of Russians via the BBC and the Voice of America.

In **Leningrad**, the army stayed off the streets and Mayor Sobchak kept his cool, warning the local coup commander, "If you lay a finger on me, you will be put on trial like the rest of the Nazis." It was pure bravado, but it worked: the general kept his forces in their barracks. That evening, Sobchak appeared on local TV and denounced the putsch – in Leningrad, it was effectively over on day one, though the citizens who gathered to defend City Hall had an anxious night awaiting tanks that never materialized. The following day, 200,000 Leningraders massed on Dvortsovaya ploschad in protest against the putsch, while the eyes of the world were on Moscow.

On Tuesday, the defenders of the White House were heartened by the news that one of the coup leaders had resigned due to "high blood pressure" (he had been drinking continuously) and the crowd grew to 100,000 in defiance of a curfew order. Around midnight, an advancing armoured column was stopped and fire-bombed on a Moscow ring road and three civilians were shot dead. Next morning it was announced that several military units had decamped to Yeltsin's side and on Wednesday afternoon the putsch collapsed as its leaders bolted. Yenayev drank himself into a stupor and several others committed suicide.

Gorbachev flew back to Moscow, not realizing that everything had changed. The same day, jubilant crowds toppled the giant statue of Dzerzhinsky which stood outside the Lubyanka in Moscow. On Friday, Yeltsin decreed the Russian Communist Party an illegal organization, announced the suspension of pro-coup newspapers such as *Pravda* and had the Central Committee headquarters in Moscow sealed up.

The failure of the putsch spelt the **end of Communist rule** and the **break-up of the Soviet Union**. In December, Ukraine voted for independence; a week later the leaders of Russia, Belarus and Ukraine formally replaced the USSR with a **Commonwealth of Independent States** (CIS); the Central Asian republics declared their intention of joining. On December 25, Gorbachev resigned as president of a state which no longer existed; that evening the Soviet flag was lowered over the Kremlin and replaced by the Russian tricolour.

New Russia

On January 2, 1992, Russians faced their New Year hangovers and the harsh reality of massive price rises, following a decree by Yeltsin that lifted controls. Initially, **inflation** was limited by keeping a tight rein on state spending, in accordance with the monetarist strategy of Prime Minister **Yegor Gaidar**, until the Central Bank began printing vast amounts of rubles to cover credits issued to state industries on the verge of bankruptcy. Inflation soared.

St Petersburg also had other concerns. On March 25, an accident at the nuclear reactor at **Sosnovy Bor**, on the Gulf of Finland, caused concern around the world. The reactor was of the same type as the one that blew up at Chernobyl and initial reports suggested that St Petersburg had been contaminated. In fact, no radiation was released, but the accident highlighted environmental worries, including the **pollution** of the city's water supply by industrial effluents discharged into Lake Ladoga and the Neva, exacerbated by the half-finished tidal barrage across the Gulf.

By December 1992, Yeltsin was forced to replace Gaidar with the veteran technocrat **Viktor Chernomyrdin**, who immediately reneged on promises to increase subsidies to industry and to restore them for vital foodstuffs (including vodka). For much of 1993 there was a **"War of Laws"** between the government and parliament, whose speaker, **Ruslan Khasbulatov**, exercised such influence over the deputies that it was suggested he had them under some form of hypnosis. Another erstwhile Yeltsin ally now in opposition was Vice-President **Alexander Rutskoy**, who denounced Gaidar's team as "boys in pink pants", and railed against the government as "scum" and "faggots".

In March 1993, Congress reneged on its earlier promise to hold a **referendum** on a new constitution. Yeltsin declared that he would hold an opinion poll anyway, and appeared on TV to announce the introduction of a special rule suspending the power of Congress and call for new elections. Yeltsin claimed to have been vindicated by 55 percent of those who voted, but the count took place in secret and the ballot papers were incinerated afterwards, so his opponents saw no reason to back down.

The uneasy stalemate lasted until September, when Yeltsin brought things to a head by dissolving Congress under a legally dubious decree. In response, **deputies occupied the White House**, refusing to budge as Yeltsin cut off their electricity and finally blockaded them in. The crisis deepened as Rutskoy gathered an armed force around the building and appeared on TV handing out guns. Who fired the first shot is still disputed, but the result was a series of battles, which lasted two days and left more than a hundred people dead. Rutskoy ordered his supporters to storm the TV centre and Yeltsin responded by ordering tanks to shell the White House into submission on October 4.

With his parliamentary foes behind bars Yeltsin turned on the local councils who had supported Congress. Councils all over Russia were abolished and new elections declared, leaving power concentrated in the hands of local mayors and officials. While Yeltsin was determined to be re-elected and rewrite the constitution, he bewildered many supporters by distancing himself from the party created to represent his government in the forthcoming elections, which bore the presumptuous name of **Russia's Choice** and campaigned as if its triumph was a foregone conclusion.

Zhirinovsky and Chechnya

The result of the December 1993 elections to the new parliament or Duma was a stunning rebuff for Russia's Choice, which won only 14 percent of the vote, compared to 23 percent for the so-called Liberal Democratic Party of **Vladimir Zhirinovsky**, an ultra-nationalist with a murky past who threatened to bomb Germany and Japan and to dump radioactive waste in the Baltic States. While Russian liberals and world opinion were aghast, evidence later emerged of systematic voting fraud in Zhirinovsky's favour, which could only have been organized at the highest level. For Yeltsin, the crucial point was that Zhirinovsky supported the new **Constitution**, giving unprecedented powers to the president, and backed Yeltsin's government in the Duma, despite his provocative rhetoric.

In **St Petersburg**, the election of a new city council in March 1994 returned only half the required number of deputies, as apathetic voters stayed at home. This allowed Sobchak to take sole command and pursue his strategy of boosting St Petersburg's international reputation by hosting conferences and the **Goodwill Games**; his fondness for ceremonies and VIPs led to him being dubbed "**Tsar Anatoly** the First". He spent much of his time on foreign trips, and his reputation also suffered from rumours that members of his family had profited from shady property deals – factors that would contribute to his electoral defeat less than two years later.

In December 1994, the Kremlin embarked on a **war in Chechnya** to subdue the breakaway Caucasian republic. The Chechens put up fierce resistance in their capital Grozny, which fell only after weeks of bombardment, leaving the city in ruins and up to 120,000 dead – including tens of thousands of Russian conscripts. Back home, the debacle was attributed to the so-called "**Party of War**", a shadowy alliance of figures within the military, security and economic ministries, whose geopolitical or personal interests coincided. It was even said that commanders deliberately sacrificed their own troops to write off hundreds of armoured vehicles, in order to cover up the illicit sale of 1600 tanks from the Soviet Army in East Germany.

As the war dragged on throughout 1995, there was a huge protest vote for the Communists in the parliamentary elections, which boded ill for Yeltsin's chances in the **Presidential election** of June 1996. Fearing the consequences of a victory by the Communist leader **Gennady Zyuganov**, Russia's financiers and journalists gave unstinting support to Yeltsin in the media. His campaign mastermind, **Anatoly Chubais**, banked on the anti-Yeltsin vote being split between Zyuganov and the ex-paratroop general **Alexander Lebed** – as indeed happened. Having gained half the vote, Yeltsin offered Lebed the post of security overlord and ordered him to end the war in Chechnya by negotiating the withdrawal of Russian forces – which he did – only to be sacked by Yeltsin soon afterwards, having served his purpose.

Yeltsin's second term

With the Communist threat dispelled, the **oligarchs** behind Yeltsin's re-election soon fell out over the remaining spoils. **Vladimir Potanin** acquired thirty percent of the world's nickel reserves for a mere $70 million and a controlling stake in the telecom giant Svyazinvest owing to the intervention of Chubais – enraging **Boris Berezovsky**, whose TV station ORT aired a 29-minute diatribe against Potanin during a news show. Along with the banking and media moguls **Vladimir Gusinsky** and **Mikhail Khodorkovsky**, and oil or gas barons such as **Roman Abramovich** (later famous abroad for buying Chelsea football club), they became synonymous with a series of scandals – including "book advances" to Chubais which were patently bribes. After Chubais had to resign as a sop to public opinion (he became boss of the electricity monopoly), Berezovsky's influence in the Kremlin grew even greater, and he was widely seen as the "kingmaker" of Russian politics.

Meanwhile, St Petersburg's 1996 mayoral election saw Sobchak ousted by his deputy following a mudslinging campaign. Though it didn't seem important at the time, one of Sobchak's protégés – an ex-KGB officer, **Vladimir Putin** – reacted to this by leaving St Petersburg politics to work in the Kremlin, where he would soon become noticed and destined for greater things.

Sobchak's successor, Governor **Vladimir Yakovlev**, found the nerve to double municipal rents and service charges, paving the way for a balanced budget. The privatization of municipal real estate yielded vast profits for speculators and corrupt officials, who were assumed to have ordered the 1997 assassination of Vice-Governor **Mikhail Manevich**, after he began investigating fraudulent city property deals. Even more shocking was the murder of **Galina Starovoitova** in November 1998. An outspoken human-rights campaigner who opposed the war in Chechnya and was untainted by corruption, she was mourned by many as the last true democratic politician in Russia.

The 1998 crash

Prime ministers and cabinets changed with bewildering frequency, as Yeltsin manoeuvred to build or neutralize coalitions in the Duma and its upper house, the Federation Council (dominated by regional governors), and find scapegoats for

Russia's economic problems. By April, 1998, Russia's foreign debt stood at $117 billion, workers were owed $9 billion in unpaid wages, and pensioners over $13 billion. With a crisis imminent, Yeltsin stunned the world by dismissing Chernomyrdin's entire cabinet and nominating 35-year-old **Sergei Kirienko** as prime minister.

His rescue plan depended on a "final loan" from the International Monetary Fund, at a time when the collapse of economies across Asia raised fears of a global crash. In August, the **ruble crashed** and many banks and businesses went into liquidation; the capitalist bubble had burst. Kirienko was replaced by the veteran diplomat and spymaster **Yevgeny Primakov**, a "safe" candidate accepted across the political spectrum, and also internationally. The US sent three million tonnes of emergency food aid, to avert the possibility of food riots over winter.

Yet the crash had some positive results. With imports so costly, shoppers switched back to domestic products, rewarding firms that survived the crisis. It also cut a few of the oligarchs down to size – though others seized the chance to snap up rivals' assets or dump all their own liabilities. By the end of the decade, these changes combined with arms sales and the rising price of gas and oil to produce a modest economic revival, which would contribute to the groundswell of support for Russia's next leader.

Yeltsin's endgame

While his government grappled with governing, Yeltsin was preoccupied with ensuring his own future – if not by running for president again in 2000, then by choosing a successor who would safeguard "**the Family**" – a term widely used to describe his inner circle of advisers and relatives, whose backroom deals with Berezovsky were the source of constant speculation in parts of the media they didn't control. With his health so uncertain that even Primakov expressed doubts as to whether Yeltsin could function as president – for which he was sacked in 1999 – Yeltsin had no alternative but to find a successor whom he could trust to guarantee the Family's security after they left the Kremlin.

Yeltsin's chosen successor emerged as suddenly and mysteriously as the apartment-block **bombings** that killed over 300 people in Moscow and other cities in September. Coming only a month after a Chechen warlord seized thousands of hostages in Daghestan, most Russians believed the government's claim that Chechen terrorists were responsible (though foreign journalists speculated that the FSB was behind the bombings), and demanded action.

It was then that the new acting prime minister, **Vladimir Putin**, made his name by pledging, "We will wipe the terrorists out wherever we find them – even on the toilet." Within weeks Russia launched a **second war in Chechnya**, using overwhelming firepower from the start. By December eighty percent of Grozny was in ruins; in Russia most greeted the city's fall as just revenge, and Berezovsky's media went into overdrive, casting Putin as the resolute, honest leader that Russia required. A new party, **United Russia** (nicknamed "Bear"), materialized overnight to back his candidacy, and was soon riding high in the polls.

The final masterstroke was **Yeltsin's surprise resignation** during his New Year message to the nation on the last night of the old millennium, when Russians would be more inclined to raise a rueful toast than ponder how power had so swiftly passed to Putin. His first decree as acting president was to grant

Yeltsin and his family lifelong immunity from arrest, prosecution or seizure of assets, and confer on Yeltsin the title of "First President" in perpetuity.

President Putin: 2000–2008

Ensconced in the Kremlin as acting president, Putin enjoyed every advantage in the forthcoming election, which his opponents tacitly conceded was a foregone conclusion. His **inauguration** on May 5, 2000, was heralded as the first peaceful democratic transfer of power in Russian history, replete with ceremonial trappings harking back to Tsarist times, invented for the occasion. His pledge to restore Russia's greatness was followed by decrees doubling military spending, increasing the powers of the security agencies and appointing seven "Super Governors" to oversee the regions. Five of these were army or ex-KGB officers, while twenty percent of the new regional governors were from the military or navy. Putin spoke openly of the need to create a **"strong vertical"** power in Russia – the *vertikal* became as much a mantra of his presidency as "all power to the Soviets" had been in the days of his grandfather (who had been a cook for Lenin and Stalin). Putin's view of Russian history embraced the Soviet, Tsarist and post-Soviet eras as equally worthwhile – symbolized by his decision to restore the Tsarist eagle as the state symbol, and the old Soviet national anthem (with revised words).

For those who feared that totalitarianism was creeping back, an early sign was the **campaign against NTV** and other elements of the Media-MOST group, which had infuriated the Kremlin by revealing human-rights abuses in Chechnya

▲ Local St Petersburg boy Putin

and casualties among Russian troops. Its owner, Gusinsky, was arrested and spent several days in Moscow's Butyurka prison, in what was seen by liberals as a warning to other media moguls, but welcomed by most Russians as a blow against the hated oligarchs. Gusinsky left Russia, soon to be followed by Berezovsky. Besides alleging that millions of dollars had been embezzled to finance Putin's election campaign, Berezovsky also implied that he had paid the Chechen warlord to invade Daghestan and thus set the stage for Putin's rise to power.

While his prestige suffered from **disasters** such as the loss of 118 men aboard the submarine *Kursk*, Putin's objectives were broadly accepted by the Duma and foreign heads of state queued up to meet him. Although Russia could only protest as Poland and the Baltic States joined NATO, the West acquiesced to Russia's human-rights abuses in **Chechnya** and Putin's claim to be fighting Islamic terrorism became easier to sell after **9/11**, when the US needed Russian help to sweep the Taliban from power in Afghanistan.

Among the achievements that Putin claimed for his first term was **reviving the economy**. Growth averaged more than five percent a year and there was a revival of light industries catering to a growing middle class. Moscow was the main locus of super-rich – boasting more dollar billionaires than New York – but St Petersburg and other cities also had their share of Russia's estimated 88,000 millionaires. By 2003, GDP was increasing by six or seven percent annually as rising oil and gas prices swelled the state's coffers and lifted the economy.

Yet **poverty** remained – and still is – endemic. While the average monthly wage is around $400, about a third of the population lives on less than a fifth of that. Alcoholism, a collapsing health system, unemployment and despair have sent male life expectancy plummeting – the average is now 58 years, less than what it was in the late nineteenth century – and abortions exceed live births. Since 1991, the population has shrunk by 5.3 million and is falling at a rate of a million a year – an unprecedented **demographic decline** for an industrialized nation in peacetime.

Putin's ability to manage the tensions arising from these contradictions rests on a tripod of power, whose most "vertical" leg consists of senior or ex-officers of the security services and armed forces, installed at the highest levels of government and business across the Federation – known as the *silovki* (from the Russian word *sil*, meaning "force"). The second is the Kremlin's control of the media, which is used to undermine any party that might crystallize discontent, and promote fake "opposition" parties. This needs the cooperation of Russia's oligarchs, for whom the *quid pro quo* is a veil drawn over how they acquired their wealth in the Yeltsin years. The rules of this *modus vivendi* were demonstrated to all when the billionaire **Mikhail Khodorkovsky**, chairman of the Yukos oil conglomerate, was arrested in his jet on a Siberian runway in October 2003. Khodorkovsky had been funding the liberal Yabloko party and looked set to challenge the Kremlin. His arrest aroused a storm of protest from foreign governments and business interests, but Russian voters were delighted, rewarding Putin's United Russia party with 222 seats in the parliamentary elections of December 2003. The Communists, meanwhile, were reduced to only 53 seats in the Duma.

Putin's re-election in March 2004 was a foregone conclusion. TV gave endless airtime to United Russia and starved other parties of publicity, while the tabloids compared one challenger to Hitler and accusing him of fathering four illegitimate children; another claimed to have been drugged and filmed in compromising positions, before fleeing to London and withdrawing from the race. Putin received 71 percent of votes cast; his nearest rival, the Communist candidate, 13.7 percent, and the only liberal just 3.9 percent. "Russia's choice: the end of democracy", was the verdict of one (pro-Kremlin) newspaper.

When similar tactics were used in **Ukraine** to secure victory for the pro-Moscow candidate, a Western-backed Orange Revolution propelled his rival, Viktor

Yushchenko, to power, while a similar Rose Revolution in **Georgia** resulted in the election of Mikhail Saakashvilli. Both leaders aspired to join the EU and NATO, so this was a strategic setback for Russia. Ominously for Putin, there were also protests in Russia over welfare cuts and corruption, with the potential to snowball. To counter this threat, the Kremlin founded its own "radical" youth movement, **Nashi** (Ours) and clamped down on NGOs in Russia throughout 2005.

By 2006 Putin was ready to strike back using the gas conglomerate **Gazprom**. On New Year's Day, it demanded a fourfold rise in the price of gas to Ukraine, which was accused of hijacking supplies destined for EU states, underscoring their reliance on Russian energy. Germany infuriated Poland by signing a deal for its own pipeline via Scandinavia (shortly after which, ex-Chancellor Schroeder joined Gazprom's board). To consolidate its grip on energy resources the Kremlin forced foreign companies to sell their controlling stakes in Russian oil and gas fields to the state oil giant **Rosneft**. The two corporations supply Europe with a third of its oil and forty percent of its natural gas. In Russia they are half jokingly described as the "only real political parties" and in 2007 were allowed to raise their own private armies.

The year's end saw Putin defuse the **succession** issue. Barred by the constitution from a third term as president, he put himself forward as prime minister and endorsed **Dmitri Medvedev** as president – approved by United Russia's majority in the Duma and by the Russian people in the elections of March 2008. That Medvedev was formerly CEO of Gazprom and Putin has hinted at becoming boss of Rosneft epitomizes the nexus of interlocking political and financial elites dubbed "**Kremlin Inc**", fusing the unbridled authoritarianism of the Soviet system with the media savvy and mega-wealth of American politics – an unbeatable combination.

Meanwhile, in St Petersburg...

As a local boy made good, Putin pulled out all the stops for St Petersburg's **tercentenary anniversary** in 2003. A staggering $1.7 billion was budgeted to cover street repairs and face-lifting; the homeless were swept off the streets; and a two-metre high, ten-kilometre-long fence was erected to hide the humble cottages and allotments between Pulkovo airport and the Konstantin Palace at Strelna, refurbished at a cost of $300 million to host the **G8 Summit** of 45 world leaders.

Meanwhile, a host of problems were ignored, unless others were willing to pay for a solution. After lobbying in vain for action, the EU stumped up $160 million to tackle sewage **pollution** from St Petersburg, which has rendered large areas of the seabed of the Gulf of Finland biologically dead. Similarly, it is largely EU funding that supports efforts to fight **Aids**; **HIV** is spreading faster than anywhere else in Europe and **heroin addiction** is spiralling. **Crime** is – statistically – falling, but cynics say that this is because corruption is so entrenched that crimes go unreported or are covered up; it's thought that most businesses either pay for "protection" (known as a *krysha*, or "roof") or are owned by organized crime.

Small wonder that Petersburgers were indifferent to the gubernatorial election, required after Yakovlev was "promoted" to the Kremlin (where his future insignificance was signalled by the award of a fourth-class medal). United Russia's candidate, **Valentina Matvienko**, Putin's "Special Envoy" in St Petersburg, was elected on a low turn-out in the autumn of 2003 and reappointed to the post after gubernatorial elections were abolished. With Putin's endorsement, Matvienko can afford to alienate her "constituents" by approving the **Gazprom Tower skyscraper** (see box on p.227), secure in the knowledge that the main "opposition" party, A Just Russia, is merely a sham created by the Kremlin to maintain an illusion of democracy.

Books

The number of books available about Russia and the old Soviet Union is vast. We have concentrated on works specifically related to St Petersburg and on useful general surveys of Russian history, politics and the arts. Publishers are detailed below in the form of British publisher/American publisher, where both exist. Where books are published in one country only, UK or US follows the publisher's name. Out-of-print books are designated o/p; University Press is abbreviated UP. Books tagged with the ⊞ symbol are particularly recommended.

General accounts, guides and illustrated books

Kathleen Berton Murrell *St Petersburg: History, Art and Architecture* (Troika, Moscow/Flint River Press, UK). Informative text by a long-term resident in Russia, although the photographs follow no apparent logical order.

⚹ **Marquis de Custine** *Empire of the Czar* (Anchor). Another vintage masterpiece, and the first book by a Westerner to get to grips with Russia, which de Custine visited during the 1830s. Waspish, cynical and indignant by turns, many of its observations are still uncannily true today.

⚹ **Arthur & Elena George** *St Petersburg: A History* (Sutton Publishing, UK). Extremely readable account of the city's history up until its tercentenary, ranging from architecture and music to intrigues and anecdotes.

Prince George Galitzine *Imperial Splendour* (Viking, UK). Palaces and monasteries of old Russia, presented by a member of the Russian nobility who lived most of his life in London, but made regular trips back to St Petersburg from the early 1960s.

Katya Galitzine *St Petersburg: The Hidden Interiors* (Hazar Publishing, UK). Written by the Prince's British-born daughter (who also founded a library in his name, see p.51), its title is a bit of a misnomer, since most of the buildings featured are well known, but Leonid Bogdanov's photographs make this an irresistible coffee-table book.

Pavel Kann *Leningrad: A Guide* (Planeta, Moscow). The last in a classic Soviet series of city guides, giving pride of place to Lenin memorial sites and the like; the 1988 edition is blissfully impervious to perestroika. You may still find copies in the city's bookshops.

⚹ **Suzanne Massie** *Land of the Firebird*; *Pavlovsk: The Life of a Russian Palace* (both Hearttree Press, US). The first is a colourful tour of pre-revolutionary Russian culture; the second sweeps over three centuries of history as embodied by Pavlovsk Palace, its inhabitants and its restorers, accompanied by wonderful illustrations.

Prince Michael of Greece *Imperial Palaces of Russia* (IB Tauris/St Martin's Press). Lavishly illustrated survey of all the major palaces in and around St Petersburg, by the "heir" to a royal family that the Greeks rejected in 1974.

⚹ **John Nicholson** *The Other St Petersburg*. Absurdity, drinking and courtyards loom large in these amusing character sketches of Leningrad as it was before capitalism changed everything. Nicholson still lives in St Petersburg and now owns *Bubyr's Guesthouse* (see p.351), where copies of this self-published book are sold. You can read excerpts online at Ⓦwww.other.spb.ru.

Colin Thubron *Among the Russians* (Penguin, UK); *In Siberia* (Chatto & Windus, UK). The first includes a chapter on Leningrad, a visit to which formed part of Thubron's angst-ridden journey around the USSR in the early 1980s; the second is as lapidary and insightful and even more gloom-inducing, given such locales as Kolyma and Vorkuta, the worst hells of the Gulag.

History, politics and society

Anne Applebaum *Gulag: A History of the Soviet Camps* (Penguin). This Pulitzer Prize-winning tome emphasizes the human cost and economic futility of the Gulag, drawing on extensive archival material.

Hugh Barnes *Gannibal: The Moor of Petersburg* (Profile). The story of Pushkin's African ancestor: a slave who became a favourite of Peter the Great, a war hero, engineer, cryptographer and scholar.

Antony Beevor *Stalingrad* and *The Fall of Berlin 1945* (both Penguin). Military history told from the standpoint of ordinary soldiers on both sides and the civilians caught in the middle. Stalingrad was one of the decisive battles of World War II, its epic scale matched by its ferocity. In 1945, the Red Army took revenge on the German capital, where isolated acts of decency were submerged in an orgy of rapine, licensed by Stalin's order and Soviet propaganda.

Bruce Clark *An Empire's New Clothes* (Vintage, UK). A provocative assessment of the *realpolitik* behind the dramas of the 1990s by *The Times*'s man on the spot, who argues that Yeltsin's "democrats" did more to lay the foundations of a resurgent Russian empire than those who accused them of selling out to the West.

Robert Conquest *Stalin: Breaker of Nations* (Weidenfeld/Viking Penguin); *The Great Terror: A Reassessment* (Pimlico/Oxford UP). The first is a short, withering biography of the Soviet dictator; the second, perhaps the best study of the Terror. In 1990, this was revised after new evidence suggested that Conquest's tally of the number of victims of the Terror was an underestimate; previously he had been accused of exaggeration.

Marc Ferro *Nicholas II: The Last of the Tsars* (Oxford UP, UK). A concise biography of Russia's doomed monarch, by a French historian who argues that some of the Imperial family escaped execution at Yekaterinburg. Most scholars reckon that the sole survivor was the family spaniel, Joy.

Orlando Figes *A People's Tragedy: The Russian Revolution 1891–1924* (Pimlico/Viking Penguin); *Natasha's Dance: A Cultural History of Russia* (Allen Lane); *The Whisperers* (Allen Lane). The first is a *tour de force* that sees the February and October revolutions and the Civil War as a continuum; the second, a magisterial survey of Russian culture; while his latest book draws on testimonies by survivors of Stalin's Terror.

Adam Hochschild *The Unquiet Ghost: Russians Remember Stalin* (Serpent's Tail/Penguin). An enquiry into the nature of guilt and denial, from the penal camps of Kolyma to the archives of the Lubyanka.

Andrew Jack *Inside Putin's Russia* (Granta, UK). Written during Putin's first term as president, it epitomizes the consensual view of Russia as a "managed democracy" of authoritarian, oligarchic rule over an impoverished majority, groping towards prosperity, legality and human rights.

John Kampfner *Inside Yeltsin's Russia* (Cassell, UK). A racy account of Yeltsin's presidency up to 1994, focusing on political crises, crime and corruption.

Dominic Lieven *Nicholas II* (St Martin's Press, US). Another, especially insightful study of the last tsar that draws comparisons both between the monarchies of Russia and other states of that period, and the downfall of the Tsarist and Soviet regimes.

Robert Massie *Peter the Great* (Abacus/ Ballantine); *Nicholas and Alexandra* (Indigo/Dell). Both the boldest and the weakest of the Romanov tsars are minutely scrutinized in these two heavyweight, but extremely readable, biographies – the one on Peter is especially good, and contains much about the creation of St Petersburg.

Andrew Meier *Black Earth: Russia After the Fall* (HarperCollins). Focuses on Putin's efforts to restore "vertical power" and Russia's prestige abroad, but also stresses the cultural tradition and the vastness of the country as crucial to an understanding of its politics and economics.

Anna Politkovskaya *Putin's Russia; A Russian Diary* (both Harvill). Two searing indictments of political corruption and state terror in today's Russia – the second covering Putin's 2004 re-election campaign and the Beslan school massacre – typifying her crusading journalism, for which Politkovskaya was murdered in 2006.

Edvard Radzinsky *The Rasputin File* (Anchor, US). This discursive biography of the "mad monk" who hastened the fall of tsarism, uses newly discovered files from the archives of the Provisional Government.

John Reed *Ten Days that Shook the World* (Penguin). The classic eyewitness account of the 1917 Bolshevik seizure of power, which vividly captures the mood of the time and the hopes pinned on the Revolution. Later made into the film *Reds*.

David Remnick *Lenin's Tomb* (Penguin/Random House). Written by the *Washington Post*'s Moscow correspondent in the early 1990s, it remains the most vivid account of the collapse of the Soviet Union, though some of its judgements seem naïve with hindsight.

Virginia Rounding *Catherine the Great: Love, Sex and Power* (Arrow). A comprehensive biography of Russia's most humane autocrat – the personification of Enlightened Despotism – and a feminist ahead of her time.

Harrison Salisbury *Black Night, White Snow* and *The Nine Hundred Days* (both Da Capo Press, US). The events of the 1905 and 1917 revolutions and the wartime Siege of Leningrad are vividly related in these two heavyweight, but extremely readable, books by an American journalist, who first visited Leningrad shortly after the lifting of the Blockade.

David Satter *Darkness at Dawn* (Yale). Satter accuses Putin (or his backers) of orchestrating the 1999 bombings that provided the pretext for the second Chechen war, to ensure Putin's election.

Simon Sebag Montefiore *Young Stalin* (Weidenfeld); *Stalin: The Court of the Red Tsar* (Phoenix); *Potemkin: Prince of Princes* (Phoenix). The first reveals how Stalin's charisma and ruthlessness were manifest at an early age; the second, the love affairs, intrigues and lifestyles of the Bolshevik magnates; while the last is the definitive biography of Catherine the Great's lover and statesman.

Robert Service *History of Modern Russia from Nicholas II to Putin* (Penguin,

UK); *Russia: Experiment with a People* (Macmillan, UK). The first is a magisterial survey of twentieth-century Russian history; the second focuses on the corruption and missed opportunities of the Yeltsin era.

Jonathan Steele *Eternal Russia: Yeltsin, Gorbachev and the Mirage of Democracy* (Faber/Harvard UP). A thought-provoking look at the birth of the new Russia, which Steele sees very much as a product of a deep-rooted authoritarian tradition.

Henri Troyat *Alexander of Russia* (Dutton, US). Study of the "Tsar Liberator", Alexander II, sympathetically profiled by the late French historian.

Peter Truscott *Putin's Progress* (Simon & Schuster). Whilst adhering to the consensual view of Putin's Russia (see Jack's and Meier's books, pp.419–420), this one contains more biographical detail about Russia's judo-loving president than the others.

Edmund Wilson *To the Finland Station* (Penguin). A classic appraisal of Lenin's place in the Russian revolutionary tradition, first published in 1940, combining metaphysics and political analysis with waspish characterization.

Culture

Anna Benn & Rosamund Bartlett *Literary Russia: A Guide* (Picador, UK). A comprehensive guide to Russian writers and places associated with their lives and works, including such famous Petersburgers as Dostoyevsky and Akhmatova, along with figures who are less well known abroad, such as the cult author Daniil Kharms.

Alan Bird *A History of Russian Painting* (Phaidon/Macmillan). A comprehensive survey of Russian painting from medieval times to the Brezhnev era, including numerous black-and-white illustrations and potted biographies of the relevant artists.

John E. Bowlt (ed) *Russian Art of the Avant Garde* (Thames & Hudson/Penguin). An illustrated volume of critical essays on this seminal movement, which anticipated many trends in Western art that have developed since World War II.

Leslie Chamberlain *The Food and Cooking of Russia* (Penguin). An informative and amusing cookbook, full of delicious – if somewhat vague – recipes.

🌂 **William Craft Brumfield** *A History of Russian Architecture* (Cambridge UP). The most comprehensive study of the subject, ranging from early Novgorod churches to Olympic sports halls, by way of Baroque palaces and Style Moderne mansions. Illustrated by hundreds of photos and line drawings.

🌂 **Matthew Cullerne Brown** *Art Under Stalin* (Phaidon/Holmes & Meier); *Contemporary Russian Art* (Phaidon, UK). The former is a fascinating study of totalitarian aesthetics, ranging from ballet to sports stadia and films to sculpture; the latter covers art in the Brezhnev and Gorbachev eras.

🌂 **Camilla Gray** *The Russian Experiment in Art 1863–1922* (Thames & Hudson). A concise guide to the multitude of movements that constituted the Russian avant-garde, prior to the imposition of the dead hand of Socialist Realism.

🌂 **George Heard Hamilton** *The Art and Architecture of Russia* (Yale UP). An exhaustive rundown of the major trends in painting, sculpture and architecture in Russia, from Kievan Rus up to the late 1990s.

Geir Kjetsaa *Fyodor Dostoyevsky: A Writer's Life* (Macmillan, UK). Readable yet scholarly, this is the best one-volume biography of Russia's most famous writer, by a Finnish academic.

Jay Leyda *Kino* (Princeton UP). A weighty history of Russian and Soviet film to the early 1980s.

Geraldine Norman *The Hermitage: The Biography of a Great Museum* (Pimlico, UK). An affectionate and engrossing history of the acquisitions, dramas and personalities that have made the Hermitage a museum in a league of its own.

Roberta Reeder *Anna Akhmatova: Poet and Prophet* (Allison & Busby, UK). Comprehensive and well-researched biography of one of the greatest poets of Russia's "Silver Age", with accounts of the artists, poets and events that influenced her life and work.

A.N. Wilson *Tolstoy* (Penguin). A highly readable biography of the great novelist and appalling family man.

Russian fiction and poetry

Anna Akhmatova *Selected Poems* (Penguin). Moving and mystical verses by the doyenne of Leningrad poets, whose *Requiem* cycle spoke for a generation traumatized by the purges.

Boris Akunin *The Winter Queen* (Random House); *Turkish Gambit* (Weidenfeld & Nicolson). Two lively historical thrillers featuring the Tsarist secret agent Erast Fandorin. One involves Masonic plots; the other is set during the Russo-Turkish war of 1877–78.

Andrei Bely *Petersburg* (Penguin, US). Apocalyptic novel set in 1905, full of *fin-de-siècle* angst and phantasmagorical imagery, by St Petersburg's equivalent of Kafka. One of the characters is a time bomb.

Fyodor Dostoyevsky *Poor Folk and Other Stories*; *The Brothers Karamazov*; *The Gambler*; *The House of the Dead*; *The Idiot* (all Penguin); *Crime and Punishment* (Penguin/Random House); *Notes from the Underground* (Penguin/Bantam); *The Possessed* (Vintage/NAL-Dutton). Pessimistic, brooding tales, often semi-autobiographical (particularly *The Gambler* and *The House of the Dead*). His masterpiece, *Crime and Punishment*, is set in Petersburg's infamous Haymarket district.

Daniil Kharms *Incidences* (Serpent's Tail, UK). Literary miniatures by the legendary St Petersburg absurdist. In his home city you can find other works in Russian, including Kharms's irreverent "Pushkin stories", illustrated with his own cartoons.

Vladimir Nabokov *Invitation to a Beheading*; *Laughter in the Dark*; *Look at the Harlequins!*; *Nabokov's Dozen*; *Speak, Memory* (all Penguin/Random House). Though best known abroad for his novel of erotic obsession, *Lolita*, Nabokov is chiefly esteemed as a stylist in the land of his birth. His childhood home, just off St Isaac's Square, is vividly recalled in his autobiographical *Speak, Memory*.

Boris Pasternak *Doctor Zhivago* (HarperCollins/Ballantine). A multi-layered story of love and destiny, war and revolution, chiefly known in the West for the film version. Russians regard Pasternak as a poet first and a novelist second.

Victor Pelevin *A Werewolf Problem in Central Russia and Other Stories*; *Omon Ra*; *The Blue Lantern: Stories* (all New Directions, US); *Buddha's Little Finger* (Viking, US); *The Life of Insects* (Penguin); *The Clay Machine-Gun* (Faber, UK). Digital-age fables by the literary voice of Russia's "Generation P", for whom Pepsi, not the Party, set the tone.

Nina Sadur *Witch's Tears and Other Stories* (Harbord Publishing, UK). Strikingly original tales of late Soviet times and afterwards, by one of the best writers in Russia today. Pain and loss are at the heart of them, whether it's the legacy of Chernobyl, emigration to Israel, or Gagarin's mother, talking to her long-dead son.

Lev Tolstoy *Anna Karenina* and *War and Peace* (Penguin). The latter is the ultimate epic novel, tracing the fortunes of dozens of characters over decades. Its depiction of the Patriotic War of 1812 cast common folk in a heroic mould, while the main, aristocratic characters are flawed – an idealization of the masses that made *War and Peace* politically acceptable in Soviet times.

Julia Voznosenskaya *Women's Decameron* (Minerva, o/p). Ten women quarantined in a Leningrad maternity clinic relate their experiences of life in the USSR. Voznesenskaya herself was jailed for her social activism.

Foreign fiction

Malcolm Bradbury *To The Hermitage* (Overlook Press, US). A witty and intriguing story interweaving St Petersburg in the time of Catherine the Great and in 1993, with French *encyclopédiste* Diderot as the central character.

Alan Brien *Lenin: The Novel* (Paladin & Morrow, o/p). A masterly evocation of Lenin's life and character, in the form of a diary by the man himself, every page exuding his steely determination and sly irascibility.

J.M. Coetzee *The Master of Petersburg* (Minerva/Penguin). A brooding novel centred on Dostoyevsky, who gets drawn into the nefarious underworld of the St Petersburg Nihilists after the suspicious suicide of his stepson.

Debra Dean *The Madonnas of Leningrad* (Harper Perennial). A pensioner stricken by Alzheimer's remembers the "memory palace" that helped her survive the Blockade.

Helen Dunmore *The Siege* (Penguin). This acclaimed novel follows a family through the terrible hardships of the first year of the Blockade.

Philip Kerr *Dead Meat* (Vintage/Bantam). An edgy, atmospheric thriller set in a mafia-infested St Petersburg, where the lugubrious detective Grushko tries to uncover the truth behind a journalist's murder.

I Allan Sealy *The Brainfever Bird* (Picador, UK). An intriguing romantic thriller that moves between St Petersburg and Old Delhi, replete with deadly viruses, international espionage and neo-Nazi thuggery.

Gillian Slovo *Ice Road* (Little, Brown). Not, as you might imagine, about the wartime Road of Life, but about Kirov's assassination, that plunged Leningrad into a vortex of fear and suffering.

Language

Language

Language

The official language of the Russian Federation is Russian (*russkiy yazik*), a highly complex eastern Slav tongue. Any attempt to speak Russian will be appreciated, though don't be discouraged if people seem not to understand, as most will be unaccustomed to hearing foreigners stumble through their language. English and German are the most common second languages, especially among the younger generation. Bilingual signs and menus are fairly common in the heart of the city, but being able to read the Cyrillic alphabet makes life a lot easier. For a full linguistic rundown, the *Rough Guide Russian Phrasebook* is set out dictionary-style for easy access, with English-Russian and Russian-English sections, cultural tips for tricky situations and a menu reader.

The Cyrillic alphabet

The Cyrillic alphabet – derived from a system invented by Saints Cyril and Methodius, the "Apostles of the Slavs" – is an obstacle that's hard to get around, and is worth trying to learn if you're going to be in Russia more than a few days. Seven of the thirty-three letters represent approximately the same sound as they do in the Roman alphabet; others are taken from the Greek alphabet, or are unique to the Slavonic languages. It's often possible to decipher the names of streets or metro stations by focusing on the letters you can recognize, but this won't get you far in other situations. Where signs are bilingual, you'll notice variations in transliterating Cyrillic into Latin script (for example "Chajkovskogo" or "Chaykovskovo" for Чайковского). In this book, we've used the English System, with a few modifications to help pronunciation. All proper names appear as they are best known, not as they would be transliterated; for example "Tchaikovsky" not "Chaykovskiy".

The list on p.428 gives the Cyrillic characters in upper- and lower-case form, followed simply by the Latin equivalent. In order to pronounce the words properly, you'll need to consult the pronunciation guide below.

Pronunciation

English-speakers often find Russian difficult to pronounce, partly because even letters that appear to have English equivalents are subtly different. On the other hand, Russian spelling is more phonetically consistent than English and the vast majority of words contain no silent letters. The most important factor that determines pronunciation is stress; if you get this wrong, even the simplest Russian words may be misunderstood. Attuning your ear to how stress affects pronunciation is more useful than striving to master Russian grammar (which shares many features with Latin).

Vowels and word stress

Unlike some Slavonic languages, the **stress** in a word can fall on any syllable and there's no way of knowing simply by looking at it – it's something you just have to

Cyrillic characters

Аа	a	Уу	u
Бб	b	Фф	f
Вв	v	Хх	kh
Гг	g*	Цц	ts
Дд	d	Чч	ch
Ее	e*	Шш	sh
Ёё	e	Щщ	shch
Жж	zh	Ыы	y*
Зз	z	Ээ	e
Ии	i	Яя	ya
Йй	y	Ьь	a silent
Кк	k		"soft sign"
Лл	l		which softens
Мм	m		the preceding
Нн	n		consonant
Оо	o	Ъъ	a silent "hard
Пп	p		sign" which
Рр	r		keeps the
Сс	s		preceding
Тт	t		consonant hard*

*To aid pronunciation and readability, we have introduced a handful of **exceptions** to the above transliteration guide:

Гг (g) is written as v when pronounced as such, for example Горкого – Gorkovo.

Ее (e) is written as Ye when at the beginning of a word, for example Елагин – Yelagin.

Ыы (y) is written as i, when it appears immediately before й (y), for example Литейный – Liteyniy.

To confuse matters further, **hand-written Cyrillic** is different again from the printed Cyrillic above – although the only place you're likely to encounter it is on menus. The chief differences are:

б which looks similar to a "d"

г which looks similar to a backwards "s"

и which looks like a "u"

т which looks similar to an "m"

learn, as you do in English. If a word has only one syllable, you can't get it wrong; where there are two or more, we've placed accents over the stressed vowel/syllable, though these do not appear in Russian itself. Once you've located the stressed syllable, you should give it more weight than all the others and far more than you would in English. We've marked the syllable to be stressed with an accent.

Whether a **vowel** is stressed or unstressed sometimes affects the way it's pronounced, most notably with the letter "o" (see below).

а – a – like the a in father

я – ya – like the ya in yarn, but like the e in evil when it appears before a stressed syllable

э – e – always a short e as in get

е – e – like the ye in yes

и – i – like the e in evil

й – y – like the y in boy

o – o – like the o in port when stressed, but like the a in plan when unstressed

ё – e – like the yo in yonder. Note that in Russia, this letter is often printed without the dots

у – u – like the oo in moon

ю – yu – like the u in universe

ы – y – like the i in ill, but with the tongue drawn back

Consonants

In Russian, **consonants** can be either soft or hard and this difference is an important feature of a "good" accent, but if you're simply trying to get by in the language, you needn't worry. The main features of consonants are:

б – b – like the b in bad; at the end of a word like the p in dip

в – v – like the v in van but with the upper teeth behind the top of the lower lip; at the end of a word, and before certain consonants like f in leaf

г – g – like the g in goat; at the end of a word like the k in lark

д – d – like the d in dog but with the tongue pressed against the back of the upper teeth; at the end of a word like the t in salt

ж – zh – like the s in pleasure; at the end of a word like the sh in bush

з – z – like the z in zoo; at the end of a word like the s in loose

л – l – like the l in milk, but with the tongue kept low and touching the back of the upper teeth

н – n – like the n in no but with the tongue pressed against the upper teeth

р – r – trilled as the Scots speak it

с – s – always as in soft, never as in sure

т – t – like the t in tent, but with the tongue brought up against the upper teeth

х – kh – like the ch in the Scottish loch

ц – ts – like the ts in boats

ч – ch – like the ch in chicken

ш – sh – like the sh in shop

щ – shch – like the sh-ch in fresh cheese

There are of course exceptions to the above pronunciation rules, but if you remember even the ones mentioned, you'll be understood.

Words and phrases

Basics

Yes	*da*	да
No	*net*	нет
Please	*pozháluysta*	пожалуйста
Thank you	*spasíbo*	спасибо
Excuse me	*izviníte*	извините
Sorry	*prostíte*	простите
That's OK/it doesn't matter	*nichevó*	ничего
Hello/goodbye (formal)	*zdrávstvuyte/do svidániya*	здравствуйте/до свидания
Good day	*dóbriy den*	добрый день
Good morning	*dóbroe útro*	доброе утро

Good evening	*dóbriy vécher*	добрый вечер
Good night	*spokóynoy nochi*	спокойной ночи
See you later (informal)	*poká*	пока
Bon voyage	*schastlívovo putí*	счастливого пути
Bon appetit	*priyátnovo appetíta*	приятного аппетита
How are you?	*kak delá?*	как дела?
Fine/OK	*khoroshó*	хорошо
Leave me alone!	*ostavte menya!*	оставте меня!
Help!	*na pómoshch!*	на помощь!
Today	*sevódnya*	сегодня
Yesterday	*vcherá*	вчера
Tomorrow	*závtra*	завтра
The day after tomorrow	*poslezávtra*	послезавтра
Now	*seychás*	сейчас
Later	*popózzhe*	попозже
This one	*éta*	это
A little	*nemnógo*	немного
Large/small	*bolshóy/málenkiy*	большой/маленький
More/less	*yeshché/ménshe*	ещё/меньше
Good/bad	*khoróshiy/plokhóy*	хороший/плохой
Hot/cold	*goryáchiy/kholódniy*	горячий/холодный
With/without	*s/bez*	с/без

Pronouns, names and introductions

Normally, you should use the **polite form** вы (*vy*, "you" plural) in conversation. The informal ты (*ty*, "you" singular) is for children, close friends and relatives (before the Revolution, the ruling classes also used it to serfs, servants and conscripts). Older Russians often introduce themselves and address others using their first name and **patronymic**, eg Maria Fyodorovna (Maria, daughter of Fyodor) or Anton Ivanovich (Anton, son of Ivan). At some stage they may suggest that you use their first name only, or begin using *ty* to each other. This is usually a good sign, but remember that such informality isn't appreciated at a business meeting (a Russian boss might call his colleagues by their first names, but they would certainly use his patronymic, too).

I	*ya*	я
you (singular)	*ty*	ты
we	*my*	мы
he, she, it	*on, oná, onó*	он, она, оно
you (plural)	*vy*	вы
they	*oní*	они
What's your name?	*kak vas zovút?*	как вас зовут?
My name is...	*menya zovút...*	меня зовут
Pleased to meet you	*óchen priyátno*	очень приятно

Getting around

| Over there | *tam* | там |
| Round the corner | *za uglóm* | за углом |

Left/right	nalévo/naprávo	налево/направо
Straight on	pryámo	прямо
Where is. . . ?	gde?	где?
How do I get to Peterhof?	kak mne popást v Petergof?	как мне попасть в Петергоф?
Am I going the right way for the Hermitage?	ya právilno idú k Ermitazhu?	я правильно иду к эрмитажу?
Is it far?	etó dalekó?	это далеко?
By bus	avtóbusom	автобусом
By train	póezdom	поездом
By car	na mashine	на машине
On foot	peshkóm	пешком
By taxi	na taksi	на такси
Ticket	bilét	билет
Return (ticket)	tudá i obrátno	туда и обратно
Train station	vokzál	вокзал
Bus station	avtóbusniy vokzal	автобусный вокзал
Bus stop	ostanóvka	остановка
Is this train going to Novgorod?	étot póezd idét v Nóvgorod?	тот поезд идёт в Новгород?
Do I have to change?	núzhno sdélat peresádku?	нужно сделать пересадку?
Small change (money)	méloch	мелочь

Questions and answers

Do you speak English?	Vy govoríte po-anglíyski?	вы говорите по-английски?
I don't speak German	ya ne govoryú po-nemétski	я не говорю по-немецки
I don't understand	ya ne ponimáyu	я не понимаю
I understand	ya ponimáyu	я понимаю
Speak slowly	govoríte pomédlenee	говорите помедленее
I don't know	ya ne znáyu	я не знаю
How do you say that in Russian?	kak po-rússki?	как по-русски?
Could you write it down?	zapishíte éto pozháluysta	запишите это пожалуйста
What	chto	что
Where	gde	где
When	kogdá	когда
Why	pochemú	почему
Who	kto	кто
How much is it?	skólko stóit?	сколько стоит?
I would like a double room	ya khochú nómer na dvoíkh	я хочу номер на двоих
For one night	tólko sútki	только сутки
Shower	dush	душ
Are these seats free?	svobódno?	свободно?
May I . . . ?	mózhno?	можно?
You can't/it is not allowed	nelzyá	нельзя
The bill please	schet pozháluysta	счёт пожалуйста
Do you have . . . ?	u vas yest?	у вас есть?
That's all	eto vsé	это всё

Signs

Entrance	vkhod	вход
Exit	výkhod	выход
Toilet	tualét	туалет
Men's	múzhskóy	мужской
Women's	zhénskiy	женский
Pull (a door)	k sebe	к себе
Push (a door)	ot sebya	от себя
Open	otkrýto	открыто
Closed (for repairs)	zakrýto (na remont)	закрыто на ремонт
Out of order	ne rabótaet	не раБотает
No entry	vkhóda net	входа нет
Danger zone	opasnaya zona	опасная зона
No smoking	ne kurít	не курить
Drinking water	piteváya vodá	питьевая вода
Information	správka	справка
Ticket office	kássa	касса

Days of the week

Monday	ponedélnik	понедельник
Tuesday	vtórnik	вторник
Wednesday	sredá	среда
Thursday	chetvérg	четверг
Friday	pyátnitsa	пятница
Saturday	subbóta	суббота
Sunday	voskreséne	воскресенье

Months of the year

January	yanvár	январь
February	fevrál	февраль
March	mart	март
April	aprél	апрель
May	may	май
June	iyún	июнь
July	iyúl	июль
August	ávgust	август
September	sentyábr	сентябрь
October	oktyábr	октябрь
November	noyábr	ноябрь
December	dekábr	декабрь

Numbers

1	odín	один
2	dva	два
3	tri	три

4	chetýre	четыре
5	pyat	пять
6	shest	шесть
7	sem	семь
8	vósem	восемь
9	dévyat	девять
10	désyat	десять
11	odínnadtsat	одиннадцать
12	dvenádtsat	двенадцать
13	trinádtsat	тринадцать
14	chetýrnadtsat	четырнадцать
15	pyatnádtsat	пятнадцать
16	shestnádtsat	шестнадцать
17	semnádtsat	семнадцать
18	vosemnádtsat	восемнадцать
19	devyatnádtsat	девятнадцать
20	dvádtsat	двадцать
21	dvádtsat odín	двадцать один
30	trídtsat	тридцать
40	sórok	сорок
50	pyatdesyát	пятьдесят
60	shestdesyát	шестьдесят
70	sémdesyat	семьдесят
80	vósemdesyat	восемьдесят
90	devyanósto	девяносто
100	sto	сто
200	dvésti	двести
300	trísta	триста
400	chetýresta	четыреста
500	pyatsót	пятьсот
600	shestsót	шестьсот
700	semsót	семьсот
800	vosemsót	восемьсот
900	devyatsót	девятьсот
1000	týsyacha	тысяча
2000	dve týsyachi	две тысячи
3000	tri týsyachi	три тысячи
4000	chetýre týsyachi	четыре тысячи
5000	pyat týsyach	пять тысяч
10,000	désyat týsyach	десять тысяч
50,000	pyatdesyát týsyach	пятьдесят тысяч

Food and drink terms

Basics

аджика	*adzhíka*	spicy Georgian relish
бутерброд	*buterbrod*	open sandwich
чашка	*cháshka*	cup
десерт	*desért*	dessert
фрукты	*frúkty*	fruit
горчица	*gorchítsa*	mustard
хлеб	*khleb*	bread
ложка	*lózhka*	spoon
масло	*máslo*	butter/oil
мёд	*myod*	honey
молоко	*molokó*	milk
мясо	*myáso*	meat
напиток	*napítok*	drinks
нож	*nozh*	knife
обед	*obéd*	main meal/lunch
овощи	*ovoshchi*	vegetables
пицца	*pizza*	pizza
рис	*ris*	rice
перец	*pérets*	pepper
плов	*plov*	pilau
пирог	*piróg*	pie
рыба	*ryba*	fish
сахар	*sákhar*	sugar
салат	*salat*	salad
сметана	*smetána*	sour cream
соль	*sol*	salt
суп	*soup*	soup
стакан	*stakán*	glass
тарелка	*tarélka*	plate
ужин	*úzhin*	supper
вилка	*vílka*	fork
яйца	*yáytsa*	eggs
яичница	*yaichnitsa*	fried egg
завтрак	*závtrak*	breakfast
закуски	*zakúski*	appetizers

Appetizers (*zakúski*) and salads

ассорти мясное	*assortí myasnóe*	assorted meats
ассорти рыбное	*assortí rybnoe*	assorted fish
бастурма	*bastúrma*	marinated dried meat
блины	*bliný*	pancakes
блинчики	*blinchiki*	*bliny* rolled around a filling and browned

брынза	*brynza*	salty white cheese
грибы	*griby*	mushrooms
икра баклажанная	*ikrá baklazhánnaya*	aubergine (eggplant) purée
икра красная	*ikrá krásnaya*	red caviar
икра чёрная	*ikrá chórnaya*	black caviar
хачапури	*khachapuri*	Georgian naan-style bread, stuffed with cheese
хачапури по-Мингрелский	*khachapuri po-Mingrelskiy*	*khachapuri* cooked with an egg in the middle
колбаса копчёная	*kolbasá kopchónaya*	smoked sausage
маслины	*maslíny*	olives
морков по-корейский	*morkov po-koreyskiy*	spicy carrot salad
огурцы	*ogurtsy*	gherkins
осетрина с майонезом	*osetrína s mayonézom*	sturgeon mayonnaise
пельмени	*pelmeni*	Siberian ravioli
салат из огурцов	*salat iz ogurtsóv*	cucumber salad
салат из помидоров	*salát iz pomidórov*	tomato salad
сардины с лимоном	*sardíny s limónom*	sardines with lemon
сельдь	*seld*	herring
селёдка под шубы	*selyódka pod shuby*	pickled herring with beetroot, carrot, egg and mayonnaise
шпроты	*shpróty*	sprats (like a herring)
столичный салат	*stolíchniy salát*	meat and vegetable salad
сыр	*syr*	cheese
ветчина	*vetchiná*	ham
винегрет	*vinegrét*	"Russian salad"
язык с гарниром	*yazyk s garnírom*	tongue with garnish

Soups

борщ	*borsch*	beetroot soup
бульон	*bulón*	consommé
чихиртми	*chikhirtmi*	lemon-flavoured chicken soup
харчо	*khárcho*	spicy beef or lamb soup
хаш	*khásh*	tripe soup, traditionally drunk as a hang-over cure
клёцки	*klyótski*	Belorussian soup with dumplings
лапша	*lapsha*	chicken-noodle soup
окрошка	*okróshka*	cold vegetable soup
постный борщ	*póstny borsch*	borsch without meat
рассольник	*rassólnik*	brine and cucumber soup
щи	*shchi*	cabbage soup
солянка	*solyánka*	spicy, meaty soup flavoured with lemon and olives
уха	*ukhá*	fish soup

Meat dishes

| азу из говядины | *azú iz govyádiny* | beef stew |
| антрекот | *antrekot* | entrecôte steak |

баранина	*baránina*	mutton/lamb
бастурма	*bastúrma*	thinly sliced, marinated, dried meat
бифстроганов	*bifstróganov*	beef stroganoff
биточки	*bitóchki*	meatballs
бифштекс	*bifshtéks*	beef steak
булкоги	*bulkogi*	spicy, stir-fried, marinated beef
чахохбили	*chakhokhbili*	slow-cooked chicken with herbs and vegetables
казы	*kázy*	pony-meat sausages
хинкали	*khinkáli*	dumplings stuffed with lamb, or beef and pork
котлеты по-киевски	*kotléty po-kíevski*	chicken Kiev
кролик	*królik*	rabbit
курица	*kúritsa*	chicken
рагу	*ragú*	stew
сациви	*satsivi*	chicken in walnut sauce, served cold
шашлык	*shashlyk*	kebab
свинина	*svinína*	pork
телятина	*telyátina*	veal
сосиски	*sosíski*	frankfurter sausages
котлета	*kotleta*	fried meatball

Fish

форель	*forel*	trout
карп	*karp*	carp
лещ	*leshch*	bream
лососина	*lososína*	salmon
осетрина	*osetrína*	sturgeon
щука	*shchúka*	pike
скумбрия	*skúmbriya*	mackerel
треска	*treská*	chub
сёмга	*syomga*	salmon
судак	*sudak*	pike perch

Vegetables and herbs

баклажан	*baklazhán*	aubergine (eggplant)
чеснок	*chisnok*	garlic
гарниры	*garniry*	any vegetable garnish
горох	*gorókh*	peas
грибы	*griby*	mushrooms
грибы с сметаной	*griby s smetanoy*	mushrooms cooked with sour cream
капуста	*kapústa*	cabbage
картофель	*kartófel*	potatoes
кимичи	*kimichi*	spicy, garlicky pickled cabbage
кинза	*kinza*	coriander
лобио	*lóbio*	red or green bean stew
лук	*luk*	onions
мхали	*mkhali*	beetroot or spinach puree with herbs and walnuts

морковь	*morkóv*	carrots
огурцы	*ogurtsy*	cucumbers
петрушка	*petrushka*	parsley
помидоры	*pomidóry*	tomatoes
редиска	*redíska*	radishes
салат	*salát*	lettuce
свёкла	*svyokla*	beetroot
толма	*tólma*	tomatoes, aubergines or vine-leaves stuffed with meat and rice
укроп	*úkrop*	dill
зелень	*zélen*	fresh herbs

Fruit

абрикосы	*abrikósy*	apricots
апельсины	*apelsíny*	oranges
арбуз	*arbúz*	watermelon
банан	*banan*	banana
чернослив	*chernoslív*	prunes
дыня	*dynya*	melon
финики	*fíniki*	dates
груши	*grushi*	pears
инжир	*inzhír*	figs
лимон	*limón*	lemon
сливы	*slivy*	plums
виноград	*vinográd*	grapes
вишня	*víshnya*	cherries
яблоки	*yábloki*	apples
ягоды	*yágody*	berries

Common terms

фаршированные	*farshiróvannye*	stuffed
фри	*fri*	fried
копчёные	*kopchonye*	smoked
маринованные	*marinóvannye*	pickled or marinated
паровые	*paróvye*	steamed
печёные	*pechónye*	baked
отварные	*ótvarnye*	boiled
овощной	*óvoshchnoy*	made from vegetables
на вертеле	*na vertele*	grilled on a skewer
с грибами	*s gribámi*	with mushrooms
солёные	*solyónye*	salted
со сметаной	*so smetánoy*	with sour cream
тушёные	*tushónye*	stewed
варёные	*varyónye*	boiled
жареные	*zhárenye*	roast/grilled/fried

Drinks

чай	*chay*	tea
кофе	*kófe*	coffee
с сахаром	*s sakarom*	with sugar
без сахара	*bez sákhara*	without sugar
сок	*sok*	fruit juice
кэфир	*kefir*	the Russian equivalent of *lassi*
квас	*kvas*	a drink made from fermented rye
мёд	*myod*	honey mead
сбит н	*sbiten*	a herbal liquor
тархун	*tarkhun*	a tarragon-flavoured drink
пиво	*pívo*	beer
вино	*vinó*	wine
красное	*krásnoe*	red
белое	*béloe*	white
бутылка	*butýlka*	bottle
лёд	*lyod*	ice
минеральная вода	*minerálnaya vodá*	mineral water
водка	*vódka*	vodka
вода	*vodá*	water
шампанское	*shampánskoe*	champagne
брют	*bryut*	extra dry
сухое	*sukhoe*	dry
полусухое	*polusukhóe*	medium dry
сладкое	*sládkoe*	sweet
коньяк	*konyák*	cognac
за здоровье	*za zdaróve*	cheers!

A glossary of Russian words and terms

Note: the accents below signify which syllable is stressed, but they are not used in the main text of this book.

bánya bathhouse

báshnya tower

bulvár boulevard

dácha country cottage

dom kultúry communal arts and social centre; literally "house of culture"

dvoréts palace

górod town

kanál canal

kassa ticket office

kládbishche cemetery

kommunálka communal flat, where several tenants or families share the bathroom, kitchen and corridor

krépost fortress

monastyr monastery or convent; the distinction is made by specifying *muzhskóy* (men's) or *zhenskiy* (women's) *monastyr*

most bridge

muzhík before the Revolution it meant peasant; it now means masculine or macho

náberezhnaya embankment

óstrov island

ózero lake

pámyatnik monument

pereúlok lane

plóshchad square
prospékt avenue
reká river
restorán restaurant
rússkiy/rússkaya Russian
rýnok market
sad garden/park
shossé highway
sobór cathedral

storoná district
teátr theatre
tsérkov church
úlitsa street
vokzál train station
výstavka exhibition
zal room or hall
zámok castle

An architectural glossary

Art Nouveau French term for the sinuous, stylized form of architecture dating from the turn of the century to World War I, called Style Moderne in Russia.

Atlantes Supports in the form of carved male Atlas figures, used instead of columns to support an entablature.

Baroque Exuberant architectural style of the seventeenth and early eighteenth centuries that spread to Russia via Ukraine and Belarus. Characterized by heavy, ornate decoration, complex spatial arrangement and grand vistas.

Caryatids Sculpted female figures used as a column to support an entablature.

Constructivism Soviet version of modernism that pervaded the arts during the 1920s. In architecture, functionalism and simplicity were the watchwords – though many Constructivist projects were utterly impractical and never got beyond the drawing board.

Empire style Richly decorated version of the Neoclassical style, which prevailed in Russia from 1812 to the 1840s. The French and Russian Empire styles both derived from Imperial Rome.

Entablature The part of a building supported by a colonnade or column.

Faux marbre Any surface painted to resemble marble.

Fresco Mural painting applied to wet plaster, so that the colours bind chemically with it as they dry.

Futurism Avant-garde art movement glorifying machinery, war, speed and the modern world in general.

Grisaille Painting in grey or other coloured monotone used to represent objects in relief.

Icon Religious image, usually painted on

wood and framed upon an iconostasis. See pp.138–140 for more about Russian icons.

Iconostasis A screen that separates the sanctuary from the nave in Orthodox churches, typically consisting of tiers of icons in a gilded frame, with up to three doors that open during services. The central one is known as the Royal Door.

Nave The part of a church where the congregation stands (there are no pews in Orthodox churches).

Neoclassical Late eighteenth- and early nineteenth-century style of architecture and design returning to classical Greek and Roman models as a reaction against Baroque and Rococo excesses.

Neo-Russian (also known as Pseudo-Russian) Style of architecture and decorative arts that drew inspiration from Russia's medieval and ancient past, folk arts and myths.

Pilaster A half column projecting only slightly from the wall; an engaged column stands almost free from the surface.

Portico Covered entrance to a building.

Putti Cherubs.

Ravelin An outlying bastion with cannons facing the curtain wall of a fortress, meant to trap attackers in a deadly crossfire – a feature of the Peter and Paul Fortress, and the Annenkron at Vyborg.

Rococo Highly florid, fiddly but occasionally graceful style of architecture and interior design, forming the last phase of Baroque.

Sanctuary (or Naos) The area around the altar, which in Orthodox churches is always screened by an iconostasis.

Stalinist Declamatory style of architecture prevalent from the 1930s up to the death of Stalin in 1953 that returned to Neoclassical and neo-Gothic models as a reaction against Constructivism and reached its "High Stalinist" apogee after World War II.

Stucco Plaster used for decorative effects.

Style Moderne Linear, stylized form of architecture and decorative arts influenced by French Art Nouveau, which took its own direction in Russia.

Trompe l'oeil Painting designed to fool the onlooker into believing that it is actually three-dimensional.

Political terms and acronyms

Apparatchiki A catch-all term to describe the Communist Party bureaucrats of the Soviet era.

Bolshevik Literally "majority"; name given to the faction that supported Lenin during the internal disputes within the RSDLP during the first decade of this century.

Cheka (Extraordinary Commission for Combating Counter-revolution, Speculation and Delinquency in Office) Bolshevik secret police, 1917–21.

CIS Commonwealth of Independent States – loose grouping that was formed in December 1991 following the collapse of the USSR. Most of the former Soviet republics have since joined, with the exception of the Baltic States, now in the European Union.

Civil War 1918–21 War between the Bolsheviks and an assortment of opposition forces including Mensheviks, SRs, Cossacks, Tsarists and foreign interventionist armies from the West and Japan.

Decembrists Those who participated in the abortive coup against the accession of Nicholas I in December 1825.

Duma The name given to three parliaments in the reign of Nicholas II, and the lower house of the parliament of the Russian Federation since 1993 (its upper chamber is called the Federation Council).

February Revolution Overthrow of the tsar in February 1917.

Five-Year Plan Centralized masterplan for every branch of the Soviet economy. The first Five-Year plan was promulgated in 1928.

FSB (Federal Security Service) The name of Russia's secret police since 1993.

GIBDD Traffic police.

GPU Soviet secret police, 1921–23.

Gulag Official title for the hard-labour camps set up under Lenin and Stalin.

Kadet Party (Constitutional Democratic Party) Liberal political party 1905–1917.

KGB (Committee of State Security) Soviet secret police 1954–91.

Kuptsy Wealthy merchant class, often of serf ancestry, that rose to prominence in the late nineteenth century.

Menshevik Literally "minority"; name given to the faction opposing Lenin during the internal disputes within the RSDLP during the first decade of the twentieth century.

Metropolitan Senior cleric, ranking between an archbishop and the patriarch of the Russian Orthodox Church.

MVD Soviet secret police from 1946 to 1954; now runs the regular police (Militia) and the OMON (see below).

Narodnaya Volya (People's Will) Terrorist group that assassinated Alexander II in 1881.

New Russians (novye russkie) Brash nouveaux riches of the post-Soviet era, mocked by countless New Russian jokes.

NKVD Soviet secret police, 1934–46.

October Revolution Bolshevik coup d'état which overthrew the Provisional Government in October 1917.

OGPU (Unified State Political Directorate) Soviet secret police 1923–34.

Okhrana Tsarist secret police.

Old Believers (Staroobryadtsy) Russian Orthodox schismatics.

Oligarchs Immensely rich and shady financiers who emerged during the Yeltsin era.

OMON Paramilitary force used for riot control and fighting civil wars within the Russian Federation.

Patriarch Head of the Russian Orthodox Church.

Petrine Anything dating from the lifetime of Peter the Great (1672–1725).

Populist Amorphous political movement of the second half of the nineteenth century advocating Socialism based on the peasant commune, or *mir*.

Purges Name used for the mass arrests of the Stalin era, but also for any systematic removal of unwanted elements from positions of authority.

RSDLP (Russian Social Democratic Labour Party) First Marxist political party in Russia, which rapidly split into Bolshevik and Menshevik factions.

SR Socialist Revolutionary.

Tsar Emperor. The title was first adopted by Ivan the Terrible.

Tsaritsa Empress; the foreign misnomer Tsarina is better known.

Tsarevich Crown prince.

Tsaraevna Daughter of a Tsar and Tsaritsa.

USSR (Union of Soviet Socialist Republics) Official name of the Soviet Union from 1923 to 1991.

Whites Generic term for Tsarist or Kadet forces during the Civil War, which the Bolsheviks applied to almost anyone who opposed them.

Travel store

ROUGH GUIDES
Complete Listing

Small print and

Index

A Rough Guide to Rough Guides

Published in 1982, the first Rough Guide – to Greece – was a student scheme that became a publishing phenomenon. Mark Ellingham, a recent graduate in English from Bristol University, had been travelling in Greece the previous summer and couldn't find the right guidebook. With a small group of friends he wrote his own guide, combining a highly contemporary, journalistic style with a thoroughly practical approach to travellers' needs.

The immediate success of the book spawned a series that rapidly covered dozens of destinations. And, in addition to impecunious backpackers, Rough Guides soon acquired a much broader and older readership that relished the guides' wit and inquisitiveness as much as their enthusiastic, critical approach and value-for-money ethos.

SMALL PRINT

These days, Rough Guides include recommendations from shoestring to luxury and cover more than 200 destinations around the globe, including almost every country in the Americas and Europe, more than half of Africa and most of Asia and Australasia. Our ever-growing team of authors and photographers is spread all over the world, particularly in Europe, the USA and Australia.

In the early 1990s, Rough Guides branched out of travel, with the publication of Rough Guides to World Music, Classical Music and the Internet. All three have become benchmark titles in their fields, spearheading the publication of a wide range of books under the Rough Guide name.

Including the travel series, Rough Guides now number more than 350 titles, covering: phrasebooks, waterproof maps, music guides from Opera to Heavy Metal, reference works as diverse as Conspiracy Theories and Shakespeare, and popular culture books from iPods to Poker. Rough Guides also produce a series of more than 120 World Music CDs in partnership with World Music Network.

Visit www.roughguides.com to see our latest publications.

Rough Guide travel images are available for commercial licensing at www.roughguidespictures.com

Rough Guide credits

Text editor: Amanda Tomlin
Layout: Dan May
Cartography: Jasbir Sandhu
Picture editor: Mark Thomas
Production: Rebecca Short
Proofreader: Karen Parker
Cover design: Chloë Roberts
Photographer: Jon Smith
Editorial: London Ruth Blackmore, Alison
Murchie, Karoline Thomas, Andy Turner, Keith
Drew, Edward Aves, Alice Park, Lucy White,
Jo Kirby, James Smart, Natasha Foges, Róisín
Cameron, Emma Traynor, Emma Gibbs, Kathryn
Lane, Christina Valhouli, Monica Woods, Mani
Ramaswamy, Joe Staines, Peter Buckley,
Matthew Milton, Tracy Hopkins, Ruth Tidball;
New York Andrew Rosenberg, Steven Horak,
AnneLise Sorensen, April Isaacs, Ella Steim, Anna
Owens, Sean Mahoney, Courtney Miller, Paula
Neudorf; **Delhi** Madhavi Singh, Karen D'Souza
Design & Pictures: London Scott Stickland,
Dan May, Diana Jarvis, Mark Thomas, Nicole
Newman, Sarah Cummins, Emily Taylor;
Delhi Umesh Aggarwal, Ajay Verma, Jessica

Subramanian, Ankur Guha, Pradeep Thapliyal,
Sachin Tanwar, Anita Singh, Nikhil Agarwal
Production: Vicky Baldwin
Cartography: London Maxine Repath, Ed
Wright, Katie Lloyd-Jones; **Delhi** Jai Prakash
Mishra, Rajesh Chhibber, Ashutosh Bharti, Rajesh
Mishra, Animesh Pathak, Karobi Gogoi, Amod
Singh, Alakananda Bhattacharya, Swati Handoo
Online: Narender Kumar, Rakesh Kumar,
Amit Verma, Rahul Kumar, Ganesh Sharma,
Debojit Borah, Saurabh Sati
Marketing & Publicity: London Liz Statham,
Niki Hanmer, Louise Maher, Jess Carter, Vanessa
Godden, Vivienne Watton, Anna Paynton, Rachel
Sprackett, Libby Jellie; **New York** Geoff Colquitt,
Katy Ball; **Delhi** Ragini Govind
Manager India: Punita Singh
Reference Director: Andrew Lockett
Operations Manager: Helen Phillips
PA to Publishing Director: Nicola Henderson
Publishing Director: Martin Dunford
Commercial Manager: Gino Magnotta
Managing Director: John Duhigg

SMALL PRINT

Publishing information

This sixth edition published June 2008 by
Rough Guides Ltd,
80 Strand, London WC2R 0RL
345 Hudson St, 4th Floor,
New York, NY 10014, USA
14 Local Shopping Centre, Panchsheel Park,
New Delhi 110017, India
Distributed by the Penguin Group
Penguin Books Ltd,
80 Strand, London WC2R 0RL
Penguin Group (USA)
375 Hudson Street, NY 10014, USA
Penguin Group (Australia)
250 Camberwell Road, Camberwell,
Victoria 3124, Australia
Penguin Books Canada Ltd,
10 Alcorn Avenue, Toronto, Ontario,
Canada M4V 1E4
Penguin Group (NZ)
67 Apollo Drive, Mairangi Bay, Auckland 1310,
New Zealand

Cover concept by Peter Dyer.

Typeset in Bembo and Helvetica to an original
design by Henry Iles.

Printed in China

472pp includes index

A catalogue record for this book is available from
the British Library

ISBN: 978-1-85828-062-2

The publishers and authors have done their
best to ensure the accuracy and currency of
all the information in **The Rough Guide to
St Petersburg**, however, they can accept no
responsibility for any loss, injury, or inconvenience
sustained by any traveller as a result of
information or advice contained in the guide.

1   3   5   7   9   8   6   4   2

Help us update

We've gone to a lot of effort to ensure that
the sixth edition of **The Rough Guide to St
Petersburg** is accurate and up to date. However,
things change – places get "discovered", opening
hours are notoriously fickle, restaurants and
rooms raise prices or lower standards. If you
feel we've got it wrong or left something out,
we'd like to know, and if you can remember the
address, the price, the hours, the phone number,
so much the better.

Please send your comments with the subject
line "**Rough Guide St Petersburg Update**"
to ℮mail@roughguides.com. We'll credit all
contributions and send a copy of the next edition
(or any other Rough Guide if you prefer) for the
very best emails.

Have your questions answered and tell others
about your trip at
ⓦcommunity.roughguides.com

Acknowledgements

The author would like to say a special thanks to Catherine Phillips for her hospitality and "Colbenzeling"; Zhenya and Natasha for wild nights, and Suzy, Jo and the two Petyas for congenial evenings. Thanks also to John Nicolson at Bubyr's Guesthouse, and Andrey Vasiliev of Novgorod's tourist office for smoothing the way. In England, thanks are due to Amanda Tomlin, for her patient, eagle-eyed editing.

Readers' letters

Thanks to all the readers who have taken the time to write in with comments and suggestions (and apologies if we've inadvertently omitted or misspelt anyone's name):

Howard Amos; Benjamin & Elena Brierley; Peter Coghill; Vicky Grainger; Stanislava Krusteva; Marie Paule Loontjens; Joe Luttrell; Louise Maher; AG Manning; Alex & Christine Moore; Duncan Naughten; Svetlana Nogai; Graham O'Neil; Andrea Royce; and Silke Tofahrn.

Index

Map entries are in colour.

W

Y

Z

INDEX

Map symbols

maps are listed in the full index using coloured text

▪▫▪▫	Province boundary	⊠	Post office
▫▫▫	Chapter division boundary	Ⓒ	Phone office
═══	Major road	@	Internet café
───	Minor road	⊞	Hospital
▥▥▥	Steps	⬓	Hydrofoil/Boat station
-----	Path	▣	Restaurants
▬▬▬	Railway	⊙	Statue/memorial
── ──	Ferry route	⚇	Fountains
───	River	⚐	Monastery
───	Wall	✿	Synagogue
▪──▪	Fence	⚑	Fortress
⊠─⊠	Gate	⛫	Monument
) (	Bridge	⚲	Church (regional maps)
⸙	Rocks	⚑	Mosque
▲	Peak	⛩	Buddhist Temple
Ⓜ	Metro station	⬭	Stadium
✈	Airport	▪	Building
🅿	Parking	⊞	Church (town maps)
★	Bus stop	⊹	Cemetery
⛽	Fuel station	▦	Park
◆	Place of interest	▨	Beach
ⓘ	Tourist office/information point	▨	Forest

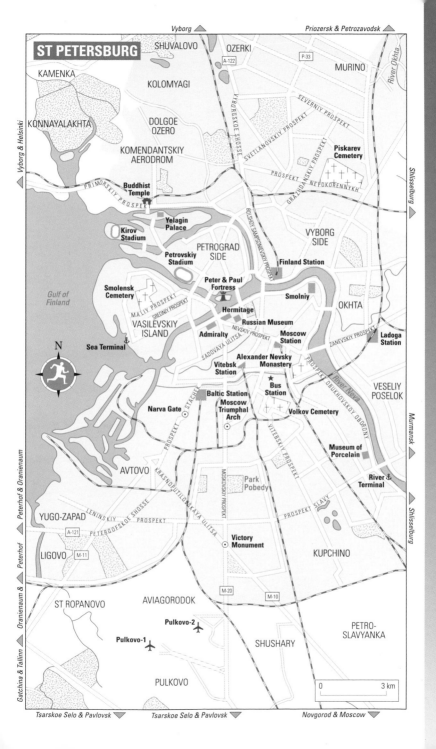

Freud's Dream Museum

Baltiyskiy dom

Gorkovskaya Ⓜ

Mosque

BOLSHAYA PUSHKARSKAYA ULITSA

BOLSHOY PROSPEKT

MALIY PROSPEKT

Artillery Museum

Alexander Park

KAMENNOOSTROVSKIY PROSPEKT

P E T R O G R A D   S I D E

ZVERINSKAYA ULITSA

KRONVERKSKIY PROSPEKT

Zoo

Petrovskiy Stadium

Prince Vladimir Cathedral

Ⓜ *Sportivnaya* PROSPEKT DOBROLYUBOVA

KRONVERKSKAYA NABEREZHNAYA

Peter & Paul Cathedral

TUCHKOV MOST

MALIY PR

Yubileyniy Sports Palace

M a l a y a   N e v a

BIRZHEVOY MOST

Peter & Paul Fortress

NABEREZHNAYA MAKAROVA

SREDNIY PROSPEKT

Rostral Columns

2-YA & 3-YA LINIYA

KADETSKAYA LINIYA

Naval Museum

Zoological Museum

Hermitage/ Winter Palace

DVORTSOVAYA NABEREZHNAYA

Vasileostrovskaya Ⓜ

V A S I L E V S K I Y   I S L A N D

4-YA & 5-YA LINIYA

6-YA & 7-YA LINIYA

University

MENDELEEVSKAYA LINIYA

Kunstkammer

Academy of Sciences

Pushkin's Apartment

ULITSA

MILLIONAYA

8-YA & 9-YA LINIYA

BOLSHOY PROSPEKT

Menshikov Palace

DVORTSOVIY MOST

Ⓘ DVORTSOVAYA PLOSHCHAD

Kapella

BOLSHAYA KONYUSHENNAYA ULITSA

10-YA & 11-YA LINIYA

Academy of Arts

Admiralty

General Staff

▲ Krasin & Sea Terminal

UNIVERSITETSKAYA NABEREZHNAYA

B o l s h a y a   N e v a

BLAGOVESHCHENSKIY MOST

Bronze Horseman

Senate & Synod

Manege

St Isaac's Cathedral

R i v e r   M o y k a

GOROKHOVAYA ULITSA

ANGLIYSKAYA NABEREZHNAYA

GALERNAYA ULITSA

KONNOGVARDEYSKIY BULVAR

KONNOGVARDEYSKIY BULVAR

MALAYA MORSKAYA ULITSA

BOLSHAYA MORSKAYA ULITSA

Rumyantsev Mansion

UL. TRUDA

POCHTAMTSKAYA ULITSA

Nabokov Museum

Mariinskiy Palace

KAZANSKAYA ULITSA

Bobrinskiy Palace

BOLSHAYA MORSKAYA ULITSA

FONARNIY PEREULOK

C a n a l

KANALA GRIBOEDOVA

New Holland

Yusupov Palace

VOZNESENSKIY PROSPEKT

G r i b o e d o v

NABEREZHNAYA

Sadovaya Ⓜ

SENNAYA PLOSHCHAD

Ⓜ *Sennaya Ploshchad*

ANGLIYSKIY PEREULOK

UL. PISAREVA

Conservatory

Railway Museum

ULITSA

MOSKOVSKIY PROSPEKT

Blok Museum

Synagogue ✡

ULITSA DEKABRISTOV

Mar...skiy Theatre

PROSPEKT RIMSKOVO-KORSAKOVA

Yusupov Garden

SADOVAYA

UL. SOYUZ PECHATNIKOV

St Nicholas Cathedral

NABEREZHNAYA KANALA GRIBOEDOVA

CENTRAL ST PETERSBURG